British Naval Supremacy and Anglo-American
Antagonisms, 1914–1930

During World War I, British naval supremacy enabled Great Britain to impose economic blockades and interdiction of American neutral shipping. The United States responded by starting to build "a navy second to none," one so powerful that Great Britain could not again successfully challenge America's vital economic interests. This book reveals that when the United States offered to substitute naval equality for its emerging naval supremacy, the British, nonetheless, used the resulting two major international arms-control conferences of the 1920s to ensure its continued naval dominance.

DONALD J. LISIO is the Henrietta Arnold Professor Emeritus of History at Coe College. His previous publications include *The President and Protest: Hoover, Conspiracy, and the Bonus Riot* (1974) and *Hoover, Blacks, and Lily Whites: a Study of Southern Strategies* (1994). He received his Ph.D. from the University of Wisconsin–Madison. Professor Lisio now lives in San Diego, California.

British Naval Supremacy and Anglo-American Antagonisms, 1914–1930

DONALD J. LISIO

CAMBRIDGE
UNIVERSITY PRESS

University Printing House, Cambridge CB2 8BS, United Kingdom

Cambridge University Press is part of the University of Cambridge.

It furthers the University's mission by disseminating knowledge in the pursuit of education, learning, and research at the highest international levels of excellence.

www.cambridge.org
Information on this title: www.cambridge.org/9781107056954

© Donald J. Lisio 2014

This publication is in copyright. Subject to statutory exception and to the provisions of relevant collective licensing agreements, no reproduction of any part may take place without the written permission of Cambridge University Press.

First published 2014

Printed in the United Kingdom by Clays, St Ives plc

A catalog record for this publication is available from the British Library.

Library of Congress Cataloging in Publication Data
Lisio, Donald J.
British naval supremacy and Anglo-American antagonisms, 1914–1930 / Donald J. Lisio (Coe College, Des Moines, Iowa).
    pages cm
ISBN 978-1-107-05695-4 (Hardback)
1. Great Britain. Royal Navy–History–20th century. 2. United States. Navy–History–20th century. 3. Sea-power–Great Britain–History–20th century. 4. Sea-power–United States–History–20th century. 5. Great Britain–Foreign relations–United States. 6. United States–Foreign relations–Great Britain. 7. Great Britain–History, Naval–20th century. 8. United States–History, Naval–20th century. I. Title.
VA454.L67 2014
359′.03094109042–dc23   2014023816

ISBN 978-1-107-05695-4 Hardback

Cambridge University Press has no responsibility for the persistence or accuracy of URLs for external or third-party Internet Web sites referred to in this publication and does not guarantee that any content on such Web sites is, or will remain, accurate or appropriate.

Contents

List of illustrations	*page* vii
Acknowledgments	ix
Abbreviations	xi
Introduction	1
1 Clashing World Interests	5
2 Washington Conference Legacy	16
3 Beatty's Japanese War Plan	36
4 Churchill's Challenge	62
5 Beatty Embraces Arms Control	94
6 The General Board's New Hope	108
7 American Arms-Control Politics	121
8 Beatty Takes Control	138
9 Combat Equivalency	155
10 Beatty's New Strategies	172
11 Conference Shocks	216
12 Hardening Positions	238
13 The Failure of the Anglo-Japanese Accord	251
14 Cabinet Crisis	269

15 Final Efforts	279
16 Breakdown and Recriminations	289
17 Conclusion	302
Bibliographical Essay	317
Index	323

Illustrations

1. HMS Kent – Note the eight 8-inch guns in four turrets. *page* 203
2. USS Pensacola – Note the ten 8-inch guns in four turrets and the ability to launch fire-control spotter aircraft. "USS Pensacola (CA-24) Underway at sea, September 1935." 204
3. Back Seat: President Woodrow Wilson; President-Elect Warren G. Harding; Front Seat: Speaker of the House Joseph Cannon; Senator Philander Knox. "Woodrow Wilson, Warren G. Harding, Philander Knox, and Joseph Cannon, in convertible, March 4, 1921." 205
4. Frank B. Kellogg, Ambassador to Great Britain shortly before his appointment as Secretary of State; Secretary of State Charles Evans Hughes. "Frank B. Kellogg and Sec. Hughes, 2/27/25." 206
5. Admiral Sir David Beatty, First Sea Lord and Chief of the Admiralty Naval Staff. "Adm. Sir David Beatty." 207
6. Winston S. Churchill, Chancellor of the Exchequer. "Winston Churchill, 10/18/29." 207
7. Foreign Secretary Austen Chamberlain, Prime Minister Stanley Baldwin, Chancellor of the Exchequer Winston S. Churchill. "[Standing, left to right: Mr. Austen Chamberlain, Prime Minister Stanley Baldwin, and Sir Winston Churchill] / Photo Central News from Underwood & Underwood." 208
8. William Clive Bridgeman, First Lord of the Admiralty. "William Clive Bridgeman, 1st Viscount Bridgeman of Leigh." 209
9. Viscount Robert Gascoyne-Cecil of Chelwood. Cecil served with Bridgeman as one of the two chief British negotiators at the Geneva Naval Conference of 1927. A third prominent member of the negotiating team, Vice Admiral Frederick Field,

	is not pictured. "Viscount Cecil of Chelwood, Robert Gascoyne-Cecil, 1864–1958."	210
10	President Calvin Coolidge; Secretary of Commerce Herbert C. Hoover.	211
11	Ambassador to Belgium Hugh Gibson; Ambassador to Great Britain Alanson B. Houghton. Gibson shared duties with Admiral Hilary P. Jones as the American negotiators at the Geneva Naval Conference of 1927. "Hugh Gibson & A.B. Houghton."	212
12	Admiral Hilary P. Jones. Jones was also chief of the American naval delegates at the Geneva Naval Conference of 1927. "Vice Adml. Hilary P. Jones, 6/23/21."	213
13	Rear Admiral Frank H. Schofield. Photo taken in 1917 when he was a captain.	214
14	Prime Minister Ramsay MacDonald and President Herbert C. Hoover. "Macdonald & Hoover, 10/5/29."	215

Acknowledgments

I have been blessed over the years by help from many institutions and individuals and I am happy to acknowledge the importance of their contributions. Generous fellowships from the National Endowment for the Humanities, the American Council of Learned Societies, and from the United States Institute of Peace, combined with the annual research stipend from the Henrietta Arnold Chair in History at Coe College, provided crucial financial support. Betty Rogers, the Head of Reference, was especially helpful in fulfilling numerous interlibrary loan requests, while all of the deans and presidents and my faculty friends during my many years at Coe have consistently been encouraging. My special thanks as well to Trustee Ed Walsh and his wife Bobbi for their support and for their establishment of the generous Donald J. Lisio Scholarship Fund for needy students.

Archivists and manuscript librarians are too numerous to mention by name, yet all historians are deeply indebted to them. I want especially to thank the professionals in Great Britain at the Public Record Office, the Churchill College Archives, the British Library, the Shropshire Archaeological and Historical Society, the Cambridge University Library, the National Maritime Museum, and the Birmingham University Library. Most important in the United States are those at the National Archives, the Library of Congress Manuscripts Division, the Naval Historical Center, the Herbert Hoover Presidential Library, the Hoover Institution, and the Naval War College.

I am grateful as well to Lewis Bateman at Cambridge University Press for his faith in the value of my manuscript and for his support of my second book when he was editor at the University of North Carolina Press. Shaun Vigil and the entire staff at Cambridge University Press have been most cordial and supportive and I owe them all a special thanks.

Others who have been helpful in the long years to publication include my good friends the late Violet and Ernest Swanson, my late father, mother, and sister, Anthony, Dorothy, and Alice Lisio, as well as late Professors David M. Pletcher and Irvin G. Wyllie. For their continuing support, I thank my sister Lila and her husband Dick Walker, my brother Dr. Arnold Lisio and his wife Dr. Anne Moore and their families, and Dave Brooks. A very special thanks to our daughter, Denise Lisio, for her computer editorial assistance.

Throughout the fifty-six years of our marriage, my lovely and talented wife, Suzanne Swanson Lisio, has enthusiastically inspired and supported my teaching and scholarship, both financially and emotionally. As an English teacher herself, Suzie employed her keen intellect and insightful skills in materially improving the three books that she carefully scrutinized and edited for me. Ours has been a joyful partnership, one blessed by two wonderful children, Denise and Steve, who became scholars devoted to public service, and, along with their spouses Warren and Christine, our grandchildren Alessandra and Andrew, of whom we are immensely proud.

Abbreviations

AC	Austen Chamberlain Papers, University of Birmingham Library, Birmingham, England
ADD MSS	Additional Manuscripts Collection, Lord Robert Cecil Papers, British Library, London, England
ADM	Admiralty Papers, Public Record Office, Kew, Surrey, England
BED	British Empire Delegation
BEDM	British Empire Delegation *Minutes*, CAB 27/350, Public Record Office
BOR	Sen. William E. Borah Papers, Library of Congress Manuscripts Division, Washington, DC
BGMN/2	Unpublished Biography of William Bridgeman, Bridgeman Papers, Churchill College Archives, Cambridge, England
BP	Earl David Beatty Papers, National Maritime Museum Greenwich, England
CAB	British Cabinet Papers, Public Record Office
CAB, NPC	Cabinet, Naval Program Committee Papers, Public Record Office
CCP	Calvin Coolidge Papers, Microfilm Series I, MF 73/1289, Library of Congress Manuscripts Division
CHAR	Winston S. Churchill Papers, Chartwell Collection, Churchill College, Cambridge University, Cambridge, England
CID	Committee of Imperial Defence Papers, Public Record Office
CP	William R. Castle Papers, Herbert Hoover Presidential Library West Branch, Iowa
DBFP	*Documents on British Foreign-Policy, 1919–1939*, Series Ia, III: *European and Naval Questions, 1927*, ed. W.L. Medicott, et al. (London: Her Majesty's Stationery Office, 1970)
EC	Executive Committee, Chief Delegates, 1927 Geneva Naval Conference

FLNA	Further Limitation of Naval Armaments Sub-Committee Papers, Public Record Office
FRUS	*Papers Relating to the Foreign Relations of the United States, 1926 – 1927*, Government Printing Office, 1927
GB	General Board, United States Navy
GBDCS	General Board Disarmament Conference Series, Record Group 80, National Archives, Washington, DC
GBM	General Board *Minutes*, Naval Historical Center, Washington Naval Yard, Washington, DC
GBR	General Board Report
GBS	General Board Study
GBUSN	General Board, Records of the Department of the Navy, National Archives, Washington, DC
GD	Hugh Gibson Diary, Hugh Gibson Papers, Hoover Institution Stanford University, Palo Alto, California
GP	Hugh Gibson Papers, Hoover Institution, Stanford University, Palo Alto, California
JP	Hilary P. Jones Papers, Library of Congress Manuscripts Division, Washington, DC
KF	Frank B. Kellogg File, Gibson Papers, Hoover Institution, Stanford University, Palo Alto, California
KP	Frank B. Kellogg Papers, Minnesota Historical Society, St. Paul, Minnesota
LC	Manuscripts Division, Library of Congress, Washington, DC
LCP	Lord Robert Cecil Papers, British Library, London, England
LCR	Lord Robert Cecil Resignation Papers, Public Record Office
MC	Microfilm Reel Number
MCDS	Memorandum of Conversation File, Department of State, Record Group 43, National Archives
MH	Sir Maurice Hankey Papers, Churchill College Archives, Cambridge University, Cambridge, England
NA	National Archives, Washington, DC
NCP	Neville Chamberlain Papers, University of Birmingham Library, Birmingham, England
NI	Records of the Office of Naval Intelligence, Record Group 39, National Archives
N.I.D.	Naval Intelligence Division, Admiralty Papers, Public Record Office
NO	Records of the Bureau of Ordnance, Record Group 74, National Archives
NWC	Naval Historical Collection, Naval War College, Newport, Rhode Island
PCF	Preparatory Commission File, Hilary P. Jones Papers, Library of Congress
P.D.	Plans Division, Admiralty Papers, Public Record Office
PP, HHPL	Presidential Papers, Herbert Hoover Presidential Library, West Branch, Iowa
PRO	Public Record Office, Kew, Surrey, England

Abbreviations

Records	Japanese Foreign Ministry, *Documents on Japanese Foreign Policy, Records of the Conference for the Limitation of Naval Armament held at Geneva from June 20 to August 4, 1927* (Nihon Gaike Junebo Kaigun Gumbi Seigen Kaigi, 1982)
RG	Record Group, National Archives
ROSKCC	Stephen Roskill Papers, Churchill College Archives, Cambridge University, Cambridge, England
SBP	Stanley Baldwin Papers, Cambridge University Library, Cambridge, England
SD	Diary of Adm. Frank H. Schofield, General Board Disarmament Conference Series VI.3, Records Group 80, National Archives
SF	William B. Shearer File, Presidential Papers, Herbert Hoover Presidential Library
SLGF	Sir Shane Leslie-Godfrey Faussett Papers, Churchill College Archives
SMP, GB	Senior Member Present, General Board
TC	Technical Committee, Geneva Naval Conference
TR	Theodore Roosevelt, Jr. Papers, Limitation of Armaments File, Manuscripts Division, Library of Congress
WBP	William Bridgeman Papers, Shropshire County Record Office, Shrewsbury, England
WBPCC	William Bridgeman Papers, Churchill College Archives, Cambridge University
WCP	Winston S. Churchill Papers, Churchill College Archives, Cambridge University

Introduction

This is a study of British insistence on preserving its naval supremacy during the 1920s and the resulting resurgence of Anglo-American naval and diplomatic antagonisms leading up to, including, and following the climactic Geneva Naval Conference of 1927. Following the end of the Great War in 1918, as Germany's mighty warships lay at the bottom of the sea and France and Italy recovered from devastating invasions, three great Allied naval powers engaged in a naval arms race to ensure supremacy in the ocean regions vital to their national security and prosperity. Japan's modern navy and its Twenty-One Demands on China challenged America's Open Door policies while its occupation of the Marshall, Caroline, and Marianas island chains threatened the ability of the United States to defend the Philippines. Much more immediate, however, was the renewed clash with Great Britain over America's doctrine of "freedom of the seas."

During World War I, but before Germany resumed unrestricted submarine warfare and the United States consequently joined the Allied Powers in 1917, the vital interests of the United States and Great Britain collided repeatedly over differing interpretations of the complex issue of neutral rights at sea. Having declared neutrality, American leaders believed that British naval blockades, interdiction of American cargoes, lengthening contraband lists, and blacklisting of American firms accused of trading with the Central Powers threatened the prosperity of the United States. British resistance to President Woodrow Wilson's interpretation of freedom of the seas eventually convinced Wilson that only a navy "second to none" could enforce America's neutral rights, and in 1916 Congress authorized the creation of the world's most powerful navy.

Not surprisingly, the British were deeply concerned with this new challenge to Great Britain's naval supremacy, especially as its diplomats failed to persuade Wilson at the Paris Peace Conference to alter his rapid naval buildup.

At first Great Britain attempted to compete in building the most powerful battleships, but the enormous expense coupled with a faltering postwar economy soon prompted it to welcome the invitation of Wilson's successor, President Warren G. Harding, to the first international naval arms-control conference. Nonetheless, while Harding and his Secretary of State Charles Evans Hughes substituted the concept of naval equality with Great Britain for Wilson's naval supremacy, the British had not forgotten that blockade and interdiction had worked well during the War and were therefore determined to preserve these strategies. Thus, at the naval arms-control conferences at Washington in 1921–1922, at Geneva in 1927, and, in the negotiations between President Herbert Hoover and Prime Minister Ramsay MacDonald before the 1930 London Conference, British diplomats cooperated with Admiralty strategists to forestall treaty provisions which would diminish Great Britain's power to impose blockade and interdiction during a future war.

This is the story of the continuation of the Anglo-American clash over freedom of the seas, one which would erupt once again in full fury at the second naval conference in 1927. The Washington Conference had succeeded in limiting capital ships – battleships, battle cruisers and aircraft carriers. But as skillful British diplomacy had stymied limitation on the numbers of auxiliary cruisers, destroyers, and submarines, the second conference, at Geneva, sought to rein in a new naval race in these powerful warships. However, high hopes for the success of the second international effort were dashed by unexpected British demands for cruiser supremacy rather than equality in the very warships best suited for blockade and interdiction. The failure of this conference prompted a bitterly disillusioned President Calvin Coolidge to switch suddenly from being a staunch advocate of naval limitation to a champion of naval supremacy. Indeed, to punctuate his disillusionment, Coolidge canceled plans to meet with Prime Minister Stanley Baldwin and the Duke of York at the 1927 opening of the "Peace Bridge" connecting Canada and the United States and instead successfully pressured Congress to build a cruiser force more powerful than Great Britain's.

This crisis in Anglo-American relations had its immediate origins in the furious reaction among naval leaders in Great Britain, the United States, and Japan to the diminution of naval power forced on them by treaties agreed to at the Washington Conference in 1921–1922. With the lessons of World War I still fresh in their minds, these naval strategists were more convinced than ever that regional naval supremacy in the ocean areas vital to national prosperity and security was being sacrificed by naïve politicians and diplomats engaged in untested, unverifiable, unenforceable, and thus totally unreliable treaties. By 1927, at the advent of the second conference, naval leaders had come to the realization that international arms-control negotiations were inherently risky and that they must therefore become more actively involved in this new experimental diplomacy.

Naval leaders understood as well that they must also become more assertive in shaping domestic naval policy. This is illustrated by the untold story of repeated clashes between Admiral Sir David Beatty, Chief of the Admiralty's Naval Staff, and former First Lord of the Admiralty and now Chancellor of the Exchequer, Winston Churchill. These clashes arose over Beatty's desire to strengthen England's postwar naval forces, most especially in the as yet unrestricted auxiliary cruisers. Alarmed by the capital ship reductions and prevented from replacing these vessels for ten years, Beatty worried over Great Britain's eroding ability to protect its Empire from future Japanese encroachments in East Asia and its equally important ability to enforce blockade and interdiction strategies against a neutral United States during a future war in Europe. Churchill agreed with Beatty on the need for naval supremacy and was enthusiastic about building the newest, most powerful 10,000-ton, 8-inch-gun cruisers. But as Chancellor of the Exchequer, he wanted to avoid asking Parliament for a tax increase to build all twenty-one of these cruisers, requested a one-year delay in beginning their construction, and thereby generated increasingly acrimonious relations with Beatty.

As a former First Lord of the Admiralty during World War I, Churchill believed that military power was based on economic capability, and, as the then current Chancellor of the Exchequer, he argued that by deploying its scarce government resources to stimulate and rebuild a faltering postwar economy, Great Britain could ensure even greater military capability in the near future. He justified this economic priority and the short naval construction delay by the absence of any imminent Japanese naval threat. Beatty's rejection of a one-year delay, however, generated a series of internal Cabinet clashes during which Beatty successfully employed threats of Admiralty resignations and skillful political infighting to achieve Cabinet approval for immediate construction, but of only sixteen rather than the twenty-one cruisers that Churchill had promised to build.

Withholding vital information was an additional means that Beatty unhesitatingly employed against the British Cabinet and against the Americans both before and during the 1927 Geneva Naval Conference. He believed that his evasive tactics were essential to keep secret strong American objections to his proposed capital ship and cruiser construction savings, proposals that were instrumental in persuading a grateful yet unwitting Cabinet to allow the Admiralty to control the negotiations at the second conference. Even more important was the imperative to prevent domestic political critics and rival foreign navies from uncovering the serious combat weaknesses in the expensive new cruisers which he had rushed into production only to discover that baffling deficiencies in the newly designed 8-inch-gun had opened the way for both the Americans and the Japanese to build superior cruisers. The shocking perception of this British naval weakness convinced him that the most effective way to prevent rival naval powers from building superior 8-inch-gun cruisers was to capitalize on the overwhelmingly popular approval for ending the naval arms race in these auxiliary warships by engineering and controlling a second international conference. At this 1927 conference, Beatty surreptitiously planned to safeguard British cruiser supremacy by substituting the less expensive 6-inch-gun for the 8-inch-gun, by outlawing the 8-inch-gun on all future warships, by securing agreement to an unlimited number of smaller British 6-inch-gun cruisers, and by offering additional capital ship and cruiser savings so compelling to American and Japanese politicians that they would override the objections of their naval advisers, just as President Harding and Prime Ministers David Lloyd George and Hara Kei had done during the Washington Naval Conference five years earlier.

The failure of Beatty's poorly planned and executed Admiralty strategy resulted in continuous disputes within the British Cabinet, punctuated by repeated threats of resignation, Churchill's skillful maneuvering, and finally, a diminution of the Admiralty's political influence. More disturbing was the serious diplomatic rift with the United States, a rift highlighted by Coolidge's success in rallying Congress to construct more 10,000-ton, 8-inch-gun cruisers than authorized by Parliament, and the consequent sudden, unexpected escalation of the naval arms race.

Digging deeply into unpublished military documents and the personal papers of these military leaders should encourage historians to evaluate more fully the military strategists who influenced interwar arms-control diplomacy. Published documents seldom reveal the most important underlying military thinking, motives, and objectives at these peace conferences, or the behind-the-scenes manipulations and deceits sometimes employed by negotiators. We need to know the degree to which military strategists at the various arms reduction conferences in the 1920s and 1930s, and perhaps since, used arms-control diplomacy as a new, more subtle, means of warfare – war at the peace table.

I

Clashing World Interests

For a brief time during World War I, the United States, Great Britain, and Japan cooperated as part of the Allied coalition against the Central Powers. This war did more than bring them together on the battlefield. The creation of the League of Nations at the Versailles Peace Conference offered glimmers of hope for future peaceful cooperation. Nonetheless, before it entered the war in 1917 and later at the Versailles Conference, the United States voiced grave concerns over imperial policies pursued by Great Britain and Japan, policies that prompted President Woodrow Wilson to begin construction of a Navy "second to none" and which drove these three allies into a continuous postwar naval arms race. Both during and after the war, each nation sought to ensure that it maintained sufficient naval supremacy in those parts of the world vital to its national and imperial interests. The resulting postwar arms race in turn gave rise to the first international arms-control conference, a novel experiment that sought to mitigate clashing world interests.

***

In the almost six years between May 7, 1915, when a single torpedo from a German submarine sank the Lusitania, and March 4, 1921, when he left office as President of the United States, Woodrow Wilson came to the unalterable conclusion that three great naval powers – Germany, Great Britain, and Japan – had threatened, albeit in different ways and in varying degrees, the current and future vital economic interests of the United States. World War I revealed the stark vulnerability of America's rapidly expanding world trade and convinced Wilson of the need for a navy "second to none," one capable of defending this expanding trade and even, if necessary, of defeating, or at the very least deterring, potential adversaries in both the Atlantic and Pacific oceans simultaneously. By July 16, 1916, a reluctant yet increasingly frightened Congress finally agreed with him. It authorized the building of a navy large enough to safeguard American shipping from submarine attacks, from the naval threat of a possibly victorious, possibly vengeful Germany, from repeated British violations of American neutral and economic rights at sea and its blacklisting of American firms engaged in neutral commerce, and from an aggressive, imperialistic Japan, whose recent occupation of the former German colonies in the central Pacific threatened America's ability to defend the Philippines, while its Twenty-One Demands made a mockery of its promises to honor the Open Door policies in China.

Wilson's naval buildup was a response to the fact that soon after the beginning of World War I both warring ententes either ignored international law governing trade by neutral nations or interpreted it to their own advantage.[1] As a neutral nation, the United States was concerned that Great Britain's evolving definitions of contraband were illegal and its use of naval blockades to enforce increasingly restrictive contraband edicts seriously infringed upon America's right to freedom of trade. German unrestricted submarine warfare was yet another unresolved flashpoint. Adding to the danger was increasing reliance on new war technologies such as the submarine, improved torpedoes, and marine minefields.[2] To allow Great Britain or Germany, or any other power, to restrict or cut off vital trade between the United States and its most valuable trading partners, with the almost certain result of either economic recession or depression, was unacceptable to Wilson.[3]

Violations of American neutrality by Germany and Great Britain were not the only causes for Wilson's frustration. Japan's actions in China and in the Western Pacific were a third worry. Just as the British, in Wilson's judgment, were openly contemptuous of neutrality laws, the Japanese were openly imperialistic. On May 7, 1915, the same day that a German submarine sank the British passenger liner Lusitania, with great loss of life, including 128 Americans, Wilson learned of Japan's Twenty-One Demands on China. Japan had wasted little time in taking advantage of the war. With the European imperialists tied down in a life-and-death struggle, they were in no position to challenge Japan's expansion in East Asia. The Twenty-One Demands violated Japan's repeated promises to the United States to honor America's Open-Door policies emphasizing the principles of equal trade and the political integrity of the Chinese government. Troubling, too, was Japan's military occupation of the German-held Marianas, Marshall, and Caroline Islands. These island groups were strategically important both to the United States and to Japan. They could be fortified with naval and air bases to form an outer perimeter to defend Japan against an attacking navy, but they also

---

[1] Arthur S. Link, *Wilson the Diplomatist: A Look at His Major Foreign Policies* (Baltimore: The Johns Hopkins Press, 1957), pp. 3, 12–23, 35–43; Kenneth J. Hagan, *This People's Navy: The Making of American Sea Power* (New York: The Free Press, 1991), pp. 249–256.

[2] Arthur S. Link, *Wilson: The Struggle for Neutrality 1914–1915*, 5 vols. (Princeton: Princeton University Press, 1947–1965), 3: 308, 589–599, 682–692.

[3] Ibid.

lay athwart the vital sea lanes which could enable Japan to interdict United States' defense of the Philippines.[4]

Wilson thus confronted two implacable imperial powers. Japan was as determined to expand its empire in East Asia as Great Britain was to improve the efficiency of its blockade of the Central Powers in Europe. Both of these nations viewed these strategies as matters of life and death. Like England, Japan was an island nation, and like England, she was convinced that safeguarding or expanding her empire guaranteed essential food, raw materials, world markets, and prosperity.[5]

Reluctantly recognizing the potential new threats from Japan in the Western Pacific as well as from Germany and England in the Atlantic, the United States Congress passed the 1916 Naval Act authorizing 156 new ships, including sixteen capital ships, generally understood to include battleships, battle cruisers, and aircraft carriers. This legislation not only vastly expanded the American navy but authorized the building of badly needed naval bases along the Pacific Coast and at Pearl Harbor, from which the navy could better defend the Philippines and its lesser vestiges of empire.[6] To reiterate the importance of

---

[4] Link, *The Struggle for Neutrality 1914–1915*, 3: 208–210, 270–272, 284–285, 306–308; Outten Jones Clinard, *Japan's Influence Upon American Naval Power, 1897–1917* (Berkeley and Los Angeles: University of California Press, 1947), pp. 131–135; John Chambers Vinson, *The Parchment Peace* (Athens: University of Georgia Press, 1955), pp. 22, 26–27; Akira Iriye, *Across the Pacific: An Inner History of American–East Asian Relations* (New York and London: Harcourt Brace Jovanovich, Harvest Book, 1967), pp. 132–135; Harold Sprout and Margaret Sprout, *Toward a New Order of Sea-Power: American Naval Policy and the World Scene, 1918–1922* (Princeton: Princeton University Press, 1946), pp. 19–20, 28–30, 35–36, 88–93. Hereafter cited as Sprout, *New Order*.

[5] Tatsuji Takeuchi, *War and Diplomacy in the Japanese Empire* (Garden City, NY: Doubleday, Doran, 1935), pp. 91–182; Clinard, *Japan's Influence*, pp. 10–13, 33, 35, 41, 44, 47, 49–51, 58–65, 76, 88–90, 107, 113–118, 127–128, 146–157, 166–167; Iriye, *Across the Pacific*, pp. 24, 64–68, 86, 97–108, 115, 120–127, 132; Rolland A. Chaput, *Disarmament and British Foreign Policy* (London: George Allen and Unwin, 1935), pp. 99–102; Sprout, *Toward a New Order*, pp. 19–20, 28–30, 64, 70–72, 90–93; Akira Iriye, *Power and Culture: The Japanese-American War, 1941–1945* (Cambridge: Harvard University Press, 1981), pp. 63–64; Akira Iriye, "Japan's Policies toward the United States" in James William Morley, *Japan's Foreign Policy: 1868–1941* (New York: Columbia University Press, 1974), pp. 414–416, 420–429, 444; Thomas H. Buckley, *The United States and the Washington Conference, 1921–1922* (Knoxville: University of Tennessee Press, 1970), p. 149; Stephen Howarth, *The Fighting Ships of the Rising Sun: The Drama of the Imperial Japanese Navy, 1895–1945* (New York: Athenaeum Press, 1983), pp. 125–130; Richard Burns and Donald Urquidi, *Disarmament in Perspective: An Analysis of Selected Arms Control and Disarmament Agreements Between the Wars, 1919–1939* (Los Angeles: California State College at Los Angeles Foundation, 1968), p. 42; Hector C. Bywater, *Sea-Power in the Pacific: A Study of the American-Japanese Problem* (Boston: Houghton Mifflin, 1921), pp. 88–91; Hector C. Bywater, *Navies and Nations: A Review of Naval Developments since the Great War* (Boston and New York: Houghton Mifflin, 1927), pp. 7–8.

[6] Link, *Wilson: Confusion and Crisis 1915–1916* (Princeton: Princeton University Press, 1964) 4: 337; George T. Davis, *Navy Second to None: The Development of Modern American Naval Policy* (New York: Harcourt, Brace, 1940), pp. 215–222, 236–237, 254; Roger Dingman, *Power*

protecting neutral trade during war, Wilson highlighted freedom of the seas as the first of his famous Fourteen Points that he hoped would influence peace negotiations. After joining the Allies in 1917, he dramatized the importance of freedom of the seas once again in December 1918, only three weeks after the war ended, by convincing Congress to pass his 1918 naval bill calling for the completion of the 1916 Naval Act, which doubled the number of capital ships to forty-four battleships and sixteen battle cruisers, for a total of over eight hundred combat ships of modern postwar design.[7] Any nation which sought to equal this new American navy would have to spend billions of dollars for an indefinite length of time to do so.

Wilson's challenge to British naval supremacy in the Atlantic and Japanese naval supremacy in the Western Pacific aroused considerable resentment. Fresh memories of the crucial success of the naval superiority which prevented the German fleet from interdicting Great Britain's vulnerable supply lines prompted Britain's Prime Minister, David Lloyd George, to vow to spend England's "last guinea to keep a navy superior to that of the United States or any other power."[8] Winston Churchill, the former First Lord of the Admiralty, reiterated this determination, proclaiming "nothing in the world, nothing that you might think, or dream of, or anyone may tell you; no arguments however specious, no appeals, however seductive, must lead you to abandon that naval supremacy by which the life of our country depends."[9] Nonetheless, with its economy devastated by the war and deeply in debt to the United States, Great Britain could ill-afford to continue what had evolved into a postwar naval race against

---

in the Pacific: The Origins of Naval Arms Limitation 1914–1922 (Chicago and London: University of Chicago Press, 1976), pp. 34, 36; Clinard, *Japan's Influence*, pp. 163–164; Woodrow Wilson, *The Papers of Woodrow Wilson, August 7–November 19, 1916*, ed. Arthur S. Link (Princeton: Princeton University Press, 1982) 38:205; David F. Trask, "Woodrow Wilson and the Reconciliation of Force and Diplomacy: 1917–1918," *Naval War College Review* 27 (1975): 25, 28, 31; Paul Kennedy, *The Rise and Fall of the Great Powers* (New York: Random House, Vintage Books, 1989), pp. 246–258, 270–272; Bywater, *Sea-Power*, p. 74; Hagan, *This People's Navy*, pp. 209, 254–256; Lloyd E. Ambrosius, *Woodrow Wilson and the American Diplomatic Tradition: The League Fight in Perspective* (Cambridge: Cambridge University Press, 1987), pp. 52, 115–116; Ian H. Nish, ed. *Anglo-Japanese Alienation 1919–1952: Papers of the Anglo-Japanese Conference on the History of the Second World War* (Cambridge: Cambridge University Press, 1982), pp. 3–5, 29; Thomas H. Buckley, *The United States and the Washington Conference*, pp. 146–147; Howarth, *Fighting Ships*, pp. 131–133; Thomas J. Knock, *To End All Wars: Woodrow Wilson and the Quest for a New World Order* (New York: Oxford University Press, 1992), pp. 155–156.

[7] Sprout, *New Order*, p. 55; Arthur Walworth, *Wilson and the Peacemakers: American Diplomacy at the Paris Peace Conference, 1919* (New York: W.W. Norton, 1986), p. 303; Christopher Hall, *Britain, America, and Arms Control, 1921–1937* (New York: St. Martin's, 1987), pp. 11–12; Ambrosius, *Wilson*, p. 52; Dingman, *Power in the Pacific*, pp. 87–88; Davis, *Navy Second to None*, pp. 241–242; Sprout, *New Order*, pp. 106, 65–66, 53–55, 58; Bywater, *Navies and Nations*, pp. 104–105.

[8] Quoted in Sprout, *New Order*, p. 62.

[9] Quoted in Burns and Urguidi, *Disarmament*, p. 7.

the prosperous United States.[10] Neither could Japan. From 1917 to 1921, Japan had tripled its naval budget. Indeed, postwar maintenance costs alone would soon claim almost one third of the nation's annual budget, prompting the Vice Minister for Finance to warn that the nation's financial position was fast becoming "hopeless," and that unless quick action was taken to cut expenses, Japan would be financially "ruined."[11]

Wilson's naval strategy soon ended in frustration. Unable to win Senate approval of the Versailles Peace Treaty, he embarked on an extensive speaking tour to generate public pressure on the Senate, but suffered a severe stroke that incapacitated him throughout the remainder of his term in office. Without Wilson at the helm, Congressional support for his "navy second to none" eroded.[12] Peace societies, church groups, women's organizations, business leaders, and journalists soon echoed a growing popular slogan that big navies meant big wars, and no warships meant no wars. In addition to reducing the fear that the current postwar naval arms race among the former allies could lead to still another world war, naval reductions, they hoped, meant lower taxes and a faster recovery from the brief but sharp economic maladies engulfing the American economy in 1921–1922. When Wilson left office in 1921, the United States had completed or authorized more new warships than all other nations combined, but soon after his departure, the American voters and their political leaders all too quickly ignored the reasons for his "navy second to none."[13]

---

[10] Paul M. Kennedy, *Rise and Fall of British Naval Mastery* (New York: Charles Scribner's Sons, 1976), pp. 259–261; Kennedy, *Rise and Fall of the Great Powers*, pp. 151–158 and preface.

[11] Asada, "Japanese Admirals," pp. 145–147; Davis, *Navy Second to None*, pp. 246, 252; Dingman, *Power in the Pacific*, pp. 122–123, 174–187; Buckley, *The United States in the Washington Conference*, p. 59; Emily O. Goldman, *Sunken Treaties: Naval Arms Control Between the Wars* (University Park: Pennsylvania State University Press, 1994), pp. 53, 65; James B. Crowley, *Japan's Quest for Autonomy: National Security and Foreign Policy, 1930–1938* (Princeton: Princeton University Press, 1966), p. 30; Takeuchi, *War and Diplomacy*, pp. 227, 229–230; Frank H. Schofield, "Incidents and Present Day Aspects of Naval Strategy," *Proceedings of the United States Naval Institute*, (May 1923), pp. 780–781; Robert A. Hoover, *Arms Control: The Interwar Naval Limitation Agreements* (Denver: University of Denver, 1980), pp. 12–13; James B. Crowley, "Japan's Military Foreign Policies" in *Japan's Foreign Policy 1868–1941*, ed. James Williams Morley (New York: Columbia University Press, 1974), pp. 23–24, 37–38; Gerald E. Wheeler, "The United States Navy and the Japanese Enemy, 1919–1931," *Military Affairs* 21 (Summer 1957): p. 67; Raymond L. Buell, *The Washington Conference* (New York: D. Appleton, 1922), pp. 138–139. Naval figures vary in these sources.

[12] Dingman, *Power in the Pacific*, pp. 91–92, 103–104, 155; Davis *Navy Second to None*, pp. 239–241, 266, 271–272; Vinson, *Parchment Peace*, pp. 62–68; Sprout, *New Order*, p. 119.

[13] Cora Rubin to Roy Baker Harris, "History of Disarmament Resolution," May 13, 1933, BOR, LC; *New York Times*, January 23, 1921; Robert G. Kaufman, *Arms Control During the Pre-Nuclear Era: The United States and Naval Limitation Between the Two Wars* (New York: Columbia University Press, 1990), pp. 23–32; Vinson, *Parchment Peace*, pp. 43, 45–46, 53, 56–57, 62–68, 83; Sprout, *New Order*, pp. 104–105, 111–115, 118, 120–121; Dingman, *Power in the Pacific*, pp. 90–94, 103 143–144; Joan Hoff Wilson, *American Business and Foreign*

Warren G. Harding, the handsome party peacemaker and orator who led the Republican Party back to the White House in 1921, began dismantling Wilson's navy. While he had promised during the 1920 presidential campaign to continue building Wilson's navy, he had also promised to cut taxes and retire the national debt. He soon discovered, however, that he could not continue to build a "navy second to none" while simultaneously lowering taxes and liquidating the national debt. To cut naval construction costs, he therefore invited the world's leading military powers to meet in Washington, DC for an international naval arms-reduction conference.

Unlike Wilson, whose wartime leadership had taught him the intimate interrelationship between military power and successful international diplomacy, neither Harding nor his Secretary of State Charles Evans Hughes would allow complex postwar diplomatic problems to trump domestic political priorities. Indeed, domestic political priorities dominated their thinking about arms control. They sought to garner both political and diplomatic success by achieving agreement to a new international naval balance of power, one which they believed would promote peace and enable the Republican Party to fulfill Harding's campaign promises to cut taxes and retire the national debt. With widespread American support for these objectives, arms reduction appeared to be smart politics and therefore smart diplomacy.[14]

While President Warren G. Harding and Secretary of State Charles Evans Hughes turned away from diplomatic realism based on military strength to a diplomacy which relied on treaties, a significant shift which was much more congenial to domestic Republican politics and priorities, British and Japanese leaders continued to respect the crucial relationship between military power and imperial objectives. Fortuitously, the new American proposals, emphasizing drastic cuts in naval construction and limitations on warship numbers, were given considerable momentum by the economic weaknesses within Great

---

Policy (Lexington: University of Kentucky Press, 1971), pp. 35, 39–40; Sprout, *New Order*, pp. 111, 120–121; Davis, *Navy Second to None*, pp. 268–269.

[14] Melvyn P. Leffler, *Elusive Quest: America's Pursuit of European Stability and French Security, 1915–1933* (Chapel Hill: University of North Carolina Press, 1979), pp. 9–15; 416–419; Merlo J. Pusey, *Charles Evans Hughes*, 2 vols. (New York: Columbia University Press, 1963), 1: 269, 181–269, 315–366; Dexter Perkins, *Charles Evans Hughes and American Democratic Leadership* (Boston: Little, Brown, 1956), pp. 3–28, 50–70; Randolph C. Downes, *The Rise of Warren Gamaliel Harding, 1865–1920* (Columbus: Ohio State University Press, 1970), pp. 140–141 272–275, 395, 562–598; Vinson, *Parchment Peace*, pp. 33–34, 69, 87, 97–98; Sprout, *New Order*, pp. 84–85, 121–124, 288–289; Robert K. Murray, *The Harding Era: Warren G. Harding and His Administration* (Minneapolis: University of Minnesota Press, 1969), p. 143; Robert James Maddox, *William E. Borah and American Foreign Policy* (Baton Rouge, Louisiana: Louisiana State University Press, 1969), pp. 90–92; Perkins, *Charles Evans Hughes*, pp. 27, 50–70; Pusey, *Hughes*, 1:174–217, 269, 323–349; Betty Glad, *Charles Evans Hughes and the Illusion of Innocence: A Study of American Diplomacy* (Urbana and London: University of Illinois Press, 1966), pp. 303, 324–327, 268, 280; Dingman, *Power in the Pacific*, pp. 148, 157–161.

Britain and Japan. While neither of these two naval powers had altered their fundamental understanding about the crucial importance of naval strength to their empires, neither of them was in an economic position to compete against continued United States naval construction. Both, therefore, intended to enhance their own imperial strategies and national security by using this novel experiment in arms control to retard America's emerging naval power. To this end, well before they arrived in Washington, DC, in 1921, each had already worked out carefully devised conference objectives.

The forthcoming conference posed the greatest challenge to Japan, whose domestic politics were destabilized by the Meiji Constitution's severe limitation on civilian control over the cabinet. Under this constitution, the leaders of the army and navy appointed their respective cabinet ministers, who were not subordinate to the civilian control of the elected prime minister and could therefore precipitate a political crisis merely by resigning, thereby forcing new elections. Every prime minister wishing to retain power was required to take requests for military appropriations much more seriously than political leaders in either the United States or Great Britain.[15] Thus Prime Minister Hara Kei had little choice but to rely on his brilliant Naval Minister Admiral Baron Kato Tomosaburo, a modest, quiet, yet highly respected leader known as a "cool, quick thinker." Tomosaburo agreed with many of his highly skeptical fellow naval officers that the United States was the most likely future threat to Japan, yet he also recognized that Japan could not win the current naval arms race against the United States and therefore tried to convince his fellow naval officers that Japan must use diplomatic means to maintain its dominance in East Asian waters.[16]

---

[15] Marius B. Jansen, *The Making of Modern Japan* (Cambridge: Harvard University Press, 2000), pp. 502, 451–452, 459, 590–600; Tatsuji Takeuchi, *War and Diplomacy*, pp. 28–29; Sadao Asada, "Japanese Admirals and the Politics of Naval Limitation: Kato Tomosaburo vs. Kato Kanji" in *Naval Warfare in the Twentieth Century, 1900–1945: Essays in Honor of Arthur Marder*, ed. Gerald Jordan (London and New York: Crane, Russak, 1977), pp. 143–145; R. P. G. Steven, "Hybrid Constitutionalism in Prewar Japan," *Journal of Japanese Studies* 3 (Winter 1977): 119, 129; Yale Candee Maxon, *Control of Japanese Foreign Policy: A Study of Civil-Military Rivalry, 1930–1945* (Berkeley: University of California Press, 1957), 72–73; Roger Dingman, *Power and the Pacific*, pp. 8–14, 49; Peter Duus, *Party Rivalry and Political Change in Taisho Japan* (Cambridge: Harvard University Press, 1968), pp. 135–142.

[16] Asada, "Japanese Admirals," pp. 142–145; Eric Lacroix, "The Development of the 'A Class' Cruisers in the Imperial Japanese Navy," Parts 1–7, *Warship International*, 1: 340, 337; Stephen Howard, *The Fighting Ships of the Rising Sun: The Drama of the Imperial Japanese Navy, 1895–1945* (New York: Athenaeum Press, 1983), p. 140; Dingman, *Power in the Pacific*, pp. 49, 51–52, 63, 180, 122; George T. Davis, *A Navy Second to None*, p. 252; William F. Trimble, "The United States Navy and the Geneva Conference for the Limitation of Armament, 1927," (Ph.D. diss., University of Colorado, 1974), p. 19; Walter LeFeber, *The Clash: U.S.-Japanese Relations throughout History* (New York: W. W. Norton, 1997), p. 138; Attaché Report, "Limitation of Armament-Japanese," October 19, 1921, Naval File, Q. Y., London and Other Conferences, Box 574, RG 45, NA.

British Prime Minister David Lloyd George also faced domestic political hazards in attempting to cut naval construction costs, primarily because the British Admiralty wielded a considerable amount of influence among powerful Conservative Party members, who generally equated naval supremacy with British security, prosperity, Empire, and world prestige. Nonetheless, chronic unemployment, declining exports, huge war debts, increasingly popular demands for government social services, especially for pensions, health, and education, convinced Great Britain's political leaders of the necessity to begin steadily slashing naval allocations. Not surprisingly, this cost cutting was met by a vigorous Admiralty counterattack.[17]

The Admiralty's campaign was conducted by the new First Sea Lord, the handsome, aristocratic war hero, Admiral of the Fleet, Sir David Beatty. Beatty's rise to the top had been meteoric. As a young commander of a British gunboat on the Nile River during the Battle of Omdurman in 1898, he had earned the Distinguished Service Order, promotion over 400 senior officers and, more importantly perhaps, the lasting admiration and friendship of Winston Churchill, one of the Army officers of the 21st Lancers who was delighted by Beatty's courage and leadership in maneuvering his gunboat at great risk to support Churchill's Lancers in their desperate battle against the Dervishes. Less than two years later, in 1900 during the Boxer Rebellion, Beatty again distinguished himself in battle and was again promoted, this time over 219 senior officers to become the youngest captain in the Royal Navy since Lord Nelson.[18]

Beatty's good fortune continued when Winston Churchill became First Lord of the Admiralty. In 1911 Churchill reinvigorated Beatty's career by appointing him as his Naval Secretary and later elevating him to commander of the prestigious Battles Cruiser Squadron. During World War I, Beatty led his

---

[17] Dingman, *Power in the Pacific*, pp. 18–31, 108, 93, 107–110, 117, 161–163; Hector C. Bywater, *Navies and Nations*, pp. 21, 24, 41, 117; Roberta Allbert Dayer, "The British Debts to the United States and the Anglo-Japanese Alliance, 1920–1923," *Pacific Historical Review* 45 (November 1976): 569; Kennedy, *British Naval Mastery*, pp. 267–274. Naval figures vary in different sources. See also Davis, *Navy Second to None*, p. 273; Chaput, *Disarmament*, p. 79; Arthur J. Marder, "The Influence of History on Sea Power: The Royal Navy and the Lessons of 1914–1918" *Pacific Historical Review* 41(November 1972): 419, 437–438; John Robert Ferris, *The Evolution of British Strategic Policy, 1919–1926* (London: Macmillan, 1989), pp. 11–13; First Sea Lord to Sir Maurice Hankey, "Memorandum by the Admiralty on Naval Aspects of a League of Nations and Limitation of Armament" December 23, 1918, ADM 116/1772/5092; Admiralty Staff Memorandum, "Freedom of the Seas," n. d. ADM 116/1772, PRO; W. H. L. [Walter H. Long], "Memorandum to the Cabinet by the First Sea Lord," 23 July 1920, Naval Building File, 1923–1925, ROSK 7/49, CCP.

[18] Winston S. Churchill, *My Early Years: A Roving Commission* (London: The Reprint Society, 1944), pp. 192, 206–208; Walter Scott Chalmers, *The Life and Letters of David, Earl Beatty* (London: Hodder and Stoughton, 1951), pp. 20–22, 26–27, 36–37, 43; Stephen W. Roskill, *Earl Beatty: The Last Naval Hero: An Intimate Biography* (New York: Atheneum Press, 1981), pp. 28, 30; Chalmers, *Beatty*, pp. xiv–xxv, 1, 20–85, 104; Roskill, *Beatty*, pp. 28–38, 51–52; Stephen W. Roskill, *Churchill and the Admirals* (New York: William Morrow, 1978), pp. 75–76.

cruisers into the battle of Heligoland Bight and the Battle of Jutland, emerging as Admiral of the Fleet Sir David Beatty, one of the navy's most popular war heroes.[19] David Lloyd George thereupon appointed him as First Sea Lord, a promotion which would make Beatty the Chief of the Naval Staff and the principal spokesman for the Admiralty's budget before the Cabinet and the Committee of Imperial Defence.[20]

Political advocacy was Beatty's strongest asset. His close association with politics and politicians while serving as Churchill's Naval Secretary had given him keen insights into the political vulnerabilities and fears of members of Parliament. He therefore regarded his own judgment on naval matters to be at least equal, if not superior, to those of politicians. Beatty's distinguished good looks, aristocratic demeanor, independent wealth, abundant self-confidence, and oratorical ability served him well in presenting himself before the cost-cutting cabinet ministers as the authentic naval war hero who constantly reminded them of the Navy's recent role in guaranteeing the security and integrity of the Empire.[21]

Despite Beatty's forceful advocacy, the Cabinet continued reducing naval expenditures. In August, 1919, it adopted the "Ten Year Rule" requiring an

---

[19] Lord Ernle Chatfield, *The Navy and Defense* (London: William Heinemann, 1942), p. 100. For Beatty's difficulties with his marriage, see Roskill, *Beatty*, pp. 202–203, 366–367; Beatty to Eugenie Godfrey Faussett, April 5, 1925, 12 July 1927, 15/6/2 and 15/6/12, SLGF, CCP. This source contains numerous letters concerning Beatty's lovers and a draft biography by Sir Shane Leslie, who was a close friend of Beatty's. For a more critical view of Beatty, see Robert K. Massie, *Castles of Steel: Britain, Germany and the Winning of the Great War at Sea* (New York: Random House, 2003), pp. 95, 675–676, 749–751; Roskill, *Beatty*, pp. 51–52, 58, 288, 335. See also Churchill to Beatty, November 11, 1924, BTY 14/4, DBP; Chatfield, *Navy and Defense*, p. 98; Beatty to My Dear Wife, July 6, 1925, BTY 17/7/21–23, BP; Roskill, *Beatty*, pp. 58, 288, 335; Chalmers, *Beatty*, pp. 107–110, 116, 124, 133, 356, 364; Chatfield, *Navy and Defense*, pp. 129–137, 140–152; Sir Shane Leslie, "Memories of Beatty," *Quarterly Review* 290 (July 1952): 456. For highly critical assessments of Beatty's leadership at the Battle of Jutland and his later efforts to alter the historical record, see especially, Roskill, *Beatty*, pp. 323–339, 187; Leslie, "Memories of Beatty," p. 458; B. Mc L. Ranft, *The Beatty Papers: Selections from the Private and Official Correspondence of Admiral of the Fleet Earl Beatty, 1902–1927*, 2 vols. (Aldershot, England: Gower, 1989) 1: 417–422; Malcolm H. Murfett, *The First Sea Lords: From Fisher to Mountbatten* (Westport, CT and London: Praeger, 1995), pp. 138–139; Massie, *Castles of Steel*, pp. 672–682.

[20] Churchill to Lloyd George, May 1, 1919, in Ranft, *Beatty*, 2: 35–36; Chalmers, *Beatty*, p. 356.

[21] Dingman, *Power in the Pacific*, p. 111; J. C. C. Davidson, *Memoirs of a Conservative*, ed. R. R. James (London: Weedenfeld and Nicolson, 1969), p. 208; Leslie, "Memories," p. 459; Murfett, *First Sea Lords*, pp. 8, 128, 378; Roskill, *Beatty*, pp. 24, 75–76, 88, 295–296, 350, 359, 371–374. Quoted in Chalmers, *Life and Letters*, pp. 396, 370, 420; Buckley, *United States and Washington Conference*, p. 25; Hankey to Beatty, April 30, 1927, BTY 14/7/5 in Roger Keyes, *The Keyes Papers: Selections from the Private and Official Correspondence of Admiral of the Fleet Baron Keyes of Zeebrugge*, ed. Paul G. Halpern, 2 vols. (London: George Allen and Unwin, 1980) 2: 214; Ranft, *Beatty Papers*, p. 70; Murfett, *First Sea Lords*, p. 139; Chalmers, *Life and Letters*, pp. 363–364, 397; Dingman, *Power in the Pacific*, pp. 111, 113; R. C. Richardson, *The Evolution of British Disarmament Policy in the 1920s* (London: Leicester University Press, 1989), p. 26.

assessment of whether England was likely to engage in any major war during the next ten years. This new rule greatly strengthened the Treasury's ability to argue against Admiralty budget demands based on theoretical future threats. The Cabinet also substituted the one-power standard for the previous two-power standard. Instead of a navy 10 percent stronger than Europe's two most powerful navies, the one-power standard only required equality with the world's most powerful navy.[22]

Recognizing that the political tide was running against them, the Admiralty reluctantly agreed to preparations for the first international arms control conference. Nonetheless, the Admiralty hedged its cooperation with boldly articulated restrictions and caveats. Fundamental to its position was its vehement opposition to the Cabinet's willingness to accept the principle of naval equality with the United States. During any future conference, the Admiralty insisted, "No opportunity should be lost in maintaining the incontrovertible fact that the naval needs of the British Empire, extending to every ocean, are infinitely greater than those of any other nation, and that although the Government has accepted the position of equality of naval strength with the United States, this is a concession to which their naval needs do not really entitle them." This was an important strategic concept that the Admiralty would maintain for many years. As Great Britain was by right entitled to a larger navy than any other power, the Admiralty emphatically insisted that the "main object" of any international arms control conference was merely "to reduce the expenditure ... on armaments" rather than to achieve either equality or limitations on the ability or the methods of making war – a position which the Admiralty would maintain in 1927 at the second naval arms-control conference in Geneva. Having articulated these two fundamental principles, the Admiralty outlined a limitation strategy that the Committee of Imperial Defence fully endorsed.[23]

The Admiralty strategy at the 1921–1922 Washington Naval Conference was, in fact, carefully crafted to retain British naval superiority and to shift any blame for failure on to other powers. It was especially intent upon avoiding any agreement to "freedom of the seas," but also intent upon placing limits on the type and number of capital ships that the United States would be allowed to build. It sought as well to secure new naval bases at Hong Kong and Singapore, which would limit the ability of the Japanese to interfere with British possessions in East Asia.[24]

---

[22] Roskill, *Naval Policy*, p. 215; Chaput, *Disarmament*, pp. 94–96; Ranft, *Beatty*, II: 75–76.
[23] "Memorandum by the Naval Staff," October 5, 1921, The Washington Conference, CID 277-B, ADM 116/3445, PRO; Committee of Imperial Defence, "Memorandum by the Standing Subcommittee, The Washington Conference on Limitation of Armaments," October 24, 1921, CID 280-B, ADM 116/3445, PRO.
[24] Ira Klein, "Whitehall, Washington, and the Anglo-Japanese Alliance, 1919–1921," *Pacific Historical Review* 41 (November 1972): 460–461, 482–483; Buckley, *United States and Washington Conference*, pp. 26–33, 60–62.

Clashing World Interests

The leaders of Great Britain and Japan agreed to accept Harding's invitation to engage in naval arms-limitation talks primarily because postwar economic imperatives and the vast new navy under construction by the United States generated political and military pressures that they could no longer avoid. In sharp contrast to their American counterparts, the political leaders and naval delegates from these two island nations understood that their navies were vital to the security and prosperity of their homelands and empires, and they were therefore able to achieve a significant degree of consensus on strategic naval negotiating objectives. Both Great Britain and Japan sent delegations to Washington, DC, to defend clearly defined supremacies which they refused to relinquish. Despite their economic woes and consequent naval vulnerabilities, the delegates from these two island empires arrived in Washington determined to make this new diplomacy of naval arms limitation a means to preserve, and, if possible, to enhance, rather than diminish, their relative naval strengths.

2

The Washington Conference Legacy

As the Washington Conference of 1921–1922 has been analyzed in great detail by reputable scholars, this chapter will concentrate on those British and American strategies and tactics which would influence the later 1927 Conference and which earlier scholars understandably either overlooked or were unable to give sufficient attention. One focus will center on the great contrasts between the pre-conference objectives of the Americans and the British. Another will examine the success with which the British skillfully maneuvered to avoid extending limits to their auxiliary class cruisers, destroyers, and submarines by conveying the misleading impression that their cruiser needs were within the range of the 450,000 tons proposed by the United States. The British also purposely omitted important improvements in battleship capabilities. In terms of the objectives sought, the diplomatic strategies employed, and the results obtained, the British were highly successful. Ironically, however, their success at the Washington Conference led First Sea Lord David Beatty to conclude that he had learned valuable diplomatic lessons on how to control and manipulate future arms control negotiations–lessons which would deepen the American sense of deception and betrayal at the 1927 Geneva Conference.

* * *

Rather than a critical analysis of existing diplomatic and military realities, Secretary of State Charles Evans Hughes's keen insight into the imperatives of domestic Republican politics was the determining factor which shaped his diplomacy. The creation of international cooperation and order, he supposed, was not unlike the creation of domestic political cooperation. Like domestic politics, Hughes believed diplomacy relied primarily on the negotiators' skillful use of adjustment, mediation, compromise, and conciliation. Earlier, President Woodrow Wilson had also begun with similar naive ideas, but the war had quickly taught him that keen assessment of military power was indispensable to successful diplomacy. Nonetheless, because Hughes understood domestic political power far better than he did the relevance of military capabilities and forward-looking strategic thinking as instruments of diplomatic success, domestic political realities and relationships became central to his thinking about American foreign policy.[1]

With Hughes' domestically oriented diplomatic approach still unknown to them, and President Warren G. Harding repeating his public insistence on building a strong navy, the General Board of the United States Navy – an advisory group of senior officers who met with the Secretary of the Navy to formulate naval policy and determine the types and characteristics of new ships – assumed that Harding, like Wilson before him, still believed as they did–that World War I had conclusively demonstrated to the United States that its vital and expanding overseas trade and possessions, and its Open Door diplomacy in China, required a navy capable of challenging both Great Britain in the Atlantic and Japan in the Pacific simultaneously. This assumption, they believed, mandated not only the building of all of the ships in the 1916 naval construction plan, but additional ones, including seven aircraft carriers, and the creation of important modern naval bases along the West Coast of the United States as well as in Hawaii, the Philippines, and Guam. These bases were crucial to enable the fleet to re-supply and to repair ships which would otherwise be required to return thousands of miles back to the United States. Naval bases had become more important because the Japanese had occupied the Marshall, the Caroline, and the Marianas island groups, which the Japanese could use during wartime to block American efforts to protect the Philippine Islands, interdict trade with China and East Asia, and thereby lessen the effectiveness of American diplomacy in East Asia.[2]

The General Board's assumptions were not politically popular. Exactly how unpopular became clear in May 1921 when President Harding and Secretary of State Hughes, with the support of congressional leaders, jettisoned the Board's

---

[1] Betty Glad, *Charles Evans Hughes and the Illusion of Innocence: A Study in American Diplomacy* (Urbana and London: University of Illinois Press, 1966), pp. 268, 280, 303, 324–327; Merlo J. Pusey, *Charles Evans Hughes*, 2 vols. (New York: Columbia University Press, 1966): 2: 455; John Chambers Vinson, *The Parchment Peace* (Athens: University of Georgia Press, 1955), pp.1, 129, 115; Dexter Perkins, *Charles Evans Hughes and American Democratic Leadership* (Boston: Little, Brown, 1956), pp. 83–86; Robert A. Hoover, *Arms Control: The Interwar Naval Limitation Agreements* (Denver: University of Colorado Press, 1980), p. 23; Raymond O'Connor, *Perilous Equilibrium: The United States and the London Naval Conference of 1930* (Westport, CT: Greenwood, 1969) pp. 9, 13.

[2] Harold and Margaret Sprout, *Toward a New Order of Sea Power: American Naval Policy and the World Scene, 1918–1922* (Princeton: Princeton University Press, 1946), pp. 145, 176. Hereafter cited as Sprout, *New Order*. See also Roger Dingman, *Power in the Pacific: The Origin of Naval Arms Limitation, 1914–1922* (Chicago and London: University of Chicago Press, 1976), pp. 95, 100, 156; Ernest Andrade, Jr., "The United States Navy and the Washington Conference," *The Historian* 31(May, 1969): 346–352; Emily O. Goldman, *Sunken Treaties: Naval Arms Control Between the Wars* (University Park: Pennsylvania State University Press, 1994), p. 53.

advice. Faced with the politically impossible dilemma of mutually exclusive promises – a "navy second to none" and drastically reducing taxes – Harding, Hughes, Secretary of the Navy Edwin Denby, Assistant Secretary of the Navy Theodore Roosevelt, Jr., and influential Republican leaders such as Senator Henry Cabot Lodge, chair of the Senate Foreign Relations Committee, and Elihu Root, the respected Republican Party's elder statesman, decided to adopt a set of domestic political assumptions to govern American foreign policy. They concurred in the easier, unproven, yet crucial assumption that Congress would never appropriate the great sums needed to complete the 1916 naval building program, build new naval bases in the Pacific, and maintain the world's most powerful navy. They agreed with Idaho Republican Senator William E. Borah's repeated public pronouncements that the surest way to cut taxes, eliminate the national debt, end the international naval arms race, reduce international tensions, and safeguard Republican harmony and political ascendancy was to abandon Wilson's navy second-to-none in favor of arms limitation.[3]

The General Board resisted these political assumptions. They rejected the claim that war between the United States and Great Britain was "unthinkable." "History consistently shows," the Board insisted, "that war between no two peoples or nations can be termed 'unthinkable.' Who, in 1830, foresaw four years of war between the North and the South? Blood relationship counted for little."[4] Nonetheless, on July 27, 1921, when Secretary of the Navy Denby, who was dominated by Hughes, ordered them to make reductions, the General Board had no choice but to begin the arduous task of crafting a new series of recommendations.

For negotiating purposes at an international naval arms control conference, the Board recommended retaining capital ships equal to the number in the British Navy, but because of the lack of naval bases and the great distances in the Pacific, a two-to-one superiority over Japan. This would require the completion of the 157 ships of the 1916 program with its 9 battleships and 6 battle cruisers still in the building stage.[5] As a result of the stalemate between Great Britain and Germany at the Battle of Jutland in 1916, naval strategists generally agreed that an attacking force needed at least a 40 percent superiority to be victorious. The General Board therefore required equality in capital ships between the United States and Great Britain with half that number allocated to Japan, or a ratio of 10:10:5 in capital ships. In auxiliary cruisers, destroyers,

---

[3] Dingman, *Power in the Pacific*, pp. 100, 156–157, 159; Pusey, *Hughes*, 2: 455, 459–460; Thomas H. Buckley, *The United States and the Washington Conference, 1921–1922* (Knoxville: University of Tennessee Press, 1970), p. 203. Hereafter cited as Buckley, *Washington Conference*.

[4] General Board to Secretary of the Navy, July 15, 1921, Subject File GB 420, Box 61, GBUSN, RG 80, NA.

[5] Andrade, "United States Navy," pp. 346–349; Dingman, *Power in the Pacific*, p. 100; Buckley, *Washington Conference*, pp. 50–52, 203; Hector C. Bywater, *Navies and Nations: A Review of Naval Developments Since the Great War* (Boston and New York: Houghton Mifflin, 1927), p. 150.

and submarines – which protected the battle fleet – the General Board recommended a 10:6 ratio against Japan, thereby providing the 40 percent superiority against its most likely future enemy.[6]

While he accepted the idea of combat equivalency ratios, Secretary of State Hughes rejected most of the General Board's recommendations on ship numbers because they were based on combat criteria, rather than on tax-saving reductions. He insisted that negotiations at the forthcoming Washington Conference must be based on the principle of "stop now." Naval ratios, therefore, would be determined on the basis of ships already afloat rather than on those currently being built or authorized to be built. In effect, Hughes decided to scrap the fifteen American capital ships already under construction, on which the General Board was relying to discourage future Japanese aggression in the Pacific and British blockade in the Atlantic. This drastic scrapping of American capital ships was essential, Hughes insisted, in order to convince the other naval powers of the seriousness of the American proposals.[7]

Despite the fact that the new American battleships were superior in armor protection and firepower to the best British warships, the General Board realized that Great Britain would still retain its naval superiority in other types of warships, the location and number of naval bases, shipbuilding capacity, the size of its merchant marine fleet, and various additional factors which were essential in determining relative naval combat strength. Nonetheless, as naval strategists generally agreed that capital ships were the single most important component in determining combat equivalency, an equal ratio in capital ships was often misunderstood by many Americans to mean naval equality.[8]

Yet, Hughes ordered the General Board to scrap all fifteen of the new capital ships under construction plus an additional fifteen already afloat, thereby reducing the number of American battleships by 50 percent. "He holds," Assistant Secretary of the Navy Theodore Roosevelt, Jr. recorded,

---

[6] W. L. Rogers to Secretary of the Navy, "Ex-German Islands in the Pacific," n.d., Box 39, TR; Theodore Roosevelt, Jr. to Ambassador George S. Harvey, March 23, 1922, *Ibid.*; Theodore Roosevelt, Jr., "My Dear Ambassador," 29 December 1921, *Ibid.*; Andrade, "United States Navy," pp. 346–349; Dingman, *Power in the Pacific*, p. 156; Buckley, *Washington Conference*, p. 52; Goldman, *Sunken Treaties*, p. 65.

[7] Pusey, *Hughes*, 2: 460–463; Glad, *Hughes and the Illusion of Innocence*, pp. 272–273; Buckley, *Washington Conference*, pp. 52–57; Dingman, *Power in the Pacific*, pp. 157–158; Andrade, "United States Navy," pp. 350–351; Sprout, *New Order*, pp. 146–147; Goldman, *Sunken Treaties*, p. 58; George T. Davis, *A Navy Second to None: The Development of Modern American Naval Policy* (New York: Harcourt, Brace, 1940), p. 300; William F. Trimble, "The United States Navy and the Geneva Conference for the Limitation of Naval Armament, 1927," (Ph.D. diss. University of Colorado, 1974), p. 22.

[8] Raymond Leslie Buell, *The Washington Conference* (New York: D. Appleton, 1922), pp. 143–144; Hector C. Bywater, *Sea-Power in the Pacific: A Study of the American-Japanese Problem* (Boston: Houghton Mifflin, 1921), pp. 12, 100–120; Buckley, *Washington Conference*, pp. 23–24. These figures are approximate and vary from source to source.

"that it could be only in this way that we could keep our people in sympathy with our undertaking."[9]

Then to ensure Senate approval of a naval limitation treaty, Hughes appointed to the American delegation the Senate's two most influential leaders, Senator Henry Cabot Lodge, chair of the Foreign Relations Committee, and Senator Oscar Underwood, the Democratic minority leader.[10] Unlike Wilson, Hughes had thus ensured that Henry Cabot Lodge would not oppose him but, like Wilson, he worried about a group of Republican Senate "irreconcilables," who had helped to defeat the Treaty of Versailles and who still distrusted him as an internationalist "League man." He worried most about Senator William Borah, a spending cutter, who generated widespread enthusiasm for the Borah resolution which demanded reductions in naval building by 50 percent and a stop to all new construction for five years. Hughes was aware that the success of the forthcoming arms control conference depended not only on winning over key senators but also on broader political agreements essential to winning Senate approval of any treaty. Some influential senators worried that Japan's Twenty-One Demands on China and her expansion into the Pacific during World War I had seriously eroded the effectiveness of the United States' Open Door Policy in China and its ability to defend the Philippines and Guam. Japan's continued military occupation of Shantung Province suggested that Japan was willing to challenge American efforts to guarantee Chinese territorial integrity and political sovereignty.[11] Nor did there appear to be any power other than the United States that was willing to challenge Japan's continued expansion, especially as the Anglo-Japanese Alliance was widely interpreted as de-facto British acquiescence to continued Japanese expansion in return for safeguarding Britain's special interests in East Asia and the Pacific. Indeed, the Alliance not only encouraged each of them to protect the other's special interests, but to come to each other's defense if a third party, such as the United States, interfered in a war in which either of them was already involved.[12]

---

[9] Theodore Roosevelt, Jr., Diary, October 24 and 25, 1921, TR; Andrade, "United States Navy," p. 345; Sprout, *New Order*, p. 168; Pusey, *Hughes*, 2: 461.
[10] Buckley, *Washington Conference*, pp. 44–47; Vinson, *Parchment Peace*, pp. 115, 137–139; Dingman, *Power in the Pacific*, p. 158; Robert Jones Maddox, *William E. Borah and American Foreign Policy* (Baton Rouge: Louisiana State University Press, 1969), pp. 88–89, 96; Richard W. Fanning, *Peace and Disarmament: Naval Rivalry and Arms Control, 1922–1933* (University Press of Kentucky, 1995), p. 9; Richard Dean Burns and Donald Urguidi, *Disarmament in Perspective: An Analysis of Selected Arms Control and Disarmament Agreements Between the World Wars, 1919–1939* (California State College at Los Angeles Foundation, 1968), pp. 14–16; John Chambers Vinson, "Hughes, Borah, and the Far East: Congressional vs. Executive Leadership," *World Affairs Quarterly* 27 (October, 1956): 269–274; Maddox, *Borah*, pp. 84–86, 96–97; Pusey, *Hughes* 2: 463.
[11] Vinson, *Parchment Peace*, pp. 24–25; Pusey, *Hughes*, 2: 456–460; Maddox, *Borah*, pp. 100–101; Buell, *The Washington Conference*, pp. 240–247.
[12] Buckley, *Washington Conference*, p. 28; Buell, *The Washington Conference*, pp. 103, 109–117, 121; Vinson, *Parchment Peace*, pp. 27, 149–150; Davis, *Navy Second to None*, pp. 246,

With Japan as America's most likely future adversary in the Pacific, Hughes understood the political necessity of securing a treaty ending the Anglo-Japanese Alliance and reaffirming the principles of the Open Door. Without such agreements, Senate opposition to drastic naval cuts was likely to be intense.[13] With these imperatives in mind, Hughes warned both Japan and Great Britain that abrogation of the Alliance was essential and invited China to the conference to challenge Japan's claims.[14] Thus, his pre-conference strategy concentrated on specific domestic political objectives essential to Senate ratification by trumping Borah on the scope and duration of the naval reductions through an expansion of the shipbuilding holiday to ten years, by scrapping thirty capital ships and thereby drastically reducing building and maintenance costs and opening the way to bigger tax cuts. Lessening Senate fears of continuing Japanese violations of the Open Door policies in China, his plan also required the abrogation of the Anglo-Japanese Alliance, and a 10:10:6 ratio which gave the United States equality with Great Britain while limiting Japan to 60 percent.[15]

On November 12, 1920, Hughes stunned the assembled delegates with the spectacular nature of his naval arms reduction proposals.[16] Great Britain and Japan had come to the Washington Conference desperately hoping to convince the United States to cut back on the fifteen powerful capital ships being built under the 1916 naval construction program. They were totally unprepared, however, for Hughes's offer to stop all building for ten years and to scrap thirty American battleships and battle cruisers, fifteen of which were 50 percent to 80 percent completed at a cost of $330,000,000, as well as scrapping fifteen older pre-Dreadnought battleships for a total scrapped of 845,740 tons.[17]

In return for scrapping the thirty new American capital ships, he asked both Great Britain and Japan to scrap a combined total of only thirty-six. He proposed that Great Britain scrap nineteen older and four new battleships for a total of twenty-three, amounting to 583,375 tons, and stop plans for the four authorized "super Hood" battle cruisers. He asked Japan not to undertake

---

250–254; Maddox, *Borah*, p. 102; J. Chal Vinson, "The Imperial Conference of 1921 and the Anglo-Japanese Alliance," *Pacific Historical Review* 31(August, 1962): 257–266.

[13] W. L. Rogers to Secretary of the Navy, "Ex-German Islands in the Pacific," n.d., Box 39, TR; Vinson, *Parchment Peace*, pp. 27–30, 149–150; Pusey, *Hughes*, 2; 456–464; Goldman, *Sunken Treaties*, p. 57; Maddox, *Borah*, pp. 102–103; Buell, *The Washington Conference*, pp. 129–134; Vinson, "Imperial Conference," pp. 262–264; M. G. Fry, "The North Atlantic Triangle and the Abrogation of the Anglo-Japanese Alliance," *Journal of Modern History* 39 (March, 1967): 46, 64; Ira Klein, "Whitehall, Washington, and the Anglo-Japanese Alliance, 1919–1921," *Pacific Historical Review* (November, 1972): 468.

[14] Buell, *The Washington Conference*, pp. 246, 249, 240–279.

[15] Maddox, *Borah*, pp. 105–106, 97–101.

[16] US Congress, Senate, 67th Cong., 2d sess., 1922, S.Doc.126, *Conference on the Limitation of Armament* (Washington, DC: Government Printing Office, 1922), pp. 41–50.

[17] Sprout, *New Order*, p. 168; Buckley, *Washington Conference*, pp. 71–72; Burns and Urquidi, *Disarmament in Perspective*, p. 14. The percentage of completion varies from source to source.

the eight battleships authorized and to scrap seven new and four old ones, amounting to 448,928 tons. The British would be allowed to retain twenty-two older capital ships totaling 604,450 tons. The United States would keep eighteen newer capital ships comprising 550,650 tons, and Japan could keep ten newer capital ships for an aggregate of 299,700 tons. The ratio in capital ships, the generally agreed upon standard for measuring offensive naval power, would be roughly 10:10:6.[18] One British observer calculated that, in one stroke, Hughes had "sunk sixty-six capital ships, more ships in fifteen minutes than all of the admirals of the world in a cycle of centuries," for a total of 1,878,000 tons.[19]

Shocked naval leaders were forced into stunned silence as waves of cheers and applause swept the Hall. Senators hailed Hughes as a national hero, and journalists were nearly unanimous in their enthusiastic support. Reaction from the world's leaders was almost equally enthusiastic.[20] Winston Churchill and his influential friend, Lord Birkenhead, for example, both of whom feared the consequences to the British navy of the emerging American naval supremacy, were exuberant.[21]

While Churchill was delighted with Hughes's proposal, his friend Admiral David Beatty was not. Several weeks before the Conference opened, Beatty had traveled to the United States to exchange informal views with American naval leaders and had informed Assistant Secretary of the Navy Theodore Roosevelt, Jr. that while he was "perfectly willing" to accept "equality of naval armaments" with the American fleet, such an agreement would require detailed negotiations because the ships of the British Navy were "largely obsolete." As only the "Hood, the Five Royal Sovereigns, and the Five Queen Marys" were "modern ships," Beatty insisted, "England can only limit and reduce within very moderate bounds" without jeopardizing the modernization of the British fleet.[22]

Beatty's concern was understandable. The newer, more powerful battleships and battle cruisers being built by the United States not only mounted bigger 16-inch guns with longer ranges, but they were more heavily armored to help

---

[18] Buckley, *Washington Conference*, pp. 55–56, 72–73; Andrade, "United States Navy," pp. 345–346; Vinson, *Parchment Peace*, p. 137; Buell, *The Washington Conference*, pp. 153–154.
[19] Glad, *Hughes and the Illusion of Innocence*, p. 270; Pusey, *Hughes* 2: 471; Buell, *The Washington Conference*, pp. 153–154; Philip Rosen, "The Treaty Navy, 1919–1937," in *In Peace and War: Interpretations of American Naval History, 1775–1984*, 2d. ed., ed. Kenneth Hagan (Westport, CT: Greenwood, 1984), p. 222.
[20] Theodore Roosevelt, Jr., Diary, November 21, 1921, TR; Glad, *Hughes and the Illusion of Innocence*, pp. 270–271; Vinson, *Parchment Peace*, p. 138; Sprout, *New Order*, pp. 155–159.
[21] William Fletcher Johnson, "George Harvey, Journalist and Ambassador," *Saturday Evening Post*, September 7, 1929; US Ambassador to Secretary of State Hughes, n.d., in London and Other Conferences, QY, RG 45, NA; Pusey, *Hughes* 2: 470–471; Buckley, *Washington Conference*, pp. 72–74, 82.
[22] Theodore Roosevelt, Jr., Diary, 24, 25 October 1921, TR.

withstand the new bombs, marine mines, and torpedoes developed during World War I. The vast majority of British capital ships were built prior to the hard lessons learned at the Battle of Jutland and were therefore no match for the post-Jutland United States and Japanese ships with their bigger guns, longer ranges, and greater protection.[23] But, despite his assurances to Theodore Roosevelt Jr., Beatty was most certainly not "perfectly willing" to grant "naval equality" to the United States.[24] Both before the Conference and for years afterward, Beatty would privately insist upon British superiority.

According to one eyewitness, Hughes's call for an immediate ten-year holiday in capital ship construction caused Lord Arthur Lee, the First Lord of the Admiralty, to turn "several colors of the rainbow" and to behave "as if he were sitting on hot coals," while it propelled Beatty forward in his chair with a look of astonishment "in the manner of a bulldog, sleeping on a Sunday doorstep, who had been poked in the stomach..."[25] Stopping most capital ship construction immediately and placing a ten-year holiday on all future construction would prevent Great Britain from modernizing her battle fleet. Rear Admiral Sir Ernle Chatfield, Assistant Chief of Naval Staff, and the entire Board of Admiralty agreed with Beatty that, in fact, Hughes' proposals were "much more favorable to the United States" because Great Britain had refrained from building battleships during the past five years. Adding an additional ten years would result in the British battle fleet becoming "distinctly inferior" to the United States fleet by 1932.[26]

Beatty logically predicted that a ten-year building holiday would have other serious adverse consequences. Rather than a steady, unhurried replacement of worn-out and obsolete capital ships, Great Britain would be required, at the end of the holiday, to engage in an extremely expensive effort to replace almost all of its old capital ships. By then, he feared, the British shipbuilding firms specializing in warships would be bankrupt, and the skilled labor required to construct the technologically sophisticated modern vessels may well have scattered, with the result that neither the shipyards nor the skilled labor could be easily replaced. This catastrophic loss of shipbuilding capability,

---

[23] *Ibid.*
[24] Some scholars have taken Beatty's professions of equality at face value. See Donald S. Birn, "The Washington Conference of 1921–1922 in Anglo-French Relations," in *Naval History: The Sixth Symposium of the US Naval Academy*, ed. Daniel Masterson (Wilmington, DE: Scholarly Resources, 1979), p. 169; Norman Gibbs, "The Naval Conferences of the Interwar Years: A Study in Anglo-American Relations," *Naval War College Review* 30 (Summer, 1977): 51.
[25] Quoted in Buckley, *Washington Conference*, p. 72.
[26] H. F. Oliver, "Memorandum by the Naval Staff: Admiralty Memorandum for the Cabinet and the CID, United States Proposals for the Reduction of Armaments," November 21, 1921, 285-B, ADM 116/3445, PRO. Oliver was the Second Sea Lord. For Chatfield's observations, see December 2, 1921, ADM 116/2149, PRO in ROSK, 7/60, ROSKCC. See also Lord Ernle Chatfield, *The Navy and Defense* (London: William Heinemann, Ltd., 1942), pp. 195–197.

Chatfield observed, ought to have been as serious a source of anxiety to the United States as it was to Great Britain.²⁷

Equally objectionable to the Admiralty was Hughes' assumption that the 10:10:6 capital ship ratio could easily be extended to auxiliary warships – "light" cruisers, destroyers, and submarines – a notion which the Admiralty claimed was "the weakest part of the U. S. scheme." As an island with a worldwide empire and extensive trade routes to protect, Great Britain needed a greater number of these auxiliary craft to protect its trade routes on which its very existence depended. The United States, on the other hand, the Admiralty claimed, "was almost independent of outside sources of supply." In a remarkable projection, the Admiralty argued that, during a war against the United States, a 10:10 ratio in auxiliaries would place England "in a dangerous position," as the United States could keep its battle fleet safely in harbor while concentrating "its whole cruiser force to attack British shipping and outlying British possessions." The United States could also make good use of the Panama Canal for "attacks on our trade in the Pacific and the Atlantic." Worse still, British cruisers could not be concentrated because they would be on patrol throughout the world, protecting vital shipping lanes. Even in peacetime Great Britain required at least 40 light cruisers and 120 destroyers in addition to those needed to fight with the main battle fleet. And, in the event of war with United States, the Admiralty noted, "a very much larger number would be required." Thus, equality in auxiliary cruisers, destroyers, and submarines was simply out of the question.²⁸

In an effort to hide the Admiralty's strong objections, Beatty often refused to give definite answers to Roosevelt's questions and instead raised troubling questions of his own. Roosevelt eventually concluded that Beatty's numerous concerns were, in fact, merely camouflage for an elaborate stalling strategy. He therefore secured Hughes's permission for a frank "informal conference with Beatty." Following this two-hour exchange, Roosevelt emerged to warn Hughes that Beatty would "have to be talked to by those in power over him or we cannot expect an agreement."²⁹

Beatty was not in a good position to bargain. With America's demand for British repayment of war debts, the expensive naval arms race, and the Anglo-Japanese Alliance causing serious tension between the United States and Great Britain, English leaders were anxious for agreements that would enhance Anglo-American relations and possibly result in both the end of the enormous expense of the naval arms race and facilitate the much-desired cancellation of their war debt.³⁰

---

²⁷ Oliver, "Memorandum by the Naval Staff," November 21, 1921, ADM 116/3445, PRO.
²⁸ Ibid.
²⁹ Theodore Roosevelt, Jr., Diary, November 16, 1921, TR; Dingman, *Power in the Pacific*, p. 199.
³⁰ Roberta Allbert Dayer, "The British War Debts to the United States and the Anglo-Japanese Alliance, 1920–1923," *Pacific Historical Review* 45 (November, 1976), pp. 576–579, 589.

The British delegation was led by Arthur Balfour, the first Earl Balfour, a former prime minister and leader of the Conservative Party from 1902 to 1911. Balfour had also served as First Lord of the Admiralty and as Foreign Secretary. As such, Balfour was highly regarded as one of England's most experienced, skillful, and distinguished statesmen. Like other British leaders, he was upset over the refusal of the United States to cancel England's huge war debt, but he prevented his irritation from interfering with his mission of ending the expensive naval arms race and improving Anglo-American relations. To this end, he overruled Beatty in order to work closely and harmoniously with Hughes.[31] Lord Arthur Lee of Fareham, the current First Lord of the Admiralty, was equally anxious for agreement and to improve relations with the United States and, not surprisingly, as the Conference proceeded, his relationship with Beatty became increasingly strained – primarily over the ten-year holiday – a strain which eventually developed into a strong mutual antipathy. Finally, when Parliament simultaneously began its own efforts to cut still deeper into naval budgets, Beatty suddenly returned home to defend the Admiralty against its Parliament critics and against charges of obstructing agreement at the Conference.[32]

But Beatty was by no means totally obstreperous. Before leaving Washington, he assisted Balfour and Lee to defeat one of Hughes' most important goals: the expansion of the 10:10:6 ratio for light cruisers, destroyers, and submarines.[33] In preparing for the Washington Conference, the Admiralty had made it crystal clear that it would negotiate equality for capital ships only. Indeed, the Cabinet and the Committee of Imperial Defence supported the Admiralty's insistence that any limitation on auxiliary warships must be based on an agreement that England's need to protect its long trade routes required that it be granted additional light cruisers and destroyers beyond those accompanying the main battle fleet. In this way, the Admiralty intended that only the auxiliary cruisers, destroyers, and submarines – which normally accompanied the main battle fleet – could be limited by the 10:10:6 ratio, or only on condition that the other naval powers agreed that England alone would be entitled to a superiority of as many as 40 additional light cruisers and 120 additional destroyers to defend its trade routes.[34]

---

[31] Ibid.; B. J. C. McKercher, *The Second Baldwin Government and the United States, 1924–1929: Attitudes and Diplomacy* (Cambridge: Cambridge University Press, 1984), pp. 15–16.

[32] Beatty, *The Beatty Papers: Selections from the Private and Official Correspondence of Admiral of the Fleet Earl Beatty, 1901–1927*, 2 vols. B. Mc L. Ranft, ed. (Aldershot, England: Gower, 1993) 2: 77 Beatty, "Memorandum to the Cabinet," December 10, 1921, ADM 116/1776 in Ibid., 2:197; Stephen Roskill, *Naval Policy Between the Wars: The Period of Anglo-American Antagonism, 1919–1929* (London: Collins, 1968), pp. 318–320, 337.

[33] Charles Evans Hughes, "Opening Address," November 12, 1920, Senate, *Conference on the Limitation of Armaments*, p. 49; Sprout, *New Order*, pp. 210–212; Goldman, *Sunken Treaties*, pp. 139–140, 115–120; Pusey, *Hughes*, 2: 470.

[34] Oliver, "Memorandum by the Naval Staff," pp. 2–3; L. of F. [Lord Lee of Fareham] to the Committee of Imperial Defence, "The Washington Conference," October 5, 1921, ADM

Balfour was undoubtedly aware that any revelation of the Admiralty's demand for substantial superiority in light cruisers and destroyers might well result in congressional pressure on Hughes to modify the American offer to scrap thirty capital ships, and he therefore carefully crafted England's negotiating strategy. His immediate goal was to create the impression that Great Britain agreed fully with all of the principles and proposals of the American offer, including the limitation of auxiliary warships. This deception was essential both to achieve the political objective of reducing tensions and creating closer ties with United States and the more immediate military goal of stopping America's emerging naval supremacy. Balfour was determined to present to the American people and to the world the deliberately misleading appearance that England was a champion of arms limitation, willing to limit all of its warships.[35]

After reassuring the Conference of Great Britain's willingness to limit all warships, Balfour then argued that while the United States was virtually invulnerable to naval attack, Great Britain's recent experience during World War I demonstrated conclusively the vulnerability of Great Britain's trade routes to submarine attack. He therefore called upon the world to abolish the submarine. At the same time, Balfour misleadingly advocated the extension of the 10:10:6 ratio to auxiliary cruisers and destroyers because, he claimed, "we think the proposition between the various countries is acceptable; we think the limitation of armaments is reasonable; we think it should be accepted; we frankly believe it will be accepted." But, then, he slyly noted, almost as an afterthought, that this 10:10:6 ratio in auxiliaries raised "questions of detail," which would have to be negotiated by technical experts, especially concerning those cruisers "not connected with or required for fleet action." Nonetheless, he reassured the Conference that these "questions of detail," did "not touch the main outline" of America's proposal.[36]

Balfour's finesse of the Admiralty's insistence on auxiliary superiority was a considerable gamble. He knew a superiority of 40 light cruisers and 120 destroyers was not a "question of detail," but one of great military magnitude, which did, in fact, "touch on the main outline" of America's intention to achieve equality in all classes of warships, and could not therefore be considered as either "reasonable" or "acceptable" to the United States. Eventually, he realized, both American and Japanese diplomats were certain to ask him for specifics concerning those auxiliary vessels "not connected

---

116/3445, PRO; "Memorandum by the Naval Staff," n.d., 277-B, ADM 116/3445, PRO; Standing Sub-Committee, Committee of Imperial Defence, "Memorandum: The Washington Conference on the Limitation of Armaments," October 24, 1921, 280-B, ADM 116/3445, PRO.

[35] Arthur J. Balfour, "Address to the Second Plenary Session," November 15 1921, Senate, *Conference on the Limitation of Armaments*, pp. 65–70.

[36] Ibid.; Sprout, *New Order*, pp. 162–164; Davis, *Navy Second to None*, p. 292; Bywater, *Navies and Nations*, p. 136; Roskill, *Naval Policy, 1919–1929*, pp. 312–313.

with or required for fleet action." Yet, for the moment, he strove to present an understated, sanguine posture.

Since one of the cardinal goals of British diplomacy was the drastic reduction of America's naval strength, Balfour could not afford to antagonize Hughes with England's hidden goal of 40 additional auxiliary cruisers and 120 destroyers. To reassure Hughes, Balfour convinced Beatty to lower the Admiralty's demand for a superiority of over 40 light cruisers and 120 destroyers to a much lower tentative total "for all purposes" of only "50 cruisers, i.e. six less than now" in the entire British fleet. But, as Balfour explained to the Committee of Imperial Defence, "we do not propose to say this at present."[37] This switch to a temporary total of only 50 cruisers for the entire British Navy would not be revealed publicly unless Balfour was pressed, and until such time, it would remain hidden from public scrutiny, in favor of a different strategy.

However, should the inevitable questions arise over his meaning of "questions of detail" for "cruisers not connected with or required for fleet action," he would be prepared to create the highly favorable impression that Great Britain was actually reducing its cruiser force by 6 ships to a total of 50 "for all purposes," rather than generate great consternation by revealing the Admiralty's insistence on a superiority of 40 cruisers and 120 destroyers.[38]

Having first reassured Hughes that Great Britain agreed to all of his objectives, including equality in auxiliary warships, and then securing Beatty's consent to only 50 cruisers "for all purposes," Balfour and Lord Lee diverted attention by focusing on the submarine menace.

The abolition of the submarine was imperative, they argued, because of the persistent and dire threat of this new weapon to England's very existence during the recent World War. Balfour had first obtained Hughes's consent to raise the issue, although Hughes had cautioned him that the other powers would not accept abolition. But as Hughes's energies, Balfour recorded, were "concentrated at the moment" on the more important "capital ship [dispute] with Japan...," Hughes accepted Balfour's reassurances, and, Balfour gladly noted, Hughes even remained "sanguine that all other details of [his] scheme [were] capable of speedy adjustment on lines agreeable to us."[39]

When, as Balfour expected, France vehemently objected to abolition of the submarine, Balfour therefore argued that, as cruisers and destroyers were essential protection against submarines, the French objection to abolition made it impossible to discuss the limitation of cruisers and destroyers "in any way."[40] Thus, as he had earlier predicted to the Committee of Imperial Defence, the

---

[37] Balfour to CID, November 28, 1921, 290-B, ADM 116/3445, PRO.   [38] Ibid.   [39] Ibid.
[40] Ibid. See also Balfour's statement, December 23, 1921, Senate, Conference on the Limitation of Armaments, pp. 285–288. For the debate on submarines, see Ibid., pp. 264–290, 303–307, 424–437. See also Buckley, Washington Conference, pp. 114–118; Pusey, Hughes, 2; 484–485; Buell, The Washington Conference, pp. 233, 212–234; Roskill, Naval Policy 1919–1929, pp. 324, 327–328; Goldman, Sunken Treaties, pp. 141, 137–139: Donald S. Birn, "Open

"Net effect of this [will] be practically to confine limitation of naval armament ... to capital ships as originally contemplated and approved by the Committee of Imperial Defence and the Cabinet."[41]

Balfour's artful dodging was successful. France raised persistent and rational objections to the abolition of the submarine, and England's refusal to compromise deadlocked the Conference. At one point the British Cabinet secretly instructed Balfour that he must insist on "our liberty to build whatever numbers and classes of cruisers and anti-submarine craft we may consider necessary to the maintenance of national and Imperial life... *Even at the cost of a complete rupture...*" of the Conference. [Emphasis mine.][42] Balfour succeeded in deflecting discussion of auxiliary ship numbers by shifting the focus to the protracted arguments over submarines, and eventually international public opinion blamed France for the Conference's failure to extend the 10:10:6 ratio to auxiliary vessels.[43] The practical effect, as Balfour had foreseen, was an agreement to limit capital ships only, exactly as the Admiralty, the Committee of Imperial Defence, and the Cabinet had originally intended – leaving Britain's auxiliary ships and other naval assets completely untouched.

Both Beatty and his Assistant Chief of Naval Staff, Admiral Ernle Chatfield, later confirmed Balfour's successful diplomacy. Beatty admitted that the issue of extending the 10:10:6 ratio to auxiliary cruisers and destroyers "was specifically avoided by the British Delegation for the reason that the number required by the British Empire was so disproportionate to those required by the USA and Japan that it was considered that it was [of] little use discussing the question with any possibility of reaching an agreement."[44] Chatfield was equally pleased with Balfour's skillful evasion, recalling that "We had successfully resisted efforts at Washington to limit our cruiser and destroyer numbers..."[45]

However, Balfour's skillful maneuver would create a serious problem at the Geneva naval arms limitation conference in 1927. In order for Balfour to avoid revealing the number of auxiliaries regarded as essential by Great Britain, he was not in a position to reject Hughes' unacceptable limit of a 450,000-ton limit for them, and the Americans therefore came away from the Washington

---

Diplomacy at the Washington Conference of 1921–1922," *Comparative Studies in Society and History* 12 (July, 1970): 310–316, 318–319.

[41] Balfour to CID, November 28, 1921, 290-B, ADM 116/3445, PRO.

[42] "Secret Dispatch Sent by the British Cabinet to Mr. Balfour, Head of the British Delegation of the Washington Conference, as revealed by Mr. Churchill, Speaking in the House of Commons in 1927," n.d., QY-London and Other Conferences, Subject File 1911–1927, Box 575, Naval Records Collection, RG 45, NA.

[43] See footnote 40.

[44] "Draft Naval Memorandum with Alterations by Beatty," May 5, 1924, in Ranft, *Beatty*, 2: 398–401. See also Churchill's statement to Parliament cited in footnote 42.

[45] Chatfield, *Navy and Defense*, p. 97.

Conference with the definite understanding that its proposal of 450,000 tons would meet all of Great Britain's needs.[46] This misperception would become crucial during the negotiations at the 1927 Geneva Conference.

The British were equally successful in securing agreement on unarmed merchantmen. With its large fleet of merchant ships, Britain was anxious to convert them in time of war for blockade and interdiction or as commerce raiders. This force could be quickly and inexpensively mobilized by mounting 6-inch guns on the faster merchant ships whose decks had already been reinforced for this specific purpose. The naval staff acknowledged that these converted merchantmen were no match for a 6-inch-gun cruiser. Yet it recognized them as effective against unarmed and unescorted enemy or neutral merchantmen, and thus as a vital component of its wartime strategy of blockading ports and intercepting contraband, a component which severely strained Anglo-American relations during the early years of the Great War and had been a major reason for Wilson's determination to build a navy "second to none." These armed merchantmen were highly advantageous to the British because neither the United States nor Japan had anything vaguely approaching the tonnage which Great Britain possessed in convertible merchant ships. Nonetheless, despite some misgivings among the other delegations, Great Britain finally carried the day when the Conference agreed that merchantmen were not to be built for quick conversion into warships, "other than the necessary stiffening of decks for the mounting of guns not exceeding 6-inch [152 millimeters] caliber," thereby ensuring their continued use for blockade and interdiction of unarmed merchantmen.[47] This was a significant and all too often overlooked victory for the Admiralty, which, like Balfour's unwillingness to challenge Hughes' 450,000-ton limit for auxiliaries, would take on greater importance at the later Geneva Conference.

Equally significant was the British success in placing a maximum limit on the tonnage and guns of light cruisers, without limiting the number allowed. Without these limits on tonnage and guns, Lord Lee worried that cruisers could evolve into highly expensive vessels "of 20,000 to 30,000 tons bristling with eight-inch guns."[48] Indeed, the Admiralty had already anticipated this possibility and had instructed the British delegation to limit future light cruisers to a maximum of 10,000 tons with 8-inch guns.[49] When the Committee of

---

[46] US, Congress, Senate, *Report of the American Delegation of the Proceedings of the Conference on the Limitation of Armaments, Submitted to the President*, 67th Cong., 2d Sess., February 9, 1922, S. Doc. 125, pp. 125, 24–25; Roskill, *Naval Policy, 1919–1927*, p. 508; Glad, *Hughes*, p. 277.

[47] "Committee on Limitation of Armaments," 13th Meeting, December 30, 1921, Senate, *Conference on the Limitation of Armaments*, p. 354. For Article 11 of the Treaty see p. 874.

[48] "Committee on Limitation of Armaments," 10th Meeting, December 28, 1921 in *Ibid.*, pp. 319–320.

[49] Beatty to Controller, November 19, 1921, ADM 116/3445/105 in Ranft, *Beatty*, 2: 195–196; E. C. [Ernle Chatfield], "Naval Staff Opinion on Cruiser Size Limit of 10,000 Tons," December 23, 1921, ADM 116/2149, PRO; William Scott Chalmers, *The Life and Letters of David Earl*

Imperial Defence expressed concern about the cost of these large cruisers, the Admiralty reminded the Committee that the British 9,500-ton Hawkins class with its 7.5-inch guns, had already set the world standard, and it was therefore reasonable to assume that rival navies would insist on building their future cruisers at least equal to, if not more powerful than the Hawkins class. Besides, the Admiralty argued, Great Britain needed the advantages of a 10,000-ton, 8-inch-gun cruiser for fighting rival cruisers, for chasing fast armed merchantmen, for its longer endurance, and for its greater sea-keeping qualities.[50]

The Washington Conference was quickly hailed as an outstanding success, yet its failure to place limits on the number of vessels in each of the auxiliary classes had long-term implications and would cause a number of persistent, difficult problems. Because of the scarcity of American bases in the Pacific and the vast distances between its Pacific possessions, and also, no doubt, because of the existence of the new British 9,500-ton Hawkins-class cruisers with their 7.5-inch guns, the General Board had, itself, been planning a 10,000-ton cruiser with 8-inch guns for two years prior to the Washington Conference.[51] The "Treaty Cruiser," as it was sometimes called, was considerably larger, more powerful, and more expensive than previous light cruisers, which had generally ranged from 3,000 to 5,000 tons. The United States was already building ten Omaha-class cruisers of 7,500 tons with 6-inch guns, but until nearly the end of World War I, auxiliary cruisers had been much smaller and less expensive ships.[52] Because the Washington Conference allowed these 10,000-ton, 8-inch-gun "Treaty Cruisers" to be built in unlimited numbers, at a time when building new capital ships was prohibited for ten years, they soon became the source of a new international arms race and, in time, generated the need for the second naval arms limitation conference which met in Geneva in 1927.

The results of the Washington Conference significantly influenced this second international parlay. While American politicians celebrated – by lowering taxes through deep cuts in naval spending and by refusing to build up to the number of naval vessels required to reach the ratios specified in the

---

Beatty (London: Hodden and Stoughton, 1951), p. 369; Roskill, *Naval Policy 1919–1928*, pp. 325–326.

[50] E. C., "Naval Staff Opinion on Cruiser Size Limit of 10,000 Tons." See also "Washington Conference Papers," n.d. 295-B, ADM 116/3445, PRO.

[51] See citations in footnotes 49 and 50. See also Norman Friedman, *U.S. Cruisers: An Illustrated Design History* (Annapolis, MD: Naval Institute Press, 1984), p. 110; Alan Raven and John Roberts, *British Cruisers of World War Two* (Annapolis, MD: Naval Institute Press, 1980), p. 105; Sprout, *New Order*, pp. 213–215; Roskill, *Naval Policy 1919–1928*, pp. 310–314.

[52] Sprout, *New Order*, pp. 312–314; "Committee on the Limitation of Armaments," 13th Meeting, December 30, 1921, *Conference on the Limitation of Armaments*, pp. 354–355. For Article 11 of the Treaty see p. 874; Christopher Hall, *Britain, America and Arms Control, 1917–1937* (New York: St. Martin's, 1987), p. 9; Bywater, *Navies and Nations*, p. 49.

Five Power Treaty – American naval strategists lamented that both the Japanese and the British had won significant military advantages. These military successes, they believed, were compounded by the popular American perception that treaty guarantees were important safeguards against a second world war, thus making a "navy second to none" an expensive waste of the taxpayers' money. None of the participating naval advisers were completely satisfied with the treaties, but it was clear that, unlike the Americans, the Japanese and British naval advisers had been much more successful in using this new experiment in diplomacy to win significant military advantages. Convinced that they had been militarily outwitted in 1921–1922, American negotiators at the second conference in 1927 would insist on either numerical equality or combat equivalency.

Japan, too, emerged from the Washington Conference with desirable military advantages. But while Navy Minister Admiral Kato Tomosaburo was negotiating in Washington, Prime Minister Hara Kei was assassinated by a right-wing extremist opposed to naval reduction – the first of two prime ministers assassinated over naval cuts between 1921–1931. Tomosaburo realized that as military expenditures already accounted for 48.7 percent of Japan's total national budget, his navy could not achieve the cherished 70 percent ratio, much less keep pace with America's rapid naval expansion, – a pace which would soon reduce the Japanese ratio to 10:5 rather than the 10:6 offered by Hughes.[53] Like Lord Balfour, Tomosaburo fully appreciated the intricate relationship between naval power, imperial imperatives, and future economic prosperity, and that diplomacy was a useful means to harmonize these objectives.

With Balfour's help, Tomosaburo agreed to a series of complex compromises which required Japan to accept a 60 percent ratio, the ten-year capital ship building holiday, an end to the Anglo-Japanese Alliance, and the ambiguously worded and unenforceable Four-Power and Nine-Power Treaties – treaties which, nonetheless, granted de facto recognition to most of Japan's recent World War I conquests and its existing domination of the Western Pacific and East Asia.[54] However, in return for these concessions Tomosaburo

---

[53] James B. Crowley, "Japan's Military Foreign Policies," in *Japan's Foreign Policy, 1868–1941* ed. James William Morley (New York: Columbia University Press, 1974), p. 41; Burns and Urquidi, *Disarmament in Perspective*, pp. 14–16; Tatsuii Takeuchi, *War and Diplomacy in the Japanese Empire* (Garden City, NY: Doubleday, Doran, 1935), pp. 233–234; James B. Crowley, *Japan's Quest for Autonomy: National Security and Foreign Policy, 1930–1938* (Princeton: Princeton University Press, 1960), pp. 27, 30; Marius B. Jansen, *The Making of Modern Japan* (Cambridge: Harvard University Press, 2000), p. 511; Sadao Asada, "The Japanese Navy and the United States" in *Pearl Harbor as History: Japanese-American Relations, 1931–1941* eds. Dorothy Borg and Shumpei Okamoto (New York: Columbia University Press, 1973), p. 190.

[54] Sadao Asada, "Japanese Admirals and the Politics of Naval Limitation: Kato Tomosaburo versus Kato Kanji," in Gerald Jordan, ed. *Naval Warfare in the Twentieth Century, 1900–1945* (New York: Crane, Russak, 1977), pp. 147–153; Dingman, *Power in the Pacific*, pp. 188,

required Hughes to prohibit the construction of American naval bases beyond Hawaii, thus forcing Hughes to break his promise to the General Board not to agree to such a demand, and thereby making it much more difficult for the American Navy to protect the Philippine Islands or to launch an invasion of Japan. Tomosaburo also gained an additional 81,000 tons for three new aircraft carriers and secured the immediate scrapping of fifteen of America's most modern and fifteen older battleships and battle cruisers, while retaining for Japan almost twice the number of modern, post-Jutland capital ships allowed to either the United States or Great Britain.[55] Indeed, despite the Prime Minister's assassination, the treaties were sufficiently advantageous to enable Tomosaburo to convince the Cabinet, the Naval General Staff, the Privy Council, and the Diet to ratify them.

Now elected to prime minister, while simultaneously retaining his position as naval minister, Tomosaburo sought to mollify his disgruntled naval colleagues by taking advantage of Balfour's success in exempting numerical limitations on auxiliary warships. To compensate for the 60 percent ratio in capital ships, he pursued the rapid expansion and increased combat capabilities of new cruisers, destroyers, and submarines.[56]

Tomosaburo advanced a two-pronged strategy featuring forty 10,000-ton, 8-inch-gun cruisers, 152 destroyers, and 78 submarines. The first phase was defensive. These newly designed warships would feature innovative combat capabilities and tactics allowing them to attack and deplete an invading American navy to rough equality before it could approach Japanese home waters. To this end he, and his successors, employed experienced German naval engineers to design Japan's newest submarines, capable of a wider cruising radius and of launching a greater number of improved, long-range torpedoes, effective up to a distance of 24 miles. During the Americans' long voyage from

---

191–192, 201; Goldman, *Sunken Treaties*, pp. 121–128; Crowley, *Japan's Quest for Autonomy*, pp. 27–30; Takeuchi, *War and Diplomacy*, p. 233; Buckley, *United States and the Washington Conference*, p. 100; Jansen, *Making of Modern Japan*, pp. 503–504, 511.

[55] Vinson, *Parchment Peace*, pp. 167–170; Jansen, *Modern Japan*, pp. 520–521; Buckley, *Washington Conference*, pp. 77, 84–87, 90–96; Pusey, *Hughes*, 2: 477, 487; Rolland A. Chaput, *Disarmament and British Foreign Policy* (London: George Allen and Unwin), pp. 104–108; Sprout, *Toward a New Order*, pp. 130, 171, 251, 266–269; Asada, "Japanese Admirals," pp. 149, 154; Naval Attache, "Report," October 19, 1921, Subject File, 1911–1927, Q.Y.-London and Other Conferences, Box 594, RG-45, NA; Dingman, *Power in the Pacific*, pp. 188–189, 203, 205; Goldman, *Sunken Treaties*, pp. 126–127; Ernest Andrade, "The United States Navy and the Washington Conference," *The Historian* 31 (May 1939): 353; Robert Gordon Kaufman, *Arms Control During the Pre-Nuclear Era: The United States and Naval Limitation Between the Two Wars* (New York: Columbia University Press, 1990), p. 61 Takeuchi, *War and Diplomacy*, pp. 237–238; Crowley, "Japan's Military Foreign Policies," pp. 29–31; Buell, *The Washington Conference*, p. 100.

[56] Peter Duus, *Party Rivalry and Political Change in Taisho Japan* (Cambridge: Harvard University Press, 1968), pp. 165–168; Asada, "Japanese Admirals," pp. 152–153, 157–158; Dingman, *Power in the Pacific*, p. 201; Buckley, *Washington Conference*, p. 100.

The Washington Conference Legacy

Hawaii, Japan would launch wave after wave of submarine torpedo attacks against the American invaders. These submarine tactics would be augmented by newly designed cruisers and destroyers, each carrying twenty-four torpedoes. Equipped with greatly improved star shells, parachute flares, and night binoculars, these warships would surprise the Americans with carefully rehearsed night attacks. Then, as the invaders approached their home waters, Japanese air superiority from nearby bases would further degrade the Americans, who lacked naval bases to repair and resupply their battered and depleted fleet. Thus, having sunk or damaged enough ships to achieve approximate combat equality, the far better trained Japanese main fleet would initiate the offensive phase of the strategy, defeat the enemy, and ensure Japan's continued dominance in the Western Pacific and East Asia. This strategy was supported by successive naval leaders and politicians throughout the 1920s, including the more peacefully oriented Foreign Minister Shedehara Kijuro.[57]

Kato Kanji, Vice Chair of the Naval General Staff and leader of the "fleet faction," – which had demanded a 70 percent ratio – remained skeptical. Kanji was bent upon "revenge" against the United States for insisting upon Japanese acquiescence to the inferior 10:6 ratio. He therefore used his influence within the Naval Staff to defeat Tomosaburo's attempt to incorporate a formal declaration in the National Defense Plan of avoidance of war with the United States. Indeed, within eight months of Tomosaburo's death in 1923, following Congressional passage of the insulting 1924 Immigration Act, which all but prohibited Japanese immigration into the United States, Kanji's vow of an "inevitable" war of "revenge" was again manifested when he and his "fleet faction" convinced the Naval Staff to plan for the conquest of the Philippines and Guam and to incorporate into the National Defense Plan

---

[57] Asada, "Japanese Admirals," pp. 157–158; Sprout, *Toward a New Order*, pp. 170–171, 175, 243–251; Fanning, *Peace and Disarmament*, pp. 154–155; Kaufman, *Arms Control During the Pre-Nuclear Era*, p. 170; Eric LaCroix, "The Development of the 'A' Class Cruiser in the Imperial Japanese Navy," *Warship International* 14: 4 (1977): 338, 360–361; John Robert Ferris, *The Evolution of British Strategic Policy, 1919–1926* (London: McMillan, 1989), p. 132; Hector C. Bywater, *Navies and Nations: A Review of Naval Developments Since the Great War* (Boston and New York: Houghton Mifflin, 1927), pp. 205, 209–210, 218–219; Hector C. Bywater, *Sea-Power in the Pacific: A Study of the American-Japanese Problem* (Houghton Mifflin Co., 1921), pp. 165–174, 193, 233–234; Ian Nish, ed., *Anglo-Japanese Alienation, 1919–1952: Papers of the Anglo-Japanese Conference on the History of the Second World War* (Cambridge: Cambridge University Press, 1982), pp. 8–9; Steven E. Pelz, *Race to Pearl Harbor: The Failure of the Second Naval London Conference and the Onset of World War II* (Cambridge: Harvard University Press, 1974), pp. 30–32, 35–38; Sadao Asada, "The Japanese Navy and the United States," in *Pearl Harbor as History*, pp. 190, 235; Goldman, *Sunken Treaties*, pp. 126–132, 182–184; Akiya Iriye, "The Failure of Military Expansionism," in *Dilemmas of Growth in Prewar Japan* ed. James William Morley (Princeton: Princeton University Press, 1971), pp. 107–108; Iriye, *Across the Pacific*, pp. 164, 175; Crowley, "Japan's Military Foreign Policies," pp. 27–28, 30–31, 41.

the operational assumption that "a clash between the United States and the [Japanese] Empire will become inevitable."[58]

Unlike Kanji, Balfour was well pleased with the outcome of the Washington Conference. Like Tomosaburo, he valued naval power as crucial to imperial success and future economic prosperity while recognizing that Great Britain's weakened economy was also unable to equal the number of the most modern and much more powerful battleships and battle cruisers under construction by the United States. He therefore worked closely with his naval advisors to secure important military advantages. Unlike Harding and Hughes, who ignored or overrode their naval advisors in order to secure their domestic political objectives, both the British and the Japanese leaders were much more intent upon achieving those naval superiorities vital to preserving their empires.

To stymie looming American superiority in capital ships, Balfour publicly and enthusiastically espoused virtually all of Hughes' major proposals, especially his offer of capital ship equality. Having ensured the immediate scrapping of thirty American capital ships, he then surreptitiously employed shrewd diplomatic maneuvers to create a deadlock over the abolition of submarines, and thereby thwarted American hopes of limiting the number of auxiliary vessels. Yet, he simultaneously managed to convince the Americans that Great Britain was willing to limit the number of its cruisers, a deliberately misleading impression that would plague the negotiations at the later 1927 Conference. Equally significant was his success in satisfying the Admiralty's insistence on the right to build and expand strategically located naval bases at Hong Kong, Singapore, Australia and New Zealand. Little noted at the time was his further success in ensuring that the decks of merchant vessels could be reinforced. This enabled the Admiralty to mount powerful, rapid-fire, 6-inch guns on these vessels, thus transforming them into dangerous commerce raiders and effective blockade vessels against unarmed merchant ships.[59]

Beatty was far less satisfied. His strong objections to the limitations on the latest capital ships and to the ten-year capital ship-building holiday eventually contributed to his recall to London, where he once again confronted politicians bent upon a new wave of naval cost-cutting. Nonetheless, despite pressure that

---

[58] Asada, "Japanese Admirals," pp. 157–159; Ferris, *Evolution*, pp. 48–49; Sprout, *Toward a New Order*, p. 263; Dingman, *Power in the Pacific*, pp. 213, 188–189; Bywater, *Navies and Nations*, pp. 142–143, 147; Pusey, *Hughes* 2: 512; Walter LaFeber, *The Clash: US-Japanese Relations Throughout History* (New York: W.W. Norton, 1997), pp. 143–146; Stephen Roskill, *Earl Beatty: The Last Naval Hero: An Intimate Biography* (New York: Athenaeum, 1981), p. 310; Stephen Roskill, *Naval Policy Between the Wars: The Period of Anglo-American Antagonism, 1919–1929* (London: Collins, 1968), pp. 565–566; Crowley, "Japan's Military Foreign Policies," pp. 27–28, 30–31, 41; George T. Davis, *A Navy Second to None: The Development of Modern American Naval Policy* (New York: Harcourt, Brace, 1940), pp. 277, 293, 301–307.

[59] Buckley, *The Washington Conference*, p. 100; Gerald E. Wheeler, "The United States Navy and the Japanese 'Enemy', 1919–1931," *Military Affairs* 21 (Summer 1957): 69; Bywater, *Nations and Navies*, p. 156.

he return home during the midst of the negotiations, his experiences at the Washington Conference and subsequent battles with cost-conscious British politicians significantly influenced his later strategy for a second naval limitation conference. Five years later, in 1927, First Sea Lord Beatty convinced himself that the skills and insights he had acquired from years of battling perfidious and shortsighted politicians had equipped him to manipulate both British and American leaders into signing a new treaty on auxiliary vessels which would be highly advantageous to the Admiralty's future war plans. Like Harding and Hughes, he would refuse to reveal his negotiating strategy prior to the opening of the 1927 Geneva Conference, and, like Balfour, he would cloak his most important objectives under reasonable rationales, while keeping those objectives secret. During these intervening five years, between 1922 and 1927, his success in forcing Great Britain's most accomplished politicians to bow to Admiralty demands convinced him that he could succeed as well against the Americans – whose diplomacy, he assumed, would continue to focus more on securing domestic political and economic advantages than on safeguarding its naval strength or defending the vestiges of America's colonial possessions in East Asia.

3

Beatty's Japanese War Plan

Beatty returned home to Britain in November 1922 while the Washington Conference was still in progress, ostensibly to defend the Admiralty from still further demands for cuts in its construction budget. This newest threat came from the recently created Cabinet Committee on National Expenditure, created by Prime Minister David Lloyd George and timed to capitalize on the upsurge of international approval for naval reduction flowing from the Washington Conference. To chair the new committee Lloyd George appointed his friend Sir Eric Geddes, a former First Lord of the Admiralty who fully agreed with the urgent need for naval budget cuts.[1] The Geddes Committee was only one of a long series of challenges which Beatty encountered between 1919 and 1927. Among the most worrisome was the abrogation of the Anglo-Japanese Alliance. This convinced Beatty that Japan would now feel free to impinge upon British possessions and trade in East Asia, and therefore Great Britain must begin to prepare for a naval war against Japan in East Asia. The key to success in this "inevitable" future war was the Admiralty's new 10,000-ton, 8-inch-gun cruiser and an expanded naval base at Singapore. However, objections to Beatty's war plan voiced by Ramsey McDonald's Labour Party in early 1924 continued when Stanley Baldwin's Conservatives returned to power in November.

Beatty's newest antagonist had once been among his most ardent champions. Winston Churchill had only recently joined the Conservative Party after many years as a leader in the Liberal Party. Both because Churchill had new responsibilities as Baldwin's Chancellor of the Exchequer and a new perspective on England's deteriorating economy, and because of the insights he had acquired

---

[1] Stephen Roskill, *Naval Policy between the Wars: The Period of Anglo-American Antagonism, 1919–1929* (Annapolis, MD: Naval Institute Press, 1976), pp. 318, 231–233, 320. The Geddes Committee reviewed the budgets of all of the military services.

as First Lord of the Admiralty during World War I, he was no longer as favorably inclined toward new naval construction as he had been three years earlier in 1922, or as sympathetic either to a new naval base at Singapore or to immediate preparations for a war against Japan in East Asia. The result was a long series of bitter debates within the Baldwin Cabinet between Churchill and Beatty over the future strategic needs of the British Empire.

***

In the midst of a rapidly deteriorating economy and rising political volubility, four different prime ministers and four different cabinets struggled between 1919 and 1926 with the perplexities and political pitfalls of shaping postwar strategic policy. This rapid rotation of leaders and cabinets hampered the emergence of a national defense consensus. Cabinets which were ill-equipped to debate strategic policy tended to rely on the recommendations of special cabinet committees, the Committee of Imperial Defence, or on the minister heading an important military department. Operating independently of one another, the Admiralty, the Treasury, the Foreign Office, and to a lesser degree other ministries, sought to convince these rotating cabinets to adopt policies and budgets which shaped strategic policy in terms which each of them considered vital. As the Admiralty had long been one of the most prestigious and politically influential, it attempted to ensure that it, rather than the Treasury, remained dominant in formulating policies affecting the financing of the Navy and its allied services, and that it, rather than the Foreign Office, determined foreign policies affecting its relationship to other navies and to the implementation of imperial strategic policy.[2]

Confronting the political challenges of this series of rotating prime ministers – especially David Lloyd George and Ramsay MacDonald, each of whom had strong views on naval and defense strategy – would have been a daunting challenge for any Admiralty leader. In this regard, Beatty's natural arrogance and narrow naval frame of reference often served him well. His aristocratic demeanor, heroic status, oratorical abilities, independent wealth, and long experience with politicians as Churchill's Naval Secretary were invaluable to him in his repeated political clashes with England's top elected leaders. Britain's worsening economy, rapidly rising unemployment, massive war debts, and increasing political volatility were matters which Beatty almost cavalierly left to the politicians to worry about. His concentration was focused almost exclusively on naval needs and on the naval strategies which he had worked out in consultation with the Admiralty's Plans Division and the Naval Staff.[3]

---

[2] John Robert Ferris, *The Evolution of British Strategic Policy, 1919–1926* (London: Macmillan, 1989), pp. xi–2, 11–13; Malcolm H. Murfett, *The First Sea Lords: From Fisher to Mountbatten* (Westport CT. and London: Praeger, 1995), pp. 131–132.

[3] For assessments of Beatty's political skills and defects, see Stephen Roskill, *Earl Beatty: The Last Naval Hero: An Intimate Biography* (New York: Athenaeum, 1981), pp. 365, 24, 35c; David Beatty, *The Beatty Papers: Selections from the Private and Official Correspondence of Admiral of*

Nonetheless, this task was compounded by the great international wave of approval for naval reductions and limitation resulting from the Washington Conference. Another handicap was the absence of any identifiable foreign naval threat. To win his recurring political battles, Beatty relied on persuading Britain's leaders of a menacing new threat arising from the folly of the Washington Conference.[4]

While the First Lord of the Admiralty, Lord Lee, remained at the Washington Conference to conclude negotiations, Beatty led the Admiralty into the budget fight against Geddes and his popular Cabinet Committee on National Expenditures. Because the American proposal of drastic cuts in capital ships was politically popular, Lloyd George and Geddes were able to throw the Admiralty on the defensive. Beatty was hampered still further by rumors that he had been recalled from the Conference because he had conspired to delay and frustrate agreement on naval reductions. Certainly Theodore Roosevelt, Jr., would have agreed with this charge, despite Beatty's vigorous denials. More importantly, Prime Minister Lloyd George was in no mood to entertain Beatty's rationale for immediately replacing warships worn-out during World War I. With the German Navy at the bottom of the sea and no foreseeable foreign naval threat in sight, Beatty and his beleaguered Admiralty Staff were facing formidable odds until Winston Churchill once again came to the rescue.[5]

Churchill had long admired the glorious fighting tradition of the British Navy, and he had identified with its brave naval officers, most especially with Beatty. After resigning as First Lord of the Admiralty in May 1915, following the disastrous Gallipoli Campaign, Churchill had resumed his Army service as a captain on the Western Front. Earlier in his career Churchill had been one of England's brave young warriors in Egypt, India, Afghanistan, and Africa.[6]

---

the Fleet Earl Beatty, ed. B. Mc. L. Ranft 2 vols. (Aldershot, England: Gower, 1989) 1: 6, 378; W. S. [William Scott] Chalmers, *The Life and Letters of David, Earl Beatty* (London: Hodder and Stoughton, 1951), pp. 83, 385; Murfett, *First Sea Lords*, pp. 8, 65, 128; Ferris, *Evolution*, p.5; Paul Kennedy, *The Rise and Fall of the Great Powers* (New York: Random House, Vintage Books, 1989), p. 279; Roger Keyes to Hamilton, May 4, 1927 in Roger Keyes, *The Keyes Papers: Selections from the Private and Official Correspondence of Admiral of the Fleet Baron Keyes of Zeebrugge, 1919–1938*, ed. Paul G. Halpern, 2 vols. (London: George Allen and Unwin, 1980), 2: 214.

[4] Chalmers, *Life and Letters*, pp. 370–371; Roskill, *Beatty*, pp. 311–312; Beatty, *Beatty Papers*, 1: 377–378 n.3; *Ibid.*, 2: 78–79; Murfett, *First Sea Lords*, pp. 131–132; Ferris, *Evolution*, xi–2; Roger Dingman, *Power in the Pacific: The Origins of Naval Arms Limitation, 1914–1922* (Chicago and London: University of Chicago Press, 1976), pp. 205–206.

[5] See footnote 3 and especially Roskill, *Naval Policy*, pp. 318, 320, 230–233; Dingman, *Power in the Pacific*, pp. 205–206.

[6] Winston S. Churchill, *My Early Years: A Roving Commission* (London: The Reprint Society, 1944), pp. 192, 206–208; Martin Gilbert, *Churchill: A Life* (New York: Henry Holt, 1991), pp. 51–131, 92, 239–320, 331–360; Stephen Roskill, *Churchill and the Admirals* (New York: William Morrow, 1978), pp. 275–276.

His love of war heroes had earlier prompted him to rescue Beatty's career when he appointed him as his naval secretary before World War I and then as commander of the prestigious Battle Cruiser fleet.[7] At the end of World War I, Churchill hailed Beatty as a hero and convinced the Cabinet to award him £100,000 in recognition of his exploits.[8] "I never cease to proclaim you," Churchill told Beatty in late 1924, when policy differences threatened their friendship, "as the inheritor of the great tradition of Nelson."[9]

Beatty had conflicting views about his former boss. Despite the fact that Churchill had rescued his career and given him prestigious command, Beatty was at times privately very critical. When angry over policy disputes, he referred to Churchill as "disgusting," as one of the "dirty dogs of the world," as "devoid of patriotism." At other times, in 1925 for example, despite their increasingly frequent arguments, Beatty pointedly reminded his equally critical yet less circumspect wife that Churchill "has been a good friend to me and has backed me many times under circumstances of great difficulty."[10]

This was one of those times. With the "Geddes Axe" about to win Cabinet approval, Churchill's return to the Lloyd George Cabinet enabled him once again to come to Beatty's defense.[11] In February 1921, as the debate became heated, Churchill convinced Lloyd George to appoint him to chair still another new cabinet committee. Rather than focus exclusively on the Admiralty, the Cabinet Committee on Defense Estimates was empowered to review cuts for all three military services.[12] Defying intense press criticism of his resistance to naval cuts, Churchill steadfastly defended Beatty's claim that Great Britain's navy must be superior to any other nation and eventually succeeded in restoring £2 million to the navy's annual budget.[13] More significant still was Churchill's Cabinet Committee on Defense Estimates' enthusiastic endorsement of Beatty's new naval defense strategy.[14]

The rapid rise of Japanese naval power during World War I and Japan's expansion into the Western Pacific, coupled with the termination of the Anglo-Japanese Alliance at the Washington Naval Conference, convinced Beatty that England must now recognize Japan as a newly emerging menace to British interests and possessions in East Asia.[15] To defend Australia and New Zealand

---

[7] Roskill, *Churchill and the Admirals*, pp. 275–279; Chalmers, *Life and Letters*, pp. 107–108.
[8] Roskill, *Beatty*, p. 293.
[9] Churchill to Beatty, November 11, 1924, BTY 14/4, BP.
[10] Beatty to Wife, July 3, 1917, February 4, 1918 in Beatty, *Beatty Papers*, 1: 444, 508; Beatty to Wife, July 6, 1925, BTY 17/7/21–23, BP; Beatty to Wife, May 12, 1912, in Chalmers, *Life and Letters*, p. 112.
[11] Martin Gilbert, *Winston S. Churchill: The Stricken World, 1916–1922* (New York: Houghton Mifflin, 1975) 4:179; Beatty to Wife, February 22, 1922 in Chalmers, *Life and Letters*, p. 371; Murfett, *First Sea Lords*, p. 131; Beatty, *Beatty Papers* 2: 78; Roskill, *Beatty*, pp. 312–313, 337–341.
[12] Roskill, *Naval Policy*, pp. 223–224, 228, 336–341.   [13] Gilbert, *Churchill* 4: 14, 769.
[14] Roskill, *Naval Policy*, pp. 336–341.   [15] Quoted in *Ibid.*, p. 279. See also pp. 278–283.

against possible Japanese attack required the development of a modern naval base at Singapore large enough to sustain the main battle fleet. In the event of war with Japan, Beatty envisioned the rapid deployment of the Mediterranean Fleet and then the Atlantic Fleet through the Suez Canal and Indian Ocean to Singapore.[16] Since the Mediterranean Fleet required thirty days and the Atlantic Fleet sixty days to reach Singapore, a strong naval presence was necessary to repel any Japanese threat, not only to secure the Singapore base for naval operations against the Japanese fleet, but also to ensure that the Japanese did not capture and make use of the Singapore base to destroy the ports and refueling depots at Colombo, Trincomali, Madras, and Rangoon or take control of the Indian Ocean with all of its valuable trade to Great Britain.[17]

Beatty returned home from the Washington Conference convinced that Japan would be Britain's future enemy. The Japanese, he argued, "were a military race from beginning to end," had won three naval wars, and despite the calm and suave reassurances from their diplomats, would inevitably challenge and encroach upon Britain's interests in China. He claimed that the commercial value of these interests was worth £300 million a year to England, yet he lamented that England was "totally incapable of defending these interests."[18] To strengthen its fleet against Japan, the Admiralty had first unsuccessfully attempted to convince the Cabinet of the need for an Anglo-French military alliance, which would allow the British to assign a greater number of warships to Asian waters.[19] Building the two new battleships allowed under the Washington Treaty and increasing production of the unlimited auxiliaries, especially light cruisers, was therefore all the more imperative. Equally crucial was building the greatly expanded, modern naval base at Singapore where Britain could quickly rally against any Japanese threat by dispatching the main battle fleet of twelve battleships, four battle cruisers, thirty-one auxiliary cruisers, eighty-one destroyers, forty submarines and ninety-seven other support vessels.[20]

With Churchill's and Birkenhead's strong support, the Cabinet Committee on Defense Estimates fully endorsed Beatty's postwar strategic naval policy for war against Japan. The Cabinet Committee agreed that Japan was now the "most likely potential enemy," and therefore building a base at Singapore large enough to service the main battle fleet was crucial to the defense of the Empire.

---

[16] *Ibid.*, pp. 294–295.
[17] *Ibid.*, pp. 294–295, 420; Rolland A. Chaput, *Disarmament in British Foreign Policy* (London: George Allen and Unwin, 1935), p. 151.
[18] Beatty, *Beatty Papers* 2: 408–409; Roskill, *Naval Policy*, pp. 348–349.
[19] Ferris, *Evolution*, p. 149.
[20] Roskill, *Naval Policy*, pp. 348–350, 290–291, 295–296. For plans to send the Main Battle Fleet to Singapore, see "Report on Naval Oil Fuel Reserves," Cabinet, Naval Programme Committee, C. P. 47 (28), CAB 24/192, PRO.

"We are deeply impressed by all that Lord Beatty has told us," the Committee concluded. On this basis, it rejected the Geddes Committee's recommendation for drastic reductions in naval personnel and succeeded in restoring £2 million to the 1922–1923 naval budget, which now totaled £65 million.[21]

An American student of British naval strategy who would later become an important negotiator at the 1927 Geneva Naval Conference fully agreed with Beatty's assessment of Japan as a future menace in East Asia and with the importance of the Singapore base. Captain Frank Schofield admired the clarity of the Admiralty's strategic thinking and the skillful manner in which the British diplomats had supported the Admiralty's strategy by exempting Singapore from the non-fortification agreement at the Washington Conference. Highly respected among American naval strategists, Schofield emphasized to his fellow American naval officers that by protecting Singapore, the British had preserved the "strategic center" of their Empire east of Suez, a base crucial to the British Fleet in the Western Pacific in the event of a war. "No Asiatic fleet" [i.e., Japanese fleet], Schofield insisted, "could ever pass Singapore towards Australia or towards the Indian Ocean if a British fleet of equal or superior strength was based or could be based on Singapore and suitably supported by that base." With undisguised admiration, Schofield pointed to the Singapore base as a prime example of the "long-standing British strategic policy – the policy of controlling narrow waters throughout the world, of controlling converged points of commerce" with adjacent naval bases, which allowed the British Navy the mobility to act anywhere in the world in defense of British interests.[22]

Beatty's new naval strategy against Japan carried with it the logical request for a larger number of modern cruisers to accompany the main battle fleet in its wartime journey to Singapore. Because the Five Power Treaty prevented the building of capital ships – battleships, battle cruisers, and aircraft carriers – for a ten-year period, and with Japan already limited to only 60 percent of British capital ships, the Washington Treaty freed the Admiralty to expand its superiority over Japan still further by building unlimited auxiliary ships. But, the Admiralty's skillful use of diplomacy at the Washington Conference in exempting auxiliaries was jeopardized by two developments which the Admiralty had not foreseen: the ever-increasing costs of these modern light cruisers and the steadily worsening British economy.

---

[21] Churchill to Beatty, October 10, 1921, in Winston S. Churchill, *Winston S. Churchill, Volume Companion* 4 Part 3, ed. Martin Gilbert (Boston: Houghton Mifflin, 1978), p. 1646; "Naval Building," Cabinet, Naval Programme Committee, 22/176, CHAR., pp. 1–2, WCP. See also Roskill, *Beatty*, pp. 312–313; Murfett, *First Sea Lords*, p. 131; Beatty to Wife, February 23, 1922 in Chalmers, *Life and Letters*, p. 371.

[22] Capt. F. [Frank] H. Schofield, "Some Aspects of the Washington Conference on American Naval Strategy," September 22, 1923, XPOD-1923-148, pp. 8–9, NWC; Roskill, *Naval Policy*, pp. 339, 342–349.

The increased cost of the new auxiliary cruiser was in large part the result of its increased combat capabilities. The prototype of the modern 10,000-ton, 8-inch-gun auxiliary cruiser – or "Treaty Cruiser," as it was sometimes called because the Washington Treaty had limited the maximum size of these auxiliary cruisers to 10,000 tons with a maximum gun-size of 8 inches – had its origin in the five British Hawkins class cruisers laid down during and immediately following World War I. Capable of 31 knots, the Hawkins class carried 7.5-inch guns, which fired shells twice as heavy as the 6-inch-gun at the maximum range of sighting. This technological increase in firepower had made almost all of the cruisers in rival navies obsolete, as they were usually not only considerably smaller, but carried only 5.5-inch or six-inch guns.[23] The superior firepower, endurance, protection, and habitability of the Hawkins class came at a greatly increased cost of over £2 million per ship, considerably more expensive than earlier smaller cruisers. As one British Admiral put it: by parading this more powerful cruiser "under their noses," during this ship's visit to Japan, England had stimulated its naval rivals to begin an even more expensive escalation of new cruisers superior to the Hawkins class.[24]

The Admiralty was well aware of this cost problem as well as the fact that it was financially impossible for England to engage in a theoretically endless round of continued escalation in cruiser sizes and gun power. The Admiralty therefore had specifically and emphatically instructed the British delegates to the Washington Conference to limit the maximum displacement of auxiliary cruisers to 10,000 tons with a maximum gun-size of 8 inches. Equally important to the Admiralty was the imperative of an unlimited number of cruisers – an objective which its diplomats had successfully achieved.[25] By limiting displacement and gun-size, and thereby slowing the rising costs of even bigger auxiliary cruisers, the Admiralty had hoped that England could afford to build a greater number of cruisers than their rivals in the years ahead.

The number of unlimited cruisers needed and the means to finance them soon became subjects of long and often bitter debates, although the characteristics of this cruiser, dictated by Beatty's new naval strategy were seldom in doubt.[26] Based on a future war with Japan and the necessity of holding

---

[23] Director of Gunnery, Minute, "Type of Light Cruisers for Dominions," May 7, 1921, P. D. 01639/21, ADM 1/8653/266; Minute, "Questions Affecting Light Cruiser Construction," June 27, 1922, G. D. 40/22, ADM 1/8653/266/23; "Cruiser Building Policy," May 6, 1937, P. D. 10926, ADM 1/9427, p.5, PRO.

[24] Fred Dreyer, Minute, June 20, 1921, "Type of Light Cruisers for Dominions," P. D. 01639/21, ADM 1/8653/266, PRO.

[25] "Questions Affecting Light Cruisers," June 27, 1922, G. D. 40/22, ADM 1/8653/266, PRO; Fred Dreyer, "Questions in Connection with Empire Naval Policy and Cooperation: Type of Light Cruisers," May 7, 1921, P. D. 01620/21 in *Ibid*. See also "Naval Staff Opinion on Cruiser Size of 10,000 Tons," ADM 116/2149/65395, PRO.

[26] "Naval Staff Opinion on Cruiser Size of 10,000 Tons," ADM 116/2149/65395, PRO. See especially Ernle Chatfield, "Questions Affecting Light Cruiser Construction," June 27, 1922,

Singapore long enough for the main battle fleet to arrive within four to six weeks, the Admiralty thought long and carefully about the capabilities of its new generation of cruisers.[27] In addition to protecting the capital ships, this new auxiliary cruiser would have to be capable of successfully fulfilling several other important combat missions. It would have to patrol alone over distant yet vital sea lanes far from British bases or help from other British warships. Sea lanes in East Asia were especially vulnerable because Australia and New Zealand lacked modern navies and, like Hong Kong and Singapore, were subject to Japan's ability to put them under quick naval threat.[28] Thus, the "Foreign Service" cruiser must be a warship able to operate with the main battle fleet, protect distant trade routes without any additional assistance, and independently harass enemy trade and lines of communication. Such a ship must also be able to defeat the largest hostile cruiser likely to be encountered, as well as have the speed to escape from larger enemy warships.[29]

In the event of war with Japan, the "Foreign Service" cruiser must fulfill, as Admiral Dudley Pound, the Director of Plans admitted, a "most difficult role."[30] Assuming that the Japanese would quickly blockade Hong Kong, Admiralty strategists not only wanted the new cruiser to protect the Singapore naval base until the main battle fleet arrived but also to interdict Japanese naval operations, lines of communication, and trade "without being brought to action by superior enemy forces."[31] To achieve all of these tasks, the cruiser must therefore be a large vessel of 10,000 tons, which would give it the very high sailing endurance of 6,500 miles. With this endurance, it could use Singapore as its base and, from it, could interdict Japanese naval operations in the surrounding area. It must also have excellent sea-keeping capabilities and speed of at least 33 to 34 knots to outrun stronger opponents. Its 8-inch, 50-caliber guns would give it the capability of fighting, alone, against most of the world's cruisers, which generally carried guns no larger than 6 inches. Its two-to-four airplanes would provide the capability for reconnaissance and for directing its longer 50-caliber guns beyond the horizon, thus making possible the destruction of enemy warships with less powerful guns well before they could get close enough to return fire.[32]

Packing all of these requirements into the new vessel created a considerable amount of anxiety among the Naval Staff. Admiralty planners worried over the new 8-inch gun, its twin-turret design, and the 8-inch shell – all of which had to

G. D. 40/22, ADM 1/8653/266/23, PRO. Ernle Chatfield was Third Sea Lord and Controller of the Navy, 1925–1928.

[27] Roskill, *Naval Policy*, pp. 404–405.   [28] *Ibid.*

[29] For one of the most complete discussions of cruiser characteristics, see Dudley Pound, "Design of Light Cruisers," September 14, 1922, P. D. 01712/22, ADM 1/8653/266, PRO. See also E. C. [Ernle Chatfield?], Minute, June 17 and June 23 1921, "Type of Light Cruisers for Dominions," P. D. 01639/21, ADM 1/8653/266, PRO and sources in footnote 26.

[30] Dudley Pound, "Design of Light Cruisers," September 14, 1921, pp. 1–12.

[31] *Ibid.*   [32] *Ibid.*

be newly designed for the larger warship. Since only a slight increase in weight made the 8-inch shell clearly superior to the 7.5-inch shell in both penetration and bursting effect, there was little debate over gun size, caliber, or shells.[33]

However, one of the new requirements deserved much more attention than it received. To increase the new gun's long-range as well as its short-range anti-aircraft capability, the Naval Staff imposed the difficult requirement that the new 8-inch guns must reach 65 degrees of elevation and be able to fire five rounds per minute.[34] Significant, also, was the fact that Admiral Sir Roger Keyes was in a hurry and wanted to rush the new 8-inch gun into production. He worried that the Japanese Furutaka class 8-inch-gun cruisers would be launched before Great Britain could match them, and he therefore pressured the gun manufacturers, responsible for the new gun design and its production process, to hasten their efforts – a fateful decision that would later prove to be important in a variety of ways.[35]

In December 1923 the Admiralty finally approved the plans for the 10,000-ton Kent-class auxiliary cruiser carrying eight of the eight-inch guns in four twin turrets. The Kent class benefited from the design experience gained from building the five earlier 9,500-ton Hawkins-class cruisers, thus resulting in greater endurance, efficiency, and comfort. Two years later, in 1925, the Admiralty revised its thinking after a prolonged and vigorous debate over protection versus speed. The modified London-class cruisers were similar to the Kent class but had faster speeds up to 34 knots, even less protection, and no torpedo tubes.[36] The Admiralty then increased its pressure for immediate authorization to build seventeen Kent-class and London-class cruisers.

Why the Admiralty needed a total of seventy auxiliary cruisers during peacetime was a closely guarded secret, which generated continuous frustration and criticism, especially from political leaders bedeviled by shrinking revenues. Many years later, this secret led one British naval scholar to complain of the "intellectual poverty" of the Admiralty's reasoning.[37] Unbeknownst to all

---

[33] Director of Gunnery, "Investigation into Performance of Up to Date 8–Inch Shell and Weights, Etc. of Pair and Single Gun 8-Inch Mountings," February 6, 1922, G. D. 40/22, ADM 1/8653/266, PRO; F. D. W., Minute, October 31, 1924, S01867/24, ADM 1/9253, PRO; Fred Dreyer, Minute, May 7, 1921, P. D. 61620/21, ADM 1/8653/266, PRO.

[34] Alan Raven and John Roberts, *British Cruisers of World War II* (Annapolis, MD: Naval Institute Press, 1980), p. 170.

[35] Director of Naval Ordinance, Minute, November 7, 1922, "Design of Light Cruisers"; R. C. [Roger Keyes], Minute, November 17, 1922, P. D. 01712/22, ADM 1/8653/266, PRO.

[36] "Modernization and New Construction," N. I. D. 7350/24, ADM 1/8655/12; "Cruisers," July 12, 1924, S01867/24, ADM 1/9253, PRO; Raven and Roberts, *British Cruisers*, pp. 116, 119.

[37] Phillips Payson O'Brien, *British and American Naval Power: Politics and Policy, 1900–1936* (Westport, CT: Praeger, 1998), p. 186; Raven and Roberts, *British Cruisers*, pp. 133, 107; Roskill, *Naval Policy*, pp. 332, 411–412; Hector C. Bywater, *Navies and Nations; A Review of Naval Developments Since the Great War* (Boston and New York: Houghton Mifflin, 1927), pp. 49–50; "Proposal Light Cruiser Building Programme," November 23, 1923, P. D. 01912/23, ADM 1/8653/266/23, PRO; Ferris, *Evolution*, pp. 136–137.

but a few, the Admiralty's reasoning was based on its highly secret war plan against Japan, the details of which were rarely revealed.[38] The plan divided the seventy cruisers into two parts: one group to sail with the battle fleet and a second group to guard England's vital trade routes throughout the world.

The number of auxiliary cruisers needed for the battle fleet was tied directly to the number of modern cruisers in the Japanese fleet. Given Japan's increased shipbuilding during World War I and its latest decision to build four new 9,000-ton, 8-inch-gun cruisers and four 7,100-ton, 8-inch-gun cruisers, it was clear that by 1929, Japan would have a total of twenty-five modern cruisers, of which eight would carry 8-inch guns. Should Great Britain be required to protect Australia, New Zealand, and the other possessions in East Asia or in the Indian Ocean from Japanese naval attack, the Admiralty insisted that the British battle fleet needed equality in modern cruisers plus an additional 25 percent to replace ships which either would fall out for repairs during the long voyage to Singapore or would become casualties of Japanese submarine attacks before the opposing fleets engaged in the decisive battle. Since Japan would have twenty-five modern cruisers in the near future, Great Britain needed twenty-five plus a 25 percent superiority, or six more, for a total of thirty-one cruisers in its battle fleet stationed in the Mediterranean Sea and able to deploy rapidly to Singapore.[39]

Since the thirty-one modern cruisers must at all times sail with the battle fleet, Great Britain also needed thirty-nine additional cruisers to protect the Empire's vital trading routes against other potential enemies in various parts of the world who might attempt to take advantage of an Anglo-Japanese war to interfere with British shipping. These additional cruisers would also fulfill another vital task. While protecting trade in Southeast Asia, they could be rapidly deployed to Singapore to protect this vital naval base until the battle fleet arrived.[40]

---

[38] Roger Bellairs, "The Total Number and Type of Cruisers Required by the British Empire," March 15, 1928, P. D. 02984/28, p. 3, ADM 116/2607, PRO. See also footnote 40.

[39] Ibid.

[40] Ibid. ; Dudley Pound, "Proposal re. Light Cruisers," October 31, 1923, P. D. 01914/23, ADM 1/8653/266, PRO; Director of Plans, "Emergency Construction Programme," December 22, 1923, P. D. 01949/23, p.3, ADM 1/8702/151, PRO; Royal Naval Staff to President, Royal Naval Staff College, March 13, 1928, P. D. 02989/28, ADM 116/2607, PRO; Neville Chamberlain to Leo Amery, December 20, 1923; Amery to Chamberlain, December 22 1923 in "Emergency Construction Programme," December, 22, 1923, P. D. 01949/23, ADM 1/8702/151, PRO. (This Admiralty memorandum was sent to Neville Chamberlain). See also Roger Bellairs' confirmation of sending the memorandum to Amery in "The Total Number and Type of Cruisers Required by the British Empire," March 15, 1928, p.3, ADM 116/2607, PRO. Bellairs insisted that "this was the only occasion on which the actual War Plan distribution of cruisers was given to a Cabinet Minister." See also Director of Plans, "Programme of Construction and Reconstruction," June 22, 1923, ADM 1/8702/151, PRO; Director of Plans, "Secret Cruiser Programme," January 29, 1924, P. D. 02053/24, ADM 1/8673/228/24, PRO; Ferris, *Evolution*, pp. 135–136;

In January 1924 Ramsay MacDonald's Labor Party took control of the government, and the new Chancellor of the Exchequer, Phillip Snowden brushed aside Baldwin's deficit-spending "brainwave" and lost no time in rejecting Beatty's demand for 70 cruisers.[41] Beatty aggressively set out to "teach them Imperialism." "It is quite extraordinary," he confided to his wife, "the amount of real ignorance that exists in their [politicians'] minds on questions of the greatest importance."[42] When MacDonald eventually agreed to build five cruisers, largely to relieve unemployment in the shipyards, Beatty claimed a "great triumph." He was delighted because, he insisted, the Admiralty had convinced "extremists of every description, pacifist, communist, socialist, etc." in the MacDonald government to vote for a strong navy.[43] Nonetheless, MacDonald dismissed the entire premise of a Japanese threat to British interests in East Asia. Rather than antagonize Japan, he insisted that British diplomacy must instead emphasize friendship. In office less than a year, MacDonald nonetheless succeeded in casting doubt on the wisdom of the Admiralty's strategic assumptions.[44]

Chaput, *Disarmament*, p. 148. The evolution of the Admiralty thinking can be traced in Director of Plans, "Proposals re. Light Cruisers," October 31, 1923, P. D. 01914/23, ADM 1/8653/266. See also Beatty's Minute approving the building schedule on November 7, 1923 in *Ibid.*; Director of Plans, "Proposed Light Building Programme," 23 November 1923, P. D. 01912/23, ADM 1/8653/266/23, PRO. On the great need for destroyers and submarines, see Roger Keyes, Minute, June, 25, 1923, "Programme of Construction and Reconstruction," December 8, 1923, P. D. 01813/23, ADM 1/8702/151, PRO; Naval Staff, "Memorandum by the Naval Staff: Cruiser Replacement Programme," January 24, 1924, P. D. 02053/24, ADM 1/8672/228/24, PRO and Minutes by Dudley Pound, Roger Keyes, and Beatty; Director of Plans, "Proposed Light Building Programme," November 23, 1923, P. D. 01912/23 ADM 1/8653/266/23, PRO; Director of Plans, "Proposals re. Light Cruisers," October 31, 1923, P. D. 01904/23 ADM 1/8653/266, PRO. Beatty's Minute approving this building program on November 7, 1923 is in *Ibid*. See also Ferris, *Evolution*, p. 136; Robert Rhodes James, *The British Revolution, 1880–1939* (New York: Alfred A. Knopf, 1977), pp. 478–480, 617; James Harold Mannock, "Anglo-American Relations, 1921–1928" (Ph.D. diss., Princeton University, 1962), pp. 140–150; Ferris, *Evolution*, p. 136; Director of Plans, "Emergency Construction Programme," December 22, 1923, P. D. 01949, ADM 1/8702/151, PRO; Director of Plans, "Proposals re. Light Cruisers: Flagships," October 31, 1923, P. D. 01914/23, ADM 1/8633/266, PRO; "Light Cruiser Construction Programme," n. d., P. D. 01970/1924, ADM 1/8672/227/24, PRO; Director of Plans, "Emergency Construction Programme," December 22, 1923, P. D. 01949/23, ADM 1/8702/151, PRO; Frederick Dreyer, Minute, June 20 1921, "Type of Light Cruisers for Dominions," P. D. 01639/21, ADM 1/8653/266, PRO; Roskill, *Beatty*, pp. 210, 219, 267; Murfett, *First Sea Lords*, pp. 132–133.
[41] For the Admiralty's defense against objections to its building recommendations, see Naval Staff, "Memorandum: Cruiser Replacement Programmes," January 29, 1924, P. D. 02053/24, ADM 1/8672/228/24, PRO; Roskill, *Naval Policy*, p. 418; Chaput, *Disarmament*, pp. 149–150; Roskill, *Beatty*, p. 340.
[42] Beatty to Wife, February 2, 1924, BTY 17/65/23–24, BP; Beatty, *Beatty Papers* 2: 272.
[43] Ramsay MacDonald to Beatty, March 20, 1925, BTY 14/9; Beatty to Wife, February 23, 1924, BTY 17/65/88–91, BP; Beatty, *Beatty Papers*, 2: 274–275; Roskill, *Naval Policy*, pp. 339, 349, 411–425, 439–444.
[44] Ferris, *Evolution*, pp. 136–137, 144, 142–146.

In November 1924, when the "extremists" were replaced by conservative cabinet ministers in the second Baldwin government, the Singapore naval base was revived, but even these conservative ministers now began to question the rapid construction of both cruisers and naval bases. Rather than a triumphant revival of imperialistic thinking, Beatty had to contend with still another new government which, while more sympathetic to the Navy's defense of the Empire, had little choice but to recognize the economic realities of a badly floundering economy.[45] Thus, Beatty's political battles were far from over.

Stanley Baldwin was a shy, nervous, lonely man, much beloved for his warm personal qualities and sterling character. His political colleagues respected his ability to maintain parliamentary support for the Conservative Party during this difficult period of political transition, which required his party to adjust to the worsening economic collapse and the increasing discontents of the mid-to-late 1920s. During the four and one-half years between late 1924, when he became prime minister for a second time, and 1929, when Ramsay MacDonald's Labour Party again toppled him, Baldwin enjoyed a margin in Parliament of 419 Conservative seats against only 151 for the Labour Party and 44 for the Liberal Party.

Yet despite this comfortable parliamentary margin, Baldwin's leadership was often criticized for its irresolution, indecision, and lack of direction. These criticisms arose in part because he preferred to wait on events to determine if a problem might resolve itself or somehow go away before taking action. He did this to prevent another party split, which had recently allowed Ramsey MacDonald to gain power, if only temporarily. Maintaining party harmony was one of his highest priorities. He accomplished this by allowing each member of his Cabinet sufficient independence and time to formulate solutions to problems affecting that particular department. Once he had a Cabinet member's recommendation, he employed his considerable political skills in guiding the Cabinet toward consensus and Parliament toward approval. His calm, friendly, sensitive and supportive ways were appreciated by his cabinet officers, but given England's multitudinous postwar problems, his collegial style and slow consensus-achieving process often resulted in sharp inter-departmental debates and consequent long delays in reaching Cabinet consensus.[46]

Baldwin's cabinet officers included some of Great Britain's most distinguished and experienced political leaders. Austen Chamberlain, for example, the Foreign Secretary, soon enhanced his reputation by successfully negotiating

---

[45] Roskill, *Naval Policy*, pp. 339, 349, 423–425, 448–464, 556; Chaput, *Disarmament*, pp. 150–153; Ferris, *Evolution*, pp. 136–137.
[46] Keith Middlemas and John Barnes, *Baldwin: A Biography* (London: Macmillan, 1970), pp. 483–506, 378–439; William Bridgeman, *The Modernisation of Conservative Politics: The Diaries and Letters of William Bridgeman, 1904–1935* ed. Philip Williamson (London: Historians Press, 1988), pp. vii–viii.

the Locarno Agreement, which sought to guarantee the security of the French, German, and Belgian borders. This won Chamberlain the 1925 Nobel Peace Prize.⁴⁷ Another luminary was Chancellor of the Exchequer Winston Churchill, who had only recently returned to the Conservative Party in 1924, after twenty years of leadership in the Liberal Party. Churchill had served in earlier Cabinet posts including the Board of Trade, the Colonial Office, the War Office, and most significantly, the Admiralty.⁴⁸

Although now an avowed Conservative, Churchill nonetheless retained his strong Liberal convictions that government ought to lead the way toward an alternative to socialism, on the one hand, and callous Conservative Party indifference to workers on the other. He championed government-financed workers insurance covering accidents, sickness, and old age; pensions for widows and orphans; and subsidies for better housing.⁴⁹ As Chancellor of the Exchequer, he recognized that to finance these reforms in 1924 he would once again have no choice but to oppose large naval budgets, as he had earlier done in 1908 for the very same reasons.⁵⁰ To accomplish these goals, he used his extensive insights acquired as the former First Lord of the Admiralty from 1911–1915 to give Baldwin advice on how to trim big Admiralty budget requests. Baldwin was delighted: "You are a Chancellor after my own heart," he exclaimed.⁵¹

Baldwin also appointed some of his close friends to his cabinet. One of these was William Bridgeman, who became the First Lord of the Admiralty. Known as "Willie" to his colleagues, Bridgeman was a short, rosy-cheeked, round-faced, balding gentleman with a drooping mustache, whose humor, honesty, and sincerity endeared him to many. Because he was an unassuming, modest person, who was a slow, bland speaker, political opponents sometimes underestimated him. Nonetheless, his long experience in politics had earlier won him his first Cabinet post as Home Secretary. But it was their close friendship and shared political beliefs and values which prompted Baldwin to elevate him into the highest circles of the Conservative Party.⁵²

---

⁴⁷ B. J. C. McKercher, *The Second Baldwin Government and the United States, 1924–1929: Attitudes and Diplomacy* (Cambridge: Cambridge University Press, 1984), pp. 6, 9–10.

⁴⁸ Martin Gilbert, *Churchill: A Life* (New York: Henry Holt & Co. Inc., 1991), pp. 164–165, 240–247, 253–254, 464–465.

⁴⁹ Ibid., pp. 152, 184, 190, 467. See also Martin Gilbert, *Winston S. Churchill: The Prophet of Truth, 1922–1939* (Houghton, Mifflin Co., 1977) 5: 65–67.

⁵⁰ Gilbert, *Churchill: A Life*, pp. 201–205, 468–469.

⁵¹ Churchill to Baldwin, December 13 and 15, 1924, CHAR 18/2, WCP; Baldwin to Churchill, December 30, 1924, in Gilbert, *Prophet of Truth*, 5: 65–70; Churchill to Baldwin, December 15, 1924, vol. 130, SBP. For Baldwin quote see Baldwin to Churchill, December 30, 1924 in Winston S. Churchill, *Winston S. Churchill: The Exchequer Years 1922–1929, Companion Volume 5* ed. Martin Gilbert (London: William Heinemann, 1979), p. 327. Hereafter cited as Churchill, *Companion Volume 5*.

⁵² J. C. C. Davidson, *Memoirs of a Conservative*, ed. R. R. James (London: Weedenfeld and Nicolson, 1969), pp. 202–209; Stephen Roskill, *Earl Beatty, The Last Naval Hero: An Intimate*

Beatty welcomed Bridgman to the Admiralty as a "dear little man," whom he liked "better than any we had had, honest and straightforward and a gentleman in the best sense." Bridgeman's strong sense of loyalty to the Admiralty soon won Beatty's "full confidence," which Beatty admitted was "more than I have ever done before" with previous First Lords.[53] But Admiralty critics were not so confident of Bridgeman's judgment and later chastised him as little more than a "voicepipe of the naval chiefs." Bridgeman's lack of experience in naval affairs and diplomacy, they would charge, rendered him compliant "to the will of the naval lords."[54] Bridgman certainly appeared to be intimidated both by Churchill, who he believed "knew so much about Admiralty business" and by Beatty, on whom he relied to combat Churchill. So long as Bridgeman acquiesced to Beatty's directions, their relationship was a harmonious one. Three years later in 1927, however, at the arms-control discussions in Geneva, when Bridgeman sought to introduce his own independent thinking, Beatty contemptuously characterized him as "weak as putty."[55]

The principal source of Bridgeman's difficulties as First Lord of the Admiralty was Winston Churchill. Churchill's relationship to the Admiralty and its leaders was a long and complex one. Even before Churchill became First Lord in October 1911, he had strongly supported British naval superiority and never wavered in that conviction. In 1912 when Germany threatened Great Britain with a vast new naval expansion, Churchill insisted on substantial increases in naval construction, and he again defended the Admiralty in 1922 when he opposed the "Geddes Axe," supported the construction of new battleships, and agreed with Beatty's new East Asian strategy based on war against Japan.[56]

Biography (New York: Athenaeum Press, 1981), pp. 349–350; Bridgeman, Diary, 1924, p. 103, WBP; William F. Trimble, "The United States Navy and the Geneva Conference for the Limitation of Naval Armament, 1927," (Ph.D. diss., University of Colorado, 1974), pp. 154–155; Bridgeman, *Modernisation of Conservative Politics*, pp. viii, 6,–7,9–10; Vice Admiral Kobayashi's description is in "Naval Notes," September 1927, ADM 1/8715/188, p. 19, PRO; Drew Pearson's impressions are recorded by Bridgeman's son in a very sympathetic unpublished biography of his father in BGMN/2, pp. 620–622, WBPCC. Hereafter cited as BGMN/2.

[53] Beatty to Wife, January 8, 1925, BTY 17/69.

[54] "Bywater Castigates British Government," *Baltimore Sun*, August 7, 1927 in Ree. 29, MF 73/1290, CC. For other critics, see Phillips Payson O'Brien, *British and American Naval Power: Politics and Policy, 1900–1936* (Westport, CT: Praeger, 1998), p. 187; McKercher, *Second Baldwin Government*, pp. 12, 187; Bridgeman, *Modernisation of Conservative Politics*. pp. 6–7.

[55] Bridgeman, Diary, 1924, p. 103, WBP; Beatty to Wife, February 5 1925 in William Scott Chalmers, ed. *The Life and Letters of David, Earl Beatty* (London: Hodder and Stoughton, 1951), pp. 405–406; Beatty to Keyes, December 12, 1927 in Roger Keyes, *The Keyes Papers: Selections from the Private and Official Correspondence of Admiral of the Fleet Baron Keyes of Zeebrugge*, ed. Paul G. Halpern 2 vols.(London: George Allen and Unwin, 1980) 2: 188.

[56] Gilbert, *Churchill: A Life*, pp. 201–205, 240–245, 253–254, 442–443; Lord Lee to Churchill, August 4, 1921 in Martin Gilbert, *Winston S. Churchill: The Stricken World, 1916–1922* (Houghton Mifflin, 1975) 4: 1575; Churchill to Beatty, October 10, 1921 in *Ibid.*, p. 1646. Beatty was grateful for Churchill's strong support. See Beatty to Wife, February 23, 1922 in Chalmers, *Life and Letters*, p. 371.

However, now that he was Chancellor of the Exchequer and economic conditions had deteriorated considerably, Churchill took a more flexible view about how and when British naval superiority was to be maintained, especially as he saw no immediate naval threat to Great Britain and because naval construction costs threatened his cherished social reforms. His efforts to limit naval construction in 1908, and again in 1924–1925, stemmed from his belief that no naval threat was immediately apparent and that important social reforms would be starved as a consequence.[57] Churchill had high personal regard for both Bridgeman and Beatty and attempted to maintain cordial relations with them, but because their naval construction demands threatened what he considered to be higher national priorities, he refused to allow either his personal regard for them or his love for the British Navy to cloud his judgment about the greater needs confronting the working people of Great Britain.[58]

As Chancellor of the Exchequer, Churchill was obligated to assess the current economic health of Great Britain and to project likely economic conditions. His analysis led him to the imperative need to adopt government policies that would stimulate economic growth. "We shall never shake ourselves clear from the debts of the past and break into a definitely larger period" of prosperity, he believed, "except by the creation of new wealth."[59] In his judgment, lowering taxes was one of the best ways to stimulate the economy. Because of the recent success of MacDonald's Labor Party, he was equally convinced that the Conservative Party must act positively to shore up the electorate's faith in capitalism by combating the ravages of skyrocketing unemployment through government-sponsored and financed unemployment insurance, old age pensions, affordable housing, and healthcare.

Churchill's call for expanded government social welfare was complicated by the conviction among professional economists, the Bank of England, Conservatives, and even some Socialists that a return to the gold standard would invigorate England's international financial position and thereby improve the economy. In a vain effort to combat this economic mindset, Churchill invited John Maynard Keynes, the noted British economist, to argue against a deflationary return to the gold standard, but Baldwin ultimately insisted on it, and Churchill reluctantly acquiesced.[60] His economic policies were hampered still further by the complex debt repayments to the United States for war loans, a source of bitterness to him, to Baldwin, and to other British leaders, all of

[57] Gilbert, *Churchill: A Life*, pp. 201–202, 240–245, 253–254.
[58] Bridgeman, Diary, 1925, p. 105, WBP; Churchill to Beatty, November 11, 1924, BTY 14/4, BP; Chalmers, *Life and Letters*, pp. 402, 408–409; David Beatty, *The Beatty Papers; Selections from the Private and Official Correspondence of Admiral of the Fleet Earl Beatty, 1902–1927*, B. Mc L. Ranft, ed. 2 vols. (Aldershot, England: Gower, 1989) 2: 225.
[59] Quoted in Gilbert, *Churchill: A Life*, p. 468.
[60] Ibid., pp. 468–469; Middlemas and Barnes, *Baldwin*, pp. 305–316; Gilbert, *Prophet of Truth* 5: 92–97, 100.

whom had unsuccessfully argued that the United States should forgive all of the war loans to all of the Allies and thereby stimulate international economic recovery.[61]

Given these political and economic realities, Churchill believed his best chance to reverse the economic decline and prevent a return to power of the socialists was to stimulate economic growth by lowering taxes and cutting spending on nonessential budget requests such as immediate naval building. He had therefore to convince the Admiralty to revise its timetable for new construction until the economy had revived. Churchill was under no illusion, however, about the Admiralty's certain opposition to any delays and the consequent intense political infighting which lay ahead. He therefore went directly to Baldwin with a political strategy designed to force the Admiralty to accept a building slowdown.[62]

Churchill's presentation to Baldwin emphasized three major concerns: the worsening state of Britain's economy, the looming threat that the Labour Party could repeat its recent electoral success, and his assessment of Beatty's war plan against Japan, all of which he believed were intimately related to one another. To provide England with a better chance for economic recovery, Churchill argued to Baldwin that it was necessary to create a stable, reliable financial plan for at least the next three years.[63] As a former Chancellor of the Exchequer himself, Baldwin undoubtedly agreed with Churchill that a plan was vital to avoid the "awful waste of chopping and changing which has marked the last three years," especially as it made no sense to "take off taxes this year in order to put them back the next year." A return to the gold standard meant that England must follow "a most strict policy of debt repayment and a high standard of credit," which by implication meant that Baldwin could not return to his earlier deficit spending for naval construction by which the first Baldwin Government in 1923, one scholar noted, "bequeathed a financial crisis to his second" government in 1925.[64] Unemployment insurance, old age pensions, health programs, better housing, and increased aid to education, Churchill assured Baldwin, could be enacted immediately but had to be paid out of current income and from increasing governmental revenues as the economy revived.

To finance these social and welfare reforms in the short run, Churchill advised Baldwin to consider cutting the naval construction costs which Baldwin

---

[61] Gilbert, *Churchill: A Life*, p. 433; Frank C. Costigliola, "Anglo-American Financial Rivalry in the 1920s," *Journal of Economic History* 37 (1977): 912, 926–934; Robert Rhodes James, *The British Revolution, 1880–1939* (New York: Alfred A. Knopf, 1977), pp. 478–479; Churchill, *Prophet of Truth*, 5: 79–82.

[62] Churchill to Baldwin, December 15, 1924, CHAR 18/4, WCP; Bridgeman, Diary, June 1925, WBP; Bridgeman, Diary, 1925 in Bridgeman, *Modernisation of Conservative Politics*, p. 179.

[63] Churchill to Baldwin, December 15, 1924, CHAR 18/4, WCP.

[64] Ibid. ; John Robert Ferris, *The Evolution of British Strategic Policy, 1919–1926* (Macmillan, 1989), pp. 158–159.

had approved in 1923, which MacDonald had then reduced from eight cruisers to five in 1924, but which, over the next three years, would cost at least £25 million and "probably more." With £25 million for naval construction, total naval costs would reach £80 million per year by 1927–1928, and this level of expenditure, Churchill warned, would "sterilize and paralyze the whole policy of the Government. There will be nothing for the taxpayers and nothing for social reform."[65]

The political costs of continued naval construction would be as disastrous, Churchill predicted to Baldwin, as the economic and social consequences. Baldwin's newly dubbed "Naval Parliament" would be continually denounced by the Labour Party, which would accuse the Conservatives of "starting up the whole armament race all over the world and setting the pace toward a new vast war." To Churchill's thinking, the Conservative Party's inability to enact crucial social welfare reforms was far more dangerous than any theoretical naval enemy because it would set a course "certain to result in a Socialist victory." Furthermore, if once again in power, the socialists would exploit the "tremendous" economic discontent, which had previously carried them into office, by cutting down and blotting out "all these Naval preparations so that in the end the Admiralty will not get the Navy programme for the sake of which your Government would have broken itself."[66]

To what purpose, he asked Baldwin, was naval construction so vital? Having himself defended the Admiralty against the "Geddes Axe," and having staunchly supported Beatty's East Asian naval strategy three years earlier, Churchill was quite familiar with the Admiralty's building rationale. He assured Baldwin that his current thoughts about the Admiralty's naval strategy were not "without experience or sympathy," yet he could no longer agree with the "wonderful staff of keen, able officers, whose minds were filled with [recent] war impressions," and who had concluded that Great Britain must begin to prepare for war against Japan. "What question is pending between England and Japan? To what diplomatic combination," he queried, "do either of us belong which could involve us against each other?"

Churchill rejected the notion that Japan could be compared to the German naval threat before World War I. "Japan is at the other end of the world" and therefore "cannot menace our vital security in any way." Furthermore, Japan was still an ally, he argued, and therefore had "no reason whatever to come into collision with us" and "every reason to avoid such a collision." Yet the Admiralty war plan involved the development of Hong Kong as a strong base for as many as twenty-one submarines "provocatively stationed there in time of peace right under the noses of the Japanese." The Admiralty would further contribute to Japanese fears by its demands for immediate construction of an expensive new modern naval base at Singapore. Simultaneous with the new

[65] Churchill to Baldwin, December 15, 1924, CHAR 18/4, WCP.   [66] Ibid.

warships construction and Singapore naval base were additional expensive demands for "reserves of stores and ammunition... rapidly completed on lavish scales" as well as "100 merchantmen... armed with six-inch guns."[67]

War with Japan, Churchill concluded, made no economic or military sense. "I do not believe there is the slightest chance of it in our lifetime," he erroneously predicted. Even if Great Britain and Japan should become involved in a dispute in China, England was in no position to go to war. Such a war would require sending the "best part of our Fleet to Singapore," leaving England "at the mercy... of every unfriendly power or force hostile to the British Empire." Not only a greatly expanded navy but also a greatly expanded army would be required to attack Japan in a war so costly, Churchill predicted, that it would "reduce us to bankruptcy." Except in the unlikely event of Japan's attack on Australia, it "would never be worth our while to do it," and, therefore, he insisted, was "not a possibility which any reasonable Government need take into account."[68]

Fully aware of the Admiralty's likely rebuttal, Churchill proposed his own line of counterattack. He advised Baldwin to request both the Foreign Office and the Committee of Imperial Defence (CID), a permanent Cabinet subcommittee responsible for assessing strategic threats and prioritizing national defense requirements, to employ the Ten-Year Rule. Passed in 1919, the Ten-Year Rule was designed to provide a carefully crafted assessment of the likelihood of war during the next ten years in order to discourage the production of weapons which would become obsolete before another conflict arose.[69]

If, as he expected, the CID and the Foreign Office concluded that no threat existed, he advised Baldwin to ask the Cabinet to relieve the Admiralty of any formal responsibility for preparing for war against Japan and instead require it "to recast all of their plans and scales and standards on the basis that no naval war against a first-class navy is likely to take place in the next twenty years," that the age at which warships were retired be prolonged, that ships scheduled as replacements "should be spread over at least three times the period specified," and that one half of the cost of these replacement ships should come from other parts of the annual naval budget. By taking these measures, Churchill believed that naval costs could be cut to £60 million by 1928–1929.[70]

Even greater savings could be achieved by a longer-term solution. Churchill knew that even if Baldwin acted on all of his recommendations, the Admiralty would fight him every year, when it submitted its annual budget. Both to lessen these bitter annual squabbles and to ensure that rival navies did not gain superiority in unlimited auxiliaries, Churchill admonished Baldwin to "seek a

---

[67] Ibid. For criticism of Churchill's assessment of Japan's intentions see Stephen Roskill, *Churchill and the Admirals* (New York: William Morrow, 1978), pp. 79–80.
[68] Churchill to Baldwin, December 15, 1924, CHAR 18/4, WCP.
[69] Gilbert, *Churchill: A Life*, pp. 485–486; Ferris, *Evolution*, pp. 158–159.
[70] Churchill to Baldwin, December 15, 1924, CHAR 18/4, WCP.

further Naval Conference at Washington or here to regulate the construction of vessels other than battleships and the rate of replacements." Churchill may well have been aware that Charles Evans Hughes had proposed limitations on all warships, but that the Admiralty had adroitly killed it.[71] Since Japan had moved ahead of Great Britain in building auxiliary warships, the wisdom of Hughes's proposal was now more apparent to Churchill. If all of his recommendations were adopted, he assured Baldwin that the Conservative Party "may be able to secure a second term of power" and with "a steady yet moderate maintenance of our armaments, the Empire will be in a far stronger position militarily, navally, financially, and socially than by any other method."[72]

Another important element in Churchill's thinking was his realization that England's future ability to provide for all the military services was dependent upon its future economic strength. What was needed, he believed, was a more comprehensive understanding of all of the major elements which contributed to national power. During this economic crisis, England had to marshal its economic, diplomatic, and political wisdom in a united and concerted effort to sustain and strengthen its military capabilities at the levels of international competition sufficient to safeguard England's strategic security. Great Britain could not achieve this coordinated effort if the Admiralty's plans for a theoretical war with Japan in East Asia were allowed to stall the essential economic recovery upon which England's future military strength depended.[73]

At first Churchill made conciliatory efforts to persuade Bridgeman of the reasonableness of his opposition to the Admiralty's expensive new building program. In addition to many of the same arguments he had presented to Baldwin, he emphasized his understanding of naval needs, his willingness to meet those needs, and the necessity of considering "whether a more moderate policy, if persevered in not for four years but for eight or nine, might not leave us in a stronger naval position."[74] He did not question the need to replace worn-out or obsolete cruisers. What he did question was the "rate of replacement."[75] Slower replacement, he argued, would provide enormous advantages to Great Britain, to the Conservative Party, and to the Admiralty.

As expected, Bridgeman rejected Churchill's reasoning. He instead suggested that their differing views were merely an interdepartmental squabble which could be ironed out through negotiations between the two departments. But Churchill refused to resolve their different perspectives at the departmental level. He instead called for a Cabinet committee on naval building. Moreover, the Cabinet, based on recommendations from the CID, must settle the question of the likelihood of war against Japan, and if the Cabinet concluded that it

---

[71] Ibid.   [72] Ibid.   [73] Ibid.; Ferris, *Evolution*, p. 176.
[74] Churchill to Bridgeman, December 15, 1924, CHAR 8/2, WCP.
[75] Churchill to Bridgeman, December 25, 1924, BGMN/3, WBPCC. See also Churchill to Bridgeman, December 25, 1924, 4629/1/1924/97, WBP.

was not likely, it must relieve the Admiralty of any responsibility of preparing for it.[76] Churchill expressed his personal sympathies to Bridgeman, who as the new First Lord of the Admiralty only days in office, must "bear the burden of this controversy at such short notice, and without having been able to shape the previous course of events." But a Cabinet decision was vital because "these new naval demands dominate the whole policy of the Government." They precluded "all possibility of relief to the taxpayer or any schemes of social betterment" and were "not warranted by any consideration of the safety of the country." And, because these Admiralty demands would doubtlessly allow the socialists to regain power, they were "deeply injurious to the political foundations of the State."[77]

Churchill wasted no time in lining up allies for the forthcoming Cabinet fight. Baldwin was his most important supporter, immediately creating the Cabinet Naval Programme Committee in December 1924. Austen Chamberlain, the Foreign Secretary, assisted him as well by informing the CID on January 5, 1925 that the prospect of war with Japan was "very remote." It would be a "great mistake," Chamberlain assured the CID, if England were to do "anything that can be read here or elsewhere as competitive building between ourselves and Japan in anticipation of a new struggle," especially as there was "no danger of war with Japan in present circumstances."[78] George N. Curzon, a previous Foreign Secretary who served on the CID and in the Cabinet as Lord President of the Council, concurred with Chamberlain, adding that Japan was pro-British and sought only cordial relations.[79] Churchill was supported as well by such staunch Cabinet allies as F. E. Smith, generally known as Lord Birkenhead, and William Joynson Hicks, the Home Secretary, and in varying degrees by other Cabinet ministers including Lord Robert Cecil, a devoted advocate of international disarmament who served as Chancellor of the Duchy of Lancaster and the Cabinet's representative to the League of Nations.[80] Thus Churchill had skillfully marshaled his arguments and his political allies well in advance of the long, bitter internal battle.

Bridgeman and Beatty were astonished by Churchill's arguments and his strong Cabinet support. Because Beatty was more experienced at confronting Churchill and because the newly appointed First Lord still had much to learn about Admiralty strategy and building programs, Beatty quickly asserted his

---

[76] See sources in *Ibid*. See also Churchill to Bridgeman, January 23, 1925, 4629/1/1925/3, WBP.
[77] Churchill to Bridgeman, January 23, 1925, CHAR 18/10, WCP.
[78] Austen Chamberlain's response is in the discussion of "Political Outlook in the Far East," January 5, 1925, 193rd Meeting of the CID, Cabinet, Naval Programme Committee, N. P. (25) 4, copy in WCP.
[79] Lord Curzon's response is in *Ibid*. See also "Cabinet Memorandum: Naval Estimates," January 29, 1925, Cabinet, Naval Programme Committee, N. P. (25) 4, pp. 362–365, WCP; Gilbert, *Prophet of Truth*, 5; 79; Ferris, *Evolution*, pp. 146, 158.
[80] Churchill to Cecil, January 20, 1925, CHAR 18/10, WCP; O'Brien, *British and American Naval Power*, p. 184.

leadership in the confrontation. He at first refused to credit that Churchill actually "believes all the rubbish he has talked."[81] Nonetheless, he knew Churchill well enough to take his challenge seriously. He suspected "that the Cabinet will try to foist what is their responsibility..." on to the Committee of Imperial Defence, which was "after all only an advisory committee."[82] Only the Cabinet, he instructed Bridgeman, could change national defense and strategic policies, and since the Cabinet had already clearly established Admiralty responsibilities to defend "our Eastern Interests," only the Cabinet, not Churchill, could alter that responsibility. This, he assured Bridgeman, "is the main question and no other."[83]

Weeks of continued debate with Churchill sapped Beatty's energies. At first he was encouraged by Churchill's good humor and lack of personal malice despite "some pretty strong things," which Beatty had hurled against the Chancellor.[84] But by early February Beatty admitted that the constant arguments took "a good deal out of me," especially, "when dealing with a man of his caliber with a very quick brain. A false step, remark, or even gesture is immediately fastened upon, so I have to keep my wits about me."[85] At one point, after he had "wrangled with Winston and his Treasury myrinidons" for four long hours, he again confessed that the "hard struggle... takes a lot out of me," especially as he had "to concentrate on gigantic figures for a prolonged period and have to battle with those whose life is spent in a maze of the figures."[86] At other times he became so discouraged that he alternatively characterized the debate as a "very bitter struggle," or as "very wearing," or "very trying," with the "continual bickering" producing a "hopeless feeling" after little progress, yet at "a considerable cost of temper and bad feeling."[87] At still other times he complained of becoming "bewildered by the change of plans and by the many proposals" to the point of being "infernally harassed."[88] But he refused to give in.

In late January 1925, Beatty saw the opportunity he had been waiting for when Churchill offered a compromise. In an effort to lower taxes, Churchill called for a stop of all cruiser construction for one year. "That extraordinary fellow Winston has gone mad," Beatty exclaimed. "Nobody outside a lunatic asylum" would accept his tax-reduction scheme. Yet to achieve it, Churchill was willing "to throw everything, all his ideas of imperialism, etc. to the winds..." Thoroughly disgusted with Churchill, Beatty charged him with

---

[81] Beatty to Bridgeman, January 8, 1925, BGMN/3, WBPCC.   [82] *Ibid.*
[83] Beatty to Bridgeman, January 8, 1925, BGMN/3, WBPCC. This is the second letter which Beatty sent to Bridgeman on the same day.
[84] Beatty to Wife, January 6, 1925, BTY 17/69, BP.
[85] Beatty to Wife, February 4, 1925 in Chalmers, *Life and Letters*, p. 405.
[86] Beatty to Wife, January 22, 1925, BTY 17/69, BP. See also Chalmers, *Life and Letters*, p. 403.
[87] Beatty to a Friend, January 23, 1925 in Chalmers, *Life and Letters*, p. 403.
[88] Beatty to Wife, February 3 and 7, 1925, BTY 17/70, BP. See also Chalmers, *Life and Letters*, p. 405.

sacrificing imperialism and the defense of the empire for paltry political advantage. But in doing so, Beatty felt certain that Churchill had sealed his own political doom. The result, Beatty predicted, would be a "split in the Conservative party." By proposing a one-year building holiday, this "silly fellow" had given the Admiralty's powerful political allies who, Beatty claimed, constituted "a very considerable portion of the Conservative Party [and] who already hate Winston like poison," the "fresh ammunition with which to destroy him."[89]

By this time in the debate, Beatty had become desperate and therefore decided that he must force Churchill into a "deadlock of a sensational kind" by bringing the Admiralty's political supporters within the Conservative Party directly into the battle. The "deadlock of a sensational kind" was nothing less than the resignation of Bridgeman and Beatty on the grounds that the Cabinet had refused to give the Admiralty the cruisers vital to the defense of the Empire. Having already cultivated Conservative party members who were staunch supporters of the Admiralty in previous battles with earlier prime ministers, Beatty was convinced that once the resignation crisis became public, he could bring the undecided Cabinet waivers to support the Admiralty by appealing to their patriotism.[90]

Bridgeman was not convinced of the wisdom of this strategy. He liked the pomp and circumstance and prestige of being First Lord of the Admiralty, and the prospect of having to resign so soon after having attained this exalted status depressed him. "Poor old Bridgeman," Beatty observed, "takes a very gloomy view and sees his job fading away from him. But I have hardened him up alot and I think he will stand firm."[91]

To prepare Baldwin for the impending resignation crisis, Beatty persuaded Bridgeman to spend still another weekend at Chequers in order to take his good friend Baldwin "for a long walk and talk sense to him."[92] Despite Bridgeman's best efforts, the Prime Minister refused to bring the controversy to the Cabinet perhaps because Churchill had demanded and finally received Admiralty estimates of building costs for the years between 1925–1929. Armed with this new ammunition, Churchill had warned Baldwin that these estimates were not limited to replacements but required new construction pushing the total annual naval budget to over £90 million by 1928–1929, almost £30 million more per year than Churchill had recommended and certain to leave no money during the next three years for housing, health, education, and other social programs. Once again Churchill questioned the necessity of quickly implementing the Admiralty's war plan against Japan on which most of the increased costs were

---

[89] Beatty to Wife, January 26, 1925 in Chalmers, *Life and Letters*, pp. 404–405. For Bridgeman's criticisms of Churchill see Bridgeman, "Memorandum by the First Lord of the Admiralty," February 5, 1925, ADM 116/2300/4925, PRO. See also "Naval Estimates" in *Ibid*

[90] See, for example, Beatty to Wife, February 5, 1925, BTY 17/70, BP.

[91] Beatty to Wife, January 26, 29, and 30, 1925, BTY 17/69, BP.

[92] Beatty to Wife, January 31, 1925, BTY 17/69, BP.

based, and, like Beatty, he too insisted that only the Cabinet could decide the issue which threatened to "dominate the whole policy of the Government."[93]

In preparation for the impending Cabinet crisis, Beatty, Bridgeman, and the Admiralty's Naval Staff drew up detailed responses to Churchill's persistent criticisms.[94] As it was impossible for them to disguise the large increases in building costs, they emphasized that both their East Asian strategy and their requests for new ships were in keeping with the recommendations made by both Baldwin and Churchill in 1922, and that the Japanese naval threat in East Asia had materially increased during the past three years. They took special aim at Churchill's belief that Great Britain had little to fear from Japan because it was a "very poor country" with few material resources, declining revenues, growing national debt, and decreasing military expenditures.[95] In a secret memorandum circulated to the members of the Naval Programme Committee, but excluded from its Minutes, the Naval Staff agreed that although Japanese military spending had decreased in 1924, Japan still devoted over one third of her entire national budget to expanding its military capability and had in fact "laid down more cruisers, destroyers, and submarines than all four other signatory Powers of the [Five Power] Treaty put together and still have 6 cruisers, 15 destroyers, and 16 submarines authorized...but not yet laid down." Indeed, Bridgeman added, Japan had recently built more warships "than the rest of the world put together..."[96]

For the Admiralty, the most important question was why. What was the motive for allocating over one-third of Japan's national budget to the military? The answer, the Naval Staff argued, was reflected in Japan's recent history, which revealed "'a race of soldiers with a mission' "to create an empire through conquest and thereby become more prosperous, more powerful, and more respected. Japan invested a high percentage of her annual national budget in military improvements because she "believes that victory in war is an efficient cause of improvement in National economy." In one generation this small island nation had defeated its giant neighbors China and Russia despite what appeared in both wars to be insuperable odds, and had propelled itself from a fourth-rate military power to a first-class one. Her great racial pride, bushido warrior code, and confidence in her national mission and destiny

---

[93] Churchill, "Navy Estimates: Memorandum by the Chancellor of the Exchequer," January 29, 1925, C. P. 39 (25), CHAR 22/28, WCP; Churchill to Bridgeman, January 23, 1925, CHAR 18/4, WCP.

[94] Bridgeman, "Memorandum by the First Lord of the Admiralty," February 5, 1925 and "Navy Estimates," February 5, 1925, ADM 116/2300/4925, PRO.

[95] Ibid. ; Churchill, "The Economic Power of Japan: Note by the Chancellor of the Exchequer," December 29, 1924, Cabinet, Naval Programme Committee, N. P. (25) 3, CHAR 22/66, WCP.

[96] See footnote 94. See also Bridgeman, "Political Outlook and the Far East: Memorandum by the First Lord of the Admiralty," March 5, 1925, Cabinet, Naval Programme Committee, N. P. (25) 5, CHAR, 22/66, WCP. This was a secret document, not included in the Naval Programme Committee *Minutes*. A copy is in CHAR 22/66, WCP.

Beatty's Japanese War Plan

encouraged her policy of continued aggressive military expansion aimed at securing safe markets, sources of raw materials, oil, and immigration outlets for her rapidly increasing population. Clearly Japan would continue "to mortgage her wealth for the improvement of her armed forces" and could be expected to use "sinister and dangerous" methods to expand in the very region where England's "stupendous" trade and militarily weak possessions were most vulnerable.[97]

Churchill remained unconvinced. After drawing the Cabinet's attention to the fact that "no attempt is made by the Admiralty to dispute the broad truth of the forecast of Naval expenditure set out by me" at over £90 million per year by 1928–1929, he turned to the broader question of evaluating foreign threats and which of the Cabinet ministers had the responsibility for assessing them. More specifically, he asked if Japan was an immediate mortal threat to Great Britain, and, if so, how probable was that threat in the foreseeable future? Should Great Britain jeopardize its chances for long-term economic recovery, he asked, to prepare for an imminent war against Japan, or could it safely afford to channel its resources for two or three years until the expected economic recovery allowed for increased naval construction without damaging vital social services and reform? These were the questions that must guide the formation of national security policy, and it was precisely these questions, Churchill charged, that the Admiralty continued to ignore.[98]

Churchill's answers to these questions were unequivocal. The degree of danger was neither great nor immediate. There was no "mortal peril" to Great Britain. Unlike Germany before World War I, which could strike directly at England's industrial power and food supply, Japan was not capable of "a physical assault so sudden and so violent" as to prevent the Empire from striking back. By waiting to determine the nature of the warships Japan was building, England could employ its greater industrial power and numerous shipbuilding yards to "build late, build fast, each one better than the last," and with these superior ships give the Admiralty a much greater advantage in war.[99] Admiral Roger Keyes, commander of the Mediterranean Fleet, countered that a strong British fleet would dampen Japanese ambitions, for "as surely as she turned China out of Korea, Russia out of Manchuria, Germany out of Tsengtau, she will turn Europeans out of China, and, in time, Asia, unless we are sufficiently strong to make it not worth her while to attempt it."[100] Churchill incorrectly reassured his friend Keyes that Japan could not do so "for at least a generation to come." But even if she did attack British

---

[97] Bridgeman, "Political Outlook and the Far East," March 5, 1925, WCP.
[98] *Ibid.* See also correspondence in CHAR 18/4, 18/5, and 18/6, WCP.
[99] Churchill, "Navy Estimates: Memorandum by the Chancellor of the Exchequer," February 7, 1925, C. P. 71 ('25), CHAR 22/30, WCP; Churchill, "Naval Shipbuilding I: Before 1925," n.d., p. 10, CHAR 22/176, WCP. See also Churchill, *Volume Companion* 5: 383–387.
[100] Keyes to Churchill, March 21 and 24, 1925, CHAR 18/8, WCP.

possessions sooner than twenty years, Churchill countered, "she would not, as was the case with Germany, have any chance of striking at the heart of the Empire and destroying its power to wage war." At best, Japan could inflict great losses on "our Australian colonies" and [our] trade, "but in three or four years we could certainly sweep the Japanese from the seas and force them to make peace."[101]

Since there was no mortal peril which threatened the ultimate ability of the Empire to defeat Japan, Churchill questioned the Admiralty's objectivity in conjuring up alarming and self-serving potential threats to the nation's security and thereby seriously distorting national strategic policy. He objected, as had Prime Minister MacDonald earlier, to the Admiralty's insistence that it, not the Foreign Office, had the right to determine both the nature and the immediacy of foreign threats. Beatty and Bridgeman had made known their opposition to the Ten Year Rule and their skepticism of the Foreign Office's ability to predict war over such a long period of time.[102] Beatty, in particular, did not trust the politicians to acknowledge and to act on any foreign threat in an expeditious manner.[103]

Churchill disagreed. He apparently assumed that Japanese military preparations, like those of Germany before World War I, would give ample warning of danger and thereby provide England the time to "build late, build fast, each one better than the last."[104] To him, the Admiralty's demand for an immediate and "disproportionate increase" in naval power stemmed not from the probability of an imminent Japanese threat so much as the Admiralty's "natural wish" to "have everything superfine and perfect, to multiply every factor of safety at every stage, and to deny themselves nothing." The possibility of a Japanese threat to Great Britain's national security, and the formulation of Britain's national strategic policy, based upon that possibility, should not, therefore, be granted to an aggressively self-serving Admiralty, but instead, to the more objective and experienced leaders in the Foreign Office, the CID, and the Cabinet. The Foreign Secretary, not the First Lord of the Admiralty, would "judge the foreign situation," and the Cabinet would "prescribe to the Admiralty," not vice versa, as Bridgeman and Beatty were demanding.[105] Ironically, the predictions of both Churchill and Beatty proved prescient.

---

[101] Churchill to Keyes, March 22, 1925, CHAR 22/68, WCP.
[102] Beatty to Bridgeman, January 8, 1925, BGMN/3, WBPCC. See both letters written by Beatty to Bridgeman on January 8, 1925. Bridgeman recalled that "Beatty and I both refused to admit that the F. O. [Foreign Office] or anyone else could predict the next war." See Bridgeman, Diary, 22 July 1925, WBP.
[103] See footnote 94.
[104] Naval Programme Committee, Second Meeting, March 5, 1925, Cabinet, N. P. (25) 2, CHAR 22/65 WCP. See especially Churchill's reassurances on p. 6. This is an important source of Churchill's reasoning.
[105] *Ibid.* ; See also "Navy Estimates: Memorandum by the Chancellor of the Exchequer, February 7, 1925, Cabinet, C. P. 71 (25), CHAR 22/30, WCP.

Japanese and German actions before World War II did give ample warning of danger and the need to "build late, build fast each one better than the last," but, as history revealed, the political leaders in the late 1930s did not act expeditiously, as Beatty had feared or Churchill had hoped. This was true both in England and the United States.

Whatever their expectations, Beatty and Bridgeman failed to win over the Cabinet. When only two cabinet ministers supported them, they prepared to carry out Beatty's "deadlock of a sensational kind." With the backing of the entire Admiralty Board, they threatened to resign, an act which Bridgeman warned Baldwin was certain to win them the support of "a very large proportion of our party."[106] Rather than risk a split within his party, Baldwin avoided an embarrassing and politically damaging fight by working out a temporary compromise. Churchill agreed to increase the Admiralty's annual naval budget from £60 million to £60.5 million and to set aside an additional £2 million on which the Admiralty could draw if absolutely necessary. To Churchill's satisfaction, the Cabinet approved his recommendation for another international arms control conference to limit auxiliary ship construction.[107] Rather than allow Beatty to charge publicly that Baldwin was "playing us [the Admiralty] false," the Prime Minister mollified Beatty by appointing a Cabinet committee to examine the still unresolved issue of future naval construction.[108] As Baldwin was careful to staff this new committee with Cabinet ministers who generally favored a strong navy, Beatty was confident that he could still defeat Churchill.[109] Indeed, he congratulated himself that he had "saved the situation."[110] "It had been a long bitter struggle," he exulted, "and we have come out of it very well and squeezed alot more out of the Chancellor of the Exchequer then he ever intended us to have."[111]

---

[106] For Bridgeman's quote threatening to resign, see Gilbert, *Churchill: The Prophet of Truth* 5: 89. Also see Bridgeman to Baldwin, February 21, 1925, in unpublished manuscript by Bridgeman's son, BGMN/2, p. 576, WBPCC; Churchill, *Volume Companion* 5: 389–390; Beatty to Wife, February 7, 12 1925, BTY 17/70, BP; Davidson, *Memoirs*, p. 212; Board of Admiralty, *Minutes*, February 11, 1925, ADM 167/71, p. 8, PRO. The Board warned that the proposed cuts made it "impossible for the Admiralty to carry out the policy of the Government..."

[107] See Cabinet Conclusion, February 12, 1925, 8 (25) and February 18, 1925, 9 (25) in CHAR 22/69, WCP. See also Robert Cecil to Churchill, February 12, 1925 and Churchill's draft of a letter to Cecil which he did not send, February 12, 1925, CHAR 22/68, WCP.

[108] Beatty to Wife, February 7, 1925, BTY 17/70, BP; Bridgeman, Diary, March 1925, p. 107, WBP; Davidson, *Memoirs*, p. 212; Ferris, *Evolution*, pp. 162–163. See also correspondence in Churchill, *Volume Companion* 5: 397–401.

[109] Beatty to Wife, February 17 and 18, 1925, BTY 17/70, BP; Chalmers, *Life and Letters*, p. 406.

[110] Quoted in Davidson, *Memoirs*, p. 215; Beatty to Wife, 17 February 1925, BTY 17/70, BP.

[111] Beatty to Wife, 18 February 1925, BTY 17/70, BP.

4

Churchill's Challenge

To placate Beatty, Prime Minister Baldwin appointed a new committee. Beatty was delighted with the strong pro-navy composition of the Cabinet Committee on Naval Construction, generally referred to as the Birkenhead Committee because it was chaired by F. E. Smith, or Lord Birkenhead. Churchill anticipated Beatty's use of elaborate charts to convince the Birkenhead Committee of Japan's imminent danger to the Empire in East Asia, a tactic he had employed earlier before Churchill's Cabinet Committee on Defense Estimates in 1922.[1] He foresaw as well that Beatty would ignore the interrelated economic and political benefits flowing from an economic revival which would continue the pro-navy Conservative Party in power and thus guarantee both Great Britain's economic ability and political will to maintain its naval supremacy. Churchill therefore decided to attack him directly on naval strategy as well as on the comparative combat effectiveness of the two navies, especially in the expensive new 10,000-ton, 8-inch-gun cruisers, which Beatty contended would soon allow Japan to establish its superiority unless England quickly matched them.

The five-month debate within the Birkenhead Committee convinced Beatty and his superior, First Lord of the Admiralty William Bridgeman that the chief cause of their inability to persuade its pro-navy Committee members of the wisdom of their Japanese war strategy and related cruiser demands was Winston Churchill. Their anger at "Winston" prevented them from acknowledging Churchill's naval sympathies and his highly advantageous promise to build all of the ships in their modified program in return for a one-year delay in the start of construction. They instead came to view him as an overbearing, ambitious politician, who only months earlier had left the

---

[1] See Chapter 3, footnotes 11–14, 21.

Liberal Party to join the Conservative Party, and who was already attempting to realign Conservative Party naval priorities. When the Committee awarded Churchill the victory, Bridgeman, Beatty, and the entire Board of Admiralty threatened to resign. Moreover, Beatty and other Conservative leaders propagated the rumor that Churchill was using his fight against the Admiralty's building needs as a smokescreen to advance a more sinister plot to bring down the Conservative Party. The former Liberal Party chieftain, therefore, needed to be taught a hard lesson about Conservative Party politics, and this dispute over cruisers offered the opportunity to give him one.

***

On March 4, 1925, the day before the first meeting of the Birkenhead Committee, Churchill warned his good friend Lord Birkenhead that he had no intention of allowing Beatty's oratorical abilities to sway the Committee by a "lecture on strategy," but would force him to give very specific details of the "actual requirements" in ships, men, oil, material, and money.[2] Churchill respected Beatty's strategic thinking and his assessment of British naval weaknesses in Southeast Asia. Both he and Lord Birkenhead had wholeheartedly supported Beatty's Japanese threat thesis in 1922, but since then, Churchill had come to question a number of its major assumptions. One of the most important was timing. "Everything really turns upon whether or not the Cabinet wish the Navy to be ready as soon as possible to put a superior fleet with all ancillaries in the Pacific" against Japan. If a quick response became Cabinet policy, Churchill conceded, "I do not think the Admiralty's requirements are excessive." In fact, if England must soon defeat Japan while simultaneously guarding its home waters and extensive trade routes, "even more," Churchill concluded, "will be needed."[3]

Churchill understood the political necessity of criticizing and undermining Beatty's strategic rationale in well-reasoned arguments that his fellow cabinet ministers and party members, who were unfamiliar with naval technicalities, could readily understand and accept. He realized as well that he could not do it alone. He therefore shored up support among the members of the Committee of Imperial Defence (CID) and the Foreign Office by reinforcing their earlier conclusion that Japan was unlikely to attack Great Britain during the next decade. Having assured himself of this important political backing, he intended to use the Birkenhead Committee's investigation of naval construction needs to highlight the more specific defects of Beatty's thinking. If he could convince his pro-naval colleagues on this Committee of the flaws in the Admiralty's

---

[2] Churchill to Birkenhead, March 1, 1925 in Winston S. Churchill, *Winston S. Churchill: The Exchequer Years 1922–1929*, Companion Volume 5 ed. Martin Gilbert (London: William Heinemann, 1979), 5: 420. Hereafter cited as Churchill, *Companion Volume 5*.

[3] *Ibid*. Beatty reveals the strong support by both Churchill and Birkenhead in Beatty to Wife, February 23, 1922 in William Scott Chalmers, *The Life and Letters of David, Earl Beatty* (London: Hodder and Stoughton, 1951), p. 371.

reasoning, he would have a more solid political basis for his budgetary challenges to the Admiralty's request for the immediate construction of cruisers, destroyers, submarines, and ancillary vessels.[4] To achieve this objective, the former First Lord of the Admiralty had been gathering naval data since December 1924 and, thus, was well-informed and highly experienced in naval debate.[5]

Cruisers were at the crux of the Birkenhead Committee debate, both because of their expense and the numbers requested. When Churchill questioned the number required and their purpose, Beatty boldly proclaimed to the Committee that cruisers were "a matter and a question which can be decided only by the Admiralty."[6] Having anticipated that Beatty would repeat the same arguments he had made before the Churchill committee in 1922, Churchill forced Beatty to draw sharp distinctions between two different types of cruiser missions. The first mission was to sail with the main battle fleet to protect the capital ships, and these cruisers must therefore be equal in size and gun power to the eight new Japanese 8-inch-gun cruisers, which had recently been authorized or were already in the building process. Since Japan had authorized eight of these new cruisers, England needed thirteen to maintain the 10:6 ratio.[7]

But, Beatty argued, the problem was not that simple. Japan also had recently built new cruisers with 6-inch and 5.5-inch guns. Twenty-five of these thirty-nine cruisers would probably be assigned to Japan's main battle fleet. Thus, merely to maintain equality, England would need twenty-five new 10,000-ton, 8-inch-gun cruisers to accompany its own main battle fleet to Singapore. Even so, these twenty-five new cruisers would constitute only a "bare minimum," as only "fools" would engage the Japanese with only twenty-five cruisers.[8]

However, Beatty merely hinted at the Admiralty's more fully developed explanation of why they would be "fools" to begin the journey to Singapore with only twenty-five cruisers. Earlier the Naval Staff had calculated that at the outbreak of a sudden Japanese attack on British possessions in East Asia, some of the twenty-five cruisers would be unavailable due to normal refitting and

---

[4] Churchill to Birkenhead, March 8, 1925 in Churchill, *Companion Volume* 5: 426. See also Churchill to my dear F. E., March 8, 1925, "Naval Committee," CHAR 18/10, WCP.

[5] See correspondence between Churchill and Bridgeman during December 1924 in BGMN/3, CHAR 18/4, CHAR 18/5, CHAR 18/6. See also Churchill to Baldwin, December 15, 1924, CHAR 18/4, WCP.

[6] Cabinet, Naval Programme Committee, "First Meeting of the Committee," March 2, 1925, N. P. (25), 1st Meeting, p. 4, CAB 27/273, PRO. Hereafter the Cabinet Naval Programme Committee will be cited as CAB, NPC.

[7] Ibid., p. 12.

[8] Ibid., pp. 14–17. See also CAB, NPC, "General Remarks: Ten Year Building Programme," March 6, 1925, N. P. (25) 7, pp. 8, 17 in ADM 1/8685/152, P. D. 02171/25, PRO. Copy is also in CHAR 22/66, WCP.

Churchill's Challenge

repair, others could be expected to fall out for repair during the long voyage, and still others might well be sunk or damaged by Japanese submarines and destroyer attacks before reaching Singapore. Japan's advantage would be increased still further because it would be fighting in home waters from nearby naval bases and could use its older, less powerful cruisers and destroyers to protect its vital trade routes with China and Korea while concentrating all twenty-five of its newest and most powerful cruisers with the main battle fleet. To compensate for these disadvantages, Great Britain must have at least a 25 percent superiority or six more cruisers, for a total of thirty-one sailing with the main battle fleet.[9]

Even with thirty-one new 10,000-ton, 8-inch-gun cruisers, many more were needed, Beatty insisted, to fulfill still another crucial purpose: to protect England's vital and extensive world trade routes. Providing minimal protection for these very distant and very long trade routes throughout the world required cruisers as swift and as powerful as the most likely Japanese cruisers to be encountered, especially as the Foreign Service cruisers must operate alone without any support from other British warships and at great distances from British naval bases.[10] These requirements mandated additional 10,000-ton, 8-inch-gun cruisers.

But unlike the calculation for numbers needed to sail with the main battle fleet, the number of trade-protection cruisers was only to a "small extent" related to the more exact corresponding number of Japanese cruisers. The Admiralty employed a new set of criteria for determining the number of trade protection cruisers: the length of the trade routes and the mass of trade on those routes. After a "very complete and thorough investigation," Beatty assured the Committee, the Naval Staff had set the number required at forty-five. Reduced considerably from the sixty-six cruisers employed in trade protection during World War I, these forty-five were a bare minimum, as they did not take into account the need for cruisers to hunt down raiders, escort troop transports, convoy merchant vessels, or provide quick replacements for the main battle fleet.[11]

Adding forty-five new cruisers for trade protection to the twenty-five for the main battle fleet brought the absolute minimum to seventy modern 10,000-ton, 8-inch-gun cruisers. Yet even these seventy would not be enough to meet all of the Admiralty's requirements. An additional six more were required, either for protection of British home waters or for the 25 percent superiority for the main fleet in its anticipated battle in Japanese home waters. Since these six additional cruisers must come from the forty-five normally assigned to trade protection, the number of cruisers available for trade protection during wartime would be

---

[9] CAB, NPC, "First Meeting," March 2 1925, pp. 17–19. See also Chapter 3, footnotes 40 and CAB, NPC, "General Remarks: Ten Year Building Programme," p. 5.
[10] CAB, NPC, "First Meeting," March 2, 1925, pp. 17–19.
[11] *Ibid.*, p. 19. See also CAB, NPC "General Remarks: Ten Year Building Programme," pp. 4, 10.

reduced to thirty-nine.[12] One hundred merchant ships equipped by the Admiralty with six-inch guns would assist the trade-protection cruisers in attacking enemy merchantmen, in hunting down raiders, and "*what is more important,*" [emphasis mine] Beatty stressed, in an echo of the intense strain in Anglo-American relations before the United States entered World War I, was the "interception of enemy trade in neutral bottoms." To accomplish all of these aims, including the blockade and interdiction of neutral merchant vessels, it was vital to replace thirty-two worn-out cruisers by 1935, when the Admiralty would have already begun scrapping its old battleships to build new ones. To complete the cruiser-building program on time, England had no choice but to build six cruisers per year until forty-five or forty-six had been built during the ten-year period between 1925 and 1935.[13]

Churchill was staggered by the Admiralty's insistence that seventy modern cruisers were an absolute minimum. In rebuttal he emphasized that this number was not based on Cabinet policy of a one-power standard, which called for a fleet only equal to that of the world's most powerful navy. It was based instead, he accused, upon the Admiralty's persistent rejection of the conclusion of the Foreign Office, the CID, and the Cabinet that there was no likelihood of a war against Japan during the next ten years.[14] Rather than an actual naval war with Japan, the most likely result of Beatty's reasoning, Churchill feared, was a naval-building race against Japan in which cruiser costs would balloon from £60.5 million to over £100 million and beyond.[15]

Churchill did not content himself with emphasizing the enormous costs of Beatty's war plan. He attacked the plan itself as one giving "all the advantages to Japan" and none to Great Britain.[16] Even if England spent the enormous sums to build all of the cruisers, the modern naval base at Singapore, and the oil depots and reserves required along the entire route to Singapore, Churchill told the Committee, Great Britain would still be exposed "to the very gravest dangers" from European or other hostile powers that could take advantage of the long absence of the battle fleet from home waters and the greatly diminished naval force left to protect the nation.[17] By contrast, the Japanese fleet could remain in its safe harbors until it decided the most advantageous time and place to attack.[18]

Instead of exposing the nation to the very grave dangers of a highly disadvantageous offensive in Japanese home waters, a safer and smarter strategy

---

[12] CAB, NPC, "Second Meeting of the Committee," March 5, 1925, N. P. (25) 2nd Meeting, p. 8, CAB 27/273, PRO.
[13] For Beatty's quote on the interception of neutral shipping, see CAB, NPC, "First Meeting," March 2, 1925, pp. 8. See also CAB, NPC, "Second Meeting," March 5, 1925, pp. 8, 11; Churchill to Bridgeman, January 19, 1925, CHAR 18/10, WCP; Churchill, *Companion Volume* 5: 349, 83.
[14] CAB, NPC, "Second Meeting," March 5, 1925, p.7.   [15] Ibid., pp. 8–10.
[16] Ibid., p. 13.   [17] Ibid., pp. 12–13.   [18] Ibid.

would delay the defense of the Empire in East Asia. By remaining calm and keeping its navy close to home, England would maximize its strengths rather than accentuate its weaknesses. Japan could not send its small navy "around the world to attack our fleet in home waters" or even in the Atlantic and Indian Oceans. Therefore, Churchill argued, England's national security would be in no immediate danger. Temporary loss of territory and trade in East Asia would not be fatal. So long as Japan could not destroy England's great manufacturing capability or stop her vital food supply, Japan could not win the war. The smarter strategy was clear enough: the decisive naval battle must not take place until Great Britain was ready to send its overwhelmingly superior battle fleet to East Asia. It made far greater sense to Churchill to wait until England's vast shipbuilding resources could launch "a fleet of almost measureless power," one which a poorer and less industrialized Japan could not hope to defeat. Rather than being able to react quickly by immediately dispatching the fleet to Singapore at the first sign of real danger, the wiser course was to realize that time was on England's side.[19]

The importance of timing was also in inherent in Beatty's own war strategy. Before the British fleet could attack Japan, a first-class, modern naval base capable of serving the battle fleet had to be built at Singapore. The Admiralty estimated that building such a complex base with all of its various docks, repair shops, and storehouses would take from eight to eleven years. Thus, Churchill told the Committee, it was obvious, therefore, that it was "impossible to base our main Battlefleet there and maintain it in an efficient state for any length of time" before 1936, or at the very earliest, 1932. Since a naval invasion was impossible until the Singapore base was completed, a slower yet steady construction of cruisers in the meantime made good naval sense and even better economic sense. Why rekindle Japanese alarm and anger, Churchill asked, and thereby ignite a financially disastrous naval arms race by the rapid construction of cruisers and a new base at Singapore, when the base could not become operational for at least eight to eleven years?[20]

Churchill sought to highlight still another flaw in Beatty's war plan. The Admiralty assigned thirty-nine modern cruisers to protect major trade routes during the war against Japan because, Beatty observed, it was "impossible to determine where the attack [on shipping] would take place."[21] But Churchill refused to accept his reasoning. He demanded to know the specific routes and locations where the trade-protection cruisers would be stationed. When at last Beatty finally revealed their dispositions, Churchill

---

[19] Ibid., pp. 13–14.
[20] Ibid., pp. 14–15. See also John Robert Ferris, *The Evolution of British Strategic Policy, 1919–1926* (London: Macmillan 1989), p. 69; Stephen W. Roskill, *Churchill and The Admirals* (New York: Wm. Morrow, 1978), pp. 79–80; Hector C. Bywater, *Navies and Nations: A Review of Naval Developments Since the Great War* (Boston and New York: Houghton Mifflin, 1927), p. 198.
[21] CAB, NPC, "First Meeting," March 2, 1925, pp. 8–9.

was incredulous: "you are actually proposing to keep a large number of cruisers in a war against Japan on the South American station, the West Indies station, the Cape station and so forth?" When Beatty defended these dispositions, Churchill countered that if Japan sent " four or five eight-inch-gun cruisers secretly away from the main fleet and fall upon one of your [smaller] squadrons, much weaker, in the West Indies or South America station or wherever it may be ... it will destroy them." Churchill's criticism, Beatty ruefully admitted, was "quite true."[22]

Moreover, rather than small weak cruiser squadrons scattered throughout the world patrolling distant trade routes during the war, Churchill proposed using convoys of slower, less expensive ships to escort merchantmen. Convoys used during World War I had proven effective and were a more economical method to ensure England's survival. Churchill may have known that Beatty had argued strenuously for convoys during the past war, but Beatty now jettisoned his former advocacy.[23] To justify the forty-five new cruisers, Beatty employed evidence which ironically emphasized how inefficient even large numbers of cruisers had been in attempting to hunt down and destroy German commerce raiders during World War I. Beatty's unwise response gave Churchill the opportunity to charge that not forty-five, not even seventy cruisers, would ever be enough to accomplish this "impossible" strategy.[24]

Sensing the momentum of his argument, Churchill reiterated that not only was Beatty attempting to accomplish the "impossible," but he was simultaneously attempting the "unnecessary." Using the one-power standard approved by the Cabinet, Churchill pointed out that the British navy was already vastly more powerful than the Japanese navy. He admonished the Birkenhead Committee to plan and budget for future naval construction based on a factual comparison of existing naval power, rather than on Beatty's hypothetical and highly disadvantageous war plan. The Washington Conference ratio of 10:6 in capital ships gave England indisputable superiority in battleships, battle cruisers, and aircraft carriers.[25] Overwhelming superiority in recently built auxiliary cruisers was equally evident, as Britain had thirty-eight to Japan's fourteen.[26] Even in the newest 10,000-ton, 8-inch-gun auxiliaries, England had authorized five, and Australia two, for a total of seven to Japan's four. In the next cruiser class below 10,000 tons, Japan had four 7,000 ton ships to England's six, four of which were new 9,500-ton Hawkins class cruisers with 7.5-inch guns. Japan gained a slight advantage in the third cruiser class

---

[22] Ibid., pp. 20, 22–23.
[23] Stephen W. Roskill, *Earl Beatty: The Last Naval Hero: An Intimate Biography* (New York: Athenaeum, 1981), pp. 70, 209–210, 267, 317. See also Churchill to Beatty, n.d., in Chalmers, *Life and Letters*, pp. 373–374.
[24] CAB, NPC, "First Meeting," March 2, 1925, pp. 8–9; CAB, NPC, "Second Meeting," March 5, 1925, p. 13.
[25] CAB, NPC, "Second Meeting," March 5, 1925, p. 13.   [26] Ibid., pp. 2–8, 13.

of ships between 5,500 tons and 4,500 tons with seventeen to England's sixteen, he acknowledged, but in the fourth class, generally below 4,000 tons, Britain had nineteen fast cruisers with 6-inch guns and Japan had none. Finally, in the smallest class were ten British cruisers with 6-inch guns against only four Japanese. Indeed, the total of all British and Australian cruisers of all sizes totaled fifty-eight, whereas Japan had only twenty-nine.[27]

Churchill's strongest argument against preparing for an imminent war against Japan was based on the reality of overwhelming existing cruiser superiority, the fact that the Singapore base could not be built in less than eight years, the inability of Japan to attack England in its home waters, and the nation's current serious internal economic and social crisis. Underlying his argument was Churchill's conviction that the future political and economic ability of the Conservative Party to protect Great Britain's military strength against the return to power of a much less sympathetic socialist government must take precedence over theoretical war scenarios. But these were not the only reasons he advised against Beatty's war plan. He next addressed alternative ways of assessing naval needs. Assuming no immediate threat of war with Japan during the next ten years, England's cruiser requirements could be reduced from seventy to fifty – the number which Beatty had accepted as temporarily sufficient "for all purposes" at the 1922 Washington Naval Conference.[28] By abandoning Beatty's war plan in favor of the findings of the CID and the Foreign Office – that no war was to be anticipated during the next ten years – and further by using Beatty's earlier figure of fifty cruisers, Churchill maintained that only sixteen cruisers would need to be replaced during the next decade, while considerable additional savings could be realized in oil storage facilities, depot ships, and other vessels required to escort the fleet to Singapore.

Should Japan suddenly begin a naval arms race, Churchill promised to match her ship for ship ensuring that England always kept "a superiority in the best ships."[29] In the unlikely event that Japan did begin such a race, Churchill suggested proposing a diplomatic trade in which Japan would stop building new cruisers in return for "no further progress at Singapore for five years." If Japan agreed, at the end of five years in 1930, Britain would have built an additional eight 10,000-ton, 8-inch-gun cruisers for a total of fifteen,

---

[27] Ibid., p. 4.
[28] For Beatty's acceptance of fifty cruisers see Cabinet, "Reduction in Limitation of Armaments: Further Limitation of Naval Armaments," July 12, 1927, C. P. 193 (27), CAB 24/187, PRO. An attachment to this source is CID, "Note by the Secretary of the Proceedings at Washington," C. P. 193, CID Paper 814-B. In this CID Paper, Balfour cites Beatty's figure of fifty cruisers at the 55th meeting of the British Empire Delegation at the Washington Conference. Churchill was obviously aware of Beatty's acceptance of fifty cruisers as he cites this figure as more realistic in CAB, NPC, "Second Meeting," March 5, 1925, p. 14. See also CAB, NPC, "Memorandum by the Chancellor of the Exchequer: Cruiser Programmes, 1927–1928," November 6, 1927, N. P. 27 (2), p. 5, CAB 27/355, PRO. See also Chapter 2, footnotes 37–38.
[29] CAB, NPC, "Second Meeting," March 5, 1925, pp. 14–16.

against only four such cruisers for Japan. Still further superiority was possible by stopping the unnecessary wearing out and scrapping of cruisers by putting them into reserve, thereby preserving and prolonging their usefulness. In this manner, by 1930, England could call out sixty-six cruisers, forty-five for trade protection and twenty-one of the best ones for the battle fleet, thus giving Great Britain "overwhelming superiority in the most modern types over Japan and... a very large numerical and qualitative superiority" in all older cruisers.[30]

However, Beatty had still another argument with which to counter Churchill. The Admiralty believed that one of the strongest arguments for the new cruisers was the revolutionary impact of its newly designed eight-inch gun. The new gun would have a longer range and its shell a deeper penetrating power than previous 8-inch guns. With its faster speed, the new cruiser could remain outside of the range of slower cruisers, and using its longer-range guns, destroy its opponents "without laying itself open to the same degree" of return fire. As the vast majority of existing cruisers had only enough armor protection to withstand a destroyer's 5-inch-gunfire, and some protection against 6-inch shells, the Naval Staff was convinced *"that the advent of the eight-inch gun ship has made not only the 6" but also the 7.5" gunships out of date, and to pit either of the two last against the first is to court disaster."*[31] [Admiralty emphasis]. Beatty assured the Birkenhead Committee therefore that Admiralty's studies demonstrated "that an eight-inch[-gun] ship is in a position to crush a 7.5-inch ship without laying itself open to be crushed in return..."[32]

The new cruiser had other important advantages. All of its guns were mounted on the centerline of the ship, which enabled them to swing to either side for a full broadside of all guns, an advantage not shared by earlier open gun-shield cruisers.[33] Admiral Roger Keyes, Deputy Chief of the Naval Staff, emphasized to the Birkenhead Committee that because the new 8-inch gun was housed in an enclosed armored turret, its crew was sheltered from nearby shell bursts, whereas most earlier cruisers with 7.5-inch and 6-inch guns had only shields in front of the gun which exposed their highly trained crews to a much greater chance of being eliminated in battle. On the basis of these additional reasons, Keyes concurred with the Naval Staff that the turreted 8-inch gun was "infinitely superior to the open shielded gun."[34]

To further buttress its case for the revolutionary impact of the new 8-inch gun, the Admiralty added still another criteria for measuring relative combat value. Greater emphasis was placed on the number and power of this new

---

[30] *Ibid.*, p. 16.
[31] CAB, NPC, "First Meeting," March 2, 1925, p. 10; CAB, NPC, "General Remarks: Ten Year Building Programme," p. 6 and Appendix B., p. 6 in CHAR, 22/66, WCP.
[32] *Ibid.*
[33] CAB, NPC, "Fourth Meeting," March 12, 1925, N. P. (25) 4th Meeting, p. 6, CAB 27/237, PRO.
[34] CAB, NPC, "Second Meeting," March 5, 1925, p. 18.

Churchill's Challenge

cruiser's guns. One of the "outstanding lessons of the last war," Beatty assured the Committee, "so far as cruisers were concerned, was that, given otherwise equal conditions, victory fell to the ship or squadron possessing the preponderance of gun power over the opponent."[35] Naval Staff studies estimated that a modern 8-inch gun could fire at ranges up to 31,000 yards, whereas the range of a 7.5-inch gun was from 2,000 to 9,000 yards shorter. Thus, given equal or faster speed, the new British 8-inch-gun cruiser could remain outside of the shorter range of the 7.5-inch-gun cruiser and use its superior gun range to sink it, without the 7.5-inch-gun cruiser getting close enough to return fire.[36]

Equally compelling to the Admiralty was the realization that all of its 7.5-inch and 6-inch guns were inferior in a range to those of the more recent American 6-inch guns. The American 6-inch gun had a range of 22,000 yards, whereas the British 6-inch gun could only reach 18,800 yards.[37] Churchill was also disturbed by this news. He was especially dispirited by Beatty's admission that the four newly built 9,500-ton, 7.5-inch gun Hawkins class cruisers were "no good against an eight-inch" and "could be destroyed quite comfortably" by Japan's new cruisers.[38]

Upon hearing this news, Churchill at first merely lamented that it was "rather a pity we spent so much money on them."[39] But after thinking about the Admiralty's use of relative combat values, he returned to the Birkenhead Committee several days later on March 9, 1925 with a blistering counterattack. He accused the Admiralty of deliberately exaggerating the relative combat value of the four Japanese 8-inch-gun cruisers under construction by simply dismissing the great fire power of Britain's six existing cruisers, "which never have been in the water until a year ago, brand-new ships, some of which cost £2,000,000 apiece, four of which are nearly 10,000 tons and which carry 7.5-inch guns, and two of which are very fast ships, with six-inch guns."[40] Yet, despite their great fire power and the great expense in building them, the Admiralty, he sneered, "tell us they are worth nothing. Brush them aside. They can be crushed instantly by an eight-inch-gun ship."[41] Keyes tried to put a better light on it by incorrectly claiming that the Admiralty had "tried very hard" to stop the 8-inch-gun cruiser at the Washington Conference, because it had foreseen that this cruiser would replicate "the situation which arose when the Dreadnought was built and made all pre-Dreadnoughts obsolete."[42] Churchill quickly rejected the Dreadnought analogy. He insisted that the four

---

[35] CAB, NPC, "General Remarks: Ten Year Building Programme," Appendix B., p. 1.
[36] Ibid.
[37] Ibid., p. 5; CAB, NPC, "General Remarks: Ten Year Building Programme," Appendix B., p. 5.
[38] CAB, NPC, "First Meeting," March 2, 1925, p. 14. [39] Ibid.
[40] CAB, NPC, "Third Meeting," March 9, 1925, N. P. (25) 3rd Meeting, p. 3, CAB 27/273, PRO. See copy in CHAR 22/65, WCP.
[41] Ibid., p. 4. See also Churchill, "Cabinet Memorandum," March 10, 1925, in Churchill, Companion Volume 5: 426–428.
[42] CAB, NPC, "Third Meeting," March 9, 1925, p. 5.

Hawkins class 7.5-inch and the two Emerald class 6-inch-gun cruisers ought to be assigned at least some combat value against the four Japanese 8-inch-gun cruisers, especially if all six were to engage in battle simultaneously against only the four Japanese 8-inch-gun cruisers. When Keyes dismissed the match-up as a "very unfair fight," Churchill erupted in biting sarcasm. The Admiralty was in effect insisting, he warned the Committee, that since these four Japanese cruisers had the theoretical capability of the new 8-inch gun, they "have only to go out and sink the whole of our fifty ships, one after another."[43]

In part because the Admiralty claimed that Japan's new 8-inch-gun cruiser could sweep the seas of all existing British cruisers, and in part because he had by now become impressed with the immense power and combat value ascribed to the new British 8-inch gun, Churchill increasingly focused his attention on it. Keyes could not tell him if the Japanese 8-inch gun would be as effective as those of the five Kent-class cruisers under construction, but he assumed that they would be, as the Japanese were "in very close touch with our armament firms..." and should therefore "have the latest eight-inch gun."[44] Dissatisfied with the Deputy Chief of Staff's response, Churchill turned to Rear Admiral Cyril Fuller, the Admiralty Controller, with the more specific question of gun range. Taking the Admiralty's estimate of 24,000 yards as the range of the Japanese 8-inch gun, rather than the 32,000 yards, which Beatty had earlier suggested would be the range of the new British 8-inch gun, Churchill pressed Fuller on his estimate of the range of the new British eight-inch gun. Fuller was evasive, pointing out that trials were under way to achieve "the biggest range" possible, but that range depended "entirely on the internal ballistics which we are working out now." Even when Churchill confronted Fuller with the Admiralty Naval Staff's own estimates which "anticipated getting at least 32,000 yards range" from the new British eight-inch guns, Fuller remained evasive. The range, he pointed out, would depend "entirely on the [gun] mountings," which were still in the design process.[45]

Nonetheless, Churchill refused to drop the range of the eight-inch gun, emphasizing that it was "an essential part of my argument." Keyes and Fuller may have more than likely suspected the familiar line of reasoning which Churchill was developing. If the range of the Japanese eight-inch gun was only 24,000 yards, whereas the range of the British gun was 32,000 yards, a difference of almost one and one-half miles, then, given equal speeds, the British cruiser could, in theory, prevent the Japanese cruiser from coming within 24,000 yards, and using its 32,000-yard range, blow the Japanese cruiser out of the water before it could ever come close enough to use its shorter-range guns. If these gun ranges were accurate, the five new British 8-inch-gun cruisers,

---

[43] *Ibid.*, pp. 7–8, 5–9.
[44] CAB, NPC, "Fourth Meeting," March 12, 1925, pp. 4–5, CAB 27/273, PRO. [45] *Ibid.*, p. 4.

not the four Japanese ships, would be clearly superior and should be awarded much higher relative combat values.

When Keyes sought to interrupt Churchill's line of reasoning by insisting that it "is absurd to talk of cruiser action at 32,000 yards," when the "real advantage" of the 8-inch gun was the destructive power "of the eight-inch projectile at a reasonable range" of not more than 15,000 yards, Churchill sprang his trap. If 15,000 yards was the more realistic range, then, he countered, "there could be no question whatever of the 7.5-inch of the [4] 'Hawkins' class being out-ranged in any practical sense by these guns in the modern Japanese cruisers."[46] Therefore, Churchill pointed out, the Committee should recognize that the Admiralty was overestimating the relative combat value of the as yet unbuilt Japanese cruisers and undervaluing the newest existing Hawkins-class British ships.

Although he retained his strong conviction that the "fundamental part of my case" rested on the fact that the Admiralty had deliberately undervalued the offensive power of six of Britain's newest existing cruisers, Churchill was nonetheless in total agreement on the importance of the newest 8-inch gun.[47] He accepted Keyes' assurance that the additional 50 pound difference between the heavier 8-inch shell and the 7.5-inch shell resulted in greater penetration, explosive, and destructive power. This was a matter of importance to Churchill, as he took personal responsibility for the failure of the British shells to penetrate German armor during World War I when he had served as First Lord of the Admiralty.[48] Because the Admiralty estimated that its new 8-inch gun would significantly out-range the new Japanese 8-inch gun, Churchill became increasingly enthusiastic about this new weapon and suggested the possibility of saving a great deal of money by refitting the six newest cruisers – the four Hawkins class and two Emerald class – with these new guns: "I think it is very important indeed that this terrific gun which we are told is absolutely unmatched among any of the other [eight-inch] guns" be fitted immediately on the large hulls of the six newest cruisers. Even at a conversion cost of £700,000 per ship, he exclaimed, it was well worth the price. It had cost £10 million to build the ships, and since the Admiralty emphasized that the new 8-inch gun was two and one-half to three times more powerful than the 7.5-inch gun, Churchill believed that by refitting the Hawkins and Emerald cruisers with the new 8-inch guns, England could more than match the offensive power of the Japanese vessels at considerably less cost than building new ships.[49]

---

[46] Ibid., p. 5.   [47] Ibid., pp. 3, 7–8.
[48] Ibid., p. 5. For Churchill's sense of personal responsibility for the failure of British shells during World War I, see Churchill to Bridgeman, November 15, 1926, WBP. Copy in BGMN/1, WBPCC.
[49] CAB, NPC, "Fourth Meeting," March 12, 1925, pp. 8–9. See also Churchill, "Cabinet Memorandum," March 10, 1925 in Churchill, *Companion Volume* 5: 426–428.

However, as it turned out, complex technical problems would eventually prevent refitting the six ships with the new gun.[50]

Churchill's abiding admiration and great expectations for this new gun were now well-known to the Admiralty, a realization that would become even more important later when the Admiralty discovered that its high expectations for this gun were so deeply disappointing that it dare not reveal its chagrin to anyone. Indeed, Churchill became so enamored with the new 8-inch-gun cruiser that it now became the only cruiser Churchill was interested in building. He accepted the Admiralty's contention that "this eight-inch-gun really created a change comparable to that when the 'Dreadnought' was introduced into the battle area," and that the Admiralty's entire case for the large number of new cruisers was based "on the striking power of the eight-inch gun."[51] For this reason, he now vehemently opposed Admiralty plans to build less powerful 6-inch-gun cruisers merely to match those already built by the Japanese. Although the 6-inch-gun cruiser cost £700,000 less than an 8-inch-gun cruiser, building the smaller cruisers made no sense to Churchill. Rather than spend £1,300,000 on 6-inch-gun cruisers, Churchill favored building the more expensive, more powerful 8-inch-gun cruisers. The Admiralty could make up the difference in cost, he advised, merely by reducing the unnecessarily large number of foreign service cruisers on station throughout the world, from the existing thirty-five to twenty-five, thereby saving "enormous" sums that could be used to build the more powerful 8-inch-gun cruiser without any "difference whatever to your security." "Who is going to attack in the three years?" he asked.[52] The 8-inch-gun cruiser was obviously the best ship for the money. Indeed, several years later he reiterated: "I am dead set against a policy of 'plenty of the weak [six-inch gun] cruisers.'"[53]

By early May 1925, Churchill's knowledgeable and well-reasoned opposition succeeded in winning significant, albeit reluctant, Admiralty concessions. The CID and the Cabinet agreed with Churchill that war with Japan was not likely during the next ten years and that further reductions in Admiralty building plans were justified.[54] Beatty and Bridgeman responded by cutting the number of cruisers to be built between 1925 and 1931 from thirty-one to twenty-one, the number of destroyers from ninety to forty-five, and the number of submarines from eighty to forty-eight. They offered as well to save

---

[50] CAB, NPC, "Sixth Meeting," May 11, 1925, N. P. (25) p. 3, CAB 27/273, PRO. Copy in CHAR 22/65, WCP. See also E. T. T. d'Egerceriel to Churchill, March 11, 1925, CHAR 22/68, WCP.
[51] CAB, NPC, "Sixth Meeting," May 11, 1925, p. 13.   [52] Ibid., p. 14.
[53] Churchill to Keyes, 6 January 1928 in Roger Keyes, *The Keyes Papers: Selections from the Private and Official Correspondence of Admiral of the Fleet Baron Keyes of Zeebrugge, 1919–1938*, ed. Paul G. Halpern 2 vols. (London: Allen and Unwin, 1980) 2: 239–241. Hereafter cited as Keyes, *Keyes Papers* 2.
[54] Churchill to Beatty, May 27, 1925, BTY 14/4, BP; W.C.B.[William C. Bridgeman], "Memorandum by the First Lord of the Admiralty: Modified Naval Construction Programme," June 18, 1925, N. P. (25) 26 in CHAR 22/67, WCP; Ferris, *Evolution*, pp. 16, 28–30,165–166, 171–172.

£500,000 per ship by reducing the size of some of the new cruisers to 8,000 tons, carrying only six, rather than eight of the new 8-inch guns. The smaller B-class cruiser would be improved with greater armor protection and the ability to carry two airplanes as spotters to increase the accuracy of its long-range guns.[55] The Admiralty achieved still further savings by extending the period of active service of cruisers from sixteen to twenty years and that of destroyers from twelve to sixteen years. Having cut £37,318,422 from naval construction over the six-year period from 1925 to 1931, and by reducing other costs for a grand total of £51 million, Beatty, Bridgeman, and the Admiralty Board were determined that these "tremendous sacrifices" would be their last.[56]

Churchill was delighted with these new savings; nonetheless he asked for one more concession. He proposed a one-year delay in building the twenty-one cruisers. This would give him the additional savings he needed to fund important welfare benefits, and, in return, he promised to finance every ship requested in the Admiralty's latest modified building program. With this one-year delay, Churchill argued, he would be able to avoid asking Parliament for a tax increase for new welfare benefits and new naval construction.[57] Merely by delaying the start of cruiser construction for one year during 1925–1926, and thereby extending completion of all the cruisers until 1931–1932, Churchill could finance all twenty-one cruisers without getting into an "absolutely disastrous" tax fight in Parliament.[58] "Everything really turns," he advised the Admiralty, "upon not having a cruiser programme this year."[59] The "difference between the First Sea Lord and myself," Churchill reiterated, "will be very largely removed if you took this [1925–1926] as a blank year," and completed the twenty-one cruisers by 1931–1932. "What is there in the condition of the world which makes it impossible to do that?" he asked.[60]

Churchill's request for a one-year delay was based partly on an important assumption, which had been reinforced by his experiences as First Lord of the Admiralty in the years immediately prior to World War I. Churchill assumed that at the first signs of Japanese efforts to challenge Britain's naval superiority or threaten British interests in East Asia, Parliament would quickly authorize construction of new warships, just as it had done to counter the Kaiser's new naval building threat before World War I.[61] At the present time, Churchill pointed out, Japan was still reeling from the disastrous impact of the 1924

---

[55] CAB, NPC, "Eighth Meeting," June 30, 1925, N. P. (25) Eighth Meeting, pp. 5–6, CAB 27/273, PRO. Copy in CHAR 22/65, WCP. See also Alan Raven and John Roberts, *British Cruisers of World War Two* (Annapolis, MD: Naval Institute Press, 1980), pp. 132–133.
[56] CAB, NPC, "Eighth Meeting," June 30, 1925, N.P. (25), pp. 3–9; CAB, NCP, W. C. B., "Memorandum by the First Lord of the Admiralty," June, 18 1925, p. 1; Lord Birkenhead, "Report: Note by the Chairman," July 13, 1925, CAB, NPC, C. P. 342 (25), p. 2. Copy in CHAR 22/69, WCP.
[57] CAB, NPC, "Eighth Meeting," June 30, 1925, pp. 3, 5–6, 11.   [58] Ibid., pp. 3, 6, 16.
[59] Ibid., p. 5.
[60] Ibid., p. 16. See also Churchill to Baldwin, June 19, 1925, CHAR 18/11, WCP.
[61] CAB, NPC, "Second Meeting," March 5, 1925, p. 6.

earthquake and consequently had cut back its naval construction to "less than one-third of what it was in 1921–1922." Churchill assured the Committee that England therefore had breathing space to concentrate on restoring its economic health, upon which the future of the Conservative Party and Great Britain's military power depended, and to do so without endangering its current national security.[62]

Timely naval construction by politicians was precisely what Beatty most distrusted, and it was this distrust which made Churchill's one-year delay "impossible." Beatty convinced himself that any delay increased the likelihood that these cruisers "may not come out at all." The reason was obvious to him. The Conservative Party had "only a certain period of office" before the next election in 1929–1930, and Beatty feared the return to power of another socialist government which would cancel those ships yet to be laid down.[63] Besides, to ask Parliament for large sums for cruiser construction on the eve of an election was in his judgment to ensure that the politicians "will not take sufficient interest in it to raise a shout when the time comes."[64]

Distrust of politicians, their unwillingness to act in a timely manner to emerging military threats, and the specter of yet another socialist government hostile to naval building were basic to Beatty's opposition to the one-year delay. Moreover, Beatty harbored deep suspicion about Churchill's motives. With Churchill's one-year delay, only seventeen of the twenty-one cruisers would be completed before the next election in 1929–1930, and this prompted Beatty to charge that "What the Chancellor has in mind really is that he disagrees with the total number of cruisers that the Admiralty consider are essential" to defend the Empire. Nonetheless, the larger issue at stake, Beatty informed the Birkenhead Committee, was no less than the Admiralty's right to determine strategic naval policy and the warships needed to implement it. Since this was at the crux of his dispute with Churchill, Beatty demanded that the Cabinet, not the Birkenhead Committee, must either support the Admiralty by immediately authorizing the construction of all twenty-one cruisers without a one-year delay, or "they must tell the Admiralty that they are incapable of doing their job and get someone else to do it for them."[65]

Churchill ignored Beatty's implied threat of resignation. Their difference, Churchill maintained, "turns on technical detail" in measuring the comparative combat effectiveness of the two cruiser fleets, and it was only a question of "degree" on which they differed.[66] More importantly, he reiterated that if "we can economize to the extent of three or four millions this year it makes all the difference..."[67] By delaying the building of four cruisers for one year,

---

[62] CAB, NPC, "Eighth Meeting," June 30, 1925, pp. 3–4. [63] Ibid., pp. 7, 13.
[64] Beatty to Wife, June 30, 1925, 17/71 BTY, BP.
[65] CAB, NPC, "Eighth Meeting," June 30, 1925, p. 8. [66] Ibid., p. 9.
[67] Ibid., p. 16. See also Churchill to King George V, April 23, 1925 in Churchill, Companion Volume 5: 463–468.

the compounded savings in future years would allow Churchill "to accept the whole of this programme exactly as it stands, without the alteration of a single vessel in it... on [the] one condition, that they begin in 1926 instead of 1925."[68] It was hardly reasonable, he scoffed, to credit the Admiralty's implication that "... with the 4 cruisers the Admiralty profoundly says 'Britannia rules the waves'; without the 4 cruisers 'We are at the mercy of Japan.'"[69]

At the start of the deliberations of the Birkenhead Committee on March 2, 1925, Beatty was confident that its pro-navy members would give him a victory, but by July 13, after almost five months and eight lengthy debates, the Committee rewarded Churchill with a significant victory. The Committee's key conclusion emphasized the "degree of urgency which should govern the [building] process."[70] The Committee accepted the one-power standard, the Foreign Office's assurance that war with Japan was not likely in the next ten years, and the CID's recommendation to proceed with the Singapore base, but not Beatty's insistence upon immediately building a navy large enough to defeat the Japanese navy in its home waters. The Admiralty's modified building program with this reduction of expenditures by £51 million and significant reduction in the number of ships was gratefully accepted. It was Churchill's reasoning rather than Beatty's fears that proved most convincing.[71] As there was "no doubt that the financial relief which would be afforded by postponing the initiation of the new programmes till next year would be substantial," the Committee "had hoped that the Treasury offer would have proved acceptable to the Admiralty." Since it had not, the crucial question now became "whether a delay of one year ... will in fact endanger our Naval position and affect the safety of the Empire."[72]

Following "a detailed examination of the relative cruiser, submarine and destroyer forces of the British and Japanese Fleets," the Committee concluded that it would limit its recommendations to the "main item in dispute, i.e., the cruiser construction."[73] The Committee did not see much difference between the seven British cruisers displacing a total of 70,000 tons, carrying fifty-six 8-inch guns, and the eight Japanese cruisers displacing 68,400 tons with exactly the same number of 8-inch guns. What was significantly different to the Committee, however, was the recent launch of six new British cruisers, which the Admiralty had underrated because they carried 7.5-inch guns and 6-inch guns rather than 8-inch guns. The Committee acknowledged the Admiralty's "strong professional opinion" about the relative combat value of the new eight-inch gun, but it concluded nonetheless that the fact that England had forty-five to Japan's twenty-one cruisers, with guns other than 8-inches, gave England

---

[68] CAB, NPC, "Ninth Meeting," July 2, 1925, N. P. (25), p. 3, CAB 27/273, PRO; Birkenhead, "Report," July 13, 1925, p. 3.
[69] CAB, NPC, "Eighth Meeting," June 30, 1925, p. 9.
[70] Birkenhead, "Report," July 13, 1925, p. 1.   [71] Ibid., pp. 2–3.
[72] Ibid., p. 3.   [73] Ibid.

"a very large superiority" until at least 1928–1929, and therefore "we cannot feel that national security will be endangered by the delay of one year in beginning the series of new programmes."[74] It specifically dismissed Beatty's fear that "political conditions...would make it dangerous to postpone" building the new cruisers and instead accepted Churchill's contention that it was fairer "to assume that the financial position of the Country will have so far improved" that it could afford to complete building the cruisers even though it had also to begin the replacement of six capital ships between 1931 and 1934.[75]

The Birkenhead Committee awarded the victory to Churchill knowing full well of Bridgeman's open mutterings about resignation. While Bridgeman allowed Beatty to carry the weight of the Admiralty's case throughout most of the debate, he entered into the fray at the end largely to reiterate Beatty's arguments.[76] He dismissed Churchill's promise to build all of the ships in the modified program – including the twenty-one cruisers – on the same grounds put forth by Beatty: that a one-year delay would allow a new government – presumably a socialist one – to cancel the remaining unbuilt cruisers before they could be laid down. The danger to the Empire, he claimed, was therefore "impossible to exaggerate," and failure to complete the cruisers," he warned, "would be most dangerous."[77] In fact, Bridgeman proclaimed that he had little choice but to interpret the Committee's rejection of the Admiralty's insistence on the immediate authorization of four cruisers in 1925–1926 as a rejection of his "essential responsibility" to defend the Empire and thereby strongly hinted that his resignation would be unavoidable.[78]

Churchill was sympathetic to Bridgeman's strong sense of ministerial responsibility. He reassured the First Lord that "I have been in the same place" in past disputes over naval building.[79] Still, it was not right, Churchill scolded him, "to try and carry through what could not be done by reasonable argument by throwing out threats of resignation and so on."[80] Churchill claimed that his years of personal experience as First Lord of the Admiralty had put him "in a position to judge very accurately of this naval manner" and that he had presented both a reasoned rationale and an acceptable political compromise which, he emphasized, gave the Admiralty all of its ships.[81]

Nonetheless, it remained unclear whether Bridgeman and Beatty would dismiss Churchill's promise to build all its warships and instead use

---

[74] Ibid., p. 4.   [75] Ibid.

[76] W.C.B. [William C. Bridgeman], "Political Outlook and the Far East: Memorandum by the First Lord of the Admiralty," March 5, 1925, CAB, NPC, N. P. (25) 5, in CHAR 22/66, WCP. Bridgeman did not refute Churchill earlier in the debate over the question of the degree of Japan's threat.

[77] CAB, NPC, "Ninth Meeting," July 2, 1925, pp. 7–8, CAB 27/273, PRO. See copy in CHAR 22/65, WCP.

[78] Ibid., p. 8.   [79] Ibid., p. 9.   [80] Ibid., p. 8.   [81] Ibid., p. 9.

Churchill's Challenge 79

the one-year delay as the justification for carrying through with their threats of resignation. The larger question in their minds was whether the Admiralty or the Treasury had the inherent responsibility and power to assess strategic naval threats and to advise the Cabinet on national security priorities.

The Birkenhead Committee's strong support of Churchill's recommendations placed Baldwin in a difficult political position.[82] Most Cabinet ministers favored Churchill's proposals, but they were anxious, as was the Prime Minister, for a compromise.[83] After several days of Cabinet discussions, Baldwin prevailed upon Churchill to modify his one-year delay by offering to begin construction of two cruisers and four gunboats in the first year and two cruisers in the second year. This modification increased costs by £600,000 in the first year and £1,200,000 in the second year, but Churchill accepted Baldwin's suggestion and contented himself with the hope of realizing "a corresponding relief in later years." Austen Chamberlain, the Foreign Secretary, who had consistently advised the Cabinet that a war against Japan was unlikely during the next ten years and who favored this modification, congratulated Churchill on the "tone and temper" of Churchill's efforts to resolve the impasse.[84]

This political impasse and consequent modification had come about because Bridgeman and Beatty had refused to accept Churchill's promise to build all of the ships in the modified program, a promise which one noted British scholar concluded was "the best naval offer ever made by the Treasury between 1919 and 1934." Instead, they had made an "empathetic protest" to Baldwin against any delay whatever.[85] Two weeks earlier on July 3, 1925, Beatty had informed the Birkenhead Committee that unless it accepted the entire modified program without any further delays in starting construction, the Baldwin Cabinet would have "to find another Admiralty."[86] There was, he believed, "no other way out."[87] Beatty was comforted by Bridgeman's unwavering resolution to resign with him. Bridgeman "has been splendid very firm and definite and has made it plain," Beatty told his wife Ethel, "that he will

---

[82] Bridgeman to My Beloved, July 15, 1925, 4629/1/1925/50, WBP; Leo Amery, Diary, July 17, 1925 in Churchill, *Companion Volume* 5: 508.
[83] For Minutes of the several days of discussions, see CAB 23/50/37 (25), July 15, 1925 and CAB 23/50/38 (25), July 16, 1925, PRO.
[84] Churchill, "Navy Estimates: New Construction Programme," July 20, 1925 in Churchill, *Companion Volume* 5: 511–512; Austen Chamberlain to Churchill, July 18, 1925 in *Ibid.*; CAB 23/50/38 (25), July 16, 1925, PRO.
[85] John Robert Ferris, *The Evolution of British Strategic Policy*, pp. 167–168; Bridgeman to Baldwin, July 18, 1925, 4629/1/1925/56, WBP. See also Bridgeman to Baldwin, July 11 and 12, 1925 in William Bridgeman, *The Modernisation of Conservative Politics: The Diaries and Letters of William Bridgeman, 1904–1935*, ed. Philip Williamson (London: The Historian's Press, 1988), pp. 185–187. Hereafter cited as Bridgeman, *Modernisation*.
[86] Beatty to Wife, July 3, 1925, BTY, 17/7, BP.
[87] Beatty to Wife, July 7, 1925, BTY, 17/71, BP.

not remain at the Admiralty unless our views are accepted and of course his Board will go with him if he goes."[88]

With Bridgeman "as firm as a rock," Beatty was cautiously optimistic about the Admiralty's chances for a Cabinet victory over Churchill.[89] His optimism was based on his belief that the Cabinet would understand that Churchill's naval policies "cut at the root of the naval policy of the Empire" and would require "the abandonment of any provisions for the defense of our Eastern Interests." The Cabinet would therefore be forced to issue "the clearest instructions on these vital questions."[90] Besides, Beatty told Bridgeman, he still could not credit that Churchill really "believes all the rubbish he has talked."[91] Furthermore, Beatty calculated, it was with the Cabinet rather than either the Birkenhead Committee or the Foreign Office that the Admiralty could most effectively exert its still considerable political influence and he therefore appealed personally to Arthur Balfour and to Baldwin.[92]

Although not as optimistic about a Cabinet victory, Bridgeman joined in support of Beatty's political battle. Repeatedly he insisted to Baldwin that any further compromise with Churchill would violate Conservative Party policy which, he claimed, had strongly supported eight cruisers for 1924 and five cruisers in each succeeding year. During the Birkenhead Committee negotiations, Bridgeman had agreed to reduce the cruisers to only four in 1924–1925 and only three in each succeeding year, but he refused to go any lower.[93] To do so, he insisted, would be "revising the Naval Policy of the Conservative Party to which I have pledged all my life – namely to keep a force in peace powerful enough to resist attack from any other nation, however small may be the probability of hostilities."[94] The one-power standard – which required Great Britain to maintain a navy equal in strength to that of its most powerful rival – was crucial to England's very survival.[95] To that point, he argued, "Once you abandoned this principle you do take risks which the country cannot afford to run," especially as "we are absolutely dependent on our existence for the control of the sea..."[96] The person responsible for abandoning this vital principle and thereby endangering the nation was Churchill.

---

[88] Beatty to Wife, July 3, 1925, BTY, 17/7, BP.
[89] Beatty to Wife, Tuesday [July 7, 1925?], BTY 17/7, BP.
[90] Beatty to Bridgeman, July, 8 1925, 4629/1/1925/12, WBP.
[91] Beatty to Wife, July 4 and 6, 1925, BTY 17/7, BP.
[92] *Ibid.*; Beatty to My Darling Tata, July 11, 1925, BTY 17/7, BP. Also see BTY 3, BP.
[93] Beatty to Wife, July 10, 1925, BTY 17/7, BP; Beatty to Wife, July 10, 1925 and Bridgeman to Baldwin in William Scott Chalmers, ed., *The Life and Letters of David, Earl Beatty* (London: Hodder and Stoughton, 1951), p. 409; Bridgeman, "Memorandum for Baldwin," n.d. [July 11 or 12, 1925?] in Bridgeman, *Modernisation*, p. 185. See also BGMN-24, WBPCC.
[94] Bridgeman, "Memorandum for Baldwin," n.d. [July 11 or 12, 1925?]; Bridgeman to Dearest Mother, July 7, 1925, 4629/1/1925/47, WBP.
[95] Bridgeman to Dearest Mother, July 2 and 7, 1925, 4629/1/1925/46–47, WBP.
[96] Bridgeman to Dearest Mother, July 7, 1925, 4629/1/1925/47, WBP.

"The influence of Winston," he warned, "is thoroughly bad and if everyone gives in to him, he will ruin our party."[97]

Bridgeman was upset as well over the realization that his determination to resign, should the Cabinet support Churchill, would put his good friend Baldwin in serious political difficulties. Twice Baldwin called him to the Prime Minister's country estate to convince him to accept a one-year delay in construction of the cruisers, but twice Bridgeman rebuffed him. He countered Baldwin's pleas by emphasizing the great need to keep skilled labor at work in the shipyards and the positive economic effect of cruiser construction on unemployment. To stop construction for one year meant further increasing the 31.1 percent unemployment in shipbuilding and encouraging still more skilled workers to leave the country for employment elsewhere. For these reasons, Bridgeman told Baldwin, "it was no use trying to get me to change my mind and it was for him to decide which course to pursue – and if he decided against me, I should go at once." And with him, Baldwin understood, would go the entire Admiralty Board and quite possibly some other influential Conservative leaders.[98] If Baldwin supported Churchill's policies, Bridgeman charged, the prime minister "was going back on his word and ruining the party..." Nonetheless, despite his threats of resignation, Baldwin still remained, Bridgeman lamented, "on the side of the economists ... though he disliked throwing me overboard..."[99]

Rather than blame his good friend Baldwin, Bridgeman vented most of his frustration on Churchill and on the Cabinet, especially after he discovered that he had the full support of only four ministers.[100] Lack of Cabinet support caused Bridgeman to become increasingly despondent and angry. "I think they [Cabinet ministers] will be mad if they refuse to do what the Admiralty experts say is essential for the safety of the country," he confided to his mother, "but some of my colleagues are such knaves and others such fools that I doubt if the wisdom of the few will prevail."[101] Bridgeman's harsh denunciation of the "knaves" and "fools," with whom he had spent long years in politics, revealed how strongly Bridgeman identified himself with his new prestigious post as First Lord of the Admiralty and the degree to which Beatty had influenced him. In the judgment of most of his fellow Cabinet ministers, a one-year delay in naval construction hardly merited the political crisis which

---

[97] Ibid. For his earlier criticisms of Churchill, see Bridgeman to Dawson, 13 February 13, 1925 in Bridgeman, *Modernisation*, p. 181.

[98] Bridgeman, "Memorandum for Baldwin: Political Case for the Admiralty," n.d. [July 11 or 12, 1925?]; Bridgeman, "Memorandum for Baldwin: Admiralty Arguments Against Postponement," n.d. [July 11 or 12 1925?], in Bridgeman, *Modernisation*, pp. 185–187; Bridgeman to Dearest Mother, July 20, 1925, 4629/1/1925/62, WBP; Bridgeman, Diary, July 22, 1925, pp. 111–113, WBP; Stephen Roskill, *Beatty*, p. 352.

[99] Bridgeman, Diary, July 22, 1925, pp. 111–115, WBP.   [100] Ibid., p. 113.

[101] Bridgeman to Dearest Mother, July 20, 1925, 4629/1/1925/62, WBP; Bridgeman, Diary, July 20–22, 1925, pp. 105–108.

would occur if he resigned, but, like Beatty, Bridgeman no longer trusted his political friends to determine national defense policy. He was amazed "that worm politicians are ready to be convinced by the amateur strategist" [Churchill] who would, upon Bridgeman's resignation, castigate him as a "traitor to my party."[102] Even if he were unexpectedly to prevail, he believed, his Cabinet "colleagues who disagree will be very resentful..." and he therefore felt that he could never again "be really comfortable in this Cabinet."[103]

With newspaper reports speculating on his imminent departure from the Cabinet, Bridgeman prepared his resignation speech, one calculated to create a political furor. Employing most of the Admiralty's arguments for cruisers, he vehemently denied that there was "no risk of war" and declined "absolutely to admit that the Foreign Office or anyone else is capable of forecasting the next war..." "The real fact is," he concluded, "that the Government have deliberately adopted the views of the amateur strategists at the Treasury rather than those of the experts who have spent their lives in the Service." He rejected the notion that "there is no danger in delay, [or] that the amateur's opinion is better than that of the experts." Moreover, he charged that the Baldwin Cabinet had "abandoned the policy of protecting our trade East of Suez." Once he explained his reasons for resigning, Bridgeman convinced himself that "No decent fellow would accept the post" of First Lord of the Admiralty.[104]

As Beatty was also preparing his resignation speech, Prime Minister Baldwin reversed course and abruptly threw his support behind the Admiralty.[105] Bridgeman was surprised, Beatty less so.[106] Beatty had been in touch behind the scenes with influential Conservative party leaders, especially, it seems, with John C. Davidson, the Parliamentary Secretary to the Admiralty.[107] Davidson was an important leader in the Conservative Party from 1927–1930.[108] He vehemently opposed Churchill's interference in naval matters, and, consequently, he had been working hard to arouse Conservative Party members against Churchill's proposals.[109] Davidson's reasons were as much political as naval. To convince wavering party members to oppose Churchill, he

[102] Bridgeman, Diary, July 22, 1925, p. 111; Bridgeman to My Beloved, July 15, 1925, 4629/1/1925/50, WBP.
[103] Bridgeman to Dearest Mother, July 17, 1925, 4129/1/1925/51; Bridgeman, Diary, July 22, 1925, p. 115, WBP.
[104] Quoted in BGMN/2, pp. 616 passim, WBPCC. See also Martin Gilbert, *Winston S. Churchill*, 8 vols. (New York: Houghton Mifflin, 1977), 5: 129; Sir John D. Kelly to Keyes, July 17, 1925 in Keyes, *Keyes Papers*, 2: 123.
[105] For an excerpt of Beatty's prepared resignation speech, see Chalmers, *Life and Letters*, pp. 374–375.
[106] Bridgeman, Diary, July 22, 1925, p. 111, WBP. See also BGMN/2, p. 595.
[107] Roskill, *Beatty*, p. 352; BGMN/2, p. 586; Hankey to Beatty, July 10 and 13, 1925, BTY 8/8, BP.
[108] J. C. C. Davidson, *Memoirs of a Conservative, J. C. C. Davidson's Memoirs and Papers, 1910–1937*, ed. Robert Rhodes James (London: Weidenfeld and Nicholson, 1969), pp. 206, 213–214, 225.
[109] Ibid., pp. 212–214.

Churchill's Challenge

propagated the sensationalistic claim that Churchill and his cohorts were merely using the cruiser dispute to hatch a sinister plot in which Baldwin's support of Churchill would trigger the resignation of Bridgeman, Beatty, and the entire Admiralty Board, and quite possibly Leo Amery, a former First Lord of the Admiralty. The ensuing political uproar would then split the Conservative Party and thereby realize the main objective of bringing down the Baldwin Government.[110]

According to Davidson, on the very eve of the Cabinet's approval of Churchill's naval recommendations, the Party's leaders convinced Baldwin that in the face of all the threatened resignations, the Party could not remain united behind Baldwin and his Cabinet. To save his leadership, Baldwin therefore decided to avoid further political damage by convincing his Cabinet to support a compromise favorable to Bridgeman and Beatty.[111]

The compromise which Baldwin imposed had important long-term consequences. Already in the midst of a national coal strike crisis, Baldwin dampened down Conservative Party squabbling by giving both Churchill and Bridgeman some measure of satisfaction, although the Admiralty believed it had won a clear victory.[112] Most significant was the abandonment of Churchill's one-year delay on all construction. Baldwin instead replaced it with a guaranteed five-year naval construction program calling for only sixteen rather than the twenty-one cruisers, which Churchill had promised to build – nine 10,000-ton and seven 8,000-ton, 8-inch-gun cruisers – along with one aircraft carrier, eighteen destroyers, and three submarines.

Churchill also won some significant concessions. He was no longer bound to his promise to build the twenty-one cruisers, which he had promised in return for a one-year delay. The Cabinet fully supported Churchill's criticism of Beatty's Japanese war plan, accepted his earlier argument for sixteen cruisers, called instead for still another Cabinet committee to investigate additional cuts in naval costs, and again reiterated its support for another international conference to limit auxiliary warships. The expensive new naval base at Singapore, which Churchill opposed, was referred to the Committee of Imperial Defence [CID], and after months of controversy, a temporary resolution scaled back its construction. With the support of the Foreign Office and the CID, the Cabinet also accepted Churchill's contention that war with Japan was not foreseeable in the next ten years and that this finding should be reviewed annually under the Ten-Year Rule.[113]

---

[110] Ibid., pp. 212–216.
[111] Ibid., pp. 210–211, 215–216; BGMN-/2, pp. 584, 591–593; Keith Middlemas and John Barnes, *Baldwin: A Biography* (London: Macmillan, 1970), pp. 330–341.
[112] *Companion Volume* 5: 514–516; Davidson, *Memoirs*, pp. 216–218; BGMN/2, pp 592–593.
[113] For Baldwin's compromise, see Cabinet Conclusion, 22 July 22, 1927, CAB 23/50/39 (25), CAB 23/50, PRO; Board of Admiralty, *Minutes*, July 22, 1925, "New Programme of Shipbuilding," No. 2075, ADM 167/71, PRO; BGMN/2, pp. 594–598; Davidson, *Memoirs*, pp. 210–216, 225;

The belief, or at the very least, the suspicion among some important Conservative Party and Admiralty leaders, that Churchill was either actively involved in, or was aiding and abetting a diabolical conspiracy to split the Party and topple Baldwin, had long-term consequences, which have not yet been fully explored. John Robert Ferris has already convincingly demonstrated the illogical and unlikely nature of the conspiracy belief.[114] Additional evidence supports his conclusion. Churchill's careful, patient, and, at times, sympathetic analysis of naval needs and policies during the Birkenhead Committee debates, his promise to build all twenty-one of the cruisers in the modified program, his willingness to compromise on the one-year delay, and his acceptance of Baldwin's final solution are inconsistent with Davidson's charge that Churchill was merely using this dispute with the Admiralty as a means to plot the Prime Minister's downfall.[115] Nonetheless, insufficient evidence to support the existence of a conspiracy should not obscure the important fact that influential leaders in the Conservative Party believed it to be true. Precisely because they believed it, propagated it, and acted on it, the conspiracy charge had an important impact on Churchill's future relationship with the Admiralty, especially in still another crisis during the 1927 Geneva Conference negotiations.

Certainly Beatty believed in the conspiracy, and he had used it to press the Admiralty's demands. On July 8, 1925, when he apparently first learned of the alleged conspiracy, he complained to his wife Ethel about the "great deal of intrigue ... principally aimed at the Prime Minister and the Admiralty." However, the bitter fight over the Admiralty's budget requests, he believed, was merely "the stalking horse" behind which the conspirators "are taking cover to assail" the Prime Minister. Rather than identify Churchill as the ringleader, Beatty accused another Cabinet minister, the "intriguing little brute" Samuel Hoare, Secretary for Air, with whom Beatty was locked in a bitter struggle over the creation of an independent naval air force. Hoare was "at the bottom of it," Beatty charged, but significantly, Churchill and Birkenhead were ready to pick up the pieces. Only two days earlier on July 6 Beatty had defended Churchill against his wife's repeated criticisms.[116] When he learned of the alleged plot on July 8, however, he immediately implicated Churchill. The conspiracy, he quickly concluded, was "whetting the appetite for more power in F. E. [Lord Birkenhead] and Winston by the suggestion that if the Admiralty are defeated it will raise such a storm as to undermine the position of the Prime Minister and be the forerunner of his fall." While Beatty refrained from accusing Churchill of hatching this plot, he certainly was willing

---

Stephen Roskill, *Naval Policy Between the Wars: The Period of Anglo-American Antagonism, 1919–1929* (London: Collins, 1968), pp. 441–453; Ferris, *Evolution*, pp. 166–168; Philip Payson O'Brien, *British and American Naval Power: Politics and Policy, 1900–1936* (Westport, CT; Praeger, 1998), p. 185; Middlemas and Barnes, *Baldwin*, pp. 330–341.

[114] Ferris, *Evolution*, p. 168.   [115] Davidson, *Memoirs*, pp. 212–216.
[116] Beatty to Wife, July 6, 1925, BTY, 17/71, BP.

to believe that Churchill knew of it and that his appetite for more power prompted him to capitalize on it. These plotters were so close to success, Beatty believed, that the "one chance the P. M. [Prime Minister] has is to stick with us and support us," for this would prevent the resignation of the entire Admiralty Board and the consequent split in the Conservative Party, whereupon the "whole country would be behind him both in the Parliament and out of it," and the conspiracy would collapse. Beatty therefore decided that he must take an active role in thwarting this skullduggery.[117]

Fearing that a Cabinet decision on the Birkenhead recommendations was imminent, Beatty wasted no time in going directly to Baldwin. It is not clear whether he advanced the conspiracy charges or merely reiterated the Admiralty Board's resignation threats, or both, but Vice Admiral Sir John D. Kelly, who served on the Board of Admiralty as Fourth Sea Lord, praised Beatty's boldness in going directly to the Prime Minister. "I think it was really a private last-minute interview that D. B. [David Beatty] had with the Prime Minister that turned the scale, especially, he added, as Baldwin was a "wobbler" who failed "to lead the Cabinet."[118] On July 10, 1925, apparently after his private session with Baldwin, Beatty reassured his wife that the Prime Minister was now "more open to entertain the Admiralty's views."[119]

It may have been at this time, in July 1925, rather than during the later 1927 Cabinet crisis, as Stephen Roskill assumed, that Sir Shane Leslie witnessed Beatty's "double pressure" on Baldwin. Although Leslie did not specify the date when the encounter took place, his recollection fits well with the corroborating 1925 evidence. As "the whole Board of Admiralty was ready to walk out," Beatty "sought Mrs. Baldwin at a London party and told her privately that in less than a month she would no longer be sleeping with the Prime Minister of England!" Thus Beatty " succeeded," Leslie concluded, "in spreading the necessary alarm."[120]

Bridgeman remained more circumspect and cautious, although, given his close association with Beatty and Davidson, he almost certainly knew of their strong belief that Churchill was conspiring to topple Baldwin.[121] Some close to

---

[117] Beatty to Wife, July 8, 1925, BTY, 17/71, BP.
[118] Sir John D. Kelly to Roger Keyes, July 27, 1925 in Keyes, *Keyes Papers*, 2: 123.
[119] Beatty to Wife, July 10, 1925, BTY, 17/71, BP.
[120] Shane Leslie, "Memories of Beatty," *Quarterly Review* 290 (July 1952): 459. Roskill admits that Leslie's evidence only created a probability that this event took place in 1927. See Roskill, *Beatty*, p. 358. An even greater probability is that no one will ever be certain of the exact time that Beatty delivered this threat, but the evidence suggests strongly that this incident took place in 1925 rather than 1927. Indeed, at the time of the 1927 Cabinet crisis, Baldwin was in Canada. In any case, regardless of the exact time, Beatty's threat illustrates the highly aggressive tactics which he was willing to employ at the highest levels of the British government.
[121] For Bridgeman's close association with Davidson, see Davidson to My Dear First Lady, July 22, 1925, 4629/1/1925/69, WBP; Bridgeman, Diary, July 22, 1925, pp. 113–115; Davidson, *Memoirs*, p. 217.

Bridgeman believed that he, too, was convinced of the reality of the plot and the danger to the Prime Minister.[122] Certainly he warned Baldwin of a serious threat. He attributed part of this threat to Churchill, whose recent return to the Conservative Party caused Bridgeman considerable misgivings. Earlier in February Bridgeman had confided to a friend his belief that Churchill had been leaking "Ludicrous propaganda [which was] grossly misleading" to the press in order to deceive the English people and ruin the Navy. On July 7, 1925, one day before Beatty alerted his wife to the plot, Bridgeman confided to his mother that the "influence of Winston is thoroughly bad and if everyone gives in to him, he will ruin our party."[123]

Bridgeman was especially discouraged because Baldwin had twice refused his request to support the Admiralty against Churchill, and Bridgeman therefore felt he had no choice but to resign his prestigious post under the most galling of circumstances. Although Bridgeman predicted that "success was impossible," he recalled that "late in the evening on July 21, party managers at last realized what it would mean to sacrifice us and the Navy to Winston [and] went to Baldwin and frightened him properly."[124]

Bridgeman and Baldwin congratulated each other on defeating the "conspirators." On July 22, 1925, the same day that Baldwin forged the Cabinet solution favoring the Admiralty, Bridgeman told him: "I allow myself to think that my obstinacy has saved you from what I believe would have been a fatal disaster for you..."[125] In recounting his role to his mother, Bridgeman dramatically exclaimed: "At the last moment the majority of the Cabinet got frightened at the row which would be created by my resignation – and came to their senses."[126] Baldwin hinted at his own shrewd political timing, while also giving some credit to Bridgeman's behind-the-scenes maneuvering: "it was you who got the parties together and I would have gladly left it to you all through, but I had to come in when I did – for appearances sake."[127]

Bridgeman was aware that besting Churchill and his allies was not without its risks. "It was really a great triumph," he chortled, "but I must be careful not to appear too cock-a-whoop as my enemies are very sick at being beaten..."[128] Churchill may well have felt downcast at seeing his hard-won victory snatched from his grasp at the very last moment. If so, he hid his

---

[122] Bridgeman] to M.B.B.[Marianne Bridgeman], July 20, 1925 in BGMN/2, p. 591. Caroline was Bridgeman's wife and Marianne was his mother.
[123] Bridgeman to G. Dawson, February 13, 1925 in Bridgeman, *Modernisation*, p. 181; Bridgeman to My Dearest Mother, July 7, 1925, 4629/1/1925/47, WBP.
[124] Kelly to Keyes, 27 July 1925, in *Keyes Papers*, 2: 123; Bridgeman, Diary, July 22, 1925, p. 115, WBP.
[125] Quoted in BGMN/2, p. 595.
[126] Bridgeman to Dearest Mother, July 22, 1925, 4629/1/1925/68, WBP.
[127] Baldwin to Bridgeman, July 31, 1925, BGMN/3, WBPCC.
[128] Bridgeman to Dearest Mother, July 22, 1925, 4629/1/1925/62, WBP; Davidson to Lady Bridgeman, July 22, 1925, BGMN/3, WBPCC; Davidson, *Memoirs*, p. 217.

disappointment.[129] Throughout the controversy Churchill had worked at maintaining cordial relations with Bridgeman and Beatty. Their insistence on turning a dispute over Admiralty expenditures and strategy into one over party unity or disunity nonetheless added a new dimension to their, by now, strained relations. The accusations that Churchill was one of the alleged conspirators certainly gave him more than sufficient reason to distrust the political tactics of the Admiralty. The mistrust was mutual. Several months later Bridgeman again revealed his abiding distrust of Churchill when he observed that as Winston was "rather openly trying to be friendly," he therefore "must be careful."[130]

Thus, a great and damaging gulf had opened between Churchill and Beatty. Beatty's opinion of Churchill had for many years fluctuated sharply. Whereas Churchill often lauded him as a great hero and had been instrumental at crucial times in saving and promoting Beatty's career, the First Sea Lord did not always think highly of Churchill. As early as 1902 Beatty confided to his wife Ethel, who harbored an intense dislike of Churchill, that she was quite right: "Winston Churchill is not nice, in fact he is what is generally described as a fraud, and to use a naval expression, all Gas and baiters."[131] At other times, especially when Churchill was promoting Beatty's career or supporting his naval budgets, Beatty considered him the good friend who had rescued his career from almost certain retirement by first appointing him as his Naval Secretary and then as commander of the prestigious Battle Cruiser Squadron before and during World War I. Churchill's strong support had continued after the War. In addition to the £100,000 award, which Churchill had sponsored in Parliament as a reward for Beatty's war services, he had backed Beatty's 1922 call for replacement battleships and endorsed his war plan against Japan.[132] But, in 1925, when Churchill felt obligated, as Chancellor of the Exchequer, to challenge the Admiralty's budget demands, Beatty's latent reservations and suspicions about Churchill surfaced once again.[133]

During the intense Birkenhead Committee debates, Beatty increasingly came to view Churchill as a political enemy whose political opportunism had led him to abandon his earlier support for Beatty's war plan against Japan and the consequent need for an immediate building program in cruisers. This became a political battle in which Beatty was determined, as he put it, to win "at all costs."[134] His contempt for politicians who meddled in Admiralty affairs

---

[129] Davidson, *Memoirs*, p. 217. Davison claimed: "I don't think that Churchill ever forgave the Admiralty."
[130] Bridgeman to MCB [Marianne Bridgeman], November 29, 1925, in BGMN/2, p. 558; Bridgeman to My Beloved, March 20, 1925, 4629/1/1925/17, WBP.
[131] Beatty to Wife, September 20, 1902 in David Beatty, *The Beatty Papers: Selections from the Private and Official Correspondence of Admiral of the Fleet Earl Beatty, 1902–1927*, ed. B. Mc L. Ranft 2 vols. (Aldershot, England: Gower, 1989–1993), 1: 11–12.
[132] See Chapter 3.
[133] Beatty to Wife, January 30, 1925 in Beatty, *Beatty Papers*, 2: 281.   [134] Ibid.

was revealed most clearly in his utter disdain for Churchill's belief that a reduction in taxes was essential to fight the ravages of the economic downturn. Churchill's argument that he could lower taxes only by cutting naval construction demands was merely, Beatty contended, a political ploy to "justify his appointment as Chancellor of the Exchequer." Equally damning was Churchill's willingness "to throw everything, all his ideas of imperialism, etc., to the winds to achieve this one thing." His new political position, Beatty lamented, had suddenly transformed him from a staunch defender of the Admiralty into one who opportunistically "attacks us with virulence, and now proclaims that a Navy is a quite unnecessary luxury." But, Beatty believed, this former Liberal Party chieftain was digging his own political grave in his newly adopted Conservative Party, as his attacks on the Admiralty had so infuriated the Party's "Die-Hards" that Beatty predicted "a split in the Conservative party" was inevitable because "a very considerable portion of the Conservative party ... already hate Winston like poison," and his continued opposition to Admiralty proposals was already "providing them with fresh ammunition with which to destroy him."[135]

Churchill was aware of Beatty's political declaration of war. As early as March 11, 1925, in the midst of the Birkenhead debates, Churchill's wife Clementine warned her husband of Beatty's indiscreet bragging about his forthcoming "'big battle with Churchill.'" Well aware of Churchill's abiding admiration of Beatty's earlier heroism, she admonished him to "stand up to the Admiralty and don't be fascinated or flattered or cajoled by Beatty." She cautioned him not to "get sentimental or too soft hearted," as Beatty "is a tight little screw and he will bargain with you and cheat you as tho he was selling you a dud horse which is I fear what the Navy is."[136]

At some point, most likely in early July 1925, about the time when the conspiracy charges against him began to circulate, Churchill called for Beatty's removal as First Sea Lord. Later, when Admiral Roger Keyes, a friend to both Churchill and Beatty, confronted Churchill with his call to oust Beatty, Churchill readily acknowledged his recommendation.[137] He had called for Beatty's removal, he informed Keyes, on the basis of policy, not personality. He had done so because Beatty was "banking so heavily on the war with Japan, which I believe to be nonsense in itself and also very bad policy on our part, that [he had become convinced] a change [must] take place." He nonetheless professed his personal regard for Beatty and reassured Keyes that "now that

---

[135] Beatty to Wife, January 26, 1925, BTY 1, BP. For an edited and significantly different version of this letter see Churchill, *Companion Volume* 5: 356. Also see Beatty to Wife, January 30, 1925 in Beatty, *Beatty Papers*, 2: 281. For the Die-Hard Coalition split in the Conservative party, see Middlemas and Barnes, *Baldwin*, pp. 338–339.
[136] Clementine Churchill to Winston, March 1, 1925 in Churchill, *Companion Volume* 5: 428–429 and Chapter 3.
[137] Churchill to Keyes, in Churchill, *Companion Volume* 5: 830.

Singapore is so satisfactorily settled for a few years to come and the new [five-year cruiser] programme agreed upon," he was content to have Beatty remain as First Sea Lord.[138]

Implicit in Churchill's willingness to retain Beatty was a subtle warning. Should Beatty reopen the Singapore or cruiser issues and again marshal the Admiralty's political supporters within the Conservative Party to defeat and defame Churchill, the Chancellor might very well renew his call for Beatty's ouster. This hint was an outward sign of a much more profound change in Churchill's thinking about Beatty. During the course of the Birkenhead Committee debates, Churchill had developed a keener insight into Beatty's defects as the peacetime leader of the Admiralty. Despite all of his efforts to educate Beatty about the seriousness of the economic weaknesses plaguing Great Britain, Beatty had chosen to encourage a political crisis over Churchill's pleas for a one-year delay in cruiser construction. It was clear to Churchill that Beatty's narrow focus on Admiralty prerogatives took precedence over regaining the economic strength on which future military preparedness depended. He was dismayed as well by Beatty's expensive, highly disadvantageous war strategy against Japan, including his illogical distribution of the trade-protection cruisers during such a war. Thus, Churchill had come away from these debates with a considerably diminished opinion of Beatty's strategic judgment and a strong distrust of his political tactics.[139]

Beatty's distrust of Churchill and his willingness to accuse him of dishonorable motives and actions continued. In August 1925, a month after the Cabinet crisis, Beatty returned to the attack when Churchill refused to fund a marriage allowance for naval officers, a goal which Beatty as First Sea Lord felt honor-bound to obtain. In turning down Beatty's request, Churchill reminded him that he had "never thought there was the slightest justification" for the naval marriage allowance and had "endeavored to express this view in repeated communications from the Treasury, largely drafted personally by myself."[140] But Beatty refused to credit Churchill's word. "That dirty dog Winston is so sick," he charged, "that he turned round and went back on his word over the marriage allowances." He made this "monstrous decision," Beatty believed, because Churchill had been forced to support Baldwin's compromise naval budget in Parliament "to save his face," and was using the marriage allowance to take revenge against the Admiralty.[141]

Beatty renewed his attack on Churchill in November 1925 in an address to the Lord Mayor's Banquet. In a thinly disguised attack on "amateur strategists," a favorite Admiralty euphemism for Churchill and his Treasury

---

[138] See also Churchill to Keyes, 16 September 1926 in Keyes, *Keyes Papers*, 2: 119. For the temporary agreement on Singapore see Roskill, *Naval Policy*, p. 463.
[139] See Chapter 3.
[140] Churchill to Beatty, August 10, 1925 in Beatty, *Beatty Papers*, 2: 302–303.
[141] Beatty to Keyes, August 6, 1925 in Keyes, *Keyes Papers*, 2: 124.

"clerks," he complained that the Admiralty had been subjected to "a campaign of ill-informed criticism so wide of the truth and so oblivious to the necessities of the Empire, that it only can be concluded that the object of the critic is political." This infamous campaign, he lectured, was not only "persistent and one-sided," but outrageously unpatriotic. "I ask is this fair play? I ask – is it patriotic to attempt to stir up in this great Service [the Navy] dissatisfaction and want of confidence in administration [leadership] for purely political or personal reasons?"[142]

Beatty was furious as well by Churchill's opposition to the Admiralty's attempt to close major dockyards such as Rosyth and Pembroke.[143] Churchill had complained directly to Baldwin that closing these dockyards made no good economic sense "when the total savings from all sources, with all the suffering [from unemployment] they entail, are far less than the £4 million a year spent on Iraq, etc." These Admiralty cutbacks lacked both economic and political sensitivity, which Churchill suggested once again highlighted the Admiralty's persistent disregard for the urgent need to use Great Britain's dwindling economic resources wisely.[144]

Beatty believed as well that Churchill was somehow involved in press leaks of the secret yet sensational Colwyn Committee report, which an infuriated Admiral Keyes denounced as "insolent venom."[145] Known officially as the Fighting Services Economy Committee, created by the Baldwin Cabinet in July 1925 at the height of the Cabinet crisis, and headed by F. H. Smith, the first Baron Colwyn, this Committee was charged with conducting an impartial investigation and making recommended economies for all of the fighting services, most especially in naval expenditures.[146] Bridgeman was "deeply hurt ... by the offensive tone of the Colwyn Report," which, he lamented "could hardly have been more offensively expressed even if written by the youngest and most self-satisfied Treasury Clerk."[147] Bridgeman had some justification for his complaint, as the Report called for substantial cuts in oil fuel reserves, officers, enlisted personnel, stores, clothing, armaments, dockyards, aircraft carriers, and Fleet airplane squadrons, without mentioning the millions which the Admiralty had already cut as a result of the Birkenhead

---

[142] Beatty, "Draft Speech for Lord Mayor's Banquet, 1925," November 9, 1925 in Beatty, *Beatty Papers*, 2: 307–309.
[143] *Ibid.*
[144] Churchill to Baldwin, September 20, 1925 in Churchill, *Companion Volume* 5: 549–550.
[145] Keyes to Bridgeman, February 23, 1926, 4629/1/1226/19 and Beatty to Bridgeman, January 19, 1926, 4629/1/1226/ 4, WBP. For those accusing Churchill of creating the Colwyn Committee, see Roskill, *Beatty*, p. 353. See also BGMN/2, pp. 598–605; Davidson, *Memoirs*, pp. 223–224. The Colwyn Committee recommendations and important correspondence are in ADM 116/2374, January 9, 1926, pp. 6–12, PRO.
[146] Davidson, *Memoirs*, pp. 223–224.
[147] Bridgeman, Draft Letter [to Baldwin?], January 15, 1926, 4629/1/1926/3 WBP.

Churchill's Challenge

debates.[148] Beatty nonetheless apparently blamed Churchill for the report and for leaking the secret document to the press.[149]

Ethel Beatty's repeated criticisms of Churchill in the elite social circles to which Beatty's status as First Sea Lord and her great wealth had opened to them, exacerbated Churchill's deteriorating relations with Beatty. In September 1926, a year after the crisis, when Churchill again learned of Ethel's outbursts denouncing him, Beatty became exasperated with his wife. Her repeated claim that half of England considered Churchill dangerous, Beatty pointed out, "made my task and work at the Admiralty much more difficult," as "I have to work with the man and when it gets to his ears, *as it has done* that my wife *continually* describes him as a Danger to the State, he very naturally ascribes that opinion to me." [Emphasis mine.][150] Nonetheless, Beatty's own denunciations of Churchill as a "dirty dog," who deliberately broke his word on marriage allowances to take revenge on the Admiralty, made no attempt to separate Churchill's policies from his character, and it is reasonable to suppose that Beatty himself may have failed to make that distinction from time to time when speaking to his wife. Little wonder then, that Churchill occasionally indulged privately in self-pity when he bemoaned that "the Navy reproach me bitterly for only criticizing and attacking their expenditures while the Air Force they say is favored and the Army is let alone. You have only to read the papers to see how cruel is the pressure to which I am subjected."[151]

Beatty's fixation on Churchill as the prime source of the Admiralty's troubles clouded his thinking and masked his own shortcomings. The Admiralty's frustration over fewer cruisers and lower budgets, allegedly perpetrated by "Winston" and by his weak-willed, short-sighted, and untrustworthy political allies, was an outward sign of a much more serious inner weakness. The Admiralty's participation in bringing about the Cabinet crisis revealed a defect of a far more serious sort. Both Beatty and Bridgeman suffered from an overblown sense of the sagacity of their political judgment – a weakness which would become even more significant and more damaging at the Geneva Naval Conference in 1927. Yet by early July 1925, Bridgeman and Beatty knew that their best arguments had failed to convince either the sympathetic members of the Birkenhead Committee or the Cabinet. The Cabinet's rejection of the immediate need to prepare for a naval war against Japan, its repeated affirmation of the Ten-Year Rule, its creation of the Colwyn Committee, and its

---

[148] Bridgeman to Baldwin, September 4, 1925; Baldwin to Bridgeman, October 16, 1925, and correspondence between Bridgeman and Colwyn in ADM 116/2374, PRO.
[149] Beatty to Bridgeman, 19 January 19, 1926, 4629/1/1926/4; copy of Beatty to Baldwin, January 19, 1926, 4629/1/1926/5, WBP. For the continuing debate between Bridgeman and Churchill, see their correspondence in CHAR 18/32, WCP.
[150] Beatty to Wife, September 30, 1926 in Beatty, *Beatty Papers*, 2: 339.
[151] See footnote 141 and Churchill to Lord Trenchard, October 11, 1925 in Churchill, *Companion Volume 5*: 555–556.

recognition of the economic necessity of accepting a substantial reduction in the number of ships were political realities fashioned after a prolonged, rational, and reasonable debate.

To their credit, Bridgeman and Beatty had indeed cut millions from their budget requests, and this had won Churchill's goodwill, but when Churchill requested a one-year delay in return for which he promised to build all twenty-one of the cruisers in the modified building program, they unwisely refused to accept his offer. Beatty and Bridgeman instead engineered an intense party squabble by repeated threats to resign, which were deliberately intended to bring about a damaging and publicly embarrassing political crisis threatening to split the Conservative party on the misleading charge that by backing Churchill, the Cabinet was failing to defend the Empire.

Rather than adjusting their naval policies to the economic and political realities on which future military strength was dependent, and thereby earning the goodwill of the Cabinet, Beatty and Bridgeman created a political climate in which there now lurked among Conservative Party and Cabinet leaders a lingering determination to avoid provoking another Admiralty resignation crisis. Bridgeman and Beatty rejoiced that they had demonstrated the Admiralty's real political clout. But it was clout of an essentially negative character, as the subsequent Colwyn Committee and its attendant negative publicity made clear.

Significant, too, was the fact that their joy in this costly political victory stemmed not from an increase in the number of cruisers to be built, or from an expanded naval budget, but merely from their victory over Churchill's one-year delay in construction. In the long run it would prove to be an unreasonably small gain paid at an unreasonably high price. When Baldwin finally pushed the compromise five-year naval appropriations bill through Parliament in 1925, his opponents roundly criticized him for caving in to an "extravagant, dictatorial and arrogant Admiralty," a view now shared by some important Conservative party leaders.[152] Admiralty critics within the Conservative Party were troubled by what they believed to be the Admiralty's unwise, damaging, and embarrassing show of power.[153] In the future, Cabinet resistance to the Admiralty's policies would be more circumspect, muted, and subtle, yet increasingly evident. The Cabinet now placed a greater reliance on the Ten-Year Rule, supported further cuts in naval spending, insisted on a peacetime rather than a war-ready fleet, rejected the Admiralty's insistence on speed in building the Singapore naval base, and again called for another international naval reduction conference to halt the escalating race in auxiliary cruisers, destroyers, and submarines.[154] Far more important, however, when next Beatty and Churchill clashed over cruisers during the 1927 Geneva Naval Conference,

---

[152] Quoted in Davidson, *Memoirs*, p. 218. See also BGMN/2, p. 596; Roskill, *Beatty*, p. 353.
[153] Ferris, *Evolution*, pp. 6, 169.   [154] *Ibid.*, pp. 166–168, 178.

Churchill would be forewarned and forearmed and therefore able to develop a much more subtle and sophisticated opposition strategy, one designed to protect himself from charges of conspiratorial opposition.

In 1926, the Colwyn Committee lashed into the Admiralty with highly publicized charges of waste and mismanagement.[155] Bridgeman and Beatty chafed under this new barrage of criticism, yet, as irritating and as damaging as these charges were, they paled in comparison to Beatty's own highly secret discovery, which, if exposed, would have undoubtedly greatly intensified criticism and greatly eroded the Admiralty's political influence. Indeed, both national security and the necessity of avoiding devastating political repercussions dictated that neither rival navies nor critical politicians at home should learn that the Admiralty's great expectations for their new highly expensive 8-inch-gun cruisers – for which they had fought so hard during the Birkenhead Committee debates – and on which they had expended so much political capital by provoking the recent Cabinet resignation crisis – had unexpectedly fallen far short of the revolutionary naval impact which the Admiralty had convinced Churchill was essential to Great Britain's continued naval superiority.

---

[155] See footnotes 146–148.

5

Beatty Embraces Arms Control

The anger, distrust, and continuing political and personal tensions generated by the still smoldering controversy over defense spending – especially about the new 10,000-ton, 8-inch-gun cruisers – made them the focus of special Admiralty anticipation. The Admiralty had paid a high political price to ensure the hurried construction of these vessels. It had rejected Churchill's offer of building all twenty-one of these cruisers in return for a one-year delay and, instead, had deliberately created a serious and damaging crisis within the Conservative Party. The lingering resentment among some influential Party leaders seemed worth the price as the Naval Staff never doubted the gun power of these new cruisers. Indeed, even Churchill became an enthusiastic supporter of the revolutionary impact that the new 8-inch guns promised. Nonetheless, despite high expectations, by October 1926, the Admiralty Naval Staff discovered serious combat deficiencies in its cherished new cruiser, and Beatty therefore searched for ways to overcome or at least minimize these defects.

Thus the wisdom of Admiral Fisher's dictum with which Churchill had repeatedly admonished the Admiralty during the Birkenhead Committee debates: "Build late, build fast, each one better than the last" – was now bitterly brought home.[1] By building first and fast rather than last and fast, the experts on the Naval Staff admitted among themselves that Great Britain had given its potential enemies the opportunity to design cruisers superior to England's latest most expensive ones. Moreover, these experts secretly concluded that British cruisers were so far along in the construction process that these serious defects

---

[1] For Churchill's admonition, see "Second Meeting of the Committee," March 5, 1925, N. P. (25) 2nd Meeting, p.6, CAB 27/273, PRO. Hereafter the Cabinet Naval Program Committee will be cited as CAB, NPC.

could not be corrected.[2] The need for a strategy to reduce the seriousness of these secret deficiencies prompted Beatty and the Naval Staff to begin considering a second arms-control conference that would severely restrict the number of 10,000-ton cruisers while prohibiting the 8-inch gun on rival warships.

* * *

Admiralty attention focused at first on the test-firing of the new 8-inch gun. The Admiralty had justified the considerable expense of this gun on the grounds that it would have an impact on future cruiser warfare equivalent to that of the offensive striking power that the earlier Dreadnoughts had had on battleship warfare.[3] Naval experts confidently expected the 8-inch-gun cruiser to be overwhelmingly superior to cruisers carrying 6-inch or even 7.5-inch guns. One Naval Staff study even asserted that one new 8-inch-gun cruiser pitted against two 6-inch-gun cruisers at 13,000 yards would put both 6-inch cruisers out of action within 40 minutes. Indeed, at any range, and especially at longer ranges, this study predicted that the new 8-inch gun would be "greatly superior to the six."[4]

In addition to the greater ranges which the longer barrel of the 50-caliber 8-inch gun was expected to achieve, the Naval Staff was enthusiastic as well about several other new design features. The new gun would have new complex mountings, which represented a very heavy part of the cost of these cruisers, and which were expected to accomplish several important combat functions. These mountings were designed to allow the gun to be elevated to as high as a 70 degree angle for anti-aircraft fire and to achieve a long distance range of 31,000 yards, the equivalent of 17 miles. Another new feature was the steel-enclosed, twin-barreled turret to protect the highly trained crew from nearby shell bursts. Moreover, all eight of these cruisers' 8-inch guns were

---

[2] See numerous reports between February and May 1926 by the Director of Naval Ordnance and Director of Naval Gunnery in ADM 1/8694/10, 188451, PRO.

[3] For complete technical details on these cruisers, see B. J. Berry, Director of Naval Construction, "Cruiser 'A' of 10,000 Tons of the 1926 Programme: Legend and Drawings for Board Approval," 8 October 1926, ADM 1/9267/S05810/26; DNC, "'A' Class Cruisers To Be Laid down in February 1927," March 2, 1926, ADM 1/9267/S01406/26; B. J. Berry, "'A' Class Cruisers: Alternative Sketches," July 13, 1927, ADM 1/9267/S04677/27 and additional detailed reports from the DNC in ADM 1/9267, PRO. See also ADM 1/8765/313 and Alan Raven and John Roberts, *British Cruisers of World War Two* (Annapolis: Naval Institute Press, 1980), p. 127; Hector C. Bywater, *Navies and Nations: A Review of Naval Developments Since the Great War* (Boston and New York: Houghton Mifflin Co., 1927), pp. 50–52; Stephen Roskill, *Naval Policy Between the Wars: The Period of Anglo-American Antagonism, 1919–1929* (London: Collins, 1968), p. 542. Roskill dismisses the Admiralty's intense focus on this gun as "some kind of obsession." For the Dreadnought analogy see Chapter 4.

[4] Tac. Sec. [Tactical Section], "Gun Armament and Protection of Small 8" Cruiser, and Comparison with 6" Cruiser," n.d., Tac. Sec. 662/20, ADM 1/8765, PRO. See also Attachments Sheet 2 and "Requirements of the Small Cruiser," n. d., Tac. Sec. 670/28, ADM 1/8765, PRO. Churchill's complaint about the Admiralty's failure to notify him of this additional expense is in Winston S. Churchill, *Winston S. Churchill: The Exchequer Years 1922–1929, Companion Volume* 5 ed. Martin Gilbert (Boston: Houghton Mifflin, 1978) p. 516. Hereafter cited as Churchill, *Companion Volume* 5.

located on the centerline of the ship, enabling them to swing to either side to deliver a simultaneous broadside with 250-pound shells at a rate of at least five rounds per minute. Against a 6-inch-gun cruiser with shorter range and shells of only 100 pounds rather than 250 pounds, the winner of such a gun battle appeared obvious.[5]

The Admiralty's great expectations suddenly plummeted in August 1925 when the new 8-inch gun on its new mounting was first tested. Instead of maintaining the high muzzle velocity of 2,900 f. s. [feet per second] required for a range of 31,000 yards, the gun could only sustain muzzle velocity of 2,775 f. s., resulting in a loss of 1,100 yards, or over two-thirds of a mile less than anticipated.[6] Naval gunnery experts worried, too, over the fact that as the gun aged with repeated firings, even greater losses in muzzle velocity and range had to be expected.[7] For six frantic months, naval ordinance and gunnery experts unsuccessfully scrambled to find a solution.[8] Despite their best efforts, these experts could not determine the exact cause of the lower-than-expected muzzle velocity. Speculations abounded. The highly expensive, heavy, and complex gun mountings required to achieve elevations from 10 degrees to 70 degrees had been designed by the Armstrong-Elwick armament firm and built by Vickers-Barrow, but, as one gunnery expert surmised, lack of coordination in the manufacturing process may have resulted in a faulty mounting with corresponding lower muzzle velocity, shorter ranges, and guns which frequently jammed.[9] Other experts blamed the solid inner tubes of the barrel which had been "extremely difficult to manufacture without flaws in the metal."[10] Without offering either specifics or examining the consequences that this great disappointment would have on Admiralty arms control policy, one British naval historian years later simply concluded that the Naval Staff had "demanded the impossible," and that in trying to meet complex technical requirements, "the designers produced the least successful armaments ever fitted to British warships in modern times."[11]

Perhaps even more frustrating was the conclusion by the Admiralty's experts that it was neither feasible nor wise to redesign the gun, its mountings, or the

---

[5] Director of Naval Ordnance, "Muzzle Velocity of 8" Guns," February 8, 1926 and attached Minutes, ADM 1/8694/10, 188451, PRO.
[6] Ibid.
[7] D.N.O. [Director of Naval Ordinance], Minute, February 8, 12, and 19, 1926 and Minutes by members of the Naval Staff, G. 0408/26, ADM 1/8694/10, 188451, PRO.
[8] Ibid. For the high cost of the gun mountings see "Memorandum for the Board," October 1927, p. 3, ADM 167/76/2391, PRO.
[9] P. H. S. Reid, "Memoir: Naval Gunnery Life, 1917–1960," pp. 9–10, in ROSK 7/30, ROSKCC.
[10] Gunnery Division, Handbook of 8-inch B. L. Mark VIII Gun on Twin Mark I Mounting, Book I, Text, 1927, Chapter 2, p. 11, ADM 186/282.
[11] Roskill, Naval Policy, p. 353. Perhaps because this information was still secret at the time he published his book, Roskill did not footnote this claim and the one reference he cited could not be located. A further search of his research notes at Churchill College did not reveal his source.

hull because eleven of the thirteen British cruisers were already too far advanced in various stages of construction. Although it was theoretically possible to redesign the gun and the mountings, the Director of Naval Construction warned that these changes would require alterations in the hull to enlarge the ship's magazine, and this, in turn, would "not be an easy matter to arrange, and if done, will encroach on the oil fuel storage to an undesirable extent." By May 1926, after months of agonizing over possible design changes, the Assistant Chief of Naval Staff ended the prolonged internal debates. Extensive trials made it clear, he concluded, that the failure to achieve the expected high muzzle-velocity was "due to the incorrect design of the gun" and that "the general design of the ships ... cannot now be altered."[12]

Beatty recognized that eleven of the thirteen new cruisers were too far advanced in their construction to allow for gun alterations. This fact had a significant impact on his naval and diplomatic strategy, an impact that has gone unrecognized. Ever since the 1916 Battle of Jutland, a battle in which his command decisions had been severely criticized, and which, in turn, had prompted him to alter the historical record, Beatty had brooded over the great loss of life in the sinking of three of his battle cruisers as against the disabling of only one German battle cruiser, which eventually sank. Immediately following the battle, and for many years afterward, he had repeatedly and bitterly lamented to a few close friends that there was "something wrong with our ships and something wrong with our system." As subsequent studies revealed, one of the most serious flaws had been in "the battle-cruiser gunnery equipment." Ten years later the problem still persisted.[13]

The Naval Staff therefore agreed to do everything possible to improve the range of the gun, but despite their strenuous efforts, this too failed.[14] Indeed,

---

[12] Director of Naval Construction, Minute, February 11, 1926, ADM 1/ 9267/S04154/25; E. C. [Ernle Chatfield?], Minute, May 5, 1926, ADM 1/8694/10, PRO. There are several additional important sources in ADM 1/8694/10, PRO.

[13] A.C.N.S. [Assistant Chief of the Naval Staff], Minute, 5 May 1926 and approval at 2,775 f.s. [feet per second] by Chief of the Naval Staff, 13 November 13, 1926, ADM 1/8694/10, PRO. See also Shane Leslie, "Memories of Beatty," *Quarterly Review* 290 (July 1952): 453–458. For Beatty's alteration of the historical record of the Battle of Jutland, see Roskill, *Naval Policy*, pp. 353, 164–167; Stephen Roskill, *Earl Beatty: The Last Naval Hero: An Intimate Biography* (New York: Athenaeum Press, 1981), p. 345; Michael J. Lyons, *World War I: A Short History* (Englewood Cliffs, New Jersey: Prentice Hall, 1994), pp. 202–203. For B. Mc. L. Ranft's commentary on the "gunnery difficulties" and the "poor showing of the battle-cruisers gunnery equipment and performance" see David Beatty, *The Beatty Papers: Selections from the Private and Official Correspondence of Admiral of the Fleet Earl Beatty, 1902–1927* 2 vols. ed. B. Mc. L. Ranft (Aldershot, England: Gower, 1989), 1: 203.

[14] The Chief of the Naval Staff officially accepted a muzzle velocity of 2,775 feet per second [f. s.] on November 13, 1926. This was attached to a Minute for the A.C.N.S. on May 5, 1926, in ADM 1/8694/10, PRO; Director of Gunnery Division, Minute, May 3, 1926, ADM 1/8694/10, PRO; Director of Gunnery Division, Minute, February 19, 1926, and May 1, 1926, ADM 1/8694/10, PRO. There are several important and highly detailed reports on muzzle velocity in this source;

from 1926 until 1938 British gunnery experts repeatedly complained of numerous difficulties with the new gun, especially from widely dispersed salvo patterns, slow rate of fire, and a variety of problems arising from the complex mountings.[15] Finally, in 1938, after twelve years of continuous efforts, gunnery experts reported that the 8-inch guns "in the Kent and London classes have now reached a satisfactory standard of reliability," with the notable exception of serious and frequent firing delays attributed to "a weakness of the mountings."[16]

During those twelve years of continuous frustration, the Admiralty worked hard at squelching internal criticism of the new guns' defects. Complaints poured in from British gunnery experts, surprised at its poor performance. "Zealous but lacking in tact," one gunnery seaman later recalled, "we bothered the authorities with bunches of defect forms." Indeed, a gunnery officer became so irate that he not only called attention to the fact that "the gun mounting design was unsatisfactory," but demanded that responsibility for its failure "should be clearly established." Rather than welcome their candor, the Admiralty quickly and sternly squelched such criticism by warning complainers that it would take "grave exception" to any further criticism, and it imposed a policy of strict secrecy. No one was to write or talk about this gun even within the secure confines of the Admiralty itself.[17]

By 1927 Hector Bywater, a respected British journalist, considered at the time to be well informed on the world's navies, complained in his new book, *Nations and Navies* that an "impenetrable screen" of "extreme secrecy" had descended on the new British 10,000-ton, 8-inch-gun cruisers, without any "apparent justification." He scoffed at the notion that British

---

Director of Gunnery, "Naval Staff Memorandum M. V. of 8-inch Guns," May 1, 1926 and "Best Muzzle Velocity for 8" Gun," n.d., ADM 1/8694/10, PRO; D.S.R., "Best Muzzle Velocity for 8" Gun, September 20, 1926, G. 0408/26 and Minutes by E.C. [Ernle Chatfield] and F.C.D., ADM 1/8694/10, PRO. Gunnery Branch, *Handbook for 8-inch B. L., Mark VIII, Gun on Twin Mark I Mounting*, Book I, 1927, G. 02613/26, pp. 6, 11, ADM 186/282.

[15] *Progress in Naval Gunnery*, 1926, CB 3001/28, pp. 22–29, ADM 186/271; *Progress in Naval Gunnery*, 1928, CB 3001/28, pp. 28–30, 82–83, ADM 186/293; *Progress in Naval Gunnery*, 1931, CB 3001/31, pp. 22–29, 61, ADM 186/309; *Progress in Naval Gunnery*, 1934, CB 3001/34, pp. 25–31, 65, ADM 186/323; *Progress in Naval Gunnery*, 1935 CB 3001/35, pp. 31–43, ADM 186/328; *Instructions for Guidance of Ordinance Artificers in Upkeep and Maintenance of 8-Inch Mark II and Mark II*Mountings*, 1935, B.R. 977, ADM 186/335; *Summary of Progress in Naval Gunnery, 1914–1936*, CB 3001/1914–1936, ADM 186/339; *Turret Gun Drill for 8-Inch B. L. Guns, Mark VIII and Mark VIII*on Twin Mark I and Mark I*Mountings*, 1937, B. R. 940, ADM 186/346; *Progress in Naval Gunnery*, 1937, CB 3001/37, pp. 36–41, ADM 186/343, PRO.

[16] The 1938 report concluded that the 8-inch gun mountings on the Kent and London class cruisers had reached a satisfactory standard of reliability with the exception of serious delays caused by a weakness in the mountings. See *Progress in Naval Gunnery*, 1938, CB 3001/38, pp. 120, 40–44, 36–41, ADM 186/349. For the names of the eleven cruisers fitted with these 8-inch guns, see p.3, ADM 186/346, PRO.

[17] Reid, "Memoir," p. 9, ROSK 7/30, ROSKCC.

"defenses were being spied upon by a host of enemy agents."[18] Admiralty officials thought otherwise. Potential enemies were in fact actively seeking information about the gun, apparently without success. Only months before the gun was test-fired in August 1925, the Director of Naval Intelligence had foiled a Japanese ploy to learn about its characteristics. Japan had for years regularly ordered some of its ships to be built by British firms, and to gain access to this new gun, it had simply placed an order for the gun and its new mountings with the private firm manufacturing them. Had the order not been intercepted, the Director warned, the Japanese would have ordered its naval experts to take copious notes on all aspects of the gun and its manufacturing process. But when informed that it could obtain another type of 8-inch gun from a British firm, which was not producing the newly designed one, the Japanese cancelled the order.[19]

The Admiralty had several other embarrassing secrets it was closely guarding. One was its "very inferior armor piercing shells," a problem which may have persisted into World War II, and it was definitely a source of considerable agony during and after World War I.[20] At the Battle of Jutland, for example, rather than taking advantage of his longer-range guns, Beatty had closed his battle cruiser squadron on the German fleet to a more effective gun range. The German gunnery officers were not so much surprised by the number of hits they received at this closer range, as by the fact that British shells literally bounced off German armor plate and turret roofs.[21] After the war ended, the Admiralty discovered that the problem stemmed from an improperly designed shell head which allowed the body of the shell to topple over on impact, "so that the base of the shell pounded against the surface of the plate," rather than the tip digging into the armor and bursting through it.[22]

The Admiralty acknowledged the seriousness of the armor-piercing-shell problem at almost the same time it clamped a lid of strict secrecy over the defects in its new 8-inch gun. Churchill knew nothing about the new gun problem, but when he discovered the shell deficiency, he unhesitatingly gave Bridgeman some advice. As First Lord of the Admiralty during the early months of World War I, Churchill confessed that he had to take responsibility for the shell's failure. He blamed himself because he had assumed that "our construction and ordnance experts were the last word in their sciences," and he had not been vigilant enough about ensuring that the shell had been properly tested. The lesson was clear to him, and he wanted it to be so for

---

[18] Bywater, *Navies and Nations*, pp. 176–177; Raven and Roberts, *British Cruisers*, p. 130.
[19] Captain J.C.C. Royles to Director of Naval Intelligence, January 30, 1925; Director of Naval intelligence to Naval Attaché, Tokyo, April 2, 1925 and Minute, N. I. D.054/25, ADM 1/8676/42, PRO.
[20] A.P.P. [Commander Anthony Pellew], "Something Wrong with Our Bloody Ships," *Naval Review* 64 (January 1976): 19–20.
[21] *Ibid.*, p. 17.   [22] *Ibid.*, p. 19.

Bridgeman as well. His own failure "only shows" he admonished Bridgeman, "one ought never to take things for granted, but probe and challenge accepted opinions to the root." Bridgeman must therefore make "a profound and searching examination into it pitilessly and patiently," as a "good stirring up always does the technical people good."[23]

Defects in the armor-piercing shells were sufficient to make Admiralty leaders nervous about any newer disclosures to Churchill. Nonetheless, a third secret elevated Admiralty anxieties to a higher level, when Beatty's loss of three large battle cruisers during World War I was finally attributed not only to poor armor-piercing shells but also to the inferior quality of British protective armor.[24] At fault were both the manufacturing process and the Admiralty's testing procedures. Each of England's few steel-plate manufacturers had its "own secret series of processes" for the intricate heating and tempering required to make the type of extremely hard steel that could withstand armor-piercing shells.[25] Testing the steel plates at the Admiralty's experimental range at Shoeburyness was critical to verifying high manufacturing standards. Yet neither the Director of Naval Ordnance, who was responsible for testing armor-piercing shells, nor the Director of Naval Construction, who was responsible for testing the armor plating, had ensured high manufacturing standards. Only in retrospect did it become clear that "one reason" for the defective British shells was that they had been tested on poor plate."[26] This, too, was probably attributable to the widespread belief, and thus lack of careful oversight among Admiralty leaders, that as Churchill had put it, "our construction and ordnance experts were [supposed to be] the last word in their sciences."[27]

By 1926, in the midst of these disturbing yet still closely held revelations, the Naval Staff also began to worry about inadequate armor protection on its new 10,000-ton, 8-inch-gun cruisers. In 1923 when the Admiralty Board approved the design of the new 8-inch-gun cruiser – which it had insisted at the Washington Conference must be limited to 10,000 tons – this tonnage restriction had forced the Board to make difficult choices. The Admiralty insisted on a powerfully offensive ship with high speeds, good living conditions, and fuel capacity sufficient for long voyages distant from supply bases. These characteristics were especially valued for combat missions in East Asia against Japan. Most prized were bigger, long-range guns and larger hulls – which enabled greater fuel capacity – expanded engine rooms, and increased speed. These features gave the new cruisers more offensive power and higher speeds to chase down or escape from enemies. However, with a 10,000-ton limit,

---

[23] Churchill to Bridgeman, November 15, 1926, BGMN/1, WBPCC.
[24] A. P. P., "Something Wrong," pp. 17–18; Roskill, *Beatty*, pp. 164–167, 186–187, 345; Leslie, "Memories," p. 453.
[25] A. P. P., "Something Wrong," p. 19.   [26] *Ibid*.
[27] Churchill to Bridgeman, November 15, 1926, BGMN/1, WBPCC.

there was not enough tonnage remaining for adequate armor protection. This cruiser would be required, therefore, to rely on its longer range, more powerful guns and high speed to remain outside of an enemy's shorter range, and be able to sink or disable the enemy before it could close the range gap. In situations where the enemy's guns outmatched the cruiser, it would use its superior speed to escape engagement.[28]

By late 1926, Admiral of the Fleet Lord Jellico, the Australian commander of British naval forces during World War I, challenged the wisdom on which this new cruiser had been designed. In his published memoirs he raised serious doubts about designing inadequately protected warships. He acknowledged that, when thinking strategically, offensive capabilities were superior to defensive ones, but British experience in World War I, especially at the Battle of Jutland, had proven, he argued, that this conventional wisdom, which emphasized offensive over defensive capabilities, did not hold true for ship design. "Ships with inadequate defensive qualities [i.e., armor protection] are no match," he concluded," for those which possess them to a considerably greater degree, even if the former are superior in gun power."[29]

All of these disappointing revelations – the defective 8-inch gun, the defective armor plate, the defective armor-piercing shell, and Jellico's warnings about the need for greater protection – had come to the full attention of Admiralty staff experts in late 1926. They reacted by keeping these defects secret while nonetheless directing "an immense volume of [internal] criticism" at the new 10,000-ton, 8-inch-gun cruisers.[30]

By October 1926, the Admiralty found itself in a serious bind of its own making. It had rushed production of a cruiser design without waiting to ascertain either the number of guns or armor protection of likely enemy cruisers. It had rejected Churchill's offer of building all twenty-one of its cruisers, agreed to in the modified construction program in return for a one-year delay, and, instead, had deliberately created a serious and damaging political crisis that had earned the Admiralty the lingering resentment of some influential Conservative Party leaders. And with the need to replace battleships and battle cruisers immediately after the auxiliary cruiser building program was completed, there was virtually no likelihood of Parliament funding a large number of additional cruisers which could compensate for the combat deficiencies of the Kent and London-class cruisers.

---

[28] See Chapter 3.
[29] Quoted in Richard W. Fanning, *Peace and Disarmament: Naval Rivalry and Arms Control, 1922–1923*, (Lexington: University Press of Kentucky, 1995), p. 15.
[30] Director of Plans, "Cruiser Building Policy," May 6, 1937, P.D. 06230/37, ADM 1/9427. This memo was a review of cruiser building policy prompted by Churchill's criticism of the Dido class cruisers which carried ten 5.25-inch guns intended for use against attacking aircraft and unarmored ships.

As early as July 30, 1926, the Assistant Chief of Naval Staff crystallized growing concerns among his Naval Staff colleagues. "The more I think on these Kent and London class cruisers," he informed them, "the more I feel uncertain if we were right in our 8" armament policy," especially as "the ships are over balanced with guns and *no* defense, just like our Lions and Invincibles were."[Emphasis his.][31] This, he suggested, presented the Admiralty Staff with a cruel dilemma and a complex problem. They were determined, on the one hand, to lay down quickly all of the cruisers approved under the recent Cabinet compromise before the perfidious politicians could again cut back the number to be built. Providing greater armor protection to a ship strictly limited to 10,000 tons would, on the other hand, require reducing the size and weight of the gun and its mounting and thereby still further reduce its range. Equally disturbing, if not more alarming, were intelligence reports that the Japanese and the Americans were considering arming their 10,000-ton cruisers with ten or twelve guns, compared to only eight on the British 10,000-ton cruisers, and only six on their 8,300 B-class cruisers. Admiralty Staff now began criticizing their new cruisers simultaneously from diametrically opposite points of view: too many guns, and therefore not enough armor protection, and too few guns, and therefore distinctly inferior in firepower to rival cruisers soon-to-be under construction.[32] Indeed, these new criticisms went well beyond the 8-inch-gun deficiencies to an even more serious level. Admiralty experts now questioned the combat effectiveness of their new cruiser design itself.

Central to the intense Naval Staff debate was the question of whether they had designed a cruiser which struck a proper balance between "fighting power" and ocean-going capabilities or one which favored ocean-going capabilities at the expense of fighting power.[33] There was little disagreement over the cruiser's excellent seaworthiness, reliability, endurance, and habitability, all of which were essential in a war against Japan in East Asia, for which the cruiser was specifically designed. The big concern, however, was its "fighting power," an Admiralty term which measured the combination of gun and torpedo armament and armor protection based on "the assumption that the greatest volume of fire is the best and that the number of assailable vital spots varies with the proportion of armor carried." Speed also was vital as the cruiser with faster or at least equal speed could chase enemy ships out of the area under control, overtake a fleeing enemy, or remain outside of the range of a more powerful enemy.[34]

---

[31] A.C.N.S. [Assistant Chief of the Naval Staff], Minute, 30 July 1926, ADM 1/92712, PRO.
[32] Director of Gunnery Division, "Investigation of the Considerations Affecting Gun Armaments and Protection of Future Cruisers," October 28, 1926, G.D. 3260/26, pp. 1–8 and Minute Sheets, ADM 1/92712, PRO. Hereafter cited as D.G.D., "Investigation."
[33] Ibid., pp. 1–2, 7.   [34] Ibid.; Director of Plans, Minute, November 8, 1926, p. 10, Ibid.

The Director of Gunnery summarized his fears candidly. The expectation that the new 8-inch gun would give Britain the essential advantage in range had already been eroded by the lower-than-expected muzzle velocity. Moreover, he now emphasized other defects of "fighting power." The first centered on the latest intelligence reports that future Japanese and American 10,000-ton cruisers might carry ten to twelve 8-inch guns. If potential enemy cruisers carried ten to twelve guns, while the British cruisers carried only six to eight guns, it clearly meant that the Kent and London-class cruisers suffered from "very marked inferiority" in firepower. In fact, as the United States Pensacola-class cruisers carried ten 8-inch guns and the Japanese Myoko-class carried ten eight-inch-guns, it was hardly necessary for him to point out that if the muzzle velocity of those nations' 8-inch guns exceeded the disappointing velocity of the new British gun, these potential rivals would be superior to Britain in both the number and the range of the guns which their cruisers carried.[35]

Alarming, too, was his conclusion on armor protection. Only by redesigning the hull or by reducing the size of the gun and its mounting, could enough weight be found either for added protection or to mount four more guns.[36] A smaller, shorter hull also meant sacrifices in habitability and seaworthiness. Even so, these ships were already so far advanced in the construction process that there was little, if any, likelihood of such drastic changes. In any case, a reduction in the size of the gun, to provide either added protection or an equal number of guns, would result in such a "very large loss of gun power," that this alternative "was not considered acceptable."[37]

Without adequate protection, the evident inferiority of these new, as yet uncompleted, British cruisers became increasingly apparent to the Director of Gunnery. Against another 8-inch gun opponent, the magazines, shell rooms, and machinery spaces of the Kent and London-class cruisers were penetrable from both a medium range of 12,000 yards and a longer range of 20,000 yards. More vulnerable still were the gun turrets. The new enclosed steel gun turrets could be penetrated by the 4 or 5-inch guns of destroyers. "Protection to these gun positions being nil," even one "lucky shot" would knock out 25 percent of the firing power of a British 10,000-ton, 8-inch-gun cruiser or

---

[35] D.G.D., "Investigation," pp. 2–5, *Ibid*. Between 1922–1929, the United States built two Pensacola-class cruisers carrying ten 8-inch guns and six Northampton-class cruisers with nine 8-inch guns. During that same period, the Japanese first built four Furutaka-class cruisers carrying only six 8-inch guns but thereafter built four Myoko-class cruisers carrying ten 8-inch guns and four Atago-class cruisers with ten 8-inch guns. See Earnest Andrade, Jr., "Arms Limitation Agreements and the Evolution of Weaponry: The Case of the Treaty Cruiser," in *Naval History: The Sixth Symposium of the U. S. Naval Academy*, ed. Daniel M. Masterson (Wilmington, DE: Scholarly Resources, 1987), p. 182.

[36] D.N.C. [Director of Naval Construction], Minute, February 1927, pp. 6, 14–15 in D.G.D., "Investigation."

[37] D.G.D., "Investigation," pp. 5–6.

33 percent of the 8,300-ton, six-inch-gun cruiser. Since there was "no solution" to the inadequate armored turrets, this British cruiser, "coming under fire of an enemy flotilla may suffer heavy casualties in the disablement of portions of her main armament." The Director of Gunnery concluded, "It would appear, therefore, that British designs do *not* meet requirements in fighting power as a whole, and that in speed they fall short of the ideal." [Emphasis his.][38]

Throughout most of 1926, reports from Naval Staff experts created a dawning realization that design flaws in the new cruiser seriously compromised its future combat effectiveness. Beginning in February 1926, with the recognition that its new 8-inch gun suffered from mystifying serious defects that defied repeated efforts for correction, the Admiralty was bombarded with more bad news. British armor plate, which remained on the ship throughout its service life, was not only poorly manufactured and inadequately tested by the Director of Naval Construction, but was of insufficient thickness, a design defect which Lord Jellico and others now argued was more important than carrying a larger number of powerful guns, even if their muzzle velocity and range had reached expectations. Revelations of unreliable armor-piercing shells, gun turrets penetrable by the much smaller 4- and 5-inch guns of destroyers, reports that Japanese and American cruisers would in the future carry ten to twelve 8-inch guns against only six to eight on British cruisers – and the acknowledgment that it was already too late to make substantial changes in eleven of the thirteen cruisers already under construction – generated an increasingly high level of anxiety within the Naval Staff. Following so closely on the heels of the Colwyn Committee's highly publicized charges of inefficiency and mismanagement, it was little wonder that the Admiralty threw an "impenetrable screen" of "extreme secrecy" over these new cruisers.[39] Secrecy was essential, not only to keep this highly damaging intelligence out of the hands of likely enemy navies, but also from domestic political leaders still smoldering from the party crisis which the Admiralty had precipitated over Churchill's request for a one-year delay in building these cruisers.

The Naval Staff's high level of anxiety was reflected in the cautionary advice from one of its experts. "We must be careful," he warned his colleagues, "not to let ourselves be 'stampeded' with regard to the designs of our 10,000-ton B-class [8300-tons with only six guns] cruisers." He cautioned them about

---

[38] *Ibid.*, pp. 3–4.
[39] *Ibid.* These criticisms are examined throughout this document. See also D.N.C. to Controller, "'A' Class Cruisers: Alternative Sketch Designs," July 13, 1927, S. 04677/27, ADM 1/9267; Director of Plans et.al., "The Design of 10,000- Ton Cruisers" and "Foreign Cruisers of 10,000 Tons," October 31, 1924, S. 0187/24, ADM 1/9253, PRO; Hector C. Bywater, *Navies and Nations: A Review of Naval Developments Since the Great War* (Boston and New York: Houghton Mifflin Co., 1927), pp. 176–177.

reports "of speeds and numbers of guns and torpedo tubes, etc." on cruisers being designed or built by rival navies. Low morale was also an important concern. "I hope for reasons of morale alone ... that we shall not be obligated to consider a gun smaller than 8" while other nations persist in mounting 8" guns."[40] Both the United States and Japan were already experimenting with triple-barreled turrets, and the Naval Staff feared that should these become feasible, rival cruisers would carry twelve guns, which would give them far greater firepower than the six-to-eight guns carried on the eleven British cruisers already under construction. This dire possibility convinced the Director of Gunnery that Great Britain should either take the two years needed to design a triple 8-inch gun turret, and presumably halt construction on its Kent and London-class cruisers until they could be fitted with the new turrets, or call an international arms control conference as the means by which the *"abolition of the 8" gun in cruisers would remove this complex problem altogether."* [Emphasis mine.][41]

The usefulness of another international arms control conference had earlier been argued by Churchill and had been adopted by the Cabinet, albeit for different reasons.[42] But prior to late 1926, when the serious defects of the new cruisers became unavoidably evident to the Admiralty Naval Staff, they had repeatedly discouraged calls for further naval limitation. Professions of willingness to cooperate were usually followed by prolonged delays, negotiating requirements seemingly calculated to discourage participation by other nations, and cautionary reasons why such conferences were dangerous to Imperial security.[43] Finally, after months of agonizing debate and delay, the Naval

---

[40] F. G. W., Minute, 16 November 1926, p. 11 in D. G. D., "Investigation."

[41] D. G. D., "Investigation," pp. 8–9.

[42] Churchill to Baldwin, December 15, 1924, vol. 130, SPB and copy in CHAR 18-4, WCP and Winston S. Churchill, *Companion Volume* 5: 307, 391. See also Keith Middlemas and John Barnes, *Baldwin: A Biography* (London: Macmillan, 1970), pp. 329–330, 722; Esme Howard to Austen Chamberlain, December 22, 1924, Cabinet Papers File, CHAR 22/30, WCP; Cecil to Churchill, "Note on Visit to America," n.d., C. P. 14 (25) CHAR 22/28, WCP.

[43] Board of Admiralty, "Board Minutes," February 11, 1925, p. 8, ADM 167/71, PRO; CAB, NPC, "First Meeting of the Committee," March 2, 1925, N.P. (25) 1st Meeting, pp. 22–23, CAB 27/273, PRO; CAB, NPC, "Second Meeting of the Committee," March 5, 1925, N. P. (25) 2nd. Meeting, pp. 9, 11, CAB 27/273, PRO; Cabinet, "The United States of America and Naval Disarmament: Note by the Secretary of State for Foreign Affairs, 12 February 1925, C.P. (87) 25 in CHAR 22/30, WCP and Cabinet, "Draft Dispatch to Sir E. Howard, February 1925, Para. 4, CHAR 22/30, WCP. In this telegram which Chamberlain reproduced for the Cabinet, Howard made it clear that the United States was "determined 'to have equality in naval strength and with its wealth is going to have it.' "In the Cabinet's draft response to Howard's warning, it was stated categorically that equality "could not be applied to the case of cruisers," but this draft response was not sent to Howard. See also Beatty to Wife, February 20, 1925, BTY 17/70/65–66, BP; Director of Plans, "New Draft Embodying Amendments to Sir M. Hankey's Request for Memorandum on International Limitation of Armaments," Part I, October 9 1925 and attached Minutes, ADM 1/8683/131; D. of T. D.[Director of Tactical Division], "Forwarding C. P. 365 (25) and Request for Memorandum on International Limitation of Armaments to be Prepared,"

Staff reluctantly agreed on the need for a second conference to reduce or eliminate the combat vulnerabilities on its newest cruisers. Nonetheless, it still insisted on superiority. Only if England's "special need" for a greater number of cruisers was agreed to by all of the other naval powers, would the Admiralty then be willing to discuss "some further limitation of the *size* of individual cruisers, *if, but only if,* accompanied by a further restriction on the *size of guns* allowed to be carried in this type of vessel" to those below 8 inches. [Emphasis mine.] Only if Great Britain were granted superiority in cruisers, would it then agree to discuss limiting the size of cruisers, and only if the 8-inch gun was outlawed.[44]

The Admiralty's central objectives in the next arms limitation conference would be reducing the size of cruisers to between 6,000–7,500 tons and outlawing 8-inch guns on the future cruisers of all nations. After a series of careful gun studies, the Admiralty had concluded that the reliable mechanically loaded and faster firing 6-inch gun was better suited to its needs than the hand-loaded, disappointing new 8-inch gun. Equally important, a 10,000-ton cruiser carrying 6-inch guns could convert the weight saved into armor protection sufficient to stop a 6-inch shell. Because the United States and Japan had yet to build all of their cruisers, the Admiralty apparently feared that if agreement at the next arms-control conference was limited only to abolishing the 8-inch gun and replacing it with the 6-inch gun, this would still allow both the United States and Japan to build 10,000-ton cruisers with armor thickness which could not be penetrated by a British 6-inch shell. To prevent such a possibility, it was essential to reach agreement on a smaller cruiser in the 6,000–7,500-ton range, which could not be so heavily armored. Both to reduce the vulnerability of their smaller, less well-armored 6-inch-gun cruisers and to bring down the cost so that Great Britain could afford to build seventy of them, the Admiralty eventually came to the conclusion that the greatest combat advantage for Great Britain was an international agreement effectively limiting maximum individual cruiser tonnage to a level which prevented them from mounting 8-inch guns and enough armor to stop a 6-inch shell. This overlooked yet vital

---

November 5, 1925 and Minutes, P.D. 02296/25 and P.D. 02164/25, ADM 1/8683/131, PRO. See also Beatty to Wife, February 20, 1925, BTY 17/70/65–66, BP; William C. Bridgeman, *Modernisation of Conservative Politics: The Diaries and Letters of William Bridgeman, 1904–1935*, ed. Philip Williamson (London: The Historian's Press, 1988), pp. 179, 203. Hereafter cited as Bridgeman, *Modernisation*. For vigorous dissent from key members of the Naval Staff to cruisers of less than 10,000 tons with 8-inch guns, see Minutes, May, 14, and May 20, 1924, ADM 1/8683/131, PRO; John Roberts Ferris, *The Evolution of British Strategic Policy, 1919–1926* (London: Macmillan, 1989), pp. 144–145.

[44] D.of T.D., Minute, August 5, 1925, p.3, P.D. 02296/25, ADM 1/8683/131, PRO; Naval Staff, "Memorandum: Limitation of Armaments, Part I" October 9, 1925, pp. 3–6 and Part II, pp. 7–8, ADM 1/8683/131, PRO; Director of Plans, "Naval Disarmament Conference: Outline of Points for the Foreign Secretary," February 14, 1925, P.D. 02161/5, ADM 1/8683/131, PRO.

Beatty Embraces Arms Control

goal now became one of the single most important reasons why the Admiralty suddenly decided to support a second naval arms-control conference.[45]

Thus, in late 1926 – only after all of the defects of their 8-inch-gun cruisers had become clear to the Admiralty – did Beatty suddenly decide to take advantage of the Cabinet's willingness to participate in another conference. He had reluctantly come to the realization that, given Great Britain's deteriorating economy, the recommendations of both the Birkenhead and Colwyn Committees, and the lingering resentments from the resignation crisis, the Cabinet would not tolerate a naval arms race requiring unlimited numbers of expensive 10,000-ton, 8-inch-gun cruisers.[46] The Admiralty's sudden, urgent desire for a new limitation conference was, in fact, motivated primarily by the desperate need to stop rival navies from building 10,000-ton, 8-inch-gun cruisers, whose guns could theoretically be superior both in number and in range, and which, if left unlimited, could, in the future, doom the entire British cruiser force to hopeless inferiority.[47]

---

[45] Director of Plans, Minute, November 8, 1926, G.D. 3260/26, p. 8, ADM 1/92712, PRO; "Limitation of Armaments," n.d., ADM 167/76, PRO. For an enlightening discussion of this continuing debate, see D.C.N.S., "Cruiser Policy," and D.of P. "Cruiser Building Policy," P.D. 06230/37, ADM 1/9427, PRO. The Admiralty would eventually propose a 6000-ton cruiser at the Geneva Naval Conference. Whether the 8-inch gun was superior to the 6-inch gun remained hotly disputed during World War II. One naval historian has argued that the 8-inch gun was superior: "in the few gun battles that did occur, such as the Java Sea battle, and the engagement off the Komandorski Islands, the superiority of the 8-inch gun over the 6-inch gun was convincingly demonstrated." See Andrade, "Arms Limitation Agreements and the Evolution of Weaponry: The Case of the Treaty Cruiser," p. 188.

[46] Stephen Roskill, *Naval Policy Between the Wars: The Period of Anglo-American Antagonism, 1919–1929* (London: Collins, 1968), pp. 502–503.

[47] "Limitation of Armaments: Memorandum by the Sea Lords for Consideration by the Board," n.d., pp. 6, ADM 167/76, PRO; Director of Gunnery, "Investigation of the Considerations Affecting Gun Armaments and Protection of Future Cruisers," November 28, 1926, pp. 1–8 and F.E.W., Minute, 14 February 1927, G.D. 3260/26, ADM 1/92712, PRO; D.C.N.S., Controller, and A.C.N.S., "Classification and Limitation of Warships," December 21, 1926, M03056/26, ADM 1/8699/118, PRO.

6

The General Board's New Hope

While the British Admiralty was discouraged by the realization that its newest cruisers suffered from serious combat deficiencies, the United States Navy's General Board remained depressed over the sudden unexpected manner in which the new Republican leaders had used the Washington Conference to scuttle its "navy second to none." Equally depressing was the enthusiastic Congressional endorsement of this drastic diminution of American naval power. Naval leaders believed that the hard lessons of World War I and the continuing importance of defending America's neutral trade in future wars had been swept aside by the wave of popular support for cutting taxes through the novel experiment in international arms-control diplomacy, an untested experiment which created the deceptively popular assumption that a 10:10:6 capital ship ratio actually provided naval equality with Great Britain and a superiority over Japan sufficient to safeguard American freedom of the seas. The realization that British battleships were superior in gun range and numbers to those in the American fleet added to the gloom.

Faced with persistent Congressional unwillingness to build new warships, the General Board concentrated on design features of its future 10,000-ton, 8-inch-gun cruisers, the heaviest auxiliary cruiser allowable under the 1922 Five-Power Treaty. According to one aircraft carrier historian, the General Board did so with "an almost obsessive insistence on increasing cruiser strength."[1] Weighing the complex and often competing combat cruiser capabilities required to support the main battle fleet, chase down raiders, escort convoys of unarmed merchantmen, and patrol alone on distant trade routes in a vessel limited to 10,000 tons was a daunting task. Nonetheless, unlike the

---

[1] C. M. Melhorn, *Two Block Fox: The Rise of the Aircraft Carrier, 1911–1929* (Annapolis MD: Naval Institute Press, 1974), p. 92.

British Naval Staff which had rushed production of its new cruisers only to discover that it was too late to correct serious flaws, the General Board took advantage of the time offered by a parsimonious Congress to design a 10,000-ton, 8-inch-gun cruiser with which it was well pleased.

***

American naval leaders were almost universal in their condemnation of what they believed to be the political, diplomatic, and strategic betrayals represented by the treaties negotiated at the Washington Conference in 1922. Harding, Hughes, and Congress had simply ignored the most basic source of tension with Great Britain prior to American entry into World War I: the insistent British claim – one never seriously challenged at the Washington Conference and still very much a part of British naval strategy – of its right to impose its interpretation of maritime belligerent rights on America neutral shipping and freedom of the seas during wartime. Harding had indeed escaped the untenable political dilemma of election promises to lower taxes and simultaneously to build a navy second to none. But he had done so by successfully perpetrating the misleading perception that a 10:10:6 ratio in capital ships and unenforceable promises to honor the Open Door Doctrine in China had sufficiently alleviated the dangers of the international naval arms race and cleared the way to less expensive paths to peace while simultaneously enhancing national security.[2]

American naval leaders were less charitable in their interpretation of the Washington Conference treaties. They charged the Harding Administration with a series of diplomatic and military failures: its unwillingness to challenge Great Britain's vehement insistence on its right to blockade all enemy ports and to interdict all neutral shipping suspected of trading in contraband with the enemy; its extremely narrow focus on capital ships as the primary basis for evaluating naval equality; its inability to extend any limit to auxiliary warships; its agreement to the prohibition of American naval bases beyond Hawaii; and its disregard of the General Board's recommendations before and during the negotiations. Taken together, these failures had sacrificed American neutral rights and freedom of the seas to the overwhelming superiority of British naval power in the Atlantic and to Japanese dominance in the Pacific.

In an era before long-range air power became a reality, a nation's navy was the single most important means to transport and to safeguard armies in distant

---

[2] SMP, GB to Secretary of the Navy, "Naval Policy: Building Program for the Fiscal Year 1924," May 31, 1922, GBS 428-2, GBUSN, RG 80, NA; SMP, GB to Secretary of the Navy, "Naval Policy: Building Program for the Fiscal Year 1926," GBS 420-2, GBUSN, RG 80, NA; Secretary of the Navy Edwin Denby to Chairman, Senate Committee on Naval Affairs, August 4, 1921, GBS 420-2, GBUSN, RG 80, NA; Richard W. Fanning, *Peace and Disarmament: Naval Rivalry and Arms Control 1922–1933* (Lexington: University Press of Kentucky, 1995), p. 8; Robert Gordon Kaufman, *Arms Control During the Pre-Nuclear Era: The United States and Naval Limitation Between Two Wars* (New York: Columbia University Press, 1990), p. 71.

foreign wars, to support those troops against hostile navies, while protecting the nation's trade. The General Board believed, therefore, that relative naval strengths could not be determined by a capital ship ratio alone. Three major components were essential in evaluating relative naval strength: warships, merchant marine, and strategically located naval bases. In all three of these categories the British Navy was clearly superior, especially as it was capable of equipping its swifter merchant vessels with 6-inch guns to prey on unarmed merchantmen, and also because of its vast number of merchant ships to sail with the fleet and to keep its strategically located naval bases well supplied and able to repair and refuel its warships. These superiorities enabled Great Britain to deploy and concentrate its numerically superior auxiliary warships in the right place at the right time for maximum combat effectiveness.[3]

The General Board pointed out that the principal result stemming from the prohibition on building capital ships for ten years was to shift international competitive building to unlimited auxiliary warships, with the predictable new race in 10,000-ton, 8-inch-gun cruisers, a vessel so much larger and more powerful than the vast majority of existing cruisers, that it was now sometimes referred to as a "junior capital ship."[4] These new cruisers, the president of the Naval War College warned, would become "almost as important ... as the introduction of the 'battle cruisers' on the [outclassed] old armored cruiser type."[5] Cruisers were essential to protect the main battle fleet against torpedo attacks by enemy cruisers and destroyers and to penetrate the enemy's outer destroyer screen safeguarding the capital ships. The new auxiliary cruisers – "junior capital ships" – could also be effective for defending unarmed merchant ships against raiders on distant shipping lanes. In this category Great Britain already had fifty-five modern cruisers of recent design and the Japanese had twenty-nine. Because the United States had emphasized the construction of destroyers during World War I to help Great Britain against German submarine attacks, the United States had under construction only ten cruisers of modern design, the Omaha 7,500-ton class carrying twelve 53-caliber, 6-inch guns.[6]

Assessing future cruiser needs, the General Board had little faith that Congress would even attempt to achieve equality in this vital category of warships. To achieve equality with Great Britain in auxiliary cruisers, even counting all ten of the Omaha class, still under construction, would require an additional forty-five, of which twenty to twenty-three must be the newest

---

[3] Hilary P. Jones to Secretary of the Navy, "Further Limitation of Naval Armaments," June 3, 1925, GBS 438-1, GBUSN, RG 80, NA.
[4] Ibid.
[5] Norman Friedman, *U. S. Cruisers: An Illustrated Design History* (Annapolis, MD: Naval Institute Press, 1984), p. 111.
[6] E. Yarnell to President, Naval War College, "Memorandum: Cruisers," January 10, 1927, UNC-25-80, NWC.

10,000-ton, 8-inch gun class to accompany the battleships.[7] The same number was required to realize an "adequate ratio" in any future conflict with Japan.[8] The General Board concluded that congressional indifference to these new challenges, meant that by the spring of 1923, rather than achieving the popular misconception of equality, the relative power of the entire United States fleet had already "sunk to a poorer second" and was "falling rapidly behind."[9]

Charged with the responsibility of protecting American trade and possessions in the Pacific, but prohibited for the next ten years from building the desperately needed naval bases beyond Hawaii, was another vexing frustration. The General Board now had to pay closer attention to the need for the battle fleet to traverse the 4,500 miles from Hawaii to the Philippines. Assuming that Japan might someday attack and occupy the Philippines and Guam, the General Board calculated that it must have air superiority to counter the anticipated air bases which the Japanese could hastily construct on the Marianas, the Caroline, and the Marshall island chains, lying athwart the sea lanes to the Philippines. At the end of 1924, however, the United States had only one experimental aircraft carrier, the *Langley*, a converted collier which had room for only twenty-five planes.[10] The 10:10:6 ratio allowed the United States five aircraft carriers to Japan's three, and although the United States was building two larger carriers, the *Lexington* and the *Saratoga*, each 33,000 tons, the General Board calculated that to ensure air superiority during the long voyage to the Philippines, it needed all five aircraft carriers to counter the three Japanese carriers and the added advantage that the Japanese would enjoy from the air bases on the three island chains, which it could quickly construct after war had been declared. Even after all three approved American carriers were eventually commissioned, they would only be able to accommodate 165 to 170 warplanes. It was obvious, therefore, that United States did not enjoy the 10:6 ratio against Japan in aircraft carriers, and this drawback became even more obvious when compared to Great Britain's six carriers.[11]

The General Board consequently pushed hard for congressional approval to build all five aircraft carriers.[12] However, this effort was hampered not only by a tax-cutting mentality in Congress but also by a heated debate over the

---

[7] SMP, GB to Secretary of the Navy, "Naval Policy: Building Program for Fiscal Year 1925," April 7, 1923, p. 7, GB 420-2, GBUSN, RG 80, NA.

[8] *Ibid.*; "Memorandum: Cruisers," January 10, 1927, UNC-25-80, and E. Yarnell, "Memorandum for the President: Cruisers," January 10, 1927, pp. 4-6, 8, UNC-1925-80, NWC. Yarnell may also have written the first document in the citation.

[9] E. Yarnell, "Memorandum for the President: Cruisers," p. 8; Senior Member GB to Secretary of the Navy, "Naval Policy," April 7, 1923, p. 5.

[10] SMP, GB to Secretary of the Navy, "Data for Secretary of the Navy's Statement to the Subcommittee on Naval Appropriations," November 3, 1924, pp. 6-8, GB 420-2, GBUSN, RG 80, NA.

[11] *Ibid.*   [12] *Ibid.*

offensive capabilities of the airplane, a debate which raged throughout the 1920s and even into the early 1930s.[13] Nonetheless, some progress was made. In April 1921, President Harding recognized the future potential of air power by establishing the Bureau of Aeronautics within the Navy Department under the energetic leadership of Rear Admiral William A. Moffett.[14] As the Japanese steadily expanded and improved its twenty-eight naval air squadrons, President Coolidge and Secretary of the Navy Curtis Wilbur announced in May 1925, that as a result of rapid advances in aircraft technology, "the new capital ship [of the future] may be an aircraft carrier similar to the *Lexington* and *Saratoga* [which would] displace the super dreadnought of today."[15] Then in 1926, Coolidge appointed his good friend, Dwight Morrow, a diplomatically adept and highly successful Wall Street banker, to head a special commission on the future of naval air power, and Congress subsequently approved a five-year program to design modern fighter and bomber planes specifically suitable to aircraft carriers, extending the number of carrier planes to be built from 350 to 1,000. Still, at this time, the combined air power of both the United States Army and Navy was less than one-third of the British and one-sixth of the Japanese air forces.[16]

Persistent worries over a variety of weaknesses, and Congress's refusal to correct those weaknesses, encouraged the General Board to focus its attention on the political and diplomatic roots of this problem. In the spring of 1923 Captain Frank H. Schofield, the tall, thin-faced, scholarly-appearing, highly respected naval strategist, boldly summarized the widespread misgivings of his fellow officers in the *Proceedings* of the United States Naval Institute. The American Navy, he charged, had suffered an overwhelming defeat at the

---

[13] See, for example, Admiral William S. Sims to Frederick W. Wile, October 16, 1924, Ms. Item 240, NWC. See also footnote 10 and correspondence in Sim's Papers, LC; Gerald E. Wheeler, "Mitchell, Moffett And Air Power," *The Airpower Historian* 8 (April 1961), pp. 79–87; Kaufman, *Arms Control*, pp. 18, 30; Ronald H. Spector, *Eagle Against the Sun: The American War Against Japan* (New York: Random House, Vintage Books, 1985), pp. 13, 17, 19.

[14] Philip T. Rosen, "The Treaty Navy, 1919–1937" in *In War and Peace: Interpretations of American Naval History, 1775–1984*, ed. Kenneth J. Hagan (Westport, CT: Greenwood, 1978), p. 225; Spector, *Eagle Against the Sun*, pp. 22–23.

[15] Curtis D. Wilbur, "A Balanced Navy," *Saturday Evening Post* (April 18, 1925), p. 10 and passim; SMP, GB, "Data for Secretary of the Navy," November 3, 1924; C. M. Melhorn, *Two Block Fox: The Rise of the Aircraft Carrier, 1911–1929* (Annapolis: Naval Institute Press, 1974), pp. 88–92; John Ferris, "A British 'Unofficial' Aviation Mission and Japanese Naval Developments, 1919–1929," *Journal of Strategic Studies* 5 (1982), pp. 417–422.

[16] Director of Naval Intelligence to President, Naval War College, "Will Japan Fight With America?" February 18, 1926, XTYG 1925–1929, RG 8, NWC; T.R.D. Mathessen, "The Logical Plan of the Orange War Plan," February 27, 1924, UNOPP 1927–1940, RG 8, NWC; Phillips Payson O'Brien, *British and American Naval Power: Politics and Policy, 1900–1936* (Westport, CT; Praeger, 1998), p. 182; Kenneth J. Hagan, *This People's Navy: The Making of American Sea Power* (New York: Free Press, 1991), pp. 275–276, 270; Gerald E. Wheeler, "The United States Navy and the Japanese 'Enemy,' 1919–1931," *Military Affairs* 21 (Summer 1957): 64–65, 74; Rosen, "Treaty Navy," pp. 229–231.

The General Boards' New Hope

Washington Conference.[17] The Navy's long cherished belief that it was "the nation's first line of defense" was no longer true. The experience at the Washington Conference made it obvious that bloodless victories won at the peace table were now the first line of defense because such bloodless victories were "sometimes equal in historical importance [to] the great [battle] decisions of war." To win these bloodless victories, however, politicians must possess both the refined sensibilities of the diplomatist and the keen insights and knowledge of the military strategist. These combined skills, Schofield argued, were essential in making the decisions vital to a nation's future strategic security.[18] Unfortunately, he concluded, American leaders, both at the Washington Conference and since that time, were lacking in these abilities and had allowed "an emotional generosity and trust in international affairs" to push aside the hard realities with which naval strategists must contend. These politicians had chosen the path of idealism rather than historical experience, experience which taught that when "pitted against commercialism and self-seeking" rivals, reliance on idealistic treaties was "bound to lose."[19]

Schofield's emphasis upon the lack of strategic sophistication among American leaders was intended to counteract the widespread popular perception that the 10:6 ratio in capital ships had given the United States naval superiority over Japan. "Sea power is not made of ships," he observed, "or of ships and men but of ships and men and bases far and wide."[20] American diplomats and politicians, he implied, had failed to grasp the great extent to which "suitably spaced, defended advance positions added to the actual naval forces present" for battle. In fact, the "great strength of the British fleet is not alone in its size but in the fact that wherever it goes a friendly, fortified harbor awaits there to receive it and supply its needs." Strategically located, fortified naval bases added great strength to a navy because they allowed ships to be moved to "the right place at the right time" for battle. Thus, the success of the British diplomats at the Washington Conference, in winning the right to build a new naval base at Singapore, testified to their superior strategic thinking.[21]

According to Schofield, the Four Power Treaty, mandating the non-fortification agreement in the Pacific, was the equivalent of a great strategic defeat for the United States and a great victory for Japan. "Had I been a Japanese naval strategist," he emphasized, "I would have done all that

---

[17] Captain Frank H. Schofield, "Incidents and Present Day Aspects of Naval Strategy," *Proceedings of the United States Naval Institute* (May 1923), p. 798.
[18] Schofield, "Incidents," pp. 799–800.   [19] *Ibid*.
[20] Captain Frank H. Schofield, "Some Effects of the Washington Conference on American Naval Strategy." Lecture delivered at the Army War College, Washington Barracks, DC, September 22, 1923, p. 1, XPOD-1923-148, Copy No. 30, NWC. See also Melhorn, *Two Block Fox*, p. 86.
[21] Schofield, "Incidents," p. 788.

I could do to keep America from fortifying further her positions in the Philippines and Guam, and of operating her naval forces there."[22] Schofield's message was clear – American politicians, acting as diplomats, had demonstrated that they lacked the strategic and naval sophistication vital to successful arms-control negotiations and therefore could not be trusted to safeguard America's strategic national interests in the future.

The discovery of glaring defects in eighteen older American battleships bolstered Schofield's charges. By concentrating on equal tonnage as a means of establishing naval equality, American negotiators had overlooked the fact that these older battleships lacked protection against air and torpedo attack and suffered from slower speeds and shorter cruising ranges because one-third of them still burned coal rather than oil. These defects, the General Board concluded, made American battleships "about thirty percent inferior" to the newer battleships built by Great Britain during and following World War I.[23]

More disturbing still was the additional discovery that the British had failed to reveal during the Washington Conference that they had increased their battleship gun elevations from a 20 degree angle to a 30 degree angle of fire. This resulted in greatly increased gun range, especially with the aid of spotter planes, which battleships now routinely catapulted into the air.[24] Given that the Washington Conference had allowed Great Britain a slightly larger number of battleships, the Chief of Naval Ordnance, Admiral Claude C. Bloch, estimated that in a duel with British battleships, at least 80 percent of the shorter-range American battleships would be damaged.[25] Later, at the 1927 arms-control negotiations at Geneva, the General Board would learn that during the Washington Conference negotiations, the British had deliberately provided "legend tonnage" of newly launched ships, rather than using the agreed-upon standard tonnage of fully equipped ones. This method had the effect of substantially underestimating the displacement and gun capabilities of its battleships on which equality was supposed to be based, thus giving Britain a 96,000-ton hidden advantage.[26]

The General Board decided, therefore, that it must elevate American battleship guns to equal the 30 degree angle of those on British battleships. In the mid-to-late 1920s naval guns, rather than airplanes or torpedoes, were

---

[22] Ibid., p. 782.   [23] SMP, GB to Secretary of the Navy, "Naval Policy," April 7, 1923, p. 6.
[24] Hector C. Bywater, *Navies and Nations: A Review of Naval Developments since the Great War* (Boston and New York: Houghton Mifflin, 1927), pp. 166–171, 169.
[25] C. S. Block to President, Naval War College, June 18, 1924, NNG 1923–1930, Gunnery Papers, RG 8, NWC. See also O'Brien, *British and American Naval Power*, pp. 181–182; William F. Trimble, "The United States Navy and the Geneva Conference for the Limitation of Armament, 1927" (Ph.D. diss., University of Colorado, 1974), pp. 48–49.
[26] Gibson to Kellogg, June 27, 1927, *FRUS*, p. 51; Schofield, Diary, June 24, 1927, SD; Trimble, "United States Navy," p. 233; William R. Braisted, "On the American Red and Red-Orange Plans, 1919–1939," in *Naval Warfare in the 20th Century, 1900–1945: Essays in Honor of Arthur Marder*, ed. Gerald Jordan (London and New York: Crane, Russak, 1977), p. 171.

The General Boards' New Hope

generally considered to be a warship's most important armaments. Few would have argued with Schofield's dictum that in a gun-battle, a warship must "hit its enemy oftener and harder than the enemy hits it, no matter at what range the battle is fought." In a naval battle, "more than in any other kind of contest, *it is the advantage at the very outset of the contest that is most important and may be decisive.*"[27] [Emphasis mine.] Until the guns of American battleships were brought to the same 30 degree angle as the British guns, this gross inequality meant that only one-third of American battleships had the range to return fire immediately against British battleships. Thus, Schofield warned, the British would have at least a three-to-one advantage and "might continue that advantage indefinitely" by using the superior speed of its oil-burning fleet to remain outside of the shorter gun-range of the slower coal-burning American battleships.[28]

Equally disturbing was First Lord of the Admiralty Leo Amery's vehement protest against the General Board's intention to elevate its battleship guns to equal those of the British battleships. Surprised by British insistence that this intention violated the Five Power Treaty, Coolidge at first refused to sanction the elevation.[29] For almost three years, from 1924 until 1927, Secretary of the Navy Wilbur engaged the British in a heated legal controversy which strained relations between the two countries.[30] In the midst of this gun-elevation controversy, Congress belatedly authorized the conversion of six coal-burning battleships to fuel oil, and once again the British voiced their outrage.[31] Nonetheless, despite vehement British protests, Congress eventually accepted the Navy's assurances that gun-elevation and conversion to fuel oil merely equaled British capabilities and neither violated the letter nor the spirit of the Five Power Treaty.[32]

During these years between the conclusion of the Washington Conference in 1922 and the start of the Geneva Naval Conference in 1927, the General Board had become progressively disillusioned with deceptive British negotiating tactics, with domestically oriented politicians acting as military strategists,

---

[27] Captain Frank H. Schofield, "Memorandum: The Gun Elevation Question," November 6, 1923, UNG 1927–1930, NWC.
[28] Schofield, "Incidents," p. 784; Schofield, "Some Effects," p. 3.
[29] George T. Davis, *A Navy Second to None: The Development of Modern American Naval Policy* (New York: Harcourt, Brace, 1940), pp. 311–312; Bywater, *Navies and Nations*, pp. 167–168, 174–175; Trimble, "United States Navy," pp. 52–53.
[30] See all of the sources in *Ibid*. See also Rear Admiral H. A. Wiley, "Memorandum for the Chief of Naval Operations," July 28, 1926, G.B. 438-1, GBUSN, RG 80, NA; Secretary of the Navy Curtis D. Wilbur to Alanson B. Houghton, January 18, 1927, G. B. 438-1, GBUSN, RG 80, NA. Houghton was the United States Ambassador to Great Britain. This is a 21-page letter which fully explains the American position.
[31] Davis, *Navy Second to None*, p. 313.
[32] Hilary P. Jones to Secretary of the Navy, "Naval Policy: Building Program for The Fiscal Year 1927," G. B. 420-2, GBUSN, RG 80, NA; Davis, *Navy Second to None*, pp. 311–313; Trimble, "United States Navy," p. 54.

with congressional parsimoniousness, and with the potentially disastrous results of the first experiment in naval arms-control diplomacy. The General Board tried to rectify some of the damage, but beyond gun-elevation and conversion to fuel oil, they were unable to alter strategic disadvantages. Nor were they able to convince Congress to build the two additional aircraft carriers or to equal the number of new 10,000-ton, 8-inch-gun cruisers being built by the British and the Japanese or to stop the new arms race in these vessels. Stymied in all of these efforts, the General Board in the mid-1920s focused much of its attention on the design features of its future cruisers, features which it believed were essential to overcome some of the disadvantages imposed on them by politicians who lacked appreciation of the need for naval strength to safeguard increasingly vulnerable international interests.

The need to develop the best possible cruiser design was heightened by the realization that while building capital ships was prohibited for the next ten years, cruisers remained unlimited in number. "Had I been a British naval strategist," Captain Schofield lectured his fellow officers, "my aim at the [Washington] Conference would [not only] have been to do away with the American battleship and battle cruiser building programs, because therein lay America's naval superiority," but also to "preserve British superiority in cruisers because with capital ships limited in numbers, the [auxiliary] cruiser became a very important item of naval strength and cruiser superiority meant naval superiority."[33]

If cruiser superiority meant future naval superiority, as Schofield claimed, it was obvious that Great Britain was the clear winner at the Washington Conference, where it had successfully blocked every effort to limit the number of cruisers, a category in which the United States was already particularly weak, in part, because it had delayed building cruisers during World War I to provide destroyers needed to combat the submarine menace and also to increase battleship production. But, following the end of World War I, Congress was no longer interested in building cruisers.[34] As a result, American cruiser strength had eroded so rapidly, Schofield lamented, that by September 1923, "even third-rate powers had us beaten."[35]

Schofield was not exaggerating.[36] Great Britain had authorized sixteen and Japan eight, while France and Italy, for example, were also building these

---

[33] Captain Frank H. Schofield, "Incidents and Present Day Aspects of Naval Strategy," *Proceedings of the United States Naval Institute*, (May 1923), p. 781.

[34] SMP, GB to the Secretary of the Navy, "Naval Policy: Building Program for the Fiscal Year 1925," April 7, 1925, p.7, G.B. 420-2, GBUSN, RG 80, NA. See also Bywater, *Navies and Nations*, pp. 178, 182–185, 196–197.

[35] Schofield, "Some Effects," p.5.

[36] Bywater, *Navies and Nations*, pp. 182–185, 196–197; Davis, *A Navy Second to None*, pp. 313–314; Norman Friedman, *U. S. Cruisers: An Illustrated Design History* (Annapolis: Naval Institute Press, 1984), pp. 108–111.

powerful 10,000-ton, 8-inch-gun cruisers.[37] The United States, by contrast, had not launched a new cruiser since 1908. Ten Omaha class cruisers with their twelve 6-inch, 53-caliber guns, carried in triple turrets on the centerline, were yet to be completed, and, in any case, were considered no match for the longer-range, more powerful 8-inch guns of rival navies.[38] More worrisome still, Congress rejected the General Board's request for sixteen 10,000-ton, 8-inch-gun cruisers in 1922. Two years later, in December 1924, it grudgingly authorized the construction of eight, but appropriated money to build only two.[39] Schofield explained that even when all ten of the less powerful Omaha class warships were commissioned, the United States would have only ten modern cruisers compared to sixty modern British cruisers and twenty-eight to thirty modern Japanese cruisers, either built or building.[40] As the United States was already outnumbered in cruisers by roughly six to one against the British and three to one against Japan, and as the General Board was "certain that attacks on convoys and on individual merchant vessels by enemy cruisers will be much more likely to occur [in a future war] than during the World War," it was clear to naval strategists that the ability of the United States Navy to protect American overseas possessions and trade had been very seriously eroded.[41]

The General Board's keen awareness of cruiser weakness, coupled with the inability to construct strategically located naval bases in the Pacific, profoundly influenced the design of its future 10,000-ton, 8-inch-gun cruisers.[42] Without naval or air bases beyond Hawaii, the General Board became unalterably

---

[37] See attached charts in Schofield, "Incidents," p. 785; SMP, GB, to Secretary of the Navy, "Data for Secretary of the Navy's Statement to the Sub-committee on Naval Appropriations," November 3, 1924, GB 420-2 GBUSN, RG 80, NA; Admiral William S. Sims to William H. Gardner, January 5, 1925, Sims Papers, LC.

[38] Friedman, *U. S. Cruisers*, pp. 106–110, 82, 136; Bywater, *Navies and Nations*, pp. 182–183; SMP, GB to Secretary of the Navy, April 7, 1925, pp. 7–8. The Admiralty reached the same conclusion. See Tac. Sec. [Tactical Section], "Gun Armament and Protection of Small 8" Cruiser And Comparison With 6" Cruiser,") n.d., p.5, Tac. Sec. 662/28, ADM 1/8765, PRO.

[39] SMP, GB to Secretary of the Navy, "Naval Policy: Building Program for Fiscal Year 1924," May 31, 1922, G. B. 420-2, GBUSN, RG 80, NA; Hilary P. Jones to Secretary of the Navy, "Naval Policy: Building Program for Fiscal Year 1926," April 18, 1924, G. B. 420-2, GBUSN, RG 80, NA; Friedman, *U. S. Cruisers*, pp. 111–112.

[40] Schofield, "Some Effects," pp. 2–4; Schofield, "Incidents," p. 785; SMP, GB to Secretary of the Navy, "Data," p.5. These figures vary slightly from source to source depending on the year cited. See for example Robert Gordon Kaufman, *Arms Control During the Pre-Nuclear Era: The United States and Naval Limitation Between the Two World Wars* (New York: Columbia University Press, 1990), p. 79.

[41] SMP, GB to Secretary of the Navy, "Naval Policy," April 7, 1923, p. 8; Schofield, "Incidents," p.785. Schofield compared the ten modern American cruisers not yet built to the combined British and Japanese total of ninety modern cruisers. See also Schofield, "Some Effects," pp. 2–4; NWC, "Comparison of Naval Forces–United States and Japan," 23–26, XTYG 1932–145, NWC; Bywater, *Navies and Nations*, pp. 185, 196–197, 201.

[42] SMP, GB to Secretary of the Navy, "Naval Policy," April 7, 1923, p. 2.

convinced that only a 10,000-ton, 8-inch-gun cruiser had the fuel capacity for the steaming radius required for a 9,800 nautical mile round-trip from Hawaii to the Philippines and the 6,800 nautical mile round-trip to Guam.[43] Assuming that the Philippine Islands were already occupied by an enemy, even an emergency fuel load – extending the new cruiser's radius to 13,000 miles – offered little reserve fuel to conduct a battle, pursue an enemy, or flee a more powerful ship.[44] Given these circumstances, increased gunpower also became an absolute essential. Whether fulfilling all the strategic and tactical demands of combat with the battle fleet, or attempting to retake the Philippines, or on lone patrol in distant waters, the greater range and destructive power of the 8-inch gun was considered crucial against the 6-inch gun carried by most of the potential enemy cruisers still in service.[45]

By April 1926 following intensive debate, the General Board modified the earlier design of the two *Salt Lake City* class cruisers. Rather than ten 8-inch guns in four turrets, the new *Northhampton* class featured nine guns in three triple turrets, two forward and one aft. With the elimination of one turret and the lengthening of the hull by 12 feet, an additional 40 to 50 feet became available to carry as many as six, rather than only four airplanes; four, rather than only two boiler rooms; more antiaircraft batteries; improved living accommodations; and a 16-inch higher freeboard, which lessened roll, increased buoyancy, and helped to keep water off the deck in rough seas.[46] The weight saved from one less gun also allowed another major benefit: greater armor protection.[47] In this class, the magazines would be protected from the 6-inch guns carried by most older cruisers. More important, the more heavily armored *Northampton* class exceeded the combat capabilities of the British *Kent* class, with one more gun, six airplanes, and one knot faster speed.[48]

The General Board was well pleased with these superior qualities. Speed had been slightly increased, magazine protection added to thwart 6-inch

---

[43] Schofield, "Incidents," p. 791; Friedman, *U. S. Cruisers*, p. 108; Captain Frank Schofield, "The General Board's Building Program," n.d., p. 6, UNC 1922-171, NWC.

[44] William F. Trimble, "The United States Navy and the Geneva Conference for the Limitation of Naval Armament, 1927," (Ph.D. diss., University of Colorado, 1974), pp. 39–40; Bywater, *Navies and Nations*, pp. 197–198; Hector C. Bywater, *Sea-Power in the Pacific: A Study of the American-Japanese Problem* (Boston: Houghton Mifflin, 1921), pp. 254–274; Friedman, *U. S. Cruisers*, pp. 108, 110.

[45] For a fascinating debate involving speed, protection, radius of action and gun power see GB, "Characteristics of Light Cruisers," *Minutes* of the General Board, 26 February 1925, pp. 9–10, 12–15, 18, 21, 25–27, 32, GBM. Hereafter the *Minutes* of the General Board will be cited as GB *Minutes*.

[46] GB, "Characteristics of 10,000-Ton Cruisers," GB *Minutes*, February 24, 1926, pp. 18–21, GBM; GB, "Characteristics of 10,000-Ton Cruisers," April 9, 1926, pp. 1–2, 4, 6, 8.

[47] GB, "Characteristics of Light Cruisers," GB *Minutes*, March 11, 1925, pp. 10–13, GBM.

[48] GB, "Characteristics of 10,000-Ton Cruisers," April 9 1926, p. 15; GB, "Characteristics of Light Cruisers," GB *Minutes*, March 23, 1928, pp. 11–12, GBM; Friedman, *U. S. Cruisers*, pp. 127, 132, 138, 141–143.

The General Boards' New Hope

shells, and the growing importance of airpower had been fully incorporated into the new design.[49]

Experts in both the Admiralty and the General Board agreed that powerful 8-inch guns with enough muzzle velocity for maximum range and high accuracy would be the essential difference between victory and defeat in the anticipated lone cruiser duels for which the 10,000-ton cruiser was, in part, designed. The General Board was delighted, therefore, when Admiral Claude C. Bloch, Chief of Naval Ordnance, reported the reality of just such an 8-inch gun. In arguing for a ten-gun rather than a nine-gun ship, he put great emphasis on the fact that the new American 8-inch guns "which we fired have given very excellent performances."[50] Test firings proved a muzzle velocity as high as 3,183 feet per second [f.s.], which at 30 degrees elevation threw a 260-pound shell 31,750 yards or eighteen miles.[51] At 40 degrees elevation, the range was 35,000 yards or 19.88 miles.[52]

Nor were these initial test results misleading. Gunnery officers continued to express this same high level of satisfaction with the gun throughout the 1920s and into the 1930s.[53] In 1931, for example, Captain H. K. Van Keuren

---

[49] GB, "Characteristics of 10,000-Ton Cruisers," April 9, 1926, pp. 14–15; GB, "Characteristics of 10,000-Ton Cruisers," GB *Minutes*, February 24, 1926, pp. 5, 15; GB, "Characteristics of 10,000-Ton Cruisers," April 9, 1926, p. 14; Buford Rowland and William B. Boyd, *U. S. Navy Bureau of Ordnance in World War II* (Washington, DC.: Government Printing Office, 1953), pp. 249–309; GB, "Characteristics of 10,000-Ton Cruisers," February 24, 1926, pp. 24–25.

[50] Tac. Sec. [Tactical Section], "Comparison of 8" and 6" Cruisers Based on Practice Results 1922–1927 Reduced by 30 Percent to Allow for Action Conditions," Sheet Z, December 4, 1928, p. 6. This report is attached to Tac. Sec., "Gun on Armaments and Protection of Small 8" Cruiser and Comparison with 6" Cruiser," n.d., Tac. Sec. 662/28, ADM 1/8765, PRO. The Tactical Section concluded that at 15,000 yards, the cruiser carrying four 8-inch guns versus the cruiser carrying six 6-inch guns would put the 6-inch cruiser out of action in 58 minutes. At 9000 yards, this would only take 18 minutes. "At any range" the report emphasized the 8-inch-gun cruiser "is greatly superior to the 6"." See also E. M. W. [E. M. Williams], "Comparisons of Two Cruisers in Size, Protection, and Speed but with One Armed with Nine 8-inch Guns and the Other with Twelve 6-inch guns," p. 3, G. B. 420-8, GBUSN, RG 80, NA. Williams concluded that the "8-inch gun cruiser for all-around work is superior to the 6-inch gun cruiser." Additional evidence on improving the American 8-inch gun can be found in Inspector of Ordnance in Charge to Chief of Bureau of Ordnance, "Erosion Rates," March 24, 1930, Entry 25, S72-4 (9), RG 74, NA. Later studies are also included in Entry 25, S72-4 (9), Box Nos. 1871–1872, 1860, 1861, 1864, 1869, RG 74, NA; Friedman, *U. S. Cruisers*, pp. 187–188, 112, 213; GB, "Characteristics of 10,000-Ton Cruisers," February 24, 1926, p. 24.

[51] Inspector of Ordnance in Charge to Chief of Bureau of Ordnance, March 24, 1930, p. 5 and Special Board on Naval Ordinance to Chief of Bureau, "Dispersion," November 1, 1926, p. 1, Entry 25, S72-4 (49), Box 1872, RG 74, NA. See also Inspector of Ordnance in Charge to Bureau of Ordnance, "Proof of 8-inch 55-cal. MK. IX, Mod. 1, 24 December 1926, S 72 – 4(13 -8"/55), Entry 25, Box 1860, RG 74, NA. See especially Round 3.

[52] GB, "Light Cruisers Nos. 37 to 41-Preliminary Design," April 9, 1930, p. 7, GBM. Rear Admiral W. D. Leahy proposed reducing the maximum range of the 8-inch gun from 35,000 to 31,500 yards.

[53] Friedman, *U. S. Cruisers*, p. 187.

informed the General Board that the 8-inch gun was "very accurate at long ranges." The commander of the Cruiser Scouting Force, Vice Admiral G. R. Marvell, was even more enthusiastic. He told the General Board that at distances from 31,500 yards or 17.81 miles to 33,600 yards or 19 miles, the 8-inch guns of the newly commissioned 10,000-ton cruisers, *Salt Lake City*, *Pensacola*, and *Northampton*, had repeatedly demonstrated "perfectly marvelous shooting."[54] In later years, after the addition of more antiaircraft batteries, the General Board informed the Secretary of the Navy that the balance of offensive characteristics of these new cruisers was "extremely satisfactory."[55] Thus, in stark contrast to the Admiralty's Naval Staff's intense frustrations with the combat deficiencies of its newest cruisers – especially the disappointing 8-inch gun – and its insistence on using the next international arms control conference to eliminate 8-inch guns on all rival warships, the United States Navy had no intention of ever eliminating its own "perfectly marvelous" new gun.

[54] GB, "10,000-Ton 8-Inch Cruisers," GB *Minutes*, June 9, 1930, p. 22, GBM.
[55] SMP, GB to Secretary of the Navy, "Characteristics of New 8-Inch Cruiser," June 20, 1931, p. 2, G. B. 420-8 (1931), GBUSN, RG 80, NA.

7

American Arms-Control Politics

Soon after World War I ended, the American public became increasingly disillusioned with the vindictive and complex nature of the Treaty of Versailles; with the bitter, prolonged political battles over the League of Nations; and with the brief but painful recession and unemployment caused by the sudden transition from a wartime to a peacetime economy. Americans found it difficult to understand, much less for American leaders to resolve, the new complexities arising from war reparations, Allied debt repayments, tariffs, currency stability, loans for European reconstruction, and the spreading civil war in China.[1] Overwhelmed by this confusing web of interrelated complexities, the Republican leaders often opted, instead, to emphasize popular domestic political and economic priorities.[2]

The great political benefits from embracing popular political demands, rather than wrestling with complex international ones, became crystal clear in 1921, when Harding scuttled his internationally oriented campaign pledge to continue building a navy second to none. In a dramatic rejection of the long-term need for such a navy, he startled Americans and the world with naval proposals at the Washington Conference that allowed him to claim credit for stopping the international naval arms race, for promoting international peace,

---

[1] Melvyn P. Leffler, *Elusive Quest: America's Pursuit of European Stability and French Security, 1919–1933* (Chapel Hill: University of North Carolina Press, 1979), pp. 4–46, 79–80; Ellis W. Hawley, *The Great War and the Search for a Modern Order: A History of the American People and Their Institutions, 1917–1932* (New York: St. Martin's, 1979), pp. 41–42; Lawrence Lafore, *The End of Glory: An Interpretation of the Origins of World War II* (Philadelphia and New York: J.B. Lippincott, 1970), pp. 1–77.

[2] Melvyn P. Leffler, "American Policy Making and European Stability, 1921–1933," *Pacific Historical Review* (May 1977): 211–216, 225; Melvyn P. Leffler, "Political Isolationism, Economic Expansionism or Diplomatic Realism: American Policy toward Western Europe, 1921–1933," *Perspectives in American History* 8 (1974): 429–430; Leffler, *Elusive Quest*, p. 81.

for reducing federal spending, for cutting taxes, and for avoiding entangling military commitments.[3]

The stunning popularity of these claims convinced many jubilant politicians that the best foreign policies were those which resulted in the best domestic political results. Increasingly, in the months ahead, policies calling for reducing taxes, protecting American jobs and profits through high protective tariffs, insistence on the repayment of Allied war debts, cutting government spending, avoiding entangling international commitments or close association with new international institutions, such as the League of Nations or World Court, and promoting peace through international arms control became popular political priorities, amounting to a new political orthodoxy. This orthodoxy set the parameters of American foreign policy in the 1920s and early 1930s, thereby making another naval limitation conference exceptionally attractive to the new president, Calvin Coolidge, his new Secretary of State Frank B. Kellogg, and to Senator William E. Borah, the chair of the powerful Senate Foreign Relations Committee.[4] But securing agreement to another conference was going to be a much more complex and difficult task than Harding and Hughes had faced in 1921. Lingering disputes from World War I and fresh suspicions arising from the perception of British duplicity at the Washington Conference alerted Coolidge and Kellogg to the challenges they might encounter in dealing with accomplished British diplomats. Nonetheless, Coolidge sent Ambassador Hugh Gibson and Admiral Hilary P. Jones as observers at the League of Nations Preparatory Commission to determine the feasibility of a second conference.

***

On August 3, 1923, Calvin Coolidge, the former Governor of Massachusetts, and current Vice President was suddenly thrust into this volatile, complex international mix by the unexpected death of President Warren G. Harding. Coolidge was strikingly unlike the imposing, handsome, gregarious Harding, who had loved to talk, or as he quaintly put it, "bloviate." Slender, with delicate features, sandy hair and blue eyes, Coolidge's taciturn nature was a startling contrast to Harding's outgoing personality.[5] "Quiet Cal," as he was dubbed, was in reality an experienced, skillful politician, who was easy to underestimate.

Foreign policy was especially challenging to him. Coolidge had no experience with diplomatic complexities and therefore relied heavily on Charles Evans Hughes until March 4, 1925, when Hughes unexpectedly resigned as Secretary of State. To replace Hughes, Coolidge selected Frank B. Kellogg who was currently serving as United States Ambassador to Great Britain.

---

[3] See Chapter 2.   [4] *Ibid.*; Leffler, "American Policy Making," pp. 211–214.
[5] Donald McCoy, *Calvin Coolidge: The Quiet President* (New York: Macmillan, 1967), p. vii; Robert K. Murray, *The Harding Era: Warren G. Harding and His Administration* (Minneapolis: University of Minnesota Press, 1969), pp. 130–132.

While presiding over the Senate as Vice President, Coolidge came to like and trust this kindly, considerate, and friendly man, who was known to temper his cantankerous outbursts with careful, cautious, common-sense judgments.[6] Kellogg had made his reputation as a wealthy corporation lawyer from Minnesota who achieved national popularity after President Theodore Roosevelt selected him to prosecute a highly publicized series of antitrust suits, including the giant Northern Securities railroad trust and Standard Oil.[7] His success in these cases elevated him to one term in the United States Senate from 1916 to 1923.

When the 68-year-old Kellogg failed to win reelection, Harding appointed him as Ambassador to Great Britain.[8] During his short tenure in London, he burnished his domestic reputation by assisting Charles G. Dawes, Owen D. Young, and Henry M. Robinson in creating the Dawes Plan, a popular postwar reconstruction effort which highlighted capital from private American banks, rather than governmental loans, to help rebuild Europe's war-ravaged economies. By the time Coolidge called his friend back to the United States to become Secretary of State in March 1925, influential members of the British Admiralty and the Foreign Office had already formed far less favorable impressions of Kellogg, impressions which would influence British diplomacy both before and during the Geneva Naval Conference in 1927.[9] Regardless of the private reservations of British officials, Coolidge and his American friends held Kellogg in high regard for his intelligence, rational approach to problem solving, and willingness to listen to advice from elder Republican Party statesmen and from the professional diplomats on the Western European desk at the State Department.[10]

Kellogg was an active Secretary of State. During his four years, he negotiated twenty-seven arbitration treaties, improved relations with Latin American nations, supported American membership in the World Court, promoted naval arms control negotiations, and avoided French pressure for a military alliance by negotiating the highly popular Kellogg-Briand Peace Pact, a pious,

---

[6] Robert H. Ferrell, "Frank B. Kellogg; Henry L. Stimson," *American Secretaries of State and Their Diplomacy*, eds. Robert H. Ferrell and Samuel Flagg Bemis (New York: Cooper Square, 1963), pp. 2–3; Richard W. Fanning, *Peace and Disarmament: Naval Rivalry and Arms Control, 1922–1933* (Lexington: University Press of Kentucky, 1995), pp. 24, 19–20, 23.

[7] Ferrell, "Kellogg; Stimson," pp. 1–8.

[8] Ibid., pp. 11–21; Charles DeBenedetti, "The American Peace Movement and the State Department in the Era of Locarno," in *Doves and Diplomats: Foreign Offices and Peace Movements in Europe and America in the Twentieth Century*, ed. Solomon Wank (Westport, CT: Greenwood, 1978), pp. 204–205.

[9] For British criticism, see Beatty to Wife, January 15, 1925, BTY 17/67, BP; British Foreign Office, "Memorandum Respecting the Future of Anglo-American Relations," 17 November 17, 1927, C. P. 292 (27) CAB 24/189, PRO; B.J.C. McKercher, *The Second Baldwin Government and the United States, 1924–1929: Attitudes and Diplomacy* (Cambridge: Cambridge University Press, 1984), p. 35.

[10] Ferrell, "Kellogg; Stimson," pp. 128–129; DeBenedetti, "American Peace Movement," p. 205.

unenforceable agreement outlawing war, which captured the world's imagination and won him a Nobel Peace Prize.[11] Nonetheless, Kellogg's tenure as Secretary of State was influenced to a considerable extent by the economic foreign policies already put in place by his predecessor, Charles Evans Hughes, and Secretary of Commerce Herbert C. Hoover and by Coolidge's acceptance of the conventional political wisdom that peacetime national defense required a military force only "large enough so that others would see that there would be a great deal of peril involved in attacking us."[12]

Given the conventional political circumstances of his time, Kellogg was more of a diplomatic realist than the toothless Kellogg-Briand Pact of 1929 suggested.[13] He privately rejected the reasoning of religiously motivated antiwar activists and kept at arm's length the more idealistic peace groups such as the Women's International League for Peace and Freedom, which lobbied for sweeping disarmament and cooperative efforts to achieve international peace and social justice. He was instead much more sympathetic to the thinking of the Carnegie Endowment for International Peace, which prided itself on recognizing international power realities.[14] To be effective, arms-control diplomacy, he believed, must be based firmly on domestic political realities and national self-interest.[15]

American foreign policy during the 1920s and continuing into the early years of the 1930s was also characterized by the overwhelmingly popular desire to avoid any entangling military alliances, while simultaneously characterized by the formulation of economic policies which served both to promote domestic prosperity and to help revive and stabilize those European economies ravaged by World War I – especially those vital to American prosperity.[16] Coolidge believed that Wilson's "navy second to none" would not only have wasted taxpayer dollars but would have destabilized the prospects for peace by perpetuating the senseless and dangerous peacetime naval arms race which

---

[11] Ferrell, "Kellogg; Stimson," pp. 84–90; McCoy, *Coolidge*, pp. 359–363. For more critical assessments see DeBenedetti, "American Peace Movement," pp. 204–210; Benjamin D. Rhodes, *United States Foreign Policy in the Interwar Period, 1918–1941: The Golden Age of American Diplomatic and Military Complacency* (Westport, CT: Greenwood, 2001), pp. 63–64, 57–71.

[12] Calvin Coolidge, "Promoting Peace Through Preparation for Defense," *Ladies Home Journal* 48 (April 1929): p. 65; Leffler, *Elusive Quest*, pp. 40–41, 62–63; Carl P. Parrini, *Heir to Empire: United States Economic Diplomacy, 1916–1923* (Pittsburgh, PA: University of Pittsburgh Press, 1969), p. 203; William E. Borah to E. A. Paddock, December 23, 1926, BOR.

[13] Fanning, *Peace and Disarmament*, pp. 82, 84.

[14] DeBenedetti, "American Peace Movement," pp. 208–213.   [15] Ibid., pp. 210–212.

[16] Parrini, *Heir to Empire*, pp.1–8, 27–28, 31, 77–88, 205–210, 259, 268; Leffler, *Elusive Quest*, pp. 24–26, 38, 55–63; Leffler, "Political Isolationism," pp. 416–422; Leffler, "American Policy Making," p. 209; Frank C. Costigliola, "Anglo-American Financial Rivalry in the 1920s," *Journal of Economic History* 37 (1977), pp. 915–916; Joan Hoff Wilson, *American Business and Foreign Policy, 1920–1933* (Lexington: University Press of Kentucky, 1971), pp. 30, 107–119; Rhodes, *United States Foreign Policy*, p. 58.

had heightened tensions both before and following World War I.[17] Rather than engage in another naval arms race, Coolidge proclaimed that "More security will be found in moderate force which menaces nobody than in great force which menaces everybody."[18] Drastic reductions in American naval forces testified to America's desire to promote peace and, therefore, he claimed, it was America's "greatest triumph" in international affairs.[19] In fact, recent charges by critics "about the destitute condition of the Navy and the deplorable plight of the army" would not deter him from enhancing the future peace of the world by making still further naval reductions.[20]

Curtis D. Wilbur, Coolidge's new Secretary of the Navy, was fully in accord with Coolidge's thinking. A former Chief Justice of the California Supreme Court, Wilbur was a graduate of the Naval Academy who favored building the United States Navy up to the strength specified in the Five Power Treaty while simultaneously supporting Coolidge's desire to call another international naval arms reduction conference to extend the 10:10:6 ratio to all warships.[21] Like Coolidge, Wilbur vigorously defended the results of the Washington Conference. Scrapping seventy-eight capital ships, he claimed, was the world's declaration of "war against war." "Never were so many or such valuable ships destroyed," he exclaimed, "never so bloodless a war; never a war so effective; and never so secure a peace following a war."[22] The new Secretary of the Navy also agreed with Coolidge that adequate national defense required a navy only large enough to deter other nations from invading the United States, a concept of national defense which was shared by highly vocal peace organizations.[23]

Given the great enthusiasm for arms control, Coolidge, Kellogg, and Wilbur agreed that calling another international naval arms control conference was a logical diplomatic and popular political initiative.[24] American congressional leaders were already convinced that European recovery was dependent upon reallocating Europe's economic resources from military to civilian investments, and arms reduction agreements were among the most obviously popular means to achieve that end.[25] Before Kellogg became Secretary of State, Congress had taken the initiative in early 1924 by passing yet another joint resolution authorizing Coolidge to call a second naval conference. This resolution may have masked a significantly increasing concern among a number of Republican

---

[17] Coolidge, 'Promoting Peace," p. 65.   [18] Ibid., p. 93.   [19] Ibid., p. 4.
[20] Quoted in McCoy, *Coolidge*, p. 364. See also George T. Davis, *A Navy Second to None: The Development of Modern American Naval Policy* (New York: Harcourt, Brace, 1940), p. 317.
[21] Phillips Payson O'Brien, *British and American Naval Power: Politics and Policy, 1900–1936* (Westport, CT: Praeger, 1998), p. 181.
[22] Curtis D. Wilbur, "The Limitation of Naval Armament," *Saturday Evening Post* (May 23, 1925), p. 17.
[23] Ibid.; Fanning, *Peace and Disarmament*, pp. 30–33.
[24] See footnotes 17 and 22; McCoy, *Coolidge*, p. 363.
[25] Leffler, *Elusive Quest*, pp. 40–41, 62–63; Parrini, *Heir to Empire*, p. 203; Borah to E. A. Paddock, December 23, 1926, BOR.

congressional leaders, who worried about reluctance to build the number of warships required to maintain the 10:10:6 ratio, and by the disturbing evidence that the United States was rapidly slipping behind Great Britain and Japan in building the newest 10,000-ton, 8-inch-gun cruisers.[26] In their judgment, either a second conference must soon limit the new naval arms race in auxiliary ships or the United States must begin its own belated building program.

Foremost among the congressional leaders championing another naval arms reduction conference was Senator William E. Borah, the aggressive, pugnacious, inflexible, yet politically perceptive chair of the powerful Senate Foreign Relations Committee.[27] "The fight for disarmament," he loved to proclaim, "was the fight for civilization."[28] But the peace dividends realized at the Washington Conference, he predicted, would soon "prove practically worthless unless ... followed up" by another international conference to restrict building in all classes of warships.[29] The failure to limit auxiliary cruisers, destroyers, and submarines was galling to him.[30] "There has never been any doubt in my mind," he complained, "that we were out-generaled in the conference of 1922," an opinion shared by American naval officers, albeit for different reasons.[31] Borah was especially suspicious of European motives. He claimed European leaders were pressing America for postwar loans and cancellation of war debts in order to build the "vast armament" programs required to promote their future imperialistic schemes and to enforce the imperialistic Treaty of Versailles.[32]

The second international naval arms-control conference, which Borah demanded, would incorporate a new code of international law guaranteeing freedom of the seas and outlawing the instrumentalities of war.[33] Like Coolidge and Kellogg, he believed that the "very best national preparedness" made it imperative for the United States to once again take the lead "to reduce the armaments of the world."[34]

---

[26] William F. Trimble, "The United States Navy and the Geneva Conference for the Limitation of Naval Armament, 1927" (Ph.D. diss. University of Colorado, 1974), pp. 66–67; Davis, *Navy Second to None*, p. 317; O'Brien, *British and American Naval Power*, pp. 108–181; Fanning, *Peace and Disarmament*, p. 17; DeBenedetti, "American Peace Movement," p. 207; Borah to A. E. Clark, September 22, 1924, BOR.

[27] Borah to C. M. Lincoln, December 21, 1923, Disarmament File 1921–1923, BOR.

[28] *Ibid.*   [29] *Ibid.*

[30] Borah to E. A. Paddock, December 23, 1926, BOR.

[31] Borah to James A. Gray, n.d., Committee on London Treaties File, BOR. For the viewpoint of American naval officers, see Captain Frank H. Schofield, "Some Effects of the Washington Conference on American Naval Strategy," September 23, 1923, Unpublished Lecture, XPOD-1923-148, NWC.

[32] Borah to Paddock, December 23, 1926, BOR.

[33] Borah to A. E. Clark, September 22, 1924, Disarmament File, BOR. Borah insisted that a second conference must establish a code of international law guaranteeing freedom of the seas and outlawing the instrumentalities of war. See Borah to S. O. Levinson, November 29, 1922, Outlawing of War File, BOR.

[34] DeBenedetti, "American Peace Movement," p. 205; Robert James Maddox, *William E. Borah and American Foreign Policy* (Baton Rouge: Louisiana State University Press, 1969), p. 179.

Kellogg, as the new Secretary of State, had no realistic choice but to take the views of the powerful peace lobbies and Borah seriously. Borah had developed a low opinion of Kellogg when Kellogg had earlier served with him on the Senate Foreign Relations Committee. Moreover, Kellogg was well aware of the difficulties which Borah, as Chair of the Senate Foreign Relations Committee, could cause him, as Kellogg had personally witnessed the damage that the Committee's previous chair, Henry Cabot Lodge, had inflicted on Wilson's Treaty of Versailles.[35] Kellogg actually had no quarrel with Borah on naval arms reduction.[36] Well before he became Secretary of State, while he was serving as Ambassador to Great Britain, he had talked with Sir Austen Chamberlain, the British Foreign Secretary, about increasing popular pressure to act upon the provision in the League of Nations Charter requiring the League to initiate comprehensive efforts to reduce all forms of warfare.[37]

Under Article Eight of the League of Nations Covenant, the League was required to promote efforts to reduce international military forces to the lowest level consistent with national defense. While vaguely worded, the obligation was clear. Finally, in October 1924, the League created a preparatory commission to arrange a general disarmament conference and requested the United States to send representatives.[38]

The League's request offered Coolidge the opportunity to satisfy the demands from the powerful peace lobbies and from Senator Borah for a second naval conference. William R. Castle, Jr., the wealthy former Harvard University Dean, and head of the State Department's Division of Western European Affairs, acknowledged the "political impossibility" of refusing the League's invitation. While Castle took a dim view of the politics practiced by the popular peace movement in America, he was attuned to the political clout wielded by these peace groups and the certainty of political "disaster for the Administration" if Coolidge refused to send representatives.[39]

When former Secretary of State Charles Evans Hughes refused to head the unofficial American delegation to the Preparatory Commission, Coolidge selected a youthful-looking diplomat who had already served nineteen years in various diplomatic posts.[40] Hugh S. Gibson was slightly built, with sharp facial features, and a quiet natural dignity. His good judgment and sense of

---

[35] Ferrell, "Kellogg; Stimson," p. 14; DeBenedetti, "American Peace Movement," 205; McKercher, *The Second Baldwin Government and the United States*, p. 52.

[36] Kellogg to Frank H. Simmons, August 17, 1927, MC 27, KP. The Library of Congress has placed Kellogg's papers on microfilm and henceforth all citations to the Kellogg papers will be to the microfilm edition cited as MC.

[37] L. Ethan Ellis, *Frank B. Kellogg and American Foreign Relations, 1925–1929* (New Brunswick, NJ: Rutgers University Press, 1961), p. 158; Trimble, "United States Navy," p. 69.

[38] Fanning, *Peace and Disarmament*, pp. 22–23.

[39] William R. Castle, Jr., Diary, January 7 and 11, 1926, CP. Earlier Castle had been skeptical of Coolidge's intentions. See Castle to Alanson B. Houghton, May 4, 1925, England file, CP.

[40] Kellogg to Gibson, April 23, 1926, Records of the Secretary of the Delegation, 1930, RG 80, NA.

humor, combined with a strong professional work ethic, had propelled him into the front ranks of the State Department's promising negotiators. Born in 1883 in Los Angeles to a devoted mother who had educated him with private tutors, then at the École Libre des Sciences Politiques in Paris, Gibson entered the diplomatic service in 1908 at the age of twenty-five, when the State Department had begun emphasizing the development of a highly professional cadre of diplomats. His sunny, optimistic nature, personal charm, and affability sometimes obscured his pragmatic realism and intellectual flexibility.[41] Gibson actually enjoyed the often tedious process of negotiation. This enjoyment arose from his deeply held conviction that the senseless nature of World War I had made it apparent that future peace depended to a considerable extent upon patient professional diplomats.[42]

Gibson's nineteen years as a diplomat made him a good choice to head the unofficial delegation to the Preparatory Commission. Having gained experience at posts in Honduras, London, Havana, and Washington DC, he was assigned in 1914 to be Secretary of the Legation in Brussels, where he soon won the gratitude of the Belgian people by attempting, albeit unsuccessfully, to save the life of Edith Cavell. Cavell was executed by a German military court for aiding British soldiers to escape from Belgium after the Germans had occupied this neutral country at the start of World War I.[43] During the war, while serving as vice chair of the American Relief Committee headed by Herbert Hoover, Gibson became known to the Belgian people, along with Hoover, as a leader in the difficult yet successful effort to feed the starving people of Belgium. During the course of this work, Hoover took a strong and abiding personal liking to Gibson. In 1926, Secretary of Commerce Hoover, who two years later would be elected the next president of the United States, praised Gibson as "one of the best Americans living."[44]

Coolidge also recognized Gibson's abilities by elevating him to be the United States Ambassador to Belgium in May 1927. Upon Gibson's arrival in Brussels, the streets were lined with smiling faces and waving handkerchiefs, as an honor guard transported him to the Royal Palace, where the King and Queen brushed aside protocol to welcome him as a hero from "the dark days when friends were needed."[45] At one of the dinners to honor him and his strikingly beautiful Belgian wife, Ywes, three hundred government officials from districts and

---

[41] Ronald E. Swerczek, "The Diplomatic Career of Hugh Gibson, 1908–1938" (Ph.D. diss., University of Iowa, 1972), pp. 1–199, 201, 231, 256–259, 289–291, 305, 364–369.
[42] Wythe Williams, "Gibson Emerges As a Fencer-Diplomat," *New York Times Magazine,* July 10, 1927, pp. 13–14.
[43] Ibid.; "Cruisers Crux," *Time Magazine,* July 18, 1927, pp. 13–14.
[44] Herbert Hoover to George H. Lorimer, April 9, 1926, Commerce Papers, HHPL. See also correspondence between Hoover and Gibson in the Gibson File, Hoover Papers, Stanford University.
[45] Gibson to Mother, May 9, 1927, GP. See also press clippings, Box 131, GP.

municipalities throughout the nation added their greetings and gratitude in an extraordinary display of affection.[46]

In 1926 Coolidge appointed him to head the American delegation to the League of Nations' Preparatory Commission. Gibson's abilities and personal charm quickly won the praises of experienced and highly critical diplomats both at the Preparatory Commission and during the 1927 Geneva Naval Conference.[47] As chief of the State Department's Western European Section, and later Assistant Secretary of State, William R. Castle, Jr., was a champion of the professionalization of American diplomacy, who often filled his diary with critical evaluations of inept colleagues, but of Gibson, he expressed "great confidence" because of his ability to infuse professional diplomacy with humor and sanity.[48]

To accompany Gibson to the Preparatory Commission, Coolidge selected Rear Admiral Hilary P. Jones, the highly respected recent president of the United States Navy's General Board.[49] With his head of snow-white hair, walrus-mustache, and sad eyes, Jones appeared more like a kindly grandfather rather than the hardened navy veteran of thirty-nine years. His father had been a colonel of artillery in Robert E. Lee's Army of Virginia, but Jones had always wanted a naval career and entered the Naval Academy at Annapolis with the top score among all of that year's applicants. His keen intelligence and considerable personal charm, a charm which even his later critics would grudgingly acknowledge, advanced him rapidly through the ranks to Commander of the Atlantic Fleet and then to Commander of the United States Fleet.[50] Significantly, while Commander of the United States Fleet, Jones's use of airplanes and aircraft carriers in fleet maneuvers distinguished him from his fellow naval officers, who had not yet grasped the growing offensive potential of these new-era combat technologies.[51]

---

[46] Williams, "Gibson Emerges," *New York Sun*, January 5, 1927.

[47] Charles Groves, "Hugh S. Gibson: Alert Guardian of America's Destiny," *Boston Globe*, August 7, 1927; Robert Cecil to Austin Chamberlain, April 6, 1927, Add Mss. 51079, LCP; "Naval Notes 1927: Vice-Admiral Kobayashi's Impression of Geneva Conference," September 22, 1927, ADM 1/8715/188, PRO; "Cruiser Crux," *Time Magazine*, July 18, 1927; Swerczek, "Diplomatic Career," pp. 200–208, 231, 256–259, 269, 289–291; Gibson to Mother, July 3, 1924, GP; Gibson to Mother, July 9 and 11, 1924, HHPL. See also additional correspondence in the Gibson Papers, HHPL.

[48] Castle, Diary, May 25 and 27, 1926; June 24, 1926; January 5, 1927, CP. See also DeBenedetti, "American Peace Movement," pp. 205–206; Trimble, "United States Navy," p. 17.

[49] Trimble, "United States Navy," pp. 79–80.

[50] Bridgeman, Diary, p. 143, BP; Drew Pearson, "Personalities at Geneva: Admiral Hilary P. Jones," *Richmond Times-Dispatch*, August 6, 1927, GP; Gibson to Kellogg, August 5, 1927, GP; Gibson to Ted Marriner, August 11, 1927, GP; Kellogg to Gibson, August 18, 1927, GP; Gibson to Jones, August 11, 1927, JP.

[51] Trimble, "United States Navy," p. 79; Pearson, "Personalities at Geneva," *Richmond Times-Dispatch*, August 6, 1927, GP.

Jones stood out in still another way. Like his close friend Rear Admiral William V. Pratt, on whom President Herbert Hoover would rely during the 1930 London Naval Conference, Jones differed with many of his fellow naval officers over the efficacy of still further naval limitation. International arms-control agreements, he believed, could be an acceptable means of safeguarding the naval security of the United States. But the results of the Washington Conference certainly suggested to him that naval leaders could not afford merely to voice their opposition to this politically popular means of reducing international tension. Naval leaders must instead take a more active and realistic role in shaping this new diplomatic device so that it did not weaken American naval strength still further.

While certainly charming, Jones neither thought nor spoke like a diplomat. His habit of plain speaking and the lack of diplomatic experience would later cause some friction at the Geneva Naval Conference in 1927.[52] He was neither an advocate of a "Big Navy," as First Lord of the Admiralty William Bridgeman would charge in 1927, nor an Anglophobe as two historians have suggested.[53] "While I am an American by birth and long tradition," he explained to Bridgeman, following the collapse of the Geneva Naval Conference in 1927, "I am an Anglo-Saxon and love and believe with a whole heart in the civilization and ideals handed down to us through the generations of the race." Indeed, in 1926, the year before the Geneva Naval Conference talks began, Jones confided to his friend Rear Admiral William V. Pratt that he would like to see a "real entente," a special relationship with Great Britain which would safeguard "Anglo-Saxon civilization." Such a military entente was crucial, he told Pratt, because the United States and Great Britain were the "only countries that do stand for civilization as we know it and that united we can carry that civilization on" to enhance the peace of the world.[54]

For all his love of "Anglo-Saxon civilization," Jones was willing to criticize as well as to extol the English. What made him "pretty hot under the collar," he admitted to Pratt, was Britain's refusal to treat the United States "as a co-equal." Irritating as well was its Admiralty's determination "to keep one leap ahead" of the United States Navy.[55] As he readied himself to sail for talks at the Preparatory Commission, Jones had already formulated his own personal mission. He would try to convince the British representatives that if they could "really at heart recognize that the United States must be treated as a co-equal," then this recognition "would go a long way toward

---

[52] "Naval Notes 1927: Vice Admiral Kobayashi's Impressions"; Pearson, "Personalities at Geneva."
[53] Jones to Rear Admiral William V. Pratt, February 1, 1926, Preparatory Commission File, JP; Editorial, *New York Times*, 16 August 1927; Fanning, *Peace and Disarmament*, p. 40; Stephen Roskill, *Naval Policy Between the Wars: The Period of Anglo-American Antagonism, 1919–1929* (London: Colliers, 1968), p. 434.
[54] Jones to Pratt, February 1, 1926, JP.   [55] *Ibid.*

straightening out questions between us" and enable the two nations to "march in international relations shoulder to shoulder."⁵⁶

As the former ambassador to Great Britain, Kellogg was also sympathetic to the British, and like both Gibson and Jones, he shared hopes for successful arms-control efforts and the recognition of the need for military realism.⁵⁷ In his instructions to Gibson and Jones, Kellogg reiterated his emphasis on the Five Power Treaty as a pragmatic model. He instructed Gibson and Jones to avoid debates on both idealistic and theoretical proposals, concentrating instead on a "practical plan which might reasonably be expected to succeed," one which the Senate might reasonably be expected to ratify, namely the extension of the naval principles and ratios already agreed upon in the Five Power Treaty to unlimited auxiliary warships.⁵⁸

Emphasis upon practical naval reductions was important for yet another reason. By 1926, congressional leaders were split over naval defense strategy. They were by now much more fully aware of the obvious strategic disadvantages imposed by the Washington Conference treaties, particularly the inability to defend the Philippine Islands and Guam and the new naval arms race in cruisers resulting from the failure to limit auxiliary warships. On the one hand, critics of these deficiencies, including the extensive Hearst newspaper chain, the American Legion, the Navy League, and a host of like-minded allies, publicized Coolidge's repeated refusals to build enough ships to maintain the 10:10:6 ratio or to keep pace with the British and Japanese in the new race in 10,000-ton, 8-inch-gun cruisers.⁵⁹ Senator Borah, on the other hand, and those in Congress opposing a renewed naval building program, not only demanded another international arms-control conference but complained that the United States had been "out-generaled" at the Washington Conference in 1922. Borah vowed, therefore, that as Chair of the Senate Foreign Relations Committee, he would insist on limiting all warships at the next conference.⁶⁰ Coolidge agreed with Borah. On January 4, 1926, he used his annual address to Congress to proclaim: "the general policy of this Government [is] in favor of disarmament and limitation of armament," insisting that this policy could not be "emphasized too frequently or too strongly." He reminded Congress that "competitive armaments constitute a powerful factor in the promotion of war," and stressed that "the necessity for lifting the burdens of taxation from

---

⁵⁶ *Ibid.*
⁵⁷ Kellogg to Secretary of War Dwight W. Davis, January 4, 1926; Kellogg to Secretary of the Navy Curtis D. Wilbur, January 4, 1926, PCF, JP. See also DeBenedetti, "American Peace Movement," pp. 208–212; Arnold Offner, *The Origins of the Second World War: American Foreign Policy and World Politics, 1919–1941* (New York: Praeger, 1957), p. 58.
⁵⁸ Kellogg to Gibson, April 23, 1926, Records of the Secretary of the Delegation, RG 80, NA.
⁵⁹ Fanning, *Peace and Disarmament*, pp. 18–20, 33–37; Hector C. Bywater, *Navies and Nations: A Review of Naval Developments since the Great War* (Boston and New York: Houghton Mifflin, 1927), pp. 272–273.
⁶⁰ Borah to James A. Gray, n.d., Committee on London Treaties File 1929–1930, BOR.

the peoples of the world by limiting armaments is becoming daily more imperative."[61]

As the American delegation made arrangements to leave for the first meeting of the Preparatory Commission in Geneva, Switzerland, other congressional members of his own party pointedly reminded Coolidge of their increasingly effective opposition to further naval cuts. Two years earlier in 1924, Congress had authorized construction of eight new 10,000-ton, 8-inch-gun cruisers, but opponents had limited funding to only two ships. But by 1926, the political tide against naval increases had begun to ebb. With significantly increasing Republican support, Congress authorized the rapid increase in carrier-based naval aviation to 1,000 planes by 1931. It also approved the modernization of American battleships allowing the conversion from coal to fuel oil, increased gun elevation to equalize the range of existing British battleships, and approved funds for the construction of three more 8-inch-gun cruisers.[62] When Coolidge opposed building the three cruisers, nineteen of the twenty members of the House Naval Affairs Committee issued a public protest, and when the Senate approved the three cruisers by a two-to-one margin, the House quickly appropriated the funds, and Coolidge reluctantly signed the bill into law.[63]

Coolidge's concern was heightened as well by a series of Anglo-American disputes which threatened to increase congressional pressure for more warships. The most serious of these disputes surfaced in early November 1925 when the British Ambassador to the United States, Sir Esme Howard, alarmed the British Foreign Secretary, Sir Austen Chamberlain, with the news that Coolidge was preparing to take legal action against Great Britain on behalf of American companies which alleged that they had suffered from the illegalities of the British blockade during World War I. Chamberlain reacted to this "thunder-clap" with a mixture of fear and indignation. "I can scarcely exaggerate the anxiety, even the dismay, which it caused me," especially because, he warned Howard, these American blockade claims "went to the root of our rights as a belligerent Power ... and ... struck straight at our naval strength and at our power to defend ourselves."[64]

---

[61] Coolidge's statement to Congress is included in the "Draft Instruction for the American Representation on the Preparatory Commission for the Disarmament Conference," pp. 1–3, PCF, JP.
[62] Philip T. Rosen, "The Treaty Navy, 1919–1937," in *In Peace and War: Interpretations of American Naval History, 1775–1984*, ed. Kenneth J. Hagan (Westport, CT: Greenwood, 1978), pp. 225–226; Trimble, "United States Navy," p. 175.
[63] Fanning, *Peace and Disarmament*, pp. 35–37; McKercher, *Second Baldwin Government*, pp. 58–60; Admiral Robert E. Coontz to Theodore Roosevelt, Jr., January 21, 1927; Roosevelt to Coontz, February 5, 1927; Coontz to Roosevelt, March 3, 1927, Coontz File, TR. See also Admiral Charles B. McVay to Roosevelt, December 15, 1927, McVay File, TR.
[64] Chamberlain to Howard, November 2, 1925; Howard to Chamberlain, October 26, 1925; Chamberlain to Howard, November 2, 3, and 4, 1925; Howard to Chamberlain November 7, 1925 in *Documents on British Foreign-Policy 1919–1939: European and Naval Questions,*

Chamberlain's alarm coincided with another current source of friction between the two nations – the repayment of war loans.⁶⁵ He predicted that when the British people learned that in addition to repaying the war loans they must also pay for blockade claims, their anger against the United States would intensify.⁶⁶ As England could not compromise on the principles on which its naval blockade strategy was based, and as popular resentment against American postwar policies were already prevalent throughout England, Chamberlain insisted that this latest American demand was too dangerous to ignore.⁶⁷ To acknowledge the validity of these claims, he stressed, would not only expose England to claims from all other neutral powers, but, more importantly, would also "destroy the basis of [our] naval power," a power which England had long cherished and on which the island nation and its Empire depended.⁶⁸

War debts and blockade claims continually ignited impassioned responses in both the countries for years following World War I.⁶⁹ Hoping to improve relations between the two nations, Coolidge listened patiently to Howard's recitation of Chamberlain's list of strong objections to the blockade claims.⁷⁰ As the argument dragged on, however, Kellogg became less and less patient. Immediately before becoming Secretary of State, Kellogg had served as the American Ambassador to Great Britain, and he was thoroughly familiar with British sensibilities about war debts and blockade rights. In March 1926, during a personal conversation with Kellogg, when Howard expressed British shock and dismay over American blockade claims, Kellogg's temper flared: "'[We] seem already to be so unpopular in England when the Chancellor of the Exchequer [Churchill] calls us Shylocks and attributes all European economic distress to us that nothing could make matters much worse.'"⁷¹

In March 1927, Howard became almost as irritated with Coolidge as he was with Kellogg.⁷² At one point when the British refused even to discuss American blockade claims, Kellogg again became angry enough to send Chamberlain a

---

Series Ia, Vol. III eds. W.N. Medlicott, et al. (London: Her Majesty's Stationery Office, 1970), pp. 861–882. Hereafter Volume III in Series Ia will be cited as *DBFP*.

⁶⁵ Alanson D. Houghton to William R. Castle, September 28, 1925, November 23, 1925; Castle to Houghton, November 12, 1925; Castle to Senator David A. Reed, April 5, 1926, CP. See also James Harold Mannock, "Anglo-American Relations, 1921–1928" (Ph.D. diss., Princeton University, 1962), pp. 209–233.

⁶⁶ Chamberlain to Howard, November 2, 1925, *DBFP*, pp. 865–866.

⁶⁷ Chamberlain to Howard, November 3 and 4, 1925, *DBFP*, pp. 867–871.

⁶⁸ Chamberlain to Howard, November 3, 1925, *DBFP*, p. 868.

⁶⁹ Castle to Houghton, November 12, 1925; Castle to David A. Reed, April 5, 1925, CP. For an excellent summary of the strained relations between the United States and Great Britain, see Mannock, "Anglo-American Relations," pp. 202–232.

⁷⁰ Howard to Chamberlain, November 7, 1925, *DBFP*, pp. 871–873.

⁷¹ Howard to Chamberlain, March 30, 1926, *DBFP*, pp. 881–882. See also Howard to Chamberlain, November 4 and 7, and March 29, 1926, *DBFP*, pp. 869–882.

⁷² Howard to Chamberlain, March 18, 1927, *DBFP*, p. 584.

protest of such an inflammatory nature that the American Ambassador to Great Britain, Alanson Houghton, refused to deliver it. Eventually William A. Borah, the powerful chair of the Senate Foreign Relations Committee who had long championed freedom of the seas, assisted Kellogg with a joint congressional resolution supporting Kellogg, whereupon Chamberlain reluctantly agreed to secret negotiations, which, in time, settled the blockade claims.[73]

As tempers flared on both sides of the Atlantic over blockade claims, Anglo-American cooperation in China disintegrated. In May 1925, the Kuomintang, the Nationalist Revolutionary Party led by Chiang Kai-shek, blamed British imperialist policies for the breakdown of the Peking Tariff Commission. This Commission was the key economic institution on which the signatories to the Nine Power Treaty had pinned their hopes for a reliable independent source of revenue vital to the political goal of building a stronger, more stable national Chinese government, one which was expected to honor the trading concessions already conceded to the foreign powers. But hatred of the special privileges for these foreign imperialist powers fueled Chinese nationalism, prompting the Kuomintang to launch an economic boycott against British goods and to revoke British trading concessions in areas it conquered.

The swiftly changing and complex nature of the Chinese revolution convinced Kellogg to hold the United States aloof from Chamberlain's requests that the United States support sanctions against the Kuomintang. Kellogg instead employed a wait-and-see approach, which increasingly led to unilateral American negotiations with the Kuomintang and consequent growing British irritation with United States.[74] Throughout 1926 and 1927, as British possessions and trading rights fell to Kuomintang control, Kellogg consistently refused British pleas to cooperate in the use of force. The dynamic complexities of the Chinese revolution and the substantively divergent interests of the United States and Great Britain in East Asia thus combined to add still another source of persistent irritation and distrust to an increasingly troubled relationship.[75]

Anglo-American relations were strained still further over disputes arising from differing interpretations of the Five-Power Treaty. The General Board of the United States Navy was particularly surprised when Great Britain vehemently protested American actions to equalize the combat capabilities of the battleship fleets. British protests seemed to confirm suspicions that they had withheld vital information during the Washington Conference negotiations, and having secretly gained unfair advantages, were now resorting to unfounded

---

[73] Mannock, "Anglo-American Relations," pp. 217–232.
[74] Emily O. Goldman, *Sunken Treaties: Naval Arms Control between the Wars* (University Park, PA: Pennsylvania State University Press, 1994), pp. 194–208, 232–233. See also an excellent dissertation by Christina A. Newton, "Anglo-American Relations and Bureaucratic Tensions, 1927–1930" (Ph.D. diss., University of Illinois at Urbana-Champaign, 1975), pp. 45–111, 238–240.
[75] See citations in *Ibid*.

legalistic and diplomatic obstructions to maintain those advantages. Equally irritating to the General Board was Coolidge's sudden order to prepare negotiating positions for the League of Nations forthcoming Preparatory Commission talks in Geneva Switzerland.[76]

The General Board complied with Coolidge's order with a heightened sense of distrust of British diplomatic wiles.[77] The gun elevation and oil conversion controversies had strengthened their conviction that, rather than conceding equality in capital ships, British military leaders and diplomats had hoodwinked American negotiators at the Washington Conference into an agreement which had guaranteed British superiority. The General Board suspected that the British would use the Preparatory Commission talks to set up yet another naval arms-control conference in which its diplomats would seek to prolong Great Britain's capital ship advantage beyond the expiration of the Five Power Treaty in 1932. They accurately predicted that the British would argue that great economic savings could be realized merely by simultaneously extending the service life and naval building holiday for all existing capital ships. Such an agreement might prevent the United States from replacing its less powerful older battleships with new ones equal to the *Nelson* and *Rodney*, two of the newest, most modern, and most powerful British battleships.[78]

With equal accuracy, the General Board predicted that just as the British had masked their capital ship superiority under the guise of a 10:10 ratio, allegedly guaranteeing capital ship equality, they would likewise work tirelessly at a new conference to prevent equality in auxiliary cruisers. In fact, the British had made no effort to hide their insistence on cruiser superiority.[79] Indeed,

---

[76] See Chapter 6. See also Secretary of the Navy to General Board, February 24, 1925, GBDCS, RG 80, NA.

[77] See reports from the Office of Naval Intelligence in "Proposed Second Limitation of Arms Conference," March 15, 1926, p. 6, GBS 438-1 (1925–1926), GBUSN, RG 80, NA. In his report to the Director of Naval Intelligence Captain L. McNamee, the Naval Attaché in London warned that British leaders would insist on "a quid pro quo twice over for anything that is sacrificed" at the next conference. See also GB, "The Situation in Great Britain," October 10, 1925, pp. 4–5, GBM. In this lengthy discussion with the General Board, Captain McNamee candidly expressed his belief that the Admiralty was "very jealous" of the United States and "probably hate us underneath" as they "attack everything that comes from America" with an especially "hostile" attitude. When Hilary Jones challenged use of the term "hatred," McNamee agreed that "jealous irritation" was a better description. The evaluation of the Admiralty's intentions by Commander J. C. Hunsaker is in GB, "The Situation and Great Britain," October 20, 1925, GBM.

[78] SMP, GB to Secretary of the Navy, "Further Limitation of Naval Armament," June 3, 1925, GBS 438-1, GBUSN, RG 80, NA. See also Captain C. L. Hussey "Notes on General Board's Preparation for a Second International Conference for the Limitation of Naval Armament," September 4, 1925, in ROSK 7/35, ROSKCC.

[79] For Jones' remark, see "The Situation in Great Britain," October 20, 1925, p. 4, GBM. Jones was referring both to the abolition of battleships and to equality in cruisers.

American naval intelligence officers stationed in Great Britain confirmed that the British would not accept the extension of the 10:10:6 ratio to these warships.[80]

Great Britain's forthright refusal to grant equality in cruisers was especially troubling to the General Board.[81] This worry was compounded by rumors of British demands to reduce the size of future cruisers to much less than 10,000 tons. A smaller cruiser would make American operations in the Pacific much more difficult as the cruiser needed to carry a large supply of fuel when operating in the Pacific where naval bases beyond Hawaii where prohibited by treaty.[82] Great Britain could compensate for the shorter cruising radius of a smaller cruiser by its world-wide system of strategically located naval bases.[83] Smaller cruisers might also appeal to the Japanese who could deploy them from nearby bases in Korea and China while using the savings to "build up her auxiliary naval forces to counteract her inferiority in capital strength."[84] Moreover, United States Naval Intelligence predicted that by 1928 Japan would already have built or have under construction a superiority of seventeen larger 10,000-ton cruisers over those of the United States and, with the savings realized from building smaller cruisers, could therefore build a greater number of these less expensive warships to enhance its offensive capabilities.[85]

The General Board's concern extended well beyond the anticipated proposals of rival powers at another conference. Far more important was the rapid erosion of American naval strength in the vessels essential to the combat effectiveness of the main battle fleet. The continuing opposition from the White House and Congress were far more serious than the anticipated difficulties of any future conference.[86]

One of the reasons the General Board was less worried about a second naval arms-control conference than it was about congressional inaction stemmed from the fact that by May 1926 the League of Nations Preparatory Commission, meeting in Geneva Switzerland, had bogged down in a tangle of disputes. Much of the wrangling was over France's continued quarrel with England over

---

[80] Alanson B. Houghton to Kellogg, February 27, 1926, *FRUS*, 1926, I: 58.
[81] *Ibid.* See also discussions with Naval Attachés cited in footnotes 77 and 78.
[82] Hilary P. Jones to Secretary of the Navy, "Construction Program for the United States Navy," January 11, 1926, GBS 420-2, GBUSN, RG 80, NA; Jones to W. V. Pratt, February 1, 1926, JP.
[83] GB, "The Situation in Great Britain," October 10, 1925, pp. 2, 8, GBM.
[84] Captain Frank H. Schofield, "Incidents and Present Day Aspects of Naval Strategy," *Proceedings of the United States Naval Institute*, (May 1923), p. 791; Frank H. Schofield, "The General Board Building Program," n.d., UNC 1922–171, NWC; Norman Friedman, *U. S. Cruisers: An Illustrated Design History* (Annapolis: Naval Institute Press, 1984), p. 108.
[85] H. R. Hein, Acting Naval Attaché to Director of Naval Intelligence, "Proposed Disarmament Conference," March 12, 1926, ONI-22-26, p. 2, in GB, "Proposed Second Limitation of Arms Conference: Trend of Thought – Japan," GBS 438-1, GBUSN, RG 80, NA; Office of Naval Intelligence, "Report," January 11, 1926, GBS 420-2, GBUSN, RG 80, NA.
[86] Jones to Secretary of the Navy, "Construction Program for the United States Navy," January 11, 1926; Kellogg to Gibson, April 23, 1926, *FRUS*, 1926, I: 85.

its future military vulnerability to German attack. The French argued that this vulnerability required security guarantees, preferably in the form of a military alliance, before arms-control and reduction could be negotiated.[87] Moreover, despite vehement opposition from the British, Americans, and Japanese, France presciently insisted that arms-control inspectors must ensure compliance before arms-control could be a trustworthy instrument of international relations. Inspection was especially important, the French correctly believed, because Germany was already violating the arms-control provisions of the Versailles Treaty in secret armament and training programs.[88]

As the Preparatory Commission talks dragged on, Gibson became increasingly troubled by the persistent undercurrent of suspicion between the former allies. The surprises and shocks of World War I were obviously etched deeply into the memories of the British, the French, and the Italians. These three nations which had been allies in World War I, were now members of the League of Nations, and had recently signed the Locarno agreements, yet they persisted in the "presumption of [future] hostilities" against one another. This persistent assumption, he lamented, generated practically "all of the obstacles to naval limitation and reduction" and thus, after almost five months of intermittent talks, the Preparatory Commission had "failed to reach agreement on any single question of importance."[89] By October, 1926, therefore, Japan's earlier informal proposal of a three-power naval conference began to gain covert support.[90]

---

[87] Edward W. Bennett, *German Reparations and the West, 1932–1933* (Princeton: Princeton University Press, 1979), pp. 93–94; Fanning, *Peace and Disarmament*, pp. 41–43.

[88] Gaines Post, Jr., *The Civil-Military Fabric of Weimar Foreign-Policy* (Princeton: Princeton University Press, 1973), pp. 7–8, 110–120, 161, 345–346; Bennett, *German Reparations*, pp. 16–20, 39–44; Arnold Wolfers, *Great Britain and France Between Two Wars* (New York: W. W. Norton, 1966), p. 39; Leffler, *Elusive Quest*, pp. 159–160.

[89] Gibson to Kellogg, September 10, 18, 30 and October 3, 1926, Kellogg File, GP. See also Kellogg to Gibson, April 22, 1926, FRUS, 1926, I: 85, 91, 93.

[90] Gibson to Kellogg, 11 June 1926, FRUS, 1926, I: 109–114; Jones to Wilbur, May 24,; July 13, October 10, 1926 and Jones to E. W. Eberle, August 14, 1926, PCF, JP; Rolland A. Chaput, *Disarmament in British Foreign Policy* (London: George Allen and Unwin, 1935), pp. 135–140; R. C. Richardson, *The Evolution of British Disarmament Policy in the 1920s* (London: Leicester University Press, 1989), p. 204; William F. Trimble, "The United States Navy and the Geneva Conference for the Limitation of Naval Armament, 1927," (Ph.D. diss., University of Colorado, 1974), p. 95; Jones to Wilbur, May 24, and July 13, 1926, PCF, JP; Jones to Eberle, August 14, 1926, PCF, JP. Eberle was Chief of Naval Operations. See also Richard Dean Burns, "International Arms Inspection Policies between the World Wars, 1919–1934," *The Historian* 35 (August 1969): 583–590; Fanning, *Peace and Disarmament*, pp. 43–45.

8

Beatty Takes Control

Beatty and the Naval Staff were more anxious than Coolidge for another naval arms-control conference. But unlike Coolidge, they kept secret that sense of urgency and the most important reasons for it. Since Great Britain was a member of the League of Nations, the Admiralty had no choice but to accept the Baldwin Cabinet's decision to appoint Robert Cecil to the League's Preparatory Commission to negotiate the general principles and guidelines for a world arms-control conference. This conference was intended to fulfill the pledge made by the signatories of the Versailles Treaty to work actively on world arms reductions. However, negotiating within the context of this new international organization, with its numerous participants and conflicting points of view, soon taxed the Admiralty's patience beyond endurance. The Admiralty's immediate need to limit the number of 10,000-ton, 8-inch-gun cruisers in rival navies required the quick convening of another conference, and to that end the Admiralty bent its energies in 1926 and early 1927.

By early November 1926, now desperate to induce the United States to participate in a second naval conference, Beatty invited Jones to London for an "urgent" meeting. Unlike Jones, who was without diplomatic experience or wile, Beatty had honed his skills in repeated clashes over naval budgets with Great Britain's most skillful political leaders. As Beatty shrewdly guessed, Jones interpreted Beatty's seeming agreement on a number of important issues as the basis for a new rapport, virtually ensuring a successful second conference and perhaps even blossoming into Jones' fond hope of an informal entente in which Great Britain and the United States would cooperate to maintain world peace.

Beatty had no such naïve illusions. He understood the meeting to have only one main purpose: to win Jones' support for another conference by charming him into the belief that the Admiralty guaranteed the principle of the equality in auxiliaries and was sympathetic to the Jones compromise method for negotiating relative naval strengths. He succeeded in doing this without revealing to Jones the secret British proposals which he intended to pursue at the forthcoming conference and which he knew would be quite unacceptable to the American navy. Yet Jones may not have been quite as naïve as Beatty assumed as he too may have had hidden motives for encouraging a second conference.

***

The cabinet minister selected by Prime Minister Baldwin to conduct League arms-control diplomacy was Lord Robert Cecil of Chelwood. Cecil gained his diplomatic experience during World War I when he served first as Under Secretary of State for Blockade and then in 1916 as the Cabinet Minister of Blockade. Throughout the war, he had worked closely with Foreign Secretary Sir Edward Grey to minimize President Woodrow Wilson's growing anger over British interference with American overseas neutral commerce. Cecil agreed with Grey that England had become so dependent on American war supplies that "a serious quarrel with the United States might have been fatal."[1] As the blockade had expanded and tightened, Cecil and Grey very carefully kept their responses to Wilson's increasing protests within the narrow confines of existing international law until eventually their patient diplomacy was rewarded when Germany, in early 1917, resumed unrestricted submarine warfare and the United States joined the Allies.[2] At this point, disputes over neutral trade were temporarily overshadowed by the need to win the war.

Sir Robert Cecil was a highly principled, sensitive aristocrat. His father, the third Marquis of Salisbury, served three times as prime minister, and Cecil's youth was filled with the excitement of Conservative politics, especially after his good friend and cousin Arthur Balfour also became prime minister. Both Cecil and his brother James were elected to Parliament, but Cecil became increasingly disillusioned, and for this reason in 1915, he accepted the position as Under Secretary of State for Foreign Affairs working closely with Sir Edward Grey on blockade policy.[3] Distinguished in appearance, Cecil was a strong-willed, highly moralistic independent thinker, and, his critics charged, temperamental, too sensitive to criticism, and autocratic.[4] Rather than relying on political pragmatism, Cecil insisted on acting on high principles.[5] At the end of World War I, for example, he resigned from the Cabinet over the disestablishment of the Welsh Church. Nonetheless, because he was an

---

[1] Viscount Cecil [Lord Robert Cecil], *A Great Experiment: An Autobiography* (New York: Oxford University Press, 1941), pp. 43, 41–46.
[2] Ibid., pp. 43–46.   [3] Ibid., pp. 25–39.
[4] Keith Middlemas and John Barnes, *Baldwin: A Biography* (London: Macmillan, 1970), p. 368; R. C. Richardson, *The Evolution of British Disarmament Policy in the 1920s* (London: Leicester University Press, 1989), pp. 210–211; B. J. C. McKercher, *The Second Baldwin Government and the United States, 1924–1929: Attitudes and Diplomacy* (Cambridge: Cambridge University Press, 1984), pp. 13–14.
[5] Cecil, *Great Experiment*, pp. 11–12.

experienced diplomat with high ideals, Prime Minister Lloyd George asked him to go to Paris as a British delegate to the Versailles Peace Conference, where he was given responsibility for League of Nations negotiations.[6]

The League of Nations commission, on which Cecil sat as the British delegate, was chaired by Woodrow Wilson. While these two men held different views on freedom of the seas, they were both deeply religious and highly principled and soon established a close working relationship based on their shared convictions expressed in the Covenant of the League of Nations and in the potential importance of the League as a new international form of government essential to the future of world peace. Like Wilson, Cecil had found a new mission in politics. He returned to England to work in Parliament for the acceptance of the League and to assume the chair of the popular League of Nations Union.[7]

When Stanley Baldwin returned to power as Prime Minister in 1924, he asked Cecil to accept the cabinet position as the Chancellor of the Duchy of Lancaster, working closely with Foreign Secretary Austen Chamberlain on League of Nations affairs. Earlier in that same year Franklin D. Roosevelt – the former Assistant Secretary of the Navy for eight years during the Wilson administration and now the president of the Woodrow Wilson Foundation – invited Cecil to the United States to confer upon him the first Woodrow Wilson Prize for Peace. During this visit he talked with President Calvin Coolidge and toured the United States for five weeks promoting the purpose and the importance of the League of Nations. Much later, in 1937, Cecil would be awarded the Nobel Peace Prize.[8]

Few Conservative Party leaders were as closely identified with the League and its principles as Cecil. His critics often referred to him as the "Dove of Peace," yet he was neither a pacifist nor an advocate of unilateral disarmament.[9] While World War I had turned him against the glorification of military values, he retained his abiding conviction in the need for an adequate national defense.[10] He agreed, for example, with the French demand for a trustworthy guarantee of military security before reaching agreements on arms reduction.[11] In the 1930s, Cecil would give strong support to Churchill's fight to re-arm Great Britain against the rising power of Adolf Hitler.[12] The "Dove of Peace" label arose in the mid-1920s because he took seriously

---

[6] Ibid., p. 61.   [7] Ibid., pp. 70–73, 100–104.   [8] Ibid., pp. 163, 143.

[9] Weston Shifnal to a friend, n.d. in W. S. Chalmers, *The Life and Letters of David, Earl Beatty* (London: Hodder and Stoughton, 1951), p. 412.

[10] Cecil to Maurice Hankey, August 24, 1925, Add Mss. 51088; Cecil to J. C. C. Davidson, December 30, 1927, Add Mss. 51165; Cecil to Viscount Hambleden, October 20, 1927, Add Mss. 51165, LCP.

[11] Cecil, *Great Experiment*, pp. 139–141; John Robert Ferris, *The Evolution of British Strategic Policy, 1919–1926* (London: Macmillan, 1989), pp. 46–47.

[12] Christopher Hall, *Britain, America and Arms Control* (New York: St. Martin's, 1987), p. 51.

Article 8 of the Treaty of Versailles which required that all League members must negotiate agreements on general arms reduction.[13]

Cecil soon became aware that few of the Conservative party leaders in the Baldwin Cabinet considered either the League or arms reduction as important as he did. In fact many were suspicious of any League policy which might interfere with British interests. Eventually, Cecil would enter the House of Lords to distance himself from Conservative Party pressures and politics.[14] In the meantime, his hopes for promoting the League within the Baldwin government were stymied by Austen Chamberlain, the Foreign Secretary, who insisted that he, not Cecil, must control Britain's policy at the League of Nations. To soften Cecil's disappointment, Baldwin gave him responsibility for representing Great Britain at all League arms-control negotiations.[15]

Cecil soon came to realize that the Baldwin Cabinet was even cooler towards League arms-control efforts than it was toward the League itself. With the lessons of World War I still vivid in their memories, the Cabinet was unwilling to embrace international arms control as a serious instrument of British foreign policy.[16] They were suspicious of the sweeping proposals emanating from League committees, treating them as peripheral, and at times, troublesome. The Admiralty was especially suspicious of vaguely worded arms-control principles crafted to achieve international consensus and therefore usually responded to League arms- control initiatives with cursory ad hoc positions intended primarily to safeguard British interests.[17]

Cabinet reaction to the League's arms-control proposals, which Cecil dutifully brought back from the League's headquarters at Geneva, varied widely. Prime Minister Baldwin often seemed indifferent, and Foreign Secretary Chamberlain worried over their impracticalities, while some influential Cabinet members voiced outright opposition.[18] The most consistent and outspoken critic was Sir Maurice Hankey. Secretary to the Cabinet and to the Committee of Imperial Defence, Hankey was in complete agreement with those military service and Cabinet ministers who viewed arms control and blockade restrictions as serious threats to Britain's military power and national security, arguing strenuously, for example, against the League's "Draft Treaty on the Limitation of Military, Naval, and Aerial Armaments" on the grounds that its restrictions were

---

[13] Cecil, *Great Experiment*, pp. 122–124.
[14] Ibid., pp. 141–147, 155; Richardson, *Evolution of British Disarmament Policy*, pp. 199, 201, 206; Middlemas and Barnes, *Baldwin*, 344.
[15] McKercher, *Second Baldwin Government*, p. 14; Richardson, *Evolution of British Disarmament Policy*, pp. 201–202, 206.
[16] Great Britain, *Parliamentary Debates* (Lords), vol. 69, No. 71, November 16, 1927, pp. 36–88.
[17] Ibid.; Richardson, *Evolution of British Disarmament Policy*, pp. 197–199, 201, 204.
[18] Great Britain, *Parliamentary Debates* (Lords), pp. 86–88; Richardson, *Evolution of British Disarmament Policy*, p. 199; Richard W. Fanning, *Peace and Disarmament: Naval Rivalry and Arms Control, 1922–1933* (Lexington: University Press of Kentucky, 1995), pp. 42–43.

"too rigid."[19] In order to respond to unexpected emergencies in far-off lands, he lectured Cecil, the British Empire must be "absolutely free to deal with them unhampered by international rules."[20]

Among the reasons for the Cabinet's reluctance to expend much time and effort grappling with the complexity of the League's various arms-control proposals was the Admiralty's open and vehement opposition. The Cabinet was well aware of the recent political crisis created by the Admiralty's threats of resignation over Churchill's proposed one-year delay in naval construction, and no one wanted to provoke another crisis over the Admiralty's opposition to League arms-control policies. In October 1924, for example, Beatty, Keyes and other Admiralty leaders complained that the League's "Protocol for the Settlement of International Disputes" would limit the fleet's need for complete freedom of action. More specifically, the Protocol threatened the vital right to blockade, especially as it was not clear about "a U. S. A. ship being subjected to visit and search."[21] Beatty was in fact furious with former Blockade Minister Cecil's participation in drafting the Protocol and support of it before the Cabinet. "I have fairly shaken up the Foreign Office and the First Lord," he fumed, because "our foolish representatives" [i.e., Cecil] at the League "have been agreeing to things at Geneva that would render the Navy impotent."[22]

Beatty's distrust of Cecil's enthusiasm for League arms-control proposals was shared by other suspicious Cabinet ministers. In 1925, when the League created the Preparatory Commission to formulate principles and methods for its future international arms control conference, Cecil's Cabinet opponents acted together to rein in the "Dove of Peace." They did so by creating within the Committee of Imperial Defence the Subcommittee on Reduction and Limitation of Armaments, staffing it with members sympathetic to the thinking of the three major military service branches and charging it with establishing negotiating guidelines for the British delegation to the forthcoming meeting of the Preparatory Commission in 1926. As Cecil was to head the British delegation, the Cabinet duly appointed him to chair the Subcommittee while simultaneously ensuring that he could not control it.[23]

---

[19] Hankey to Cecil, February 8, 1927, CAB 21/305, PRO; Richardson, *Evolution of British Disarmament Policy*, pp. 197–201, 204; Great Britain, *Parliamentary Debates* (Lords), pp. 86–88.

[20] See sources in *Ibid*.

[21] Beatty, Minute, October 14, 1924 and Keyes, Minute, October 11, 1924, in "Report by Director of Plans on His Visit to Geneva," September 25, 1924; "Peace Protocol: Diary of Events," ADM 1/8672/224/24, P. D. 02092/24. See also ADM 1/8659/73, G. P. (24), pp. 1–5, PRO.

[22] Beatty, "Memo"[?], October 1924, quoted in Chalmers, *Life and Letters*, p. 400.

[23] Cecil, *Great Experiment*, p. 171; Richardson, *Evolution of British Disarmament Policy*, p. 202; Ferris, *Evolution the British Strategic Policy*, pp. 10–11; Rolland A. Chaput, *Disarmament in British Foreign Policy* (London: George Allen and Unwin, 1935), p. 137; Stephen Roskill, *Naval Policy Between the Wars: The Period of the Anglo-American Antagonism, 1919–1929* (London: Collins, 1968), p. 444; "Note by Secretary of the Committee of Imperial Defence," 29 July 1925, ADM 1/8683/131/25, M 01943/25, PRO.

Like Secretary of State Kellogg and the American Navy's General Board, the majority on the CID subcommittee had little patience with vague language, broad principles, or intriguing but impractical theories of arms control. Subcommittee members wanted, instead, to examine how a particular principle or method would impact the specific combat effectiveness of a specific military service before deciding whether or not it was acceptable, and certainly before it was submitted for Cabinet consideration. They were frustrated by the current practice whereby League commissions would agree to a Treaty of Mutual Assistance or a Draft Protocol, for example, and then challenge member nations either to accept it or reject it. Instead of League-initiated proposals, they preferred, if required to do so, to advance their own principles and methods for League consideration. In late 1925, at a subcommittee meeting, Vice Admiral Sir Frederick L. Field, Deputy Chief of the Naval Staff, pointedly warned Cecil that unless the Preparatory Commission defined its military terms more precisely, there could be no possibility of agreement on any arms-control proposal.[24]

Fields' pointed criticism did not mean, as Cecil often apparently assumed, that the Admiralty was bent on opposing another arms-control conference. In fact, by mid-July 1926, after almost a full year of secretly failing to correct the 8-inch guns on its expensive new cruisers, the Admiralty abruptly yet silently changed its thinking about the usefulness of a second international naval conference. Moreover, by this time, the Naval Staff was willing to admit that replacement of worn-out ships and the maintenance of the fleet would soon require an annual budget of £80 million a year, an amount which would make it "increasingly difficult" to gain Cabinet approval.[25]

Rather than revealing its defective 8-inch gun to potential future naval enemies, or exposing itself to a wrathful Churchill, who still harbored high expectations for this expensive gun, the Naval Staff recognized the wisdom of emphasizing economic reasons for its sudden interest in another international arms limitation conference. After months of agonizing indecision, Beatty therefore finally decided to attempt to minimize this major cruiser weakness by encouraging another conference in which Great Britain would surprise the world by insisting upon the future elimination of the 8-inch gun on all British and rival warships.[26]

To ensure the success of this hidden objective, Beatty demanded that the Admiralty, not the Foreign Office, must control both the British negotiating

[24] Committee of Imperial Defence, Sub-Committee on Reduction and Limitation of Armaments, "Minutes of Meeting," November 28, 1925, ADM 1/8678/74/25, PRO.
[25] D.C.N.S. [Deputy Chief of the Naval Staff], Controller, and A.C.N.S. [Assistant Chief of the Naval Staff], "Classification and Limitation of Warships," December 21, 1926, M 03056/26, ADM 1/8699/118, PRO.
[26] Beatty forwarded these recommendations to the Board of Admiralty for its consideration. See C.N.S. [Chief of the Naval Staff] to Board in *Ibid.*

strategy and the negotiators at the next conference. It was not clear to what extent Bridgeman was made aware of the seriousness of the 8-inch gun defect, but he agreed with Beatty on the Admiralty's control of the British delegation, and in late July 1926 surprised and delighted Cecil by suddenly reassuring the "Dove of Peace" that the Admiralty was making a "reasonable effort" to arrange another conference. But, Bridgeman warned, Cecil must not reveal the Admiralty's secret initiative.[27]

The Admiralty's emphasis on reducing naval expenditures was deliberately intended to obscure its two most important conference objectives: the elimination of the 8-inch gun and – contrary to the Washington Conference principle of naval equality between the United States and Great Britain – the continuation of a clear superiority in British cruisers. Indeed, frustration with the inadequacies of the 8-inch gun were so intense by late 1926 that the Director of Gunnery Division admitted to his Naval Staff colleagues his fervent hope that the "abolition of the eight [inch] gun in cruisers" by means of an international arms-control conference "would remove this complex problem altogether."[28] Such a conference must limit individual cruiser tonnage, thereby preventing it from carrying guns beyond 6 inches.[29] Moreover, the Admiralty insisted that, as the Washington Conference had recognized the "special needs of the British Empire for an adequate number of cruisers to protect its trade routes" [i.e., a superiority in cruiser numbers], it would only negotiate a limitation of cruisers within this acknowledged context of British "special needs."[30]

The method to be employed in the negotiations was equally explicit. It rejected the total tonnage method which allowed each nation freedom, within a specified tonnage limit, to build whatever warships it needed during the life of the treaty. The Admiralty insisted that participating nations must agree to divide their warships into classes with strict limits on the exact maximum numbers, the exact maximum tonnage, and the exact maximum armament of each ship within each class. Cecil objected to the highly technical nature of these

---

[27] Bridgeman to Cecil, July 26, 1926, Add Mss. 51098, LCP.
[28] Director of Gunnery, "Investigation of the Considerations Affecting Gun Armaments and Protection of Future Cruisers," November 28, 1926, G. D. 3260/26, ADM 1/92712. This quote is located on the last page of this long memorandum.
[29] See footnote 25. A 7,500 ton 6-inch-gun cruiser was recommended in "Limitation of Armaments: Memorandum by the Sea Lords for Consideration by the Board," January 24, 1927, Corrected Copy, ADM 167/76, PRO. On June 9, 1927, the Director of Plans recommended a 6-inch-gun cruiser of between 8,000 to 7,000 tons. See D. of P. to D. C. N. S., "Geneva Conference: Outstanding Questions," June 9, 1927, P. D. 02868/27, ADM 118/3371, PRO. At the 1927 Geneva Conference, the Admiralty would reduce the weight to 6,000 tons.
[30] See especially "Limitation of Armaments: Memorandum by the Sea Lords for the Consideration of the Board," January 24, 1927, Corrected Copy, p. 6, ADM 167/76, PRO. See also Lord Cecil [?], "Limitation and Reduction of Armaments: Notes on Admiralty Policy," July 1926, Add Mss. 51098, LCP.

restrictions, but the Admiralty overrode him.[31] It cited the introduction of the Dreadnought class of battleships prior to World War I as justification for its position. Great Britain could not afford to allow rival naval powers to delay construction once again, until Great Britain had already built its fleet, only to discover that these rivals had then built larger and more powerful ships or had used all of its tonnage to build submarines.[32]

The principle reason for the Admiralty's intense dislike of the total tonnage method was the fear that rival nations could use it to build ships which could make British ships obsolete. Under the total tonnage method, the Admiralty believed, a rival nation would be encouraged to wait until Great Britain had built all of its ships within a class, whereupon the rival could build fewer but more heavily armored ships with more powerful guns and thereby "inevitably revert to the cut-throat policy of building larger and larger vessels." Thus, the "old competition in naval armaments would be revived in the worst form and the purpose of the disarmament conference negated." Despite its support by smaller naval powers the total tonnage method provided "no practicable basis for compromise" and could not achieve "any practical results" within a reasonable amount of time.[33]

Cecil agreed with the Admiralty's reasoning but was unaware of its increasingly acute sense of urgency over the necessity for an immediate naval conference.[34] While Cecil patiently went about the difficult task of promoting a general consensus on principles and methods and was willing to consider compromises on a wide variety of proposals necessary to reach such a consensus, the Admiralty contemptuously dismissed this diplomatic approach. In the Admiralty's opinion the "sole result" of attempting to divine "ideal" principles and methods of arms limitation was merely "to delay indefinitely the consideration of specific measures for the limitation of armaments of any or either kind." It was vital to continued British naval dominance to put a tight cap on the ability of rival navies to build 8-inch-gun cruisers, and to do so as soon as possible. Timing was vital. If the Admiralty could achieve a tight cap on the 10,000-ton 8-inch-gun cruiser in 1927, it would still have time to switch its 1928 building schedule to the construction of more numerous

---

[31] See footnotes 25, 28–29. For Cecil's criticisms of the Admiralty's rejection of broad disarmament principles, see Great Britain, *Parliamentary Debates* (Lords), pp. 85–88.

[32] O. M. [Sir Oswyn Murray], "Secret Memorandum Circulated to the Board as a Foreword to the Memorandum on Limitation of Armaments," January 24, 1927, ADM 167/76, PRO. Hereafter cited as O. M., "Secret Memorandum." See also Hector C. Bywater, *Navies and Nations: A Review of Naval Developments Since the Great War* (Boston and New York: Houghton Mifflin, 1927), p. 270.

[33] O.M. "Secret Memorandum," January 24, 1927, ADM 167/76, PRO. Murray was Secretary to the Board of Admiralty.

[34] Cecil to My Dear Jim, March 30, 1927, Add Mss. 51086; Lord Salisbury to My Dear Bob, April 9, 1927, Add Mss. 51086, LCP. Salisbury was Cecil's brother who agreed with Cecil that the total tonnage method was unacceptable.

6-inch-gun cruisers. Moreover, all of these cruisers must be built before it began the still more expensive process of replacing as many as fifteen capital ships during the ten-year period from 1931 to 1941. With naval building costs continuing to escalate, the British economy stagnating, and the Colwyn Committee's public criticisms still reverberating in the press, Admiralty leaders decided to intervene directly in the negotiations at the Preparatory Commission.[35]

Cecil was shocked and dismayed in April 1927, when he discovered that the Admiralty was giving "direct instructions to their representatives here [at the Preparatory Commission] ... which they expect me to obey." He complained to Foreign Secretary Austen Chamberlain that the Admiralty was conducting its own negotiations, advancing its own policies, and expecting Cecil to support them without ever consulting with him. He was especially exasperated by the persistent Admiralty refusal to consider reasonable compromises put forth by other League nations. "If anything is to be done," he complained, "it must be done exactly in their way," as these Admiralty representatives at the Preparatory Commission seemed to believe that "any concession is a sign of weakness unworthy of a Briton."[36] Cecil's brother, James, who served the Cabinet as Lord Privy Seal, and who sat on the CID Subcommittee, which he chaired in Cecil's absence, entirely agreed: "They always give the impression either that they cannot argue or that one is not worth arguing with, but that in any case they do not intend to abandon any part of their view."[37]

Cecil was deeply disturbed by what he considered to be the Admiralty's unwavering opposition to reasonable compromises.[38] He felt humiliated by the British Admirals at the Preparatory Commission who, he claimed, openly negotiated with the Americans, created the impression that they attached very little importance to the Commission's efforts, and by their actions, suggested that he did not have the confidence of the Cabinet.[39] Cecil certainly had good

---

[35] O. M., "Secret Memorandum," January 24, 1927, pp. 2–3, ADM 167/76, PRO. The Sea Lords pointed out that at the Preparatory Commission talks "a numerically strong group" of nations opposed "any attempt to limit naval armaments by classes of vessels."; "Limitation of Armaments," n.d., ADM 167/76. This memorandum for the Board of Admiralty's consideration stressed the urgent need to convene another conference as soon as possible. For many volumes on the Admiralty's careful analysis of each Preparatory Commission meeting, see "Preparatory Commission Minutes and Summaries," ADM 116/2530; ADM 116/2598 and ADM 116/3372, PRO.

[36] Cecil to Austen Chamberlain, April 6 and 12, 1927, Add Mss. 51079; Cecil to Bridgeman, November 22, 1927, Add Mss. 51099, LCP; Cecil to Austen Chamberlain, April 6, 9, and 12, 1927, Add Mss. 51079, LCP; Cecil to My Dear Jim, April 8, 1927, Add Mss. 51086, LCP.

[37] Marquis of Salisbury to My Dear Bob, April 16, 1927, Add Mss. 51086, LCP.

[38] See footnotes 35, 36; Cecil to Chamberlain, March 15, 1927, DBFP, p. 98; Cecil to Bridgeman, November 22, 1927, Add Mss. 51099; R. C. [Robert Cecil] to My Dear Jim, April 8, 1927, Add Mss. 51086, LCP.

[39] R. C. [Robert Cecil] to My Dear Willie [William Bridgeman], March 10, 1927, 4629/1/1927/22, WBP.

cause for his complaints. But he misinterpreted the Admiralty's unwillingness to confide in him as evidence of its opposition to another conference. In reality, the Admiralty had already decided that because of the pressing need to finalize its 1928 cruiser-building schedule quickly, it could not allow the Preparatory Commission the luxury of lengthy theoretical talks in the vain hope of arriving at some idealistic agreement on a universal arms-control method. Instead, the Admiralty must take the initiative to advance "those methods which proved successful at Washington – namely, the putting forward of concrete proposals by one power as a basis for discussion." If Cecil could not convince the French and the Italians to accept the Admiralty's method of naval limitation, the Admiralty was anxious to abandon the League's Preparatory Commission efforts and instead invite the United States and Japan to a three-power conference.

But the Admiralty would not reveal all of its hidden objectives, either to the Cabinet or to rival naval powers. As Hughes had not revealed the United States proposals before convening the earlier Washington Conference, Beatty and Bridgeman felt free to use the same surprise tactic. Indeed, secrecy was essential, as the Admiralty was convinced that "any leakage in regard to the proposals which this country is ready to put forward will result in the advantage to be gained being entirely lost."[40] The "advantage to be gained" was the anticipated great wave of world public approval for Great Britain's enormous cost reductions resulting from additional limitations on capital ships as well as auxiliary cruisers, destroyers, and submarines. This wave of international approval was crucial to stifle any opposition to the elimination of the 8-inch gun on all future warships. Beatty and Bridgeman were convinced that world public opinion would force American and Japanese politicians to accept their proposals or appear to their constituents, and to the world, as callous obstructionists.[41]

Public approval had been an important factor in the success of the first conference, but Admiralty assumptions about the certainty of overwhelmingly favorable public pressure on American and Japanese politicians was risky, especially as the Admiralty would demand a superiority in smaller cruisers as well as the elimination of America's new highly accurate 8-inch gun. Nonetheless, Beatty and Bridgeman had astutely read the anxieties and fears of British politicians. Rather than risk another battle with the Admiralty, Baldwin and his Cabinet concluded that it was politically safer and far less acrimonious to bow to the Admiralty's demand that it, rather than the Foreign Office, control Great Britain's negotiations at a second international naval arms-control conference.

After several months of discussions at the Geneva Preparatory Commission, Admiralty naval experts had convinced Jones that they were reasonable men

---

[40] "Limitation of Armaments," n.d., pp.1–4 ADM 167/76, PRO; O.M., "Secret Memorandum," January 24, 1927, ADM 167/76, PRO.
[41] See Chapter 10.

with whom he could arrange a "practical" method of harmonizing American limitation methods and divergent strategic needs with those of the British.[42] Throughout the summer of 1926, Jones had bluntly informed the British of the American need for auxiliary equality, especially in 10,000-ton 8-inch-gun cruisers to defend its Pacific possessions as well as to safeguard a volume of imports almost equal to that imported by Great Britain.[43] Encouraged by the responses of Admiralty representatives to his "practical" compromise, he traveled to London to explain his ideas directly to Beatty and Bridgeman. By September 10, 1926, he informed Secretary of the Navy Wilbur that he no longer saw "grave difficulty" in reconciling British and American limitation methods because the British were now "gradually seeing that their method of limitation by numbers and our method of limitation by tonnage and classes may well merge into each other in the final consideration." Indeed, a few days later he canceled a vacation to work "on harmonizing our formulae."[44]

Jones' compromise plan was based on the idea of combat equivalency. He accepted the British insistence on dividing auxiliary warships into three distinct classifications: cruisers, destroyers, and submarines. Each of these classes was limited first by the total number of tons allowed for the entire class and second by the maximum tonnage and armament of each ship within each class. To allow for some flexibility while simultaneously reducing the fear of unpleasant surprises, Jones divided the maximum tonnage limit for each class into discretionary and non-discretionary categories. Each of these two categories within each class would be assigned a percentage of the total tonnage

---

[42] Jones to Wilbur, September 10, 1926, pp. 8–9, 11, PCF, JP; Jones to E. W. Eberle, August 14, 1926, PCF, JP; Jones to Alan W. Dulles, September 13, 1926, PCF; Jones to Wilbur, July 21, 1927, Wilbur File, JP. See also Gibson to Castle, September 30, 1928, p. 6, Castle File, GP; Gibson to Castle, September 30, 1928, Castle File, GP; Gibson to Kellogg, September 16, 1926; Kellogg to Gibson, September 18, 1926, FRUS, 1926, I: 109–118.

[43] Jones to Eberle, August 14, 1926, PCF, JP; Admiralty Naval Staff [?], "Memorandum on International Limitation of Armaments sent to Mr. Hankey for Circulation to the CID," October 9, 1925, ADM 1/86/83/131. This memorandum was designated as Most Secret, and numerous members of the Naval Staff added their Minutes. It was approved by Bridgeman on October 13, 1925. See also GB, "The Situation in Great Britain," October 20, 1925, p. 3, GBM; United States Shipping Board, "Quantities and Value of the United States Exports and Imports For the Fiscal Year Ended 30 June 1925 by Deep Sea Shipping," February 20, 1926, PCF, JP; Jones to Wilbur, July 13, 1926, PCF, JP; Jones to Wilbur, September 10, 1926, pp. 11–12, PCF, JP; Jones to Alan Dulles, September 13, 1926, PCF, JP; Jones to Andrew T. Long, September 23, 1926, PCF, JP.

[44] Jones to Wilbur, September 10, 1926; Jones to Dulles, September 13, 1926, PCF, JP; Jones to Wilbur, July 21, 1927, Wilbur File, JP; Jones, "Memorandum," November 10, 1926, PCF, JP. This is Jones's memorandum detailing his talk with Beatty. See also Jones to Eberle, August 14, 1926, p. 3, PCF, JP and [Jones], "Untitled Memoir," n.d., PCF, N.D. File, JP. This is an important document in which Jones recalls his experiences on the Preparatory Commission and at the 1927 Geneva Conference. Its authenticity and accuracy is collaborated by numerous other sources cited in the study. See also Gibson to Castle, September 30, 1928, p. 6, Castle File, GP; Cecil to Chamberlain, April 8, 1927, DBFP, pp.202–203.

allotted to that class. Within the discretionary category, a nation was free to meet its unique strategic needs by building ships of varying sizes, but these ships could not exceed the agreed upon maximum limit on the size and armament for warships within that class. The percentage of ships built under the non-discretionary category, however, would be strictly limited by the treaty in size, gun, and number. Thus the non-discriminatory tonnage category acted to reduce the risk of sudden surprises, such as the earlier introduction of the German Dreadnought battleships, by ensuring that each nation would be required to build a fixed percentage of its ships with similar combat capabilities and in exactly the same numbers.[45] As Jones was by now convinced that the British would have little difficulty in translating his compromise method into reliable numbers, he eagerly responded to Beatty's "urgent" invitation to meet in London.[46]

On November 8, 1926, two days before Jones arrived in London, Captain W. A. Egerton, the Admiralty's Director of Plans, recorded the motives behind Beatty's two urgent telegrams beckoning Jones back to London. Egerton sought to bolster the Admiralty Naval Staff's sagging morale with the reassurance that "as a result of the conference on Limitation of Armaments *to be held shortly*, a further limitation in the maximum [cruiser] tonnage will be made in conjunction with a *smaller maximum caliber of gun*." [Emphasis mine.] Egerton's revelation left no doubt that the purpose of the Admiralty's invitation to Jones was to win his support for a second conference in which the Admiralty intended to minimize the combat vulnerabilities of its latest cruisers.[47] This secrecy left diplomats, both British and American – including Cecil, Chamberlain, and Gibson – completely in the dark as to the Admiralty's most important objectives. It also gave Beatty the freedom to fire up the diplomatically

---

[45] Jones, "Memorandum," February 21, 1927, PCF, JP. This memorandum is the most complete explanation of Jones's compromise plan. In 1926 he wrote of his efforts at "harmonizing" the differing methods of limitation by tonnage and by numbers without providing much detail. It was not until February 1927 that Jones offered a much more refined and elaborate exposition of his earlier thinking.

[46] Jones to Captain Adolphus Andrews, April 19, 1927, JP; Jones, "Memorandum," November 10, 1926, PCF, JP. Jones made it explicitly clear to Beatty that all of the future United States cruisers would be of 10,000 tons. He had earlier repeatedly rejected Admiralty pressure to adopt the 6-inch gun rather than the 8-inch gun on these cruisers. See also Jones to Wilbur, July 21, 1927, Wilbur File, JP and Jones to Eberle, August 14, 1926, p. 3, PCF, JP; Jones to Admiral W.V. Pratt, February 1, 1926, PCF, JP; Gibson to Castle, September 30, 1928, Castle File, GP.

[47] Jones, "Untitled Memoir," n.d., p. 4, PCF, N.D. File, JP. Jones apparently wrote this working draft soon after the 1927 Conference failed. It contains valuable details not found elsewhere. See also Jones, "Memorandum," November 10, 1926, PCF, JP. Hereafter cited as Jones, "Memorandum." For Egerton's quotation see W. A. Egerton, "Minute," November 8, 1926, Minute Sheet No. 10–11 in Directory of Gunnery, "Investigation of the Considerations Affecting Gun Armaments and Protection of Future Cruisers," October 28, 1926, P.D. 3206/26, ADM 1/92712, PRO. For Cecil's objection to secrecy, see Cecil, "Memorandum," September 24, 1926, in *DBFP*, p. 397.

inexperienced and decidedly Anglophile Jones with the false hope that his American compromise method had real promise as a basis for reconciling their differing limitation approaches at a second international conference.

The negotiating styles as well as the priorities of the two naval leaders were quite different. Jones was a plainspoken sailor without much political or diplomatic experience who stated his views with often unguarded clarity. "I have been very persistent," he reported to his friend and Chief of Naval Operations Admiral Edward W. Eberle, "in stating to our British friends that ... a thoroughly open and above board spirit, keeping nothing up our sleeves ... should govern [the negotiations and thereby] arrive at acceptable results." The British, Jones had been led to believe, had "adopted the same attitude." Indeed Jones' fondest hope was that a second conference would have far greater ramifications than merely limiting auxiliary warships. Only eight months earlier he had confided to his friend Admiral William V. Pratt that Great Britain's unwillingness to accept naval equality was the only obstacle to an informal yet "real entente" between the two "Anglo-Saxon civilizations." As naval equals, the two nations could finally evolve policies enabling them to "march in international relations shoulder to shoulder" in defense of the "civilization and ideals handed down to us through the generations of the race."[48]

Earlier, in 1921, Beatty had expressed a vague hope for "a union between the English-speaking nations of the world."[49] But, this thought was far from his purpose in calling Jones to London.[50] Since that time, Beatty had acquired a much higher level of political and diplomatic sophistication. Fashioning finely nuanced distinctions which softened or even evaded underlying purposes were skills which Beatty had honed at the cabinet level of British politics in debates with Churchill and Ramsay MacDonald and, to a lesser extent, during the many months of negotiations at the Washington Conference in 1921–1922. Much to Jones' later chagrin, Beatty now made good use of these skills to accomplish his hidden objectives.

Beatty immediately reassured Jones of exactly what Jones most needed to hear before he could recommend another conference to Coolidge: "that there could be no question between the two countries as to general policies, and that they [the British] would bring up no question as to our [United States] equality in naval armaments." When Jones asked Beatty if naval equality meant that Great Britain accepted the extension of the 10:10 ratio to auxiliaries,

---

[48] Jones to Eberle, March 17, 1927, JP. Gibson agreed. See Gibson to Kellogg, September 16, 1926, *FRUS*, 1926, I: 109–114.

[49] Jones to Pratt, February 1, 1926, PCF, JP. For Beatty's profession of equality, see ADM 116/667/5846, PRO and Norman Gibbs, "The Naval Conferences of the Interwar Years: A Study in Anglo-American Relations," *Naval War College Review*, 30 (Summer, 1977), p. 51.

[50] See Chapter 5.

Beatty Takes Control

Beatty reassured him that "there would [also] be no question raised as to our [United States] right to equality in all categories of warships."[51]

Beatty's repeated assurances of equality assuaged Jones' initial worry. He further reassured Jones by dismissing as "intolerable" any suggestion of modifying the Washington Conference Five-Power Treaty limiting the tonnage and armaments of capital ships, thus allaying one of the General Board's greatest worries. Indeed, Jones immediately reported to Secretary of State Kellogg, that Beatty was "very insistent" that no changes could be permitted until after the expiration of the Treaty. Taking Beatty at his word, Jones believed this promise ensured that they would avoid the complex problems already agreed upon at the Washington Conference and therefore allow the second conference to concentrate exclusively on extending the 10:10:6 ratio to cruisers, destroyers, and submarines.[52]

Once he had established a friendly and agreeable rapport, Beatty skillfully proposed the manner in which equality in auxiliary cruisers would be realized. He began by reiterating what Jones had heard from the Admiralty's naval representatives at the Preparatory Commission: that as an island nation dependent upon overseas sources of supply for its very survival, Great Britain was justified in requiring a larger number of cruisers to protect its worldwide trade routes and lines of communication. But, he hastened to add, that need did not preclude equality in cruisers. By way of illustration, he casually suggested that if the United States determined that it needed 200 cruisers, Great Britain would not object but would merely claim the right to build the same number.[53] Thus, Beatty cleverly intimated that, to his way of thinking, equality could only be achieved if the United States was willing to match the number needed by Great Britain, not by a treaty arbitrarily restricting the number required for British security. What he deliberately left out of his illustration was the number and characteristics of cruisers which Great Britain would propose.

Jones should obviously have pressed Beatty for some idea of cruiser numbers and combat characteristics, but he failed to do so. The fact that both of these knowledgeable naval leaders neglected these questions was important. Several considerations may account for Jones's failure. Beatty had promised not to alter the Five-Power Treaty which already established maximum cruiser combat characteristics. Moreover, only four years earlier at the Washington Conference, Beatty had agreed to Britain's need for only fifty cruisers. Jones may also have relied on the fact that Cecil had earlier reassured Gibson, albeit erroneously, that the Admiralty was in favor of "a considerable eventual reduction" in the number of its cruisers. Thus, when Beatty "seemed to agree," that his compromise method could become the basis for a successful negotiation, Jones

---

[51] Jones, "Memorandum," November 10, 1926.   [52] Ibid., p. 2.   [53] Ibid., p. 1.

took this to mean that Beatty was encouraging him to develop his combat equivalency plan in greater detail.[54]

More immediately worrisome to Jones was Beatty's surprise proposal to cut naval costs by reducing the maximum size of capital ships and cruisers, a major change to the Five-Power Treaty which Beatty had only minutes earlier promised not to alter. Cecil had raised this same suggestion in September, but Gibson had refused to respond as the General Board was adamantly opposed.[55] Jones carefully explained to Beatty the reasons why the United States was firmly opposed to this alteration of the Five-Power Treaty. He emphasized the need for increased armor protection against air and submarine attacks which could only be achieved with battleships of 35,000 tons and cruisers of 10,000 tons. Unknown to Jones, the Admiralty's Naval Staff had reached the same conclusion and for exactly the same reasons.[56]

In his earnest efforts to dissuade Beatty with reasons for American opposition to reopening the tonnage limits on capital ships and cruisers, Jones may have revealed more information than was wise. He felt compelled to explain candidly and "in detail why we required certain characteristics in all of our units."[57] Jones' "open and above board" diplomacy gave Beatty a welcome source of intelligence, quite possibly about the number and reliability of the new 8-inch guns to be placed on future American auxiliary cruisers.[58] Such candor was in keeping with Jones' great desire to establish a deeper more trusting relationship with the British Navy and the great importance which he placed upon avoiding the troubling misunderstandings that would poison such a relationship in later years, as the gun elevation and fuel conversion controversies had so recently threatened.[59]

When Beatty avoided discussion of the Jones compromise limitation ideas, and merely promised to have them studied, Jones should have become much more acutely aware of Beatty's evasive tactics. Jones had been explaining his ideas to Vice Admiral Aubrey Smith and to other Admiralty representatives at the Preparatory Commission for several months, and Beatty was therefore doubtlessly well briefed on them.[60] When Jones explained the nature of this

---

[54] *Ibid*. Also see Gibson to Kellogg, September 30, 1926, KF, GP.
[55] Gibson to Kellogg, September 30, 1926, KF, GP.
[56] Jones, "Memorandum," November 10, 1926, p. 3; Naval Staff, "Limitation of Armament: New Draft," November 9, 1925, p. 5, ADM 1/8683/131, PRO.
[57] Jones, "Untitled Memoir," n.d., p. 5, PCF, N. D. File, JP.
[58] Director of Gunnery, "Investigation of the Considerations Affecting Gun Armaments and Protection of Future Cruisers," October 28, 1926, Minute Sheet 11, G. D. 3260/26, ADM 1/92712, PRO.
[59] Jones to Eberle, 17 March 1927, JP. See also Gibson to Castle, September 30, 1928, p. 7, Castle File, GP. Gibson agreed about the importance of candor and was later bitterly critical of the British delegates both at the Preparatory Commission and later at the Geneva Conference in 1927 for their lack of candor.
[60] See footnotes 42–44.

compromise to Beatty, he stressed that it was intended to limit "the percentage of maximum tonnage units" – i.e., 10,000-ton, 8-inch-gun cruisers "in order to reconcile the English preference for specific size, armament and numbers in a class with the American preference for total tonnage." He was convinced that his compromise would bridge the differences between their two methods and offered the best hope for success at a second conference, especially as the non-discretionary category would allow the Admiralty to build the larger number of smaller cruisers it repeatedly demanded. Yet Beatty again skillfully eluded any definite response when he "seemed to agree" but only promised to study the compromise. Thus, Jones made a serious mistake by not eliciting a more definite response from Beatty, both about the concept of auxiliary combat equivalency and about the number and combat characteristics of the cruisers that Britain would require – before he recommended that Coolidge call another conference.[61]

Immediately following his meeting with Beatty, while the details of the meeting were still fresh in his mind, Jones went directly to the American Embassy to write a long memorandum to Secretary of State Kellogg. Jones revealed his lack of experience as a diplomat and his susceptibility to Beatty's skillful evasions by reassuring Kellogg that the discussion with Beatty had been "very open and frank with no beating around the bush or jockeying for position."[62] Jones' underestimation of Beatty arose in part from his lack of diplomatic experience, but also from his desire to pave the way for a closer relationship between the two countries. Almost equally naïve was his further assurance to Kellogg that Beatty had "made no suggestion as to a necessary predominance of British Sea power."[63] He accepted Beatty's word as a fellow naval officer and gentleman, stressing to Kellogg Great Britain's unqualified endorsement of the Washington ratio for all categories of American and British vessels.[64]

Beatty was unfazed by his evasions. He was determined to maintain British naval superiority and thereby ensure the successful defense of the British Empire against all political and military adversaries. By keeping his motives and proposals secret until the conference actually began, he counted on world public approval of the Admiralty's proposals, coupled with the continued desire of American politicians for cutting naval expenses, to generate the intense political pressure needed to induce American compliance and thereby put even greater pressure on the Japanese politicians to follow suit. He believed that Hughes had proven the success of this strategy at the Washington Conference in 1921–1922. This time, however, Beatty would set the agenda and spring the surprises, and this time the politicians would bow to his demands.

---

[61] Jones, "Memorandum," November 10, 1926, p. 3.
[62] Ibid.   [63] Ibid.   [64] Ibid.

Jones may also have had his own secret reasons for recommending America's participation in another conference. It is likely that Jones believed that the American navy had everything to gain and nothing to lose by participating, especially as Beatty had already pledged that the new treaty would concede America's right to equality in auxiliary vessels. Congress had authorized so few new cruisers since the Washington Conference that the United States Navy stood to benefit whether the conference succeeded or failed. On the one hand, if the conference limited cruiser numbers, this could stop the current United States trend of falling farther and farther behind rival navies, while perhaps providing some time to catch up. If, on the other hand, Great Britain demanded too many cruisers and thus caused the conference to fail, angered congressional champions of a stronger American navy – with renewed evidence of a continued British threat to American neutral rights on the high seas – could more effectively bring pressure on Coolidge for an expanded cruiser-building program. With either result, the American navy could benefit substantially.

9

Combat Equivalency

Jones returned to Washington, DC to develop a more expansive version of his combat equivalency compromise that would grant Great Britain an even larger number of less powerful cruisers in return for a smaller number of more powerful American cruisers. His more elaborate and flexible scheme emphasized approximate combat equivalency in all three classes of auxiliaries. Not surprisingly, the General Board questioned his optimism and rejected his plan.

His disappointment was compounded when he returned to London in March 1927. Four months after having first outlined his initial equivalency plan to Beatty, the Admiralty's evasiveness and unwillingness to discuss his ideas caused him considerable unease. Based, in part, on his recommendation, Coolidge had already issued his call for another international naval conference. Jones therefore alerted the General Board to the likelihood of difficult negotiations.

Coolidge's acceptance of combat equivalency as an alternative to the General Board's insistence on mathematical equality created several problems for Secretary of State Kellogg. Kellogg was well aware of the General Board's distrust of Admiralty negotiating tactics, and its opposition to the idea of combat equivalency in auxiliaries. It was equally clear to him that Congress would not consent to build up to the sixty-four cruisers in the British fleet, but would nonetheless insist on an agreement guaranteeing the treaty right to equality. Moreover, after Coolidge had invited the five Washington Treaty powers to a second conference, the British unexpectedly insisted on the right to modify the principles of naval limitation agreed upon at Washington in "important ways." Faced with these difficult obstacles and equally difficult uncertainties, Kellogg admitted to Secretary of the Navy Curtis Wilbur that British demands for a larger number of cruisers than Congress was likely to authorize necessitated the adoption of a negotiating strategy which might well have "certain disadvantages" for the United States Navy.[1]

***

By the time Jones returned to the United States in November 1926, after several months of talks at the Preparatory Commission, he believed that he was thoroughly familiar with the differing strategic needs as well as the differing limitation methods proposed by the five major naval powers. These talks had clearly outlined the differences between the American and Japanese preference for total tonnage and the British insistence on a method specifically restricting the maximum tonnage, gun-caliber, and number of ships within each class. Following his encouraging meeting with Beatty, he had convinced himself that his equivalency approach would provide the practical breakthrough needed to reconcile the much wider variety of purposes, sizes, and gun power which characterized auxiliary vessels, especially cruisers, and which made limiting them much more difficult than capital ships, whose tonnage more closely correlated with gun size and armament.[2]

After his November meeting with Beatty, Jones realized that his original equivalency plan might not be flexible enough to satisfy the Admiralty.[3] He decided therefore to expand it by devising a carefully crafted alternative which might overcome the General Board's insistence upon exact mathematical equality, a plan requiring a reasonable approximation of combat equivalency, most particularly in the cruiser class where the greatest disparities and disagreements were likely to arise.[4]

Fundamental to his expanded combat equivalency formula were several crucial assumptions. Perhaps most fundamental was his conviction, one shared by many leaders in Great Britain and the United States, that war between these two democratic nations was so remote as to be all but unthinkable.[5] Having agreed on the importance of this crucial assumption, Jones and Gibson acknowledged the generally accepted consensus that there was no "scientifically accurate method of establishing exact" equality, especially not in the difficult category of auxiliary warships, which varied widely in function and therefore in tonnage and armament.[6] Jones' equivalency approach assumed, as well, that Great Britain and Japan would honor the principles which the five major naval powers had already agreed to at the Washington Conference, a negotiating condition which Beatty had already acknowledged in their November meeting.[7]

---

[1] Jones, "Memorandum," November 10, 1926, p. 3, PCF, JP; Kellogg to Wilbur, March 23, 1927, GBDCS V: 4 Miscellaneous Papers, RG 80, NA.
[2] See Chapter 8.   [3] Jones, "Memorandum," November 10, 1926, p. 1.
[4] See footnote 11 and Allen Dulles to Gibson, August 31, 1927, Dulles File, GP.
[5] Gibson to Castle, September 30, 1928, pp. 5–6, Castle File, GP; Jones to W. V. Pratt, February 1, 1926, PCF, JP; Howard to Chamberlain, July 29, 1927, DBFP, pp. 708–709; Castle, Diary, July 10, 1927, CP.
[6] Gibson to Castle, September 30, 1928, pp. 5–6, Castle File, GP; Jones to Eberle, March 17, 1927, JP.
[7] Jones, "Memorandum," 10 November 1926, p. 1.

Combat Equivalency   157

The Five-Power Treaty had approved cruisers of 10,000 tons and 8-inch guns, a maximum limit which Great Britain had honored in building its newest cruisers.[8] Moreover, Jones had repeatedly explained to Admiralty representatives in Geneva and to Beatty in London that the United States' strategic weakness in naval bases in the Western Pacific required it to build 10,000-ton cruisers to achieve maximum steaming radius. For these reasons, he had repeatedly warned the British that the General Board would not agree to severe restrictions on these larger cruisers or agree to build smaller 6-inch-gun cruisers with less steaming radius.[9] Since Jones knew that Admiralty leaders were well aware of these facts and yet still enthusiastically pushed for a second naval conference, he assumed, further, that they were open to some form of compromise.

He believed that the key to success depended upon a secret, informal agreement with the Admiralty to accept his combat equivalency method as the basis for negotiations prior to the opening of the conference. Since Japan appeared to be especially anxious for further limitation, and had called for a three-power conference, Jones apparently believed that the Japanese would immediately recognize that his alternative method allowing for a greater number of smaller cruisers would be as advantageous to Japan as it was to Great Britain. A greater Japanese defense capability did not alarm Jones because – as the United States had no intention of attacking Japan – the likelihood of war with Japan would not arise unless Japan first attacked American possessions in the Pacific. Moreover, Jones' surreptitious attempts to get prior British approval of his method strongly suggests that he hoped to confront Japan with a united Anglo-American front, leaving Japan little choice but to accept his combat equivalency plan as the basis for negotiation, or to bear the brunt of world disapproval for a failed conference. What Jones was unaware of was the fact that Beatty was actively preparing for a British naval war against Japan in its home waters and would not countenance a compromise which could actually increase the number of Japan's cruisers.

The greatest immediate difficulty confronting Jones was how to justify a superiority of British cruisers to the General Board, which had already rejected British claims to superiority on the basis that American overseas trade was equal to Great Britain's.[10] His task was complicated by the fact that cruisers performed widely varying functions as fighting ships of the main fleet, scouts, escorts, commerce raiders, and submarine chasers. Cruisers, therefore, ranged from 10,000 tons to less than 3,000 tons, and even as low as 600 tons, thus making it much more difficult to measure combat equivalency based primarily on individual ship tonnage alone.[11] In an effort to overcome these difficulties,

---

[8] See Chapter 5.   [9] See Chapter 8.
[10] H. A. Wiley, SMP, GB to Secretary of the Navy, April 25, 1927, pp. 6–8, GB 438, GBR, RG 80, NA.
[11] Jones, "Memorandum," February 21, 1927, PCF 1927, JP. See also Allen Dulles to Gibson, August 31, 1927, Dulles File, GP. Jones left untitled his February 21, 1927, working copy of his

Jones proposed to the General Board three different alternatives by which a reasonable equivalency might be achieved.[12]

His first equivalency alternative was a slight variation on the total tonnage method which France, Italy, Japan, and the United States had favored at the Preparatory Commission, but which Great Britain had rejected. This method, strongly favored by the General Board, merely limited the total tonnage of a class, thus giving each nation complete freedom to determine the size and number of ships that could be built within that tonnage limit. Since the British currently had sixty-four cruisers totaling 387,410 tons, Jones assumed, for purposes of illustration, that the British would want at least sixty cruisers of the latest design, and a total tonnage limit of 400,000 tons, an increase of ten cruisers beyond the fifty which Beatty and Lord Balfour had indicated that Great Britain required at the Washington Conference four years earlier.[13]

Jones' second alternative was closer to his original method proposed to Aubrey Smith at the Preparatory Commission discussions in Geneva and to Beatty in London. It featured discretionary and non-discretionary categories. Once again, for the purposes of illustration, Jones assumed a British need for sixty cruisers and a total cruiser limit of 400,000 tons. In the non-discretionary category, he suggested restricting the maximum cruiser size to between 10,000 and 8,000 tons, the maximum gun-size to 8 inches, and the maximum number of these larger cruisers to 50 percent of the total cruiser tonnage for this class, or 200,000 tons. The number of ships would, therefore, vary from twenty 10,000-ton, 8-inch-gun cruisers to as many as twenty-five British ships if all were limited to 8,000 tons (totaling 200,000 tons). The remaining 200,000 tons would fall under the discretionary category, which would allow the British to build, for example, an additional forty 5,000-ton, 6-inch-gun cruisers – a tonnage which Lord Cecil had informed Gibson was the cruiser size which the Admiralty believed would cut costs and increase numbers most efficiently.[14]

---

combat equivalency plan. I have described it in this footnote as a "Memorandum," and it hereafter will be cited as such.

[12] *Ibid.*

[13] Churchill, "Cabinet Memorandum: Cruiser Programmes, 1927–1928," November 6, 1927, in Winston S. Churchill, *Winston S. Churchill: The Exchequer Years 1922–1929, Companion Volume 5*, ed. Martin Gilbert (London: Wm. Heinemann, 1979), 5: 1093, 1089–1095; CAB 4/16/815B, 6 July 1927, PRO; Hector C. Bywater, "Bywater Castigates British Government," *Baltimore Sun*, July 26, 1927, CCP. For a different interpretation see Christopher Hall, *Britain, America and Arms Control, 1921–1937* (New York: St. Martin, 1987), p. 42; Stephen Roskill, *Naval Policy Between The Wars: The Period of Anglo-American Antagonism, 1919–1929* (London: Collins, 1968), p. 508.

[14] Jones, "Memorandum," February 21, 1927, pp. 5–6; Jones to Secretary of the Navy, January 11, 1926, GB 420–2, GBUSN, RG 80, NA. At the Geneva Conference Gibson cited the tonnage authorized by Parliament in 1925 as the total tonnage required by Great Britain and on which the United States had based its calculation of British needs. See "Informal Meeting of Delegates, Wednesday, August 3 at 10:00 P.M.," Ex. 110.1, 1927, Box 439, RG 43, NA.

The third alternative awarded a "discount" to a nation willing to build smaller cruisers with 6-inch guns. The discount allowed a tonnage "credit" by evaluating these smaller ships at less than their actual tonnage, thus allowing a larger number of ships in this class to be built. As Jones explained it, "the tonnage of such smaller cruisers, with guns smaller than the maximum size, would be evaluated at less than full [tonnage] value in computing the allowed [total] tonnage" for that class. By building smaller ships only capable of mounting shorter-range guns, a nation could earn additional total tonnage and significantly increase the number of ships it could build in that class.

Jones was intrigued with the flexibility of this third alternative. It allowed the United States to build all of its 400,000 tons in 10,000-ton, 8-inch-gun cruisers, while meeting the British demand for a significantly larger number of cruisers with smaller guns. On the one hand, if the United States used all of its 400,000-ton limit to build forty 10,000-ton, 8-inch-gun cruisers – a highly unlikely event given congressional parsimony – it could not be entitled to any discount and would be limited to forty cruisers. On the other hand, Jones explained, if the British built only twenty 10,000-ton, 8-inch-gun cruisers and ten 7,500-ton, 6-inch-gun cruisers to equal the American Omaha class, Britain could build the remaining tonnage in 4,000-ton, 6-inch-gun cruisers, and, with the discount, actually construct fifty of these ships for a total cruiser force of eighty ships constituting 475,000 tons – compared to forty American cruisers totaling 400,000 tons. Jones considered this to be well above the 450,000-ton limitation which Lord Balfour and Beatty had indicated at the Washington Conference or the 458,000 tons authorized by Parliament in the 1925 Birkenhead five-year building program. Even in the unlikely event of a war between them, the British would have eighty cruisers to the American forty. One might argue, therefore, that this great numerical superiority in Britain's faster firing 6-inch-gun cruisers virtually ensured that the British would be at least a match against the Americans, especially at ranges where cruiser gunfire was most effective and where a 6-inch shell could penetrate the armor of a 10,000-ton, 8-inch-gun cruiser.

Jones was open, as well, to differing British alternatives. He did not expect that the three he outlined would remain unchanged at the negotiating table. He fully expected that the British and the Japanese would bargain for combinations even more suitable to their needs. Nonetheless, he remained firmly convinced that "a combination of these applications ... if properly applied, will produce a method that will bring about a positive reduction and limitation of armaments that will allay all suspicion and doubt during the life of any agreement."[15]

---

[15] Jones, "Memorandum," February 21, 1927, PCF, 1927, JP; GB, "Memorandum: Study No. 4," June 2, 1927, PP, Foreign Affairs Disarmament Series, HHPL; Jones to Adolphus Andrews, April 19, 1927, JP.

Jones' optimism and diligence had a profound impact on Gibson. The two men had worked closely and harmoniously together for months at the Preparatory Commission, and Gibson had developed the highest respect for the naval expertise of his fellow delegate.[16] While Jones put his naval staff to work on the details of his three revised combat equivalency alternatives before placing them for consideration before the General Board, Gibson took the initiative for winning over Coolidge and Kellogg. The president was eager for another conference, but Secretary of State Kellogg was much more skeptical. Gibson was able nonetheless to present them with an intriguing diplomatic scenario.[17]

Both Lord Cecil and Foreign Minister Chamberlain had assured Gibson that if the United States was willing to allow the Admiralty an undetermined yet larger number of cruisers, the prospects for a limitation agreement, based on the principle of equality, were encouraging.[18]

Gibson relayed this message to Coolidge who trusted Gibson's judgment and therefore welcomed his enthusiastic reassurances. Even Assistant Secretary of State William Castle, who was skeptical of arms control and quick to criticize shortcomings in his fellow diplomats, was impressed with Gibson's presentations. "It is always pleasant to see Hugh Gibson's cheerful face," he noted, and to know that not only had Gibson put both "sanity and humor" into the Preparatory Commission talks, but had also conducted the tricky arms control negotiations "in such a manner as to bring the United States out with flying colors as the leader in plans for real disarmament."[19]

By the middle of January 1927, Coolidge and Gibson were engaged in extensive, highly detailed, yet unrecorded working sessions. As these discussions progressed, Gibson's respect for Coolidge climbed steadily. He was pleased to discover that the president had followed the Preparatory Commission talks closely, had a "clear idea of our problems," and was willing to "put in as much work as may be necessary" in order to "get something accomplished."[20] Coolidge was likewise impressed with Gibson. Within weeks he elevated Gibson to be Ambassador to Belgium, which Gibson considered an "ideal post," as he was already immensely popular in Belgium for his relief work with his good friend Herbert Hoover during World War I, and because he was married to a Belgian. More important, this post would enable him to devote a good deal of his time to a variety of forthcoming international arms

---

[16] Gibson to Kellogg, September 30, 1926, pp. 5, 13–14, Kellogg File, GP; Cecil, "Memorandum," September 24, 1926, *DBFP*, pp. 396–397.
[17] Gibson to Kellogg, September 30, 1926, Kellogg File, GP.
[18] *Ibid.*; Jones to Kellogg, September 10, 1926, PCF, JP. Jones was optimistic prior to his meeting with Beatty on November 10, 1926, and even more so following this meeting. For Beatty's encouragement see Jones to Kellogg, November 10, 1926, PCF, JP.
[19] Castle, Diary, January 5, 1927, CP.
[20] Gibson to Mother, January 13, 1927, HHPL. Gibson observed that Coolidge "*can* talk when he wants to." [Emphasis his.]

control conferences in which he was intensely interested and to which Coolidge intended to designate him as the American representative.[21]

Secretary of State Kellogg was initially far less convinced of the prospects for another conference's success than either Coolidge or Gibson. As the former Ambassador to Great Britain, Kellogg may have been more wary of what might lie behind the charming words and manners of British diplomats. He had recently been struggling with the continuing strain in Anglo-American relations over the fuel oil modernization and the elevation of guns on American battleships, the bitter exchanges over blockade claims, and his unwillingness to be drawn into British retaliatory schemes against the boycott of foreign goods by Chiang Kai-shek and the Kuomintang in China.[22]

Kellogg's caution may also have stemmed from the skepticism voiced by Assistant Secretary of State Castle and by the American Ambassador to Great Britain, Alanson Houghton.[23] While Castle was very favorably impressed with Gibson's diplomatic skills, he nonetheless refused to take Gibson and Jones' assurances of British intentions at face value. He suspected that professions of interest in another naval conference were nothing more than a public relations ploy by unnamed "insincere and militaristic" nations, which wanted to reap public approval, but who would then subtly block any progress while making the United States "the goat." Houghton was equally skeptical. He reiterated his earlier warning that the Admiralty had no intention of granting naval equality in auxiliary ships and would actually become furious if the United States ever attempted to keep pace with British naval building.[24]

However, more than reassurances from Gibson and Jones lay behind Coolidge's decision to call another conference. In December 1926, Coolidge had sent a message to Congress defending his cuts in defense spending in which he castigated his critics as adherents of a "cult of disparagement."[25] Coolidge was well aware that since 1923, Congress had inserted clauses in naval appropriations bills to express repeatedly its desire for another conference to end the naval race in cruisers and to limit all auxiliaries. But, by 1927, the alarming acceleration in cruiser building by Great Britain and Japan, and the increasingly evident American inferiority in these ships had convinced Congress to rectify this deficiency to some degree.[26] In early January, as his talks with Gibson

---

[21] Gibson to Mother, February 4, 1927, HHPL. See also Belgium Appointment File, GP.
[22] Kellogg to Houghton, May 2, 1927, MC 25, KP; Esme Howard to Chamberlain, March 10, 1927, *DBFP*, pp. 581–583; Castle, Diary, January 5, 1927; Castle to Houghton, January 7, 1926, England File, CP; Richard W. Fanning, *Peace and Disarmament: Naval Rivalry and Arms Control, 1922–1933* (Lexington: University Press of Kentucky, 1995), p. 47.
[23] Castle, Diary, January 5, 1927, CP; Castle to Houghton, January 7, 1926, England File, CP.
[24] Houghton to Castle, February 16, 1926, England File; Castle, Diary, January 4, 1927, CP.
[25] "Message of the President of the United States," December 7, 1926, *FRUS*, 1926, I: xxiii–xxviii.
[26] Philip T. Rosen, "The Treaty Navy, 1919–1937," in *In Peace and War: Interpretations of American Naval History, 1775–1984*, ed. Kenneth J. Hagan (Westport, CT: Greenwood, 1978), pp. 225–226; Fanning, *Peace and Disarmament*, pp. 35–37.

began, Coolidge had stopped Congress from funding three cruisers which it had authorized in 1924. He succeeded in preventing funding in the House of Representatives, where his Republicans had a fifty-vote majority, yet won by only two votes. When the Senate disregarded his opposition by approving the construction by a two-to-one margin on January 24, 1927, the House quickly reversed course, and to avoid continuous intra-party squabbling, Coolidge signed the cruiser bill into law.[27] Under pressure from Congress to build more cruisers, Coolidge secured unanimous approval from his Cabinet on February 1, 1927 and on February 10 issued his formal invitation to the five naval powers that had ratified the Washington Conference treaties to attend a second naval conference limiting auxiliary ships.[28]

Before returning to Geneva for the second round of the Preparatory Commission talks, Gibson spent weeks in secret unrecorded meetings with Coolidge, Kellogg, and Secretary of the Navy Curtis Wilbur.[29] Kellogg now paid much closer attention to Gibson's presentations, so much so that the more skeptical Assistant Secretary of State, Castle, may have become somewhat envious and thus complained: "the only person for whose advice he [Kellogg] cares anything at all is Hugh Gibson, and that is only because Hugh is new."[30] In retrospect, Kellogg's own skepticism may well have been almost equal to Castle's. But for now, Kellogg dutifully accepted Coolidge's decision that the British demand for superiority in the number of cruisers could be reconciled in ways which were worth some risks.[31]

In return for a treaty limiting auxiliaries, Coolidge and Kellogg were willing to give the British a superiority in the number of cruisers. Thus, Kellogg informed Secretary of the Navy Wilbur that the exact number of ships must consequently be a "variable," dependent "for the time being [on] the national needs of the British."[32] Allowing the British the number of ships it needed, Kellogg claimed, was justified as a means of realizing the higher political goal of ending international competitive naval building and thereby dampening "the spirit of suspicion and hostility to which it gives rise and the obvious opportunity it offers to jingoes in each country to accuse the other countries of hostile designs."[33]

---

[27] Fanning, *Peace and Disarmament*, pp. 36–37; Howard to Chamberlain, March 10, 1927, DBFP, pp. 581–583.
[28] Fanning, *Peace and Disarmament*, p. 47; Castle, Diary, January 15, and March 9, 1927, CP.
[29] Gibson to Mother, January 13 and 31, 1927; February 4, 10, and 11, 1927, HHPL.
[30] Castle, Diary, January 25, 1927, CP.
[31] Kellogg to Wilbur, "Memorandum," March 23, 1927, GBDCS V: 4, Miscellaneous Papers, RG 80, NA.
[32] *Ibid.* See also Kellogg to Herrick, February 3, 1927, *FRUS*, 1927, I: 9; Joseph C. Grew, "Memorandum by the Undersecretary of State," February 24, 1927, *FRUS*, 1927, I: 22–23. Herrick was Ambassador to France.
[33] Kellogg to Wilbur, "Memorandum," March 23, 1927.

The still secret willingness of Coolidge and Kellogg to allow the British to keep all of its existing sixty-four cruisers, rather than reducing this number, was a crucial concession, which scholars have overlooked. Kellogg informed Wilbur that should the British want to retain all of their sixty-four cruisers, the United States would accept their current total tonnage of 387,410 tons as the cruiser limit at the conference.[34] These sixty-four cruisers were fourteen more than the fifty that Beatty had stated was the Admiralty requirement at the Washington Conference and, though still unknown to the Americans, only six less than the more recent, highly secret Admiralty goal of seventy cruisers needed for the anticipated war against Japan.

Another overlooked American concession was perhaps even more significant. No American leader expected Congress to authorize sixty-four peacetime cruisers. This meant that Congress was not likely, short of war, to equal Britain ship-for-ship, and this changed the reality, if not the theoretical principle, of naval equality. Rather than persist in continuing the popular misconception that the 10:10 ratio meant actual naval equality, Coolidge and Kellogg were ready to accept a treaty giving the United States the "right" to build-up to the British strength in cruisers, destroyers, and submarines.[35] Thus, British agreement to a treaty specifically granting the United States the right to equality was crucial. Political symbolism and future legal rights to equality, therefore, would trump existing naval strength.

Somewhat disturbing, however, was the slow British response to Coolidge's invitation. This prompted Kellogg to instruct Allison Houghton, the American Ambassador to Great Britain, to emphasize to Foreign Secretary Chamberlain that President Coolidge would recognize Britain's "special interests" and therefore did not require the British to reduce the number of their present cruisers, only to agree to some definite limitation figure. More risky was Coolidge's further concession that, because the United States still hoped to induce France and Italy to join the negotiations, Houghton was to inform the British that Coolidge had "no intention to bar the door to any proposal that might be made."[36] Having gained this important concession, the British Cabinet also insisted that the conference must be allowed "to consider to what extent the principles adopted at Washington can be carried further, *either as regards the ratio in different classes of ships between the various Powers, or in other important ways.* [Emphasis mine.]"[37]

---

[34] Ibid. [35] Ibid.
[36] Kellogg to Houghton, February 21, 1927, *FRUS*, I, p. 17; Kellogg to Ambassador in France [Herrick], February 3, 1927, *FRUS*, 1927, I: 49; Grew to Houghton, February 21, 1927, *FRUS*, 1927, I: 17; Howard to Chamberlain, February 16 and 17, 1927, *DBFP*, pp. 574, 576.
[37] Chamberlain to Howard, "Memorandum," February 25, 1927, *DBFP*, p. 578; CAB, *Proposed Answer to Invitation from President of the United States to a Conference on Naval Disarmament* in Appendix, CAB 23/54/10 (27), PRO. See also CAB, "Further Limitation of Naval Armaments: Proposals of the Government of the United States (Communicated by the American Ambassador in London), February 10, 1927, C. P. 59 (27), CHAR 22–185, WCP; R. C. Richardson,

Worried about the intentions underlying British insistence on the right to alter the principles agreed upon at the Washington Conference as well as in "other important ways," Kellogg instructed Jones to stop in London in early March 1927 on his way back to the resumption of the Preparatory Commission talks in Geneva.[38]

In anticipation of his arrival, Chamberlain asked Bridgeman to give Jones "as much of your confidence as you can" even though it "might be a little embarrassing to you."[39] However, when Jones arrived in London on March 4, 1927, neither Bridgeman nor Beatty would reveal British intentions for the forthcoming conference or the meaning of "in other important ways." Equally significant was the failure to discuss or even to mention Jones' combat equivalency method, which Jones had outlined to Beatty almost four months earlier. These glaring evasions awakened Jones to the realization that British diplomacy was not as open and frank as he had assumed. Absent any response to his combat equivalency method, the pointed remark by Admiral Sir Frederick Field, the Deputy Chief of the Naval Staff, that England "would require an advantageous position in cruisers" clearly upset Jones.[40]

Field's remark could hardly have come as any surprise to Jones. The British had made their claim to superiority to him repeatedly in 1926, and Jones' compromise combat equivalency alternatives were designed to accommodate a superior number of British cruisers. However, Field's remark was made within a context of repeated evasions which led Jones to suspect a subtle dismissal of his combat equivalency method. Jones promptly warned Field that the United States "could not accept a position of inferiority in any category of vessels" and that equivalency "would be the *sine qua non* of any agreement to which we would ascribe."[41] Jones' emphasis on inferiority was significant. Although he was willing to grant the British superiority in cruiser numbers, his equivalency method was nonetheless designed to ensure that this concession would not result in combat inferiority for the United States. Later Jones recalled emphasizing his warning to Field that any American delegates who agreed to "a position of inferiority would deserve to be hung, drawn, and quartered."[42]

The degree to which Jones was upset became clear when he sent his "special request" to Chief of Naval Operations E.W. Eberle to appoint Frank Schofield, recently promoted to Rear Admiral and chief of the War Plans Division, to the

---

The Evolution of British Disarmament Policy in the 1920s (London: Leicester University Press, 1989), p. 121; William F. Trimble, "The United States Navy and the Geneva Conference for the Limitation of Naval Armaments, 1927," (Ph.D. diss., University of Colorado, 1974), p. 120; Hall, *Britain, United States, and Arms Control*, p. 41.

[38] Jones to Kellogg, March 9, 1927, GBDCS V: 4, Miscellaneous Papers, RG 80, NA.
[39] Chamberlain to Bridgeman, February 25, 1927, 4629/1/1927/19, BP. See also copy in WCP.
[40] Jones to Kellogg, March 9, 1927, p. 4; Secretary of the Navy to General Board, March 11, 1927, GBDCS VIII, 3 Party Conference, RG 80, NA.
[41] Jones to Kellogg, March 9, 1927, p. 4.
[42] Jones, "Untitled Memoir," n.d. p. 7, PCF, N. D. File, JP.

General Board's special staff of experts preparing the General Board's proposals for the forthcoming conference. Schofield was well known as a scathing critic of inept American arms control diplomacy and an admirer of the manner in which British diplomats had secured naval advantages at the Washington Conference. Intensely suspicious of the Admiralty, Schofield would accompany the American delegation to the international conference at Geneva and, in the course of the negotiations, become a highly influential adviser.[43]

Despite his disappointment and growing suspicions, Jones remained cautiously optimistic. While the British had avoided any mention of his compromise ideas during his talks with Bridgeman, Field, and Beatty in March 1927, these leaders had not specifically ruled out his combat equivalency method. Since Jones had made it crystal clear to them that the Americans would only negotiate on the basis of either combat equivalency, or the General Board's insistence on numerical equality, he clung to the hope that once the Conference began, the British would begin to bargain over some variation of his flexible alternatives.[44]

Even as late as the middle of April 1927, two months before the Conference began, Jones persisted in his hope that the British would ultimately be accommodating. Although the "British still talk limitation by numbers," rather than equivalency, they had given him the distinct impression that they were "ready to accept a combination of our thesis and theirs," and therefore "we ought to be able to come to an agreement" and eventually bring the Japanese around.[45] But, as Secretary of State Kellogg was about to discover, convincing the General Board to adopt the Jones combat equivalency compromise was as difficult as convincing the Admiralty.

The member of the General Board's special staff who best exemplified the Board's distrust of the Admiralty was Frank H. Schofield.[46] Few naval officers who had read his published lectures on the disadvantages of the Washington Conference treaties would have forgotten Schofield's scathing criticisms of American politicians and diplomats, or his warning that ignoring naval realities in negotiating arms control treaties could "equal in historical importance the great [battle] decisions of war."[47] Having served as a naval adviser to the American delegation to the Washington Conference, Schofield would accompany Jones to the Geneva Conference, where Jones relied heavily on his "clear thinking, profound knowledge of naval affairs, and clear-cut analysis of all problems."[48] Indeed, Jones' "special request" that Schofield be appointed to

---

[43] Jones to Eberle, March 21, 1927, JP.
[44] Jones to Kellogg, March 9, 1927, GBDCS V: 4, RG 80, NA; Jones to Eberle, March 17, 1927, JP.
[45] Jones to Adolphus Andrews, April 19, 1927, JP Jones was delighted that Captain Adolphus Andrews had agreed to join the American delegation to the Geneva Disarmament Conference.
[46] See Chapter 6 and Jones to Eberle, March 21, 1927, JP. [47] See Chapter 6.
[48] Jones to Secretary of the Navy, August 18, 1927, GBDCS VI: 6, Miscellaneous Papers, RG 80, NA.

the American negotiating team underscored the depth of his new suspicion – a suspicion which was far more significant than later historians have recognized.[49]

Most immediately troublesome for Kellogg was the General Board's categorical rejection of the Jones combat equivalency compromise.[50] This rejection was based upon its fundamental distrust of the British rationale for a greater number of cruisers. The British "plea to guard commerce," the General Board insisted, masked "the equally important missions which they [cruisers] have of denying the sea to enemy commerce and controlling neutral commerce." Cruiser usefulness in guarding British shipping was in fact "inseparably linked" to controlling and blockading neutral shipping. Moreover, since peacetime "requires no guarding of commerce," the General Board reasoned that only "war alone" could make "such demands on naval vessels." It was clear, therefore, that Great Britain's claim to a larger number of cruisers than the United States had less to do with protecting its trade routes in peacetime than with its preparations for some future war in which these cruisers would again interdict American neutral trade. Realism dictated, therefore, that whenever any nation increased its number of warships, the combat capabilities and uses of these ships must be the measure by which the United States evaluated them.[51]

The General Board also worried about the fast British merchantmen equipped to carry 6-inch guns and therefore highly effective in interdicting unarmed neutral commerce. Had the General Board known of the Admiralty's highly secret wartime strategy to deploy 164 armed merchantmen during a war against Japan and that it planned to station some of them off American ports,

---

[49] Fanning, *Peace and Disarmament*, pp. 5, 8; Robert Gordon Kaufman, *Arms Control During the Pre-Nuclear Era: The United States and Naval Limitation Between the Wars* (New York: Columbia University Press, 1990), Kaufman makes no mention of Schofield, and Fanning does not evaluate Schofield specific criticisms or the significance of Jones' special request for his appointment. See also Trimble, "The United States and the Geneva Conference," pp. 117–121; Frank H. Schofield, "Incidents and Present Day Aspects of Naval Strategy," *Proceedings* of the United States Naval Institute (May 1923), pp. 798–800. For Schofield's estimates of British and Japanese war plans, see William R. Braisted, "On the American Red and Red-Orange Plans, 1919–1939," in *Naval Warfare in the Twentieth Century, 1900–1945: Essays in Honor of Andrew Marder*, ed. Gerald Jordan (London and New York: Crane Russak, 1977), pp. 191–192.

[50] SMP, GB to Secretary of the Navy, "Further Limitation of Naval Armament: The Capital Ship Question," May 13, 1927, GB 438, Foreign Affairs, PP, HHPL. Complete sets of the General Board's recommendations to the Secretary of the Navy are in HHPL and NWC, 1927, Conference, RG 8 XPOD, NWC. See also Records of the Chief of Naval Operations, Intelligence Division, C-96, RG 83, NA and GBDCS VI: 1, Three Power Conference, 1927, RG 80, NA; SMP, GB to Secretary of the Navy, "Further Limitation of Naval Armament: General Consideration of National Policies," April 21, 1927, pp. 5–6, April 22, 1927, p. 3, GB 438, Foreign Affairs, PP, HHPL and GBDCS VI: 1, 3 Power Conference, 1927 RG 80, NA; Jones to William Howard Gardiner, April 2, 1924, JP; Michael K. Doyle, "The U. S. Navy and War Plan Orange, 1933–1940: Making Necessity a Virtue," *Naval War College Review*, 29 (Winter 1977), pp. 56–58.

[51] SMP, GB to Secretary of the Navy, "Further Limitation of Naval Armament: General Consideration of National Policies," April 21, 1927, pp. 5–6.

they would have become even more concerned.[52] The deployment of British cruisers varied. For example, one plan assigned four cruisers to North America and Newfoundland, one to the Panama Canal, and four to the Philippine Islands. Another plan put three cruisers and six armed merchantmen off San Francisco and one cruiser and four armed merchantmen off the Panama Canal. The purpose of these distributions remained secret, yet would have appeared obvious to the General Board and was challenged by Churchill, who professed to be baffled by the intent of this strategy.[53]

In order to give the United States "at least an equal opportunity for success in a war" against either Great Britain or Japan, the General Board was equally adamant about the size and number of guns its cruisers should be allowed to carry. The Board had no knowledge of the Admiralty's defective 8-inch gun or its plans to eliminate this gun at the forthcoming conference, believing instead that the British would not propose any reduction in "the maximum caliber of gun from the eight-inch set by the Washington Conference."[54] Its reasoning for equipping all of its new cruisers with as many new 8-inch guns as possible was based on the American gun's proven long-range accuracy and power. The impact from its 8-inch shell, the General Board revealed, was so great that it could sink many of the less well armored battleships currently in the American fleet. Sinking battleships with this new 8-inch-gun cruiser was possible because it "could operate beyond the range of many" of the existing "capital ships," while safely bringing the enemy's "capital ships under effective fire."[55] Indeed, the General Board was so well pleased with the "very high effectiveness

---

[52] SMP, GB to Secretary of the Navy, "Further Limitation of Naval Armament: Cruisers," April 25, 1927, pp. 8, 10–13, Foreign Affairs, PP, HHPL. For the number of merchantmen which the British were planning to equip with six-inch guns during wartime see footnote 53.

[53] For Churchill's challenge see Chapter 4. See also Neville Chamberlain to Leo Amery, December 20, 1923; Amery to Chamberlain, December 22, 1923 in "Emergency Construction Programme," December 22, 1923, P. D. 01949/23, ADM 1/8702/151, PRO. This Admiralty memorandum was sent to Neville Chamberlain. Roger Bellairs confirmed sending the memorandum to Amery in "The Total Number and Type of Cruisers Required by the British Empire," March 15, 1928, p. 3, ADM 116/2607, PRO. Bellairs insisted that "this was the only occasion on which the actual War Plan distribution of cruisers was given to a Cabinet Minister." See also Director of Plans, "Programme of Construction and Reconstruction," June 12, 1923, ADM 1/8702/151, PRO and Director of Plans, "Secret Cruiser Programme," January 29, 1924, P. D. 02053/24, ADM 1/8673/228/24, PRO; Director of Plans, "Proposals re. Light Cruisers: Flagships," October 31, 1923, P. D. 01914/23, ADM 1/ 8683/266 PRO; "Light Cruiser Construction Programme," n.d., P. D. 01970/1924, ADM 1/8672/227/24, PRO.

[54] See footnote 52.

[55] Ibid., pp. 6–7. Schofield maintained "that the 8-inch gun is more than double the usefulness for general naval purposes of the 6-inch gun." The Schofield conclusion is in paragraph 16 of a document fragment found in Miscellaneous File, JP. For British battleship supremacy see "Memorandum," January 13, 1927, Attaché Reports 1886–1939, Intelligence Division, Chief of Naval Operations, RG 83, NA; Frank H. Schofield, "Memorandum: The Gun Elevation Question," November 6, 1923, NWC 1923–1930; President, Naval War College to General Board, "Battle Range Studies Against Red Fleet," June 19, 1924, NWC.

of their [eight-inch] gunfire at long-range" and the "very great maneuverability" of the 10,000-ton cruisers, that it predicted that these newest warships would "have a controlling influence in battle" against battleships. Thus, the General Board ruled out any plan which would grant "to any power a total tonnage in the cruiser class that exceeds the tonnage allowed to us."[56]

The General Board's suspicions of the Admiralty's intentions at a second conference were bolstered by a sensational news story in *The New York Times*.[57] Edwin L. James, a reporter who had earlier covered the negotiations at the Preparatory Commission in Geneva, somehow gained access to the Admiralty's highly secret negotiating strategy, which Bridgeman, Beatty, and Baldwin were attempting to keep under tight wraps, and which had not yet been revealed to either the Committee of Imperial Defence or to the British Cabinet.[58] James' warning of Admiralty surprises, including a demand for a 6,000- to 7,000-ton limit on cruisers, reinforced the earlier advice offered by American Ambassador Alanson Houghton, who opposed a second conference and who stressed the Admiralty's determination to retain its naval supremacy.[59]

Warnings from Houghton, James, and the General Board tempered Kellogg's optimism.[60] Throughout much of May 1927, the month preceding the opening of the Geneva Conference, Kellogg worked closely and harmoniously with his team of naval conference experts. With their guidance he poured over the Board's comprehensive studies, rationale, and conclusions. Following a series of conferences with these experts, Kellogg developed, as Jones recalled, "an astonishing grasp of the fundamentals of our naval policy."[61] By the end of May, Kellogg fully understood and supported the strategic reasoning, if not all of the recommendations of the General Board, telling Coolidge that he had come to value the expertise of his naval advisors on all "technical" questions.

---

[56] SMP, GB to Secretary of the Navy, "Further Limitation of Naval Armament: The Capital Ship Question, May 13, 1927, p. 13; SMP, GB to Secretary of the Navy, "Further Limitation of Naval Armament: Cruisers," April 25, 1927, p. 7.

[57] *The New York Times*, 12 May 1927.

[58] Plans Division, "Limitation of Armaments: Memorandum by the Naval Staff," April 14, 1927, P. D. 02832/27, ADM 1/8715/188, PRO. See also Beatty, Minute, April 13, 1927 and Bridgeman, Minute, April 21, 1927, ADM 1/8715, PRO. Another secret document to which James might have had access was Plans Division, "Limitation of Naval Armaments: Admiralty Proposals," May 6, 1927, P. D. 02832/27, ADM 1/8715/188, PRO. This document was labeled "Secret" and was circulated among the Naval Staff only six days before the James article appeared. The meeting at which these proposals were revealed to the CID did not take place until May 20, and Bridgeman presented them to the Cabinet on May 25, 1927.

[59] Houghton to Castle, February 16, 1926; Castle to Houghton, May 2, England File, 1927; Castle Diary, January 4, 1927, June 5, 1927, CP.

[60] Kellogg to Houghton, May 2, 1927, MC 25, KP; Kellogg to Coolidge, May 30, 1927, Series I, MF 73/1289, Reel 28, CCP.

[61] Jones, Untitled Memoir," n.d., p. 8, N. D. File, JP.

Kellogg's concentration, patience, and tact paid handsome dividends. Before the American delegation left for the second naval conference in Geneva, Kellogg received an unexpected and unusually high compliment. In the presence of Secretary of the Navy Wilber, Admiral Frank Schofield, the outspoken critic of previous naval arms control diplomacy, was heard to remark loudly to Undersecretary of State Castle: "I am inclined to believe that Mr. Kellogg is one of the best secretaries of the Navy this country has ever had."[62] Schofield's praise was significant because it openly expressed the naval delegates' new-found confidence in the Secretary of State's judgment, a confidence which arose from the final negotiating position, which Kellogg now fully endorsed and which Coolidge approved.

Between April 25, 1927 – when it had first rejected Jones' combat equivalency proposal – and June 1, the General Board tacitly altered its negotiating terms. In a memorandum entitled "Study No.1: Proposals for the Geneva Conference," the Board now made no mention of its prior objections to negotiating on the basis of combat equivalency.[63] Instead, it limited its objectives to the need to refrain from any changes to the Five-Power Treaty, the extension of the ratios agreed upon at the Washington Conference to auxiliary vessels, the use of total tonnage as the basis of limitation, and the desirability of keeping total tonnage for cruisers, destroyers, and submarines as low as possible. Total limits of 250,000 to 300,000 tons for all cruisers; 200,000 to 250,000 tons for destroyers; and 60,000 to 90,000 tons for submarines, along with a detailed transitional building and scrapping plan, completed the main features of its latest proposals.[64] The apparent reason for dropping its opposition to combat equivalency becomes clear, however, by closely examining the final negotiating position ordered by Kellogg and Coolidge.

At a meeting with Coolidge on June 1, 1927, Kellogg, Wilbur, Gibson, Jones, and Schofield agreed upon the final American negotiating strategy. Overlooked by scholars is the crucial fact that Coolidge pointedly asked each of the naval members present whether they believed the United States Navy would wholeheartedly back a treaty based on combat equivalency. According to Ted Marriner, Chief of the State Department's Division of Western European Affairs, who was also present at this meeting, their "replies were all in the affirmative."[65] Coolidge then emphasized to the delegates that the

---

[62] Castle, Diary, June 5, 1927, CP.
[63] SMP, GB, "Memorandum Prepared by Direction of Senior Member Present, General Board: Proposals for the Geneva Conference," June 1, 1927, Foreign Affairs, PP, HHPL. See also SMP, GB to Secretary of the Navy, "Further Limitation of Naval Armament: Summary of Conclusions," GB 438, Foreign Affairs, PP, HHPL.
[64] See sources cited in footnote above.
[65] Theodore Marriner, "Memorandum by the Chief of the Division of Western European Affairs," June 1, 1927, FRUS, 1927, I: 42. This is an exceptionally important document as it clearly

preferred negotiating method of the American delegation was Jones' combat equivalency. In endorsing Jones' method, he expressed the hope, in words similar to those used by Jones, "that a *combination limitation by tonnage and numbers* could possibly be worked out which would be satisfactory in all probability to both Powers, as it would give Britain the scope [i.e., larger numbers] she desires for building smaller cruisers." [Emphasis mine.][66] On the following day, June 2, Kellogg specifically authorized the flexibility Gibson needed to negotiate an agreement based on combat equivalency. Rather than the General Board's rigid insistence on total tonnage, Coolidge and Kellogg promised to "leave to your discretion the *method* and the manner" by which these negotiating aims would be achieved. [Emphasis mine.][67]

The American negotiating strategy had evolved during the month of May into an understanding which the naval experts accompanying Gibson and Jones to the Conference could wholeheartedly embrace.[68] At no time did the General Board actually approve of combat equivalency as an acceptable basis for negotiation, but it dropped its open opposition to it, and thereby gave it a chance to succeed. Thus, a tacit compromise had emerged. If the British eventually negotiated on the basis of some variation of combat equivalency, Coolidge and Kellogg gave the delegates the discretion to alter the method and manner by which Great Britain was granted numerical superiority in smaller cruisers.[69] But should Great Britain reject combat equivalency, and instead attempt to take advantage of America's existing naval weaknesses, especially in cruisers, Coolidge, Kellogg, and the American delegates would support the General Board's insistence on the "total tonnage" method and on strict numerical equality in all auxiliary classes.

Coolidge had much to gain and little to lose from this strategy. Two alternative outcomes appeared likely. If the British agreed to some acceptable form of combat equivalency, Coolidge and Kellogg would reap the political rewards in Congress and with the voting public for ending the auxiliary

establishes Coolidge's and Kellogg's acceptance of the Jones combat equivalency compromise as the initial basis for negotiations.

[66] *Ibid.*
[67] Kellogg to Gibson, June 2, 1927, *FRUS*, 1927, I: 45.
[68] See footnote 65 and Castle, June 5, 1927, CP; Ethan L. Ellis, *Frank B. Kellogg and American Foreign Relations, 1925–1927* (New Brunswick, NJ: Rutgers University Press, 1961), p. 167.
[69] See sources in footnote cited above and Jones, "Untitled Memoir," p. 8; Dulles to Gibson, August 31, 1927, Allen Dulles File, GP. Dulles recalled that "even before he [Jones] went to Geneva," he had devised plans "to arrive at a parity of combat strength by making certain tonnage allowances in the case of vessels carrying six-inch guns and allowing any nation which desires a six-inch gun type of vessel to build up to a greater tonnage than the country which might utilize its tonnage with eight-inch gun vessels." Dulles thus supports Jones claim that before the American delegates left the United States for the opening of the 1927 Geneva Conference, they were united behind his compromise plan, on which he still hoped to base the negotiations. This also supports the important memorandum by Theodore Marriner cited in footnote 65 above.

arms race and reducing the need for immediate and future increases in naval spending. If, on the other hand, the British pulled an unpleasant surprise – as Houghton and James had warned – and as the General Board suspected – by refusing to negotiate on the basis of combat equivalency, and by rejecting the General Board's alternative of strict numerical equality, Coolidge could call for a dramatic end to the negotiations yet still reap credit for having made a good-faith effort to end the naval arms race. Moreover, peace groups would then have far less political traction for mounting an effective opposition against Coolidge's subsequent acquiescence to congressional demands to build the additional cruisers needed to ensure America's freedom of the seas. The president could thereby avoid a serious split within his own party, retain the popular mantle of a leader who had called the second conference, and even if the conference failed, still earn the gratitude of those demanding a more resolute naval building program. Which of these two scenarios would emerge depended in large part on what the British would propose at Geneva, but, in either case, Coolidge would gain added respect for his efforts and thereby enhance his political popularity.

10

Beatty's New Strategies

During the six months between August 1926 and February 10, 1927, when Coolidge surprised the Admiralty by quickly issuing his invitation to a second arms limitation conference, Beatty skillfully initiated important changes in British naval policy. These changes have largely gone unnoticed, and deserve more careful scrutiny. In January 1927, he delighted England's political leaders by suddenly and unexpectedly reversing Admiralty policy from an indirect yet persistent opposition to international arms reductions to a strategy calling for the immediate convening of a second naval conference. This shrewd political move, Beatty believed, must however be accompanied by an equally brilliant diplomatic one. At the second conference the Admiralty would astonish the world, as Hughes had done at the Washington Conference, with cost reductions certain to win overwhelming world approval and thereby make it difficult, if not impossible, for the Americans and the Japanese to reject them. Both Beatty and Bridgeman assumed that Coolidge and Kellogg were weak, even spineless politicians, who had called the conference primarily to gain popular 1928 reelection slogans. With world attention focused on them at the bargaining table, they would therefore cave in under Admiralty pressure and, like Harding and Hughes, overrule their naval advisers.

The eagerness with which Prime Minister Baldwin and his Cabinet endorsed the Admiralty's proposals enabled Beatty to soften Churchill's reservations and to win approval for control of the diplomatic negotiations at the forthcoming conference. However, when presenting their new strategy and objectives to the Committee of Imperial Defence and to the Cabinet, Beatty and Bridgeman resorted to important omissions. These tactics won the Admiralty control of the negotiations, but would adversely impact the negotiations at Geneva and later result in considerable turmoil within the Cabinet. Beatty justified these tactical omissions because he believed that he had been forced into fighting two unconventional yet related types of strategic warfare simultaneously: the long, seemingly endless political battle at home against Cabinet Ministers who were effectively sabotaging preparations for the eventual war to stop Japan from encroaching on highly lucrative British possessions in East Asia, and the approaching diplomatic offensive against the United States over naval equality and freedom of the seas, doctrines which threatened England's ability to interdict neutral commerce in the Atlantic and on world trade routes during future wars. Success at the bargaining table, he hoped, would enable him to win both of these wars.

***

Beatty achieved his first objective with relative ease. He was materially assisted in this effort by Parliament's recent decision requiring a new budgetary method by which the yearly funding for the three major military service branches would be submitted to Parliament as one combined military budget or estimate. This new method forced each of the services – the Navy, the Army, and the new Royal Air Force – to negotiate among themselves the amounts which they would require and then to combine all of their requests into one military budget recommendation. Given the intensity of the rivalry among the service branches for funding, a rivalry which was exacerbated by Parliament's determination to cut military costs still further, Beatty's naval supporters argued strenuously for his continuation as First Sea Lord, at least until the first budgetary battle had been concluded. Only Beatty, they argued, possessed the intimate familiarity and skills needed to negotiate the numerous pitfalls and intricacies required to hammer out a budget with the Army and, most especially, with the aggressive leaders of the newly created Royal Air Force, let alone the equally certain difficulties expected in the complex give-and-take of parliamentary budget politics.[1]

On August 31, 1926, in response to prompting by his good friend, Vice Admiral Sir Roger Keyes, Beatty outlined a plan to secure the extension of his tenure as First Sea Lord. Rather than give up his post in November to Admiral Sir Charles Madden, Bridgeman's well-known choice to succeed him, Beatty instructed Keyes to write directly to Bridgeman and to Winston Churchill, subtly arguing the necessity for extending him as First Sea Lord. Only in this way, Beatty suggested, could the Admiralty make good use of his political experience as well as his expertise in negotiating ways to cut wasteful spending while simultaneously protecting Britain's naval strength.[2]

Keyes promptly contacted Churchill and Bridgeman. Perhaps to Keyes' surprise, Churchill warmly supported Beatty's extension. Churchill admitted

---

[1] Beatty to Keyes, August 21, 1926 and Keyes to Bridgeman, September 8, 1926 in William Scott Chalmers, *The Life and Letters of David, Earl Beatty* (London: Hodder and Stoughton, 1951), pp. 335–337; Stephen Roskill, *Earl Beatty: The Last Naval Hero: An Intimate Biography* (New York: Athenaeum, 1981), p. 355.
[2] Beatty to Keyes, August 31, 1926, in Chalmers, *Life and Letters of David, Earl Beatty*, pp. 335–336.

that during the Birkenhead Committee fights, when Beatty was "banking so heavily on a war with Japan," Churchill had favored summarily removing him as First Sea Lord. But following the 1925 resolution of the cruiser building program and the later compromise on slowing the rate of construction of the Singapore naval base, he had "entirely changed" his opinion. "On every personal ground," Churchill assured Keyes, "I have always wished Beatty to remain and now I am glad to say public as well as private considerations flow together."[3]

Bridgeman was much less enthusiastic. According to Captain John D. Kelly, the Fourth Sea Lord, Beatty's ploy generated significant tensions. Kelly complained that "little Bridgeman" failed to exhibit "anything like the keenness" to retain Beatty, as did Kelly and other Beatty supporters on the Naval Staff. He noted especially that "some politicians" were actively engaged in "a good deal of intriguing" against Beatty's extension.[4] Beatty indirectly suggested the intensity of this behind-the-scenes struggle by crediting his retention to the direct intervention of King George V.[5] Whatever his reservations may have been, Bridgeman eventually acquiesced graciously in approving the extension, whereupon Prime Minister Baldwin appointed Beatty to chair the Chiefs of Staff subcommittee to hammer out a joint services budget proposal.[6]

Having secured his extension as First Sea Lord, Beatty began implementing his second major objective. He now suddenly and unexpectedly reversed course from foot-dragging opposition to naval reductions to a new policy actively embracing them. Persistent political pressures, fueled by a steadily worsening economy, calls for deeper cuts in naval spending voiced by highly-placed Parliamentary critics, and denunciations by the Colwyn Committee of wasteful naval spending had combined to put the Admiralty on the political defensive. The Naval Staff had repeatedly deflected many of these irritants by plausible counterarguments, long delays, and either compliance or periodic opposition accompanied by outbursts of righteous indignation.

But now, in November 1926, the Naval Staff acknowledged two new realities: an increasingly faltering economy unable to finance the more expensive cruisers and the real possibility that rival navies would build 10,000-ton

---

[3] Churchill to Keyes, September 16, 1925, in Winston Churchill, *Winston S. Churchill: The Exchequer Years 1921–1925, Companion Volume 5* ed. Martin Gilbert (London: William Heinemann, 1979) 5: 830. Hereafter cited as Churchill, *Companion Volume 5*. See also Stephen Roskill, *Naval Policy between the Wars: The Period of the Anglo-American Antagonism, 1919–1939* (London: Collins, 1968), p. 464.

[4] John D. Kelly to Keyes, September 12, 1926 and Keyes to Hamilton, May 4, 1927 in Roger Keyes, *The Keyes Papers: Selections from the Private and Official Correspondence of Admiral of the Fleet Baron Keyes of Zeebrugge, 1919–1939* ed. Paul G. Halpern 2 vols. (London: Allen and Unwin, 1980), 2: 189, 216; Keyes to Bridgeman, September 8, 1926 in Chalmers, *Life and Letters of David, Earl Beatty*, pp. 337–338.

[5] Roskill, *Earl Beatty*, p. 355.   [6] Chalmers, *Life and Letters of David Earl Beatty*, pp. 380–381.

cruisers carrying a larger number of longer-range and more accurate 8-inch guns, thereby making the newest British cruisers even more inferior than their disappointing shorter range guns already rendered them. It was crucial, therefore, to restrict the ability of rival nations to build 8-inch-gun cruisers. This combat deficiency remained a closely guarded secret to be kept at all costs from rival navies and from Parliamentary critics, who would certainly use it to good political effect as further evidence of shockingly wasteful inefficiency.[7]

The defective 8-inch gun solidified the Naval Staff's support for a second conference. Taking the political offensive, Beatty now decided that the most effective defense against all of these persistent political and military pressures was a dramatic new policy. Rather than continue the Admiralty's increasingly unpopular resistance to these criticisms, he seized the political initiative and delighted the Baldwin Cabinet by his unexpected call for drastic cuts in naval spending.[8]

As the Admiralty had already implemented many of the sharp economic cuts demanded by the Colwyn Committee, Beatty concluded that the smartest way to safeguard British naval superiority was a treaty which reduced the size and number of warships in the world's rival navies.[9] This diplomatic strategy was based solidly on economic realities and Britain's secret cruiser weaknesses, a strategy certain to win the gratitude of the Cabinet and the Parliament.[10]

Recalling Churchill's earlier opposition to 6-inch-gun cruisers during the 1925 Birkenhead Committee disputes, Beatty anticipated that his sudden shift from the 8-inch- to the 6-inch-gun cruiser was certain to arouse Churchill's sharp scrutiny. During the Birkenhead Committee debates, Keyes had convinced Churchill that the new and at that time still untested 8-inch gun "really created a change comparable to that when the 'Dreadnought' was introduced

---

[7] See Chapter 5.
[8] D.C.N.S. [Deputy Chief of the Naval Staff], Controller, and A.C.N.S. [Assistant Chief of the Naval Staff] to C.N.S. [Chief of the Naval Staff], "Classification and Limitation of Warships," December 21, 1926, M03056/26, ADM 1/8699/118; "Limitation of Armaments: Memorandum by the Sea Lords for Consideration by the Board," n.d., ADM 167/76, PRO. See also A.D.P.R. Pound to Keyes, April 13, 1927, in Keyes, *Keyes Papers*, 2: 213; R. C. Richardson, *The Evolution of British Disarmament Policy in the 1920s* (London: Leicester University Press, 1989), pp. 119–120; Roskill, *Naval Policy between the Wars*, p. 499; Philip Payson O'Brien, *British and American Naval Power: Politics and Policy, 1900–1936* (Westport, CT: Praeger, 1998), pp. 186–187; D.C.N.S., Controller, and A.C.N.S. to C.N.S., "Classification and Limitation of Warships," p. 1; Pound to Keyes, April 13, 1927, in Keyes, *Keyes Papers*, 2: 203.
[9] Director of Plans, "British and Japanese Cruiser Strength," August 15, 1927, P. D. 02905/27, ADM 1/8711, PRO.
[10] D.C.N.S., Controller, and A.C.N.S. to C.N.S., "Classification and Limitation of Warships," pp. 1–8; "Limitation of Armaments," n.d., pp.1–4, ADM 167/76, PRO. Some historians have accepted the Admiralty's economic justifications as the primary motive for British willingness to participate in another conference. See O'Brien, *British and American Naval Power*, p. 198; Roskill, *Naval Policy between the Wars*, p. 499.

into the battle area."[11] Like the American General Board, Churchill too had been greatly impressed with the 8-inch gun's potentially revolutionary destructive power, and like the General Board, he saw no good naval or economic sense in building cruisers with much less powerful and shorter-range 6-inch guns.[12]

When Churchill supported Beatty's extension as First Sea Lord, he did so in the belief that Beatty had shelved his strategic plan for war against Japan. In fact, Beatty held tenaciously to his conviction that seventy cruisers were essential because of the virtual inevitability of a future Anglo-Japanese war fought in waters near Japan. To reach seventy cruisers, he therefore proposed building only fifteen 10,000-ton, 8-inch-gun cruisers, while adding thirty-five new 7,500-ton, 6-inch-gun cruisers for a total savings of over £16 million during a ten-year period.[13]

To soften Churchill's expected objections to the smaller 6-inch- gun cruisers, Beatty and the Naval Staff put their greatest emphasis on the enormous savings the Admiralty hoped to achieve by re-opening negotiations on capital ships. By extending the life of battleships from twenty to twenty-six years, reducing the size of new battleships from 35,000 tons allowed under the Five-Power Treaty to 28,000 tons with guns from 16 to 13.5 inches, and by reducing aircraft carriers from 27,000 tons to 25,000 tons and replacing their 8-inch guns with 6-inch guns, the Admiralty claimed it could reduce total replacement building costs during the decade 1930–1940 from £71.5 million to £38.5 million. This £33 million savings in capital ships, when added to the £16 million savings garnered by building smaller cruisers, came to a minimum of at least £49 million. Further savings were promised by reductions in the numbers and extending the life of destroyers and submarines. These savings, Beatty believed, would so warm the hearts of politicians, especially Churchill, that little serious opposition to the switch to 6-inch-gun cruisers was expected.[14]

---

[11] D.C.N.S., Controller, and A.C.N.S. to C. N.S., "Classification and Limitation of Warships," p. 3; O.M. [Oswyn Murray], "Secret Memorandum Circulated to the Board as a Foreword to the Memorandum on the Limitation of Armament," January 24, 1927, p. 6, ADM 167/76, PRO. Hereafter cited as O.M., "Secret Memorandum." The Sea Lords noted that the size of the new cruiser would depend upon "the size of the gun carried." The maximum caliber of gun was to be six-inches. See also Plans Division, "Limitation of Armaments: Admiralty Proposals," May 6, 1927, P. D. 02832/27, p. 2, copy in ROSK 7/36, ROSKCC; Director of Plans, "Limitation of Armaments: Memorandum by the Naval Staff, n.d. P.D. 02832/27, pp. 3–7, ROSK 7/36, ROSKCC; Director of Plans, "Limitation of Naval Armaments: Aircraft Carriers and Cruisers," May 10, 1927, P.D. 02851/27, ADM 116/3371, PRO.

[12] See Chapter 4; Churchill to Keyes, January 6, 1928, *Keyes Papers*, 2: 191, 239–241. For the General Board's insistence on the 8-inch gun, see Chapter 6.

[13] Beatty, "Geneva Conference on the Limitation of Armaments: Meeting with the Sea Lords on 22 July 1927," in ROSK 7/36, ROSKCC; Plans Division, "Limitation of Armament: Cruisers," March 17, 1927, p. 4, P.D. 02807/27, ADM 116/3371, PRO; O.M., "Secret Memorandum," p. 7.

[14] O.M., "Secret Memorandum," pp. 4–7.

While confident that the Cabinet would applaud the Admiralty's cost-cutting proposals, Beatty and his representatives at the Preparatory Commission were well aware that as soon as the Admiralty revealed these proposals at the second conference, the Americans would raise immediate and very serious objections. Gibson and Jones had repeatedly made it clear to British naval representatives that the purpose of the next conference was primarily to extend the 10:10:6 ratio to all auxiliary vessels, not to reopen the still hotly controversial capital ship issues that had been agreed upon at the Washington Conference – but which were now the principal means by which the Admiralty intended to achieve drastic cost reductions.[15] The General Board was still smarting from the heavy-handed manner in which Harding and Hughes had forced the scrapping of so many of its partially completed new battleships, while at the same time allowing the British to achieve battleship superiority by building the *Nelson* and the *Rodney*, the two biggest, most modern and most powerful battleships in the world. Equally obvious to the British was the General Board's public position that, rather than extend the building holiday, it would not agree to continued British supremacy in capital ships beyond the termination of the Five-Power Treaty in 1932. Nor could the General Board have forgotten the very recent, prolonged, and bitter disputes arising from strenuous Admiralty and Foreign Office objections when the General Board had sought to equalize combat capabilities for its battleships by elevating guns and converting from coal to oil.[16]

The Admiralty's Naval Staff therefore set to work devising public rationales to present to the Committee of Imperial Defence, the cabinet, and the next international conference.[17] Several vital facts would not be revealed. These omissions included the Admiralty's need for a minimum of seventy cruisers for a future war against Japan, the defective 8-inch gun on its newest cruisers, and its determination to eliminate that gun from the ships of its rivals. The Naval Staff therefore floated an idea first presented by Lord Lee in 1925 when he was First Lord of the Admiralty. Rather than five cruisers for every three battleships, he had suggested that the number of cruisers allocated to each navy ought to be "in proportion to the amount of commerce carried under its flag and to the extent of its trade routes."[18] As Lord Lee's idea had the effect of providing a rational justification for British superiority in smaller, 6-inch-gun

---

[15] *Ibid.*, pp. 1–6. See also Chapters 7 and 9.   [16] See Chapter 6.
[17] O.M., "Secret Memorandum," pp. 1–4; Board of Admiralty, "Minutes of Meeting 27 January 1927," pp. 1–3, ADM 167/75; Richardson, *Evolution of British Disarmament Policy*, pp. 119–120; Roskill, *Naval Policy between the Wars*, p. 499.
[18] American Naval Intelligence in London reported on Lord Lee's suggestion in late April 1925. See C. L. Hussey, "British Agenda," April 30, 1925, in "Notes on General Board's Preparation for a Second International Conference for the Limitation of Naval Armament," September 4, 1925 in ROSK 7/35, ROSKCC.

cruisers, the Admiralty's Director of Plans used it to devise a formula which quickly won the support of the Naval Staff.

The "ton-mileage" rationale provided a badly needed public justification for cruiser superiority. The Director of Plans maintained that by "multiplying the tonnage at sea on defined ocean routes by the length of the routes to be traversed from port to port, a factor which may be termed 'ton-mileage' is obtained." He calculated that England's world-wide ton-mileage trade totaled 27,229,492,000 whereas the United States' total ton-mileage only came to 12,379,311,000. Japan's was much less at 3,757,721,000, a total only slightly higher than the ton-mileage for France and Italy. Assuming two cruisers to protect every 1,000,000 ton-miles, the number of cruisers required by Great Britain for trade protection came to fifty-four, but the United States was only entitled to twenty-five, and Japan, France, and Italy only seven each. Thus, when the fifty-four British cruisers needed for trade protection were added to the twenty-five cruisers needed for the battle fleet, the total number of British cruisers required was seventy-nine. By contrast, the United States only needed twenty-five cruisers for trade protection and twenty-five for the battle fleet for a total of fifty, while Japan required only seven for trade protection and fifteen for its battle fleet, for a total of twenty-two. France and Italy would have to settle for a maximum of sixteen each.[19]

Beatty fully endorsed the Naval Staff's strong support of the "ton-mileage" method as a basis for negotiation at the second international naval conference. "This is very good from our point of view," but, he warned," we shall have difficulty in making the Powers swallow it."[20] To bolster its superiority claims, therefore, the Naval Staff argued as well that neither the United States nor Japan faced the very real security risk that the vital Mediterranean trade route posed for Great Britain. The Mediterranean Sea was "the vital artery through which the life blood of the Empire flows," yet it was flanked by France and Italy. The potential of these navies to interdict British trade made it "impossible for the Government of Great Britain and the Dominions to be indifferent in regard to the number and type of vessels maintained by these two powers," and therefore these realities further justified a larger number of British cruisers than those needed by either the United States or Japan.

Despite the Naval Staff's satisfaction with its latest justifications for a superior number of cruisers, it nonetheless recognized another problem in convincing its naval rivals to accept its trade protection rationale. By reducing the size of the gun, which future cruisers could carry, to 6-inches, the Naval

---

[19] The most complete explanation of "ton-mileage" is in Director of Plans, "Limitation of Armament: Cruisers," March 17, 1927, pp. 2–4, P.D. 02807/27, ADM 116/3371, PRO. See also Plans Division, "Limitation of Armaments: Memorandum by the Naval Staff," April 14, 1927, P.D. 02832/27, pp. 8–9, ADM 1/8715/188, PRO.

[20] Beatty, Minute, March 19, 1927, in Director of Plans, "Limitation of Armament: Cruisers," March 17, 1927, p. 1.

Staff conceded that this would allow critics to highlight England's ability to equip its larger number of fast merchant vessels with 6-inch guns during war, thereby quickly and inexpensively augmenting Great Britain's naval power. Admiralty experts correctly argued that a merchant vessel armed with a 6-inch gun could not successfully engage a 6-inch-gun cruiser. Nonetheless, the Admiralty would not tolerate any effort to place restrictions on its ability to deploy armed merchant vessels with 6-inch guns during war. These armed merchantmen were a crucial component in Great Britain's ability to impose blockades and to interdict neutral shipping in time of war, and the Admiralty therefore would refuse to discuss any proposal to reduce the size of the gun on these merchantmen or the number of its merchant vessels already designated for quick conversion during wartime.[21]

While the Admiralty would later argue that the smaller 6-inch-gun cruiser qualified it as a defensive rather than an offensive vessel, its initial public rationale at the 1927 Geneva Conference would stress significant economic savings, which could only be realized by reducing the size of capital ships and 10,000-ton cruisers, and also by extending the service life of these vessels. With these objectives and rationales strongly supported by the Naval Staff, Beatty turned to the task of convincing the Cabinet that the Admiralty, not the Foreign Office, must be in complete control of the negotiations at the forthcoming conference.

Beatty was well aware that he must first win over Churchill before presenting his strategy to Prime Minister Baldwin and the Cabinet. To avoid a repetition of Churchill's great skill in refuting Admiralty arguments, as he had repeatedly demonstrated during the 1925 Birkenhead Committee debate, Beatty arranged through his good friend and close associate Admiral Roger Keyes, currently serving as the commander of Britain's main battle fleet in the Mediterranean, to invite Churchill to join the fleet on its maneuvers. Beatty knew that Churchill relished such opportunities and that once under the spell of this inspiring fleet, the Chancellor of the Exchequer was more likely to be in a congenial frame of mind. Keyes then pitched the Admiralty's conference strategy promising great savings in annual naval budget requests. In return, a delighted Churchill pledged to ensure that the British fleet would not "fall behind" the United States and that Great Britain would maintain its "proper proportion of cruisers."[22]

---

[21] Plans Division, "Limitation of Armaments: Memorandum by the Naval Staff," 14 April 1927, pp. 1-2, P.D. 02832/27, ADM 1/8715/188, PRO. See also Hector C. Bywater, *Navies and Nations: A Review of Naval Developments Since the Great War* (Boston and New York: Houghton Mifflin, 1927), pp. 268–269; D.C.N.S., Controller, and A.C.N.S. to C.N.S., "Classification and Limitation of Warships," December 21, 1926, p. 4; O.M., "Secret Memorandum," p. 6; T. H. Binney, Minute, July 29, 1927, P. D. 02896/27, ADM 116/3371, PRO.

[22] Keyes to Bridgeman, January 14, 1927, WBPCC.

By early February 1927, soon after his return from fleet maneuvers, Churchill cheerfully informed Baldwin and the Cabinet Standing Committee on Expenditure that the Admiralty "had voluntarily agreed to postpone their new building programme for seven months," thus ensuring that no "new ships would be laid down until February 1928."[23] Churchill predicted that this unexpected gift of a building delay, for which he had unsuccessfully fought so hard during the Birkenhead Committee crisis in 1925, would reduce forthcoming naval expenditures by £3,420,000.[24] Two months later, on April 14, 1927, when he learned of the Admiralty's detailed proposals to limit capital ship expenditures and extend the building holiday beyond its termination in 1932, he enthusiastically blessed the initiative as "more admirably broad-minded than those put forward by any Board of Admiralty," one which might even "result in a definite halt in shipbuilding."[25] With Churchill in full support, Beatty had jumped an important hurdle.

Winning Prime Minister Baldwin's approval took longer. The Prime Minister had several reasons to react with greater caution. A year earlier, in 1925, Beatty and Bridgeman had created considerable consternation by threatening to create a split within the Conservative Party over the Birkenhead Committee's recommendation for a one-year delay in naval construction.[26] Moreover, by the time the Admiralty had informed Baldwin of its proposals, in mid-February 1927, Coolidge had already issued invitations to a second naval conference focused exclusively on limiting auxiliaries.[27] Baldwin therefore needed time to consider these developments, especially as he remained wary of involving himself in another round of negotiations with the United States or another battle with the Admiralty.[28]

Baldwin's reluctance arose from vivid memories of the 1925 Admiralty-induced resignation crisis and from his antipathy toward the United States over its insistence on British repayment of war loans.[29] Whether his wariness stemmed from his prior dealings with the Admiralty, from his smoldering

---

[23] CAB, "Cabinet Standing Committee on Expenditures: Minutes," February 10, 1927, in Churchill, *Companion Volume 5*: 944.
[24] Ibid.
[25] CAB, NPC, "Naval Shipbuilding," n.d., p. 10, CHAR 22/176, WCP.
[26] See Chapter 4.
[27] Fanning, *Peace and Disarmament: Naval Rivalry and Arms Control, 1922–1933* (Kentucky: University Press of Kentucky, 1995), pp. 47, 52; Robert Gordon Kaufman, *Arms Control During the Pre-Nuclear Era: The United States and Naval Limitation Between the Wars* (New York: Columbia University Press, 1990), p. 108.
[28] Baldwin received the Admiralty's proposals for a second conference on 15 February 1927. See "Limitation of Naval Armaments," SBP. See also Philip Payson O'Brien, *British and American Naval Power: Politics and Policy, 1900–1936* (Westport, CT: Praeger, 1998), p. 188.
[29] Keith Middlemas and John Barnes, *Baldwin: A Biography* (London: Macmillan Company, 1970), pp. 375, 398–399; James Harold Mannock, "Anglo-American Relations 1921–1928," (Ph.D. diss., Princeton University, 1962), pp. 140–162.

resentment toward the Americans, from a reputed disinterest in naval affairs, or from some combination of the three is not clear, but Baldwin's consistent aloofness from such an important diplomatic endeavor was significant. From the outset of the Admiralty's proposals to him and continuing throughout the negotiations, he refused to take any political risks or to expend any political capital in promoting a second conference. Later, when the negotiations were in serious danger, he brushed aside Foreign Secretary Chamberlain's fervent pleas that he remain in England to guide the Cabinet's increasingly unruly deliberations. Instead, he distanced himself still further by embarking upon a scheduled tour of Canada – leaving his Cabinet to untangle what had become a complex diplomatic nightmare.[30]

Baldwin's reasons for maintaining his aloofness will most likely remain murky. He was well-known, however, as an accomplished political strategist who weighed his options carefully before either acting or declining to act.[31] Given his political suspicions of both the Admiralty and the Americans, his aloofness may have simply reflected his calculation that it was politically safer to allow the Admiralty to proceed with its conference strategy, unhindered either by him or his Cabinet because – whatever the outcome of the conference – he stood to gain politically. By approving all aspects of the Admiralty's initiative without any political interference from him or his Cabinet, he avoided giving the Admiralty an excuse for another resignation crisis, maintained internal party unity, and created the perception of supporting diplomatic efforts to lessen international tensions through naval limitation, a politically popular position both domestically and internationally. If the Admiralty succeeded in securing naval reductions, Baldwin would reap the gratitude of the British voters. Should the Conference fail, the blame could be placed on the Americans, or the Japanese, or both, for their unwillingness to appreciate the reasonableness of Great Britain's proposals. Even so, as all Conservative Party leaders would be well aware that the Cabinet had given the Admiralty complete freedom to shape and conduct the negotiations, the Admiralty therefore would share in the blame for failure, thus weakening its clout within the Conservative Party and rendering it less of a political threat in future budget battles. By allowing Beatty and Bridgeman to control the negotiations from start to finish, and by remaining benignly supportive, but aloof, Baldwin may have calculated that he had much to gain from a successful conference, while in the event of failure, he could cast the blame upon two disagreeable antagonists – the Americans and the Admiralty.

---

[30] Chamberlain to Baldwin, July 22, 1927, SBP; Richardson, *Evolution of British Disarmament Policy*, pp. 206–207.

[31] Middlemas and Barnes, *Baldwin*, pp. 483–505; O'Brien, *British and American Naval Power*, p. 188; William Bridgeman, *The Modernisation of Conservative Politics: The Diaries and Letters of William Bridgeman, 1904–1935*, ed. Philip Williamson (London: Historians Press, 1988), pp. vii–viii.

Whatever his reasons, Baldwin did not suggest any alternatives either to the Admiralty's conference strategy or to its specific proposals. Instead, he merely acquiesced to the Admiralty's objectives, including its insistence on total control of the negotiations, and on maintaining strict secrecy until the conference convened.[32] Thus, on March 9, 1927, when Robert Cecil requested permission to outline the Admiralty's proposals to Hugh Gibson, both Baldwin and Bridgeman strictly forbade him on the convenient grounds that the Cabinet had not yet given its approval.[33]

Significant also was the acquiescence of the Foreign Secretary Austen Chamberlain. After undoubtedly discussing this important diplomatic endeavor with Baldwin, he, too, bowed to Admiralty insistence on secrecy and control of all aspects of the negotiations. Like Cecil, Chamberlain worried about the possible negative consequences of keeping the details of the proposals a closely guarded secret. In early March 1927, when Admiral Hilary Jones arrived in London, hoping to get a positive Admiralty response to his combat equivalency proposals before journeying on to the resumption of the Preparatory Commission talks in Geneva, Chamberlain suggested that Bridgeman give Jones "as much of your confidence" as possible.[34] But Bridgeman ignored Chamberlain's advice, perhaps because he and his Admiralty colleagues were still smarting over the Ten Year Rule, which adversely impacted naval budgets by empowering the Foreign Office to determine the likelihood of war within the next decade, or simply because of the Admiralty's distrust of militarily naïve diplomats interfering in naval matters.[35] In any case, Bridgeman had no intention of sharing the Admiralty's proposals with Jones in advance of the conference, especially as he was aware that Jones would almost certainly reject the British proposals and immediately report his displeasure to Washington.[36]

Bridgeman, Beatty, and later historians as well, underestimated the impact of the Admiralty's insistence on secrecy. Jones had outlined his combat equivalency proposals to Admiralty representatives at Geneva several months earlier and had explained them again to Beatty in November 1926, at which time, Jones believed, Beatty had "seemed to agree" and had promised

---

[32] Cecil to Baldwin, March 9, 1925; Baldwin to Cecil, March 9, 1925; Cecil to Baldwin, March 10, 1925, SBP.
[33] Bridgeman to Cecil, February 8, 1927; Cecil to Bridgeman, February 9, 1927, 51098, LCP; Cecil to Bridgeman, March 10, 1927, 4629/1/1927/22, WBP. Beatty and Bridgeman carefully considered the policy of secrecy. See especially Minutes by Beatty, Egerton, and Bridgeman in M 01052/27, ADM 1/8715/188, PRO.
[34] Chamberlain to Bridgeman, February 25, 1927, 4629/1/1927/19, BP.
[35] See Chapter 9. See also B. J. C. McKercher, *The Second Baldwin Government and the United States, 1924–1929: Attitudes and Diplomacy* (Cambridge: Cambridge University Press, 1984), pp. 11–12.
[36] Bridgeman to Cecil, February 8, 1927, 51098, LCP.

to study them.³⁷ Jones was not the only one concerned about the Admiralty's ominous silence.³⁸ Both Chamberlain and Cecil had already advised Bridgeman and Baldwin of the wisdom of sharing the Admiralty's proposals with the Americans in advance of the conference.³⁹

The Admiralty's Director of Plans, Captain W. A. Egerton, also pointedly warned that the strategy of secrecy was likely to cause serious difficulties. He reminded his Naval Staff colleagues that the United States had repeatedly refused to re-open negotiations on capital ships. Since this was the Admiralty proposal which would generate most of the savings, one so enthusiastically anticipated by Churchill and the Cabinet, Egerton courageously warned of likely American rejection.⁴⁰

Egerton's warning was prescient. Surprised by the Admiralty's re-introduction of capital ship limitation – especially in light of the settlement of that issue at the Washington Conference in 1922 – Egerton cautioned that both American and Japanese diplomats would quite likely reserve their responses until their governments had time to consider it. Meantime, Egerton predicted that the Powers could reasonably be expected to press for continuing the negotiations on the question of the number and size of cruisers. This new focus would shift world attention away from the great savings to be realized through capital ship reductions to the more contentious one of cruiser tonnage, armaments, and numbers. The anticipated acrimony would deflate the enthusiastic world reaction, which Beatty and Bridgeman were counting upon to pressure the American and Japanese politicians into accepting the complete package of Admiralty proposals. To avoid this likelihood, Egerton advised that rather than springing a series of complete surprises at the opening of the Conference, the Admiralty ought to reveal its proposals "in general terms" before the talks began.⁴¹

Beatty brushed aside Captain Egerton's concerns. "There is no doubt that the United States scored tremendously at Washington by withholding her proposals for a Naval Holiday until the first public session," Beatty

---

³⁷ Jones, "Memorandum," November 10, 1926, PCF, JP. See also Tadashi Kuramatsu, "The Geneva Naval Conference of 1927: The British Preparation for the Conference, December 1926 to June 1927," *The Journal of Strategic Studies* No. 1, 19 (March 1996), pp. 104–121. I agree with the author on several important points concerning the Admiralty's insistence on secrecy. However, Kuramatsu is unaware of Beatty's reasons for hiding the weaknesses of his latest cruisers from the Cabinet, of Beatty's prior discussions with Jones, of Jones' combat equivalency proposal which would allow the British superiority in cruiser numbers, or of the reasons for Beatty's refusal to inform the Cabinet of crucial American objectives outlined to him by Jones. Kuramatsu accepts the Admiralty's cost-saving rationale as the sole motivation for the Admiralty's sudden decision to pursue a second conference.
³⁸ Jones to Eberle, March 21, 1927, PCF, JP; Jones to Secretary of the Navy, 17 August 1927, GBDCS VI, Miscellaneous Papers, RG 80, NA.
³⁹ See footnotes 33 and 34.
⁴⁰ W. A. Egerton, Minute, April 8, 1927, ADM 1/8715/188, PRO.   ⁴¹ Ibid.

retorted. The First Sea Lord reminded his Naval Staff colleagues that as an active participant at the Washington Conference, he had personally witnessed how effectively the United States had used this surprise tactic which, he reminded them, "caught the imagination of the world and made it difficult for any Power to oppose" the American proposals. Presenting Great Britain's own surprise, Beatty assured the Naval Staff, "would be of greatest advantage to us" because Great Britain would thereby dramatically demonstrate "to the World evidence of an earnest endeavor to limit naval armaments and expenditures."[42]

Bridgeman was not as quick to dismiss Egerton's warning. He acknowledged that Egerton had highlighted "a difficult problem."[43] Nonetheless, after consulting with colleagues, including some in the Foreign Office, Bridgeman fully supported Beatty's strategy and agreed "that we should aim at a public conference and refrain from communicating our proposals to anyone until we make them at the Conference."[44] Prime Minister Baldwin and the influential Sir Maurice Hankey, the longtime Secretary to the Committee of Imperial Defence and to the Cabinet, agreed. Both of them advised Bridgeman to "get the approval of the CID [Committee of Imperial Defence] and the Cabinet, but ... not circulate this policy in writing" to either body because "there may be leaks."[45] Thus, in contrast to Chamberlain, Cecil, and Egerton, who favored some advance notice of the proposals, Baldwin, Hankey, Beatty, and Bridgeman agreed on the presumed advantages of secrecy. They agreed further that to safeguard that secrecy, the Admiralty should make its presentations to the CID and to the Cabinet "by word of mouth," a method which had the effect of making careful assessment of the Admiralty's proposals more difficult.[46]

The Committee of Imperial Defence was far more likely to offer a critical evaluation of the Admiralty's proposals than was the full Cabinet, but on May 20, 1927, when Bridgeman made his oral presentation to the CID, he gave that Committee relatively little time to think about its details.[47] In keeping with Baldwin's and Hankey's earlier advice, Bridgeman apparently avoided distributing written copies of the Admiralty's negotiating terms to the CID. He justified this unusual procedure by explaining that the Admiralty was "particularly anxious" to maintain the strictest secrecy until the opening "moment" of the first public session.[48]

---

[42] Beatty, Minute, April 13, 1927, M 01052/27, ADM 1/8715/188, PRO.
[43] Bridgeman, Minute, April 14, 1927, M 01052/27, ADM 1/8715/188, PRO.
[44] Bridgeman, Minute, April 21, 1927, M 01052/27, ADM 1/8715/188, PRO.
[45] Bridgeman, Minute, April 25 and 26, 1927, M 01052/27, ADM 1/8715/188, PRO.
[46] Ibid. [47] Ibid.; Richardson, *Evolution of British Disarmament Policy*, p. 122.
[48] Kuramatsu, "The Geneva Naval Conference of 1927," pp. 112–113, 116; Richardson, *Evolution of British Disarmament Policy*, p. 122; CID, "Minutes of the 227th Meeting, May 20, 1927," CAB 2/5, PRO. The Secretary of the CID Sir Maurice Hankey noted in the Minutes that following Bridgeman's introductory remarks, Bridgeman "proceeded to lay before the

Beatty's New Strategies

Bridgman's oral presentation emphasized the Admiralty's strategic objectives. The first had already been achieved through the cooperation of the Foreign Office. Coolidge's call for merely extending the 10:10:6 ratio on capital ships to cruisers, destroyers, and submarines, Bridgeman complained, had been too narrowly restrictive as it "dealt with the question of ratio only" and failed therefore to "effect real economies." To circumvent Coolidge's narrow focus on auxiliaries, the Admiralty had worked with the Foreign Office to obtain American and Japanese consent to a "wider reference," which, he claimed, opened the door to negotiations on capital ships savings.[49] However, Bridgeman was either unaware of or conveniently omitted Jones' explicit warnings to Beatty opposing any capital ship revisions of the Five-Power Treaty. Moreover,

---

Committee" the Admiralty's "original recommendations." At this point Hankey inserted into the Minutes this parenthetical note: "Details of the Admiralty's proposals were subsequently circulated as C. I. D. Paper No. 808-B." However, he did not clarify if the Admiralty's "original recommendations" were "subsequently circulated" during the meeting or at some time following the meeting. It is difficult to believe that proposals of such importance to British diplomatic success at a highly publicized international conference would not have been put before the CID in writing and with sufficient time for careful consideration. Yet Hankey informed the Cabinet that the Admiralty's presentation to the CID had been made orally. In the "Provisional Minutes of the 227th Meeting of the Committee of Imperial Defence Held on May 20, 1927," C. P. 159 (27), CAB 24/187, PRO Hankey explicitly stated that the "First Lord and the First Sea Lord communicated *orally* [emphasis mine] to the Committee of Imperial Defence full details of the recommendations which they proposed to present to the forthcoming Naval Conference at Geneva with representatives of the United States of America and Japan on the subject of the reduction and limitation of Naval Armaments." This method of oral presentation was in keeping with Baldwin's and Hankey's earlier recommendation. (See footnote 45) To avoid any "preliminary publicity," Hankey noted, they had stressed the necessity of "strict secrecy." The CID approved the Admiralty's proposals that same day, May 20, 1927.

This evidence has led historian R. C. Richardson to conclude that as Bridgeman "was allowed to present the scheme to the CID only by word of mouth," it was "impossible for the CID to undertake a detailed study of the scheme and its possible ramifications" and resulted therefore in "only a cursory examination" before the CID approved it that same day. I was initially skeptical that responsible British leaders, such as Foreign Secretary Chamberlain who sat on the Committee, would have allowed such a diplomatically slipshod procedure. Nonetheless, I too have come to the same conclusion as Richardson. While Richardson did not provide a detailed analysis of the confusing and ambiguous nature of the "cursory examination" or its ramifications at the later Geneva Conference, as I have, we are nonetheless in agreement that the CID and the Cabinet allowed the Admiralty to secure approval of its own proposals based merely on the information which the Admiralty wished them to hear and with virtually no time for careful scrutiny and analysis. Indeed, even if, in the unlikely event, that a written document had been presented to the CID, the internal evidence still supports the conclusion of a "cursory examination." See Richardson, *Evolution of British Disarmament Policy*, p. 122. Hankey later noted that the "full Minutes [of the May 20 CID meeting] were not circulated until the 24th June 1927, when ... the need for close secrecy had passed." This notation can be found on the bottom of the first page of CID, "Minutes of the 227th Meeting, 20 May 1927."

[49] CID, "Minutes of the 227th Meeting, May 20, 1927, p. 1, CAB 2/5, PRO.

the Americans had reluctantly agreed to this "wider reference," but only to induce France and Italy to participate.[50]

Beyond some adjustment to French and Italian ratios, the General Board was not willing to consider either a sweeping revision of capital ship tonnage and armaments, or the extension of the building holiday, suspecting that the British would once again, as they had at the Washington Conference, fail to be forthcoming about their superior battleship characteristics.[51] Following so soon after the prolonged, bitter dispute – lasting almost three years – during which the Admiralty had sought to prevent the Americans from equalizing the combat characteristics of British battleships, Bridgeman nonetheless assured the CID and the Cabinet that the United States was ready to reconsider the issue of capital ships.[52] Moreover, as France and Italy had, by this time, already refused to join in the negotiations, the only reason for American consent to reopen this contentious issue had already been obviated.[53] When it was determined that there was no longer any possibility that France and Italy would participate, Coolidge should have withdrawn his consent to "a wider reference," but he neglected to do so.

American and Japanese agreement to reconsider "a wider reference," Bridgeman emphasized, cleared the way for the Admiralty to offer significant savings.[54] Bridgeman assured the CID that during the ten years from 1931 to 1940, the Admiralty's proposals could cut £33 million in capital ship expenditures and £16 million in cruisers for a savings of at least £49 million, a figure which he hoped to increase after the Three-Power Conference agreed on destroyer and submarine reductions.[55] To realize these great savings, Bridgeman asked that the British delegation be granted "a certain latitude in dealing with details," while promising to refer any "big question of principle" directly to the Cabinet.[56]

Historians have correctly criticized the lack of a more open, probing process by which the participating nations clarified points of agreement and disagreement in advance of their meeting in Geneva. This certainly was one of the major

---

[50] Joseph C. Grew, "Memorandum by the Undersecretary of State," March 10 1927, *FRUS*, I, 1927, pp. 26–27; Japanese Embassy to the Department of State, "Memorandum," March 11, 1927, *FRUS*, I, 1927, p. 27; Chamberlain, Minute, February 12, 1927, in" Memorandum by Mr. Campbell," *DBFP*, Ia, Series III: 571.

[51] For a copy of Coolidge's invitation, see CAB, "Further Limitation of Naval Armaments: Proposals of the Government of the United States," February 10, 1927, C. P. 59 (27), CHAR 22-185, WCP. See also Chapter 6 and Fanning, *Peace and Disarmament*, pp. 47–48.

[52] See Chapter 6.

[53] Ambassador to Italy to Secretary of State, February 21, 1927, *FRUS*, I, 1927, pp. 14–15; Castle, "Memorandum by the Chief of the Division of Western European Affairs," February 22, 1927, *FRUS*, I, 1927, 18–19; Robert William Dubay, "The Geneva Naval Conference of 1927: A Study of Battleship Diplomacy," *Southern Quarterly* (January 1970): 184–185. For the General Board's opposition to any alteration of the Five-Power Treaty see Chapter 9.

[54] CID, "Minutes of the 227th Meeting, May 20, 1927," p. 1, CAB 2/5, PRO.

[55] Ibid.   [56] Ibid.

causes of the Geneva Conference's failure. But what historians did not detect were the underlying reasons for keeping Admiralty objectives secret and its withholding of almost certain American objections from its own CID and Cabinet.[57] Since £33 of the £49 million in savings which Bridgeman projected was based on extending the capital ship holiday and on future reductions in capital ship tonnage and armament, the First Lord of the Admiralty and the First Sea Lord promised enormous savings, but, for example, omitted any mention of repeated American objections to the reintroduction of the long-settled capital ships issues.[58]

This was not the only time Beatty had withheld or suppressed unwelcome information. According to Beatty's biographer, British naval historian Stephen Roskill, Beatty had also sought to escape public exposure of his alleged errors as commander of the Battle Cruiser Squadron at the Battle of Jutland during World War I by unsuccessfully attempting to suppress embarrassing criticism.[59]

More successful was his refusal to inform the CID and the Cabinet of the Jones combat equivalency offer and of his decision to reject it. Jones had made it abundantly clear only weeks earlier, in March 1927, to Deputy Chief of Naval Staff Sir Frederick Field that in the event that his combat equivalency method was rejected, the Americans would insist on strict numerical equality in all classes of auxiliary vessels. Nonetheless, Beatty blithely proceeded to outline proposals which he knew would meet with stiff American opposition, if not outright rejection, yet he refused to share this knowledge with British politicians.

The root of Beatty's evasive tactics stemmed largely from his unwillingness to reveal to the CID and the Cabinet the Admiralty's desperate determination to achieve a treaty eliminating the 8-inch gun on all future cruisers and his knowledge that the American navy was all but certain to reject this objective. However, if he had revealed this knowledge to the CID and to the Cabinet, he might have been forced into accepting responsibility for the startling combat

---

[57] See for example Fanning, *Peace and Disarmament*, pp. 52, 64, 77–80; Kaufman, *Arms Control During the Pre-Nuclear Era*, pp. 108–111; Peter Calvocoressi, Guy Wint, and John Pritchard, *Total War: The Causes and Courses of the Second World War*, 2 vols. 2d ed. rev. (New York: Pantheon Paper Edition, 1989), II: 692–694.

[58] CID, "Minutes of the 227th Meeting," pp. 1–2; Jones, "Memorandum," November 10, 1926, p. 3, PCF, JP. Beatty first raised the possibility of reducing the size of cruisers but Jones objected on the grounds that maximum tonnage was necessary for radius of action and protection against underwater and air attacks. When Beatty then suggested "reduction in the size of battleships," Jones countered "with the same reasoning," stating clearly that he was "not in favor of such reduction."

[59] David Beatty, *The Beatty Papers: Selections from the Private and Official Correspondence of Admiral of the Fleet Earl Beatty, 1902–1927*, 2 vols. ed. B. Mc L. Ranft (Aldershot, England: Gower, 1989) I: 110–111, 201–205; II: 419–428; Stephen Roskill, *Earl Beatty*, pp. 187, 222, 323, 325–327; Sir Shane Leslie, "Memories of Beatty," *Quarterly Review* 290 (July 1952): 449–452; John Robert Ferris, *The Evolution of British Strategic Policy, 1919–1926* (London: Macmillan, 1989), pp. 185–186.

deficiencies of Britain's expensive new 8-inch-gun cruisers. There was also the risk that angry politicians would leak this secret and thereby alert rival navies. To evade these possibilities, he instead emphasized the prohibitive expense of continuing to build the larger cruisers required to carry 8-inch guns. At the same time, he kept secret Jones' repeated insistence on mounting the American version of its highly successful 8-inch-gun on all of its future cruisers.

To further bolster his case against continuing to mount the 8-inch gun on British cruisers, Beatty incorrectly informed the CID that the Admiralty "had always been rather against" 10,000-ton cruisers carrying 8-inch guns, and that the British delegates to the Washington Conference in 1921–1922 had only consented to these cruisers after "it had been forced on them at Washington."[60] The United States had, in fact, favored this cruiser, but as First Sea Lord and as one of the British delegates to the Conference, Beatty knew that the Board of Admiralty had also strongly supported these 10,000-ton, 8-inch-gun cruisers. If his memory was faulty, Beatty could easily have checked the Admiralty's 1921 instructions to the British delegation, explicitly insisting on the right to build 10,000-ton, 8-inch-gun cruisers. The Admiralty's demand was predicated, in part, on its recognition that rival navies would require the right to equal or exceed the 9,500-ton, 7.5-inch guns of the British Hawkins class cruisers already in service.[61] Four years later in 1925, Beatty was still so bent upon rapidly building these more powerful cruisers that he had provoked the cabinet crisis resulting in construction of fourteen of these 10,000-ton, 8-inch-gun-cruisers by 1927, with two more planned for 1928.[62]

Beatty was well aware that equally unacceptable to the Americans was the Admiralty's proposal for a second category of smaller cruisers, "unlimited" either by number or by ratio, and restricted to carrying only 6-inch guns. Again without informing the CID of certain American opposition, Beatty contended that by limiting the number of 8-inch-gun cruisers to the 10:10:6 ratio, Great Britain would be better able to build a larger number of unlimited and less expensive 6-inch-gun cruisers necessary to protect its extensive, worldwide trade routes.[63]

His trade route justification, already rejected by the Americans at the Preparatory Commission talks, would be presented at the Conference's initial public session "before the ears, so to speak, of the whole world" because "it would show our proposals were genuine and not prompted by bellicose

---

[60] CID, "Minutes of the 227th Meeting," pp. 2–3. See also Chapter 2, footnotes 49–51.
[61] Chapter 2. [62] See Chapters 4 and 5.
[63] Throughout the summer of 1926, Jones had repeatedly informed Admiralty representatives at the Preparatory Commission that the United States would insist upon the 8-inch gun and reject the 6-inch gun for its cruisers. See Jones to Curtis D. Wilbur, July 21, 1927, Wilbur File, JP. See also Chapters 8 and 9. Jones had repeatedly insisted on limiting the number of cruisers within a framework of either combat equivalency or numerical equality. See Jones, "Memorandum," November 10, 1926, PCF, JP.

motives." So compellingly obvious was the unique British need for an unlimited number of smaller cruisers to protect its more extensive trade routes that Beatty could not envision "any valid argument" in opposition to it.[64]

Equally important, if not more so, was Beatty's refusal to inform the CID and the British Cabinet of the reasons for the strong and repeated American opposition to his 6-inch-gun cruiser proposal.[65] American naval representatives at the Geneva Preparatory Commission talks had consistently rejected Admiralty calls for smaller cruisers with 6-inch guns.[66] Cruisers smaller than 10,000 tons, the Americans had pointed out, could not carry enough fuel to traverse the vast distances of the Pacific Ocean, where the United States had been prohibited by the Washington Conference from building refueling bases.[67] Whether Jones, in his enthusiasm for an open and aboveboard diplomacy, had revealed to the British delegates the General Board's delight in its new, highly accurate, long-range, 8-inch gun is not known, but, in any case, the excellent performance of this gun was yet another reason for vehement American opposition to smaller cruisers, which lacked sufficient tonnage to carry it.[68]

Beatty admitted to the CID that because Coolidge intended the Conference to place some restriction on all auxiliaries, the Admiralty's desire for an unlimited number of smaller cruisers would pose a "difficult problem." Robert Cecil, Great Britain's chief negotiator at the Preparatory Commission, who was present at the CID meeting and who had consulted frequently with Jones and Gibson, pointedly emphasized that such a category of unlimited cruisers would be totally unacceptable to the Americans and the Japanese. However, Beatty reassured the CID that Great Britain would be flexible on this issue, implying that the unlimited small cruiser proposal could be used as a bargaining chip. He suggested, for example, that Great Britain, might forego its demand for an unlimited number of smaller cruisers, but only in return for an agreement on limiting capital ship and big cruiser expenditures.

Despite his impression of a willingness to use unlimited cruisers as a bargaining chip, Beatty was intent on securing a treaty right to numerical superiority in these smaller cruisers. He would demand an open session during the Conference in which each nation must offer a public justification for the precise number, tonnage, and gun size of its smaller cruisers.[69] At this point, Great Britain would introduce its "ton-mileage" formula to calculate small cruiser needs, a formula which would entitle the United States to only 3.6 cruisers for every 5 for Great Britain, and entitling Japan to only 1.5. Thus, the British-proposed small-cruiser ratio would be 5:3.6 with the United States and 5:1.5

---

[64] CID, "Minutes of the 227th Meeting," p. 3. See also Naval Staff, "Limitation of Armaments: Memorandum by the Naval Staff," April 14, 1927, pp. 7–9, P. D. 02832/27, ADM 1/8715/188, PRO. This memorandum was identified as having been "Printed As CID 808-B."
[65] See footnote 63. [66] Ibid. [67] See Chapter 6. [68] Ibid.
[69] CID, "Minutes of the 227th Meeting," pp. 2–3.

with Japan. Using this formula, the British would be entitled to 70 cruisers while the United States would be limited to only 47 and Japan to only 21.[70]

This risky effort to justify British superiority in smaller cruisers was called into question from time to time and in varying yet confusing degrees by Chamberlain, Churchill, and even Bridgeman.[71] Recalling his earlier conversation with Gibson at Geneva, Chamberlain bluntly informed his colleagues "that the United States would not in any case accept a [cruiser] limit which was less than ours."[72] Later, apparently in response to Chamberlain's warning, Bridgeman offered the vague assertion that "the Admiralty would not take a grave view if the United States built up to their limit."[73] Bridgeman's questionable reassurance may account for Chamberlain's, otherwise inexplicable, conclusion that he had "no criticisms to make" of the Admiralty's proposals.[74] Nonetheless, as Bridgeman did not specify the United States' "limit," his meaning could not have been clear to the CID. Yet no one asked for clarification. The importance of Bridgeman's confusing statement and the lack of any call for elaboration would later become important during the Geneva Conference, when Bridgeman would remind his colleagues that since no one had objected to his assertion that "the Admiralty would not take a grave view if the United States built up to their limit," he had understood this to mean that the CID, and later the Cabinet, had thereby authorized him to offer the United States a treaty guaranteeing the right to parity, a view strongly supported by Cecil, but not by other members of the CID, and certainly not by Beatty.[75]

As Beatty undoubtedly anticipated, Churchill felt compelled to acknowledge that he did " not feel satisfied" with the Admiralty's claim to an unlimited number of smaller cruisers. Churchill first called the CID's attention to the Admiralty's persistent argument for an absolute minimum of seventy cruisers, the number which the Admiralty had advanced during the Birkenhead Committee debates in 1925 to justify its war plans against Japan, and was now using to justify trade protection, based on its new "ton-mileage" formula. Churchill had vigorously opposed the seventy cruisers as prohibitively expensive and unnecessary either for a theoretical and unnecessary war with Japan or for trade protection.[76] Rather than take on Beatty directly, as he had in 1925, however, Churchill instead asked him a revealing question: would the

---

[70] Naval Staff, "Limitation of Armaments: Memorandum by the Naval Staff," April 14, 1927, pp. 7–8; Naval Staff, "Limitation of Naval Armaments: Admiralty Proposals," May 6, 1927, p. 3, P.D. 02832/27, ADM 1/8715/188, PRO; Director of Plans, "Considerations Affecting Cruisers for Trade Routes," May 3, 1927, P. D. 02846/27, ADM 116/2607, PRO.
[71] CID, "Minutes of the 227th Meeting," pp. 1–6.   [72] Ibid., p. 2.
[73] Ibid.   [74] Ibid.
[75] Cecil to Chamberlain, July 17, 1927, 51097, pp. 156–160, LCP; "Notes on Lord Cecil's Speech in the House of Lords on 16 November 1927, on the Subject of His Resignation," (Hansard Vol. 69, No. 71, Cols. 8–100), pp. 4–5, in CAB 21/297, PRO. These "Notes" are probably Maurice Hankey's gloss of Cecil's speech.
[76] CID, "Minutes of the 227th Meeting," p. 3.

Admiralty remain satisfied with seventy cruisers if the United States and Japan used the unlimited category of smaller cruisers to build a number equal to those in the British fleet? Beatty then replied that seventy "would not be sufficient for our purpose." By forcing this reply, Churchill required Beatty to make two very important admissions. First, Beatty thus made it abundantly clear to the CID that he had no intention of conceding cruiser parity to the United States. Equally clear was Beatty's claim to the possibility of an even greater number of future British cruisers, which, in turn, cast some degree of doubt on the considerable annual savings which the Admiralty had promised, and which Churchill had praised.[77]

Bridgeman further confused the issue of using trade route justification for small cruiser superiority with his reminder that "America would not agree that the defense of our trade required a larger number of cruisers than the protection of American trade." But, he quickly added, the United States "would however accept the argument of relative length of coastline," a dubious and baffling claim which the CID also allowed to go unchallenged and unexplained.[78]

At this point Lord Balfour, the Lord President of the Council and England's highly skilled chief negotiator at the 1921–1922 Washington Conference, offered his advice. He reinforced the Admiralty's justification of British cruiser superiority by reminding the CID that the Empire's cruiser requirements "were largely governed by the fact that our territories were broken up and scattered in all parts of the world." Perhaps to promote harmony, Churchill agreed with Balfour. Carefully avoiding further dissent over the divisive issue of unlimited smaller cruisers, Churchill added that "our food supply was in itself an outstanding factor which differentiated us" from other naval powers.[79] Taking quick advantage of Churchill's apparent olive branch, Beatty offered what appeared to be a compromise, although a highly unlikely eventuality. The Admiralty, he promised, would remain open to limiting smaller cruisers "provided that thereby the smaller Powers [France and Italy] would be forced to accept a limitation on the number of submarines and destroyers" – a condition which Lord Balfour had insisted upon at the Washington Conference to prevent any limitation on cruisers, and which, as Beatty was well aware, had been rejected by France and Italy both at the Washington Conference and at the more recent Preparatory Commission talks in Geneva.[80]

Reminded that France and Italy would not, in any case, attend the upcoming Geneva Conference and therefore would remain free to build unlimited numbers of cruisers, destroyers, and submarines, Beatty offered still another unlikely reassurance. Although the British delegates to the Conference "would start on the principle that it is undesirable for us to impose any limit on the number of small cruisers," the delegates would be free to accept some limitation

[77] CID, "Minutes of the 227th Meeting," pp. 3, 5.   [78] Ibid.   [79] Ibid.
[80] Ibid., pp. 5–6.

if the United States and Japan agreed to all of the Admiralty's other proposals on capital ships and 10,000-ton, 8-inch-gun cruisers, destroyers, and submarines.[81]

Apparently satisfied with Beatty's appearance of reasonableness, Chamberlain advised the CID that the exact details of the Admiralty's proposals "could be safely left to the British delegates to deal with in accordance with the circumstances which might arise in the course of the Conference."[82] Baldwin immediately agreed. Having remained silent throughout the cursory CID discussion, the Prime Minister apparently sought to avoid the reemergence of controversy over cruiser numbers by instructing Bridgeman to provide the Cabinet with only an "outline of the proposals ... without necessarily going into detail in regard to actual numbers."[83] The CID then agreed to recommend the adoption of the Admiralty's negotiating proposals to the Cabinet with the added stipulation "that the British delegates should be given a reasonable latitude in regard to details."[84] On May 25, 1927 the Cabinet approved Bridgeman's oral presentation of the Admiralty's negotiating proposals.[85]

The CID's strikingly passive, cursory, and occasionally confused discussion of the Admiralty's proposals on May 20, 1927, becomes more apparent when compared to the extensive 1925 Birkenhead Committee debates and to the searching examination of the Admiralty by the Colwyn Committee following the resignation crisis. Rather than offering probing analyses, three of the CID's most knowledgeable participants – Churchill, Cecil, and Chamberlain – each raised warnings, but then quickly retreated. Each of them could have elaborated upon serious flaws in the Admiralty scheme, yet each declined. Most of the discussion merely endorsed Admiralty desires, Admiralty justifications, and the reasonableness of the Admiralty's negotiating positions.

Absent from the Admiralty's presentation of its demands, and from the CID's discussion of them, was any serious consideration of America's special needs. This absence was a stark contrast to the offer by American leaders, a compromise specifically tailored to accommodate Great Britain's need for a larger number of cruisers. Coolidge, Kellogg, Jones, and Gibson rejected the General Board's demand for strict numerical parity in all categories of auxiliary warships as the principal negotiating strategy. Instead, they adopted Jones' flexible combat equivalency method as a reasonable alternative. If accepted by the British, one variation of this method would permit the British to build twice the number of cruisers than was likely to be authorized by Congress. Moreover, Jones had made clear to Beatty the American need for the larger cruisers to protect the Philippines and Guam against the very same potential enemy which Beatty was intent upon confronting. While the Americans were sensitive to the needs of the British Empire, Beatty refused to inform the CID of

[81] Ibid.   [82] Ibid.   [83] Ibid.   [84] Ibid.
[85] Richardson, *Evolution the British Disarmament Policy*, p. 122.

the importance which the General Board placed on the plausibility of a Japanese threat to American possessions in East Asia.

The unwillingness of the CID and the Cabinet to challenge or at least critically examine the Admiralty's proposals stemmed, at least in part, from the desire to avoid a repetition of the 1925 resignation crisis and, in part, from the great benefits that the savings from the extension of the capital ship building holiday and cruiser proposals would confer upon England's deteriorating economy. The CID was also undoubtedly influenced by Beatty's professed yet carefully hedged willingness to be flexible in using the smaller cruiser category as a bargaining chip. Nonetheless, still another, unspoken factor influenced the CID: Beatty's assumption, shared by influential British political leaders, that Coolidge and Kellogg were weak politicians who would override the General Board's objections to Admiralty demands in order to reap immediate political gains. Much, then, depended on whether this assessment of the American President and Secretary of State was as shrewd and insightful as Beatty's reading of British politicians.

The cabinet minister least favorably impressed with Beatty's and Bridgeman's judgments was Robert Cecil, Viscount of Chelwood and Chancellor of the Duchy of Lancaster. As the Cabinet's chief arms-control negotiator and a devotee of the League of Nations, Cecil had worked conscientiously at the League's Preparatory Commission negotiations hammering out various disarmament proposals, which a highly suspicious Cabinet and Admiralty repeatedly rejected as idealistic and impractical.[86] Cecil complained to Baldwin and Chamberlain about the Admiralty's insistence on devising and implementing its own foreign policy at the Preparatory Commission without ever consulting him, while nonetheless expecting his support.[87] Cecil's brother James, the Marquis of Salisbury and the Cabinet's Lord Privy Seal, who substituted for his brother by chairing the CID subcommittee on arms control when Cecil was negotiating in Geneva, agreed with his brother's criticism.[88] The Admiralty, James acknowledged, "always gave the impression either that they cannot argue or that one is not worth arguing with, but that in any case they do not intend to abandon any part of their view."[89]

During the May 20, 1927 CID meeting which approved all of the Admiralty's negotiating proposals, Cecil remained silent until compelled to challenge an important shift in Admiralty policy. Only months earlier, he pointed out, the Admiralty's proposals to the Preparatory Commission had insisted on strict

---

[86] See Chapter 8; Cecil to Baldwin, August 9, 1927, SBP; Cecil to Chamberlain, May 16, 1927, April 9, 1927, AC 54/95, AC; J.C.C. Davidson, *Memoirs of a Conservative*, ed. R. R. James (London: Weidenfield and Nicolson, 1969), p. 202.

[87] See Chapter 8; Cecil to Chamberlain, April 9 and 12, 1927, March 15, 1927, Add Mss. 51079, LCP; Cecil to Bridgeman, March 10, 1927, BGMN/1, WBPCC.

[88] See sources in footnote above.

[89] Marquis of Salisbury to my dear Bob, April 16, 1927, Add Mss. 51086, LCP.

limitations on the maximum tonnage, gun size, and numbers of all warships in all major auxiliary categories.[90] The Admiralty's sudden and totally unexpected introduction of a new category of cruisers allowing for an unlimited number of 7,500-ton, 6-inch gun ships would, he implied, certainly alarm both the Americans and the Japanese, who were participating in the Preparatory Commission talks and were consequently familiar with the Admiralty's earlier demand for strict limitation on numbers in all auxiliary categories.[91] Aware as well of American insistence on some form of naval equality, Cecil advised the CID to abandon the unlimited cruiser category and to remain consistent by stating forthrightly the precise number of cruisers Great Britain required. When none of his CID colleagues supported his recommendations, and Beatty appeared willing to compromise by implying that he would use the unlimited cruiser category as a bargaining chip to gain agreement on capital ship savings, Cecil lapsed into resigned silence.[92]

Cecil's lack of spirited opposition certainly did not arise from any sudden trust in Beatty or the Admiralty. What, then, accounts for his refusal to challenge Beatty more forcefully on this vital issue? There are several possibilities. Cecil may have concluded that Beatty's promise to use the unlimited cruiser demand as a bargaining chip in exchange for an agreement on capital ships was the best that he could expect from the Admiralty. He may also have been reassured somewhat by the adoption of Chamberlain's suggestion that the delegates would be given "reasonable latitude in regard to details."[93] Finally, based on his own previous experience with Baldwin's and Chamberlain's tolerance of the Admiralty's insistence on formulating its own naval foreign policy, Cecil may have concluded that he must simply accept the reality of the Admiralty's much more powerful political influence within the CID and the Cabinet.[94]

Much more puzzling was Cecil's agreement, however reluctant, to become a leading member of the British delegation to the Conference, a delegation which he knew would be dominated by Admiralty policy and representatives. Cecil distrusted the Admiralty's professed willingness to compromise. Why, then, did he agree to become one of England's two chief negotiators, a responsibility which obligated him to promote the Admiralty's proposals, which the CID and the Cabinet had approved and therefore had become the official British

---

[90] CID, "Minutes of the 227th Meeting, May 20, 1927, pp. 1–2, CAB 2/5, PRO. See also Richardson, *The Evolution of British Disarmament Policy in the 1920s*, p. 207.

[91] CID, "Minutes of the 227th Meeting, May 20, 1927, pp.1–3.

[92] *Ibid.* For Cecil's conviction that he lacked the support of Cabinet colleagues see Cecil to Chamberlain March 15 and April 6, 1927, Add Mss. 51079; Cecil to Earl of Onslow, April 5, 1927, Add Mss. 51099, LCP.

[93] CID, "Minutes of the 227th Meeting, May 20, 1927," p. 6. The Naval Staff did foresee the necessity for some compromise. See Naval Staff, "Limitation of Armaments: Memorandum by the Naval Staff," April 14, 1927, p. 5, P.D. 02832/27, ADM 1/8715/188, PRO.

[94] See footnote 87.

negotiating objectives?[95] Cecil's own later explanation following the collapse of the Conference, while somewhat self-serving, was nonetheless significant. He recalled that although he "had not really very much approved of the Admiralty policy," he had consented to serve on the delegation because Baldwin and Chamberlain had "pressed" upon him that it would appear strange if the Cabinet's chief arms-control minister was absent from the delegation. More importantly, they had assured him that they were "prepared to make concessions."[96] Cecil still doubted his usefulness, but as Baldwin and Chamberlain "thought differently," he had ultimately "yielded to their opinion," but only after they had finally convinced him "that agreement was almost certain."[97]

Given the fact that Cecil was well known as a man of great personal integrity, moral rectitude, and high principles, his claim that Baldwin and Chamberlain had assured him that "agreement was almost certain" requires serious consideration, even though he offered this excuse after he had resigned from the Baldwin Cabinet on the highly publicized grounds that the Cabinet as well as the Americans must share in the responsibility for the failed negotiations at Geneva. Cecil had accepted Baldwin's and Chamberlain's assurance of a successful Conference at face value, in part, because they were two leaders for whom he had the greatest respect. Indeed, they were so convincing that Cecil even made a personal last-ditch effort to convince the French to join the talks. Stopping in Paris on his way to the Conference, he informed Paul Boncour, who had served with him on the Preparatory Commission, "that the Naval Conference would succeed, [and] would help considerably the [Commission's] general disarmament work," but Boncour remained skeptical.[98]

Assuming that Cecil's recollection was accurate, and that Baldwin's and Chamberlain's reassurance of success was sincere, the question arises as to how Baldwin and Chamberlain could have come by the unrealistic assumption that "agreement was almost certain." Unfortunately, there is no single document which can answer this question. Nonetheless, these three British leaders

---

[95] B. J. C. McKercher, *The Second Baldwin Government and the United States*, p. 65; Philip Payson O'Brien, *British and American Naval Power*, p. 190.

[96] Cecil to Edward [Lord Irwin], September 27, 1927, Add Mss. 51084, LCP; Viscount Cecil [Lord Robert Cecil], *A Great Experiment: An Autobiography* (New York: Oxford University Press, 1941), p. 185.

[97] Cecil explained to the House of Lords: "Accordingly when I was asked by the Prime Minister and the Foreign Secretary to go with my right hon. Friend Mr. Bridgeman to the Three-Power Conference I doubted I could be of any use. As, however, my colleagues thought differently I *yielded to their opinion particularly as it was believed that agreement was almost certain* and I thought such an agreement would help the larger [League of Nations Preparatory Commission] negotiations." [Emphasis mine.] See Great Britain, *Parliamentary Debates* (Lord's), vol. 69, 16 November 1927, pp. 88–89. See also Cecil to Baldwin, August 9, 1927, SBP; Cecil, *Great Experiment*, p. 185: CAB, "Lord Cecil: Resignation of: from Conservative Government in 1927," CAB/A./42, CAB 21, PRO.

[98] See sources in footnote 96. See also Chapter 8.

were not the only ones to rely on this assurance. Jones was also encouraged to accept it, and he, in turn, enthusiastically convinced Coolidge and Kellogg. Thus, as political leaders in both London and Washington approved the Conference based on this same assumption, it is too important for historians to dismiss their unwarranted optimism as mere naïveté or the result of a lack of careful preparation, although both are also relevant criticisms.[99]

There was an additional reason – one which deserves more careful analysis. From what source did Jones, Coolidge, Kellogg, Chamberlain, Baldwin and Cecil acquire their shared conviction that "agreement was almost certain"? The evidence strongly suggests that Beatty was that source. Soon after the Naval Staff's conclusion that its persistent efforts to correct the defects of the new 8-inch gun had all failed, Beatty called Jones to London for an "urgent" meeting in early November 1926. At this meeting he convinced Jones of the Admiralty's determination to reach an acceptable compromise based on the principle of naval equality. Elated by Beatty's reassurances, Jones immediately recorded this conversation in a long memorandum. He was especially pleased with Beatty's repeated reassurance that "there could be no question between the two countries as to general policies, and that they [the British] would bring up no question as to our equality in naval armaments...in all categories of warships." Beatty had also promised to study Jones' combat equivalency plan, with which Beatty "seemed to agree." Jones had also carefully explained to Beatty the reasons why the United States would strongly oppose Beatty's suggestion of reductions in the size and armaments of capital ships.[100]

With Jones on board, Beatty then embarked on a successful behind-the-scenes campaign to win Churchill's strong support based largely on the suggestion which Jones had firmly rejected – the projected savings from extending the capital ship building holiday as well as reductions in the size and armaments of these vessels. After Coolidge issued the invitation to this second conference, Beatty and Bridgeman outlined their negotiating strategy to Baldwin, who avoided another confrontation with the Admiralty by approving it – including the importance of keeping its contents a closely guarded secret.[101] The evidence strongly supports the conclusion, therefore, that in order to ensure participation in the Conference, Beatty very deliberately perpetrated assurances of a successful outcome both to American and British leaders. He did so because he desperately needed to limit the alarming naval vulnerabilities arising from

---

[99] Richardson, *Evolution of British Disarmament Policy*, pp. 121–122; Richard W. Fanning, *Peace and Disarmament: Naval Rivalry and Arms Control, 1922–1933* (Lexington: University Press of Kentucky, 1995), pp. 77–80; Robert Gordon Kaufman, *Arms Control During the Pre-Nuclear Era: The United States and Naval Limitation Between the Two World Wars* (New York: Columbia University Press, 1990), pp. 88–89, 108–111; Arnold A. Offner, *The Origins of the Second World War: American Foreign Policy and World Politics, 1917–1941* (New York: Praeger, 1975), p. 78.
[100] See Chapter 8.   [101] See footnotes 95–100.

the defective 8-inch gun and a steadily weakening economy, and also because he believed that he had devised a winning negotiating strategy.

It is clear, as well, that Beatty successfully manipulated Jones and to a lesser extent Baldwin, Churchill, and Cecil. What is not entirely clear is whether Beatty had briefed Bridgeman – a politician – on the startling defects of the 8-inch gun and the imperative military reasons for eliminating this gun on all rival warships at the forthcoming conference.[102] In any case, to gain Cabinet approval, he and key members of the Naval Staff emphasized great economies and their willingness to compromise, but kept secret their knowledge of the Americans' insistence on arming all of their cruisers with 8-inch guns and the reasons for the Admiralty's uncompromising determination not merely to restrict but to eliminate all 8-inch guns. To convince the Americans, Beatty promised "naval equality," while hiding his intention to reject combat equivalency, to propose a category of unlimited smaller cruisers capable of carrying only 6-inch guns, to make significant changes to the capital ship agreement, and to revive the demand that the United States justify cruiser equality by proving that it had an equal number of lengthy trade miles to protect. Beatty kept these objectives secret for another important, albeit unstated, reason: that if Jones became aware of these secret objectives, he would immediately inform the General Board, which, in turn, would put great pressure on Coolidge and Congress to reject British overtures before the conference convened.

While political leaders in London and Washington wanted to believe that "agreement was almost certain," Roland Campbell, a British diplomat, who had spent many years at the British Embassy in Washington, was more realistic. As early as mid-February 1927, only days after Coolidge had issued his invitation to the Conference and about the same time the Admiralty was presenting its proposals to Baldwin, Campbell warned Chamberlain and his Foreign Office colleagues that the success of the Conference "*appears to turn on our own naval policy.*" Crucial to success was the necessity that the Admiralty reduce the number of cruisers "below its projected requirements." The Americans, Campbell predicted, were "weak in cruisers, [and] would bring the upmost pressure to bear on us in that category, for, *if we persist in*

---

[102] The fact that Bridgeman would later support the "modus vivendi" allowing the Americans to mount the 3-inch gun on their cruisers until 1931 suggests that Bridgeman may not have had the heightened sense of the Naval Staff's pressing need to eliminate this gun on all future warships. As Beatty was vehemently opposed to Bridgeman and Cecil's "modus vivendi," it is possible that Bridgeman – a politician – had been sold on the political and economic reasons for substituting 6-inch-gun cruisers for the more expensive 8-inch-gun cruisers, but had been kept in the dark about the military reasons for eliminating this gun. In any case, there is no clear evidence to establish that Bridgeman was aware of the military importance of this secret goal. For Bridgeman's support of the "modus vivendi," see Chapter 14. See also R. H. Campbell, "Memorandum," February 12, 1927 in *DBFP*, Ia, III: 570–571 and McKercher, *Second Baldwin Government*, p. 25.

our refusal to reduce, irrespectively of ratio, the conference would surely collapse."[103] [Emphasis mine.]

Sir Esme Howard, the charming and talented British Ambassador to the United States, who enjoyed a close working relationship with Foreign Secretary Chamberlain, also worried about cruisers. Like Campbell, Howard also had many years of experience in Washington, and like Campbell, he, too, sounded the alarm. He warned Chamberlain of Coolidge's recent difficult political tussle over cruisers with congressional Republican leaders, including the powerful and influential Speaker of the House, Nicholas Longworth. Under considerable pressure from his own congressional Republicans, Coolidge had bowed to the will of Congress by signing the recent $26,650,000 cruiser bill because, Howard noted, the President's initial opposition to it had already "borne witness to his desire for economy," while Coolidge's invitation to an international conference "had made clear that the Administration was prepared to take the initiative in the direction of fleet reduction" to stop the escalating arms race. By signing the cruiser bill, Coolidge had avoided a split within his own party. But serious problems remained, and Howard especially worried about the Admiralty's cruiser demands. Should Coolidge's efforts to limit all cruisers at the international conference fail, he predicted, "it will be difficult for Congress to resist demands on the part of the big navy advocates for an increase in fleet strength which would place the United States on a parity with any other Power."[104]

Warnings from British diplomats as well as from Jones and Gibson of the vital necessity of conceding some form of cruiser equivalency were nonetheless subsumed by a set of faulty assumptions which clouded the thinking of important British decision makers in the months prior to the Conference. Basic to all of these assumptions was the belief that Coolidge's invitation was primarily a political ploy to placate competing domestic political factions. On the one hand, Coolidge sought to neutralize a perceived threat to his political leadership from Congressional leaders demanding a second conference, while, on the other hand, he sought to simultaneously pacify those demanding a more robust cruiser-building program.[105]

Roland Campbell reinforced Howard's assessment that Coolidge was using a second naval limitation conference for domestic political purposes. While Campbell predicted the failure of the Conference if the Admiralty did not reduce its cruiser requirements, he also argued that Coolidge had issued the invitation primarily for the political ammunition it would give him a year later during his reelection campaign in 1928. Campbell believed that Coolidge was attempting to solve a domestic political conundrum by the transparent and

---

[103] R. H. Campbell, "Memorandum," February 12, 1927, *DBFP*, Ia, III: 570–571. See also McKercher, *Second Baldwin Government*, p. 25.
[104] Howard to Chamberlain, March 10, 1927, *DBFP*, Ia, III: 602–604.
[105] McKercher, *Second Baldwin Government*, pp. 55–61.

"simple expedient of transforming it into an international one." Just as the Republicans had "profited enormously" as a result of the Washington Conference in 1921–1922, so also would Coolidge, "whose electioneering cupboard is bare."[106]

Campbell was not alone in this perception. Other knowledgeable diplomatic analysts were also convinced of the paramount importance of domestic politics motivating Coolidge. Sir J. Tully, the British Ambassador to Japan, for example, confided to Chamberlain that the Japanese Minister for Foreign Affairs had suggested that Coolidge's call for a quick conference was "dictated by American domestic politics."[107] Teddy Roosevelt, Jr., who had been an active participant as Assistant Secretary of the Navy during the Washington Conference, agreed. He characterized Coolidge's initiative as "a political gesture for home consumption."[108] Churchill later summarized the consensus among many British leaders when he rhetorically asked his Cabinet colleagues in July 1927: "After all who called the Conference? Who called it for political motives? Who is most interested in producing something that can be hawked about the American political platforms in 1928 as an English submission to American parity, i.e., supremacy?"[109]

This widespread assumption that Coolidge needed the conference for political advantage in 1928 lead to an even more important British assumption: that Coolidge was therefore vulnerable to British pressure at the negotiating table, especially as the Admiralty was offering a limitation package which allowed Coolidge to trumpet dramatic savings in capital ships, an end to the race in expensive 10,000-ton, 8-inch-gun cruisers, and the prospect of still further savings on destroyers and submarines. The Admiralty was convinced that its proposals would be irresistibly alluring to Coolidge precisely because agreement would fill his bare election cupboard with the campaign slogans he desperately needed to win reelection. Even as the negotiations were collapsing in late July 1927, British leaders clung desperately to this fundamental negotiating assumption. Churchill, for example, held that despite appearances, Coolidge would eventually cave in. "It may well be," he reminded the Cabinet, "that the American Government in their *anxiety for some sort of agreement* will gradually conform to our view." [Emphasis mine.][110]

---

[106] Campbell, "Memorandum," February 12, 1927, p. 570.
[107] J. Tilley to Chamberlain, February 13, 1927, *DBFP*, Ia, III: 572.
[108] Theodore Roosevelt, Jr., to R. E. Koontz, March 5, 1927, Koontz File, TR, LC.
[109] Churchill, "Cabinet Memorandum: Cruisers and Parity" July 2, 1927, in Churchill, *Companion Volume* 5: 1034.
[110] *Ibid.* McKercher accepts this view. He stated: "Coolidge's subsequent efforts to secure naval disarmament were geared solely to making a favourable impression on American voters and had little to do with allaying the fears that disarmament meant to other Powers." See McKercher, *Second Baldwin Government*, pp. 59, 55–59.

Beatty was among those who were singularly unimpressed with Coolidge. The First Sea Lord had attempted to talk to Coolidge during a long train ride while Coolidge was still Vice President, possibly at the time of the Washington Conference in 1921–1922. Although sharing a train compartment with Beatty during the journey, Coolidge characteristically had little to say. The First Sea Lord recalled that Coolidge had sat "bolt upright" in a "very tall hat" without "hardly uttering a word." This uncomfortable encounter with "Silent Cal" prompted Beatty to ridicule Coolidge, comparing him to a sailor's parrot: "E don't say much, but he thinks alot."[111]

Because of Coolidge's desire to preserve and promote cordial Anglo-American relations, leaders in the Foreign Office were somewhat less critical. They were, nonetheless, disdainful of Coolidge's seeming indifference to foreign policy. They were frustrated, for example, by his reluctance to offer his own assessments of important foreign-policy issues. They suspected, therefore, that he was almost totally focused on domestic political imperatives and possibly both ignorant of and indifferent to world affairs.[112]

Foreign Office disdain of Coolidge was reinforced by his selection of Frank B. Kellogg to replace the dynamic and impressive Charles Evans Hughes as Secretary of State. At the time of Hughes' resignation in 1925, Kellogg was serving as United States Ambassador to Great Britain, a post to which Coolidge had appointed him following Kellogg's defeat for reelection to the United States Senate from Minnesota. During Kellogg's short tenure in London, Foreign Secretary Austen Chamberlain and his colleagues in the Foreign Office formed a decidedly unfavorable view of Kellogg's capabilities. They were critical of Kellogg's inexperience in foreign affairs and consequent tendency to rely on the advice of subordinates. Chamberlain characterized him as "'a somewhat tired man who had lost his power of grip and decision.'"[113] British diplomats viewed the sixty-eight-year-old Ambassador as aged, nervous, irritable, vacillating, and unable to grapple with problems decisively. Indeed, they expected these deficiencies to worsen as he encountered his far more exhausting responsibilities as Secretary of State.[114]

Some months later, following the failure of the Geneva Naval Conference, British diplomats became even more critical of Kellogg. In November 1927, a British Foreign Office assessment lamented that when Kellogg became Secretary of State, he accepted anti-British propaganda and was "weak, irritable and [a] not too friendly politician lacking the courage required...to espouse firmly

---

[111] Chalmers, *The Life and Letters of David, Earl Beatty*, p. 368.
[112] McKercher, *Second Baldwin Government*, pp. 50–51.
[113] Quoted in *Ibid.*, p. 35. See also Howard to Chamberlain, March 30, 1926, *DBFP*, Ia, III: 881.
[114] Foreign Office, "Memorandum Respecting the Future of the Anglo-American Relations," November 17, 1927, A6768/133/45, C. P. 292 (27), CAB 24/189, PRO; McKercher, *Second Baldwin Government*, pp. 34–35, 51.

the cause of Anglo-American friendship."[115] British disdain was undoubtedly exacerbated in 1928 when Kellogg engineered the Kellogg-Briand Pact outlawing war as an instrument of international diplomacy, a pact which many nations felt compelled to sign, and which, eventually, won Kellogg the Nobel Peace Prize.

Beatty fully agreed with the Foreign Office's disparaging assessment of Kellogg. He doubted if Kellogg would have "any success" as Secretary of State because he lacked both the capacity and the strength for the enormous amount of work required by his new post. Beatty predicted that Coolidge had made "a great mistake," as the President "thinks he can do it himself [function as both President and Secretary of State] and keep the old man [Kellogg] as a figurehead."[116] Beatty now intended to take advantage of that mistake. Thus, well before the news of the defective 8-inch gun compelled him to confront unpleasant British naval realities, and to use another conference to minimize them, Beatty had already formed a thoroughly disparaging opinion of Coolidge and Kellogg, a view which convinced him that these men would bow to British naval demands in order to secure immediate domestic political advantage.

Still another important assumption, upon which Beatty was particularly counting, was the expectation that the British announcement of the extension of the capital ship-building holiday and other great savings at the opening session of the Conference would generate an enormous wave of world public exultation.[117] Because Beatty assumed that Coolidge and Kellogg were weak, vacillating, and under-informed diplomatic neophytes, concerned only with reaping domestic political advantage, he assumed further that they would be overwhelmed by the sheer force of world approval of the British proposals. Rather than resisting this overwhelming pressure, America would, as Gibson had assured Chamberlain, content itself with the mere legal right to build up to equality in the future. This capitulation would allow the Coolidge Administration to emerge as the champions of peace and tax-reduction during the 1928 reelection campaign.

Until shortly before the opening of the Conference in mid-June 1927, the Admiralty's strategy was proceeding exactly as Beatty and Bridgeman had planned. Its hasty adoption by the CID and the Cabinet reassured the Admiralty of its continuing political and diplomatic influence. However, according to Beatty, when violent eruptions at Chinese and Egyptian ports required the dispatch of British warships to Shanghai, Alexandria, and Port Said, Baldwin refused to allow Beatty to attend the Conference, instead ordering him, as First Sea Lord, to remain in London to direct naval operations

---

[115] Foreign Office, "Memorandum Respecting the Future of the Anglo-American Relations," November 17, 1927.
[116] Beatty to Wife, January 15, 1925, BTY17/69, BP.
[117] Beatty, Minute, April 13, 1927, Minute Sheet No. 2, M01052/57, ADM 1/8715/188, PRO.

in China and Egypt and to consult with him daily.[118] Beatty had counted on personally orchestrating British negotiations at Geneva, but he now had no choice but to ask Sir Frederic Field, his Deputy Chief of Naval Staff, who had attended the Preparatory Commission talks, to accompany Bridgeman and Cecil.[119]

More than these uprisings may have been at work in keeping Beatty at home. As early as April 1927, well before the uprisings, Chamberlain recorded that the Foreign Office had recommended Bridgeman, Cecil, and Vice Admiral Field, but not Beatty, to represent Great Britain at the Conference.[120] Foreign Office lack of enthusiasm may have arisen from the perception that Beatty had obstructed the talks at the Washington Conference in 1921–1922 and had been recalled to London to smooth the path to agreement. Certainly, during the 1925 Cabinet crisis, he had proven to influential Conservative party leaders that he could be an obstinate, uncompromising political manipulator, lacking in diplomatic finesse. In any case, whatever Baldwin's reasons for retaining Beatty in London, this decision was a major disappointment to him, which seriously hampered his plan to control the negotiations.

As the British delegates prepared to leave for Geneva, Beatty confessed to some trepidation. Rather than continue the fiction that "agreement was almost certain," Beatty finally admitted that the British delegation would encounter substantial American opposition, so much so in fact, that he "did not envy them in their task."[121] More worrisome was the Cabinet reaction to the outrage he expected from the Americans. The "principle difficulty," he consoled himself, would be "the Cabinet at home."[122] Since he was forced to remain in London, he could, at least, deal directly with any presumed Cabinet defections during the acrimonious negotiations. At the same time, he expected to control the British naval delegates at Geneva, as he had "fairly tied them up so they cannot decide any important question ... [on] their own but have got to refer it to me first."[123] Beatty was determined that he, not Bridgeman and Cecil, would decide what constituted a "reasonable latitude in regard to details."

---

[118] Beatty to Wife, June 14 and 22, 1927 in Chalmers, *Life and Letters*, pp. 413–414.
[119] Stephen Roskill, *Naval Policy between the Wars*, p. 358.
[120] Chamberlain to Howard, April 5, 1927 in *DBFP*, Ia, III: 588–589.
[121] Beatty to Wife, June 17, 1927 in Chalmers, *Life and Letters*, p. 414.   [122] *Ibid.*
[123] *Ibid.*

FIGURE 1. HMS Kent – Note the eight 8-inch guns in four turrets.
Source: National Maritime Museum, Greenwich, London. Courtesy of National Maritime Museum, Greenwich, London.

FIGURE 2. USS Pensacola – Note the ten 8-inch guns in four turrets and the ability to launch fire-control spotter aircraft. "USS Pensacola (CA-24) Underway at sea, September 1935."
Source: Official US Navy Photograph from the collections of the US Naval Historical Center, September 1935. Courtesy of Naval History and Heritage Command, Washington, DC.

FIGURE 3. Back Seat: President Woodrow Wilson; President-Elect Warren G. Harding; Front Seat: Speaker of the House Joseph Cannon; Senator Philander Knox. "Woodrow Wilson, Warren G. Harding, Philander Knox, and Joseph Cannon, in convertible, March 4, 1921."
Source: National Photo Company Collection (Library of Congress), March 4, 1921. Courtesy of the Library of Congress Prints and Photographs Division, LC-USZ62-126309.

FIGURE 4. Frank B. Kellogg, Ambassador to Great Britain shortly before his appointment as Secretary of State; Secretary of State Charles Evans Hughes. "Frank B. Kellogg and Sec. Hughes, 2/27/25."
Source: National Photo Company Collection (Library of Congress), [19]25 February 27. Courtesy of the Library of Congress Prints and Photographs Division, LC-DIG-npcc-26794.

FIGURE 5. Admiral Sir David Beatty, First Sea Lord and Chief of the Admiralty Naval Staff. "Adm. Sir David Beatty."
Source: Bain News Service, publisher, [between ca. 1910 and ca. 1915]. Courtesy of the Library of Congress Prints and Photographs Division, LC-DIG-ggbain-17741.

FIGURE 6. Winston S. Churchill, Chancellor of the Exchequer. "Winston Churchill, 10/18/29."
Source: National Photo Company Collection (Library of Congress), October [=9]29 18. Courtesy of the Library of Congress Prints and Photographs Division, LC-DIG-npcc-17934.

FIGURE 7. Foreign Secretary Austen Chamberlain, Prime Minister Stanley Baldwin, Chancellor of the Exchequer Winston S. Churchill. "[Standing, left to right: Mr. Austen Chamberlain, Prime Minister Stanley Baldwin, and Sir Winston Churchill] / Photo Central News from Underwood & Underwood."
Source: Underwood & Underwood, 1925. Courtesy of the Underwood & Underwood/ Library of Congress Prints and Photographs Division, LC-USZ62-111781.

FIGURE 8. William Clive Bridgeman, First Lord of the Admiralty. "William Clive Bridgeman, 1st Viscount Bridgeman of Leigh."
Source: Lafayette (Lafayette Ltd), December 10, 1926. Courtesy of the National Portrait Gallery, London.

FIGURE 9. Viscount Robert Gascoyne-Cecil of Chelwood. Cecil served with Bridgeman as one of the two chief British negotiators at the Geneva Naval Conference of 1927. A third prominent member of the negotiating team, Vice Admiral Frederick Field, is not pictured. "Viscount Cecil of Chelwood, Robert Gascoyne-Cecil, 1864–1958."
Source: Harris & Ewing, c 1919 Sept. 5. Courtesy of the Library of Congress Prints and Photographs Division, LC-USZ62-83296.

FIGURE 10. President Calvin Coolidge; Secretary of Commerce Herbert C. Hoover. *Source*: [Orphan.] Courtesy of the Herbert Hoover Presidential Library, West Branch, Iowa.

FIGURE 11. Ambassador to Belgium Hugh Gibson; Ambassador to Great Britain Alanson B. Houghton. Gibson shared duties with Admiral Hilary P. Jones as the American negotiators at the Geneva Naval Conference of 1927. "Hugh Gibson & A.B. Houghton."
Source: Bain News Service, publisher, [no date recorded on caption card]. Courtesy of the Library of Congress Prints and Photographs Division, LC-DIG-ggbain-39105.

FIGURE 12. Admiral Hilary P. Jones. Jones was also chief of the American naval delegates at the Geneva Naval Conference of 1927. "Vice Adml. Hilary P. Jones, 6/23/21."
Source: National Photo Company Collection (Library of Congress), June 23, 1921. Courtesy of the Library of Congress Prints and Photographs Division, LC-DIG-npcc-04460.

FIGURE 13. Rear Admiral Frank H. Schofield. Photo taken in 1917 when he was a captain.
Source: [Unavailable.] Courtesy of the Yates County History Center, Penn Yan, NY.

FIGURE 14. Prime Minister Ramsay MacDonald and President Herbert C. Hoover. "MacDonald & Hoover, 10/5/29."
Source: National Photo Company Collection (Library of Congress), October 5, 1929. Courtesy of the Library of Congress Prints and Photographs Division, LC-DIG-npcc-17850.

11

Conference Shocks

The Geneva Naval Conference convened on June 20, 1927 at a large U-shaped table in the famous Glass Room of the League of Nations headquarters.[1] With world attention focused on this dramatic international event, the Admiralty expected a swift tidal wave of popular support which would compel a weak-willed Coolidge to accept its cost-cutting proposals. As these hopes quickly faded, Bridgeman sought Japanese support, only to discover that the Japanese were quite content to exploit the widening rift between Great Britain and the United States. After eight frustrating days of attempting to force consideration of his capital ship proposal, Bridgeman

---

[1] The composition of the delegations elicited extensive commentary. See Bridgeman, Diary, June-August 1927, p. 143, WBP; Castle, Diary, April 27, and May 11, 1927, CP; Richard W. Fanning, *Peace and Disarmament: Naval Rivalry and Arms Control, 1922–1933* (Lexington: University Press of Kentucky, 1995), pp. 48–49, 53–56, 58, 77; Christopher Hall, *Britain, America and Arms Control, 1921–1937* (New York: St. Martin, 1987), pp. 44, 100; B. J. C. McKercher, *The Second Baldwin Government and United States, 1924–1929: Attitudes and Diplomacy* (Cambridge: Cambridge University Press, 1984), pp. 65–67; Kellogg to My Dear Ambassador, May 2, 1927; Kellogg to Coolidge, May 27, 1927, MC 25, KP; Houghton to Kellogg, February 21, 1927, FRUS, 1927, I: 20–21; Grew to Herrick, March 12, 1927, FRUS, 1927, I: 28–29; Cecil to Baldwin, March 28, 1927, SBP; Cecil to Chamberlain, April 12, 1927, DBFP, Ia, III: 221; Gibson to Kellogg, April 14, 1927, FRUS, 1927, I: 35–36; Kellogg to Houghton, April 22, 1927, FRUS, 1927, I: 37–38; Chamberlain to Cecil, May 4, 1927, Add Mss. 51079, LCP. See also CID, "Minutes of the 222nd Meeting," March 4, 1927, pp. 6–7, CAB 45, PRO; Castle, Diary, April 27, 1927, CP; Office of Naval Intelligence, "Geneva Conference (1927) For the Limitation of Naval Armaments-Japanese Delegates," June 1927, Records of the Chief of Naval Operations, Intelligence Division, C-9-b, Box 146, NA; Sadao Asada, "The Japanese Navy and the United States" in *Pearl Harbor As History: Japanese-American Relations, 1931–1941*, eds. Dorothy Borg and Shumpei Okamoto (New York: Columbia University Press, 1973), pp. 225–227. For additional confidential intelligence reports on the backgrounds and predilections of the Japanese delegates see Jones, PCF 1927, LC; William F. Trimble, "The United States Navy and the Geneva Conference for the Limitation of Naval Armament, 1927," (Ph.D. diss., University of Colorado,

reluctantly unveiled the Admiralty's demands for an unlimited number of smaller 6-inch-gun cruisers, for strict limits on the 10,000-ton, 8-inch-gun cruisers, and for the elimination of the 8-inch gun on all future warships. With this latest surprise, negotiations deteriorated as the Americans came to suspect that the Admiralty's demands were based upon its determination to achieve naval supremacy and its anticipation of a future conflict over freedom of the seas.

This suspicion quickly hardened into an abiding mistrust. American naval delegates now repeatedly violated the Conference rule to keep the daily discussions secret by systematically leaking British proposals to American reporters. As the implications of these proposals became clearer, Coolidge and Kellogg threatened to terminate the negotiations unless Great Britain explicitly and publicly acknowledged the American right to parity. On June 29, as the British Cabinet labored to devise cleverly worded language intended to avoid such an acknowledgment, Bridgeman and Cecil issued a press release affirming the right of the Americans to a treaty guaranteeing equality in all classes of warships, thus pleasing the Americans while generating growing confusion and anger in London. This confusion was the direct result of the conflicting and unresolved positions taken at the earlier May 20 meeting of the Committee of Imperial Defence (CID).

* * *

Hugh Gibson, the chief of the American delegation, opened the first plenary session with proposals which were hardly surprising. He emphasized the necessity for ending the competitive naval arms race in auxiliaries by reducing these forces to the lowest level consistent with a nations' defense. This could be accomplished by agreeing to a limit of 300,000 tons on

---

1974), pp. 151–155; Kellogg to My Dear Ambassador, May 2, 1927, MC 25, KP; Kellogg to Coolidge, May 27, 1927, MC 26, KP; Kellogg to Coolidge, May 27, 1927, *FRUS*, 25 May 1925, I: 40–41; Castle, Diary, June 5, 1927, CP; Gibson, Diary, May 25, 1927, HHPL; Kellogg to My Dear Clara, June 2, 1927, MC 26, KP; Robert Gordon Kaufman, *Arms Control During the Pre-Nuclear Era: The United States and Naval Limitation Between the Wars* (New York: Columbia University Press, 1990), p. 79; Kellogg to Jones, June 2, 1927, Kellogg File, JP; Gibson to Jones, April 27, 1927, Gibson File, JP; Jones to Eberle, March 21, 1927, JP; Jones to Secretary of the Navy, August 17, 1927 GBDCS, VI.6, Miscellaneous Papers, GBUSN, RG 80, NA. In Miscellaneous Papers are Jones' letters of commendation to the Secretary of the Navy on each of the naval officers accompanying the delegation. For a complete list of the delegates, see 1927 Conference, 100 General, Box 438, RG 43, NA; Castle, Diary, June 5, 21, and 28, 1927, CP; Kellogg to Dulles, April 20, 1927, MC 25, KP; Gibson to Theodore Marriner, August 11, 1927, Marriner File, GP. For critics of the American delegates, see Bridgeman, Diary, July-August 1927, p. 143. Shearer was also critical of Dulles. William B. Shearer newspaper article in the *New York American*, October 23, 1927 in Newspaper Clippings File, GP; Kellogg to Coolidge, July 22, 1927, MC 27, KP; Gibson to Mother, June 1, 1927, GD; SMP, GB, "Proposals for the Geneva Conference: Study No. 1," June 1, 1927, GB 438, in PP, Foreign Affairs, Disarmament Series, HHPL. There are a number of General Board studies in this box.

cruisers, 250,000 tons on destroyers, 90,000 tons on submarines and by extending the 10:10:6 ratio to these vessels.[2]

First Lord of the Admiralty William Bridgeman shocked the Americans, however, with his opening address. It called for great economic savings by prolonging the life of capital ships from twenty to twenty-six years, by extending the current capital ship building holiday from ten to sixteen years, and by expanding the service life of cruisers to twenty-four years, destroyers to twenty years, and submarines to sixteen years. Further savings would be realized by reductions in gun caliber for all capital ships and cruisers and by applying the 10:10:6 ratio to a drastically curtailed number of 10,000-ton, 8-inch-gun cruisers. Additional economies would flow from limiting all future cruisers to 7,500 tons with a maximum gun size of only 6 inches. However, as he pointedly refrained from placing a limit on the number of these smaller, less powerful cruisers, the American delegates became increasingly anxious.[3]

As expected the two chief Japanese delegates, Admiral Viscount Minoru Saito, the former Minister of the Japanese Navy, and Viscount Ishii Kikijuro, Japan's top diplomat, merely suggested shorter service life for all auxiliaries and gently hinted at the need for a ratio greater than 60 percent.[4]

Bridgeman was delighted with American surprise and disappointment. He reassured Baldwin that the Americans had committed "a great political blunder by calling the Conference merely to help them in electioneering." They had also "greatly irritated the Japs" by restricting their ratio to 60 percent,

---

[2] League of Nations, *Records of the Conference for the Limitation of Naval Armament Held at Geneva from June 20 to August 14, 1927*. Copies of these Records were published by the League of Nations, the United States Department of State, the United States Senate (United States Congress, Senate, 70th Cong., 1st. sess., 1928, S. Doc. 55) and by the Japanese Foreign Ministry, *Documents on Japanese Foreign Policy*, Nihon Gaiko Junebu Kaigun Gumbi Seigen Kaigi, 1982. My page number citations are from *Documents on Japanese Foreign Policy*. (Hereafter cited as *Records*). For the Conference Committee structure and personnel see *Records*, pp. 17–21; Kellogg to Coolidge, June 17, 1927 MC 28 CCP; Schofield, Diary, June 20, 1927, SD; "Verbatim Report of First Plenary Session," in 1927 Geneva Naval Conference, Records of the Conference, 110.1 Executive, Box 439, RG 43, NA. A complete set of the conference minutes is in RG 43, NA. See also Gibson to Kellogg, June 20, 1927, FRUS I: 46–47. These tonnages were based on the General Board's recommendations. See SMP, GB, "Proposals for the Geneva Conference: Study No. 1," June 1, 1927, GB 438, in PP, Foreign Affairs, Disarmament Series, HHPL.

[3] *Records*, pp. 21–23; Bridgeman to Chamberlain, June 20, 1927, *DBFP*, Ia, III: 605–609; R. C. Richardson, *The Evolution of British Disarmament Policy in the 1920s* (London: Leicester University Press, 1989), p. 123; Rolland A. Chaput, *Disarmament in British Foreign Policy* (London: George Allen and Unwin, 1935), pp. 155–158; Philip Payson O'Brien, *British and American Naval Power: Politics and Policy, 1900–1936* (Westport, CT: Praeger, 1998), pp. 190–191; Hall, *Britain, America and Arms Control*, p. 45.

[4] *Records*, pp. 23–24; Chaput, *Disarmament in British Foreign Policy*, pp. 159–160; Robert A. Hoover, *Arms Control: The Interwar Naval Limitation Agreements* (Denver: University of Denver Press, 1980), pp. 82–84.

Conference Shocks 219

and the Americans could not reject the Admiralty's much more economical and "practical proposals" without making "great fools of themselves."[5] Beatty was equally pleased, agreeing that Bridgeman's opening "broadsides" had "taken a great deal of wind out of their [American] sails."[6]

The Admiralty's opening "broadsides" had unintended consequences. Immediately recognizing the significance of the absence of any limitation on smaller cruisers, a chagrined Kellogg complained to Coolidge that Gibson and Jones "had been talking for months with the British during the Preparatory Commission and at the Admiralty in London" and "had no reason to think [that] the British proposals [would] contain no limitation" on smaller cruisers. Revealing a much stiffer backbone than the Admiralty had anticipated, Kellogg concluded that the United States had offered " a clean-cut, straight limitation based on the same ratio as the Washington Treaty and if other countries do not wish to come in, our shirts are clean."[7]

While Kellogg was keenly disappointed, Jones was "entirely outraged." Well before Coolidge called the Conference, he had repeatedly rejected the Admiralty's capital ship proposals. It could hardly escape the "notice of even a child," he charged, that extending the Five-Power Treaty's capital ship building holiday from ten to sixteen years was intended to "freeze us into a position of inferiority... from which it would be impossible for us to escape in view of the existence of the *Nelson* and *Rodney*" battleships. Equally galling was the fact that he had thoroughly discussed the 6-inch gun with the British "all last summer" and had repeatedly explained the reasons why smaller cruisers mounting 6-inch guns were unsuitable to American needs, especially in the Pacific.[8]

During the first week of negotiations Admiralty strategies increasingly went awry. As Captain Edgerton had predicted, the Americans refused to discuss capital ships until an agreement on cruisers was reached.[9] At the same time, the Americans warded off pressure from the Japanese for an increased ratio and from the British for a second plenary session to argue the reasonableness of their proposals to the world and thereby put pressure on Kellogg and

---

[5] Bridgeman, Diary, June-August 1927, p. 149; Bridgeman to Maurice, June 21, 1927, 4629/1/1927/48, WBP; Bridgeman to Baldwin, June 21, 1927, SBP; Bridgeman, Diary, June-August 1927, p. 149; Bridgeman to Sire [King George V], June 20, 1927, ROSK; Standfordham to Bridgeman, June 24, 1927, BGMN 1, WBPCC.
[6] Beatty to Bridgeman, June 23, 1927, BGMN 1, WBPCC and in 4629/1/1927/49, WBP; Beatty to Wife, June 21, 1927, BTY 17/77, BP.
[7] Kellogg to Coolidge, June 22, 1927, MC 28, KP; Castle to Coolidge, June 22, 1927, CCP; Gibson to Mother, June 23, 1927, HHPL.
[8] Jones to Wilbur, July 21, 1927, Wilbur File, JP and sources cited in Chapter 8.
[9] Edward Sander to Kellogg, June 22, 1927, MC 28, CCP; Gibson, "Memorandum of Conversation," June 22, 1927, pp. 2, 4–6, Department of State, RG 43, NA. The Memorandum of Conversation File, Box 440, Department of State, RG 43, NA is hereafter cited as MCDS; Gibson to Kellogg, June 27, 1927, *FRUS*, I, 1927: 60–61.

Coolidge.[10] Gibson and Jones instead repeatedly sought to direct the talks toward Jones' combat equivalency method, but Bridgeman and Admiral Sir Frederick Field, the principal Naval Staff delegate, repeatedly rebuffed them.[11] This in turn reinforced the suspicion that the underlying aim of an unlimited number of smaller British cruisers was not economy, but a superiority which would enable the Admiralty to interdict American neutral trade during a future war.

Bridgeman's efforts to pressure the Americans by dangling the prospect of a higher ratio before the Japanese was stymied by the determined opposition from Australian and New Zealand representatives within the British delegation at Geneva and by Churchill in London.[12] Bridgeman's bargaining ability decreased still further when Admiral Field had to admit that at the Washington Conference the British had used the much lighter measure of legend rather than standard tonnage to disguise the actual tonnage of their capital ships, thus adding 63,000 tons to their 33,000-ton advantage, for a superiority of 96,000 tons and an effective ratio against the Americans of 13:10 rather 10:10.[13]

---

[10] Jones to William Howard Gardiner, April 2, 1924, Gardiner File, JP; Jones, "Memorandum," June 23, 1927, PCF, JP; SMP, GB to Secretary of the Navy, "Further Limitation of Naval Armament: General Consideration of National Policies," April 21, 1927, pp. 2–3, 4, 6; SMP, GB, "Memorandum: Study No. 1: Proposals for the Geneva Conference," June 1, 1927, both in PP, Foreign Affairs, Disarmament Series, HHPL; Schofield, Diary, June 21, 1927, SD.

[11] Gibson, "Memorandum of Conversation," June 23, 1927, pp. 2–4 MCDS; Gibson to Kellogg, June 24, 1927, *FRUS*, 1927, I: 54–55; Jones, "Japanese and British Proposals," PCF, 1927, JP; Curtis D. Wilbur to Allison Houghton January 18, 1927, 431–1, GBUSN RG 80, NA. See also George T. Davis, *A Navy Second to None: The Development of Modern American Naval Policy*, (New York: Harcourt, Brace, 1940), p. 322; Fanning, *Peace and Disarmament*, p. 58; R. C. Richardson, *The Evolution of British Disarmament Policy in the 1920s* (London: Leicester University Press, 1987), p. 126; Schofield, Diary, June 22, 1927, SD; Executive Committee, "Minutes," June 24, 1927, pp. 47–53; Gibson to Kellogg, June 23 and 24, 1927, *FRUS*, 1927, I: 51–53, *Records*; Kellogg to Gibson. June 24 and 25, 1927, *FRUS*, 1927, I: 53–54; TC, "Minutes," June 28 1927, pp. 82–84, *Records*. Jones stated that the British "figure represented at first at Washington by the American Delegation was accepted by the British and was considerably smaller than this." Jones also argued that Balfour "had agreed to the figures proposed by the United States." See also Bridgeman to Chamberlain, June 23 and 26, 1927, *DBFP*, Ia, III: 613–614, 617; BED, "Minutes," June 21, 1927, pp. 2–3, BEDM; Beatty to Keyes, June 26, 1927 in Roger Keyes, *The Keyes Papers: Selections from the Private and Official Correspondence of Admiral of the Fleet Baron Keyes of Zeebrugge, 1919–1938*, ed. Paul G. Halpern 2 vols. (London: George Allen and Unwin, 1980), 2: 223–224.

[12] Bridgeman to Chamberlain, June 22, 1927, *DBFP*, Ia, III: 611; Bridgeman to Baldwin, June 21, 1927, SBP, BED, "Minutes," June 21 and 22, 1927, BEDM; Churchill, "Naval Shipbuilding: IV-Geneva Conference, 1927," p. 11, CHAR 22/176, WCP.

[13] TC, "Minutes of the Technical Committee," June 22, 1927, pp. 70–72, *Records*. Lord Balfour had in fact specifically requested an agreement on the exact meaning of tonnage as the measurement by which to evaluate the combat capabilities of capital ships. This agreement was essential, he argued, in order to avoid "a controversy arising as to what ton was intended, how the measurement was to be made, and whether the measurement had been properly and honestly reached." The delegates agreed with Lord Balfour and adopted standard tonnage displacement.

Bridgeman diminished his leverage still further on June 28 when he finally had to reveal the Admiralty's insistence on sixty 7,500-ton, 6-inch-gun cruisers, a limit of fifteen 10,000-ton, 8-inch-gun cruisers to equal the number of new British cruisers, and the elimination of the 8-inch gun on all future warships, thereby asking the Americans to accept total British cruiser demands of 600,000 tons rather than their limit of 300,000.[14]

While members of the American delegation remained outwardly calm, the naval advisers within the delegation reacted with smoldering indignation and a prevailing sense of betrayal. Rather than stopping the cruiser arms race, Great Britain appeared intent on escalating it. Kellogg, too, was indignant. He ordered that Gibson "should ... not sign a treaty increasing British cruiser tonnage by about seventy-five percent and requiring us to triple our effective cruiser strength." Should the British continue to insist on these terms, Kellogg was confident that American public opinion "would more than justify failure to conclude a treaty."[15] Equally significant, Kellogg's thinking now edged much closer to that of the General Board's belief that the purpose of such an escalation could only mean that the British viewed the United States as a future threat and that Great Britain's real objective was the cynical use of arms-control diplomacy to ensure its own naval supremacy. Indeed, Kellogg informed

---

See U. S., Congress, Senate, Doc. No.126, *Conference on the Limitation of Armament*, 67th Congress, 2d. sess., (Washington, D.C.: Government Printing Office, 1922), pp. 306–307. Chapter 1, Article 2 of the Five Power Treaty repeatedly specified standard displacement. See pp. 872–874 and Gibson to Kellogg, June 27, 1927, *FRUS*, 1927, I: 58–59; Schofield, Diary, June 24, 1927, SD; Jones, "Memorandum: The British and Japanese Proposals," June 23, 1927, PCF, JP.; William F. Trimble, "The United States Navy," p. 233; William R. Braisted, "On the American Red and Red-Orange Plans, 1919–1939" in *Naval Warfare in the Twentieth Century, 1900–1945: Essays in Honor of Arthur Marder*, ed. Gerald Jordan (London and New York: Crane, Russack, 1977), p. 171; Schofield, Diary, June 24, 1927, SD; Jones, "Memorandum: The British and Japanese Proposals."

PCF, 1927, JP. See also Frank H. Schofield, "Memorandum: The Gun Elevation Question," November 6, 1923, UNG 1923–1930, NWC; Rear Admiral C. C. Bloch, "Memorandum," January 13, 1927, in Chief of Naval Operations, Intelligence Division, Attaché Reports 1886–1939, E-12-C, RG 38, NA; Jones to Alanson Houghton, January 14, 1927, Houghton File, JP; Schofield, "Gun Elevation Question," November 6, 1923 and Bureau of Ordnance, "Memorandum," January 13, 1927; Director of Naval Intelligence, "Maximum Range of Main Battery Guns," July 18, 1924 both in Chief of Naval Operations, Intelligence Division, Naval Attaché Reports 1886–1939, E-12-C, 17216, RG 38, NA; C.C. Bloch, to President Naval War College, General Board, and Chief of Naval Operations, "Battle Range Studies Against Red Fleet," June 19, 1924, Miscellaneous Items 240, NWC.

[14] TC, "Minutes," June 28, 1927, pp. 83–87, *Records*.

[15] Kellogg to Gibson, June 24, 1927, *FRUS*, 1927, I: 55–56; Kellogg to Gibson, June 25 and 28, 1927 in MC 28, CCP; Gibson to Kellogg, June 27, 1927, *FRUS*, 1927, I: 59–61. For press speculation see, for example, ADW [?], "Memorandum of Conversation with Mr. Sharkey," June 28, 1927, MCDS. Sharkey was the Associated Press representative and generally deemed reliable. Cecil denied this and other speculations. See Cecil to Chamberlain, July 2, 1927, Add Mss. 51079, LCP. See also Howard to Kellogg, June 27, 1927, *FRUS*, 1927, I: 61–62; Kellogg to Gibson, June 28, 1927, *FRUS*, 1927, I: 64.

Coolidge that British claims to capital ship economy were "quite likely" mere camouflage to ensure their own continued battleship superiority. Coolidge agreed with Kellogg's analysis. "Your position," he reassured Kellogg, "seems to me correct and satisfactory."[16]

The growing American perception that British demands at Geneva were based on the likelihood of future hostilities with the United States alarmed Sir Esme Howard, the British Ambassador in Washington. Howard warned Chamberlain that rather than waste "time, money, and energy" in a naval race which the United States could easily win and which served to feed suspicions of a war, one which would be "ruinous for us" and for the British Empire, Chamberlain should intervene in the negotiations to reassure the Americans that "a corner stone" of British foreign policy rested on the conviction that "no war between us is possible." By so doing, Chamberlain could scotch the growing suspicion that the United States was a "potential enemy," a "very silly impression" created by the Admiralty, which was by now already widely accepted in the United States. Well aware of the Admiralty's likely reaction, Chamberlain merely informed Bridgeman of Howard's concern.[17]

As Chamberlain undoubtedly expected, Bridgeman dismissed Howard's warning as "sheer nonsense" and simply "ridiculous."[18] He agreed with Beatty's complaint that "those d----d Yanks are very tiresome and ridiculous and very sensitive" as well as a "very slippery lot." Unlike Beatty, who also blamed Prime Minister Baldwin's ignorance of the Empire and lack of courage in supporting the Admiralty, Bridgeman placed all of the blame for the stymied negotiations on the Americans.[19] Beneath his calm exterior, Bridgeman privately castigated them as "most obstructive," suspicious, jealous, and malicious, "very conceited," "very stupid," and "mostly second-rate men [who] do not understand naval affairs well enough to discuss them intelligently." In sharp contrast to this "self-satisfied race," he claimed that "the British race is the only one you can trust fully to play the game."[20] Rather than admit that the Admiralty's pre-conference secrecy had stoked American suspicions, as both Cecil and William Tyrell, the British Undersecretary of State for Foreign Affairs, privately acknowledged, Bridgeman convinced himself that American obstinacy stemmed from the fact that their "eyes are fixed as

---

[16] Coolidge to Kellogg, June 30, 1927, MR 28, CCP and *FRUS*, 1927, I: 64. On American resistance to capital ship reductions see Trimble, "United States Navy," pp. 209, 203–205, 215–217.

[17] Howard to Chamberlain, 23, 27, 28 June 1927, *DBFP*, Ia, III: 614–615, 619–621.

[18] Bridgeman to Sir Esme Howard, June 24, 1927, *DBFP*, Ia, III: 616–617.

[19] Bridgeman to Chamberlain, June 23 and 26, 1927, *DBFP*, Ia, III: 613–614, 617; BED, "Minutes," June 21, 1927, pp. 2–3, BEDM; Beatty to Keyes, June 26, 1927 in Keyes, *The Keyes Papers*, 2: 223–224; Beatty to Wife, June 21, 1927, BTY 17/77, BP; Beatty to Keyes, June 23, 1927, BTY 17/77, BP; Beatty to Keyes, June 26, 1926, in Keyes, *Keyes Papers*, 2: 223.

[20] Bridgeman to Baldwin, June 21 and 25, 1927, SBP; Bridgeman to Maurizio Mio, June 27, 1927, 4629/1/1927/54, WBP; Bridgeman to Dearest Mother, July 2, 1927, 4629/1/1927/53, WBP.

much on their own electioneering tactics at home as upon the success of the Conference here."[21] He vowed to King George V that he would not "give way on every point in order to help Coolidge to win his election."[22]

Focused on American "electioneering" and convinced of British justification for a superior number of cruisers to protect vulnerable trade routes, Bridgeman seriously misjudged the American reaction both to the nature of the Admiralty's proposals and the surprising manner with which he had presented them. Far less obvious to him than American "electioneering" was the changing attitude of the American naval advisers. Beneath their cordial demeanor lingered smoldering memories and resentment of the recent and prolonged controversies over British failure to reveal inequalities in capital ship gun elevations and fuel oil capabilities at the Washington Conference and their vehement opposition to later American efforts to equalize these inequalities. To these old wounds was now added the most recent revelation of still another hidden British advantage, one amounting to 96,000 tons, or a 13:10 capital ship ratio, thus making a mockery of presumed equality. This evidence reinforced their long-held suspicion of deliberate British duplicity at the first naval conference. When added to the British rejection of Jones' combat equivalency compromise, the unexpected effort to extend this 96,000-ton capital ship advantage from ten to sixteen years, the demand for a total of sixty cruisers carrying only 6-inch guns, the strict limit of only fifteen 10,000-ton, 8-inch-gun cruisers to equal those already built by the British, and the elimination of the marvelous new American 8-inch gun on all future warships, the American naval delegates now felt justified in disregarding the agreement to conduct the negotiations in secret. Convinced that the American navy was once again betrayed by British duplicity, the naval delegates initiated their own secret publicity campaign to educate Congress and the voters to what they perceived to be yet another very real danger to American national security.

On June 3, 1927, more than two weeks before the Conference opened on June 20, British Ambassador to the United States Sir Esme Howard became concerned over a swelling chorus of warnings in American newspapers. Howard cited in particular a story in the *New York Times* by Wythe Williams, who repeated the same fears over British demands for 6,000-ton cruisers carrying only 6-inch guns, which another newspaper reporter, Edwin L. James, had earlier warned against in his revelations of the Admiralty's secret negotiating strategy on May 12.[23] Williams was even more critical than James. He argued that this British proposal was a deliberate "trick" designed to obscure the extensive number of swift merchant vessels which the British could

---

[21] See sources in footnote 20 and Cecil to Sir William Tyrrell, June 24, 1927, Add Mss. 51079, LCP; W. T. [William Tyrrell] to Cecil, June 27, 1927, Add Mss. 51079, LCP; Viscount Cecil, *A Great Experiment: An Autobiography* (New York: Oxford University Press, 1941), p. 85; Fanning, *Peace and Disarmament*, pp. 60–61.

[22] Bridgeman to Sire, June 27, 1927, in ROSKCC. [23] See Chapter 9.

quickly outfit with 6-inch guns during wartime, which could fulfill some of the most important functions of cruisers in blockading ports, and which the United States Congress would not equal in number. Williams also reinforced the *Chicago Tribune* criticism that if Great Britain was in fact a friendly ally with no hostile intentions toward United States, it ought to agree to dismantle its naval bases in the Caribbean, which threatened vital American trade routes. What particularly worried Howard was the fact that these and similar warnings in the American press not only championed the views of the "advocates of a great Navy," but were "almost the only [press] comment of any kind beyond a friendly article in the *Christian Science Monitor*."[24]

This flurry of American press criticism also worried some of the British delegates assembling in Geneva. On June 19, the day before the Conference opened, Sir Joseph Cook, the representative from Australia, highlighted the importance of winning over American public opinion quickly before the "press draw their own conclusions possibly to our disadvantage."[25] At first Bridgeman refused to worry, basking instead in self-congratulatory confidence over the persuasiveness of his opening statement on July 20 at the first plenary session.[26] Admiral Sir Frederick Field, on the other hand, wasted no time in marshaling the British press to attack the American naval proposals as an elaborate reelection ploy. According to Gibson, Field proceeded to assure newsmen that the American proposals "were gotten out merely for internal political purposes and were not naval proposals of a serious nature," but, rather, were "composed of generalities" which "could not be put into practice."[27]

British reporters accepted Field's assurances. Aided by Sir Arthur Willet, chief of the Foreign Office's news department, the British press rallied behind Field's characterizations of the American proposals. Obviously unaware of Beatty's earlier promises of equality to Jones, or of Jones's combat equivalency proposal which allowed for a greater number of smaller British cruisers, the British Navy League, echoed the Admiralty's insistence on the need to defend Great Britain's long trade routes and denounced the American call for equality in cruisers as "grossly unfair." This characterization was reinforced by the *London Times* and other British newspapers. Gibson's opening address to the Conference, they agreed, had failed to make a convincing case for cruiser equality.[28]

Field's harsh criticism and the immediate eruption of British press rejection of cruiser equality greatly disturbed Gibson. He later came to the conclusion

---

[24] Howard to Chamberlain, June 3, 1927, *DBFP*, Ia, III: 603–604; Richard W. Fanning, *Peace and Disarmament: Naval Rivalry and Arms Control, 1922–1933* (Lexington: University Press of Kentucky, 1995), p. 56.
[25] For expressions of British anxiety, see BED, "Minutes," June 19, 1927, BEDM.
[26] See footnote 5.   [27] Gibson to Kellogg, June 21, 1927, MC 28, CCP.
[28] *The New York Times*, June 23, 1927; Skinner to Kellogg, June 27, 1927, MC 28, CCP.

that the Admiralty had conducted a "systematic campaign of abuse and distortion," which it fed to the British press throughout the negotiations at Geneva. Whereas the British press recorded "every word uttered by Bridgeman, Cecil, Jellico, Field and others," he lamented, it refused to print "a single American text" and instead only occasionally included "a brief and sometimes misleading [American] quotation." Regardless of the accuracy of Gibson's later recollection, his belief in the persistence of this pattern during the negotiations convinced him that the British delegation was directing a successful and "consistent effort" to "control the British press." He confessed his bewilderment, however, over "how it was possible [for the British] to effectively clamp a censorship on the whole American viewpoint." Gibson concluded that in an "amazing" series of speeches, "Bridgeman, Jellico, Balfour, and others" conducted "the most shocking campaign of abuse of a friendly government ever carried out by responsible cabinet officers."[29]

The American delegation at Geneva and the Department of State in Washington, DC, worked at influencing the American press at least as much as their British counterparts. Soon after the Conference began, Assistant Secretary of State William B. Castle convinced Kellogg to hold regular news briefings for reporters.[30] Angered and surprised by the British demands, the Secretary of State frequently used these briefings to pass on the substance of Gibson's confidential telegrams while reassuring reporters that the American negotiating positions had the solid backing of the General Board. Kellogg and Castle were assisted by J. Theodore Marriner, chief of the State Department's Western European Affairs Division. Acting in harmonious consort for the delegates at Geneva, these State Department officials supplied the American press with a steady stream of information favorable to the American naval viewpoint.[31] Indeed, the success of this close-working relationship with the State Department, the delegates at Geneva, and the General Board confirmed Schofield's earlier assessment of Secretary of State Kellogg as "one of the best Secretary's of the Navy this country has ever had."[32]

As the cascade of American press criticisms increased, British expectations of overwhelming public pressure on Coolidge and Kellogg quickly faded. The British began blaming this disappointing setback on the diabolical American negotiators and their press allies. Cecil joined wholeheartedly with Bridgeman in castigating the American reporters. He eventually came to believe that the American proposals were "so inferior to ours" that they "had no

---

[29] Gibson to Castle, September 30, 1928, Castle File; Gibson to Ted Marriner, August 11, 1927, Marriner File; Gibson to Hugh Wilson, May 29 and 31, 1928, Wilson File; Gibson to Allen Dulles, November 25, 1927, Dulles File, GP.

[30] Castle, Diary, June 23, 1927, CP.

[31] Ibid. Compare the frequent news reports in the New York Times, for example, to Gibson's telegrams to Kellogg throughout the Conference.

[32] See Chapter 9, footnote 63.

recourse except to pretend" that the British proposals harbored "some dark and deadly design against American security." Indeed, Cecil undoubtedly agreed with Bridgeman's claim that American reporters had "immediately set to work to read into our plans all sorts of Machiavellian devices for retaining [naval] superiority."[33]

The American press was not their only culprit. Bridgeman and Cecil agreed as well that the continuing hostile American press reaction was fueled by wealthy American "industrial concerns," which, Bridgeman correctly believed, "were working tooth and nail against any agreement of any kind."[34] Cecil charged American steel and iron manufacturers with financing the hostile press campaign.[35] More specifically, their suspicion eventually centered on a flamboyant American lobbyist as the chief source and disseminator of anti-British press distortions.[36]

William B. Shearer was one of the most controversial and colorful lobbyists of his day. Much is known about him because in 1929 when Coolidge's successor, Herbert Hoover, revitalized naval arms-control diplomacy, he initiated numerous investigations of Shearer by the Federal Bureau of Investigation, the State Department, the United States Naval Intelligence, and Congress. The resulting sensational scandal transformed Shearer from a lobbyist posing as a journalist at the 1927 Geneva Conference into a disreputable tool of greedy industrialists, who had used him to subvert important international peace negotiations for their own selfish interests.[37] Shearer's critics – both British and American – viewed him as an unscrupulous agent of big American steel and ship-building corporations, bent upon defeating arms-control diplomacy while simultaneously inflaming public anger over British demands and thereby increasing political support for building new American warships.[38]

Shearer rejected these characterizations. He saw himself as a patriot fighting naïve pacifists who were promoting still further cuts in American naval forces and thereby gravely endangering future American national security. This view was shared by influential naval officers who often supplied Shearer with classified information.[39]

Shearer was a tall, handsome man with a charming personality who impressed people with his fashionable clothes, intelligent and easy

---

[33] Cecil to Sir William Tyrrell, June 24, 1927, 51079, Add Mss., LCP.
[34] Bridgeman, Diary, June-August 1927, p. 151, WBP.
[35] Cecil repeatedly made this charge. See, for example, BED, "Minutes," June 24, 1927, BEDM; Cecil to Hunter Miller, December 12, 1927, Add Mss 51099, LCP.
[36] Frank S. Bright to Herbert Hoover, September 11, 1929, SF; Stephen Roskill, *Naval Policy between the Wars: The Period of Anglo-American Antagonism, 1919–1929* (London: Collins, 1968), p. 508.
[37] See, for example, *The New York Times*, "Hoover Turns the Light on the Lobbies," September 25, 1929; *The New York Times*, September 25, 1929; *The New York Times*, October 2, 1927 and October 1, 1929.
[38] See sources in footnote above.   [39] Ibid.

conversation, and exceptionally well-informed naval data, much of it still classified as secret.[40] Using his considerable talents as a salesman, Shearer secured press credentials as a journalist for the *New York Illustrated News* and quickly became friendly with American reporters covering the Geneva Preparatory Commission talks in 1926 and the naval conference in 1927. Reporters valued him in 1927 as a reliable source for their news stories and for his inside information on the thinking of the American naval delegates.[41]

Others familiar with Shearer's activities had a much less favorable impression of him.[42] Investigations by Scotland Yard, the Federal Bureau of Investigation, the Department of Justice, United States Naval Intelligence, and the Pinkerton Detective Agency led to the unanimous conclusion that Shearer was a thoroughly disreputable character.[43] Scotland Yard characterized him as a "notorious associate of international crooks," whose skill at robbery and card-cheating never left enough evidence to bring formal charges against him.[44] As early as 1918, the Pinkerton Detective Agency concluded that he was "an all around crook and card shark," who regularly operated on large ocean liners, where he ingratiated himself with wealthy families and succeeded in "fleecing" those whom he "enticed into card games." This "shrewd, smart swindler" was assisted by his wife who, like him, was "a very smart talker" and "a confidence" expert. However, these and other allegations of criminal activity were dropped for lack of evidence.[45]

By 1924 Shearer had forged a new career as a highly publicized and exceptionally well-informed opponent of the Washington Conference treaties and of any further naval reductions.[46] Throughout 1924 Shearer attracted attention by his consistent criticism of Congress for its failure to authorize actual capital ship equality with Great Britain and to maintain the 10:6 ratio with Japan. In April 1924, for example, the *New York Times* featured lengthy and highly detailed articles based on secret naval data supplied by Shearer about American inadequacies in battleships, cruisers and submarines.[47] Budget-cutting members

---

[40] A.F.C., "Backstage in Washington," *Outlook and Independent*, p. 16, SF; "W.F. Shearer or William B. Shearer (Also known as Schlarer, Roscovey, Sear, and Nevin)," n.d., SF; Lawrence Ritchey to Captain Alfred W. Johnson, September 5, 1929, SF; John Lord O'Brian to Samuel M. Shortridge, September 18, 1929, SF; Fanning, *Peace and Disarmament*, pp. 66–67.

[41] Wythe Williams, "Shearer's Methods at Naval Parlays," *New York Times*, September 16, 1927.

[42] Fanning, *Peace and Disarmament*, pp. 65–67.

[43] See numerous detailed reports from these investigative agencies in SF. See also John Lord O'Brian to Herbert Hoover, September 28, 1929, and reports from J. Edgar Hoover, the head of the FBI in SF.

[44] See "W.F. Shearer or William B. Shearer," in SF.

[45] Mr. Webster, "In Re: William B. Shearer, Paris, London, and New York," March 30, 1918, SF.

[46] Curtis D. Wilbur to Senator Frederick Hale, December 13, 1924, SF; Captain W. R. Sayles to My Dear Lang, June 5, 1925, SF. See collection of newspaper articles written by or about Shearer, SF. Among these are articles from *The New York Times*, April 27, 28, and 29, 1924 and *The Washington Post*, December 18, 1924.

[47] *The New York Times*, April 24 and 27, 1927.

of the House and Senate naval committees denounced Shearer's claims, but when the Navy Department refused to deny the validity of his statistics, the editors of the *New York Times* praised Shearer "for rendering a service to the country" by awakening the public to these national security weaknesses.[48] Shearer again attracted notoriety, first by claiming that Japan was preparing for war against United States, and then by threatening a lawsuit to prevent the scrapping of the battleship *Washington*.[49] This sensational news prompted the *Washington Post* to feature Shearer in a lengthy article in which Shearer claimed that his expenses were being paid by William Randolph Hearst, owner of a number of American newspapers.[50]

Shearer's new-found prominence as a publicist and lobbyist received a major boost from rumors that President Calvin Coolidge invited him to a private meeting at the White House.[51] When Secretary of the Navy Curtis Wilbur heard of this meeting, he became furious. He ordered an extensive investigation into the "leaks" of naval secrets to Shearer who, he acknowledged, was "in close touch with certain officers at the War College, and a host of friends among the line officers of the service," two of whom Wilbur court-martialed for supplying Shearer with secret intelligence.[52] Wilbur denounced Shearer as a "spy" and a liar, but despite Wilbur's fury, Shearer's reputation as a "naval expert" with impeccable sources was now well-established.[53] This new reputation was significantly enhanced by news reports that Coolidge had indeed consulted Shearer about American naval inferiority and by a feeble White House denial that although Coolidge had met privately with Shearer, they had not discussed naval weaknesses.[54]

In 1926 Shearer appeared in Geneva at the Preparatory Commission talks where his activities soon prompted Jones to complain to the Chief of Naval Operations that Shearer was "posing as a naval expert and an authority on the United States naval affairs." Jones was undoubtedly irritated as well by Shearer's denunciations of the arms control diplomacy which was reported in the *New York Times*. "Only the United States," Shearer charged, "has bowed to the impractical, dangerous appeal of the pacifists and the mean appeal of the economists, neither of whom realize the dangers into which they are dragging the country." As the former president of the General Board, Jones was

---

[48] *The New York Times*, editorial, "Our Naval Deficiencies," April 28, 1924, SF.
[49] *The New York Times*, December 10, 1926, SF.
[50] Albert Fox, "Shearer, Agitating Navy Investigation," *Washington Post*, December 18, 1924, SF.
[51] Albert Fox, "President Confers with Naval Expert Who Criticizes Ratio," *Washington Post*, December 12[?], 1924, SF.
[52] "Inquiry into Leak of Navy Secrets Ordered by Wilbur," *Washington Post*, December 18, 1924, SF. See also FBI report [?], "William Baldwin Shearer," SF and *The New York Times*, November 15, 1924.
[53] Wilbur to Senator Frederick Hale, December 13, 1924, SF. See also Henry Stimson to John Lord O'Brian, September 29, 1930, Department of State Decimal File, 500 A 15 ai/16, NA.
[54] Wilbur to Hale, December 15, 1924, SF.

understandably irritated by Shearer's further claim that "only the United States [was] pleading for disarmament," as "not one European power or nation [was] willing to make any sacrifice which would jeopardize its security," especially not Great Britain, which would never voluntarily surrender its naval superiority through an arms limitation treaty.[55]

Perhaps to Jones' surprise, A. P. Hepburn, the Director of Naval Intelligence, to whom Jones directed one of his complaints, was far less irritated with Shearer. Hepburn warned Jones not to trust Shearer, citing several extensive investigations of Shearer's background. Nonetheless, he strongly hinted that as Shearer's loyalty was not in question, he might someday prove useful to the Navy. Several officers who "have known him personally," Hepburn reassured Jones, attested to Shearer's devotion to the Navy, amounting to "something of the nature of a mania which might possibly be turned to some account if the circumstances ever permitted the employment of such an erratic and unusual type of character."[56] Jones apparently avoided contact with Shearer during both the 1926 Preparatory Commission talks and the 1927 Geneva Conference. Nonetheless, in 1927, after the British surprised Jones by first refusing to discuss his combat equivalency plan, and then by demanding an unlimited number of smaller cruisers, several of the naval advisors on the American delegation concluded that "the circumstances" had indeed changed.[57]

Few reporters were fooled by Shearer's flimsy cover as a reporter for the *New York Illustrated Press*.[58] While they easily guessed that he was a lobbyist, they may not have known that his big salary and even bigger expense account was bankrolled by several major naval defense contractors including Bethlehem Steel, Newport News Shipping, and Brown Boveri Electric Corporation.[59] Shearer concentrated his attention on American reporters, routinely inviting them, Wythe Williams recalled, to delicious home-cooked dinners at his "sumptuous apartment in the exclusive Champel quarter of Geneva, where in precise staccato tones he dictated clearly and thoroughly an opinion on the disadvantages for the United States" of the British proposals. For seven weeks Shearer supplied these reporters with "daily reports of the previous [secret] session's proceedings," complete with "a tremendous amount of elaborate data, written and tabulated for public consumption, in which he vividly explained such matters as gun calibers

---

[55] "Says America Only Is Ready to Disarm," September 9, 1926, SF.
[56] Jones to Chief of Naval Operations, August 16, 1926; A. J. Hepburn to Jones, September 15, 1926, JP.
[57] *Ibid.*
[58] See reports from John Lord O'Brian to Senator Samuel Shortridge, September 18, 1929, SF.
[59] John Lord O'Brian to Herbert Hoover, September 17 and 23, 1929, SF; J. Edgar Hoover to Lawrence Richey, September 18, 1929, SF; E.G. Grace to Herbert Hoover, September 9, 1929, SF.

and elevations, tonnage and, in fact, every technical intricate detail that came under the investigation of the Conference."[60]

Shearer's lobbying was undoubtedly influential. Reporters especially valued his statistical information and his ability to explain the relevance of intricate technical proposals, which the delegates had agreed to keep strictly confidential.[61] Nonetheless, Shearer was less influential than later critics supposed. His intensely anti-British diatribes had little impact on the thinking of most reporters. Williams recalled that Shearer's weekly memos elaborating his personal views were "so violently and tactlessly anti-British that this form of Shearer propaganda fell completely flat."[62]

Understandably, neither Bridgeman nor Cecil believed that Shearer's anti-British diatribes "fell completely flat." More important, neither of them fully understood the extent to which the American naval delegates were conducting their own surreptitious public-relations war.[63] As they suspected, the principal outlet for passing on reliable statistics and the American naval point of view on proposals before the Conference to news-hungry reporters was, in fact, William Shearer. Since the daily proceedings of the Conference were officially secret from the press and limited to official communiqués, which were often bland and of limited news value, the appearance in the American press of confidential statistics and technical disagreements recently discussed by the delegates made it obvious that a good deal of clandestine leaking was under way. The source of the leaking, however, was disputed.[64]

Aware of British suspicions, Gibson and Jones kept their distance from Shearer and, in response to British complaints, denied any implication in the leaks.[65] The American naval delegates also denied leaking. Gibson, and

---

[60] Wythe Williams, "Shearer's Methods," *The New York Times*, September 16, 1927; Wilson to Richey, September 26, 1929, SF; John Lord O'Brian to Herbert Hoover, October 12, 1929, SF; John Lord O'Brian to Dear Mr. President, October 12, 1929, SF; Herbert Bayard Swope to George E. Akerson, September 9, 1929, SF.

[61] "American Navy Men Named As Working with Shearer," *The New York Times*, September 27, 1929; Theodore Marriner to Mr. Beck, September 19, 1929, SF; "William Baldwin Shearer," n. d., SF.

[62] Wythe Williams, "Shearer's Methods," *The New York Times*, September 16, 1927.

[63] Bridgeman, Diary, June-August 1927, p. 151; Bridgeman to My Beloved, July 14, 1927, 4629/1/1927/86 and Bridgeman to Dearest Mother, July 15, 1927, 4629/1/1927/89, WBP; Cecil to Chamberlain, July 2, 1929, Add Mss. 51079, LCP; *The New York Times*, July 15, 1927. Although Cecil complained of American press distortions, he makes no mention of the American delegates as sources of leaks to the press. See also Roy Atherton to Secretary of State, October 15, 1929, Department of State, Decimal File, 500A 15ai/32, RG 59, NA.

[64] A. F. C., "Back Stage in Washington," *Outlook and Independent*, p. 16, SF; "William Baldwin Shearer," n.d., SF; William T. Beck to Mr. Richey, September 26, 1929 and accompanying telegram from the American Legation, Bern, Switzerland, September 24, 1929, SF.

[65] See sources in footnote above. See also Jones to Chief of Naval Operations, August 16, 1926, JP; "William Baldwin Shearer," n.d., SF; Gibson to Kellogg, July 2, 1927, MC 28, CCP; Gibson to Kellogg, July 12, 1927, *FRUS*, 1927, I: 96; Bridgeman to Baldwin, July 4, 1927, SBP; Schofield,

Schofield blamed French official observers who sat in on the confidential discussions, and who were known to be highly critical of arms limitation, generally, and of the Conference in particular.[66] Nonetheless, both Gibson and Jones appreciated the strong support of the American press during the negotiations.[67] Neither of them expressed any displeasure with the reporters' favorable treatment of the American negotiating proposals or with their criticisms of the British demands.[68]

Admiral Frank Schofield was the principal delegate leaker. Schofield's diary entries, recording his meetings with Shearer, made this abundantly clear, although he sometimes also used Captain J. M. Reeves to spread the word among reporters.[69] Schofield met as well with Drew Pearson and other American journalists.[70] Immediately upon hearing Bridgeman's opening statement on June 20, and continuing as the British slowly revealed their insistence on an unlimited number of smaller 6-inch- gun cruisers and their vehement opposition to the 8-inch gun, Schofield characterized this verbal diplomatic combat at the peace table as a new form of warfare, which he fervently believed would have very direct consequences on future naval battles. Schofield was not alone in this perception. The entire American delegation understood his reasoning, and whether or not they agreed with him, Schofield was bolstered by his knowledge that Coolidge, Kellogg, the General Board, Gibson, and Jones were deeply dismayed by the British proposals, and that they also were bent upon achieving a treaty which realized actual equality or at the very least, a reasonable combat equivalency.[71]

Well-known in American naval circles as an outspoken critic of the Washington Treaties, Schofield wasted no time in utilizing Shearer and other American reporters to counteract the crafty "reasonableness" of the British arguments. On June 21, the day following Bridgeman's opening speech, Schofield met with Shearer.[72] Three days later on June 24, he again met with Shearer to explain that the Japanese proposal for 700-ton submarines was not as defensive as was claimed, because these submarines could carry enough fuel to allow the British to cross the Atlantic and the Japanese to operate as far as the Philippines.[73] Schofield recognized that the importance of a technical detail,

---

Diary, July 1 and 5, 1927, SD. See also telegram enclosed in William Bush to Lawrence Richey, September 20, 1929, SF.
[66] Gibson to Kellogg, July 2, 1927, MC 28, CCP; Bridgeman to Baldwin, July 4, 1927, SBP; Schofield, Diary, July 1 and 5, 1927, SD.
[67] Jones to William H. Gardner, July 8, 1927, Gardner File, JP; Schofield, Diary, June 21 and July 6, 1927, SD; Gibson to Kellogg, July 14, 1927, MC 28, CCP.
[68] See sources in footnote above.
[69] Schofield met repeatedly with Shearer. See Schofield, Diary, June 21, 24, 26, and 30, and July 6, 8, and 20, SD. See also Theodore Marriner to Mr. Beck, September 19, 1929, SF.
[70] Schofield, Diary, June 26 and 30, 1927, SD; *The New York Times*, 17 September 1929.
[71] Schofield, Diary, July 20, 1927, SD.   [72] See sources in footnote 69.
[73] Schofield, Diary, June 24, 1927, SD.

such as the range of a 700-ton submarine, would have been unfamiliar to reporters, and therefore its significance would be unlikely to be communicated to the American public. Indeed, as the British demand for an unlimited number of small cruisers hardened, and nerves began to fray, Schofield made it abundantly clear to the American delegation that the details of the negotiations must be made known to the press in order to inform and influence American public opinion.[74] "I believe that this business of keeping everything comparatively secret from the Press is not working in our interests," he complained. Yet, for the record, he continued to deny that he and others in the American delegation were leaking the contents of secret Conference discussions and interpreting their meaning for American reporters.[75]

In addition to Schofield's own diary entries recording his meetings with Shearer, further evidence emerged after the Conference had ended. Gibson complained bitterly of Schofield's persistent disobedience by feeding Shearer secret information.[76] As a professional diplomat, Gibson had worked hard to secure an agreement, and following the collapse of the talks, he charged that Schofield met with Shearer "nearly every day in [his] office and at the hotel." In his discussions with the American delegates, Gibson recalled, Schofield had exhibited a consistent "hard-boiled" antagonism toward the British proposals. But Schofield was not the only culprit. Gibson also criticized the other American naval advisors who, he believed, had adopted Schofield's antagonistic attitude. Gibson left no doubt that naval officers in the American delegation were as deeply engaged as the British in the press war.[77]

As the confident British expectation of overwhelmingly favorable American public opinion toward British proposals faded, the flaws in the Admiralty's poorly crafted and poorly explained negotiating strategy became increasingly clear and increasingly troublesome to the members of the CID and Cabinet. Indeed, with negotiations deadlocked over American demands for assurances of equality, and the Admiralty's equally adamant determination to prevent that equality, Bridgeman and Cecil in Geneva and chagrined Cabinet Ministers in London began working at cross-purposes.

By June 29, nine days after the Conference opened, Bridgeman and Cecil had come to the realization that Coolidge and Kellogg were threatening to terminate the negotiations unless Great Britain publicly acknowledged the right to parity in naval strength. The crucial problem, they believed, had come down to the question of parity.[78] Both Kellogg and Assistant Secretary of State Castle were indeed puzzled over Great Britain's refusal to admit parity in

---

[74] Schofield, Diary, July 6, 7, and 8, 1927, SB.   [75] Schofield, Diary, July 5 and 7, 1927, SB.
[76] Gibson to Theodore Marriner, November 25, 1927, Marriner File, GP.   [77] Ibid.
[78] BED, "*Minutes* of the Fourth Conference of British Delegations," June 29, 1927, p. 3, BEDM. Copies of these minutes can also be found in ADM 116/2609, PRO and in LCP. See also Bridgeman, Diary, June-August 1927, p. 149, WBP and BED, "*Minutes* of the Fifth Conference of British Delegations, July 31, 1927, p. 2, BEDM.

Conference Shocks

smaller cruisers, especially as Castle noted, "we have continually been assured that this was thoroughly understood." British insistence on seventy cruisers, he complained, was "no limit at all and will lead to furious building." "Of course we cannot make any such agreement as this," he lamented, but "I think if we do not the world will clearly understand where the trouble lies" and might even "drive the Japanese [delegates] into our arms again." It now appeared to him that the Admiralty was "running the show for England without much assistance from the Foreign Office."[79]

Secretary of State Kellogg's persistent pressure for a public acknowledgment of cruiser parity finally convinced Howard, the British Ambassador to the United States, to warn Chamberlain that the United States will "only continue [the] conference on [the] basis of parity in all units." To drive home his message to the Foreign Secretary, Howard stressed that it was already "very noticeable that practically all the press, even papers most friendly, now comment on our failure to agree to [the] principle of parity ... to which they evidently attach the greatest importance."[80] Sir William Tyrrell, the Permanent Undersecretary of State for Foreign Affairs, was embarrassed and perplexed by Howard's warning. He believed that parity had in fact been the agreed-upon basis for the negotiations, and he had assured the American Embassy in London that "the principle of parity ... has been recognized and he [Tyrrell] was of the opinion that Bridgeman was quite aware of this."[81]

Alarmed by Howard's warning of impending failure, Tyrrell brought the issue directly to Baldwin and the entire Cabinet. Tyrrell first presented the Ministers with Howard's repeated warnings that Kellogg insisted that parity was the "agreed upon" basis for calling the conference and the only one acceptable for continuing it.[82] He then read excerpts from the May 20 meeting of the Committee of Imperial Defence emphasizing Chamberlain's "opinion that the United States would not in any case accept a limit which was less than ours" – even while professing that it was unlikely that they would actually build up to that limit. He also quoted Bridgeman's seeming agreement with Chamberlain to the effect "that the Admiralty would not take a grave view if the United States built up to their limit." Based on these quotations, Tyrrell concluded that the Foreign Office and the Admiralty representatives at the CID meeting had been in basic agreement on a treaty granting parity to the United States.[83]

---

[79] Castle, Diary, June 29, 1927, CP.
[80] Howard to Chamberlain, June 28, 1927, *DBFP*, Ia, III: 621.
[81] Quoted in Sterling to Kellogg, June 27, 1927, MC 28, CCP. See also Richardson, *The Evolution of British Disarmament Policy*, pp. 123–124.
[82] CAB, "Minutes," June 29, 1927, CAB 23/55/37(27), MC 82, PRO.
[83] *Ibid*. While the Cabinet Minutes do not specifically indicate that it was Tyrrell who introduced these statements, the context strongly supports my belief that Tyrrell was the logical one to have done so.

During this lengthy Cabinet debate on June 29, Baldwin again refused to be drawn into the controversy, but once it became clear to Churchill that the great savings from capital ship reductions and the expanded capital ship building holiday had been sidetracked, and that Field had finally unveiled the Admiralty's revived demand for seventy cruisers, Churchill became alarmed. "I have never been convinced," he told his Cabinet colleagues, "that our present Admiralty scheme of seventy cruisers is the minimum compatible with security and I doubt the exactness of the methods of calculation" used by the Admiralty to arrive at so high a number.[84] It was obvious to him that the Admiralty had never informed either the CID on May 20, 1927 or the Cabinet that it would attempt to secure international sanction for seventy cruisers. Without a corresponding decrease in capital ship expenditures, the cost of such a large number of cruisers would clearly threaten Churchill's efforts to secure tax relief and greater social services during the continuing depression. But Churchill was careful not to dwell on these objections.

He emphasized instead his agreement with the Admiralty's opposition to parity in smaller cruisers. Great Britain, he argued, must refuse to be "netted in a scheme of parity with the United States in cruisers and other ancillaries" because there "can really be no parity between a Power whose Navy is its life and a Power whose Navy is only for prestige." If Great Britain agreed to parity with United States, he proclaimed, it was effectively conceding naval supremacy and quite unnecessarily so. Echoing back to his argument made during the Birkenhead Committee debates in 1925, Churchill advised that the best way to maintain British supremacy was to lull the United States into a slower cruiser-building program by retarding Great Britain's own construction of new warships. Indeed, the United States cruiser fleet was already "so far inferior to our own" that they could build ten new cruisers "without calling for any additional exertions on our part." He advised the Cabinet, therefore, that Great Britain should instead "set the slowest [building] pace possible and not be afraid of a sudden [yet temporary] advance in United States construction as long as we have a good lead."[85]

To support the Admiralty, Churchill simply disregarded Howard's warnings of impending failure. He instead recalled lingering resentments which had arisen during and since World War I. Rather than fret about "unjust American irritation," the Cabinet ought to remember "all the concessions which we made at the Washington Conference in giving up the naval supremacy we had so long enjoyed, in parting with our faithful Japanese ally, and subsequently in paying them [the United States] these enormous [war debt?] sums." But these painful concessions, he charged, "have only resulted" in still greater American

---

[84] Churchill, "Memorandum by the Chancellor of the Exchequer," 29 June 1927, C.P. 189 (27), CAB 24/187 and WCP.
[85] Ibid.

Conference Shocks 235

demands while the Americans do "nothing for us in return, but exact their last pound of flesh."[86]

The Americans' insistence upon and the Admiralty's vehement opposition to parity in smaller cruisers presented the Cabinet with a sudden unexpected dilemma. On the one hand, the Cabinet wanted to realize the great savings from the capital ship proposals and therefore wanted to secure agreement to these savings. On the other hand, it had no stomach for another political crisis over Admiralty charges that by agreeing to parity the Cabinet had given away British naval supremacy. In an effort to resolve this conundrum, Lord Balfour, who had been England's chief negotiator at the Washington Conference in 1921–1922, soft-pedaled his earlier belief that the Cabinet had supported the treaty right to parity as the basis for the Conference and offered a hurriedly worded compromise in an effort to bridge the gap between the Foreign Office and the Admiralty.[87]

Balfour suggested that the Cabinet send instructions to Bridgeman, which, in effect, denied the principle of parity without publicly admitting the denial. The public statement would avoid any mention of parity, but merely support the Admiralty's insistence that each nation had the right to build the number of cruisers it needed. The United States could build a lesser number, but it would not be obligated to build up to the number required by Great Britain. Nonetheless, its treaty right to build an equal number of smaller cruisers was not specifically acknowledged.

Balfour's cloudy wording was important primarily for the confusion and dissent which it soon generated. Anxious for a way out of the parity conundrum, the Cabinet accepted Lord Balfour's wording and instructed Bridgeman to announce immediately that: "For diplomatic reasons we think it most desirable to say publicly and at once ... that while we mean to build cruisers up to our needs, we lay down no conditions limiting cruisers to a smaller number. Do you see any objection?"[88]

Sir Maurice Hankey, the Secretary to the Cabinet, immediately saw a number of objections. Following the meeting, he criticized the Cabinet's "rather incoherent" discussion, which led to the ambiguous and confusing adoption of Lord Balfour's instruction. He complained both to Balfour and Baldwin that this confusing message threatened to muddle the Admiralty's negotiating strategy. To clarify that strategy, as he understood it, Hankey divided it into two stages. In the first stage Great Britain had already emphasized its capital ship proposal and strict limitation of 10,000-ton, 8-inch-gun cruisers based on the 10:10:6 ratio. In the forthcoming second stage all additional cruisers were to be

---

[86] Ibid. [87] CAB, "Minutes," 29 June 1927, CAB 23/55/37(27), MC 82, PRO.
[88] Ibid. See also Richardson, *Evolution of British Disarmament Policy*, pp. 129–130; William F. Trimble, "The United States Navy and the Geneva Conference for the Limitation of Naval Armament, 1927," (Ph.D. diss., University of Colorado, 1974), pp. 245–246.

reduced to a maximum of 7,500 tons with 6-inch guns, but with no limitation in numbers and no concession to parity.[89]

Beatty was also "very concerned." On the following day, June 30, he complained directly to Baldwin about "the possibility of our being forced into issuing a communiqué to assuage the feelings of the United States" over the right to parity. The negotiations at Geneva, he assured the Prime Minister, were "very much in our favour," and he therefore urged Baldwin to maintain the policy of "Silence is Golden." Like Hankey, he believed that the strategy he had outlined "to the CID in your room at the House of Commons is bearing fruit." Baldwin must therefore avoid "falling in with the plans of the [American] obstructionists" with unnecessary Cabinet pronouncements. If another communiqué became necessary, he instructed Baldwin, the Prime Minister should use the one which Beatty would dictate.[90]

While Beatty reminded Baldwin that the Admiralty was in charge of the negotiations, Bridgeman and Cecil had already concluded that silence on the right to parity was no longer an option.[91] Cecil was the first to reassure Gibson. Cecil was puzzled as to how such an "unfortunate misunderstanding" had arisen as the "British Delegation had not knowingly done anything to dispute ... [America's] right to parity."[92] Bridgeman then delivered the same reassurance, quickly agreeing to Gibson's suggestion that a personal statement to the Associated Press would ensure the widest circulation in the United States.[93] At 9:30 that evening, June 29, apparently either before the Cabinet's confusing instruction arrived in Geneva, or because Bridgeman and Cecil failed to grasp its hidden intention to evade granting the Americans a treaty right to parity, the First Lord met with a reporter from the Associated Press to authorize a text in which he stated that "Great Britain has no intention of contesting the principle of parity between the naval strength of the United States and Great Britain." He specifically denied that that Great Britain "was asking for supremacy" and insisted instead that "we have never disputed the American claim for parity." Although he pointed out that "our special needs demand a higher number in certain types of vessels," Great Britain nonetheless did not deny "the right of the United States to build up to an equal figure in any type of warship which she thought necessary." He concluded by acknowledging the perception that the *Rodney* and the *Nelson* battleships had allegedly given Great Britain "some superiority," but he was confident that if the United States adopted the

---

[89] Hankey to Balfour, June 29, 1927, SBP. Hankey evidently sent a copy of this letter to Baldwin. See also Hankey, "Points in Lord Cecil's Minute on which confirmation is lacking: Summary," n.d., pp. 5–7, CAB 21/297, PRO.
[90] Beatty to Baldwin, June 30, 1927, SBP.
[91] Richardson, *Evolution of British Disarmament Policy*, p. 206.
[92] Gibson, "Memorandum of Conversation: Lord Cecil" June 29, 1927, MCDS.
[93] Gibson, "Memorandum of Conversation: Bridgeman" June 29, 1927, MCDS.

British proposals on capital ships, "a reasonable adjustment of replacement tables" could be agreed upon.[94]

Both Bridgeman and Cecil were very pleased by their public promise.[95] Neither believed that the press acknowledgment of an explicit treaty right to parity differed in any significant way from the Cabinet's latest instruction. Bridgeman merely intended to acknowledge that the Americans had the treaty right to build up to the much higher number of smaller cruisers required by Great Britain.[96] Nonetheless, his promise contradicted the intent of Balfour's too cleverly worded subterfuge, created immediate consternation in London, and ultimately led to an increasing American sense of having been cynically manipulated.

---

[94] Ibid.; Gibson to Kellogg, June 29 and 30, 1927, MC 28, CCP; Bridgeman, "Log," June 29 and 30, 1927, BDGM/ Folder 4, WBPCC; BED; "Minutes of the Fifth Conference of British Delegations, p. 1, BEDM; Gibson to Kellogg, June 30, 1927, FRUS, 1927, I: 65; Richardson, Evolution of British Disarmament Policy, p. 124.

[95] Bridgeman to My Beloved, 30 June 1927, 4629/1/1927/56, WBP; Bridgeman to Chamberlain, 30 June 1927, DBFP, Ia, III: 629–630; Cecil to Chamberlain, July 2, 1927, Add Mss. 51079, LCP and DBFP, Ia, III: 633.

[96] Bridgeman to Maurizio Mio, June 27, 1927, 4629/1/1927/54, WBP; Bridgeman to My Beloved, June 30, 1927, 4629/1/1927/56, WBP. See also Gibson, "Memorandum of Conversation: Bridgeman," June 29, 1927, MCDS and Bridgeman to Chamberlain, 30 June 1927, DBFP, Ia, III: 631.

12

Hardening Positions

Bridgeman's parity promise forced the Cabinet into an increasingly confusing diplomatic quagmire. Beatty refused to allow Bridgeman's parity assurance to go unchallenged. He insisted that the Cabinet reinterpret the meaning of Bridgeman's statement, while hinting at resignation if the Cabinet failed to bow to his demands. The Cabinets' effort to placate Bridgeman, Beatty, and Churchill simultaneously was complicated on July 4 when Jones exacerbated already strained Anglo-American relations by his refutation of the Admiralty's major arguments in a carefully planned "Independence Day" speech. On the following day, tensions escalated when he announced that all future American cruisers would be 10,000-ton, 8-inch gun ships. Bridgeman and Beatty immediately denounced this as an "ultimatum." Already disappointed and frustrated by the implied Cabinet criticism of his public promise of parity, and by the unwillingness of the Americans to accept the Admiralty's proposals, Bridgeman privately vented his increasingly intense frustration, while Beatty used the "ultimatum" to prod the Cabinet into a tougher negotiating stance.

To avoid these time-consuming and complex disputes, the Cabinet ordered the Committee of Imperial Defence to formulate appropriate responses. Once again Beatty was able to dominate the contentious internal debate in London. Bowing to his will, the CID ordered Bridgeman not to make any concessions, but instead to launch an immediate publicity counterattack emphasizing the "offensive" nature of the American determination to build only 8-inch-gun cruisers.

Tentative agreements on destroyers, submarines and exempt classes of very small warships were encouraging.[1] However, Prime Minister Baldwin had

---

[1] For progress on tentative agreements for destroyers, submarines and exempt classes of smaller warships see TC, "Minutes," June 27–30, July 1, 1927, *Records*, pp. 74–99, 103, 109, 141–142:

taken seriously Howard's warning that "the United States government feels that they can only continue [the] conference on [the] agreed basis of parity in all units."² He therefore instructed Howard to reassure Kellogg that the British Cabinet fully supported Bridgeman's parity statement to the Associated Press and that Great Britain "did not dispute or contest in any way [the] claim of the United States to absolute parity and that they [the Cabinet] agreed that [the] Geneva negotiations should be conducted on that basis." However, Baldwin had not consulted Beatty, and the First Sea Lord would have none of it. Upon hearing of Baldwin's instruction to Howard, Beatty successfully demanded that Baldwin rescind this reassurance before Howard had time to deliver it to Kellogg and to allow Beatty to address the Cabinet on its obligation to support the Admiralty's original negotiating strategy.³

At the July 4 Cabinet meeting, Beatty instructed the ministers that Bridgeman's press statement had been "misinterpreted."⁴ Rather than a willingness "to accept parity in all classes," he claimed, Bridgeman had not intended to include the smaller cruisers needed for trade protection but only the fifteen 10,000-ton, 8-inch-gun cruisers needed to accompany the main battle fleet.⁵ Beatty's reinterpretation was immediately challenged, most probably by Chamberlain, who argued that Bridgeman had been "most precise" in granting America's claim to parity in all classes of auxiliaries.⁶

Refuting both the Prime Minister and the Foreign Secretary, Beatty insisted that the Cabinet had approved the Admiralty's negotiating strategy outlined in the May 20 meeting of the Committee of Imperial Defence. This strategy required that in the event that the United States, as expected, demanded parity in all cruisers, the British delegates would insist that all parties publicly reveal the exact number of cruisers needed "and why they required them." "This procedure," he explained, "would put the representatives of the United States in a difficulty as it would be hard for them to justify, on strategic grounds, anything like the same numbers as we required." It was obvious, therefore, that the Americans were attempting to "lead us into a trap" by using

---

Schofield, Diary, 24, 27, 29, 30 June 1927, SD. See also Chamberlain to Howard, July 1, 1927 and Howard to Chamberlain, July 2,1927, *DBFP*, Ia, III: 631–632.
² Howard to Chamberlain, June 28, 1927, *DBFP*, Ia, III: 621.
³ CAB, "Minutes" 38 (27), July 4, 1927, CAB 23/55, PRO; Chamberlain to Cecil, July 5, 1927, Add Mss. 51079, LCP. See also R. C. Richardson, *The Evolution of British Disarmament Policy in the 1920s* (London: Leicester University Press, 1989), pp. 124–125, 206.
⁴ Churchill, "Memorandum by the Chancellor of the Exchequer: The Naval Conference," June 29, 1927, C.P. 189 (27), CAB 24/187, PRO; CAB, "Minutes" 38 (27), July 4, 1927, CAB 23/55, PRO. See also copy in CHAR 22/182, WCP.
⁵ *Ibid.*
⁶ *Ibid.* The Minutes did not identify the challenger but Chamberlain's letter to Cecil on the following day strongly suggests that Chamberlain raised the objection. See Chamberlain to Cecil, July 5, 1927, 54/88 and Cecil to Chamberlain, July 2, 1927, 54/87, AC; Chamberlain to Cecil, July 5, 1927, Add Mss. 51079, LCP.

press agents in Geneva to draw "a red herring" of distortions over Bridgeman's meaning of parity.[7]

Beatty assured the Cabinet that very real dangers could be avoided by refusing to be drawn into the American parity "trap." The first danger arose from the Admiralty's need for seventy cruisers as an absolute minimum to protect trade. Cabinet approval of parity in these smaller 7,500-ton, 6-inch gun trade cruisers would require great increases in American cruiser construction, thus giving the Americans the excuse to alert the world that the British cruiser demands "had only resulted in increased armaments."[8] Moreover, Bridgeman was already aware of a second danger. If the Americans did build seventy cruisers, he warned, "Japan would demand 50 in which event the Admiralty would require more than 70 cruisers," a prospect which undoubtedly further alarmed Churchill. Even more dangerous, Beatty claimed, was the fact that parity would give the United States naval supremacy. By securing parity in all cruisers, he insisted, "the American navy really obtained a great superiority, since British cruisers had to be spread for the protection of our world-wide communications, whereas the American cruisers could be concentrated at any point," presumably to challenge a British blockade or even to accompany the American battle fleet in its attack on the British fleet.[9]

This very important claim has not been given the emphasis it deserves. Both Beatty and Churchill argued strenuously that equality in both cruiser classes meant United States superiority. Moreover, this important claim went unchallenged by the Cabinet. Churchill and Beatty were in agreement on the necessity to retain superiority, but for totally different reasons. Churchill agreed with Beatty about the need to maintain superiority in cruisers but not because he accepted the Admiralty claim that lonely cruisers patrolling distant trade routes must protect against and chase down elusive commerce raiders. Churchill had long been on record favoring convoys during wartime, a bait-the-trap tactic which had proven effective during World War I. It also allowed for a greater concentration of cruiser forces, required far fewer cruisers at far less cost, and, because merchantmen traveled at slower speeds, allowed the transfer of tonnage from additional boiler rooms, for faster speed, to armor plate for greater protection.[10] He undoubtedly agreed on the need for cruisers to enforce blockades and for interdicting trade in wartime, but he called the Cabinet's attention to the fact that the United States cruiser fleet was "so far inferior to our own" that they could build ten cruisers without Great Britain losing its superiority or even being required to respond during this lengthy construction process. Besides, he predicted, the American taxpayer would soon force Congress

---

[7] CAB, "Minutes" 38 (27), July 4, 1927, CAB 23/55, PRO.   [8] *Ibid.*   [9] *Ibid.*
[10] For Churchill's argument for convoy cruisers, see Chapter 4.

to cut back construction, and thus, he implied, Beatty's grave dangers were more theoretical than real.[11]

Churchill disagreed with Beatty for yet another important reason. He still suspected that Beatty's motive for seventy to seventy-five cruisers was less for the protection of trade routes than a future war against Japan, a theoretical threat which currently did not exist and was put forth at the very time when the British economy and taxpayers desperately needed tax cuts and expanded social services. Future budget battles were undoubtedly an unspoken consideration as well. Churchill must have been acutely aware that once the Cabinet authorized seventy to seventy-five British cruisers, without having first secured the great savings from a new capital ship agreement, the Admiralty would once again use this authorization in future budget battles. Thus, while Churchill agreed with Beatty that Great Britain must not be "netted in a scheme of [cruiser] parity with the United States," he did so with a suspicious eye on the Admiralty's ploy of using the Conference to win Cabinet approval for seventy to seventy-five cruisers and the consequent likelihood of another future political crisis over construction costs.[12]

The Cabinet had good reason to fear another resignation crisis, as Beatty now warned the Ministers that if they reduced cruisers below seventy "the Admiralty could not guarantee the protection of the trade routes." As this was the same justification which he had used to bring about the 1925 resignation crisis, his veiled threat could not have passed unnoticed by either Baldwin or the Cabinet.[13]

Rather than reignite his continuing battle with Churchill over seventy cruisers, Beatty instead focused his wrath on Bridgeman, demanding that the Cabinet repudiate Bridgeman's parity promise to the Associated Press. This clearly upset Foreign Secretary Chamberlain, who had kept his diplomats at some distance from this dramatic international conference, most probably at Baldwin's request. However, Chamberlain had become increasingly irritated by Beatty's diplomatic clumsiness as evidenced by his "extreme sensitiveness to the use of the word 'parity'," and by his claim that Bridgeman's clearly stated promise to the Associated Press had somehow been "misinterpreted." Even more upsetting to Chamberlain was Beatty's insistence that the Cabinet inform the Americans of Bridgeman's diplomatic ineptness. Rather than "do actual harm" by repudiating the promise, Chamberlain advised the Cabinet instead to instruct Bridgeman to correct the "misinterpretation" through informal conversations with the Americans

---

[11] Churchill expressed these views in a memorandum which he completed on June 29 and sent to the Cabinet. See Churchill, "Memorandum by the Chancellor of the Exchequer: The Naval Conference," June 29, 1927, C.P. 189 (27), CAB 24/187, PRO.

[12] Ibid.

[13] CAB, "Minutes" 38 (27), July 4, 1927, CAB 23/55, PRO. See also Richardson, *Evolution of British Disarmament Policy*, p. 125.

in Geneva.¹⁴ The Cabinet ultimately concluded that it "must support" the wording of Bridgeman's public promise to the Americans. Chamberlain then informed Cecil that "to use any other language in Washington than that which you have used in Geneva was unthinkable."¹⁵

The Cabinet's instructions to Howard, therefore, attempted a delicate political and diplomatic balancing act. To forestall a possible breakdown in negotiations, the Cabinet accepted Chamberlain's advice by ordering Howard "to confirm to the United States government [the] statement made by Mr. Bridgeman and Lord Cecil to Mr. Gibson at Geneva...," a statement which clearly conceded parity in all classes of cruisers.¹⁶ At the same time, the Cabinet also attempted to placate Beatty by instructing Howard to reiterate the Admiralty's insistence on building cruisers "to our own needs."¹⁷ Finally, it sought, as well, to clarify the meaning of Balfour's vague instruction which the Cabinet had sent to Bridgeman on June 29. Howard was now told to inform Secretary of State Kellogg that "we lay down no conditions of limiting *American* cruisers to a smaller number."¹⁸ [Emphasis mine.] This was intended to clear the way for the eventual revelation of an essential feature of Beatty's strategy: the requirement that the United States must first publicly justify an equal number of smaller cruisers before Great Britain could grant parity in this class, a need which the Admiralty stubbornly maintained could not be justified to the world or to the American people and would therefore require Coolidge to bow to the combination of Admiralty and American domestic political pressure to accept a lesser number of smaller cruisers.

The Cabinet attempted, as well, to placate Churchill by insisting on capital ship savings. It further instructed Howard to place great emphasis on the "strong hope" that the United States would "withdraw any objection" to the discussion of the question of capital ships. Rather than attempting to weaken the Washington Treaty, the "sole objective" of the British capital ship proposal, the Cabinet asserted, was merely to extend the agreement further into the future without any disturbance to the already existing capital ship balance and with great savings to all.¹⁹

By July 4 as the Admiralty's assurance of a quick and easy agreement evaporated, the Cabinet struggled to dampen smoldering internal dissension by simultaneously placating Chamberlain and Beatty. It first sought to keep alive the dimming possibility of an international agreement by supporting

---

[14] Chamberlain to Cecil, July 5, 1927, Add Mss. 51079, LCP. See reprint in *DBFP*, Ia, III: 637–639. Chamberlain's response to Beatty during the July 4 Cabinet meeting is revealed in this letter to Cecil.
[15] Ibid.
[16] CAB, "Minutes" 38 (27), July 4, 1927, Appendix, CAB 23/55, PRO. A copy of the Cabinet's telegrams to Howard was included in the Minutes.
[17] Ibid.   [18] Ibid.
[19] Ibid. See also Richardson, *Evolution the British Disarmament Policy*, p. 125.

Bridgeman's public promise of parity. It did so in the hope that the second stage of Beatty's strategy might yet succeed: that when the United States could not justify an equal number of smaller cruisers, American public opinion would shift away from parity in favor of significant reductions in naval spending and that this shift would give Coolidge the political cover he needed to accept the Admiralty's demands. It was a slim hope, yet it had the virtue of allowing time for the Admiralty's strategy to bear fruit and, therefore, appeared to be the safest political option.

Aware of increasing British insistence upon a second plenary session to generate stronger world and American political pressure on Coolidge and Kellogg, Jones launched a preemptive verbal counterattack at the Independence Day celebration at the Hotel Beau Rivage. Although unauthorized and unofficial, the contents of Jones' July 4 address were almost certainly approved by members of the American delegation, as his major arguments were all too obviously refutations of the British justifications advanced at the first plenary session and reiterated during subsequent negotiations.[20]

Jones' speech took aim at the major Admiralty arguments. In return for sacrificing its Navy "second to none," the United States at the Washington Conference had "asked only for parity" with Great Britain in auxiliary tonnage and only at the lowest level consistent with national defense.[21] Naval equality was justified by America's rapidly expanding industrial development and its corresponding expansion of trade throughout the world. This trend foretold an "obvious destiny," necessitating new world markets, foreign sources of raw materials, and the ability to protect overseas trade. Indeed, the transportation by sea of America's enormous trade from its Atlantic Coast to its Pacific Coast was alone "practically equal" to the total foreign sea commerce of Great Britain and was as vital to American survival as overseas trade was to Great Britain.[22]

On July 5, Field responded to Jones' obvious shot across the bow by implicitly yet unmistakably rejecting any possibility of considering Jones' combat equivalency proposal, a rejection he would reiterate four days later on July 9. The offensive power of "30 cruisers of 10,000 tons with eight-inch guns," he pointedly claimed, "was far greater than twice the number of six-inch-gun cruisers of half the individual displacement." Thus, Field made it quite clear that Jones' equivalency plan, which allowed for twice the number of British 6-inch-gun cruisers than the number of American 8-inch-gun cruisers, was not acceptable.[23] The entire American delegation now unanimously supported Schofield's insistence that the time had come to present "a very strong, straight-forward statement" making the American negotiating position

---

[20] Jones, "Our Interest in Seapower and Its Equitable Distribution: An Address at Geneva," July 4, 1927, Speeches File, JP.
[21] Ibid.   [22] Ibid.
[23] TC, "Minutes," July 5, 1927, p. 109, Records; EC, "Minutes," July 9 1927, p. 63, Records. See also Chamberlain's quote in the New York Times, July 28, 1927.

"perfectly clear."[24] Since the British had clearly rejected his combat equivalency compromise, Jones agreed "to set forth the [alternative] position of the American delegation very plainly," a position which Bridgeman and Beatty would henceforth refer to as "the ultimatum."[25]

Jones softened his rebuttal with two significant concessions. He offered a treaty until December 31, 1936, which reluctantly increased American cruiser tonnage by 100,000 tons from the limit of 300,000 to a more expensive 400,000 tons. He agreed also to divide cruisers into a larger class and a smaller one. However, rather than limit the 10,000-ton, 8-inch-gun cruisers to only fifteen to accompany the battle fleet, as the British proposed, the United States required twenty-five of these cruisers. The ten Omaha-class 7,500-ton cruisers, carrying 6-inch guns, would be included in the remaining 150,000 tons, but the United States must retain "full liberty" to arm all of the smaller class vessels with 8-inch guns. Nonetheless, Jones added significantly, the United States would agree to lower its number of twenty-five larger cruisers if the British came down to 400,000 tons or less. This offer, Jones concluded, "should be construed as our maximum effort to meet the British viewpoint." If Great Britain continued to insist on a total cruiser tonnage beyond 400,000, the United States would regard such a claim "as so ineffective a limitation as not to justify the conclusion of the treaty at this time."[26]

According to Schofield, Jones privately worried that his statement was "nearly in the terms of an ultimatum." Schofield admitted that "the terms were a little rough," although in accordance with Kellogg's explicit instructions not to go beyond 400,000 tons in cruisers, a crucial point which Gibson had required Jones to make crystal clear.[27] Nonetheless, Bridgeman was furious. He railed against it as "outrageous," as "a monstrous thing," and as a "purely political menace without a note of warning."[28] When Gibson assured him that Jones' proposal was not intended as an ultimatum, Bridgeman privately accused Gibson of "an absolute falsehood."[29] Only after his anger subsided would Bridgeman console himself with the hope that the "ultimatum" was only "a big bluff, bred of the self-satisfaction engendered by [Jones'] Independence Day [speech]."[30]

---

[24] Schofield, Diary, July 4, 1927, SD.
[25] TC, "Minutes," July 5, 1927, pp. 109–110, Records; Bridgeman, Diary, June-August 1927, WBP.
[26] TC, "Minutes," July 5, 1927, pp. 109–110, Records.
[27] Schofield, Diary, July 4, 1927, SD. For Kellogg's instructions see Olds to Gibson, July 2, 1927, FRUS 1927, I: 69. See also Kellogg to Charge in Great Britain, July 5, 1927 and Kellogg to Gibson, July 6, 1927, FRUS 1927, I:70, 73.
[28] Bridgeman, "Report to King," July 7, 1927, 4629/1/1927/70, WBP. This appears to be a rough draft which was not sent. See also Bridgeman to My Beloved, July 6, 1927, 4629/1/1927/64, WBP.
[29] Bridgeman, Diary, June-August 1927, WBP.
[30] Bridgeman to My Beloved, July 5, 1927, 4629/1/1927/64, WBP.

Bridgeman's intense irritation arose from a variety of causes. Immediately following his parity concession statement to the Associated Press, his self-congratulatory mood evaporated upon learning of Beatty's disapproval. Also discouraging was Baldwin's willingness to allow Beatty to reinterpret Bridgeman's "misunderstood" parity promise to the Cabinet.[31] Alerted to serious trouble within the Admiralty and the Cabinet, Bridgeman instructed his wife to spread the word to "everyone at home that we are the only people with any practical ideas and are waging a stubborn war" against the Americans, who "only came here to establish parity and don't really care a damn about economy" because, he later added, "they are so disgustingly rich that they care little about what they spend."[32] Adding to his chagrin was the suspicion that the Foreign Office might "be going behind our backs to Washington" to avoid "a deadlock."[33]

The looming specter of failure prompted Bridgeman to pour out his intense frustration in private letters to his family. To his son he lamented that the Americans "are a quite impossible people if they are a people at all."[34] He convinced himself that "Winston would burst with fury if he were here," yet he worried about those at home, like Churchill, who professed to be unconcerned about a collapse.[35] While King George V, for example, expressed sympathy for Bridgeman's plight, agreeing that the American "demand for parity with us in all ships was unreasonable," he nonetheless appeared to agree with Churchill, when he advised Bridgeman that should the Americans "choose to build an unnecessarily huge fleet of cruisers why not let them do so? Their public will soon get tired of paying the bill."[36]

Adding to the frustration was the belief shared by both Bridgeman and Cecil that the Americans thoroughly distrusted them. Bridgeman complained that the Americans "obstructed all progress" by blocking savings from his capital ship reductions, while "all their journalists were let loose to detect diabolical intentions in our simple and straightforward proposals."[37] He placed most of the blame on Jones, "who, while personally most friendly," was determined not to make a "single concession." Cecil, too, was perturbed. He interpreted Gibson's repeated refusals to discuss negotiations privately at Cecil's rented villa on Lake Geneva as additional evidence of distrust. The Americans, Cecil noted, "love to represent themselves as

---

[31] Bridgeman to My Beloved, July 2, 1927, 4629/1/1927/58; Bridgeman to My Beloved, July 4, 1927, 4629/1/1927/63, WBP.
[32] Bridgeman to My Beloved, July 2, 1927, 4629/1/1927/58, WBP.
[33] Bridgeman to My Beloved, July 4, 1927, 4629/1/1927/63, WBP.
[34] Bridgeman to My Dear Son, July 6, 1927, 4629/1/1927/62, WBP.
[35] Bridgeman to My Beloved, July 6, 1927, 4629/1/1927/64, WBP.
[36] Stamfordham to Bridgeman, July 3, 1927, 4629/1/1927/61, WBP.
[37] Bridgeman, "Confidential Memorandum," July 1, 1927, ROSK 7/36, ROSKCC.

a simple generous people who are always cheated by the phenomenally skillful and unscrupulous English or Continental Machiavelli." While "they do not nowadays dislike an Englishman as such, they listen to him with suspicion, and the better case he makes the more they distrust it."[38]

The Jones "ultimatum" gave Beatty the opportunity to use it to the Admiralty's advantage. In the July 6 Cabinet meeting, Beatty ignored Bridgeman's suggestion that the "ultimatum" might be a "bluff" and that the Americans had expressed a willingness to reduce its claim of twenty-five 10,000-ton, 8-inch-gun cruisers in return for a British reduction to 400,000 tons. He charged, instead, that the Americans "had come to the Conference not to confer but to present us with an ultimatum," designed to ensure American naval supremacy.[39] Perhaps to bolster the Admiralty's claim to an absolute minimum of seventy cruisers, he predicted that Congress would hurriedly build twenty-five additional 10,000-ton, 8-inch-gun cruisers during the five years of the treaty, and another eleven by 1936, a prediction of thirty-eight new cruisers, which ignored the reality of powerful congressional opposition to accelerating the cruiser arms race.[40]

But Beatty did not walk away from this July 6 meeting with a complete victory. The Cabinet ultimately approved Beatty's insistence that its cruiser proposal must continue to be divided into two categories: a 10,000-ton, 8-inch gun class limited by the 10:10:6 ratio and a smaller, unlimited class of 6-inch-gun cruisers, the number of which each nation would be free to determine according to its security needs. However, he was challenged, most likely by Churchill, about American press reports that the Admiralty was negotiating on the basis of 600,000 tons of cruisers, a figure which would allow the Admiralty to build fifteen 10,000-ton, 8-inch-gun cruisers and sixty 7,500-ton, 6-inch-gun cruisers for a total of seventy-five cruisers. Beatty undoubtedly astonished the Ministers by claiming that the Cabinet had approved 600,000 tons in their "Report of Lord Birkenhead's Committee on Cruisers." On this important point, however, the Cabinet not only withheld its approval, but recorded that "Any emphasis on the 600,000 tons aggregate of our Cruiser Programme was deprecated." To avoid rehashing the 1925 Birkenhead debate, the Cabinet then ordered the Committee of Imperial Defence to deal directly with all future Geneva negotiating problems

---

[38] Bridgeman to Baldwin, July 10, 1927, July 1, 1927, SBP; Bridgeman, "Memo," July 11, 1927, ROSK 7/36, ROSKCC; Viscount[Lord Robert] Cecil, *A Great Experiment: An Autobiography* (New York: Oxford University Press, 1941), p. 145.

[39] CAB 39 (27), 6 July 1927, CAB 23/55 in CHAR 22/182, WCP.

[40] *Ibid.* How Beatty arrived at a figure of thirty-six rather than thirty-three American cruisers is unclear. Congress had only authorized eight 10,000-ton, 8-inch-gun cruisers. When the eight were added to Beatty's presumption that Congress would build five per year for five years, the total American cruisers would be thirty-three. See also CID, "Minutes: Cruisers," Doc. 815-B, July 6, 1927, CAB 24/187, PRO.

and to review the Admiralty's Conference strategy in greater detail on the following day.[41]

When the CID met the next day, July 7, Chamberlain raised the specter of a complete collapse.[42] He suggested that a promising way out of this "impossible position" was to capitalize on the American "olive branch" of "incorporating in the Treaty [the] cruiser building programmes of the three Powers up to 1936." Beatty admitted that a building program approach was a "possible solution" to the "immediate difficulty," but he quickly rejected it. When the treaty expired, the same problem would emerge, he argued, in quite possibly "a more acute form, because Great Britain would then have to put forward proposals for an increase in her number of cruisers, which would probably be regarded as provocative."[43]

Rather than back Chamberlain's solution, Churchill skillfully supported Beatty's refusal to accept any limitation on the number of smaller cruisers, thereby avoiding any claim that he was again opposing the Admiralty and bringing about another resignation crisis.[44] He instead disparaged Chamberlain's worry over a failed Conference.[45] To become entangled in an undesirable set of conditions and limitations would be much worse, Churchill advised his CID colleagues, "than a breakdown of the Conference."[46] Following a Conference failure, he predicted, the Americans would launch a cruiser-building frenzy until the great costs dampened their initial ardor.[47]

Churchill's scenario alarmed the Foreign Secretary. Chamberlain cautioned that a Conference failure was "deplorable" for several reasons. An increase rather than a decrease in naval forces would undermine rather than strengthen the League of Nations' fledgling experiment in arms- control diplomacy. Equally deplorable would be the necessity of convincing the British people to build against the United States, at best a "very difficult" task indeed and one which "would make our relations with that country very delicate." Reflecting the warnings from Sir Esme Howard, Chamberlain refuted Churchill's claim that American public opinion would react negatively against the additional cruiser costs, especially if it appeared that Great Britain was at fault for refusing to accept tonnage limitations in smaller cruisers. But then Chamberlain quickly backed off his implicit challenge to an unlimited number of small cruisers. He advised instead that Great Britain must concentrate on convincing the world that its unlimited number of smaller cruisers "had no aggressive role" and were "purely defensive," whereas the Americans' demand for the larger aggressive cruisers with the bigger, more destructive guns would threaten world peace.[48]

---

[41] CAB 39 (27), "Minutes," July 6, 1927, CAB 23/55, PRO. See especially Baldwin's telegram to Bridgeman in Appendix III. See also Richardson, *Evolution of British Disarmament Policy*, pp. 128–129.
[42] CID, "Minutes of the 228th Meeting," 7 July 1927, p. 2, C.P. 193 (27), CAB 24/187, PRO.
[43] Ibid., pp. 1–2.   [44] Ibid.   [45] Ibid., p.2.   [46] Ibid.   [47] Ibid.   [48] Ibid., pp. 2–3.

Doubtlessly agreeing with Chamberlain's advice to shift the blame to the Americans, Beatty defied Churchill by again focusing the CID's attention directly on the contentious issue of seventy cruisers. He recalled that during World War I, eighty to ninety cruisers and old battleships had been inadequate to protect trade, and therefore, the current request for only fifteen cruisers for the battle fleet and forty-five cruisers to protect trade had reduced the margin of trade security to the "vanishing point." He rejected as fallacies the American suspicion that armed merchantmen could substitute for cruisers, as well as Churchill's 1925 claim that "no nation can expect to maintain in peacetime the numbers of cruisers required in wartime." Unless Great Britain could defend its trade routes at the very outset of war, Beatty contended, she would quickly be "reduced to starvation" because armed merchantmen were "quite incapable of fighting cruisers successfully." Challenging Churchill to contradict him, he emphasized that seventy cruisers had been "fully substantiated by the Admiralty," and had been placed before the Conference because it "has formed the approved policy of His Majesty's Government for the last two years."[49]

He then dictated the terms for continued negotiations. The "only way out of the present impasse," Beatty insisted, was to instruct the British delegates that the American proposals were "unacceptable," to refuse to make any counter-proposals, to drop any consideration of total tonnage or total number of small cruisers, to insist on a strict limitation of 10,000-ton, 8-inch-gun cruisers using the 10:10:6 ratio, and to limit the size and guns of the unlimited category of smaller cruisers while extending their service lives.[50]

Like Chamberlain, Churchill also declined to argue over Beatty's negotiating demands, but he could not allow Beatty's claim that the government had agreed to seventy cruisers to go unchallenged. Such a figure, he objected, "has never been accepted." Neither was it legitimate for Beatty to "compare present needs with pre-war figures," nor to claim the necessity "to protect and patrol every one of our trade routes in the event of war," as those routes needing protection were currently unknown and "would depend on the circumstances of the conflict." Having made his opposition to seventy cruisers quite clear, Churchill then carefully backed away from confrontation, explaining that he "did not wish to open an argument on this question at the present time." His refusal to challenge Beatty's control of the negotiations masked a more sophisticated mode of opposition. After two weeks of negotiation at Geneva, it was abundantly clear to him that the Admiralty's demand for an unlimited number of smaller cruisers or even its minimum of seventy to

---

[49] CID, "Memorandum by Lord Beatty, communicated verbally to the Committee of Imperial Defence at its 228th Meeting held on July 7, 1927," Doc. 818-B, C.P. 193 (27), CAB 24/187, PRO. This memorandum is in Appendix V. The "Minutes of the 228th Meeting" reveal that Beatty read this memorandum to the members of the CID.

[50] Ibid.

seventy-five cruisers was totally unacceptable to both the United States and Japan, and, if pursued, as Beatty demanded, could only lead to a collapse of the Conference and a major political defeat for the Admiralty – a prospect quite acceptable to Churchill.[51]

By refusing to send Bridgeman any new instructions or to endorse Chamberlain's suggestion of a building plan to 1936, the CID capitulated completely to Beatty's terms for continuing the negotiations.[52] It reiterated Great Britain's "special position" on cruisers by quoting directly from Balfour's public justification of that "special position" at the Washington Conference in 1921–1922 and instructed the delegates to deny any "arrogant desire for maritime supremacy" or any charge that Great Britain was attempting to deny parity, a charge which it claimed was "wholly without foundation." Bridgeman was also required to reiterate the right of the United States to build cruisers "in numbers sufficient" to ensure its national security while simultaneously insisting that Great Britain would never "voluntarily surrender its right to live" by accepting a treaty denying it the larger number of cruisers required to protect its overseas trade.[53] Beatty's definition of the meaning of parity had now become apparent. The United States had a right to parity, but could only realize it, Beatty claimed, by building up to the number of cruisers needed by Great Britain. However, the Americans did not have the right to a treaty which either limited or guaranteed parity in all warships, as this could prevent Great Britain from building the number of smaller cruisers it needed for the future.

The July 7 meeting of the CID was significant for another reason. Sensing the increasingly distinct possibility of failure, its members began thinking of arguments clearly intended to place the blame on the United States. Chamberlain, for example, now suggested that Great Britain ought to emphasize that the "American proposals were monstrous" because they resulted in "an increase rather than a decrease of armaments."[54] Both Amery and Lord Balfour agreed with this line of attack. Amery wanted greater stress placed on Chamberlain's argument that "the 10,000-ton-cruisers possess powers of offense, while the smaller cruiser was designed purely for defensive purposes," a line which the British delegation would push vigorously in the days ahead, and which the Americans would dismiss as transparent sophistry.[55] Amery advised, as well, that the British delegates must begin manipulating the negotiations to make it appear that the Conference was in danger of failing "as a result of a conflict between America and Japan on the subject of the ratio."[56]

To place the blame on the United States and Japan more effectively, the CID agreed that the British propaganda must be improved immediately. Lord

---

[51] CID, "Minutes of the 228th Meeting," July 7, 1927, pp. 4–5, C.P. 193 (27), CAB 24/187, PRO.
[52] Ibid., p. 5.   [53] Ibid.   [54] Ibid., p. 2.   [55] Ibid., pp. 3–4.   [56] Ibid., p. 4.

Birkenhead was quite dissatisfied with "the apparent ineffectiveness of our propaganda at Geneva as compared with that of America." The CID therefore instructed Bridgeman to act quickly to counter the "gross misrepresentations" spread by the American newspapers.[57]

---

[57] *Ibid.*, p. 5 and Appendix IV. See also Baldwin to Bridgeman, July 7, 1927, 4629/1/1927/71, WBP; "Mr. Grigg note on Message from Winston Churchill," July 9, 1927, SBP; Gibson to Kellogg, July 6, 1927, *FRUS* 1927, I: 74–75.

13

The Failure of the Anglo-Japanese Accord

By July 8 the growing hostility between American and British delegates opened the way for the patient and hitherto circumspect Japanese to offer a series of compromises. The Japanese delegates remained focused on improving their auxiliary ratio while keeping the cruiser tonnage – especially the 10,000-ton, 8-inch gun category – as low as possible. At first Bridgeman dismissed their overtures, but when they surprised him by supporting the American compromise of 8,000-ton cruisers carrying 8-inch guns as an alternative to the British preference for 7,500-ton cruisers with 6-inch guns, Bridgeman quickly changed course. To stymie what appeared to be a budding alliance, he now put forth a building program scheme incorporating overage cruisers and thereby increasing the combined British tonnage in cruisers and destroyers to 660,000 tons.

Although this scheme, which soon became known as the Anglo-Japanese Accord, diverged significantly from the instructions of his Admiralty colleagues in London, the First Lord became enthusiastic because he believed it offered the best way to reach an agreement by combining the virtues of the total tonnage method favored by the United States and Japan with the British insistence on revealing the exact number and combat characteristics of the ships to be built during the life of the treaty.

The Anglo-Japanese Accord quickly generated intense opposition. Bridgeman's unilateral decision to delay the publicity counterattack – intended to emphasize the offensive purpose underlying American insistence on mounting 8-inch guns on all of its cruisers – irritated members of the CID and prompted Churchill to complain directly to Baldwin.[1] Much more important was the opposition of Kellogg and Coolidge, who were willing to allow the

---

[1] Churchill to Baldwin, July 11, 1927, in Winston S. Churchill, *Winston S. Churchill The Exchequer Years 1922–1929, Companion Volume 5* ed. Martin Gilbert (London: William Heinemann, 1979), 5:1028 Hereafter cited as Churchill, *Companion Volume 5*.

Conference to fail rather than to consider any cruiser proposal beyond 400,000 tons. Beatty was equally adamant in his opposition to Bridgeman's acceptance of the principle of total tonnage. For the second time Bridgeman angered Beatty: first by publicly promising to honor the principle of parity in all warships, and now, by his willingness to negotiate on the basis of total tonnage. He was also deviating from the second stage of Beatty's negotiating strategy requiring the Americans to address the ton-mileage formula for establishing trade route protection and thereby revealing to the world that America's cruiser needs were much lower than Great Britain's. Thus, in addition to the rift between United States and Great Britain, an increasingly serious one developed between the British delegates in Geneva and their colleagues in London.

At this point Baldwin ordered Bridgeman and Cecil to return to London where they came to the full realization that Beatty and Churchill were prepared to allow the Conference to fail. To forestall this increasingly likely possibility, they put forth a "modus vivendi" scheme allowing 8-inch guns on smaller cruisers. Churchill at first supported their initiative, but, as Churchill, Bridgeman, and Cecil were unaware of the Admiralty's vehement opposition to the 8-inch gun, this promising scheme merely intensified friction within the Cabinet.

***

The CID had good reason to be concerned about the effective propaganda offensive by the American naval delegates.[2] On July 8, after noting a "growing edge" in the discussions between the American and British delegates, Schofield met with a reporter from the *Chicago Daily News* with whom, he admitted, he "talked freely" about naval tactics and strategy as well as "the fallacies in some of the British published articles regarding our needs." Schofield then spent an hour with Shearer before going to bed, leaving it to Captain Reeves and Commander Train to brief Wythe Williams of the *New York Times*.[3]

The sense of betrayal felt by the American naval delegates became increasingly evident on July 9. The emotional "edge" on the previous day, noted by Schofield, flared again when Field angrily dismissed Jones' counterproposal for twenty-five 10,000-ton, 8-inch gun cruisers. Field dismissed it as unintelligible, Cecil castigated it as nonsense, and Bridgeman characterized it as an "ultimatum."[4] In response American naval delegate leaks to American reporters escalated substantially.[5]

Jones too now became a leaker. On July 13 a newspaper reporter for both the American *Christian Science Monitor* and the British *Westminster Guardian* informed Jones that through his access to private British press briefings, he had reliable "inside information" that the Admiralty had never intended to concede naval equality. Jones responded by revealing that in his private meetings prior to the conference "with Mr. Bridgeman, Lord Beatty and Admiral Field ...

---

[2] See Chapter 12.   [3] Schofield, Diary, July 8 and 9, 1927, SD.
[4] *Ibid.*; Bridgeman to Baldwin, July 9, 1927, SBP.
[5] *The New York Times*, July 10 and 11, 1927.

The Failure of the Anglo-Japanese Accord

I represented to all of them that the recognition of equality ... would be a sine qua non of any agreement that might be reached," and that Beatty had reassured him of equality, but that excessive British cruiser demands had now made equality "impossible."[6]

Appalled that the secret negotiations were compromised by an increasing cascade of leaks, the Cabinet increased pressure on Bridgeman to combat the Americans' "violent press campaign." But there was little he could do against what he believed to be an unholy alliance of American "political bosses who have their eyes on the next election" and lavish spending, big steel lobbyists who were causing "a lot of damage" by feeding sensation-seeking American reporters with misinformation and distortions. Lengthy British rebuttals at the second plenary session failed to diminish the flow of critical press reports, in part, because the American leakers were convinced that their information was accurate. Indeed, shortly after the conference failed, Kellogg lauded the American press for its "intelligent presentation of the news" and concluded that the reporters at Geneva had done "a very good job."[7]

The rapid deterioration of relations between the Americans and British provided the opening for the Japanese to advance their own agenda. Although Bridgeman characterized Japanese diplomacy as "very silent" and often "wrapped in obscurity," he expected that the growing strain in Anglo-American negotiations would soon encourage Japan to squeeze "the most she could for herself out of our differences of opinion."[8] The Japanese had good reason to exploit these differences. The British were insisting on building an unlimited number of smaller cruisers, and the Americans had countered by threatening to build twenty-five of its most powerful cruisers, both of which would directly threaten the viability of the Japanese naval strategy of relying on auxiliaries to offset the disadvantages of their 10:6 ratio in capital ships.

However, the Japanese delegates were hampered by their own internal challenges. On the one hand, the Naval Vice Minister, who sent the delegates instructions without seeking prior approval from the Prime Minister and Cabinet, was pressuring them to secure a higher ratio, preferably an increase from 60 percent to 70 percent. This demand was strongly supported by the

---

[6] Jones, "Memorandum," July 13, 1927, PCF, JP. This is the only evidence of Jones' use of the press.

[7] Bridgeman to My Beloved, July 14, 1927, 4629/1/1927/86, WBP; EC, "Minutes," July 8, 1927, pp. 57–60, *Records*; *The New York Times*, July 4, 1927; Bridgeman to Dearest Mother, July 15, 1927, 4629/1/1927/86, WBP; BED, "Minutes of the Ninth Conference of the British Delegations," July 14, 1927, BEDM; *The New York Times*, July 2 and 10, 1927; Ronald Campbell to Sir Robert Vansittart, June 30, 1927, FO371/12672/W6610/61/98, PRO. Vansittart believed Campbell's report "sums up the psychology very concisely." For Kellogg's quotation see *The New York Times*, July 27, 1927.

[8] Bridgeman to My Beloved, July 5, 1927, 4629/1/1927/64; July 6, 1927, 4629/1/1927/67, WBP; Bridgeman, Diary, June-August 1927, WBP.

officers of the Japanese Navy and by the nation's newspapers. On the other hand, as Japan was still recovering from a devastating 1923 earthquake and from the more recent financial collapse only months earlier in 1927, Premier Tanaka was determined not to raise taxes and needed therefore to keep naval costs as low as possible. These conflicting pressures put the delegates in a delicate situation. Tradition required that if Japan achieved a higher ratio, the nation was honor-bound to build up to the maximum naval strength allowed under the treaty, and this, in turn, would require unpopular tax increases. The Japanese delegates therefore were genuinely interested in achieving a slightly higher ratio – from 10:6 to approximately 10:6.6 – to placate their fellow Japanese naval officers, but not one high enough to require new taxes.[9]

Unable to interest Bridgeman in lowering British tonnage requirements, the Japanese were finally able to capture his attention on July 8 by unexpectedly supporting the American willingness to consider a smaller cruiser class of 8,000 tons with 8-inch guns. To counter what appeared to be on emerging alliance, Cecil favored offering the Japanese a 70 percent ratio, but, over the next few days, Bridgeman proposed a scheme intended to lure Ishii and Saito into an Anglo-Japanese accord. In return for restricting the 10,000 ton, 8-inch-gun cruisers to twelve for Great Britain and the United States and eight for Japan, Bridgeman offered to reduce the number of British active duty cruisers from seventy-five to sixty-six, for a combined total tonnage in cruisers and destroyers of 550,000 tons, and to allow Japan a 65 percent ratio in cruisers and a 70 percent ratio in submarines. All future cruisers would be limited to 6,000 tons mounting 6-inch guns. However, to achieve seventy to seventy-five British cruisers, he exempted 20 percent of all existing over-age cruisers, due to be scrapped after twenty years of service, thus increasing total British tonnage to as much as 660,000 tons.[10]

---

[9] Ian Nish, ed. *Anglo-Japanese Alienation, 1919–1952: Papers of the Anglo-Japanese Conference on the History of the Second World War* (Cambridge: Cambridge University Press, 1982), pp.10–16, 31–32, 35–38; Richard W. Fanning, *Peace and Disarmament: Naval Rivalry and Arms Control, 1922–1933* (Lexington: University Press of Kentucky, 1995), pp. 21–22, 38–39, 53–54; Asada Saito, "The Japanese Navy and United States," in *Pearl Harbor As History: Japanese-American Relations 1931–1941* eds. Dorothy Borg and Shumpei Okamoto (New York: Columbia University Press, 1973), pp. 227–228; MacVeagh to Kellogg, June 29 and 30, 1927, MC 28, CCP; Schofield, Diary, July 6, 1927, SD; Gibson, "Memorandum of Conversation," July 1, 1927, GP; Bridgeman to Baldwin, July 10, 1927, p. 3, SBP; Gibson to Kellogg, July 6 and 7, 1927, *FRUS*, 1927, I: 77–78, 80. For the evidence that the Japanese Naval Vice Minister acted without Cabinet involvement, see Tadashi Kuramatsu, "The Geneva Naval Conference of 1927: The British Preparation for the Conference, December 1926 to June 1927," *The Journal of Strategic Studies* No.1, 19 (March 1996), p. 116, n. 81.

[10] "Informal Meeting of the Delegates," July 6, 1927, pp. 113–114 *Records*; EC, "Minutes," July 8, 1927, p.59, *Records*; Gibson to Kellogg, July 12, 1927, *FRUS*, 1927, I: 100–101; Bridgeman to Baldwin, July 12, 1927, SBP; Kellogg to Coolidge, July 8, 1927, MC 28, CCP; Bridgeman, Diary, June-August 1927, WBP; Bridgeman, "Report to King," July 7, 1927, 4629/1/1927/70, WBP; Schofield, Diary, June 29, 1927, July 6, 1927, SD; Gibson to Kellogg,

Bridgeman's Accord merged the total tonnage method favored by the United States and Japan with the British method requiring exact numbers and exact characteristics of combat vessels in each class. To obviate the Admiralty's principal objection to total tonnage, each nation was required to publish its building plans to 1936, specifying in detail the exact number and types of ships to be built during the life of the treaty. Bridgeman and Cecil anticipated that this transparency could alleviate the Admiralty's suspicion that total tonnage was merely a disguise to gain an unfair advantage, whereby rival nations could wait until Great Britain had built its quota of ships before using all of their tonnage to build a larger number of smaller, but much more powerful ones.[11]

While the Japanese delegates were initially favorable to this Anglo-Japanese Accord, they were eventually instructed to object to the enormous increase in total tonnage. The Americans, on the other hand, wasted little time in rejecting it. Kellogg was appalled at 660,000 tons and would not agree to go beyond the absolute limit of 400,000 tons in cruisers. He stressed that the "President called the Conference for [the] purpose of limitation of armaments, not to lay [the] foundation for world-wide naval expansion" and could not "understand why the British government finds it necessary to create so large a sea force when the United States and Japan are the only countries against which there is any necessity for building large navies" and when neither "British safety, nor British trade routes, nor British foreign possessions can possibly be endangered" by either the United States or Japan. Nor did Kellogg agree with the British claim to "great [capital ship] economies," as there could be no savings until 1931–1932, when the Washington Treaty allowed for a resumption of capital ship building. Moreover, an increased American "building program of cruisers [required to equal the seventy-five projected by Great Britain] and the cost of their maintenance would more than offset any possible economies in battleships."[12]

Coolidge agreed. The President was unwilling to accommodate the British further. Both Kellogg and Coolidge simply dismissed British demands that the Americans use the ton-mileage formula to justify their cruiser numbers to the world. What "is needed," Coolidge told Kellogg, "is not excuse or soft

---

July 6, 7, and 8, 1927, FRUS, 1927, I: 76–77, 80–81,89–98; EC, "Minutes," July 9, 1927, pp. 61–67, Records. Schofield, Diary, 12 July 1927, SD.

[11] Bridgeman to Baldwin, 19 July 1927, SBP; BED, "Minutes of the Sixth Conference of the British Delegations," July 7, 1927, pp. 5–6, BEDM; BED, "Minutes of the Seventh Conference of British Delegations," July 10, 1927, BEDM; Bridgeman to My Beloved, July 5, 6, 9 1927, 4629/1/1927/64, 67,69, WBP; Schofield, Diary, July 7, 9, 1927, SD; Schofield "Conversation between Rear Admiral Schofield and Captain Egerton," July 7, 1927, MCDS. See also Gibson to Kellogg, July 9, 1927, FRUS, 1927, I: 89–91.

[12] Gibson to Kellogg, 7, 9 July 7 and 9, 1927, FRUS, 1927, I: 80, 89; Gibson to Kellogg, 7 July 1927, FRUS, 1927, I: 80–81. This is the second telegram sent on this date. See also Kellogg to Gibson, July 8, 1927, FRUS, 1927, I: 82–83.

words but [a] clear strong statement of [the] American position. Let blame fall where it may." To punctuate his disillusionment, Coolidge announced that he would not attend the opening ceremony of the so-called "Peace Bridge" linking Buffalo, New York and Canada, where he was to meet with the Prince of Wales and Prime Minister Baldwin.[13]

For a brief time, the Anglo-Japanese Accord raised hopes for a breakthrough, especially among the Japanese and British delegates. This hope prompted Bridgeman to delay his propaganda counteroffensive until after the second plenary session. In the meantime, while the British delegates continued "working hard for the six-inch gun" and the Americans continued to insist on "the right to eight-inch guns," the Anglo-Japanese Accord generated consternation in London.[14]

Details of the Accord alerted Churchill to new dangers to the British Treasury. He warned Baldwin and Chamberlain that the Admiralty must not be allowed to increase cruiser numbers beyond those authorized in 1925. Baldwin immediately became alarmed, fearing that Churchill's intervention could bring about another Conservative Party crisis. He was especially irritated by Churchill's insistence on communicating his opposition directly to Bridgeman. "I couldn't stop Winston from sending you a message, which I thought a work of supererogation," he apologized to Bridgeman, "but he has whacked himself into a panic about the whole thing."[15] When Churchill then took his complaint directly to the entire Cabinet, Baldwin selected Churchill, Beatty, Chamberlain, Balfour, and Cecil's brother James, the Marquis of Salisbury, to serve with him on a new subcommittee of the Committee of Imperial Defence, thereby insulating the Cabinet from these increasingly disrupting and emotional disputes.[16]

---

[13] Kellogg to Gibson, July 9, 1927, *FRUS*, 1927, I: 89. Kellogg quoted from Coolidge's telegram to him. See also Castle, Diary, July 10, 1927, CP.

[14] For the Admiralty's instructions to Field on the importance of the 6,000 ton, 6-inch-gun cruisers, see Admiralty to Flint, July 10, 1927, ADM 116/3371, PRO; Beatty, "Minute," July 10, 1927 in Director of Plans, "Naval Limitation and Disarmament: Geneva Conference 1927," P. D. 02909/27, ADM 116/3371, PRO. See also A.D.P.R. Pound to Keyes, 13 July 1927 in Roger Keyes, *The Keyes Papers*: Selections from the Private and Official Correspondence of Admiral of the Fleet Baron Keys of Zeebrugge, 1918–1938, 2 vols., ed. Paul G. Halpern (London: George Allen and Unwin, 1980), 2: 224–225; BED, "Minutes of the Eighth Conference of British Delegations," July 11, 1927, pp. 2–3, BEDM; BED, "Minutes of the Ninth Meeting of the British Delegations," July 14, 1927, p. 3, BEDM; Kellogg to Gibson, July 19 and 21, 1927, *FRUS*, 1927, I: 116–117, 122–123; Bureau of Construction and Repair, "Memorandum to Captain McBride: Comparison of 6-Inch and 8- Inch Guns," July 20, 1927, GBS, GBDCS.

[15] Churchill to Baldwin, July 11, 1927, in Churchill, *Companion Volume* 5: 1028; Chamberlain to Bridgeman, July 11, 1927, *DBFP*, Ia, III: 666; Baldwin to Bridgeman, July 12, 1927, 4629/1/1927/81, WBP; Bridgeman to Chamberlain, July 12, 1927, *DBFP*, Ia, III: 674.

[16] CAB, "Minutes," July 13, 1927, C.P. 40(27), CAB 23/55, PRO. Although the Cabinet minutes did not specifically identify Churchill as the Minister who made these objections, the nature of the objections and the context in which they were made makes it almost certain that it was

When the Further Limitation of Naval Armaments Subcommittee began meeting on July 14, Beatty took the initiative by denouncing the Anglo-Japanese Accord for giving Japan a much higher ratio in cruisers and thereby putting Great Britain in a "very dangerous position."[17] More dangerous still, Beatty warned, was the concept of a total tonnage limit for the entire cruiser category allowing the United States to build up to parity in smaller cruisers.[18] Should the Cabinet force the Admiralty "to sign a document definitely accepting parity with the United States" in these smaller cruisers, he once again pointedly hinted at resignation, as such a treaty would leave the Admiralty no choice but "to say quite definitely" that it could no longer protect "the territories of the Empire from invasion."[19]

Seizing this opportunity, Churchill quickly joined Beatty in opposition to the "fatal" consequences of granting parity to the United States in the smaller cruisers. He dismissed Balfour's and Chamberlain's cautions against explicitly denying parity and instead supported Beatty's warning that the smaller cruisers had now become the central issue. Parity in these warships, he argued, "meant supremacy for the United States" and "inferiority" for Great Britain. Rather than allow the Americans "to obtain supremacy so easily," Great Britain should make clear the enormous expense of achieving equality by requiring the United States to build up to the number needed by Great Britain. This would entail a cost so onerous to the American taxpayer, Churchill confidently predicted, "that within two or three years a great reaction would set in... against such a policy."[20]

Rather than meandering wildly between contradictory and confusing positions, as some Admiralty critics charged, Churchill was carefully evolving a skillful strategy. Supporting Beatty whenever possible, rather than opposing him directly as he had done in 1925, was crucial to opening the way to a safe political avenue from which he could sabotage the Admiralty's cruiser ambitions without again arousing Baldwin's fear of another resignation crisis. Without a new capital ship agreement, the substantial savings – which had motivated Churchill to support the negotiations – had all but evaporated. Avoiding the vast expenditures for new ships had been Churchill's rationale in 1925, and it remained his single most important motivation in July 1927. The major difference in his latest struggle with Beatty's cruiser ambitions was the fact that he had learned from his mistakes in 1925 and had evolved a more subtle strategy to achieve what he believed to be a much more immediate national priority. By temporarily aligning himself with Beatty on the grounds of protecting the Empire's naval supremacy, a supremacy which he fervently

---

Churchill. See also CID, "Minutes of the 229th Meeting," July 14, 1927, CAB 2/5, PRO; FLNA, "Minutes," July 15, 1927, L.N.A. (27), CAB 27/350, PRO; R. C. Richardson, *The Evolution of British Disarmament Policy in the 1920s* (London: Leicester University Press, 1989), p 131.

[17] CID, "Minutes of the 229th Meeting," p. 7.   [18] Ibid.   [19] Ibid.   [20] Ibid., pp. 9–10.

supported, he could much more safely advocate a slower cruiser-building pace compatible with England's worsening economy.[21]

Beset by opponents both in London and at the bargaining table, Bridgeman privately vented his rage. The Jones "ultimatum" requiring twenty-five 10,000-ton, 8-inch-gun cruisers set him to muttering "extremely pungent remarks in his own gruff way," while castigating Jones to King George V as a ludicrous old man whose "head is one of quite impenetrable density."[22] He was furious as well with both Howard and Chamberlain for interfering in the negotiations. He had suspected that the Foreign Office would intervene and his suspicion was confirmed by reports of a dinner on a hot rainy evening on July 9 in Washington, DC.

This dinner was attended by the British Ambassador Sir Esme Howard, Secretary of State Kellogg, Assistant Secretary of State Castle, and Secretary of Commerce Herbert Hoover, who would soon succeed Coolidge as President of the United States and would revive these negotiations in 1929 to achieve an agreement at the London Naval Conference in 1930. The purpose of the dinner was to impress upon Howard the inability of the Americans to understand why Great Britain needed such a large number of cruisers, especially as the German Navy was at the bottom of the sea, and the United States and Japan were pressing for reductions rather than increases. Hoover succinctly summarized the American perception with his observation that there was "sufficient common sense in the world to sneer at a conference that pretended to limit and actually doubled the size of fleets." Kellogg was equally pointed, suggesting that the Admiralty was not only dictating British negotiating terms but did not bother to consult with the Foreign Office.[23]

Howard's subsequent warning prompted Chamberlain to meet twice with Baldwin, Balfour and Beatty, but nothing substantive emerged from these talks, other than to infuriate Bridgeman. Upon hearing of the dinner and Howard's warning, Bridgeman complained to the Foreign Secretary that "negotiations simultaneously in two places is most dangerous," and to Baldwin

---

[21] For a more critical view of Churchill's seemingly contradictory arguments, see B. J. C. McKercher, *The Second Baldwin Government and the United States, 1924–1929: Attitudes and Diplomacy* (Cambridge: Cambridge University Press, 1984), p. 11; Richardson, *Evolution of British Disarmament Policy*, p. 130.

[22] RHC [R. H. Campbell] to My dear Gerry [G.H. Villiers], July 10, 1927, pp. 4–5, FO 371/12673, PRO; Bridgeman to Sire [King George V], July 11, 1927, ROSK 7/36, ROSKCC; Stanfordham to Bridgeman, July 14, 1927, BGMN 1, WCP.

[23] Bridgeman to My Beloved, July 9, 1927, 4629/1/1927/74, WBP; RHC [R. H. Campbell] to My dear Gerry, July 10, 1927, pp. 4–5; Bridgeman to My Beloved, July 9, 1927, 4629/1/1927/74, WBP; Bridgeman to Baldwin, July 9, 1927, SBP; Bridgeman, "Memorandum," July 1, 1927, ROSK 7/36, ROSKCC; Castle, Diary, July 10, 1927 CP. For Bridgeman's worries over Foreign Office interference, see Bridgeman to My Beloved, July 4, 5, 6, 9, and 11, 1927, 4629/1/1927/64–67, 74 77 WBP; Kellogg to Gibson, July 13, 1927; Houghton to Kellogg, July 7, 1927, *FRUS*, 1927, I: 78–79, 102–103; Kellogg to Gibson, July 9, 1927, *FRUS*, 1927, I: 89; Castle, Diary, July 10, 1927, CP.

The Failure of the Anglo-Japanese Accord

that Chamberlain and Secretary of State Kellogg "seem to be in a panic that we are going to break up in confusion" because of the mistaken "notion that there is a Admiralty policy and a F.O. [Foreign Office] policy." He cautioned Baldwin that if Chamberlain were allowed to come to Geneva, it would be interpreted "as a sign that I have been pursuing a violent policy at the dictation of the Admirals," and that if he were put in such an "intolerable position," he threatened to "go home and retire." Bridgeman then instructed his wife to contact Baldwin through personal friends to suggest that his resignation "would rouse great fury in a large section of our party if I were superseded and everyone would feel sure the Navy was being given away." The only "very serious rocks ahead," he confided to her, were American insistence on the 8-inch gun and "interference of the Home Government." Taking no chances, Baldwin thereupon instructed Chamberlain that Howard was "not to make any further suggestions" to Kellogg unless specifically instructed to do so.[24]

When Beatty received the complete draft of the Anglo-Japanese Accord, his concern escalated. He warned the subcommittee that it was clear to him that the British delegates were "on the verge of acknowledging the right of the United States of America to parity in Cruisers and for Japan to build up to sixty-five percent of our figure," both of which were intolerable. Once Great Britain "accepted the principle [of parity], it would be impossible," he contended, "to escape from it in any renewal of the Treaty," and, he predicted, this would mean "actual superiority to America for all time." With the support of the subcommittee, Beatty quickly modified the Anglo-Japanese Accord to allow Great Britain to retain all of its cruisers up to twenty-four years of age, while requiring the United States and Japan to scrap their cruisers after sixteen years of service, thereby guaranteeing British cruiser superiority to 1945. Rather than sink into inferiority against the United States and an "insufficient superiority" against Japan, Beatty declared that he "would prefer to see the Conference breakdown, even with the onus on us." On July 18, therefore, Baldwin made it clear to the British delegates that parity was unacceptable. Any limit on smaller cruisers, he instructed them, could "only be a temporary expedient ... for the next few years and not the acceptance of a principal that the needs of [the] United States and ourselves in small cruisers are equal."[25]

As both Bridgeman and Cecil had worked diligently with the Japanese to arrive at the Accord, they were dismayed at the news of the subcommittee's

---

[24] Bridgeman to Baldwin, July 14, 1927, SBP; Bridgeman to Chamberlain, July 13, 1927, *DBFP*, Ia, III: 676; Bridgeman to Cecil, July 12, 1927, Add Mss. 51099, and 51098, LCP;
Bridgeman to My Beloved, July 13 and 15, 1927, 4629/1/1927/83 and 91, WBP Chamberlain to Howard, July 16, 1927, *DBFP*, Ia, III: 688.

[25] FLNA, "Minutes," July 28, 1927, L.N.A. (27) 2nd Meeting, CAB 27/350, PRO; Chamberlain to Bridgeman, July 18, 1927, *DBFP*, Ia, III: 695.

capitulation to Beatty's modifications, a capitulation Cecil immediately challenged. One day earlier, on July 17, he had bluntly reminded Chamberlain that he and Bridgeman had already publicly pledged Great Britain to parity in all classes of warships, because without this pledge, the Conference would have ended abruptly, and if the pledge were now retracted, "we should be rightly accused of vacillation amounting almost to sharp practice." He warned that he could "conceive no more disastrous termination of the present conference" than if Great Britain suddenly claimed that *"we are not really prepared to accept the principle of parity...but that we only accepted it if it meant we might have a larger number of smaller cruisers"* than the United States. [Emphasis mine.][26] R. H. Campbell, the secretary to the British Delegation, also alerted the Foreign Office that the Americans would "never sign anything that does not give them now, and at once, paper parity with us."[27] Bridgeman was equally succinct. "Any attempt now to go back ... on parity," he warned Baldwin, "seems to me impossible."[28]

In response to these warnings from Cecil, Campbell, and Bridgeman, Chamberlain made a desperate effort to convince the subcommittee that Great Britain had in fact repeatedly agreed to parity and must not now reverse its promise. To bolster his argument, he read Cecil's letter of July 17, cited Campbell's warning, and pointed explicitly to two telegrams in which he, himself, had also stated his understanding that Great Britain would not object if the United States built up to parity in smaller cruisers. On June 30, for example, Chamberlain had instructed Howard to assure Kellogg that "His Majesty's Government has never disputed American claims to parity ... or [the] right to build up to [an] equal figure in any type of man-of-war."[29] By refusing to accept a treaty based on the principle of parity in smaller cruisers, Chamberlain implied, Great Britain would ensure the failure of the Conference.[30] But, when Beatty and Churchill adamantly rejected the advice of Bridgeman, Cecil, Campbell, and

---

[26] Cecil to Chamberlain, July 17, 1927, *DBFP*, Ia, III: 693–695; Cecil to Chamberlain, July 17, 1927, Add Mss. 51079, LCP; Bridgeman, Diary, June-August 1927, WBP; Cecil to My dear Jim, July 18, 1927, Add Mss. 51086, LCP.

[27] Campbell to Villiers, July 17, 1927, *DBFP*, Ia, III: 691–692.

[28] Bridgeman to Baldwin, July 19, 1927, *DBFP*, Ia, III: 697; Cecil to Chamberlain, July 17, 1927, AC 54, AC.

[29] FLNA, "Minutes," July 19, 1927, L.N.A. (27), 3rd Meeting, CAB 27/350, PRO; Howard to Chamberlain, June 30 1927, *DBFP*: 628; Bridgeman to Chamberlain, June 30, 1927, *DBFP*: 629–630.

[30] FLNA, "Minutes," July 19, 1927, L.N.A. (27) 3d Meeting, CAB 27/350, PRO; Ray Atherton to Dear Mr. Ambassador [Gibson], August 23, 1927, GP. Atherton was an American diplomat in the London Embassy who defended Chamberlain's efforts. See also Richardson, *Evolution of British Disarmament Policy*, pp. 132–133; Trimble, "The United States Navy And the Geneva Conference for the Limitation of Naval Armament, 1927 (Ph.D., diss.: University of Colorado, 1974), pp. 295, 302.

Chamberlain, Baldwin ordered the delegates to return to London for immediate consultations.[31]

Before Bridgeman and Cecil departed for London on July 19, they were already aware of the formidable obstacles to the Anglo-Japanese Accord. Gibson again made it clear to Bridgeman that while he favored some sort of an agreement, the Accord's additional tonnage in over-age cruisers and the elimination of the 8-inch gun on the smaller cruisers were unacceptable.[32] Beatty had categorically rejected the Accord because of its acceptance of total tonnage, parity with the United States in the smaller cruisers, and the 10:10:6.5 ratio for Japan.[33] Nonetheless, Bridgeman and Cecil continued to insist that the Anglo-Japanese Accord was still a viable basis for negotiation, and this unrealistic assessment would later complicate their discussions in London.

Bridgeman was furious over the recall as he charged that it left the negotiations "free for the machinations of all our enemies, and the probability of a satisfactory agreement is a good deal more remote in consequence."[34] Chamberlain and Howard were high on his list of irritants. Much later, in 1929, Bridgeman complained that "the expression of any strong opinion by the Sea Lords was a red rag" to Chamberlain, who was "no judge at all of men or their motives." British Ambassador to the United States Esme Howard was no better, as he, too, had interfered in the negotiations. Suspecting that his letters to his wife were being opened, Bridgeman finally resorted to using personal friends to communicate his thoughts directly and privately to Baldwin.[35]

Bridgeman's suspicions about Churchill's interference were based on more solid evidence. Before Bridgeman and Cecil arrived in London, Churchill issued a long secret memorandum to the Cabinet that sought to convince his fellow Ministers of the benefits of refusing parity to the United States. Churchill agreed with the Americans that cruiser strength "can only be measured in relation

---

[31] FLNA, "Minutes," July 19, 1927; Baldwin to Bridgeman, July 19, 1927, *DBFP*, Ia, III: 698. See also CAB 23/55/41 (27) and I. Kirkpatrick, "Minute," in FO 371/12672 W 6845/16/98, PRO. For various evaluations of the recall see Richardson, *Evolution of British Disarmament Policy*, pp.128, 132–133, 206–207; Roskill, *Naval Policy*, p. 509; Fanning, *Peace and Disarmament*, p. 74; McKercher, *Second Baldwin Government*, pp. 73–74; Trimble, "The United States Navy," pp. 295, 302; Christopher Hall, *Britain, America and Arms Control, 1921–1937* (New York: St. Martin, 1987), p. 47.
[32] BED, "Minutes of the 10th Conference of the British Delegations," July 19, 1927, p. 1, BEDM; Gibson to Kellogg, 19 July 1927, *FRUS*, 1927, I: 117–119.
[33] See footnotes 17–19.
[34] Bridgeman to Dearest Mother, July 24, 1927, 4629/1/1927/100; Bridgeman to My very dear Son, July 26, 1927, 4629/1/1927/99, WBP.
[35] Bridgeman, Diary, November 1929, reproduced in the unpublished biography by Bridgeman's son, pp. 615, 648, BGMN/2, WBPCC; Bridgeman to My Beloved, July 12, 1927, 4629/1/1927/80, WBP. Bridgeman's suspicions that his mail was being opened and his use of intermediaries are in the unpublished biography, pp. 645–646, 648, BGMN/2, WBPCC.

to other Powers."³⁶ In contrast to Beatty's emphasis on the absolute need for seventy cruisers, he pointed out that Beatty had admitted that naval strength was relative to the power of rival navies when he stated categorically that if the United States built beyond the forty-seven, which the Admiralty calculated America needed for security, then the Admiralty would require even more than seventy cruisers. Convoys, protected by "more powerful guns than the hostile cruisers," Churchill still insisted, were a smarter and more economical strategy. Great Britain should allow the United States to spend enormous amounts of money building 10,000-ton, thinly-clad, 8-inch-gun cruisers, whereupon the British could then quickly build "convoy cruisers," which were much more heavily armored and with even larger guns. This strategy was viable, however, only "as long as we remained free" of parity restrictions.³⁷

Churchill opposed parity for still another reason. The fundamental flaw with parity, and thus with the negotiations in Geneva, he charged, was that it was based on the utterly false notion that "war with the United States was 'unthinkable.'"³⁸ Such a war would, of course, be both "foolish and disastrous," he admitted, but parity would "put ourselves in the power of the United States," allowing the Americans "to give us orders" because it could starve Great Britain "into obedience." It was time, therefore, for Great Britain to "draw up our own charter of the freedom of the seas" and "right to live."³⁹

Churchill also wholeheartedly agreed with one of the fundamental assumptions on which the Admiralty based its negotiating strategy. He charged that Coolidge had called the Conference for "political motives" so that "English submission to American parity, i.e., supremacy" could be "hawked about the American [political] platforms in [the] 1928" election.⁴⁰ "They risk nothing, we risk everything," he exclaimed. Churchill was irritated as well by his belief that the Americans were attempting "to buy the sovereignty of the seas by mere money power," while at the same time demanding such drastic reductions in tonnage that they "do not even expect to have to cash the cheque."⁴¹ They could, of course, build a superior fleet "from the 15 millions a year war indemnity which they are extracting ... from the German people," but not before so alarming the Japanese as to reinvigorate "the Anglo-Japanese association."⁴²

Churchill's argument that the Cabinet must carefully consider the possibility of future conflicts with United States before it granted cruiser parity was in harmony with the thinking of Beatty and the Board of Admiralty. On July 22 Beatty won the Sea Lords' unanimous support to his unalterable conviction that by conceding cruiser parity to the United States, England would "sink to

---

³⁶ Churchill, "Memorandum: Cruisers and Parity," July 20, 1927, in Churchill, *Volume Companion* 5:1030.
³⁷ Ibid., p.1031.   ³⁸ Ibid., p. 1033.   ³⁹ Ibid.   ⁴⁰ Ibid., p. 1034.   ⁴¹ Ibid.
⁴² Ibid. See also Philip Payson O'Brien, *British and American Naval Power: Politics and Policy, 1900–1936* (Westport, CT: Praeger, 1998), pp. 188, 192–193, 195–196.

The Failure of the Anglo-Japanese Accord

inferiority and would surrender that control of the sea by which alone we had hitherto existed."[43] Admiral Keyes, the current commander of the British battle fleet in the Mediterranean, was more explicit. He assured Churchill that if ever Great Britain were at war and the United States "set out in convoys to force her trade and maintain the Freedom of the Seas for neutrals," he prayed that the government would "allow the British Fleet" to spring into action as "Nothing in the world would possibly please me more than to be in command of such an undertaking."[44]

Despite Churchill's admonition to allow the Conference to fail rather than grant parity, the Further Limitations of Naval Armaments Subcommittee concluded instead that to break up the Conference would result in "evil consequences ... too obvious to need recapitulation."[45] Following an "exhaustive discussion," the Subcommittee decided to present two alternative strategies to the full Cabinet. First, Great Britain would not "quarrel with" [the Americans], but neither would it agree to a treaty right to equality in smaller cruisers. It would instead merely reject the implied American claim "that [equality in] numerical tonnage meant...equality of sea power," or that a "simple mathematical formula" for smaller cruisers was possible "since equal numbers with unequal needs do not give equal security."[46]

Beatty produced the second alternative, "Scheme B," which divided cruisers into two classes. It limited the number of 10,000-ton, 8-inch-gun cruisers to twelve for Great Britain and for the United States and eight for Japan and extended their service life from sixteen to twenty years. Another category limited all other cruisers to a maximum of 6,000 tons with 6-inch guns and stipulated that "as no true basis has been discovered" for establishing parity in this second category of cruisers, the decision on their numbers would be left open for a future conference. Although the small cruisers would remain unlimited, Great Britain was willing to accept the recommendations of the Technical Committee on the size, armament, and service life of destroyers and submarines. However, if a satisfactory basis for determining total tonnage proved elusive, they too would remain unlimited until a later conference. Finally, if the United States should reject this second alternative, the Conference "would be allowed to break down."[47]

Chamberlain was appalled by Beatty's willingness to allow the Conference to fail. He warned Baldwin that while Churchill and Birkenhead supported "Scheme B," Cecil had assured him that not only would the Americans and the

---

[43] Board of Admiralty, "Meeting of Sea Lords," July 22, 1927, ROSK 7/36, ROSKCC.
[44] Keyes to Churchill, January 20, 1928, in Keyes, *The Keyes Papers*, 2: 239.
[45] CAB, "Note on the Present Position of the Geneva Conference," July 21, 1927, p. 3, C.P. 211 (27), CHAR 22/185, WCP. See also FLNA, "Minutes," July 21, 1927, L.N.A. (27) 4th Meeting, CAB 27/350, PRO.
[46] CAB, "Note on the Present Position of the Geneva Conference," pp. 3–5.
[47] Ibid., pp. 6–8.

Japanese reject it, but that "if Beatty's scheme is our last word," Cecil, and quite possibly Bridgeman, would not return to Geneva. The Subcommittee decided, therefore, to provide Bridgeman and Cecil with a fallback position.[48] This third alternative required each nation to declare the number of smaller cruisers it intended to build to 1936. If the United States insisted on an equal number and Japan agreed to an acceptable ratio of 10:10:6, Great Britain would not object. However, the delegation was to make it "unmistakably clear that this offer is made without admitting any principle that can be quoted as a precedent in any renewal of the Treaty, and that after 1936, we reserve the right to approach the question with complete freedom."[49]

Chamberlain was by now more worried than ever. Still unaware of the almost certain rejection of the Anglo-Japanese Accord by both the Americans and the Japanese, he complained to Baldwin that "it would seem to me that the position of our delegates would be made almost impossible." If Great Britain repudiated the Anglo-Japanese Accord, which even Field believed was "a fairly satisfactory basis for agreement," but which Beatty and Churchill now criticized as "fundamentally vicious and incapable of being the basis of a settlement," Chamberlain warned Baldwin that the ramifications of the Conference failure would extend well beyond a major defeat for international arms control diplomacy. In the event of a failure, he foresaw "the last chance of any political cooperation with either Japan or the U.S.A. in China and the Far East ... as absolutely ruined."[50] For these reasons, he pleaded with Baldwin to remain in London, as no one other than the Prime Minister had "sufficient authority to direct the Cabinet." Indeed, he concluded, "Balfour, Churchill, and I all think that it is impossible that you should leave with these questions unsettled, and we hold, however regrettably, that your visit to Canada must be abandoned or postponed."[51]

On the morning of July 22, before the full Cabinet met later that afternoon, Beatty convened the Board of Admiralty to inform the Sea Lords of "two distinct misunderstandings" that the British delegates had made at Geneva.[52] The first mistake was Bridgeman's concession of parity to the United States in all vessels. This he characterized as "very difficult to understand" and "entirely unacceptable." While he softened his criticism somewhat by citing the "ambiguous wording of certain [i.e., Balfour's] telegrams," he nonetheless stressed to the Sea Lords that rather than accept parity in all cruisers, and the resulting naval inferiority, he would "prefer to break up the Conference, and to bear the onus," especially as the American insistence on parity was "smothered in political considerations" rather than legitimate naval needs.[53]

The delegation's second major mistake arose from Bridgeman's stratagem to eliminate Jones from the negotiations by allowing junior naval delegates to

[48] Ibid.   [49] Ibid.   [50] Chamberlain to Baldwin, July 22, 1927, SBP.
[51] Ibid.
[52] Board of Admiralty, "Meeting of the Sea Lords," July 22, 1927, p. 1.
[53] Ibid., p. 2.

The Failure of the Anglo-Japanese Accord

propose a compromise. The resulting Anglo-Japanese Accord compounded the parity blunder by agreeing to a total tonnage scheme which increased Japan's ratio from 60 percent to 65 percent in cruisers and destroyers.[54] Despite Cecil's claim that Field had supported the 65 percent, Beatty had ascertained from Field, whose illness had kept him in Geneva, that he had only entertained it as a basis for discussion.[55]

In explaining the alternatives which the Subcommittee would present to the full Cabinet later that afternoon, Beatty stressed to the Sea Lords the Subcommittee's failure to anticipate the consequences of an agreement extending to 1936. Beatty had not voiced his principle objection to this 1936 agreement, most likely because of the uproar it would have provoked, but he had no such hesitation before the Sea Lords. He warned his colleagues that a future Board of Admiralty would discover that by 1936, a new government, presumably dominated by Socialists, would have replaced the Conservatives. This new government, he predicted, would dismiss the Admiralty's requests for new ships as mere "Jingoism," much as the earlier MacDonald government had done in 1924. To embody as a treaty right, either the principle of parity or a 10:10:6.5 ratio for Japan, for even a short time, he warned, would tie the hands of future Boards of Admiralty "for all time." This was true because the politicians in the new government would be "prepared to sacrifice...the Country's birth-right," just as some of the current Cabinet Ministers were preparing to do. As expected, the Sea Lords unanimously endorsed Beatty's analysis, rejected the two Subcommittee alternatives, and agreed that it must offer its own modification of the Anglo-Japanese Accord.[56]

Later, when Baldwin convened the full Cabinet on the afternoon of July 22, the Ministers determined that Beatty's "Scheme B" was not viable. This decision rested upon recent communications both from Kellogg and from the Dominion representatives at Geneva. Chamberlain informed the Cabinet of Kellogg's warning on July 21, that the "United States Government could not possibly give way on the point of [the 6,000 ton] six-inch-gun cruisers" because "the lack of naval bases" in the Western Pacific would render these vessels incapable of protecting "American merchant marine in time of war," and therefore, the Senate would never ratify such a treaty. Kellogg had also explicitly instructed Howard that Great Britain must acknowledge that the United States had the right to arm its cruisers with 8-inch guns. Kellogg's objection was reinforced by Lord Salisbury's report that the Dominion representatives at Geneva had also recently concluded that 6,000-ton, 6-inch-gun cruisers were incapable of defending them.[57]

---

[54] Ibid. pp. 2–3.
[55] Ibid. p. 3; Field to First Sea Lord, July 23, 1927, in Appendix. [56] Ibid., pp. 4–6.
[57] CAB 43(27), "Minutes," July 21, 1927, pp. 1–2, CAB23/55, PRO; Kellogg to Gibson, July 21, 1927, FRUS, 1927, I: 122–123; Howard to Chamberlain, July 21, 1927, DBFP, Ia, III: 699; Richardson, Evolution of British Disarmament Policy, p. 133.

Faced with these revelations, the Cabinet scrapped the Subcommittee's alternatives. After a vigorous debate, it decided that the negotiations ought to be continued on the basis of the Anglo-Japanese Accord, but with the caveat that the building of smaller cruisers was to be limited to "the next few years" – generally understood to mean 1931 – but without committing Great Britain to parity in this class. Beatty refrained from opposing this decision while skillfully securing permission for the Sea Lords to examine the Anglo-Japanese Accord "in order to bring it into conformity with the indispensable requirements of Imperial Defence." The Cabinet therefore authorized him to present his revisions of the Anglo-Japanese Accord to them at a 5:00 p.m. meeting on July 25.[58]

With the nature of the British negotiating positions still very uncertain, Baldwin ignored Chamberlain's plea and instead secured the Cabinet's blessing of his Canadian trip.[59] Some historians questioned his decision to leave, as did Bridgeman, Chamberlain, Churchill, and Balfour at the time.[60] At least one knowledgeable historian has suggested that even if Baldwin had remained, he could not have saved the Conference.[61] This judgment appears to be quite defensible. Baldwin was undoubtedly aware of the Admiralty's determination to continue dominating the negotiations, and that failing to achieve Cabinet approval of its objectives, the Board of Admiralty would again threaten to resign, thereby bringing on another political crisis within the Conservative Party. This possibility was a greater danger to his leadership than merely allowing the Admiralty to kill the negotiations with terms unacceptable to the United States. It was equally clear to Baldwin that his Cabinet Ministers were deeply divided and that some – such as Churchill, Birkenhead, and Beatty – were already willing to allow the Conference to fail. By taking himself out of the country in the midst of this crucial debate, Baldwin skillfully allowed blame for the failure to fall on Beatty and the Admiralty. Moreover, his departure freed him from the intensifying acrimony, which without his restraining presence, now burst forth within the rudderless Cabinet.

Bridgeman and Cecil were acutely aware of the increasing likelihood that the Cabinet would bow to the Admiralty's refusal to support their promise of parity in all vessels, and that a Conference failure was becoming increasingly acceptable to influential Ministers. They therefore refused to wait passively while the Admiralty modified their Anglo-Japanese Accord. On July 23, apparently without consulting Beatty, Bridgeman and Cecil pushed forward their own compromise. Their plan highlighted the centrality of the 8-inch gun. It was by now evident to them that both the Americans and the Dominion

---

[58] CAB, "Minutes," July 22, 1927, pp. 2–4. [59] Ibid., p. 5.
[60] Chamberlain to Baldwin, July 22, 1927, SBP; Keith Middlemas and John Barnes, *Baldwin: A Biography* (London: Macmillan, 1970), pp. 370, 376.
[61] Richardson, *Evolution of British Disarmament Policy*, p. 207.

The Failure of the Anglo-Japanese Accord

representatives would reject 6,000-ton cruisers with only 6-inch guns, as only two days earlier, on July 21, Kellogg had made clear his insistence on the 8-inch gun. They therefore advanced a "modus vivendi" compromise to 1931, allowing 8-inch guns on the smaller auxiliary cruisers. The larger 10,000-ton, 8-inch-gun cruisers would be strictly limited in number to twelve, twelve, and eight, with some compensation to the Americans for the four British 9,500-ton, 7.5-inch Hawkins-class cruisers and the four Japanese Furutaka 8-inch-gun cruisers. Since negotiating this equalization process would require a degree of flexibility, Cecil and Bridgeman required "a certain amount of liberty" on the 8-inch-gun issue.

Bridgeman and Cecil argued forcefully before the Subcommittee that their "modus vivendi" compromise to 1931 offered considerable advantages to Great Britain. As the Japanese did not intend to lay down any 8-inch-gun cruisers before 1931, and as they had already agreed to grant Great Britain a significant number of over-age cruisers, these concessions justified an offer of a 6.5 ratio for Japanese in cruisers and destroyers. More important, neither the Japanese nor the Americans could hope to build beyond their respective ratios before 1931–1932, when the Washington Conference treaties terminated, and another international naval arms control conference would be convened. Moreover, their "modus vivendi" compromise would clearly stipulate that Great Britain was not bound by any implied precedents and would be free to negotiate new terms in 1931–1932.[62] At the same time, Cecil confided to Chamberlain that unless the language in the new British proposal was less offensively worded, it "was bound to lead to a recrudescence of all the bitterest controversy," and he, therefore, would refuse to return to Geneva and would resign from the Cabinet.[63] Finally, if the Cabinet withdrew its promise of parity, Cecil and Bridgeman asked the Cabinet to make an authoritative statement to Parliament explaining its reasoning for this change "to our own people," as this would appear to be less embarrassing to them [Cecil and Bridgeman] and "less of a challenge to the U.S.A."[64]

When Bridgeman and Cecil presented their "modus vivendi" proposal to the Further Limitation of Naval Armaments Subcommittee on July 23, they were delighted by Churchill's enthusiastic support.[65] Churchill explained that their compromise "to a large extent met my anxieties about the United States because it is not physically possible for that Power to build up to parity

---

[62] FLNA, "Memorandum by Mr. Bridgeman and Lord Cecil," July 23, 1927, in Appendix to L.N.A. (27) 6th Meeting, CAB 27/350, PRO. See also Cecil to Bridgeman, February 17 and 23, 1928, 4629/1/1928/104 and 110; Bridgeman to Cecil, March 30, 1928, 4629/1/1928/109; Bridgeman to Cecil, April 17, 1928, 4629/1/1927/111, WBP.

[63] Cecil to Chamberlain, July 24, 1927, AC 54/90, AC.

[64] FLNA, "Memorandum by Mr. Bridgeman and Lord Cecil," July 23, 1927, CAB 27/350; J. C. C. Davidson to Baldwin, July 27, 1927, in Churchill, *Companion Volume* 5: 1037–1038.

[65] Cecil to Baldwin, August 9, 1927, LCR.

with us" by 1931.⁶⁶ To Bridgeman, Cecil, and Churchill, this modus vivendi appeared to be a reasonable means to save the Conference – in part, no doubt, because they were unaware of the Admiralty's steadfast determination to eliminate the 8-inch gun. However, as Baldwin had already departed, and as the Cabinet remained hostage to the Board of Admiralty's unspoken yet very real threat of resignation, Beatty and his Sea Lords had no intention of allowing either Churchill or the Delegates to interfere with the Admiralty's own modification of the Anglo-Japanese Accord.

⁶⁶ W.S.C. [Winston S. Churchill], "1931 or 1936," July 26, 1927, CHAR 22/182, WCP.

14

Cabinet Crisis

The debates on July 25 and 26 resulted in victories for Beatty and Churchill and bitter disappointment for Bridgeman and Cecil. During the July 25 morning session of the Cabinet's Further Limitation of Naval Armaments Subcommittee, Beatty upset Bridgeman and Cecil by rejecting their modus vivendi. Churchill also became upset when Beatty revealed the Admiralty's demand for as many as twenty-eight new cruisers by 1936. To counter the Admiralty's new building proposal, Churchill first supported Bridgeman and Cecil's modus vivendi compromise, but when Beatty rejected it, Churchill countered by reviving his 1925 idea of a naval holiday. This holiday, he argued, would also extend to 1931 and would benefit all three powers. But, as he no doubt expected, neither Beatty nor Bridgeman would accept what they deemed to be the Chancellor's latest outrage. When Beatty instead presented the Admiralty's modification of the Anglo-Japanese Accord, Bridgeman dutifully supported it. After still another emotional debate on July 26, the majority of the Cabinet adopted the Admiralty's modified Anglo-Japanese Accord, a proposal which Cecil correctly predicted would doom any chance of an agreement with the United States.[1]

***

The modus vivendi compromise which Bridgeman and Cecil put forth to the Subcommittee on July 25 highlighted the crucial importance of the 8-inch gun. Their proposal allowed the United States to mount 8-inch guns on all of its cruisers until 1931 and thereby keep alive the hopes for an interim treaty until a more comprehensive agreement could be achieved at a future conference in 1931 or 1932, after the Washington Conference treaties had expired. Churchill supported their proposal because he did not believe that the United States could

---

[1] Cecil to Baldwin, August 9, 1927, CAB 21/297, PRO.

build enough 8-inch-gun cruisers between 1927 and 1931 to overcome British naval superiority in these warships. His support momentarily encouraged Cecil to believe that a breakthrough was imminent.

But Beatty was not about to allow these politicians to dictate to the Admiralty. He complained that if Great Britain adopted the modus vivendi, the Admiralty would be forced to continue building its smaller cruisers with 8-inch guns in order to avoid the risk that the seventeen British 6-inch-gun cruisers, which would be built between July 1927 and 1931, would be "rendered obsolete ..." by "a refusal on the part of the United States of America and Japan to limit their future small cruisers to guns of six-inch caliber."[2] To avoid this potential danger, Beatty insisted on immediately limiting the size and gun caliber of the smaller cruisers to 6,000 tons with 6-inch guns. He therefore informed the Subcommittee of the Admiralty's determination to prevent the United States or Japan from building cruisers with 8-inch guns beyond the twelve, twelve, and eight in number.[3]

Alarmed by Beatty's revelation of the Admiralty's intention to press for as many as twenty-eight new cruisers by 1936, and acutely aware that Bridgeman's support of the 1931 modus vivendi would quickly erode without Beatty's approval, Churchill hurriedly put forward an alternative plan. Without Baldwin to restrain him, and with the support of Chamberlain, who chaired the Cabinet in Baldwin's absence – and who was desperately seeking ways to avoid the diplomatic consequences of failure – Churchill was able to present his new plan for a naval building holiday to 1931.[4]

Churchill highlighted his building holiday scheme by citing a welter of evidence establishing Great Britain's existing cruiser superiority. This superiority supported the reasonableness of Bridgeman and Cecil's modus vivendi, which, he argued, could be used to save the Conference. By allowing the United States time to build up to the twelve 10,000-ton, 8-inch-gun cruiser limit, the three naval powers could further enhance the likelihood of an agreement simply by not building any of the smaller cruisers during the five-year naval holiday, thus ending the acrimonious deadlock over the size and gun-caliber of these vessels. Adjustments, of course, would be necessary to allow the United States to equal the Hawkins and Furutaka class cruisers. In the meantime, Great Britain would cease work on one 10,000-ton, 8-inch-gun cruiser, already being built, and postpone one more not yet laid down.[5]

---

[2] FLNA, "Minutes," July 25, 1927, L.N.A. (27) 5th Meeting, CAB 27/350, PRO. For the purpose of clarity, the arguments during the two meetings of the Further Limitation of Naval Armaments Subcommittee on July 25 are presented as having been offered in a single meeting.
[3] *Ibid.*
[4] J.C.C. Davidson to Baldwin, July 27, 1927 in Winston S. Churchill, *Winston S. Churchill: The Exchequer Years 1922–1929, Companion* Volume 5 ed. Martin Gilbert (London William Heineman, 1979), 5: 1037–1038. Hereafter cited as *Churchill, Companion Volume 5*.
[5] FLNA, "Minutes," July 25, 1927; W. S .C. [Winston S. Churchill], "Draft Memorandum," n.d., CHAR 22/182, WCP. For another copy see Churchill, "Cabinet Memorandum," July 25, 1927 in

Churchill contended further that his new cruiser-building holiday offered several other important advantages. It would appeal to the United States because it allowed the United States to concentrate its expenditures on overcoming its inferiority in 10,000 ton, 8-inch-gun cruisers. The Japanese would be pleased because Prime Minister Tanaka had repeatedly appealed for a considerable reduction in naval costs. It would simultaneously eliminate the controversy over the Japanese demand for a 6.5 ratio in smaller cruisers and enable these delegates to save face by agreeing to postpone that decision until 1931 or 1932. His cruiser building holiday would therefore enable Great Britain to avoid the controversies inherent in the Anglo-Japanese Accord, eliminate the need to grant a 6.5 ratio to Japan, postpone the dispute over the size and gun caliber of smaller cruisers, and realize great economies without sacrificing British naval superiority.[6] Moreover, he concluded, the Admiralty's latest expensive 10,000-ton, 8-inch-gun cruisers, had "virtually discarded armor" and were, therefore, a class of vessels unworthy of "the vast sums being spent on them or the dangerous antagonisms they have aroused." Indeed, he was no longer "convinced [that] we have been well advised to count so much upon this very costly but frail type [of cruiser] or that they could ever constitute trustworthy foundations of our sea power."[7]

Churchill's cruiser building holiday helped to drive Bridgeman back into Beatty's camp. While he still half-heartedly favored Cecil's ardent desire for a modus vivendi on small cruisers to 1931, several factors undermined his continued support for it. Bridgeman understood that Beatty's staunch opposition meant that the Sea Lords would never consent either to the modus vivendi or to Churchill's interference with the Admiralty's plan to build as many as twenty-eight additional cruisers by 1936. As he and the entire Board of Admiralty had threatened to resign in 1925 over Churchill's request for even a one-year delay, it was obvious that they would not tolerate one lasting four-years.[8] Bridgeman therefore abandoned the modus vivendi, acquiesced to Beatty's modification of the Anglo-Japanese Accord, but adamantly

---

Churchill, *Companion Volume* 5: 1035–1036. In his calculations, Churchill included two 10,000-ton, 8-inch-gun cruisers built by the Dominions.

[6] FLNA, "Minutes," 25 July 1927.
[7] Churchill, "Three Fallacies," n.d., CHAR 22/182, WCP.
[8] Churchill, Working Draft of Speech, n.d., CHAR 22/182, WCP. The memorandum begins with this sentence: "I think it necessary to place on record..." It is not clear whether Churchill made this presumably oral presentation to the Subcommittee on July 25 or to the Cabinet on July 26. This is a carefully articulated summary of his position and a biting criticism of the Admiralty's judgment. Given Churchill's formidable oratorical abilities and political infighting skills, it would have been uncharacteristic of him had he not presented these thoughts to both the Subcommittee and the Cabinet. See also Chapter 4 and Cecil to Bridgeman, February 23, 1928, 4629/1/1928/110, WBP.

rejected pressure to admit that he had exceeded his instructions by promising parity to the Americans.[9]

With Bridgeman safely back onboard, Beatty redoubled his pressure on the Cabinet to reject the 1931 modus vivendi and instead to accept his modification of the Anglo-Japanese Accord. Two principal overarching considerations, which he could not reveal to the Cabinet, dominated his thinking. The first was the necessity of limiting the vulnerabilities of Britain's latest cruisers by severely restricting the mounting of 8-inch guns by rival navies. The second was his growing conviction that the Conservative Party would soon lose control of the government and that a coalition more hostile to the high costs of maintaining British naval supremacy would replace it. Three days earlier, on July 22, Beatty had confided to the Sea Lords his belief that Baldwin's pro-navy government could not long survive and that "certain Ministers were prepared to sacrifice everything in order to reach final agreement at the Conference." Should the Sea Lords agree to Churchill's holiday, the Board of Admiralty would be forced to contend with a new Cabinet which lacked the political will to restart the stalled building program. Thus, he argued, if the Sea Lords accepted either parity in smaller cruisers or a 6.5 ratio for Japan, the new government would be unwilling to alter such an agreement, and the Board of Admiralty "should be tied for all time."[10] Indeed, Beatty's prediction of the looming political defeat of the Conservative Party and its replacement by one less sympathetic to the Admiralty's building ambitions became a reality in 1929, when Ramsay MacDonald again became Prime Minister.

With these unspoken fears in mind, Beatty presented the Admiralty's latest decisions both to the Subcommittee and to the full Cabinet on July 26. He first dismissed Churchill's justification for a cruiser building holiday to 1931. Many of England's existing cruisers were so badly "war-worn," he pointed out, that they were in a relatively dilapidated condition compared to Japan's newer postwar cruisers. Great Britain therefore did not enjoy the overwhelming superiority that Churchill's statistics suggested, and consequently, Britain must replace these old cruisers regardless of the outcome of the Conference.[11]

---

[9] For Bridgeman's fury over the Subcommittee's criticisms of his negotiations at Geneva, see William Bridgeman, *The Modernisation of Conservative Politics: The Diaries and Letters of William Bridgeman, 1904–1935*, ed. Philip Williamson (London: Historian's Press, 1988), pp. 208–209.

[10] Board of Admiralty, "Meeting of the Sea Lords," July 22, 1927, p. 4, ROSK 7/36, ROSKCC.

[11] Beatty first presented his modification of the Anglo-Japanese Accord to the Subcommittee. See FLNA, "Minutes," July 26, 1927, L.N.A. (27) 6th Meeting, CAB 27/350, PRO. This meeting took place during the evening of July 25 but the Minutes are dated July 26. See CAB, "The Geneva Conference on the Reduction and Limitation of Naval Armaments: Note by the Secretary," July 26, 1927, C.P. 212 (27), CAB 24/188, PRO. Beatty then presented his modification to the full Cabinet on July 26, 1927. See CAB 44 (27), "Conclusions of Meeting on July 26, 1927," CAB 23/55, PRO. See also R.C. Richardson, *The Evolution of British Disarmament Policy in the 1920s* (London: Leicester University Press, 1989), pp. 134, 207.

He disposed of Bridgeman and Cecil's 1931 modus vivendi, as well, arguing that if the United States and Japan refused to accept 6-inch guns in 1931 when the modus vivendi terminated and instead continued building cruisers with 8-inch guns, the seventeen new British 6-inch-gun cruisers built between 1927 and 1931 would become instantly obsolete. Thus, Bridgeman's and Cecil's modus vivendi would force the Admiralty to continue building 8-inch-gun cruisers at a cost of £250,000 more than a 6-inch-gun cruiser, and, therefore, the modus vivendi was "very uneconomical."[12] For these reasons, the Sea Lords "expressed a strong preference" for continuing the negotiations based on the Admiralty's modification of the Anglo-Japanese Accord extending to 1936.[13]

Yet this modification was surprising. Beatty now informed the Cabinet that the Board of Admiralty had reversed its earlier opposition and instead accepted Bridgeman's offer of a 6.5 ratio for Japan, the total tonnage method for cruisers, destroyers, and submarines, and the transfer of cruiser and destroyer tonnage from one category to another. This sudden and otherwise inexplicable reversal only made sense as a transparent effort to win Japanese support at the Conference table and thereby cast the blame for rejecting it on the United States. Indeed, Beatty ensured American rejection by adding that all of the smaller cruisers must be restricted to 6,000 tons with 6-inch guns – which Cecil had warned was totally unacceptable to the United States. To realize his cherished seventy cruisers, Beatty also required the retention of an additional 25 percent of the total tonnage in over-age cruisers and destroyers, thus increasing the total tonnage in the cruiser-destroyer-submarine combined categories from 500,000 to 590,000 tons for Great Britain and the United States and from 325,000 to 385,000 tons for Japan. In return for this offer, the United States and Japan must agree to the Admiralty's capital ship building holiday and reductions.[14]

---

[12] CAB 44 (27), "Conclusions," July 26, 1927, pp. 4–5.
[13] *Ibid.*, pp. 3–5,7. On page 7 the Cabinet made it clear that it took "full responsibility for the possible consequences resulting from an insufficiency of Cruisers and Destroyers to safeguard our communications *in the event of simultaneous difficulties in Europe and in the Far East as apprehended by the Naval Members of the Board of Admiralty.*" [Emphasis mine.] This clearly establishes that, despite the abbreviated nature of the Minutes, Beatty clearly articulated the need to prepare for a future war against Japan. It also establishes that the Cabinet rejected buildings plans based on this fear as the Minutes also revealed the conclusion that "the Government could not provide against every conceivable contingency" and therefore took responsibility if the nation was inadequately prepared for "simultaneous difficulties." On July 22 Beatty had complained to the Sea Lords that the Cabinet was inclined to forget the difficulty of the problems with which the Admiralty was faced in wartime, especially as Great Britain was "surrounded by potential enemies who were taking no part in this Conference." Beatty's remarks are found in Board of Admiralty, "Meeting of the Sea Lords, 22 July 1927, p. 5, ROSK 7/36, ROSKCC. See also Richardson, *Evolution of British Disarmament Policy*, p.134; Rolland A. Chaput, *Disarmament in British Foreign Policy* (London: George Allen and Unwin, 1935), p 162.
[14] CAB 44 (27), "Conclusions," July 26, 1927, pp. 7–8.

While no detailed official records were kept of the stormy Cabinet debates on July 26, Churchill had prepared arguments which he undoubtedly used at some point during these heated exchanges. His strategy was two pronged. He first denounced the Admiralty's "monstrous fallacies" upon which the Admiralty was basing its "unreal" negotiating strategy at Geneva.[15] Following these denunciations, Churchill then reversed course to support much of the Admiralty's modified Anglo-Japanese Accord. Equally significant was his abandonment of his naval holiday building scheme allowing the United States to build 8-inch-gun cruisers to 1931. More surprising, he abandoned his insistence on equipping British cruisers with the 8-inch gun and instead adopted the Admiralty's argument for restricting all smaller cruisers to 6-inch guns. His sudden abandonment of the modus vivendi infuriated Cecil, who believed that Churchill had switched to the 6-inch gun in order to kill the Conference.[16]

Churchill's new tactic enabled him first to denounce the Admiralty and then to support it, but not before putting the entire Cabinet on notice that if Japan only intended to build a few more cruisers, as its low tonnage requests at Geneva indicated, then regardless of what a treaty might allow, as Chancellor of the Exchequer, he could not support the Admiralty's demand for twenty-seven or twenty-eight new cruisers to be built between 1927 and 1936. Rather, he informed the Cabinet, Great Britain should "build no more ships then we think necessary on a detailed survey of the situation [from] year to year."[17] Indeed, after the Conference failed, to the Admiralty's later chagrin, Churchill's resolve was one to which he would steadfastly adhere.[18]

Churchill's denunciations of the Admiralty, before he skillfully switched to supporting Beatty's modified Anglo-Japanese Accord, are important to understanding the otherwise confusing nature of the Cabinet debate and his effective opposition to the Admiralty's building ambitions after the Conference failed. The first fallacy of the Admiralty's thinking that he denounced was the Admiralty's sudden willingness to grant a 6.5 ratio to Japan. Recalling the Birkenhead Committee debates during which Beatty had justified the Admiralty's demand for a minimum of seventy cruisers on the likelihood of a future war with Japan in East Asia, Churchill charged that the Japanese request for a combined total tonnage of only 315,000 tons for both cruisers and destroyers had been so low that it had actually alarmed the Admiralty's delegates at Geneva, who began "beseeching the Japanese to claim the right to build more cruiser tonnage." The British delegates had urged this higher Japanese tonnage, he believed, in order to justify the "fictitious Anglo-Japanese war scare," on which the Admiralty based its claim for seventy to seventy-five "indispensable" and

---

[15] Churchill, "Three Fallacies."   [16] Cecil to Salisbury, July 31, 1927, Add Mss. 51086, LCP.
[17] Churchill, "1931 or 1936?" July 26, 1927, CHAR 22/182, WCP. Churchill accused Beatty of suddenly switching from favoring 1931 to insisting upon 1936.
[18] Churchill to Bridgeman, October 28, 1927; Churchill to Douglas Hogg, 14 November 1927 in Churchill, *Companion Volume* 5: 1075–1077 and 1101–1103.

expensive cruisers and on which it had "extorted the last four annual cruiser programmes." According to Churchill's view, these contradictory policies of increasing the Japanese ratio to 6.5, while demanding more cruisers to fight Japan "have never yet been exposed to the glare of the public eye."[19]

Churchill also charged the Admiralty with a second fallacy, centering on Bridgeman's public pledge of parity. This American demand had only arisen because the Americans had become alarmed at the rapid British cruiser buildup, which the Admiralty had justified on the basis of the same "fictitious Anglo-Japanese war scare." To stop this new arms race, the United States had called for a "disarmament" conference in which it demanded "absolute numerical parity in all classes with us." Absolute numerical parity, promised by Bridgeman, was exceedingly dangerous, however, because if England ever conceded, or if the United States ever built up to parity, it would "become a Monroe Doctrine." Echoing Beatty, Churchill claimed that parity would condemn Great Britain "to permanent naval inferiority." To adhere to Bridgeman's promise of parity, therefore, would be "as big a mistake with America in principle" as abrogating the Anglo-Japanese Alliance had been in practice.[20]

Churchill further contended that the Admiralty's third fallacy highlighted its "unreal" negotiating strategy based on seventy cruisers. To illustrate this unreality, he reiterated his belief that "70 cruisers are not an absolute standard for the British Empire." The question of the number of cruisers actually needed, he repeated, was "relative" to the strength of rival navies, a negotiating principle particularly pertinent in light of Japan's request for a much lower tonnage in cruisers and destroyers than even the United States. The Admiralty's latest justification for these seventy cruisers, based on the protection of trade routes, was equally fallacious. Trade routes could not be realistically protected by cruisers, Churchill assured the Cabinet, because not even a five-to-one superiority would suffice against a raider, as demonstrated during World War I by the German raider *Emden*, which had only 4.1-inch guns. A totally different strategy, based on slower, more heavily armored cruisers specifically designed to protect convoys, he believed, was the best alternative to the costly and thinly armored cruisers already built by the Admiralty.[21]

Having thoroughly castigated the Admiralty, Churchill then offered yet another compromise, which he hoped would "remove the principle Admiralty objection to [an agreement ending in] 1931."[22] Churchill offered to support a treaty which severely restricted the 8-inch gun, but which allowed the continued building of smaller cruisers limited to 6-inch guns, provided, he implied, that the Cabinet agreed not to build "more warships than we think necessary

---

[19] Churchill, "Three Fallacies." [20] *Ibid.*
[21] *Ibid.* For Churchill's elaboration on his arguments, see the sources cited in footnotes 8 and 17. See also Churchill, "1931 or 1936?" and Bridgeman to Baldwin, July 18, 1927, in *DBFP*, Ia, III: 695.
[22] Churchill, "1931 or 1936?"

on a detailed survey of the [naval] situation from year to year." By adopting a yearly review of building needs, the nation could thereby avoid "the risk of our having wasted our money on vessels subsequently outclassed" by rival 8-inch-gun cruisers.[23]

As he undoubtedly expected, because of the Admiralty's objection, the Cabinet refused to support his "year-to-year" alternative, yet Churchill had laid down his marker. He severely chastised the Admiralty's cruiser design and negotiating strategy, reiterating his steadfast determination to prevent wasteful naval building regardless of what a treaty might permit. At the same time he avoided the political hazards of continued opposition by abandoning Cecil's cherished modus vivendi, accepting the smaller 6-inch-gun cruiser, and by joining with the majority in the approving the Admiralty's modified Anglo-Japanese Accord.[24]

Churchill's arguments may have appeared confusing to some observers at the time, but in retrospect, his intent was clear. He first challenged and criticized the Admiralty, articulated alternative negotiating possibilities, and when these were rejected, ultimately supported the Admiralty's modified Anglo-Japanese Accord. This strategy enabled him to justify his opposition to the Admiralty's building ambitions, while simultaneously offering consistent support of British naval supremacy, a support which obviated the charge that he was precipitating still another resignation crisis.

Admiral Pound failed to appreciate the twists and turns of Churchill's versatile and imaginative political intellect. He complained to Keyes that during the week of July 19 to July 26 "Winston produced wild schemes in the way of Naval holidays etc. etc. and often a whole day was spent by Lord B [Beatty] in getting these schemes turned down." Pound believed Churchill to be a politician who was "as usual absolutely unreliable – one moment he would be all on the side of the Admiralty and at other times, but less often, a d---d nuisance to us, to say the least of it." Pound suspected that Churchill generally sided with the Admiralty only "when Birkenhead was at the Cabinet meetings." "Once or twice when Birkenhead was away," he observed, "Winston was quite off the rails." Nonetheless, Pound acknowledged that "On the whole he was helpful."[25]

Beatty was less critical of Churchill. He, too, recalled the "hard struggle" during the week of debates. But he hinted that his latest struggle was waged within the Cabinet against those who were attempting to save the Conference. He congratulated himself that he was able to "defeat the pacifists in our

---

[23] *Ibid.*
[24] Churchill, "Three Fallacies"; Cecil to Baldwin, August 9, 1927, pp. 5–7, SBP; Cecil to Edward [Lord Irwin], September 29, 1927, Add Mss. 51084, LCP.
[25] Pound to Keyes, August 6, 1927, in Roger Keyes, *The Keyes Papers: Selections from the Private and Official Correspondence of Admiral of the Fleet Baron Keyes of Zeebrugge, 1919–1938*, 2 vols., ed. Paul G. Halpern (London: George Allen and Unwin, 1980), 2: 225.

Government who would have given everything away rather than have the Conference breakdown." This candid admission confirmed that, by July 26, Beatty preferred a breakdown rather than concessions which "would have given everything away." In any case, he agreed with Pound about Churchill's helpfulness. He concluded, "Luckily Winston and Birkenhead took the right line, and so we were able to scotch the weak ones."[26]

The Cabinet's decision on July 26 to reject the 1931 modus vivendi proposal, to repudiate Bridgeman's promise of parity, and to support the Admiralty's modification of the Anglo-Japanese Accord, heightened the conviction within the Cabinet of an impending failure at Geneva and generated intense personal animosities.[27] Beatty castigated "that lunatic Cecil" as the leader of the Cabinet pacifists.[28] Admiral Pound was equally critical of Cecil, whom he dismissed as "undoubtedly very clever but is a peace fanatic and as you know cannot be trusted a yard in anything to do with his [peace] hobby."[29]

Bridgeman and Cecil were also bitter. In his diary Bridgeman poured out his disappointment over the weak support offered by Chamberlain and Balfour, complaining that neither one of them had offered vigorous opposition to Churchill or Lord Birkenhead.[30] Rather than placing most of the blame on Beatty and the Admiralty, Cecil seemed to concentrate on Churchill for abandoning his support of the 1931 modus vivendi because, he shrewdly observed, Churchill wanted to "wreck the negotiations."[31]

Beatty's implied criticisms of Bridgeman and Cecil were certainly unfair. Rather than being pacifists, they had attempted to nurture the slim possibility of an agreement based on a modus vivendi on small cruisers to 1931, which would have allowed 8-inch guns and, which Churchill even argued, would not immediately threaten British naval supremacy.[32] Unwilling to admit that they had exceeded the Cabinet's confusing instructions on parity or return to Geneva with a proposal which explicitly withdrew their promise of parity in all warships, Bridgeman and Cecil threatened to resign. To avoid this embarrassment, the Cabinet authorized Chamberlain to inform Parliament that the Cabinet took the responsibility for explicitly rejecting parity in smaller cruisers.[33]

---

[26] Beatty to Keyes, August 6, 1927, in Keyes, *Keyes Papers*, 2: 225.
[27] Neville Chamberlain, Diary, July 30, 1927, NC 2/22, NCP; Cecil to Salisbury, July 31, 1927; CAB 44 (27), "Conclusions of the Meeting on 26 July 1927," pp. 7–8 and Appendix I, CAB 23/55, PRO; Richardson, *Evolution of British Disarmament Policy*, pp. 134, 206–207.
[28] Beatty to Keyes, September 9, 1927, in Keyes, *Keyes Papers*, 2: 228.
[29] Pound to Keyes, August 10, 1927 in Keyes, *Keyes Papers*, 2: 228.
[30] Bridgeman, Diary, June-August 1927, WBP.
[31] Cecil to Salisbury, July 31, 1927, LCP; Cecil to Baldwin, August 9, 1927, SBP.
[32] Cecil to Salisbury, July 31, 1927, LCP; Churchill, "Cabinet Memorandum," July 25, 1927, in Churchill, *Companion Volume* 5: 1035–1036; Churchill, "1931 or 1936?," July 26, 1927, WCP.
[33] J. C. C. Davidson to Baldwin, July 27, 1927 in Churchill, *Companion Volume* 5: 1037–1038; CAB 44 (27), "Conclusions," July 26, 1927, p. 7 and Appendix I; Neville Chamberlain, Diary, July 30, 1927, NC 2/22, NCP.

Nonetheless, Cecil warned the Cabinet that, should the Conference fail as a result of the Admiralty's rejection of parity, the 8-inch gun on the small cruisers, and the modus vivendi to 1931, he reserved the right to resign in protest.[34]

Conservative Party members were well aware of these debates and worried about the explosive nature of the furor. J. C. C. Davidson, for example, wrote to Baldwin that he "was very frightened" by the emotional intensity of the exchanges and confessed that without the Prime Minister's steady hand, he had felt "as though we were sitting on the edge of a volcano."[35] Nonetheless, the Cabinet's decision on July 26 averted another Admiralty resignation crisis by once again rejecting alternative negotiating strategies suggested by Bridgeman, Cecil, and Churchill and by supporting the Admiralty's modification of the Anglo-Japanese Accord.

Still, despite the Cabinet's backing, it was obvious that the Admiralty had suffered a severe setback. Its fundamental underlying assumption, that Coolidge was a weak-willed politician, who was merely seeking a reelection issue and would bow to the Admiralty's unrelenting demands, now lay in tatters. Coolidge was, in fact, content to "let the blame fall where it may," and it was obvious to the Cabinet that most, if not all, of the blame for the confusing and unsuccessful British negotiating strategy must fall upon the Admiralty. While the Cabinet avoided still another resignation crisis by assuming public responsibility for rejecting parity, and thereby inducing Bridgeman and Cecil to return to Geneva, the Ministers were by now well aware that the Admiralty's conduct of the negotiations had been woefully inadequate and embarrassingly disappointing.

---

[34] Cecil to Edward [Lord Irwin], September 29, 1927, LCP; Cecil to Baldwin, August 9, 1927, p. 6, SBP.
[35] J. C. C. Davidson to Baldwin, 27 July 1927; Richardson, *Evolution of British Disarmament Policy*, pp. 134, 206–207, and 234 footnote 6.

15

Final Efforts

Before Bridgeman and Cecil returned to Geneva to resume negotiations on July 28, the American delegates had already rejected the essential features of the Anglo-Japanese Accord, a decision supported by Coolidge, Kellogg, and the General Board. Prospects for a compromise were dampened still further when the Japanese delegates received instructions to demand a ratio of 70 percent rather than 65 percent. More depressing still was Chamberlain's presentation to Parliament, revealing the Cabinet's repudiation of Bridgeman's public promise of parity for all warships and its adoption of the Admiralty's elaborate justification for denying parity in the smaller cruisers. A brief ray of hope emerged when Gibson softened American rejection of the British modification of the Anglo-Japanese Accord by suggesting that if Great Britain could accept 8-inch guns on the smaller cruisers, he could see "no insuperable obstacles" to some sort of agreement. But Beatty refused to allow 8-inch-guns on any future warship. Gibson's olive branch nonetheless prompted another round of proposed compromises featuring a 7-inch gun, several variations of a political escape clause, Cecil's revival of a naval holiday to 1931, and still another Japanese proposal. Yet despite these efforts, the Admiralty held firm against the 8-inch gun, and, ultimately, a deeply frustrated Cabinet in effect chastised the Admiralty for its embarrassing diplomatic failure and granted Churchill the means by which he could effectively counter future Admiralty building ambitions.

***

Between July 20 and July 27, while the British delegates were in London debating with the Cabinet, Gibson and Jones became increasingly convinced that the Anglo-Japanese Accord did not offer a satisfactory basis for

America's continued participation in the negotiations.¹ Kellogg was equally pessimistic, agreeing with them that a compromise lasting only until 1931 was not feasible, as it was "impossible for the [State] Department to predict what Congress will do."² They nonetheless agreed on several issues which could conceivably keep the negotiations alive in the event that the consultations in London allowed for greater British flexibility. Based on the General Board's latest studies, Jones informed Secretary of the Navy Wilbur that if the British would agree to 8,300-ton, 8-inch-gun cruisers for the smaller class, the American delegation would be "disposed to grant Japan a small concession" on a slightly higher ratio, and, recommend that Great Britain and the United States consider 400,000 tons in cruisers and 225,000 tons in destroyers.³ To reassure the British, an escape clause would guarantee the right of each of the parties to terminate the treaty if any development "materially threatened its national interests." Gibson believed that this escape clause "might assist materially in obtaining British ratification."⁴

Despite these efforts to keep the negotiations alive, Kellogg was resigned to the likelihood of failure. In reviewing the negotiations for Coolidge, he complained about the immediate lack of trust generated by Great Britain's "exorbitant" cruiser tonnage, about the "more difficult problem" of Britain's insistence on severely limiting the number of 10,000-ton, 8-inch-gun cruisers while demanding an unlimited category of smaller cruisers restricted to 6,000 tons with 6-inch guns, and about the much publicized yet false British claims to great savings. He pointed out to Coolidge that Great Britain's economy claims were merely "camouflage" to detract from their "demand for an enormous tonnage of cruisers." For these reasons he doubted whether either the United States Navy or the Senate could ultimately agree to these British terms.⁵

Like Kellogg, Coolidge worried about hidden British motives. The President was well pleased with the positions taken by his negotiators at Geneva, with Kellogg's reasoning, and with the terms which they had offered to the British. "We have made a perfectly straightforward and candid presentation," Coolidge reassured Kellogg, and "I do not think we should deviate from it," but instead "leave others with the responsibility of its rejection." The President stressed that "We should *by all means* keep our right to build such 10,000-ton cruisers as we wish and arm our vessels with such *eight-inch guns* as we wish." [Emphasis mine.] Indeed, in words strikingly similar to those privately

---

¹ Gibson to Kellogg, July 18, 1927, *FRUS*, 1927, I: 109–111, 113–115; Gibson to Kellogg, July 23, 1927, *FRUS*, 1927, I: 127–132; Gibson to Mother, July 23, 1927, GP, HHPL; Jones to Wilbur, July 21, 1927, Wilbur File, JP.
² Kellogg to Gibson, July 27, 1927, *FRUS*, 1927, I: 135–136.
³ Jones to Wilbur, July 21 1927, Wilbur File, JP; Gibson to Kellogg, July 22, 1927, *FRUS*, I: 130–131.
⁴ Gibson to Kellogg, July 23, 1927, *FRUS*, 1927, I: 131–132; Kellogg to Gibson, July 25, 1927, *FRUS*, 1927, I: 132–133; Kellogg to Coolidge, July 22, 1927, MC 27, CCP.
⁵ Kellogg to Coolidge, July 22, 1927, MC 27, CCP and *FRUS*, 1927, I: 124–127.

expressed by Churchill, Coolidge concluded: "I am not in favor of the six-inch gun and small cruiser proposals."[6]

When the British delegates returned to Geneva on July 28 insisting upon 6,000-ton, 6-inch-gun cruisers, a severe limit on 10,000-ton, 8-inch-gun cruisers, and a 6.5 ratio for Japan, the hope for a successful compromise all but vanished. This prevailing gloom deepened when Admiral Kobayashi explained that the Japanese delegates now faced a very difficult dilemma. His delegation was under considerable pressure to obtain a 70 percent ratio and had in fact been "censored" for agreeing to discuss a 65 percent ratio.[7] But even if a 70 percent ratio were granted, he continued, when it was combined with the higher-than-expected British tonnage demands, it would force Japan to increase its building well beyond its current budget. Since Japanese tradition required that the nation must build up to the maximum armament allowed under a treaty, the result would be "no limitation at all." To realize both Great Britain's unexpectedly high tonnage demands and a higher Japanese ratio of between 65 and 70 percent would require an increase in taxes, which Premier Tanaka was determined to avoid. The Japanese delegates were, therefore, caught in a difficult bind between the popular support for the Naval Ministry's demand to increase the ratio to 70 percent and the Prime Minister's need to reduce military spending following the devastating earthquake in 1923 and the Japanese financial panic of 1927. For these reasons, the Japanese supported the American desire for as low a combined tonnage as possible.[8]

Adding to the growing sense of futility was Kellogg's swift rejection of Chamberlain's lengthy justification to Parliament for withdrawing parity in smaller cruisers.[9] His equally swift rejection of the British modification of the Anglo-Japanese Accord misled Bridgeman and later historians into thinking that Chamberlain's repudiation of parity in smaller cruisers had caused the Americans to reject the Accord. This erroneous impression may have arisen because Kellogg pointedly informed American reporters that the British

---

[6] Coolidge to Kellogg, July 25, 1927, MC 28, CCP and *FRUS*, 1927, I: 133–134; Richard W. Fanning, *Peace and Disarmament: Naval Rivalry and Arms Control, 1922–1933* (Lexington: University Press of Kentucky, 1995), pp. 74–75.

[7] Gibson to Kellogg, July 22, 1927, *FRUS*, 1927, I: 130–131; Schofield, Diary, 21, 23 July 1927, SD. See also Fanning, *Peace and Disarmament*, p. 75. For the Navy Vice Minister's direct orders to the Japanese delegates at Geneva see Tadashi Kuramatsu, "The Geneva Naval Conference of 1927: The British Preparation for the Conference, December 1926 to June 1927," *The Journal of Strategic Studies* No.1, 19 (March 1996), p. 116, footnote 81.

[8] Schofield, "Conversation between Rear Admiral Schofield and Captain Toyoda," July 22 and 23, 1927, MCDS; Schofield, Diary, July 22 and 23, 1927, SD.

[9] Mr. Chilton to Chamberlain, July 28 and 29, 1927, *DBFP*, Ia, III: 702, 706; "Statement Made in Parliament, 27th July, 1927," Appendix I, ADM 116/2609, PRO; Kellogg, "Draft Response to Chamberlain's Speech to Parliament," July 28, 1927 MC27, KP; Houghton to Kellogg, July 28, 1927, *FRUS*, 1927, I: 136; William F. Trimble, "The United States Navy and the Geneva Conference for the Limitation of Naval Armament, 1927" (Ph.D. diss., University of Colorado, 1974), p. 318.

modification was worse than the original Accord. Coolidge reinforced this conclusion in his own press conference by stressing the unnecessarily large tonnage demanded by the British as well as the need to resolve the issues of the size of the guns and the cruisers to carry them. In fact, even before Chamberlain's public repudiation of parity in smaller cruisers, both Kellogg and Coolidge had already concluded that the United States would not compromise on the right to build 8-inch-gun cruisers with sufficient tonnage to carry this gun.[10]

Perhaps encouraged by the Japanese insistence on lower total tonnage, Gibson informed the British delegates that he "could hold out no hope of agreement" unless the British could accept the 8-inch gun, and, without that, there was "no useful purpose to be served by discussing other features of the [latest] British proposal."[11] Nonetheless, he suggested that if the British could make concessions on the 8-inch gun, he was willing to negotiate adjustments of the British modifications of the Anglo-Japanese Accord, as he "did not regard any of them as insuperable."[12]

Realizing that Gibson would not compromise on the 8-inch gun, but would be willing to negotiate on all other aspects of the Admiralty's modification of the Accord, Bridgeman and Cecil redoubled their efforts to convince the Cabinet to revise its terms.[13] The possibility of saving the negotiations also prompted the Japanese to reconsider their own preference for the 8-inch gun.

---

[10] Bridgeman to King George V, August 6, 1927, ROSK 7/36, ROSKCC; Fanning, *Peace and Disarmament*, p. 75; L. Ethan Ellis, *Frank C. Kellogg and American Foreign Relations, 1925–1929* (New Brunswick, NJ: Rutgers University Press, 1961), p. 177; Stephen Roskill, *Naval Policy Between the Wars: The Period of Anglo-American Antagonism, 1919–1929*, (London: Collins, 1968), p. 510. For Kellogg's response, see Mr. Chilton to Chamberlain, July 29, 1929, *DBFP*, Ia, III: 706. Coolidge's statement to the press is in Kellogg to Gibson, July 29, 1927, *FRUS*, 1927, I: 139–140.

[11] Gibson to Kellogg, July 28, 1927, *FRUS*, 1927, I: 136 and in CCP; Gibson [?], "Meeting of the Delegates Held at Monsieur Sugimura's house at 3:30 PM on Thursday, July 28th," p. 3, MCDS; Bridgeman, "Log," July 28, 1927, BGMN 1, WBPCC. See also R. C. Richardson, *The Evolution of British Disarmament Policy in the 1920's* (London: Leicester University Press, 1989), p. 136; Roskill, *Naval Policy Between the Wars*, pp. 511–512.

[12] Gibson [?], "Meeting of Delegates at Monsieur Sugimura's House," p. 4. For the full text of the modified Anglo-Japanese Accord, which deliberately excluded the consideration of capital ship reduction, see Bridgeman to Chamberlain, 28 July 1928, *DBFP*, Ia, III: 702–703. See also BED, "Minutes of the Eleventh Conference of British Delegations," July 28, 1927, CAB 27/350, PRO. Estimates of the total tonnage required by Great Britain vary from source to source. See for example Roskill, *Naval Policy Between the Wars*, p. 511 and Philip Payson O'Brien, *British and American Naval Power: Politics and Policy, 1900–1936* (Westport, CT.: Praeger, 1998), pp. 193–194.

[13] Bridgeman, "Log," July 28, 1927, BGMN 1, WBPCC; Bridgeman to Chamberlain, 29 July 1927, *DBFP*, Ia, III: 704–705; Cecil to Baldwin, August 9, 1927, SBP; Bridgeman to Cecil, April 17, 1928, 4629/1/1928/111, WBP. See also Bridgeman to Cecil, n.d. [February 23, 1928?], 4629/1/1928/ 104 and 110; Bridgeman to Cecil, March 30, 1928, 4926/1/1928/109, WBP; Richardson, *Evolution of British Disarmament Policy*, p. 135.

Final Efforts

If Great Britain and the United States could reach a gun compromise, the Japanese promised to accept it, although Count Ishii warned that as the new British terms now required 90,000 tons of submarines rather than the 70,000 tons, to which Great Britain and the United States had earlier agreed, Japan would require 70,000 rather than 60,000 tons.[14]

Cecil and Bridgeman now proposed two separate gun compromises for the Cabinet's consideration. These two proposals differed significantly both in their nature and in the seriousness with which they were offered. Cecil was far more intent upon reviving his modus vivendi allowing for 8-inch guns to be mounted on all cruisers until 1931. He argued that this was "a solution [which] would be even now accepted."[15] As an alternative to the modus vivendi, Cecil also strongly supported lowering the gun caliber to 7 inches and, following the collapse of the Conference, would later vociferously argue that the fact that Bridgeman had suggested the 7-inch gun to the Cabinet was proof of the First Lord's support.[16]

What Cecil later overlooked was the fact that Bridgeman's suggestion had been carefully qualified. "The only alternative I can see," he had informed the Cabinet, "is an attempt at compromise on [a] gun between six-inch and 7.5-inches which would eliminate [the] argument with which [the] Americans are obsessed about armed merchantmen."[17] However, Bridgeman simultaneously alerted the Cabinet that Rear Admiral A. D. Pound, the Assistant Chief of the Naval Staff who replaced the ailing Field, had forwarded his own dissent over the 7-inch gun directly to the Admiralty, and that Bridgeman therefore had advised the Cabinet to "Please see [the] Admiralty on [this] subject," a clear signal of his willingness to abide by the Admiralty's decision.[18]

In response to the urgency of these alternative proposals, the Cabinet hastily assembled to consider them, and, as usual, invited Beatty to offer his judgment. Pound asked Beatty if the Admiralty would consider "some gun intermediate between six-inch and eight-inch, such as seven-inch."[19] Not surprisingly Beatty was unalterably opposed both to Cecil's modus vivendi and to the 7-inch gun. On the one hand, he argued, designing a new 7-inch gun would be "highly inconvenient and incurred increased tonnage and expense," while Cecil's modus vivendi, on the other hand, would force Great Britain to accept the principle of an 8-inch gun on future cruisers, thereby forever committing Great Britain to this principle.[20] Pound therefore obediently accepted Beatty's

---

[14] Gibson [?], "Meeting of Delegates at Monsieur Sugimura's House," pp. 4–6.
[15] Cecil to Chamberlain, July 29, 1927, *DBFP*, Ia, III: 705–706.
[16] Cecil to Bridgeman, March 25, 1928, 4629/1/1928/106, WBP.
[17] Bridgeman to Chamberlain, July 29, 1927, *DBFP*, Ia, III: 705.
[18] *Ibid.* Bridgeman later admitted that the 7-inch gun compromise was "originally my own idea," but "I always said it must depend upon the Admiralty experts view as to its feasibility..." See Bridgeman to Cecil, April 17, 1928, 4629/1/1928/111, WBP.
[19] CAB 46 (27), "Cabinet Conclusions," July 29, 1927, p. 1, CAB 23/55, PRO.   [20] *Ibid.*

direction. Nonetheless, the Cabinet was not willing to preclude the 7-inch gun. Neville Chamberlain, the Minister of Health, believed that he was able to keep the issue of the 7-inch gun alive to the extent that the Cabinet could reexamine it if the Americans were to offer such a solution.[21]

The General Board soon precluded this possibility. By August 1 its special committee on naval ordinance concluded that although a 7-inch gun could be mounted on an 8,000-ton cruiser, allowing for four centerline triple turrets, the 8-inch gun was still far superior both in rapidity of fire and destructive impact.[22]

Despite the eventual rejection of the 7-inch gun as a possible conference-saving alternative, British delegates continued to debate its usefulness. Both Cecil and Sir Joseph Cook, the Australian delegate, attempted to use Bridgeman's admission that the Japanese delegates "were getting very upset at the prospect of a breakdown of the conference" to convince Admiral Pound to alter his opposition to the 7-inch gun. Pound then offered a much clearer and more convincing explanation for the Admiralty's opposition. Rather than merely claim inconvenience and added expense, as Beatty had done in the Cabinet discussion, Pound went beyond these two reasons to point out that the Admiralty "never had a seven-inch gun and consequently would be faced with considerable expense on new designs and new type of ammunition, etc."[23]

Pound's fear of designing a new gun was significant. Unknown to either Cecil or Cook, the still secret, central, and decisive military reason for the Admiralty's push for the current arms control conference, and its steadfast refusal to allow the Americans to mount the 8-inch gun on its future cruisers, was the Admiralty's failure to design and manufacture an effective 8-inch gun. To risk designing a new 7-inch, so soon after this still mysterious failure, made no sense to Admiral Pound and to his Naval Staff colleagues, especially as they already possessed reliable 6-inch guns, which could be more inexpensively mounted on smaller cruisers and merchantmen.[24]

Cecil became so upset over the Admiralty's seemingly flimsy reasoning about the expense and inconvenience of designing a 7-inch gun that he was prepared to resign, but not before he offered a "political clause," which would put the "question of the eight-inch or six-inch gun in suspense" at least "until the United States proved that they really intended to go ahead and build a number of the 8-inch-gun cruisers beyond the agreed quota." Still unaware of why the Admiralty was steadfastly determined to eliminate all 8-inch guns on all future warships, Cecil argued that this political clause would

---

[21] Neville Chamberlain, Diary, July 30, 1927, NC 2/22, NC; Captain V. A. Kimberly, Special Board on Naval Ordinance to Chief of Bureau of Ordnance, August 1, 1927, 480–482, RG 80, NA.
[22] Kimberly to Chief of Naval Ordinance, August 1, 1927, 480–482, RG 80, NA.
[23] BED, "Minutes of the Twelfth Conference of British Delegations," August 1, 1927, pp. 3–4, CAB 27/350, PRO.
[24] Ibid.

"be regarded in the nature of a modus vivendi and not as an admission of principle," and therefore allow Great Britain to cancel the treaty if the United States decided to continue building 8-inch-gun cruisers beyond its permitted ratio.[25]

Pound vehemently opposed Cecil's political clause because it would have the "same disadvantages" as the modus vivendi ending in 1931, which, in effect, would either force the Admiralty into a cruise-building holiday until the Americans had equaled the British number of 8-inch-gun cruisers, or run the risk of building smaller 6-inch-gun cruisers from 1927 to 1931, which would be outclassed if the United States elected to continue building 8-inch-gun cruisers "beyond their agreed-upon quota." Nonetheless, perhaps to placate Cecil, Bridgeman supported this revised political clause, and the delegates voted to propose it to the Cabinet, while allowing Pound to send his own telegram opposing it.[26]

Sensing impending collapse, the Japanese delegates opened secret talks with Schofield to explore still another compromise. Its principal feature was a cruiser-building holiday until 1931 during which Great Britain and Japan would pledge not to lay down any auxiliary vessels not already authorized or needed for replacement, thus giving the United States the opportunity to equal Great Britain's 8-inch-gun cruiser tonnage. The United States would be permitted to build smaller cruisers of 8,000 tons rather than 8,300 tons, but as the gun caliber was deliberately omitted, it would be free to equip these vessels with 8-inch guns. In return, the Japanese proposed that the United States would agree to limit its 10,000-ton, 8-inch-gun cruisers to twelve for itself and Great Britain and to eight for Japan, thus increasing the Japanese ratio to 66 percent in these warships. To avoid surprises, future building plans for each nation would be agreed upon, and a political clause would allow for "readjustment" in the event of new threats.[27]

Both the Americans and the British, in effect, rejected the latest Japanese proposal. Schofield was at first willing to consider it, but only if the United States was allowed to build more than twelve 10,000-ton, 8-inch-gun cruisers and was guaranteed smaller cruisers of 8,300 tons with 8-inch guns. Kellogg doubted whether the British would allow the 8-inch gun while Bridgeman dismissed it as "a trap...to save America's face," especially as it allowed for 8-inch guns on the smaller cruisers. Bridgeman therefore "never took it very seriously."[28]

---

[25] Ibid., pp. 4–5. See also Cecil to Salisbury, July 31, 1927, August 1, 1927, Add Mss. 51086, LCP; Richardson, *Evolution of British Disarmament Policy*, pp. 135–136.

[26] BED, "Minutes of the Twelfth Conference of British Delegations," p. 6.

[27] Kellogg to Coolidge, July 29, 1927, *FRUS*, 1927, I: 138–139; Schofield, "Conversation Between Rear Admiral Schofield and Captain Toyoda," July 29, 1929, MCDS; Schofield, Diary, July 29, 1927, SD; Kellogg to Coolidge, August 3, 1927, *FRUS*, 1927, I: 148–150; Bridgeman to Chamberlain, 2 August 2, 1927, *DBFP*, Ia, III: 717–718.

[28] Schofield, Diary, August 1 and 2, 1927, SD; Bridgeman to My Beloved, August 2, 1927, 4629/1/1927/110, WBP; Bridgeman to Cecil, November 22, 1927, Add Mss. 51099, LCP; Jones,

During the August 3 meeting of the Cabinet, pent-up emotions burst forth in a flurry of resignation threats.[29] At the center of the heated debate was Cecil's decision to resign if the Cabinet rejected the 7-inch gun.[30] After Cecil's brother James, Lord Salisbury, read Cecil's resignation telegram to the Cabinet, Neville Chamberlain recorded that the Cabinet erupted in a furious debate characterized by "stormy scenes with threats of resignation."[31] Foreign Secretary Austin Chamberlain, who, in Baldwin's absence, was chairing the meeting, confirmed his brother Neville's recollection. At one time he recorded, "I had four resignations threatened, three of them actually in my hands."[32] Chamberlain blamed Baldwin for leaving in the midst of the unsettled negotiations. "I told the P.M.," [Prime Minister], he lamented, "that it was not safe for him to leave till the Geneva Conference was over, and he will never go that far afield again if I can prevent it." Cecil's brother agreed that the emotional debate was "very long and very difficult," but he ascribed most of the blame to "several threats of resignation on the Winston side."[33]

To allow tempers to cool, the Cabinet met again on the following day, August 4, when Admiral Sir Charles Madden, who had succeeded Beatty as First Sea Lord on July 30, presented a highly detailed memorandum vigorously opposing a treaty which would force the British into a building holiday to 1931 on the grounds that it was "wholly favorable" to the United States. He also opposed the latest Japanese compromise and the American limit of 400,000 tons because that would reduce the essential number of cruisers needed by Great Britain from seventy to only forty-seven, and thereby placed "Great Britain in a position of inferiority to the United States on the high seas," while fulfilling "exactly the wishes of the U.S.A. delegates." Much more surprisingly and without elaboration for this important change, he withdrew the Admiralty's offer of a 6.5 ratio for Japan.[34] As word had arrived shortly before the August 4 meeting that the United States had rejected the latest Japanese proposal, the Cabinet was able to forgo any detailed discussion of Madden's memorandum.[35] Nonetheless, a significant new policy emphasis

---

"Memorandum: Japanese Proposal, August 1, 1927," PCF, JP; Gibson to Kellogg, July 31, 1927, *FRUS*, 1927, I: 142–145; Kellogg to Gibson, August 2, 1927, MC28, CCP. See also Kellogg to Gibson, July 19, 1927, *FRUS*, 1927, I: 116–117 and Kellogg to Gibson, July 25, 1927, *FRUS*, 1927, I: 132–133.

[29] CAB 47 (27), "Meeting of the Cabinet," August 3, 1927, pp. 1–4, CAB23/55, PRO.

[30] Cecil to Salisbury, July 31 and August 1, 1927, Add Mss. 51086, LCP. See also Richardson, *Evolution of British Disarmament Policy*, pp. 135–136, 206–207.

[31] Neville Chamberlain, Diary, July 30 and August 3–4, 1927, NC 2/22, NC.

[32] Austen Chamberlain to My Dear Ida, August 7, 1927, AC 5/1/427, AC.

[33] Salisbury to Cecil, August 3, 1927, Add Mss. 51086, LCP. See also Richardson, *Evolution of British Disarmament Policy*, pp. 206–207, 136.

[34] CAB 48 (27), "Meeting of the Cabinet," August 4, 1927, Appendix I, CAB23/55, PRO.

[35] Ibid., p. 1.

Final Efforts

emerged from this meeting, one which has been overlooked and deserves greater recognition.

With the obvious failure of the negotiations and with emotional resignations threatening the stability of the Cabinet, the Ministers turned their ire against the Admiralty. To forestall still another Admiralty-induced crisis, the Cabinet continued to support the Admiralty's negotiating demands. But, on August 4, as the Third Plenary Session formally closed the Geneva Conference, the Cabinet signaled its displeasure by creating a Cabinet Inquiry into the question of future naval construction, an inquiry which would rely on Churchill's criteria of the relative strengths of other naval powers rather than on the "absolute needs" calculation demanded by the Admiralty.[36] Three weeks later, on August 25, the Cabinet Ministers sought to alleviate public anxiety over the renewed threat of a continuing naval arms race by creating a Cabinet Committee to examine the "large programme of cruiser construction," to "ascertain what readjustments could be made" in future naval construction, and to reconsider the number of 10,000-ton, 8-inch-gun cruisers already authorized.[37]

The Cabinet's creation of a new committee to slow down cruiser construction was a clear defeat for the Admiralty and a satisfying victory for Churchill.[38] In still another highly detailed attack on the Admiralty's justification for seventy cruisers, Churchill argued that the evidence gathered at the Conference of low Japanese tonnage requirements had "exploded the 'Japanese menace' and with it the whole basis" of the Admiralty's unjustifiable demands for an "immense increase" in cruisers.[39] More important still was the Admiralty's diplomatic ineptness. This ineptness had enabled Churchill to execute a series of deft political maneuvers. By supporting Beatty's insistence that parity in smaller cruisers meant naval inferiority for Great Britain, he had steadfastly supported the Admiralty's insistence on naval supremacy, thereby aligning himself with Beatty and those Cabinet Ministers and Conservative Party members opposed to Cecil and his allies. While continuing to challenge the need for seventy cruisers and briefly entertaining Cecil's cruiser-building holiday to 1931, he had nonetheless consistently championed naval supremacy

---

[36] CAB 48 (27), "Meeting of the Cabinet," August 4, 1927, p. 3, CAB 23/55, PRO.

[37] CAB 49 (27), "Meeting of the Cabinet," August 25, 1927, p. 12, CAB 23/55, PRO.

[38] CAB 48 (27), "Meeting of the Cabinet," August 4, 1927. The agenda of the Cabinet minutes for August 25 revealed that Churchill was the most likely one to have raised these issues.

[39] Churchill, "Material For the Study of Future Programme of Naval Construction," n.d., pp. 3, 5, CHAR 22/176, WCP. This fourteen-page document is attached to another secret fifteen-page memorandum, apparently also distributed to the Cabinet, entitled "Naval Shipbuilding" in which Churchill marshals an impressive array of evidence attacking Admiralty shipbuilding policy since 1925, during the 1925 Birkenhead Committee crisis, and at the Geneva Conference. For the MacDonald Government's efforts to restrain naval building see Committee on the Fighting Services, "Naval Construction Programme," July 6, 1929, CP, 198 (29), CAB 24 (29), WCP and Roskill, *Naval Policy Between the Wars*, pp. 558–559.

and ultimately supported the Admiralty's most important negotiating demands. Thus, neither the Sea Lords nor their supporters in the Conservative Party could charge Churchill with undermining British naval strength as they had done in 1925 during the Birkenhead Committee political crisis. The Cabinet's decision to create a new cabinet committee to ensure the moderation of cruiser construction heralded the decline of the Admiralty's prestige and political influence within the Baldwin Cabinet, a decline which would continue under Ramsay MacDonald's Labour Party Government in 1929. Churchill had successfully fought a long, intricately complex political battle to emerge simultaneously as a champion of British naval supremacy and the Admiralty's continuing nemesis.

16

Breakdown and Recriminations

The breakdown of the negotiations sparked a number of emotional responses and shed a good deal of light upon the underlying complexities of the second international effort at arms-control diplomacy. The American leaders were furious over what they charged was deliberate British duplicity. They believed the Admiralty had purposely misled Jones and Gibson in order to induce Coolidge to call the Conference, where they intended to spring their unpalatable surprises. British duplicity, they believed, had continued throughout the negotiations, heightened by the prohibition of the 8-inch gun on all future warships, by previously hidden cruiser demands, and by the Cabinet's withdrawal of Bridgeman's public promise of parity in smaller cruisers.

British leaders were also indignant. They accused the United States of refusing to admit that Great Britain's long supply lines entitled it to cruiser superiority. The Americans, they continued to believe, had called the Conference for mere domestic political purposes, to aid in Coolidge's 1928 reelection campaign, and to achieve naval equality "on the cheap" by requiring unacceptable reductions in British naval strength.

Significant, as well, was the recurring mistrust over British blockade practices during World War I. American insistence on a navy which could protect its trade from future British interference appeared as relevant in 1927 as it had been in 1916, when Woodrow Wilson convinced Congress to build a navy "second to none." Admiralty demands at Geneva appeared to the Americans to be explicable primarily in terms of British insistence on naval supremacy to enforce future blockades.

***

Worried that a failure would be disastrous for future arms-control progress, Kellogg sought advice from Coolidge on the advisability of requesting an adjournment to allow tempers to cool and to reassess negotiating positions. After he had consulted with the Navy, Kellogg reported to Coolidge that the

General Board unanimously rejected the terms of the modified Anglo-Japanese Accord, as it would require the United States "to expend over five hundred million dollars to attain parity in cruiser tonnage and would require us to build a type of cruiser which we do not need." Kellogg preferred freedom of action to build the "ten thousand ton cruisers which we do need."[1] Coolidge agreed. But he rejected Kellogg's suggestion of an adjournment as it would probably promote "continued recrimination with little prospect of [a] better result." Instead, he ordered Kellogg to prepare a firm statement ending the negotiations.[2]

The British Ambassador to the United States, Sir Esme Howard, emphasized another, more fundamental reason. He believed that the underlying problem was the lingering American resentment over British blockade practices during World War I. He informed Chamberlain of his conviction that the Americans were insistent on parity "because they believed that some day – not far off – Great Britain will be involved in a European war ... and will then have again to conduct a blockade," and they are determined "never again to allow American ships to be brought into British ports for examination or American goods to be subject to rationing systems." The Americans therefore believed that they must have "the means to be ready in the next naval war ... to protect neutral rights to the uttermost."[3]

Howard was clearly upset over the impending rupture in Anglo-American relations.[4] Chamberlain was equally worried.[5] Both of these British diplomats had hoped to avoid still another bitter quarrel with the United States.[6] Bridgeman, however, was far less concerned. He worried more about Cecil who was "getting rather agitated at the idea of a possible break-down, and trying very hard to invent some way out of our difficulties." Like Churchill and Beatty, Bridgeman preferred "no result" to "some ill-considered" and therefore "bad agreement," especially as he believed Cecil was ready to "make almost any compromise." He became especially upset when Cecil refused to help him prepare a closing argument for the last plenary session which would throw the blame for the failure on the Americans.[7] Cecil reminded

---

[1] See the four telegrams sent by Kellogg to Gibson, July 29 and 30, 1927, MC 28, CCP; Kellogg to Coolidge, July 29, 1927, MC 28, CCP; Castle, Diary, August 2, 1927, CP. For an excellent summary of the wide variety of explanations offered by historians for the failure of the Conference, see William F. Trimble, "The United States Navy and the Geneva Conference for the Limitation of Naval Armament, 1927," (Ph.D. diss., University of Colorado, 1974), pp. 148, 183–184, 350–356, 360–386, 446–448.
[2] Kellogg to Coolidge, July 29, 1927, MC 28, CCP; Kellogg, "Conversation Between Secretary Kellogg and the President," July 29, 1927, MC 28, CCP; Kellogg to Gibson, July 30, 1927, CCP and FRUS, 1927, I: 141. Kellogg quotes Coolidge in this telegram.
[3] Howard to Chamberlain, August 3, 1927, DBFP, Ia, III: 723–725.   [4] Ibid.
[5] Chamberlain to Howard, August 2, 1927, DBFP, Ia, III: 718–719.
[6] Ibid. See also footnote 3.
[7] Bridgeman to My Beloved, July 30, 1927, 4629/1/1927/105, WBP; Bridgeman, "Log," July 31, 1927, BGMN 1, WBPCC; Bridgeman to My Beloved, August 3, 1927, 4629/1/1927/111, WBP; Bridgeman to My Dearest Mother, August 2, 1927, 4629/1/1927/109, WBP.

Bridgeman that he had agreed to come to Geneva to get an agreement, not to argue over technical naval details, and he therefore refused to help "prepare the ground for a [future] disagreement."[8]

Without Cecil's help, Bridgeman struggled with this speech, declaring it "more difficult" than any speech he had yet made at the Conference.[9] What bedeviled him most was the attempt to reconcile Great Britain's earlier proposals, including his public promise of parity in all warships, with "our new proposals," especially as "the connection of the two must be proved to show our consistency."[10] This task was difficult because the Cabinet had withdrawn his parity promise and also because, at one point, the Admiralty's modification of the Anglo-Japanese Accord had suddenly switched from steadfast opposition to total tonnage and tonnage transfer between categories to acceptance of these principles, and from a 60 to a 65 percentage for Japan. Then, with equal suddenness, following the rejection of its modified Anglo-Japanese Accord, the Admiralty withdrew its sixty-five ratio offer. Bridgeman fretted, too, because he had no clear idea of "what line the Americans are going to take" and because he was convinced that the Americans "never give a straight answer to any questions," making it impossible to "trust them one yard," and "impossible to deal with."[11] His anger extended to the Cabinet as well for recalling the delegation in order "to tie our hands very closely" and thereby "making it impossible for us to come to an agreement." If the Cabinet had granted to the British delegates the discretion it had promised, and "if we had been left alone," Bridgeman believed that he could have secured "a fairly satisfactory agreement."[12]

Bridgeman's closing plenary speech made no effort to reconcile Great Britain's earlier proposals with its "new proposals." He instead simply ignored the inconsistencies while alluding only vaguely to the Cabinet's rejection of his public promise of parity in all warships. He emphasized the oft-repeated geographical need for an unlimited number of trade-protecting smaller cruisers, denied that there had been any "concealment of our needs" prior to the Conference, and attempted to suggest that Great Britain had actually reduced its cruiser needs when one compared 70 cruisers to Great Britain's 114 cruisers "just before the war." Repeatedly placing great emphasis upon the reasonableness of British proposals, he focused as well on his allegation that the United States was far less reasonable than the British on several key points of dispute. He complained that the United States had refused to discuss the great savings offered by Great Britain's capital ship proposal, had ignored the tentative

---

[8] Bridgeman to Cecil, July 30, 1927; Cecil to Bridgeman, July 31, 1927, Add Mss. 51099, LCP.
[9] Bridgeman to My Beloved, July 30, 1927, 4629/1/1927/105, WBP.
[10] Bridgeman to My Beloved, July 31, 1927, 4629/1/1927/106, WBP.
[11] Ibid.; Bridgeman to Dearest Mother, August 2, 1927, 4629/1/1927/109, WBP.
[12] Bridgeman to Dearest Son, August 1, 1927, 4629/1/1927/107, WBP.

agreement on destroyers and submarines achieved by the Technical Committee, and had made cruisers the crux of the failure to reach an agreement.[13]

By emphasizing the "marked disagreement" over cruisers, Bridgeman highlighted the central role of the 8-inch gun. The breakdown resulted, he contended, because the Americans were "unwilling to put a limit, within the total tonnage, to the number of cruisers carrying eight-inch guns." He professed to be baffled over American "reasons for demanding so many large cruisers or so many with weapons of such high offensive power as the eight-inch gun." American insistence on mounting the 8-inch guns rather than the 6-inch guns on smaller cruisers, he informed the world, would have resulted in "a considerable increase in the offensive strength of the fleets of the world," thus violating the principle of non-competition, which "could have no other effect than that of "increasing rather than decreasing naval offensive capabilities.[14]

Bridgeman also blamed the Americans for breaking two crucial pledges. He first alleged that the American delegates to the Preparatory Commission had agreed that total tonnage would be determined by "a proper division of classes and a maximum fixed by each type."[15] Gibson had, in fact, expressed his personal sympathy with this approach and had suggested a possible compromise between the British method of limitation – based on classes, maximum vessel tonnage, guns within a class – and the total tonnage method preferred by France, Italy, the United States, and Japan.[16] Jones had agreed with Gibson that a compromise was possible and had offered his combat-equivalency proposal as a means to reconcile these two methods of limitation.[17] What Bridgeman ignored was the fact that Beatty had secretly consented to consider Jones's compromise before the Conference was called, but then he had refused to discuss it or even refer to it specifically after the Conference convened, whereupon the Americans reverted to the General Board's insistence on the total tonnage method and numerical equality.[18]

The second pledge broken by the Americans, Bridgeman claimed, was Gibson's assurance that if the British and the Japanese could work out an

---

[13] Bridgeman, "Address to Third Plenary Session," August 4, 1927, *Records*, pp. 35–38. Influential members in the Foreign Office approved of Bridgeman's efforts to cast the blame for the failure of the Conference on the Americans. See FO 371/12673, W 7277/61/98; W 7287/61/98; W 7328/61/98, pp. 136–138, 147–148, 201–204, PRO. See also Stephen Roskill, *Naval Policy Between the Wars: The Period of Anglo-American Antagonism, 1919–1929* (London: Collins, 1968), p. 513 and Tadashi Kuramatsu, "The Geneva Naval Conference of 1927: The British Preparation for the Conference, December 1926 to June 1927," *The Journal of Strategic Studies* No.1, 19 (March 1996), p. 116. Kuramatsu argues that: "The truth was that the Americans simply would not accept anything less *than* 'a navy second to none.'"

[14] Bridgeman, "Address to Third Plenary Session," *Records*, pp. 35–38.   [15] *Ibid.*, p. 38.

[16] *Ibid.* See also Bridgeman, Diary, June-August 1927, WBP and Chapter 15.

[17] See Chapter 9.   [18] See Chapters 8 and 9.

agreement, the American delegates would make it "complete."[19] Bridgeman maintained that the English had made a "great effort" to "put our requirements into a form which had been acceptable to the Japanese," the terms of which Chamberlain had explained to the world in his statement to Parliament on July 27, only to have the Americans reject it.[20]

In concluding his plenary address, Bridgeman used the American rejection of the Anglo-Japanese Accord as evidence of American perfidy. Convinced that the Japanese and the British could not reconcile their tonnage differences, and no doubt hoping to throw the blame on them, Gibson had unwisely offered a vague promise to make an Anglo-Japanese agreement "complete." This open-ended promise was a blunder. At the time Gibson apparently had assumed that all of the parties understood that he had not altered his repeated insistence upon a limit of 400,000 tons for all cruisers and the right to mount 8-inch guns on these cruisers. What Bridgeman neglected to acknowledge was that the Admiralty's modification of the Anglo-Japanese Accord had rejected Gibson's two key requirements, thus making American acceptance virtually impossible.[21]

Speaking for Japan, Admiral Viscount Saito wisely recalled the two compromises put forth by Japan and outlined in great detail the original Anglo-Japanese Accord. He denied any Japanese responsibility for the collapse by pointing out that the failure of these proposals resulted from "apparently insoluble" differences between the United States and Great Britain.[22] The "main difficulty," Saito stressed, was the tonnage and gun caliber of cruisers, issues with which Japan was still "not entirely in accord with those of the British delegation," but which Japan had nonetheless sought to resolve through practical compromises.[23] Having laid the blame for the failure upon the United States and Great Britain, while highlighting Japan's two attempts to mediate the differences, Saito closed his brief address with the hope that future talks would be more successful.[24] What he left unsaid was the Japanese Naval Ministry's last-minute insistence on a 70 percent ratio, a demand which neither the United States nor Great Britain could accept.

Gibson's response to Bridgeman reflected the sentiments of Kellogg, Castle, and Coolidge who had carefully read, added to, and approved his address.[25] Gibson articulated all of the reasons why the United States could not accept

---

[19] Bridgeman, "Address to Third Plenary Session," p. 37. For Gibson's statement, see Gibson, "Supplementary Statement," Second Plenary Session, July 14, 1927, *Records*, p. 34.
[20] Bridgeman, "Address to Third Plenary Session," pp. 37–38.
[21] Gibson, "Supplementary Statement," p. 34.
[22] Admiral Viscount Saito, "Address to Third Plenary Session, *Records*, p. 41.
[23] Ibid., pp. 41–42. [24] Ibid. p. 42.
[25] Gibson to Kellogg, July 28 and 29, and August 1, 1927; Kellogg to Gibson, July 30, and August 1 and 3, 1927; Kellogg to Coolidge, July 30, and August 4, 1927; Coolidge to Kellogg, July 30, 1927, MC28, CCP; Castle, Diary, 2 August 2, 1927, CP; Gibson to Mother, August 4, 1927, GP, HHPL.

British terms, while subtly placing great emphasis on freedom of neutral commerce in wartime. Arguing that America's request for a lower cruiser tonnage was clear evidence of its desire to reduce offensive capabilities, Gibson agreed that cruisers were indeed at the heart of the breakdown. Only after the Conference had convened, he charged, had the British suddenly insisted upon seventy cruisers, leaving the United States unable to understand "why, in a time of profound peace," the British had laid claim to a "naval expansion of an absolute and even a vital necessity."[26] The United States, he pointed out, "never contested" the British need for a larger number of cruisers and had even consented to discuss both the number of 10,000-ton cruisers and a secondary class of cruisers, provided that these smaller cruisers were also allowed to carry the 8-inch gun agreed upon at the Washington Conference.

Gibson dismissed Bridgeman's claim that the United States' proposals would increase rather than decrease offensive naval power. He belittled British insistence on "very strictly" limiting larger cruisers with 8-inch guns on the grounds that they were "offensive" warships, while defining the unlimited number of British 6,000-ton, 6-inch-gun cruisers as "defensive." He countered their argument with the fact that the British had led the auxiliary arms race by building eleven of these offensive cruisers, whereas the United States had laid down only two and would have "none that will be afloat for approximately two years." He challenged, as well, the British claim that the 6,000-ton, 6-inch-gun cruiser was defensive, intended merely to protect British commerce. This overlooked the fact that these same warships "must in time of war effectively deny the sea to others." Their use in blockade and trade interdiction was therefore self-evident. Less self-evident were persistent British efforts to force the abandonment of the 8-inch gun on smaller cruisers, which the United States needed to protect its neutral shipping against 6-inch gun blockade vessels. The British purpose in abandoning the 8-inch gun became clear, Gibson contended, when one read Lord Jellico's able presentation of the "great part in the late war" played by converted British merchant ships outfitted with 6-inch guns. The United States, therefore, was compelled to consider the possible uses of the 6-inch gun in a future war. The advantages to Great Britain became even more obvious, Gibson observed, when one recognized that Great Britain had "approximately 888,000 tons of fast merchant ships, capable of being readily converted into cruisers, and armed with 6-inch guns" whereas the United States had only "188,000 tons of such ships."[27]

Gibson next attacked the British claim to great economic savings. "Economy can only be realized," he argued, "by reduction of total tonnage." Rather than realizing savings by reducing the size of ships, as the British suggested, Gibson contended that "the larger the unit size of vessels the greater is the economy,

---

[26] Gibson, "Address to Third Plenary Session," *Records*, p. 42.   [27] *Ibid.*, p. 43.

both in the initial construction and in operations and maintenance."[28] Considering the issue of total tonnage alone, the British had not only abandoned the 450,000 tons in surface vessels which it had supported at the Washington Conference, but with its new demand for 25 percent in over-age ships, the British had pushed its total tonnage requirements to 737,000 tons, of which 426,000 tons would be in cruisers. Such large tonnage did not support their claims of economy.

After reiterating still further obstacles to agreement, Gibson concluded his address by reminding the world that the United States had offered an escape clause allowing quick cancellation of the treaty if Great Britain believed that the United States cruisers threatened its security. This was offered in the same spirit of the "statement recently made by the British Foreign Secretary to the effect that war between the British Empire and the United States was already outlawed in the hearts of both nations." With the conviction that "war between them is unthinkable," Gibson ended his address with the hope that the realization of naval limitation and real economy would still be possible at some future conference.[29]

Gibson's plenary speech greatly disturbed Bridgeman, who became increasingly bitter in the days following the collapse of the Conference. In his diary he confided his belief that the Americans were primarily responsible for the failure as their "real object" was to "try to get 'parity' cheap by forcing us to give up the numbers [of cruisers] we require for security and also," he pointedly conceded, "to prevent us from intercepting contraband in wartime."

Bridgeman refused to acknowledge that he and Beatty had misjudged Coolidge. Still convinced that the president's motives for calling the Conference stemmed from the imperatives of American domestic reelection politics, Bridgeman persisted in his belief that Coolidge had acted merely "to get a good election cry ... by saying that they had not only made a further peace move but also twisted the British Lion's tail by making him reduce his cruiser strength." The Americans, Bridgeman concluded, "never meant to agree to any other terms" but their own, and they had arrived at the Conference "with very little preparation and hardly any knowledge of the problem of limitation."

Near the end of the Conference, Bridgeman had also become exasperated by Beatty's continuous interference. When asked to extend Beatty as First Sea Lord until the Conference concluded, Bridgeman refused, later lamenting that he would have been successful if the delegation "had been left alone."[30] Thus, Beatty was once again forced out in the midst of the negotiations, as he

---

[28] *Ibid.*, p. 44.
[29] *Ibid.*, pp. 44–45. For a more critical assessment of Gibson's speech see B. J. C. McKercher, *The Second Baldwin Government and United States, 1924–1929: Attitudes and Diplomacy* (Cambridge: Cambridge University Press, 1984), p. 76.
[30] Bridgeman, Diary, June–August, 1927, WBP. See also Bridgeman to Chamberlain, August 6, 1927, FO 371/12674/W 8063/61/98, PRO.

had been at the Washington Conference.³¹ Upon retiring on July 30, Beatty claimed to agree with Bridgeman that it was time for "fresh blood and a new outlook on the many naval problems" confronting the Admiralty. But, still not trusting Bridgeman, he could not resist a parting shot, warning Bridgeman that "We have gone as far as it is possible to go," as any further concessions "would jeopardize the fate of the Empire and it would be better to bust the Conference than to do that."³²

Ironically, despite his embarrassing failure to achieve the Admiralty's negotiating objectives, Beatty congratulated himself for having prevented the Americans from somehow jeopardizing "the fate of the Empire." He congratulated himself as well for succeeding in "the hard struggle to defeat the pacifists in our Government who would have given everything away rather than have the Conference breakdown."³³ The pacifist uppermost in his mind was, of course, Lord Robert Cecil, whose modus vivendi would have allowed the Americans to continue building 8-inch-gun cruisers to 1931, thus apparently jeopardizing "the fate of the Empire" by giving "everything away."

Beatty blamed not only the Americans and the "weak ones" in the Baldwin Cabinet but the British delegates as well. He excused Field for allowing the tangled British negotiations to "get as bad as it was" on the grounds that Field was "very ill." He was less charitable toward Bridgeman and venomous in castigating Cecil. Bridgeman's failure to carry out the Admiralty's negotiating stratagems, Beatty confided to Keyes, was directly attributable to his character. "Little Bridgeman is really not up to dealing with the wiles of others," he charged, because he was "too simple and too lazy." He confessed that the "Geneva business was a dreadful affair," yet congratulated himself again, contending that had he not "been pretty strong on the Downing Street Front that lunatic Cecil would have sold the pass." Beatty had remained strong because "Little Bridgeman was like putty in his [Cecil's] hands and got all twisted up and made statements which we could not support."³⁴

Admiral Pound, who had replaced Field at Geneva, was also critical of both Bridgeman and Cecil. He agreed with Beatty's characterization of Cecil, whom he denounced as a very clever "peace maniac who could not be trusted a yard in anything to do with his [peace] hobby." He charged, as well, that Cecil had done "all he could" to make commitments which he could then present to the Cabinet as a "fait accompli."³⁵

---

³¹ Beatty to Bridgeman, July 29, 1927, BGMN 1, WBPCC; Board of Admiralty, "Minutes," July 29, 1927, ADM 167/75, PRO. See also Chapters 2, and 3.
³² Beatty to Bridgeman, July 29, 1927, BGMN 1, WBPCC.
³³ Beatty to Keyes, August 6, 1927 in Roger Keyes, *The Keyes Papers: Selections from the Private and Official Correspondence of Admiral of the Fleet Baron Keyes of Zeebrugge, 1919–1938*, 2 vols. ed. Paul G. Halpern (London: George Allen and Unwin, 1980), II: 225.
³⁴ Beatty to Keyes, September 9, 1927, in *Ibid.*, p. 228.
³⁵ Pound to Keyes, August 10, 1927, in *Ibid.*, pp. 226–227.

Breakdown and Recriminations

On August 4, as the Conference concluded, Cecil submitted his resignation to Baldwin in a letter which he intended to publish. Sir Maurice Hankey, the Secretary to the Committee of Imperial Defence and also to the Cabinet, assisted by Lord Balfour, took the lead in blocking publication. According to Hankey, Balfour was insistent that Baldwin "ought on no account to advise the King to permit publication ... in its present form."[36] They claimed that Cecil's letter not only contained inaccuracies but would have "a deplorable effect in America, Germany, France, and elsewhere," as it would be "quoted as proof that the British Government does not want disarmament" and thereby "have an adverse effect on the whole foreign-policy of the country."[37] The publication of Cecil's letter, "moreover, would be a breach of the Privy Counselor's oath and disastrous to the whole system of Cabinet Government."[38] Baldwin agreed, and Hankey therefore began a long negotiation forcing Cecil to make changes to no less than five drafts of the letter before eventually approving its publication.[39]

Hankey, Balfour, and Baldwin required Cecil to eliminate his more sensational charges. They particularly objected to Cecil's claim of the "pernicious" opposition of the Admiralty to arms control and to the Cabinet's "very little interest in the success or failure" of the Preparatory Commission.[40] More serious were Cecil's complaints blaming the Baldwin Cabinet for the failure of the Conference. On the question of parity, Cecil incorrectly charged that the Cabinet had given the delegates "full authority to accept the American point of view," which "in our minds and in those of the other negotiators meant what is now called 'mathematical equality'."[41] The Cabinet had reinforced this understanding of parity, he claimed, in a telegram to the delegation "directing us to agree to parity, which as a matter of fact we had already done" and which the Cabinet later withdrew.[42]

Cecil acknowledged that the dispute over cruisers was less clear-cut. While he admitted that the Admiralty had advised the delegates to avoid a limit on the number of smaller cruisers, if possible, he claimed that the Cabinet had, nonetheless, granted the delegates "discretion" and had approved the CID's recommendation that "it may be necessary to accept some limiting figure [on smaller cruisers] so as to avoid a departure from the principle of limiting all classes of displacement, armament and numbers." Then, after the delegates

---

[36] M. P. A. Hankey to Baldwin, "Lord Balfour's Views," August 28, 1927, pp. 3–4, LCR. For Cecil's resignation letter, see Cecil to Baldwin, August 9, 1927, SBP. Hankey's report to Baldwin is a fourteen-page document that seeks to refute much of Cecil's version of events.

[37] Hankey to Baldwin, "Lord Balfour's Views," pp. 3–4.   [38] *Ibid.*, p. 5.

[39] For Cecil's redrafts of his resignation letter, see CAB21/297/PRO.

[40] Hankey, "Points in Lord Cecil's Minute on Which Confirmation is Lacking: Summary," n.d., CAB21/297, LCR; Cecil to Baldwin, August 9, 1927, pp. 2–3, SBP.

[41] Hankey, "Points in Lord Cecil's "Minute," p. 104. See also Cecil to Lord Edward Irwin, September 29, 1927, Add Mss. 51084, LCP; Cecil to Baldwin, June 29 and August 9 1927, SBP.

[42] Cecil to Baldwin, August 9, 1927, pp. 3–4.

had painstakingly negotiated the Anglo-Japanese Accord as a basis for discussion, and it appeared "that we were well on the road to an agreement," with the only question yet to be resolved being "whether these smaller cruisers were or were not to be allowed to carry an eight-inch gun," the Cabinet suddenly demanded the recall of the delegation to London.[43]

Cecil was not totally at odds with the Admiralty's cruiser objectives. At Geneva he had loyally supported the length of trade routes justification and the need for a greater number of smaller British cruisers. As the Blockade Minister during World War I, he fully understood the argument for a sufficient number of cruisers to enforce blockade strategy in a future war. He agreed as well with the argument that it would "be a great misfortune," as he put it, to increase offensive naval power by mounting the 8-inch gun on these smaller cruisers. But, perhaps because he was unaware of the defective British 8-inch gun, and, because he believed a successful treaty was crucial to advancing future League of Nations arms-control efforts, he vigorously dissented from the Admiralty's insistence on prohibiting the 8-inch gun on these smaller American cruisers, warning that such a prohibition would result in the "catastrophe" of a failed Conference.[44] Privately he lamented that if the Cabinet had been serious about its profession of no war against the United States, it would not have allowed the Conference to fail over the relatively "unimportant" possibility of granting "a little excess of cruiser strength" to the United States. Indeed, the Cabinet's adherence to the principle of equality with America, he believed, would also have kept "our naval experts in order" during the negotiations. Instead, by allowing the Admiralty to dictate arms-control policy generally and the negotiations at Geneva specifically, the Cabinet had effectively granted the Admiralty "an altogether unconstitutional position" of dominance.[45]

---

[43] Ibid., p. 3. See also Chapter 10.
[44] Cecil to Baldwin, August 9, 1927, p. 4. See also Cecil to Thomas Lamont, November 2, 1927, pp. 32–34. 51144, LCP; Cecil to Chamberlain, August 16, 1927, AC54/95, AC. The meaning of a "little" excess of cruiser strength is not entirely clear, but the evidence strongly suggests that Cecil was referring to gun power rather than numbers. He was aware that the American Congress was unlikely to build up to the number of British cruisers. Moreover, in order to secure a treaty, he advocated allowing the United States to build smaller 8-inch-gun cruisers at least until 1931, and possibly even to 1936. In the meantime, while the Americans attempted to equal the number of existing British 8-inch-gun cruisers, the Admiralty's overwhelming lead in these cruisers would enable it to safely commence building its smaller 6-inch-gun cruisers. However, if the Americans continued to mount 8-inch guns on their smaller cruisers after the treaty expired, as Beatty suspected, the resulting difference in gun power could not be easily dismissed as "little." Nonetheless, Cecil characterized this theoretical possibility as "unimportant" because he was convinced that war between the two nations was so unlikely that the Cabinet would have been justified in overriding exaggerated Admiralty's fears.
[45] Cecil to W. A. Egerton, August 30, 1927, Add Mss. 51165, LCP; Cecil to Edward [Lord Irwin], September 29, 1927, Add Mss. 51084, LCP.

While Hankey, Balfour, and Baldwin prevented Cecil from revealing his most sensational charges in his published letter of resignation, he was nonetheless able to articulate those previously censored charges in his address to the House of Lords in November 1927. He exaggerated the significance of the Anglo-Japanese Accord, which was unacceptable to the Americans, and therefore had not cleared the path, as he claimed, to an agreement. Nonetheless, his charge that the Cabinet had reversed its promise of equality resonated with American leaders, who basically agreed with Cecil's judgment that the Cabinet was guilty of deliberate duplicity, rather than with Hankey's more charitable conclusion that the Cabinet was merely an unwitting victim of a "genuine" misunderstanding arising from a vaguely worded telegram.[46]

Kellogg certainly agreed with Cecil. Although the British had promised parity to Jones before the Conference began, the Secretary of State confided to Coolidge that the British obviously "intended not to grant it," as every proposition they offered at Geneva "was intended to deprive the United States of an equal, effective navy." Jones had confirmed to Kellogg that "the British went back on everything they had agreed to with him in London" prior to Coolidge's calling the Conference. What angered Kellogg the most was the British insistence on increasing rather than reducing cruiser tonnage despite the absence of any "possible threat to the British Government, her commerce or her possessions." Because the British had refused to disclose its tonnage demands prior to the Conference, Kellogg unsuccessfully sought to avoid any personal responsibility by concluding that there was no way the United States could have prevented the failure.[47]

Both Chamberlain and Sir Esme Howard agreed with Kellogg in placing at least part of the blame on the Admiralty's refusal to reveal its tonnage requirements in advance of the Conference. Howard was acutely embarrassed by Kellogg's criticism to the effect that, if Howard had told Kellogg that the British would ask for more than 450,000 tons of auxiliary vessels – which Kellogg insisted the British had indicated would meet their needs at the earlier Washington Conference – the United States "would never have issued the invitation." "No doubt a great mistake was made," the Foreign Secretary admitted, "in entering upon such a Conference without a preliminary exchange

---

[46] Great Britain, *Hansard's Parliamentary Debates*, (Lords) 69 (1927): 86–109. See copy in CAB21/297, LCR. See also [Hankey], "Notes on Lord Cecil's Speech in the House of Lords on 16 November 1927 on the Subject of His Resignation, "n. d., pp. 1–19, but especially pp. 5–7, CAB 21/297, PRO. For the claim of a "genuine misunderstanding," see Hankey [?], "Points on Lord Cecil's Minute," p. 8; Viscount [Robert] Cecil, *A Great Experiment: An Autobiography* (New York: Oxford University Press, 1941), pp. 184–188. Cecil agreed with Churchill in his opposition to seventy cruisers. Cecil to Sir Herbert Richmond, 30 November 30, 1929, Add Mss. 51099, LCP.

[47] Kellogg to Coolidge, August 10, 1927, MC 28, CCP. Copy in *FRUS*, 1927, I: 157–159; Kellogg to Coolidge, August 4, 1927, *FRUS*, 1927, I: 155–156. Kellogg included his statement to the press.

of ideas and for this I must take a share of the blame." Chamberlain told Howard that he had been "more worried about the Geneva Conference than about anything which has occurred since I took Office." He confessed further that he had misjudged "the rigidity of the American attitude." Both of these diplomats were embarrassed, as well, by the fact that this important international negotiation had been taken out of their hands and given to the Admiralty.

Despite his admission of responsibility, Chamberlain nonetheless placed most of the blame on the United States. The Americans would only agree to a treaty, he claimed, which "twisted the Lion's tail," as they "are a terrible lot of people to deal with and Gibson is a mean and untruthful twister," who had ordered the American press "on the first day [of the Conference] to discredit and misrepresent our proposals." Chamberlain supported Bridgeman's interpretation of the failure. The Foreign Secretary indirectly forewarned Howard to avoid any criticism of Bridgeman, who was "a really good fellow" and whose sterling character "gives him an extraordinary influence with our party." Chamberlain instead unfairly and inaccurately cast the blame on Gibson by accepting Bridgeman's assessment that Gibson was "too small a man" to handle the responsibilities of controlling his naval delegates, and had even failed to give his own State Department a "full or even a fair picture of the British case and attitude."[48]

In contrast to Chamberlain, Churchill placed the blame squarely on an unwise Admiralty strategy. No doubt delighted that the Admiralty's diplomatic blundering had convinced the Cabinet to act on his recommendation to create a special committee to review all future naval construction, he was nonetheless chagrined by the Admiralty's persistent claims to great savings in building smaller cruisers with 6-inch guns, complaining that no sooner than "these weak ships are built," the Admiralty "will begin to disparage them" as "valueless" when compared to "the new [more powerful] American and Japanese types."[49] A year after the conference ended, Churchill was still in the dark over the reason for the Admiralty's continued insistence on the 6-inch gun and elimination of the 8-inch gun, confiding to Baldwin that the 1927 Geneva Conference was "the worst blunder we have committed and we did it with our eyes open..."[50]

Churchill's anxiety reached new levels in early 1929. On February 7, he requested a special Cabinet meeting to address the American decision to

---

[48] Howard to Chamberlain, August 2, 1927, *DBFP*, Ia, III: 720; Chamberlain to Howard, August 10, 1927, *DBFP*, Ia, III: 729–731. See also Chamberlain to Bridgeman, August 5, 1927, BGMN 1, WBPCC.
[49] Churchill to Bridgeman, October 28, 1927, in Winston S. Churchill, *Winston S. Churchill: The Exchequer Years 1922–1929, Companion Volume 5*, ed. Martin Gilbert (London: William Heinemann, 1979) 5: 1075–1077. Hereinafter cited as Churchill, *Companion Volume 5*.
[50] Churchill to Baldwin, September 30, 1928 in Churchill, *Companion Volume 5*: 1352–1354.

Breakdown and Recriminations

build fifteen new 10,000-ton, 8-inch-gun cruisers. Once again denouncing a policy of premature building, he reiterated the wisdom of waiting until potential enemies had built their ships before quickly building more powerful ones, especially as these latest American cruisers "would render obsolete our existing Cruisers."[51] By adopting a policy of delayed building until the combat characteristics of the American cruisers became known, Great Britain could "incorporate all of the recent technological improvements" into superior ships while in the meantime demonstrating "to the world a more pacific policy."[52]

As a nation "does not build war ships for fun," Churchill privately lamented, it was "certainly stupid deliberately to make weapons which will be outmatched" by rivals, especially as it was "painful to me to see our hard-earned money invested so unfruitfully" on weak 6-inch-gun cruisers, which would be forced to encounter stronger enemy vessels, with the result that the British ship would sink "beneath the waves with all her crew." While Churchill justified his strong convictions on the grounds that he had long "studied naval affairs under the highest authorities and with all the secret information," ironically the defects of the Admiralty's 8-inch gun – for which he had such high hopes – remained unknown to him.[53] Still unaware of the secret reasons for the Admiralty's desperate efforts to prevent rival navies from continuing to mount this gun on their warships, Churchill insisted that rather than continuing to build the smaller 6-inch-gun cruisers, the 10,000-ton, eight-inch-gun cruisers were "best for our finance, for our foreign-policy, and for our naval power."[54]

---

[51] Cabinet Conclusion, February 7, 1929, CAB 23, NO. 60, PRO.   [52] *Ibid.*
[53] Churchill to Sir Douglas Hogg, November 14, 1927, in Churchill, *Companion Volume* 5: 1102, 1101–1103.
[54] Churchill to Bridgeman, October 28, 1927, in *Ibid.*, p. 1077.

17

Conclusion

This study of the 1927 Geneva Naval Conference and events leading up to it adds to our understanding of international relations and arms-control diplomacy in the 1920s by revealing that underlying the political, economic and diplomatic arms-control rationales of the time were less apparent behind-the-scenes struggles to preserve strategic naval supremacies in a world of competing empires.

Out of the clash of empires during World War I came the desire for a better world. However, inhibiting that yearning were acrimonious disputes among the victors over the Treaty of Versailles, the League of Nations, reparations, freedom of the seas, repayment of war loans, and economic competition. In 1921 President Warren G. Harding and his Secretary of State Charles Evans Hughes captured the world's attention when they revived hope for a safer world by initiating the first international naval arms-control conference. In sharp contrast to Harding and Hughes' disregard of warnings from their naval advisors, British and Japanese delegates at the Washington Naval Conference of 1921–1922 consulted closely with their naval staffs to safeguard naval supremacies in those ocean regions essential to their future security and prosperity.

British leaders had not forgotten that their navy had contributed significantly to victory in World War I by keeping most of the German fleet bottled up in the North Sea while simultaneously blockading and interdicting neutral trade to the Central Powers. As imperialists they also valued the importance of protecting the continuous stream of trade flowing from their worldwide colonies, especially as England's postwar economy steadily worsened. At both the Washington and Geneva Conferences, British delegates therefore collaborated closely with their naval strategists on proposals fostering supremacy in the Atlantic Ocean and the Mediterranean Sea. With memories of World War I still fresh in their minds, they knew that the vital trading routes in these two ocean regions would be most vulnerable during a future war, especially against a European enemy such as Germany, which was close enough geographically to threaten England's industrial wartime capabilities.[1]

Another hard lesson of World War I emphasized the economic power of neutral nations in determining victory or defeat. The British worried that during a future European war, the United States would again remain neutral and, with a vastly more powerful navy, use this force to continue trading with its prewar customers. This posed a serious threat, as the British navy would be dispersed in blockading the enemy's European ports, in engaging the enemy's fleet, and in protecting the British Empire's far-flung global trading routes. Taking advantage of this disbursement, the United States could concentrate its cruiser force to escort its merchantmen, easily overwhelm British blockades, and thereby significantly strengthen an enemy's war-making capabilities. At both the Washington and Geneva Conferences, therefore, British negotiators articulated rationales which effectively masked the more fundamental goal of denying, or, at the very least, significantly degrading America's ability to overcome future British blockades and its seizure and interdiction of neutral trade.[2]

Just as the British Empire required naval supremacy on its trade routes in the Atlantic Ocean and Mediterranean Sea, Japanese imperialists focused on supremacy in the waters of Southeast Asia, most especially, but not exclusively, in the seas surrounding Japan, Korea, and Manchuria. This regional supremacy necessitated a navy strong enough to impose its control over weaker neighbors and to defeat a naval enemy challenging its recently acquired empire, as Russia had done in 1904–1905.[3] To safeguard that regional supremacy, the Japanese sought a 70 percent ratio at both the Washington and the Geneva Conferences.[4] Thus, like the British, Japanese foreign policy nurtured the fundamental strategic imperative of naval supremacy in specific ocean regions vital to its empire and thus to its future prosperity.

For a brief period, from 1916 to 1921, the United States was equally intent upon naval supremacy. A combination of British blockade and interdiction of American neutral shipping and German submarine warfare between 1914 and 1916 had imposed heavy losses on America's increasingly important export trade. The outcry from American businessmen enabled President Woodrow Wilson to convince Congress that the futility of his repeated diplomatic protests and mediation efforts required the United States to begin building the world's most powerful navy, one large enough to protect American neutral rights in the Atlantic and the Pacific simultaneously. Wilson understood that the capital ships of his "navy second to none" could not be built fast enough to have an immediate impact during World War I. However, this vast armada could be ready for rapid deployment during a future war to prevent any nation from

---

[1] See Chapters 1–4.   [2] See Chapter 13.   [3] See Chapter 2.   [4] See Chapters 2 and 15.

blockading America's trade, interdicting its unarmed commercial merchant vessels, or imposing unilateral contraband restrictions, all of which could again threaten to plunge the American economy into recession or depression. Such a navy could also inhibit Japan from again challenging the American Open Door Policy by resurrecting its Twenty-One Demands on China or casting covetous eyes on Guam and the Philippines.[5]

At the conclusion of World War I, following the United States Senate's rejection of the Treaty of Versailles and the League of Nations, Harding promised during his 1920 presidential election campaign to enforce freedom of the seas by completing Wilson's "navy second to none."[6] But, by 1921, severe economic downturns pressured all three major naval powers to cut naval expenses. Ignoring his campaign promise to build Wilson's navy – already well on its way to completion – as well as the advice of his naval advisors on the General Board, President Harding and his Secretary of State, Charles Evans Hughes, decided that the nation could not sustain enormous naval expenditures while simultaneously fulfilling Republican campaign promises to lower taxes and to retire the national war debt. Rather than continue the expensive postwar naval race among the Allies, they argued, America should instead adopt a more enlightened foreign policy by inviting the world's naval powers to the first international arms control conference in Washington DC.[7]

At this Conference in 1921–1922, Harding and Secretary of State Hughes shocked their naval rivals by proposing to scuttle all capital warship building programs. World peace, they proclaimed, would be better served by lowering the strengths of all major navies to defensive levels. This defensive strategy could be quickly implemented, simply by scrapping large numbers of capital ships, by a ten-year capital ship building holiday, by agreement to naval equality between Great Britain and the United States, by Japan's acceptance of a 60 percent ratio, and by lesser ratios for France and Italy. More dramatic than these drastic reductions was the immediate outpouring of press and popular political support which helped propel the Conference to a series of treaty agreements.[8]

Both Great Britain and Japan were greatly relieved by America's turning away from naval supremacy. Neither of them had the economic strength to continue the furious building necessary to keep pace with Wilson's "navy second to none." But, while paying lip service to the highly popular notion of maintaining the lowest number of ships consistent with national defense, neither was willing to surrender their respective ocean supremacies. Instead, they took advantage of this new experiment in arms control diplomacy to negotiate treaties which sought to enhance their own supremacies.

---

[5] See Chapter 1.   [6] See Chapter 2.   [7] *Ibid.*   [8] *Ibid.*

British negotiators were the most successful. Working harmoniously with their naval advisors, they prevented any limitation on the number of "auxiliary" warships – which accompanied the main fleet and served a variety of additional purposes. Britain also obtained the right to arm converted merchant vessels with 6-inch guns – all of which were essential to blockade and interdiction. They further secured the right to build new naval bases, especially at Singapore, and thereby safeguarded Great Britain's ability to maintain supremacy on the Atlantic and Mediterranean trading routes and, to a lesser extent, in Southeast Asia.[9]

The Japanese were somewhat less successful, primarily because Great Britain and the United States restricted them to a 60 percent ratio rather than their cherished wish for a 70 percent ratio in the capital ships needed to defeat a naval challenge to its regional supremacy. Nonetheless, in return for accepting a 60 percent ratio, Tomosaburo considerably hampered any future American threat to Japanese regional dominance by forcing Hughes to agree to prohibit new American bases beyond Hawaii. Vast ocean distances and lack of naval and air bases made it much more difficult for the American navy to enforce the Open Door policies in China, to protect the Philippines and Guam, or to retaliate against Japanese aggression against American possessions. Tomosaburo returned to Japan to become Prime Minister and to launch an immediate auxiliary shipbuilding program featuring innovative combat capabilities and tactics to compensate for the lesser ratio in capital ships.[10]

Focus on British and Japanese respective ocean supremacies was obscured by the popular American assumption that capital ship equality with Great Britain and a 40 percent advantage over Japan were sufficient to guarantee freedom of the seas in the Atlantic and the Open Door policies in the Pacific – thus making continued naval building a waste of taxpayers' money and a destabilizing threat to world peace. This widespread popular notion became an important component in a newly emerging American political orthodoxy which severely restricted American foreign policy options in the 1920s and 1930s. Disillusioned by World War I and its vengeful Treaty of Versailles, Republican politicians adopted a set of interlocking assumptions based, in part, on the widespread belief that the Washington treaties enabled the United States to stop its naval construction yet still achieve its foreign policy aims with reasonable economy and safety.[11]

Eschewing the acquisition of additional colonial possessions and entangling military alliances, Presidents Harding, Coolidge, and Hoover encouraged foreign policy initiatives fostering the rapid expansion of overseas trade and sources of raw materials. Secretary of State Charles Evans Hughes cooperated with Hoover's revitalized and innovative Department of Commerce to assist private American bankers in financing European economic recovery and in

---

[9] See Chapter 2. [10] *Ibid.* [11] See Chapters 2 and 7.

promoting what some have since identified as an informal commercial global empire, one dependent on unimpeded access to the world's markets.[12] This continually expanding importance of freedom of the seas to American foreign policy startled the British in 1925 when Coolidge supported the right of American ship owners to sue Great Britain for neutral rights violations during World War I.[13]

Coolidge's decision created consternation in London. The resurrection of this unresolved dispute caused Foreign Minister Austen Chamberlain great "anxiety, even dismay." He immediately recognized the threat to blockades and interdictions and thus to British naval supremacy in the Atlantic. Coolidge's challenge, he lamented, "went to the root of our rights as a belligerent Power ... and ... struck straight at our naval strength in our power to defend ourselves." Indeed, either to acknowledge the right of the United States to freedom of the seas, or to relinquish Great Britain's right to blockade and interdict neutral shipping during wartime, he feared, might well "destroy the basis of [British] naval power."[14] Later, the sudden resumption of American naval building, following the breakdown of the Geneva talks, convinced Chamberlain that any attempt by Great Britain to enforce blockade and interdiction on American shipping in a future European conflict "would make war between us 'probable.'"[15]

First Sea Lord David Beatty – once strongly supported by former First Lord of the Admiralty Winston Churchill, who now served as Chancellor of the Exchequer – also worried about Great Britain's ability to impose future blockades. In retrospect, it is clear that Beatty's sudden desire for a second arms-control conference arose from internal weaknesses threatening Great Britain's naval supremacy.[16] The first and most immediate weakness was the still closely held secret that his newest 10,000-ton, 8-inch-gun auxiliary cruisers were so woefully inadequate in gun range, armor, and number of guns that they were only suitable to sail under the protection of the longer-range guns of the main battle fleet. Unable to match the combat capabilities of the 10,000-ton, 8-inch-gun cruisers being built by rival navies, and unwilling to expose this embarrassing knowledge to Churchill or to the Cabinet, especially as antagonisms lingered over the damaging political fight to hurry their construction in 1925, Beatty therefore purposely decided to use a second

---

[12] *Ibid.*   [13] See Chapter 7.   [14] *Ibid.*
[15] A. C. [Austen Chamberlain], "Belligerent Rights at Sea and the Relations Between the United States and Great Britain," October 26, 1927, C. P. 258 (27), CAB 24/189, PRO; Esme Howard to my dear Tyrrell, September 15 and 22, 1927, C.P. 258 (27), CAB 24/189, PRO. See also R. L. Craigie, " Memorandum Respecting the Possibilities of an Anglo-American Agreement Regulating the Exercise by Either Power of Its Belligerent Right to Intercept Private Property at Sea," October 17, 1927, C.P. 258 (27), CAB 24/189, PRO; A.C. [Austen Chamberlain], "Belligerent Rights at Sea," November 14, 1927, C.P. 286 (27), CAB 24/189.
[16] See Chapters 5 and 10.

conference at Geneva in 1927 to prevent rival navies from continuing to build their superior 8-inch-gun cruisers.[17]

To minimize this secret cruiser weakness, Beatty therefore carefully crafted a behind-the-scenes political and diplomatic initiative. He disguised his military motives by offering the economically beleaguered British Cabinet substantial savings in both current and future construction costs. Beatty's switch from prolonged resistance to naval cuts to a sudden and unexpected embracing of naval economies convinced a delighted Cabinet to approve his demand that he control the negotiations at the Geneva Conference. His diplomatic strategy, he reassured the Cabinet, would realize enormous savings by convincing the other major naval powers to extend the capital ship building holiday, to restrict construction of 10,000-ton, 8-inch-gun cruisers, to outlaw the 8-inch gun on all future warships, and to build all future auxiliary cruisers in an unlimited category of smaller, less expensive 6-inch-gun cruisers.[18] Crucial to success, however, were his equally erroneous expectations of a great outpouring of favorable public approval which would successfully pressure weak-willed, electioneering America politicians to again override the advice of their naval advisers, just as Harding and Hughes had done at the Washington Conference.

Equally risky, if not more so, were secret objectives which Beatty carefully kept hidden from the Americans prior to the opening of the Conference. After the talks began in Geneva, Beatty rejected any treaty right to equality in smaller cruisers and refused to negotiate on the basis of combat equivalency.[19] Especially irritating to the Americans was his insistence on strictly limiting the number of 10,000-ton, 8-inch-gun cruisers, an unlimited number of 6-inch-gun cruisers, and the abolishment of 8-inch guns on all future warships. To stiffen resolve against an outpouring of American objections, Beatty warned the Cabinet that should Great Britain allow the United States equality in the smaller cruisers, especially those large enough to mount 8-inch-guns, the Americans could take advantage of British disbursement of its naval forces during the next European war by concentrating its 8-inch-gun cruisers and overwhelm the outnumbered 6-inch-gun cruisers and armed merchantmen enforcing British blockade and interdiction strategies. Equality in cruisers, he insisted, meant supremacy for the United States, inferiority for Great Britain, the resignation of the entire Board of Admiralty, and, as the Ministers were well aware, yet another political crisis within the Baldwin Cabinet and the Conservative Party.[20]

Surprised by Beatty's sly attempt to use the negotiations at Geneva to extract tacit Cabinet approval for a large increase in cruiser tonnage, Churchill responded with his own surreptitious political strategy. As Chancellor of the Exchequer, and as a former leader in the Liberal Party who had only recently joined the Conservatives, Churchill had to protect himself from a repetition of

[17] See Chapter 10.   [18] *Ibid*.   [19] See Chapters 12–14.   [20] See Chapters 13 and 14.

the unsubstantiated yet damaging 1925 charge that his persistent opposition to the Admiralty's budget demands, especially for a large increase in expensive new cruisers in preparation for a war against Japan, was part of a clandestine plot to force the resignation of the entire Board of Admiralty, thereby splitting the Conservative Party and bringing down the Baldwin Government. Rather than allow a repetition of this charge by again openly opposing Beatty, Churchill instead repeatedly supported Beatty's insistence on cruiser supremacy. Indeed, as he had long been in agreement with the First Sea Lord on naval supremacy, Churchill enthusiastically reassured the Cabinet that granting parity in cruisers would "put ourselves in the power of the United States," by allowing the Americans "to give us orders and even to starve Great Britain" into obedience. It was time, he declared, for Great Britain to "draw up our own charter of freedom of the seas."[21]

Churchill understood that his call for a British "charter of freedom of the seas" would be welcomed by the Admiralty and its allies in the Cabinet, the Parliament, and the Conservative Party. Indeed, the response by Admiral Sir Roger Keyes, a staunch Beatty ally, reflected the underlying yet intense rivalry between the British and American navies. Delighted with Churchill's defense of British naval supremacy, he inadvertently lent some weight to Chamberlain's later anxiety over the danger that future blockades risked an Anglo-American war. Keyes assured Churchill that if the United States "set out in convoys to force her trade and maintain the freedom of the seas for neutrals," he prayed that the government would "allow the British Fleet" to spring into action as "nothing in the world would possibly please me more than to be in command of such an undertaking."[22]

Churchill's purpose, of course, was not to encourage a war against the United States, but simply to reiterate Beatty's recommendation that a failed conference was preferable to agreeing to an American treaty right to cruiser equality. By rejecting this right and simply allowing the Geneva Conference to fail, Churchill advised the Cabinet, Great Britain would preserve her existing cruiser superiority and blockade capabilities without the need to raise taxes for additional cruiser construction. Naval supremacy, he argued, not equality based upon unreliable arms-control panaceas, must continue to govern British foreign policy.[23]

In retrospect, despite his artful twists and turns, Churchill's unarticulated yet prescient strategy becomes clear. By supporting Beatty's negotiating demands, he protected himself from a resurgence of disloyalty charges by Admiralty supporters within the Conservative Party. Moreover, with keen political foresight, he understood that he could contribute significantly to an embarrassing Admiralty failure simply by mustering support within the Cabinet for the Admiralty's rejection of America's treaty right to cruiser equality. He foresaw

---

[21] Ibid.   [22] See Chapter 13.   [23] Ibid.

as well that as this likelihood became more and more evident, the Cabinet's embarrassment and frustration with Admiralty diplomatic ineptness would steadily increase. Indeed, this frustration became especially painful when Bridgeman and Cecil forced the Cabinet to announce in Parliament that the Cabinet, not the Admiralty, must bear the responsibility for withdrawing Bridgeman's promise of equality in cruisers. Thus, by supporting Beatty's negotiating demands, Churchill not only successfully protected himself against Admiralty critics, but simultaneously undermined the slim hopes for an agreement at Geneva and, with the collapse of the negotiations, severely weakened the Admiralty's political clout with the highly disappointed and disillusioned Ministers. Indeed, when the Conference failed, rather than approving an increase in the number of smaller cruisers, the Cabinet instead awarded Churchill a long-delayed yet satisfying victory over the Admiralty by creating a special committee to scale-back cruiser construction.[24]

For differing reasons, Japan was also willing to allow the 1927 arms-limitation conference to fail. Despite its delegates' initial willingness to negotiate on the basis of the Anglo-Japanese Accord, the Japanese Naval Ministry rejected the Accord's promise of an improved ratio, demanding instead the explicit guarantee of 70 percent, considered essential to its regional supremacy in Southeast Asia. This significant switch was little noticed at the time, perhaps because Admiral Makoto Saito, the Japanese spokesman at the last plenary session, emphasized Japan's repeated willingness to compromise while subtly placing the blame for the breakdown on the irreconcilable disputes between the United States and Great Britain.[25]

Coolidge's response was more clearly expressed by his actions than by his words. The surprises during the Geneva Conference had erased the naïveté so evident when Coolidge had trusted Jones' assurance of Beatty's promise of equality and had therefore rushed to call a second conference without first carefully probing potential points of conflict. From an ardent champion of naval limitation, who had fought vigorously to prevent Congress from funding three cruisers in late 1926, he suddenly emerged eight months later as a determined commander-in-chief bent upon naval supremacy. To this end, Coolidge threw his political support behind a House Naval Affairs authorization for twenty-five new 10,000-ton, 8-inch-gun cruisers, five aircraft carriers, nine destroyer leaders, and thirty-two submarines for a total of seventy-one ships at an estimated cost of $725 million. With eight 10,000-ton, 8-inch-gun cruisers already authorized, these thirty-three new cruisers represented seventeen more than Parliament had approved under the 1925 Birkenhead building compromise, and would ensure cruiser superiority over Great Britain and Japan by 1936. The House passed the bill by 287 to 58.[26] But persistent

---

[24] *Ibid.* See also Chapters 13–16.   [25] See Chapters 15 and 16.
[26] William F. Trimble, "The United States Navy and the Geneva Conference for the Limitation of Naval Armament, 1927," (Ph.D. diss., University of Colorado, 1974), pp. 388–389, 394–401,

and determined lobbying by peace organizations delayed Senate action for several months until the announcement of a tentative Anglo-French Accord. This Accord severely limited 10,000-ton, 8-inch-gun cruisers, permitted an unlimited number of smaller 6-inch-gun auxiliary cruisers, and succeeded only in reigniting Congressional concern over British supremacy and blockade intentions. Coolidge now renewed his pressure on the Senate to join the House, and on February 7, 1929, Congress approved a less expensive program of one aircraft carrier and fifteen of these new cruisers, bringing the total to seven more than Parliament had approved in 1925.[27]

Coolidge's switch in 1927 was certainly dramatic, yet there is very little convincing evidence that lobbyists or systematic leaks to the press from naval delegates accounted either for the breakdown of the Conference or for the sudden determination by Coolidge and Congress to renew the drive for naval equality, if not supremacy. American public opinion was undoubtedly influenced by press criticisms of English demands, but Secretary of State Frank B. Kellogg and his emissary Hugh Gibson were convinced that American press criticisms, including the clandestine activities of Shearer and Schofield, had no discernible impact on the day-to-day negotiations. Kellogg adamantly denied that press reports had influenced either him or the negotiating objectives of the United States.[28] Gibson agreed. When Sir Esme Howard complained to Kellogg over biased American reporters, Gibson countered that American press reports were "less partial and more exact than the British," whose press was under constant pressure from the British delegation and whose news reports and editorials "consistently misrepresented" the American positions.[29]

Regardless of the validity of the charges and countercharges of press influence, Admiralty surprises at the negotiating table were clearly more important

---

427–439; Richard W. Fanning, *Peace and Disarmament: Naval Rivalry and Arms Control, 1922–1933* (Lexington: University Press of Kentucky, 1995), pp. 88–95; Coolidge, "Message of the President of the United States," December 6, 1927, *FRUS*, 1927, I: vii–viii.

[27] Trimble, "United States Navy," pp. 394–401: Fanning, *Peace and Disarmament*, p. 91; See also George T. Davis, *A Navy Second to None: The Development of Modern American Naval Policy* (New York: Harcourt Brace, 1940), p. 331.

[28] Kellogg to Castle, September 23, 1927, State Department, Decimal File, 500 A/15A1/39, RG 19, NA; Houghton to Kellogg, July 23, 1927, CCP; Kellogg to American Mission, July 12, 1927; Gibson to Kellogg, July 14, 1927, CCP; Kellogg to Gibson, June 26 and July 11, 1927, *FRUS*, 1927, I: 57, 93; Gibson to Ted Marriner, August 11, 1927, Marriner File, GP; Hugh Wilson to Gibson, May 29, 1928, Wilson File, GP; Gibson to Castle, September 30, 1928, Castle File, GP. See also Wilson to Lawrence Ritchey, September 26, 1929 and Frank S. Bright to Hoover, September 11, 1929, Shearer File, PP, HHP; Robert Gordon Kaufman, *Arms Control During the Pre-Nuclear Era: The United States and Naval Limitation Between the Two Wars* (New York: Columbia University Press, 1990), pp. 116–117; Stephen Roskill, *Naval Policy Between The Wars: The Period of Anglo-American Antagonism, 1919–1929* (London: Collins, 1968), p. 508.

[29] Gibson to Kellogg, July 25, 1927, CCP.

Conclusion

in fostering growing American disillusionment.[30] Effectively withdrawing First Lord of the Admiralty William Bridgeman's public promise of parity, demanding a greater number of smaller 6-inch-gun cruisers, refusing to allow the latest weapons technology represented by America's highly prized 8-inch gun on all future warships, and requiring the new unexpectedly higher British total tonnage were infinitely more instrumental in convincing American negotiators, the public, and Congress that Great Britain had never intended to fulfill its promises of limitation or of extending the principle of equality to all American auxiliary vessels, and was, instead, cynically using the Geneva Conference to enhance its naval supremacy.

The prolonged Congressional debate over the renewed drive for naval supremacy highlighted two opposing foreign policy options. One reemphasized that if the United States insisted on freedom of the seas to protect its rapidly expanding informal commercial empire, it must equal, if not surpass, British capital and auxiliary ship forces. This policy tacitly acknowledged that only military power could guarantee future American security. But for many, the validity of this lesson, most recently learned during World War I, was neither diplomatically nor fiscally acceptable. Only after some months of bitter internal wrangling and only after the British announced the Anglo-French Accord on unlimited 6-inch-gun cruisers, did the Senate finally succumb to Coolidge's relentless pressure for cruiser supremacy.[31]

***

Passage of the new cruiser legislation energized the advocates of a second option. Of this group, none was more adamant than Herbert Hoover, the new president of the United States. During the summer of 1927, when the Geneva negotiations were floundering, then Secretary of Commerce Hoover had met three times with Sir Esme Howard in vain brainstorming efforts to rescue the talks.[32] Now, in March 1929, the newly inaugurated president met repeatedly with his good friend Hugh Gibson for extensive consultations to determine the reasons underlying the failed effort and to devise ways to revive the negotiations.[33] As the chief spokesman and principal negotiator at the Geneva talks, Gibson was well aware of the pitfalls in arms control negotiations, yet he remained convinced that a second world war could only be averted by persistent arms-control initiatives.[34]

---

[30] See Chapters 11, 13, and 15. See also Kellogg to Castle, September 23, 1929, November 6, 1929, State Department, Decimal File, 500 A15A1/39, RG 59, NA.
[31] Trimble, "United States Navy," pp. 394–401; George T Davis, *A Navy Second to None*, p. 331.
[32] Howard to Chamberlain, July 29, 1927, *DBFP*, Ia, III: 708–709.
[33] The best source for Hoover's extensive conversations with Gibson at the White House is Gibson's Diary. See Gibson, Diary, February 22 and 25, 1929; March 20, 28, and 30, 1929; and April 2 1929. See also Herbert Hoover, *The Memoirs of Herbert Hoover: The Cabinet and Presidency, 1920–1933*, 3 vols. (New York: Macmillan Company, 1952), 2: 340.
[34] Gibson to Mother, December 10 and 12, 1929, GP, HHPL.

Hoover agreed.³⁵ As a young partner in a British mining firm, Hoover had lived in London for many years, and as president he was determined to heal the breach in Anglo-American relations.³⁶ Influenced no doubt by his earlier talks with Sir Esme Howard as well as his confidential talks with Gibson, he had no difficulty concurring with Gibson's recommendation that civilian control of a third conference was the key to success. Naval considerations must not again be allowed to trump more important diplomatic objectives. As Secretary of Commerce, he had vigorously promoted the rapid expansion of an informal commercial empire, which he had championed as Secretary of Commerce, but like Harding and Hughes, he hoped to protect it with treaties rather than naval supremacy.³⁷ Equally clear was the necessity for detailed agreements reached at the highest levels well in advance of the conference opening. To revive interest in arms control, Hoover and Gibson set international diplomacy buzzing with their announcement of a new "yardstick," suggesting that the Americans had discovered a breakthrough virtually guaranteeing the viability of another round of talks.³⁸

The yardstick which Gibson announced at the resumption of the Geneva Preparatory Commission talks in 1929 succeeded in dramatically reviving interest in a third conference. In reality, it merely at first repackaged Jones' combat equivalency idea.³⁹ As a highly successful engineer prior to becoming president, Hoover was convinced that scientific engineering principles must be adapted to solve complex national and international problems.⁴⁰ He therefore became an enthusiastic promoter of a yardstick which could be more

---

[35] Hoover, *Memoirs: Cabinet and Presidency*, pp. 338–361. French Strother to Gibson, June 13, 1929, Strother File, GP. Strother was a close personal friend of Hoover's who characterized Hoover's arms-control efforts as "close to his heart."

[36] Hoover, *Memoirs: Cabinet and Presidency*, p. 340.   [37] *Ibid.*, p. 341.

[38] Herbert Hoover, "Memorial Day Address at Arlington National Cemetery," May 30, 1929, in Herbert Hoover, *Public Papers of the Presidents: Herbert Hoover 1929*, 6 vols. ed. James B. Rhodes (Washington DC: Government Printing Office, 1974), 2: 164–165; Hoover to Jones, June 14, 1929, Foreign Affairs, Great Britain, PP, HHPL; Dulles to Secretary of State, June 20, 1929, State Department, Disarmament File, PP, HHPL; Stimson to Hoover, June 24, 1929, State Department, Decimal File, 500.A 15/1027, Capital Offices, NA; Gibson to Dawes, June 28, 1929, London Naval Conference, Preliminary Talks and Negotiations File, GP. For the British consideration of the yardstick, see FO 371/13521 and ADM 116/3371, PRO. See also Christina E. Newton, "Anglo-American Relations and Bureaucratic Tensions, 1927–1930," (Ph.D. diss., University of Illinois, 1975), pp. 169–171, 185, 187, 205–206; Raymond O'Connor, *Perilous Equilibrium: The United States and the London Naval Conference of 1930* (New York: Greenwood Press, 1969), pp. 18, 25, 34, 44.

[39] Hoover to Secretary of the Navy, June 14, 1929; Jones to Secretary of the Navy, June 18, 1929, Washington Conference 1921–1925 File, JP; Castle, Diary, May 6–7, 1929, CP; O'Connor, *Perilous Equilibrium*, pp. 27, 34.

[40] Ellis W. Hawley, *The Great War and the Search for a Modern Order: A History of the American People and Their Institutions, 1917–1933* (New York: St. Martin's Press, 1979), pp. 54–55, 68, 70, 100–104, 178–180; Joan Hoff Wilson, *Herbert Hoover: Forgotten Progressive* (New York: HarperCollins Publishers, 1975), pp. 36–37.

mathematically exact than the one proposed by Jones at the 1927 Conference. He hoped thereby to achieve combat equivalency through the creation of a scientifically precise formula bringing American and British cruisers into a politically acceptable ratio approximating naval equality. To this end he ordered the General Board to devise such a formula.[41] But try as it might, the reluctant and skeptical General Board finally informed Hoover that complex cruiser variables made it impossible to arrive at a reliable formula, and the yardstick was eventually dropped as a negotiating tool by both the Americans and the British. This failure greatly disappointed and vexed Hoover, but he kept this failure under wraps lest it dampen hopes for another conference.[42]

Hoover's determination to improve Anglo-American relations by successfully concluding a treaty extending equality to auxiliary ships was championed by the new British Prime Minister Ramsay MacDonald. Like Hoover, MacDonald agreed that civilian control of the negotiations was the key to success and pressured the Admiralty to accept a temporary equality based on a limit of fifty cruisers, the number which Beatty had cited at the Washington Conference.[43] Having pleased the Americans with a limit of fifty cruisers, MacDonald steadfastly supported the Admiralty objectives which it had failed to realize at Geneva. In preliminary negotiations he rejected Hoover's call for freedom of the seas, for neutral rights for neutral ships, for exempting food ships in time of war, and for selling British naval bases in the Caribbean, which threatened approaches to the Panama Canal, in exchange for credit against England's war debts owed to the United States.[44] While MacDonald was willing to allow the United States between fifteen to eighteen new 10,000-ton, 8-inch-gun cruisers to equal the existing British cruiser strength, he succeeded in achieving a significant continuity with the Admiralty's demands at the 1927 Geneva Conference by inserting into the 1930 London Naval Treaty the Admiralty's continued insistence on the strict limitation of the 8-inch gun, on restricting all future cruisers to 6-inch guns, and on the extension of the capital shipbuilding holiday until 1936.[45]

---

[41] Jones to Gibson, June 11, 1929; Jones, "Memorandum for the Secretary of the Navy," May 28 and 29, 1929, Jones File, GP. The second memorandum of May 29, 1929 outlines Jones' idea on the yardstick. See also Castle to Kellogg, April 6, 1929, England File, CP; O'Connor, *Perilous Equilibrium*, p. 25.

[42] O'Connor, *Perilous Equilibrium*, pp. 34, 42–44; General Board to the Secretary of the Navy, June 10, 1929, PP, Disarmament File, HHPL.

[43] Hoover, *Memoirs: Cabinet and Presidency*, p. 341; O'Connor, *Perilous Equilibrium*, pp. 40–41. For Admiralty reactions see A. V. Alexander to MacDonald, July 15, 1929 and Charles Madden to Dear First Lord, July 12, 1929 in PRO 30/69/267, PRO; Craigie, "Minute," June 2, 1929, FO 371/13520/A3662, pp. 169–171, PRO.

[44] Hoover, *Memoirs: Cabinet and Presidency*, pp. 345–347; O'Connor, *Perilous Equilibrium*, pp. 22, 48–51; Davis, *A Navy Second to None*, pp. 327, 332–333.

[45] Kaufman, *Arms Control During the Pre-Nuclear Era*, pp. 125–138; Fanning, *Peace and Disarmament*, pp. 106–118, 124–128.

Crucial to the success of the London Naval Treaty of 1930 was the political accord agreed upon by Hoover and McDonald in November 1929 at Hoover's woodland retreat on the Rapidan River in Virginia. It was here that the two leaders agreed on the fundamental negotiating principle which had been rejected by both the Admiralty and the General Board during the 1927 Conference: that avoiding war between the United States and Great Britain must be the bedrock political principle underlying the forthcoming naval negotiations. MacDonald delighted a joint session of Congress with a dramatic reiteration of the enduring friendship between the two nations, a speech which did much to pave the way for Senate approval of the new conference and its eventual ratification of the London Naval Treaty in 1930.[46]

While Hoover and MacDonald's limit on fifty cruisers and the mutual pledge to avoid war eased American anxieties over British naval supremacy, Japanese politicians faced a much more difficult task. During the three years between 1927 and 1930, especially with the onslaught of the Great Depression, discontent within the Japanese "fleet faction" reached a fever pitch. Hoover recognized the importance of placating Japan by sending William R. Castle as the United States Ambassador to Japan, where Castle worked hard to convince the Japanese that they had nothing to fear from America. However, despite his seeming success with Japanese politicians and diplomats, Castle had much less success in persuading Japan's naval officers.[47]

At the Washington Conference Admiral Kato Kanji – the leader of the "fleet faction" who had steadfastly, yet unsuccessfully, opposed Kato Tomosaburo's acceptance of the 60 percent ratio – had not forgotten his vow that "as far as I am concerned, war with America starts now. We will take revenge on her. We will." Indeed, in 1923 when Tomosaburo attempted to incorporate a formal declaration of avoidance of war with the United States into Japan's unofficial National Defense Policy, Kanji successfully substituted the "fleet faction" policy which emphasized that "a clash between the United States and the [Japanese] Empire will become inevitable."[48]

Late in the negotiations at the Geneva Conference in 1927, the Navy Ministry instructed the Japanese delegates to withdraw consideration of a 65 percent ratio, and instead to continue negotiating for 70 percent.[49] This demand reemerged in 1930 with even greater urgency, and although the 1930 Treaty granted Japan a much improved ratio, it was no longer acceptable to a rapidly growing, fanatically militaristic clique, which retaliated against Prime Minister Hamaquchi Osachi's success in ratifying the Treaty by assassinating him.[50] In the next year, 1931, the Japanese

---

[46] Castle, Diary, October 7, 1929, CP.
[47] See Castle correspondence, speeches, and press releases in Japan File, CP, HHPL.
[48] See Chapter 2.   [49] See Chapter 15.
[50] Davis, *A Navy Second to None*, pp. 342–345.

Army expressed its own discontent with civilian restraints by initiating its unauthorized expansion into Manchuria.[51]

As the Great Depression deepened, and the vision of an American global commercial empire dimmed with the erection of higher tariff barriers and imperial preferences, Congressional concerns about competing naval supremacies continued to languish. Throughout his four years as president, Hoover declined to build up to the 1930 London Naval Treaty limits, refusing to lay down even one additional warship.[52] Convinced that the money was needed to fight the Depression at home, he unsuccessfully attempted to rescue the collapsing negotiations at the 1932 Geneva Disarmament Conference by offering to cut American military forces by 25 to 33 percent.[53]

Hoover's successor, President Franklin D. Roosevelt, for eight years the Assistant Secretary of the Navy during the Wilson Administration, continued American participation in international arms- control diplomacy. Between 1933 and 1939 Roosevelt had completed a total of 106 new warships, but he, too, failed to build the American fleet to the levels authorized by the 1930 London Treaty, joining instead with Great Britain and France to extend limitation in the 1936 London Naval Treaty.

Despite increasingly ominous signs, hopes of including all of the major naval powers in limitation treaties continued to propel international diplomacy. By December 1934, a 70 percent ratio was no longer acceptable to the Japanese navy, and, when the United States and Great Britain made it clear that they would not agree to increase Japan's naval ratio beyond 70 percent to full equality, which would have seemingly guaranteed Japan's regional naval supremacy, Japan formally announced that it would terminate the Washington and London treaties. Nonetheless, hopes persisted. In 1935 British political leaders negotiated a naval treaty with Hitler, which, as history revealed, he never intended to honor.[54]

* * *

Negotiations at Geneva in 1927 reflected the lessons garnered by Beatty, Schofield, and Kato Kanji during World War I and at the Washington Conference. During the course of the 1920s, these naval strategists realized that the growing political popularity and long-term military consequences of this experimental diplomacy of arms limitation required them to adopt increasingly clandestine tactics. Under the cover of seemingly plausible rationales, as well as the lofty panaceas favored by politicians and disarmament enthusiasts, British and Japanese military advisors channeled the negotiations both at the Washington Conference and at the Geneva Conference to incorporate

---

[51] Arnold A. Offner, *The Origins of the Second World War: American Foreign Policy and World Politics, 1917–1941* (New York: Praeger Publishers, 1975), p. 96.
[52] Davis, *A Navy Second to None*, pp. 254–255, 364–365.
[53] Ibid., pp. 355–391. Kaufman, *Arms Control during the Pre-Nuclear Era*, pp. 175, 197, 184.
[54] See sources in footnotes 52 and 53.

vital military priorities. At the 1927 Geneva Conference the Americans also incorporated unarticulated military priorities into their negotiating goals. The importance of realizing these military priorities at the Geneva Conference convinced Beatty that he was justified in deceiving the British Cabinet, the Americans, and the Japanese about underlying Admiralty objectives. Thus, the arms-control negotiations of the 1920s were by no means devoid of military realism, albeit a realism which was often hidden below the surface.

The underlying persistence of imperial priorities and naval supremacies during the Washington Conference of 1921–1922 and the Geneva Conference of 1927 requires scholars to focus more carefully on the hitherto underutilized yet voluminous military records and private correspondence and memorabilia of military advisors at the arms-control conferences during the 1930s. We need to understand to what degree these advisors succeeded either in keeping hidden their secret military objectives from their civilian leaders or convincing civilian leaders to incorporate secret military imperatives into these negotiations – as they had, in varying degrees, in 1921–1922 and again in 1927 – and to what degree these military imperatives affected the outcomes. Indeed, in 1927 political leaders in London, Tokyo, and Washington agreed with their military advisors – albeit for different reasons – that diplomatic failure was preferable to military disadvantage.

More sharply focused on the intricate relationship between navies and empires, these wary rival military strategists acted on the realization that arms-control diplomacy must be understood as another dimension of warfare – war at the peace table.

Bibliographical Essay

One of the principal temptations in researching the voluminous materials available on arms-control conferences between the wars is to rely too heavily on the highly informative yet surprisingly incomplete published documents. So voluminous are these published sources that one can receive the erroneous impression that they are sufficient for a highly detailed understanding. The exclusion of emotional, personal, or embarrassing expressions creates the impression of highly rational and unemotional diplomatic exchanges. Yet this study reveals that the examination of private, unpublished correspondence and records adds vital facts, emotional emphases, and more importantly, secret negotiating motives and objectives not found in official publications. For this reason, careful reading of the unpublished personal papers and correspondence of the principal leaders and negotiators as well as the official but unpublished documents is essential to our understanding, especially of the 1927 Geneva Naval Conference.

Another temptation arising from too heavy a reliance upon published sources is to assume that because the chief spokesmen at these conferences were usually civilians, their military advisers must have played a secondary role in formulating policy goals and in conducting the negotiations. But the 1927 Geneva Conference offers a cautionary tale. The Admiralty was able to dominate the negotiations to a far greater degree than scholars have recognized. To discover the most revealing evidence of the Admiralty's motivations and objectives in arranging the Conference and in conducting the negotiations, one must look to its highly technical unpublished Admiralty documents at the Public Records Office, Kew, London, England.

The Admiralty's lengthy technical reports, studies, and recommendations on which its negotiating strategy was based are scattered throughout a variety of record groups. The Naval Staff's adamant determination to use the 1927 Conference to eliminate the 8-inch gun can only be found in its numerous technical reports on cruisers. Most revealing is the Director of Gunnery's "Investigation of the Considerations Affecting Gun Armaments and Protection of Future Cruisers," in ADM 1/92712. The Gunnery Division's yearly handbooks on the unsatisfactory performance of the 8-inch gun between 1925 and 1938 are in ADM 186. Essential, as well, are my numerous citations in Chapters 11 and 16 to Admiralty record groups ADM 1/8694, ADM 118 and ADM 167. Included in these numerous reports are the "minutes" by members of the Naval Staff offering their insightful reactions and recommendations. Their sense of urgency for an immediate international conference to eliminate the 8-inch gun differs markedly from the British delegation's public economic rationale and casts an entirely different light on our understanding of hidden Admiralty motivations and objectives.

The intricate interrelationship between the perception of military realities and political and economic constraints is revealed most clearly in the prolonged 1925 Birkenhead Committee disputes over the Admiralty's insistence upon building new 10,000-ton, 8-inch-gun cruisers. Understanding the issues and the positions taken by Churchill, formerly First Lord of the Admiralty and then currently Chancellor of the Exchequer, and by the Admiralty during these debates and the subsequent resignation crisis is crucial to understanding the Admiralty's ability to dominate the negotiations at the Geneva Conference in 1927, as well as Churchill's strained relationship with the Admiralty and its objectives between 1925 and 1927. Many of the documents can be found in Cab 27/273 and in the personal papers of Winston S. Churchill at Churchill College, Cambridge University. The confused discussion in the Committee of Imperial Defence on May 20, 1927 is in Cab 2/5. Cabinet discussions and decisions throughout the negotiations can be found in Cab 23/55 while the important records of the Cabinet Naval Programme Committee are in Cab 27/355. Fascinating debates in the Further Limitation of Armaments Subcommittee and the *Minutes* of the British Empire Delegation at the Conference are in Cab 27/350, Public Record Office, Kew, London. Copies of many of these documents are also in the Winston S. Churchill Papers.

Unpublished documents are also essential to our understanding of the personal relationships among the principal leaders. Beatty's stormy confrontations with Churchill, his contempt for politicians, and his criticisms of individual political leaders are revealed in his letters to his wife and to a lesser extent, to Admiral Roger Keyes. This private correspondence reveals his determination to dominate the political leaders during the 1925 resignation crisis and later in setting the terms of the negotiations and in maintaining control of those terms at Geneva and London in 1927. One should also consult his correspondence with Roger Keyes in *The Keyes Papers: Selections from the Private and Official Correspondence of Admiral of the Fleet Baron Keyes of Zeebrugge* (London: George Allen and Unwin, 1980), edited by Paul G. Halpern. Other important letters are in published collections edited by B. Mc. L. Ranft, William Scott Chalmers, Philip Williamson and Martin Gilbert. Stephen Roskill's biography of Beatty, *Earl Beatty: The Last Naval Hero: An Intimate Biography* (New York: Athenaeum, 1981) adds importantly to our knowledge of this pivotal figure.

As an historian as well as the most prominent British political leader in this story, Winston S. Churchill was acutely aware of the value of preserving documentable evidence. His collection of private correspondence and important government papers is indispensable in untangling his intricate political maneuverings in London, both prior to and during the negotiations. As a former First Lord of the Admiralty, Churchill's personal relations and repeated clashes with First Sea Lord Beatty, his abiding keen interest and fulsome knowledge of naval matters, and his willingness to link strategic military thinking with economic and political realities are crucial to an understanding of the dynamic politics of British arms-control diplomacy between 1925 and 1927. It is only through his private papers that one is able to understand the evolution of the clever counter-strategy which he employed against Beatty during the 1927 Conference. Many, but by no means all, of the important Churchill letters and documents are reproduced in *Companion Volume 5* of Martin Gilbert's monumental published collection cited in the footnotes.

British frustrations during the negotiations are most clearly revealed in the private letters and diary of First Lord of the Admiralty William C. Bridgeman. These letters are essential to understanding his role in the 1925 resignation crisis, his distrust of Churchill, his confusion over parity, his relations with Gibson and Jones, his efforts at compromise, and his growing displeasure with Beatty's dominance. These important documents are located in the Shropshire County Record Office, Shrewsbury, England. The Churchill College Archives also has a much smaller collection of Bridgeman's letters and an unpublished biography apparently written by his son. Much less complete but occasionally useful is *The Modernisation of Conservative Politics: The Diaries and Letters of William Bridgeman, 1904–1935* (London: The Historian's Press, 1988), edited by Philip Williamson.

The collection of private letters of Lord Robert Cecil of Chelwood at the British Library, London, is yet another example of the crucial importance of private personal communications. Like Bridgeman, Cecil was candid in expressing his views, especially about the Admiralty's dominance over arms-control negotiations, both before and during the Geneva Conference. His complaints to Prime Minister Stanley Baldwin and to Foreign Secretary Austen Chamberlain are especially helpful in untangling the confusion which bedeviled the relations between the delegates at Geneva and the Cabinet in London. The voluminous papers detailing his resignation following the Conference, and his charges before the House of Lords, must be interpreted cautiously. Yet, despite refutations of his reasons for resigning by Sir Maurice Hankey and Lord Balfour, these private and public complaints and subsequent correspondence with Bridgeman are highly revealing.

The correspondence of Prime Minister Stanley Baldwin at Cambridge University Library and of Foreign Secretary Austen Chamberlain and his brother Neville at the University of Birmingham Library fill in important parts of the story. Much of the correspondence to Austen Chamberlain is from Cecil, but Chamberlain reveals his own frustrations with the Americans, with Baldwin, and with Cabinet resignation threats during the last days of the negotiations. Neville Chamberlain confirms the tumultuous nature of the Cabinet debates in early August.

The voluminous unpublished records of the United States Department of the Navy are located in four separate locations: at the National Archives and at the Washington Naval Yard in Washington, DC, at the National Archives at College Park, Maryland, and at the Naval War College in Newport, Rhode Island. These four repositories contain essential data pertaining to the arms-control conferences of the 1920s and 1930s. The National Archives in Washington, DC, is the repository for the General Board's Disarmament Conference Series, which contains the voluminous records of the 1927 Geneva Naval Conference in Record Group 43. These records include correspondence, reports, charts, and memoranda prepared for the Secretary of the Navy and are an invaluable source for American naval thinking. But a more complete understanding emerges from research into the General Records of the Department of the Navy (Record Group 80), Records of the Office of Chief of Naval Operations (Record Group 38), Records of the Bureau of Ordnance (Record Group 74), and Records of the Office of Naval Intelligence (Record Group 39), all of which are housed in the National Archives in Washington, DC. Collectively, these sources provide one with the overwhelming sense of inferiority felt by United States naval leaders relative to Great Britain, the inadequacy of their resources for protecting American interests throughout the world, especially in the Pacific, their strenuous efforts to convince civilian leaders to strengthen naval forces, and the motives underlying the publicity war which the American naval delegates surreptitiously waged throughout the Geneva Conference. These resources are helpful also in understanding why Coolidge and Kellogg came to accept the General Board's assessment of naval weakness and its insistence on parity.

Valuable, too, are the highly informative *Minutes* of the General Board, its equally valuable *Hearings*, and the correspondence with the Secretary of the Navy, which are located at the Naval Historical Center, Washington Naval Yard, Washington, DC. These *Minutes* and *Hearings* and the various collections at the Naval War College in Newport Rhode Island are especially important to an understanding of the development of the American 10,000-ton, 8-inch-gun cruiser, the enthusiasm expressed over the success of the new American 8-inch gun, and the inability to penetrate the veil of secrecy which had descended upon the British 10,000-ton, 8-inch-gun cruiser.

The records of the Department of State at the National Archives in Washington, DC, contain unpublished correspondence and memoranda of conversations in the Decimal File of Record Group 59. Fortunately, the *Papers Relating to the Foreign Relations of the United States, 1927* reproduces most of the essential communications passing between Geneva and Washington both during the Preparatory Commission talks and the Geneva Conference. Nonetheless, as complete and as valuable as this published source appears to be, it must be supplemented by equally important unpublished correspondence and memoranda in the Frank B. Kellogg and Calvin Coolidge papers. The Calvin Coolidge Papers at the Library of Congress, Manuscripts Division, and the Frank B. Kellogg Papers at the Minnesota Historical Society in St. Paul, Minnesota, are available on microfilm and, although neither collection is extensive, each contains documents essential to this study.

Much more informative and voluminous are the unpublished materials in the Hilary P. Jones Papers at the Library of Congress in Washington, DC. His letters and memoranda to members of the General Board and to the Secretary of the Navy enable us to comprehend an entirely new and more meaningful dimension to the negotiations, especially the importance of his combat equivalency compromise plan, which has been overlooked. In his letters we discover his strong Anglophile sentiments coupled with an equally strong determination for naval equality. As President of the General Board prior to the Conference, Jones gives valuable insights into the thinking of the top echelon of the United States Navy and his own brand of open diplomacy. His appointment of Rear Admiral Frank H. Schofield to the American delegation, his private meetings with Beatty, his Fourth of July Speech, and his growing disillusionment over Beatty's evasive tactics are all essential to this story and are not found in other sources.

Even more voluminous are the papers of Hugh Gibson. Located at the Hoover Institution Archives at Stanford University, this collection preserves the correspondence, diary, memoranda of conversations, reports, telegrams, extensive newspaper clippings, and official documents which Gibson retained throughout his long career. It is difficult to exaggerate the importance of this collection. His diary entries, for example, detail his extensive consultations with Secretary of State Kellogg and President Coolidge prior to the Conference and his growing admiration for their studious concentration and understanding of American naval weakness. This judgment was confirmed in the diary of William R. Castle, the Assistant Secretary of State, who recorded Frank Schofield's pointed comparison that Kellogg was "one of the best secretaries of the Navy this country has ever had." Despite Coolidge's hasty calling of the Conference, Gibson enables us to understand that before the delegates left for Geneva, both Coolidge and Kellogg had made a decided effort to balance political and military considerations in approving the Jones combat equivalency plan as a negotiating alternative to the General Board's insistence on numerical parity.

A number of smaller private collections should also be consulted. The papers of William R. Castle located at the Herbert Hoover Presidential Library in West Branch, Iowa, give a somewhat jaundiced insider view of Kellogg, Gibson, Coolidge and the progress of the negotiations at Geneva. The papers of the Senator William E. Borah and of Theodore Roosevelt, Jr., at the Library of Congress offer important domestic political details. Especially interesting is Roosevelt's conviction that Beatty would have to be recalled to London in order for the Washington Conference to succeed. The William B. Shearer papers at the Herbert Hoover Presidential Library are an invaluable source for the publicity war which raged throughout the Geneva Conference. The diary of Rear Admiral Frank H. Schofield at the National Archives in Washington, DC, records the intensive behind-the-scenes publicity activities of the American naval delegates and the reactions of these naval delegates to British and Japanese proposals. His article, "Incidents and Present Day Aspects of Naval Strategy," in the *Proceedings* of the United States Naval Institute and his unpublished lecture, "Some Effects of the Washington Conference on American Naval Strategy," at the Naval War College in Newport, Rhode Island reveal his convictions about the naïveté of American negotiators, his admiration of the British and Japanese diplomats, who, acting on the advice of their naval delegates, thereby protected their vital strategic interests at the Washington Conference, and his abiding determination not to allow another arms-control conference to further weaken American naval forces.

I am deeply indebted to the large number of historians whose excellent scholarship on arms-control diplomacy was essential to my understanding of this complex subject. Several scholars have analyzed more than one conference in a single volume. They were confronted with an overwhelming mass of documents, private collections, and shifting contexts. Despite the disadvantage of such an approach, their willingness to tackle this formidable task and the clarity of their writing places all historians in their debt.

Robert Gordon Kaufman, *Arms Control During the Pre-Nuclear Era: The United States and Naval Limitation Between the Wars* (New York: Columbia University Press, 1990) is a thoughtful analysis of arms-control conferences between 1921–1936. Richard W. Fanning, *Peace and Disarmament: Naval Rivalry and Arms Control, 1922–1933* (Lexington: University Press of Kentucky, 1995) adds significantly to our understanding, especially of the influence of peace lobbies on arms-control diplomacy in the 1920s and 1930s. Another useful one-volume study is Christopher Hall, *Britain, America, and Arms Control 1921–1937* (New York: St. Martin, 1987). While largely passing over the 1927 Conference, Emily O. Goldman's, *Sunken Treaties: Naval Arms Control Between the Wars* (University Park: Pennsylvania State University, 1994) blends historical content and context with arms-control theories in an intellectual analysis of the possibilities and pitfalls for present-day arms-control diplomacy. The three volumes by Stephen Roskill cited in the footnotes and his collection of naval documents at the Churchill Archives are especially useful. John Robert Ferris, *The Evolution of British Strategic Policy, 1919–1926* (London: Macmillan, 1989) provides both background and context. British arms-control efforts are discussed in R. C. Richardson, *The Evolution of*

British Disarmament Policy in the 1920s (London: Leicester University Press, 1989). Richardson's excellent study highlights the confusion within the British Cabinet during the 1927 Conference. William F. Trimble, "The United States and the Geneva Conference for the Limitation of Naval Armament, 1927," (Ph.D. diss., University of Colorado, 1974) is a careful narrative limited only by the resources available to him at the time, but with a very useful summary of various historical interpretations of the 1927 Conference. Finally, Roger Dingman, *Power in the Pacific: The Origin of Naval Arms Limitation, 1914–1922* (Chicago and London: University Press of Chicago, 1976) is an excellent study emphasizing the primacy of domestic politics in arms-control diplomacy.

I wish also to acknowledge the contribution of Tadashi Kuramatsu, "The Geneva Naval Conference of 1927: The British Preparation for the Conference, December 1926 to June 1927," *The Journal of Strategic Studies*, No.1, 19 (March 1996), pp. 104–121. Although we differ significantly on Admiralty and American motives and objectives, I am indebted to him for the knowledge that Japan's Naval Vice Minister was dictating negotiating strategy at Geneva without conferring with the civilian cabinet.

Scholars interested in pursuing this subject will also benefit from consulting the histories, cited in the footnotes, of the following historians: Ernest Andrade, Sadao Asada, Richard Burns and Donald Urquidi, Thomas H. Buckley, Raymond Leslie Buell, Rolland A. Chaput, Betty Glad, B.J.C. McKercher, Philip Payson O'Brien, and Ron Swerczek.

Index

Admiralty, British
 alternate limitation methods, 144
 armed merchantmen, 29, 66
 blacklisting, 1, 6
 blockade, 1–3, 6
 building schedule, 45–46, 66, 74
 contraband, 6
 Coolidge's political motives, 199–200
 cruiser superiority, 2, 4, 24–25, 42, 135, 144, 157, 178
 decline of political influence, 4, 278
 defective armor and armor-piercing shells, 99–101
 demands seventy cruisers, 45–46
 eight-inch gun, 29, 43, 70–73, 93–96, 98, 103–106, 143, 221
 interdiction, 1–3, 66
 League of Nations, 138, 141
 limitation strategy, Washington Conference, 14
 necessity of public approval, 147, 201
 regional supremacy, 2, 5
 rejection of total tonnage standard, 252
 resignation threats, 61, 63, 85
 secret war plan against Japan, 43, 45, 58–59, 62
 six-inch gun, 70, 106, 256
 special needs, 23, 65, 106, 143–144, 163
 surprise proposals, 143–144, 217
 ton-mileage method, 178
 trade-route protection, 24, 45, 67
 urges second conference, 138, 143

American neutral trade, 6, 108, 303–304
 blockade, 303
 Geneva Naval Conference, 16
 regional supremacy, 2, 5, 303
 Washington Naval Conference, 2, 14, 108–109, 304
Amery, Leo, 115, 249
Anglo-Japanese Accord
 Bridgeman's offer, 254–255
 modified, 273–274
 opposition to, 251
 US rejection of, 279–280
Anglo-Japanese Alliance, 20–21, 36
Australia, 45, 53, 220
auxiliaries, tentative agreement on, 238

B-class cruisers, 75, 102
Baldwin, Stanley, 47–48
 importance of Canadian trip, 2, 266
 political strategist, 47, 83, 86, 147, 181, 256
 secrecy, 182, 184
 parity promise withheld, 239–240
Balfour, Arthur, 25, 34, 235
 450,000-ton limit on auxiliaries, 28
 auxiliary ship deception, 27
 confusing telegram, 235
 Hughes, Charles Evans, 25
 justification for British cruiser superiority, 26
 "questions of detail," 26–27
 submarine, abolition of, 27
 Washington Conference, 25–29

323

Battle of Jutland
  Beatty alters record, 187
Battleship controversy, 114–116, 135
Beatty, Adm. David, 3, 273
  anger at Churchill, 39, 56, 88–91, 276
  Anglo-Japanese Accord, modification of, 265–266, 273–274, 279–280
  appearance of reasonableness, 191–192
  assessment of Kellogg, 172, 193, 201
  assurance of success, 151
  assurances to Jones, 138–139, 150
  Baldwin defied, 239–240
  Beatty's secret objectives, 3–4, 25, 107, 139, 143, 147, 164, 177, 183
  Bridgeman's character, 49, 57
  British Empire, 7
  building holiday, 23, 41
  Churchill's Naval Secretary, 12
  Conservative Party split, 57, 84–85
  control of British delegates at Geneva, 3, 144, 179, 202, 307
  criticism of politicians, 76, 87
  criticizes Bridgeman, 239, 264, 295–296
  cruiser supremacy, 191, 248
  defeats pacifists, 46, 276, 296
  defective British eight-inch gun, 93, 107, 188
  denounces Anglo-Japanese Accord, 259, 261, 265
  diplomatic strategy, 4, 150, 175, 307
  distrust of Cecil, 142, 265, 277, 296
  distrust of Churchill, 39, 87–91
  East Asian strategy, 41
  equality equals superiority, 240
  evasive tactics, 3, 152–153, 187
  extension of tenure, 173–174
  First Sea Lord, 12
  friendship with Churchill, 12
  Japanese expansion, 39–40
  naval equality, 22–23, 25, 150
  offers 6.5 ratio to Japanese, 273
  omissions to Cabinet, 177, 187–189, 193
  opposes cruiser parity, 191, 264, 307
  outlaw all eight-inch guns, 3, 106, 144, 187, 221
  parity, definition of, 249
  postwar strategic naval policy, 40, 76, 175
  propagates conspiracy charge, 84
  rejection of Bridgeman's parity promise, 239, 241, 264
  rejects modus vivendi, 252, 269–270, 273, 283
  ridicule of Coolidge, 172, 193, 200–201
  secrecy, importance of, 104, 143–144, 147, 149, 182–184, 187–188, 197
  secret initiative, 144, 307
  seven-inch gun, rejected, 284
  seventy cruisers, 44, 65, 176, 248
  six-inch-gun 6,000-ton cruiser, 263, 265
  socialist fears, 272
  threatens Mrs. Baldwin, 85
  threats of resignation, 3–4, 63, 79, 85
  ton-mileage method, 178
  total tonnage, opposes, 252, 257, 265
  trade route rationale, 241
  ultimatum, use of, 246
  unlimited smaller cruisers, 247–248
  urgent invitation to Admiral Jones, 138, 149
  urges unlimited six-inch gun cruisers, 4, 188
  war hero, 12–13
  war plan against Japan, 40, 64–65, 157
  Washington Conference, 21, 25, 28, 35
Beatty, Ethel:
  denounces Churchill, 91
Bethlehem Steel, 229
Birkenhead Committee, 62–70, 72–74, 76–78
  Churchill's victory, 62, 78
Birkenhead, Lord, 55, 63, 84, 250
  See also F.E. Smith
Bloch, Adm. Claude C. 119
  eight-inch gun success, 119–120
Borah, Sen. William E.
  arms limitation, 18
  blockade, 133
  criticizes Treaty of Versailles, 126
  failure of Washington Conference, 126
  freedom of the seas, 18, 126, 134
  Kellogg, low opinion of, 127
  limit on all warships, 131
  reduction demanded, 126
  Senate Foreign Relations Chair, 122, 126
Bridgeman, William C., 254
  American electioneering, 218, 223
  American perfidy, 293
  anger and mistrust of Churchill, 78, 81, 85–86, 261
  Anglo-Japanese Accord, 254, 255, 261
  Associated Press statement, 236
  Beatty's tenure, 173–174, 295
  blames Gibson, 292, 295
  blames Jones, 245, 258
  castigates Americans, 222, 245, 253
  closing plenary speech, 291
  critical of Cabinet, 81, 245, 291

Index

critical of Coolidge, 223, 295
eight-inch gun, 144, 292
First Lord of the Admiralty, 48
Foreign Office, suspicious of, 245, 258, 261–262
hostile press, 226
Japanese diplomacy, 49, 253
misjudges Coolidge, 223, 295
modus vivendi, 254, 267, 269, 271
omissions to Cabinet and CID, 184, 186–187, 192
opposes Beatty, 260, 295
oral presentation to CID, 184, 190–191
parity promise, 236, 260
plot to topple Baldwin, 85–86
political judgment criticized, 48–49, 91–92
recalled to London, 261
resignation threatened, 61, 78, 81
right-to-parity promise, 217, 238, 249
seven-inch-gun compromise, 283
split with Cecil, 291
supports secrecy, 182, 184
ultimatum, 244–245, 258
"wider reference," 185
Brown, Boveri Electric Corporation, 229
Bywater, Hector, 98

Cabinet, British
Beatty's omissions to, 177, 182–189, 192, 196–197
Committee on cruiser construction, 287
compromise on parity, 241–243
crisis, 83, 91, 286
explosive debates, 278
instructed Balfour, 28
ire against Admiralty, 92, 287
League of Nations arms control, suspicious of, 141
modification of Anglo-Japanese Accord, 277–278
naval construction inquiry, 287
Naval Programme Committee, 55
parity repudiated, 277, 279
rejects 600,000 tons, 246
resignation threats, 4, 286
Cabinet Committee on Defense Estimates, 39–40, 62
endorses Beatty's postwar naval policy, 39
Japan most likely potential enemy, 40
rejects Geddes Committee naval cuts, 41
Cabinet Committee on National Expenditure, 36, 38
Cabinet Committee on Naval Construction. See also Birkenhead Committee
Campbell, Roland, 198
Coolidge reelection campaign, 198
predicts failure of Conference, 197–198, 260
Capital ship-building holiday, 21
Carnegie Endowment for International Peace, 124
Castle, William R., Jr., 127, 129, 161
Ambassador to Japan, 314
British proposals, 233
Gibson, 160, 162
League of Nations, 127
peace movement, 127
skeptical of British, 161
Cecil, James, 146
Cecil, Robert, 139, 193
Admiralty instructions, opposition to, 145–146, 193
Admiralty's unconstitutional dominance, 298
"agreement was almost certain," 195–197
American right to parity, 236, 299
Article 8 Treaty of Versailles, 141
Balfour, 139, 297, 299
blames Cabinet, 297
Blockade Minister, 139
Chancellor of the Duchy of Lancaster, 55, 140, 193
Churchill blamed, 273, 277
critical of Americans, 245, 252
"Dove of Peace," 140
eight-inch gun, 266, 283
Gibson's distrust, 245
Hankey, Maurice, 297, 299
high principals, 139
hostile American press, 225
House of Lords, address to, 299
League arms control proposals, 142–143
League of Nations Union, 140
May 20 CID meeting, 193
modus vivendi, 267–270
Nobel Peace Prize, 140
political clause, 284
Preparatory Commission, 193
recommendations to CID rejected, 146
refuses closing plenary argument, 290
resignation charges, 297, 299
resignation, 277, 286, 297

Cecil, Robert (cont.)
  seven-inch gun proposed, 283
  sharp practice, 260
  Sub-Committee on Reduction and Limitation of Armaments, 142
  warns against secrecy, 184
  Woodrow Wilson Prize, 139–140
  Woodrow Wilson, 139–140
Chamberlain, Austen, 132
  accepts responsibility for failure, 300
  Baldwin's Canadian visit, 264, 286
  blames Admiralty, 299
  Blames Baldwin, 286
  blames Gibson, 300
  blames United States, 300
  bows to Admiralty, 182
  caution against secrecy, 184
  Cecil, 140, 146
  Conference failure deplored, 299
  critical of Kellogg, 127, 200
  defensive cruisers, 247
  embarrassed by failure, 299
  four resignations threatened, 286
  Kuomintang, 134
  Locarno Agreement, 48
  "monstrous" American proposals, 249
  Nobel Peace Prize, 48
  opposes blockade claims, 132–133, 306
  parity promise withdrawn, 281
  risk of future war, 308
  supports Anglo-Japanese Accord, 264
  supports Bridgeman's parity promise, 241, 260
  warns of collapse, 247, 260, 263
Chamberlain, Neville, 284
  resignation threats recorded, 286
Chatfield, Adm. Ernle, 28
Chicago Daily News, 252
Chicago Tribune, 224
Christian Science Monitor, 252
Churchill, Winston
  Admiralty fallacies, 274–275
  Admiralty nemesis, 288
  Anglo-Japanese Accord, 256
  Beatty's political tactics, 79–80, 82–85, 87–88, 173–176
  Beatty's removal, 88
  building holiday, 23, 41, 269–270
  Chancellor of the Exchequer, 3, 36
  Conservative Party, 50, 52, 57
  convoys, 68, 240, 262
  Coolidge's political motives, 199, 262
  criticizes war against Japan, 51–52, 59–60, 63, 65–67, 241
  cuts to naval construction, 51, 241
  defends Admiralty, 39, 49, 246
  denigrates Japanese threat, 3, 66–67, 176
  economic priority, 3, 50, 54
  First Lord of the Admiralty, 3, 36, 49
  industrial power, 3, 54
  John Maynard Keynes, 50
  Labour Party, 52
  Liberal convictions, 48, 50–51, 55
  Liberal Party, 36
  modified Anglo-Japanese Accord, 274
  modus vivendi, 267–270
  naval supremacy, 2, 8, 49, 69–70, 234, 308
  one-year delay, 3, 75, 92
  opposes parity, 234, 241, 247, 257, 262, 308
  opposes seventy cruisers, 66, 68, 235, 248
  opposes six-inch gun cruisers, 74, 176, 300–301
  opposes unlimited smaller cruisers, 53, 191
  prescient strategy, 248, 257
  priority of economic strength, 3, 51, 54
  rate of ship replacement, 54, 275, 300
  responsibility for shell failure, 100
  Singapore base, 53
  skillful strategy, 4, 248, 257, 274, 276, 287, 307–308
  social and welfare reforms, 51–52
  supports Beatty's extension, 173, 179
  supports eight-inch gun, 72–73, 94, 175
  Ten-Year Rule, 53
  three major concerns, 51
  war with the United States, 262
  worst blunder, 300
  year-to year building alternative, 276
Churchill, Clementine
  warns against Beatty, 88
CID See Committee of Imperial Defense
Colwyn, Lord. See also F. H. Smith
Colwyn Committee
  charges waste and mismanagement, 93
  demands cuts in naval spending, 90, 92
Coolidge, Calvin, 122
  British cruiser superiority, 162, 222
  calls 1927 Conference, 155, 161–162
  cancels Baldwin meeting, 256
  concessions to British, 163
  Congress, 161
  disarmament, 131
  endorses combat equivalency, 170
  ends negotiations, 290

Index

Gibson, 160, 162
insists on eight-inch gun, 280
naval limitation, 132, 161
naval supremacy, 2, 309–310
opposes Anglo-Japanese Accord, 255
opposes six-inch-gun cruisers, 281
Preparatory Commission, 132, 135
rejects adjournment, 289
right to build 10,000-ton, eight-inch-gun cruisers, 281
switch to cruiser superiority, 309–310
tacit compromise with General Board, 169
Committee of Imperial Defense
Beatty's omissions, 177, 185–189, 191
confused discussion May 20, 192
League arms control proposals, 143
propaganda initiative, 249
reasonable latitude on details, 192
Subcommittee on Reduction and Limitation of Armaments, 142
unlimited smaller cruisers, 248
unwillingness to challenge Admiralty, 192–193
See also Further Limitation of Naval Armaments Subcommittee
Congress, United States
10,000-ton, eight-inch-gun cruisers, 4
1916 Naval Act, 1, 5, 7
1918 Naval Act, 8
1929 naval construction, 310
cruiser construction, 132
joint resolution on blockade claims, 134
modernization of battleships, 132
naval defense strategy, 131
convoys
Beatty opposes, 68, 241
Churchill advocates, 68, 240
Conservative Party
Admiralty's political power, 60–61, 83
critics of Admiralty, 92
fear of resignation crisis, 63, 82, 86
cruisers
10,000-ton, eight-inch-gun cruisers, 3, 30, 42, 100, 306
6,000-ton, six-inch-gun cruiser, 106, 223, 265
7,500-ton, six-inch-gun cruiser, 106
auxiliary cruisers, 2
battle cruisers, 2
combat missions, 43, 64
combat weaknesses, 3, 72, 101–104
Emerald Class, 73

fighting power, 102–104
Furutaka Class, 44, 267, 270
Hawkins Class, 30, 42, 44, 71
increased costs, 41
Kent Class, 44, 101, 118
London Class, 44, 101
Myoko Class, 103
Northampton Class, 118
Omaha Class, 30, 110, 117
Pensacola Class, 120
Salt Lake City Class, 118
trade route protection, 24
Washington Conference approves unlimited number, 28
Curzon, George N., 55

Director of Gunnery
abolition of eight-inch gun, 105–106
defects of British eight-inch gun, 103
recommends second naval conference, 105–106
Dreadnought, 71–74
Davidson, J.C.C.
angry Cabinet debates, 278
claims sinister plot, 83
Conservative Party, 83
opposes Churchill, 83
Denby, Edwin, 18

Eberle, Adm. E. W., 164
Edgerton, Capt. W. A., 149
challenges strategy of secrecy, 149, 183
limitation of cruiser tonnage and gun size, 149
warnings verified, 183
Eight-inch gun
250-pound shell, 96
centerline, 70, 96
combat deficiencies of British, 3, 73, 94–95, 98
combat value, 70
complaints about, 96, 98
disappointing British muzzle velocity, 96
elevation, 95
excellent performance of American gun, 119–120
mountings defective, 95
range, 71, 73, 95
redesign efforts, 96, 98
revolutionary impact, 95, 157
rounds per minute, 96
secrecy, 98
superior to six-inch and 7.5-inch guns, 70

Federal Bureau of Investigation, 226, 310
Ferris, John Robert, 84
Field, Adm. Frederick L., 202, 252
  advantageous position in cruisers, 164
  criticism of Preparatory Commission, 143
  marshals British press, 224
  rejects combat equivalency, 243
Fighting Services Economy Committee
  See also Colwyn Committee
Five-Power Treaty, 31, 131, 134
Fleet Faction, Japan, 33, 253, 314
Foreign Office, 53
  critical of Kellogg, 123, 200
  disdain of Coolidge, 200
  recommends Field, 202
  Ten-Year Rule, 74
Four-Power Treaty, 31
Fourteen Points, 8
France, 1
  arms-control inspections, 137
  opposition to submarine abolition, 27
  seeks guarantees of security, 137
Freedom of the Seas, 1–2, 6, 18, 126, 134, 302
Fuller, Adm. Cyril, 72
Further Limitation of Naval Armaments Subcommittee
  Anglo-Japanese Accord, 259
  created, 257
  three alternative strategies, 263–264

Geddes, Eric, 36, 38
  Geddes Committee, 36
    See also Cabinet Committee on National Expenditures
General Board, United States Navy
  10,000-ton cruiser, 108, 117, 168
  10:10:6 ratio, 19, 21, 108
  armed merchantmen, 110, 166
  arms limitation, 134
  blockade, 109
  British duplicity, 223
  combat equivalency, 166, 169
  Congressional weakness, 10, 112, 116, 136
  criticisms of Washington Conference, 108–110
  cruiser design, 108, 110, 117
  disillusionment, 108–109, 115
  eight-inch gun success, 118–120, 167, 256
  elevation of battleship guns, 114
  fuel oil conversion, 115
  Geneva negotiating objectives, 169
  Great Britain's cruiser superiority, 110, 116, 135, 166

naval equality, 18, 171
naval policy, 17
naval strategy, 17, 116
need for aircraft carriers, 17, 111, 116
Pacific bases, 17–18, 111, 117, 136
Preparatory Commission, 135–136
rejection of strategy, 19, 166
rejects seven-inch gun, 284
relative naval strengths, 19, 110
tacit compromise, 170
total tonnage, 168, 170
German Navy, 1
Gibson, Hugh, 127–129
  Ambassador to Belgium, 128
  blockade, 294
  blunder, 279, 282, 293
  British press, 224
  Castle, 160–161
  closing plenary address, 293, 295
  Coolidge, 160
  diplomatic posts, 128
  Hoover, 128, 160
  Kellogg, 162
  Preparatory Commission, 122, 128–129, 137
  rejection of Anglo-Japanese Accord, 279
  Schofield, 232
  Shearer, 232
  Wilbur, 162
Guam, 17, 304

Hamaguchi, Osachi, 314
Hankey, Maurice
  arms control, 141
  criticizes Cabinet, 235
  supports secrecy, 184
  two-stage strategy, 235
Harding, Warren G.
  calls Washington Conference of 1921-1922, 2, 11, 121, 302
  campaign pledge, 10, 17, 121
  cut taxes, 10, 122
  naval equality, 2
  political orthodoxy, 122, 305
  priority of domestic politics, 10, 121, 304
  Wilson's Navy, 10
Hawkins Class cruisers. See Cruisers
Hearst, William Randolph, 228
Hepburn, Adm. A. P., 229
Hicks, William Joynson, 55
Hoare, Samuel, 84
Hoover, Herbert C., 2
  1930 London Conference, 2, 312, 315

Index

1932 Geneva Disarmament Conference, 315
effort to save 1927 Conference, 257, 311
Gibson, 128, 312
Howard, 258
London Naval Treaty, 2, 313
MacDonald, 2, 313
yardstick, 312–313
Houghton, Alanson, 134
opposes second conference, 168
warns of Admiralty supremacy, 161, 168
Howard, Esme, 132, 198
Admiralty cruiser demands, 198, 222, 299
blames Admiralty, 299
blockade claims, 133
Conference failure, 289
Coolidge, 133
freedom of the seas, 290
future hostilities, 222, 290
Kellogg, 133
neutral rights, 290
parity essential, 198
warns of failure, 258
House Naval Affairs Committee, 132
Hughes, Charles Evans, 2, 122, 127
Anglo-Japanese Alliance, 21
diplomatic naïveté, 16
domestic political priorities, 10, 16, 304
scraps capital ships, 19, 21, 302

Italy, 1
Ishii Kikijuro, 218

James, Edwin L., 168, 223
Japan
1930 London Treaty, 315
advocates three-power conference, 137
Anglo-Japanese Accord, 251, 254
British eight-inch gun, 98–99
compromise efforts, 251, 253–256, 285, 293, 309
Empire, 7
financial crisis, 9, 11
Manchurian invasion, 315
Marshall, Caroline, and Marianas Islands, 1, 6
Meiji Constitution, 11
menace to British, 64
National Defense Plan, 33
naval budget, 9
regional supremacy, 2, 5, 302–303
seventy percent ratio, 253, 305
terminates treaties, 315
Twenty-one Demands on China, 1, 6

Japanese delegates
avoid tax increases, 281
higher ratio, 254
secret talks, 285
support eight-inch gun, 254
Japanese Naval Vice Minister
bypasses Japanese Cabinet, 253
demands seventy-percent ratio, 253, 309
Fleet Faction, 33, 253, 314
instructions to delegates, 253
Jellico, Adm. John R., 101
Jones, Adm. Hilary P, 129–131
Adm. Frederick Field, 164
Anglo-American front, 157
Anglo-Saxon civilization, 130, 150
appoints Adm. Frank Schofield, 164–165
Beatty's assurances, 150–151
British duplicity, 223
combat equivalency, 148, 220
compromise plan, 148–149
crucial assumptions, 156–157
diplomatic inexperience, 130, 147–148, 150, 152–153
discount, 159
emphasis on equality, 130, 151
entente with Great Britain, 130, 150
equivalency alternative, 158–159
expanded combat equivalency formula, 155–157, 159–160
Gibson, 160
July 4 address, 238, 243
memorandum to Kellogg, 153
Preparatory Commission, 122, 129
press leaker, 252
rejects Anglo-Japanese Accord, 279
rejects British proposals, 219
rejects cruiser inferiority, 164
secret Anglo-American agreement, 157
secret reasons, 154
serious mistake, 153
Shearer, 228
ultimatum, 238, 244, 252
US General Board Chair, 129

Kanji, Adm. Kato, 33, 314
Kei, Hara, 4
assassinated, 31
relies on Tomosaburo, 11
Kellogg, Frank B, 122–124
Ambassador to Great Britain, 122
Anglo Japanese Accord rejected, 255, 279, 290

Kellogg, Frank B (cont.)
  arms control, 126
  blames Great Britain, 221, 280-281, 299
  blockade claims, 133
  British cruiser superiority, 162
  caution about second conference, 161-162
  China, 134
  combat equivalency, 155, 169
  criticisms of, 126, 172, 193, 200-201
  diplomatic realist, 124
  effort to save Conference, 258
  future hostilities with Great Britain, 222
  grasp of naval fundamentals, 168
  Howard, 133
  Kellogg-Briand Pact, 124
  lack of limits on smaller cruisers, 219, 281
  news briefings, 225, 253
  Nobel Peace Prize, 124
  proposes adjournment, 289
  Schofield's praise of, 169
  urges practical plan for Preparatory Commission, 131
Kelly, Vice Admiral John D.
  criticizes Baldwin, 85
  praises Beatty, 85
Kent Class cruisers. See cruisers
Keyes, Adm. Roger, 59, 70, 88, 173
  anticipates U. S. blockade breaking, 263, 308
  rushes production of British eight-inch gun, 3, 44
Keynes, George Maynard, 50
King George V, 245
Kobayashi, Adm. Seizo
  censored, 281
  difficult dilemma, 281
Kuomintang, 134

Labor Party, 36
League of Nations, 5, 121, 302, 304
  Article 8 of Covenant, 127
  Robert Cecil, 141-142
  Preparatory Commission, 142
Lee, Arthur, 25, 38
legend tonnage, 114, 220
Leslie, Shane, 85
Lloyd George, David, 4, 36-37
  British naval supremacy, 8
  cuts naval construction, 12, 38
Lodge, Henry Cabot, 20, 127
London Class cruiser. See cruisers
London Conference, 1930, 2, 315

London Times, 224
London Treaty, 1930, 313

MacDonald, Ramsay, 37, 46-47, 52
  1924 Government, 36, 46
  agrees to fifty-cruiser limit, 313
  civilian control, 313
  continuity with Admiralty demands, 313
  dismissed Japanese threat, 46
  Hoover, 313
  opposed food ship exemptions, 313
  opposed sale of naval bases, 313
  policy to avoid war with United States, 314
Madden, Adm. Charles, 173, 286
Marvell, Vice Adm. G.R.
  "perfectly marvelous" eight-inch gun, 120
Mariner, Ted (J. Theodore), 225
  Coolidge endorses combat equivalency, 169
Meiji Constitution, 11
merchantmen
  as commerce raiders, 29, 66
  with six-inch guns, 179
modus vivendi, 267-269, 271

National Defense Acts of 1916 and 1918, 5, 7-8
Naval Staff, British
  anxiety over its cruisers, 95-107
  defective eight-inch gun, 104, 175
  economic rationale, 143
  limits cruisers and guns, 105-106
  superiority in cruisers, 45, 177-178
Naval supremacy
  Great Britain, 1-2, 8, 14, 29, 302, 304
  Japan, 11, 14, 302-303
  United States, 2, 5-6, 9, 303-304
Navy League, 224
Newport News Shipping, 229
New York Illustrated News, 227
New York Times, 223, 227-228
Nelson, HMS, 135, 177, 219, 236
Nine-Power Treaty, 31, 134
Northhampton Class cruisers. See cruisers
New Zealand opposes higher Japanese ratio, 220
Neutral rights, 1, 6

Omaha Class cruisers. See cruisers
One-power standard, 14, 66
Open Door policy, 1, 17, 20, 109, 304

Index

Panama Canal, 24
Paris Peace Conference, See Versailles
peace societies, 9
Philippine Islands
   inability to defend, 1, 7
Pinkerton Detective Agency, 227
Pound, Adm. D. P. R.
   criticism of Cecil, 277, 296
   opposes political clause, 285
   opposes seven-inch gun, 283–284
   Winston's wild schemes, 276
Pratt, Adm. William P., 130
Preparatory Commission
   League of Nations, 127
   tangle of disputes, 136

Reeves, Captain J. M., 231, 252
Rodney, HMS, 135, 177, 219, 236
Roosevelt, Franklin D.
   1936 London Naval Treaty, 315
   Assistant Secretary of the Navy, 140, 315
   naval building, 315
   Woodrow Wilson Prize, 140
Roosevelt, Theodore, Jr.
   Beatty's stalling strategy, 24, 38
   Coolidge's political gesture, 199
Root, Elihu, 18
Roskill, Stephen, 85

Saito, Makato
   Anglo-Japanese Accord, 293
   casts blame for failure, 293
   denies Japanese responsibility, 293
   mediates differences, 293
   seventy percent ratio, 218, 253, 293, 305
Salt Lake City Class cruisers. See cruisers
Schofield, Adm. Frank H.
   Admiralty strategic thinking, 41, 113
   bloodless victories, 113
   British superiority, 113–116
   critical of Washington Conference, 113
   definition of sea power, 113
   Four-Power Treaty, 113
   meetings with reporters, 252
   meetings with Shearer, 231–232
   on politicians, 113
   praise of Kellogg, 169
Scotland Yard, 227
Shearer, William B., 226–232
   anti-British, 230

   criticism of Congress, 227
   disreputable character, 227
   lobbyist for defense contractors, 229
   meeting with Coolidge, 228
   self-defense, 226
shells, British defective, 100
Singapore
   naval base, 36, 83
   war with Japan, 41, 67
Smith, Vice Adm. Aubrey, 158
Smith, F.E.
   See also Birkenhead, Lord
Smith F. H.
   Fighting Services Economy Committee chair, 90
   naval budget cuts, 90
   See also Colwyn Committee
Snowden, Philip
   rejects seventy cruisers, 46
submarine, 1–2

Tanaka, Giichi, 254
tentative agreement on auxiliaries, 238
Ten-Year Rule, 13, 91
   Admiralty opposition to, 55, 60, 182
   Churchill's support of, 53, 60
Tomosaburo, Adm. Kato, 11, 305
   compromise at Washington Conference, 31–32
   innovative combat tactics, 33
   seventy-percent ratio, 31
   sixty-percent ratio, 31
   two-pronged strategy, 32–33
ton-mileage method, 178, 189, 252
total-tonnage method, 158
trade protection, 24, 166
trade routes, 191
Train, Harold C., 252
treaty right to equality, 163
Twenty-one Demands, 1, 6, 304
Tyrell, William
   parity agreed to, 233
   presentation to Cabinet, 233
Tully J., 199

United States Naval Intelligence, 226
Underwood, Oscar, 20

Van Keuren, Capt. H. K.
   accuracy of eight-inch gun, 119–120
Versailles Peace Conference, 1, 5, 302

war at the peace table, 4, 316
Washington Conference, 1921–1922, 2, 14, 16–36
Westminster Guardian, 252
Wilbur, Curtis D., 125
　defense of Washington Conference, 125
　denounces Shearer, 228
　Gibson, 162
Willet, Arthur, 224
Williams, Wythe
　6,000-ton cruisers, 223
　British trick, 223
　reports on Shearer, 229–230
Women's International League for Peace and Freedom, 124
Wilson, Woodrow
　1916 Naval Act, 5–6
　1918 Naval Act, 8
　freedom of the seas, 1–2, 8, 304
　"navy second to none," 1, 5, 9, 303